Fodor's

CHINA

S0-BOE-438

Thomas
Cook
Bureau de Change
FANDA
PERFUME COSMETIC PHARMACY
PRINCE JEWELLERY & WATCH CO.
CHINA PRODUCTS CO.
France Japan
FASHION SQUARE
SONY
NIKON
BOSE
ALPINE
QUAD

# WELCOME TO CHINA

China—old and new—is a feast for the senses. The vast, awe-inspiring landscapes run the gamut from river deltas, subtropical jungles, and deserts to pulsing megacities with space-age skylines. Tranquil palaces and fog-wrapped mountain peaks evoke the Taoist philosophers of yesteryear. Hong Kong's and Beijing's dizzying modernity exhilarates city culture vultures. Full of diverse peoples and traditions, this fast-changing country reveals its riches to travelers who seek them out, from foodies on a quest for the best dumplings to explorers trekking the Silk Road.

## TOP REASONS TO GO

★ **Great Wall:** China's most iconic fortification delivers postcard-perfect views.

★ **Tiger Leaping Gorge:** Breathtaking mountain scenery rewards adventurous hikers.

★ **Architecture:** Futuristic skyscrapers vie with dynastic compounds to dazzle the eye.

★ **Food:** The vibrant flavors of authentic Chinese cuisine are a gourmand's delight.

★ **Imperial History:** Terracotta Soldiers and ancient temples take you back 5,000 years.

★ **Cities:** Beijing's Olympic makeover, Hong Kong's harbor, Shanghai's art-deco splendor.

# Fodor's CHINA

**Publisher:** Amanda D'Acierno, *Senior Vice President*

**Editorial:** Arabella Bowen, *Executive Editorial Director*; Linda Cabasin, *Editorial Director*

**Design:** Fabrizio La Rocca, *Vice President, Creative Director*; Tina Malaney, *Associate Art Director*; Chie Ushio, *Senior Designer*; Ann McBride, *Production Designer*

**Photography:** Melanie Marin, *Associate Director of Photography*; Jessica Parkhill and Jennifer Romains, *Researchers*

**Maps:** Rebecca Baer, *Senior Map Editor*; David Lindroth and Mark Stroud (Moon Street Cartography), *Cartographer*

**Production:** Linda Schmidt, *Managing Editor*; Evangelos Vasilakis, *Associate Managing Editor*; Angela L. McLean, *Senior Production Manager*

**Sales:** Jacqueline Lebow, *Sales Director*

**Marketing & Publicity:** Heather Dalton, *Marketing Director*; Katherine Fleming, *Senior Publicist*

**Business & Operations:** Susan Livingston, *Vice President, Strategic Business Planning*; Sue Daulton, *Vice President, Operations*

**Fodors.com:** Megan Bell, *Executive Director, Revenue & Business Development*; Yasmin Marinaro, *Senior Director, Marketing & Partnerships*

Copyright © 2014 by Fodor's Travel, a division of Random House LLC

**Editorial Contributors:** Sky Canaves, Gareth Clark, Sophie Friedman, Daniel Garber, Kit Gillet, Julie Grundvig, Dana Kaufman, Doretta Lau, Samantha Leese, Ami Li, Maloy Luakian, Tom O'Malley, Adrian Sandiford, Dorothy So, Jason Spotts, Kate Springer, Sander Van de Moortel, Amy Wu

**Editors:** Róisín Cameron, Mark Sullivan

**Production Editor:** Jennifer DePrima

8th Edition

ISBN 978-0-7704-3209-6

ISSN 1070-6895

## SPECIAL SALES

PRINTED IN THE UNITED STATES

10 9 8 7 6 5 4 3 2

# CONTENTS

# ABOUT THIS GUIDE

### Fodor's Recommendations

Everything in this guide is worth doing—we don't cover what isn't—but exceptional sights, hotels, and restaurants are recognized with additional accolades. **Fodor's**Choice★ indicates our top recommendations. Care to nominate a new place? Visit Fodors.com/contact-us.

### Trip Costs

We list prices wherever possible to help you budget well. Hotel and restaurant price categories from **$** to **$$$$** are noted alongside each recommendation. For hotels, we include the lowest cost of a standard double room in high season. For restaurants, we cite the average price of a main course at dinner or, if dinner isn't served, at lunch. For attractions, we always list adult admission fees; discounts are usually available for children, students, and senior citizens.

### Hotels

Our local writers vet every hotel to recommend the best overnights in each price category, from budget to expensive. Unless otherwise specified, you can expect private bath, phone, and TV in your room. For expanded hotel reviews, facilities, and deals visit Fodors.com.

### Restaurants

Unless we state otherwise, restaurants are open for lunch and dinner daily. We mention dress code only when there's a specific requirement and reservations only when they're essential or not accepted. To make restaurant reservations, visit Fodors.com.

### Credit Cards

The hotels and restaurants in this guide typically accept credit cards. If not, we'll say so.

**Top Picks**

- ★ **Fodor's**Choice

**Listings**

- ✉ Address
- 📨 Branch address
- ☎ Telephone
- 📠 Fax
- 🌐 Website
- 📧 E-mail
- 🎟 Admission fee
- 🕒 Open/closed times
- [M] Subway
- ✥ Directions or Map coordinates

**Hotels & Restaurants**

- 🏨 Hotel
- 🛏 Number of rooms
- 🍽 Meal plans
- 🍴 Restaurant
- ✍ Reservations
- 👔 Dress code
- 💳 No credit cards
- [$] Price

**Other**

- ⇨ See also
- ☞ Take note
- ⛳ Golf facilities

# EXPERIENCE CHINA

# WHAT'S WHERE

*Numbers refer to chapters.*

**2 Beijing.** *Beijing is in massive flux, and the construction never stops. Feel the ancient pulse beneath the current clamor.*

**3 Beijing to Shanghai: Hebei, Shandong, Anhui, Jiangsu.** *Discover a cultural and natural treasure trove— Huang Shan peaks are islands in a sea of clouds, and canal-laced Suzhou is the Venice of the Orient.*

**4 Shanghai.** *In the 1920s Shanghai was known as the Whore of the Orient, but we like to think of her as a classy lady who knows how to have a good time. The party stopped for a few decades after the revolution, but now Shanghai is back in swing.*

**5 East Coast: Zhejiang, Fujian.** *Fujian's Xiamen is an undiscovered pearl, with all the history, culture, and infrastructure of more popular tourist magnets. Zhejiang's Hangzhou is known for scenic West Lake, immortalized in Chinese poetry.*

**6 Hong Kong.** *A city of contrasts—east and west, old and new, work hard and play harder. Long nights of barhopping are offset by tai chi sessions at dawn.*

**7 Pearl River Delta: Guangzhou and Shenzhen.**

The word "engine" is used metaphorically to describe the Pearl River Delta region, but the vibrations are still palpable here in China's industrial hub.

**8 Southwest: Guangxi, Guizhou, Yunnan.** *The mountains are high and the emperor is far away. If you're looking to take a walk on the wild tribal side, then any or all of these three regions should be high on your to-visit list.*

**9 Sichuan, Chongqing.** *China's latest industrial revolution is happening in faraway Sichuan and Chongqing, where the nearby Three Gorges Dam (in Hubei), while hotly debated, remains a stunning sight.*

**10 The Silk Road: Shaanxi, Gansu, Qinghai, Xinjiang.** *Distant and mysterious, this was ancient China's lifeline to the outside world. Visit the country's last remaining walled cities—Xi'an is fascinating for its cultural and its historical importance.*

**11 Tibet.** *The roof of the world is not the most accessible place, but that's changing thanks to the train line connecting Lhasa to major cities throughout China.*

# QUINTESSENTIAL CHINA

### Art for Art's Sake

China may be careening through the 21st century at breakneck speed, but the Chinese are immensely proud of their artistic heritage and traditional folk arts have not been forgotten. Every region of China is rich in local arts and craft traditions. In the north, delicate designs are painstakingly cut from rice paper and hung from windows and doors during festivals and weddings. In the east, Suzhou is as famous for its elegant silk embroidery as it is for its gardens, and nearby Huang Shan is a wonderful place to discover bamboo weaving. Yunnan is known for its painted clay figurines, Chengdu for its sweet sugar paintings, Fujian for its colorful hand puppets. Everywhere you go you'll see fluttering overhead one of China's oldest pastimes: kite flying, dating all the way back to 475 BC.

### Be Moved

Getting there is often half the fun, and in China there are limitless ways to travel from point A to point B. China already has the world's longest high-speed rail network, and has plans to add many new lines in the coming years. But there's more than just trains. Sightseeing in Chongqing? Cross the Yangtze or Jialing rivers in an old-school cable car. Horses are the best way to get around in the beautiful countryside surrounding Songpan in Sichuan. If you're flying into Shanghai's Pudong Airport, take the superslick maglev train into town at speeds of more than 260 miles per hour. China's crown jewels of passenger transport belong to Hong Kong, where it's normal to get around by light rail, bus, taxi, trolley, boat—it even has the longest covered outdoor escalator system in the world.

Chinese culture is rich, diverse, and will hit you like a ton of bricks. Keep an open mind while you're traveling, because this will be an experience of a lifetime.

### China Beyond the Han

The Han are far and away the dominant ethnic group in China, but there is surprising ethnic diversity, from the Muslim Uighurs in Xinjiang to the Dai and Hani of Xishuangbanna. Officially there are 56 ethnic groups, including the nomadic Mongols, that make up the great Chinese nation. Though small in number relative to the Han, the minorities have historically been a force to be reckoned with. Rulers of the last dynasty (the Qing) were Manchus. Though Chinese history is rife with examples of intertribal war and Han incursion into non-Han territory (Tibet being the latest and most famous example), the revolution, in theory, leveled the playing field. Traveling through areas less dominated by the Han Chinese offers views of the country far different from the usual Beijing-Shanghai–Three Gorges tour.

### All the Tea in China

For a vast majority of the Chinese people, the day begins and ends with tea. Whether it's being savored in a delicate ceremonial porcelain cup or slurped out of a glass mason jar, you can bet that the imbiber takes tea consumption seriously. Ask a Chinese person about the best tea and the answer will very likely depend on where they're from. The highly prized Pu'er tea has a dark color and heavy, almost earthy flavor. It gets its name from the region of southern Yunnan Province where it's grown. Fujian produces the best oolong teas, thanks to the high mountains and favorable climate. Oolong is usually served with much ceremony. Perhaps the most expensive tea in China is a variant of green tea from the Longjing ("Dragon Well") region of Hangzhou. Longjing tea is served in clear glasses, so one can watch the delicate dance of the long, thin leaves as they float to the top.

# IF YOU LIKE

### Contemporary Art

China has one of the most vibrant, eclectic, and often downright avant-garde art scenes this side of Paris. Beijing is arguably the center of China's contemporary art scene, and it's in China's capital that well-known artists like sculptor Wang Guangyi (who blends propaganda and icons from the cultural revolution for what some consider cynical effect) and painter Feng Mengbo (whose hallmarks include mixing oil painting and computer graphics) ply their trades.

**Dashanzi 798 Art District, Beijing.** This former military warehouse complex in Beijing's Chaoyang district houses dozens of galleries and the workshops of many of the city's up-and-coming artists.

**Suzhou Creek Art District, Shanghai.** In a renovated factory area on Suzhou Creek, more than 120 art galleries and studios are open to the public. Some of Shanghai's top artists have studios here, including the contemporary art collective Liu Dao and world renowned artists Zhou Tiehai and Xu Zhen.

**Guangdong Museum of Art, Guangzhou.** Denizens of the Pearl River Delta, though normally thought of as caring more about making money than art, have a number of museums and galleries worth visiting. This museum is well respected throughout China.

**Museum of Contemporary Art, Shanghai.** MOCA is the first nonprofit independent contemporary art museum in China. It showcases cutting-edge contemporary art from China and around the world.

### Bicycling

In the not-too-distant past, China was known as "The Bicycle Kingdom," but as cars become more popular, the iconic sea of bicycles that once filled the avenues of Beijing and Shanghai is drying to a trickle.

But this doesn't mean that bicycling enthusiasts should lose heart. While the two-wheeled herd has thinned out considerably, you'll hardly be riding alone. Most hotels will be able to help you out with bicycle rentals, or a brand-new Flying Pigeon (the bike of China) should only set you back a few hundred yuan.

**Beijing.** Though notorious for its bad air and traffic gridlock, the capital is still our favorite urban bicycling ground. Its wide avenues and impossible-to-maneuver-by-car back alleyways make it an ideal city to tour by bicycle.

**Xi'an.** The city center is small enough to make it perfect for exploring by bike. For a unique experience, take a tour on top of the city wall, the only one left fully intact in all of China.

**Shanghai.** The Pearl of the Orient is also two-wheel friendly, though you'll be asked to dismount and walk along the Nanjing pedestrian area.

**Chengdu.** The spiciest city in China is also as flat as a Ping-Pong table, which makes it one of our favorites for exploring by bike.

### Treasure Hunting

For anyone who loves to shop, China is heaven on earth. Along with the glitzy department stores found in big cities, vibrant street markets and pedestrian shopping areas are found everywhere and can be terrific places to hunt for bargains. Every region of China has a specialty, whether silk embroidery in Suzhou, mud figures in Beijing, Longjing tea in Hangzhou, or stuffed tiger toys in Xi'an. Popular souvenirs include Chinese silk, jade, and wood carvings—travelers never come

home disappointed. The rule of the land is to bargain hard and bring an extra bag for your loot.

**Panjiayuan Antiques Market, Beijing.** If you have a hankering for a scroll, jade bracelet, embroidery, or even a musical Mao alarm clock, this is the place. On weekends, Beijing's most popular spot for kitsch is teeming with shoppers on the lookout for a well-fought bargain. Haggle fiercely and doubt any claims that the Ming-style vase you desire is the real thing.

**Duolun Lu, Shanghai.** Spend a pleasant afternoon strolling along Duolun Lu's pedestrian street in Shanghai's historic Hongkou District, once the home of aspiring writers Lu Xun and Mao Dun. Browse through the numerous bookstores, galleries, and curio shops, and when you're done you can relax over a cup of tea at one of the many restored teahouses.

**Temple Street Night Market, Hong Kong.** Locals and tourists alike frequent this lively night market for its festive atmosphere and outdoor dining. Hundreds of vendors vie for your attention, selling everything from silk scarves to bamboo backscratchers. Most people come here for the party rather than the merchandise, but it's still a good spot to find a treasure or two.

**Suzhou Arts and Crafts Museum, Suzhou.** Housed in a restored courtyard, this museum is a terrific place to purchase authentic arts and crafts, including jade, silk embroidery, and sandalwood carvings. In the adjoining workshop watch artisans at work shaping lattice fans and transforming blocks of jade into delicate figurines.

Adventurous Dining

Much has been written about the cuisine of China, and for a very good reason—it's some of the best (and most varied) on the planet. Most visitors will be happy to stick with such well-known dishes as Peking duck or kung pao chicken, but for those who want a culinary walk on the wild side, might we suggest a few less well-known regional favorites?

**Huang Shan Stone Frog, Anhui.** Stone frog soup is a delicacy of Huang Shan, famous for its simple, rustic cuisine. Hefty-sized black frogs are collected from the rivers around the mountain and served in a clear soup mixed with bamboo shoots, mushrooms, and ham. Locals claim the frogs will cure bad eyesight, strengthen bones, and increase energy. What's better for a day scaling the peaks of Huang Shan?

**Yak-Butter Tea, Yunnan, Tibet.** This beverage is ubiquitous throughout both Tibet and the higher mountain regions of Yunnan Province. Thick and tangy, the main ingredients of yak butter tea are yak butter, tea, and salt. Though its adherents drink it by the gallon, considering it delicious and healthy, unsuspecting imbibers have likened its flavor to melted blue cheese, or even wood polish.

**Thousand-Year-Old Eggs, Guangdong.** Preserved eggs are a Cantonese specialty made from coating duck or chicken eggs in a potent mixture of lime, salt, ash, and clay for up to a month until the egg whites turn dark brown and the yolks become green, smelling faintly of ammonia. With a jelly-like consistency, this pungent delicacy is often served with congee or pickled ginger to make it less edgy.

# CHINA
# TOP ATTRACTIONS

China has racked up a total of 43 United Nations World Heritage Sites. Given the country's huge tourism numbers, sites can be overrun at peak travel times, but it doesn't take much to get away from the crowds.

## Forbidden City

(A) Sitting at the heart of Beijing across from Tiananmen Square, the nearly 500-year-old Forbidden City is one of the world's most impressive imperial compounds. For the emperors and their courts, this moat-encircled complex was literally their city within a city, featuring 1,000 buildings covering more than 7.8 million square feet. Today the Forbidden City is home to the Palace Museum and its world-class collection of priceless paintings, bronzes, pottery, and documents that once belonged to the Qing imperial collection.

## Temple of Heaven

(B) The Temple of Heaven—known in Chinese as the Altar of Heaven—was once where Ming and Qing emperors made sacrifices to heaven. The emperor and his court visited the Temple of Heaven twice each year to perform ceremonies with the hope of ensuring a good harvest—even a minor mistake could spell disaster for China. The complex was built in the early 15th century by the Yongle Emperor, who was also behind the construction of the Forbidden City.

## Great Wall

(C) The Great Wall of China is one of the country's most iconic structures, as well as one of the world's most ambitious engineering projects. Originally intended to prevent invasion by nomadic tribes north of China, the wall was an imperial obsession for more than 1,000 years, beginning in the 5th century BC. Built primarily of stone and rammed earth, the

wall stretches 5,500 miles (8,850 kilometers) from its easternmost point on the Bohai Sea to its western terminus at Lop Nur in Xinjiang.

### Old Town of Lijiang

**(D)** The Old Town of Lijiang is renowned for its winding cobblestone streets, charming wooden homes, and clear, fish-filled mountain streams. The area has been home to the Naxi people (with their unique culture and architecture) for eight centuries. One of China's most popular destinations for domestic or international travelers, Lijiang is visited by millions each year. UNESCO has raised concerns that over-commercialization is affecting the site's heritage value, but it is still a must-visit destination for many tourists.

### Yunnan Three Parallel Rivers Protected Areas

**(E)** Northwest Yunnan is one of the world's biodiversity hot spots, primarily owing to the steep river valleys through which the upper reaches of the Yangtze, Mekong, and Salween rivers flow. These protected areas contain unforgettable scenery, including the awe-inspiring Tiger Leaping Gorge and hundreds of varieties of rhododendrons, and rare animals such as the red panda and snow leopard.

### South China Karst

**(F)** Spread across the southwestern regions of Yunnan, Guizhou, and Guangxi, the South China Karst area is recognized for the diversity of its limestone scenery. The Stone Forest, outside of Yunnan's capital Kunming, is the best-known site in this group, featuring stone spires and strangely shaped monoliths that boggle the mind. A stony paradise for shutterbugs, Stone Forest and the other South China Karst sites are very popular, but still large enough to allow you to find your own quiet corner to take photos or just marvel at these improbable wonders.

# CHINA'S WORLD HERITAGE SITES

## Emei Shan

(G) Mist-shrouded Emei Shan is located in lush southern Sichuan Province. Emei Shan is one of China's four sacred Buddhist mountains. Emei's seemingly endless stone paths are usually hiked over one or two days. Hikers on Emei go there for the luxuriant and diverse foliage, the charming, run-down monasteries, the occasional waterfall, and the gangs of Tibetan macaques roaming its slopes. Emei's peak is best seen at dawn, when the sun rises from a sea of clouds.

## Mogao Caves

(H) The northwestern city of Dunhuang in Gansu Province was once an important stopover on the Silk Road that connected China with Europe via Central Asia. Along with bringing traders and goods in from the West, the Silk Road also brought Buddhism. The Mogao Caves near Dunhuang were first established more than 2,300 years ago as places for Buddhists to practice their faith. Over time, the caves grew into a complex of nearly 500 temples featuring astonishingly well-preserved Buddhist painting and architecture collected during a 1,000-year period.

## Terracotta Warriors

(I) The Terracotta Army at the mausoleum of the first Qin Emperor is one of the biggest archeological discoveries in the last half century. In 1974 farmers discovered pits with thousands of life-size statues of soldiers, horses, chariots, musicians and acrobats—their find instantly captured China's—and the world's—imagination. The army was commissioned by Qin Shihuang, China's first emperor, and buried with him in the early 3rd century with the hope that the warriors would protect him in the afterlife. Each 6-foot-tall statue is believed to have been modeled after a living human from the emperor's time.

## Potala Palace

**(J)** The Potala Palace is one of the world's most impressive buildings. Looking out over the valley below, its 13 stories house more than 1,000 rooms with countless shrines and statues throughout. Prior to serving as the residence of Dalai Lamas, the Potala was originally used by the historic Tibetan king Songtsen Gampo as a retreat for meditation. Its first palace was begun in the 7th century, with construction finishing in 1645. The Potala suffered during the 1959 uprising that led to the current Dalai Lama's fleeing Tibet, and also was at risk during the Cultural Revolution, but this great building still stands tall today, a monument to the greatness of Tibet's past.

## Summer Palace

**(K)** In Beijing's northern suburbs, the Summer Palace is where many an emperor went to escape his virtual imprisonment within the city center's Forbidden City. A peaceful retreat with a tranquil lake, a hill with scenic views of the city below, and a fantastic collection of gardens, statues, and pagodas, the Summer Palace is a great place to take a break from Beijing without actually leaving the city.

## Chengde Mountain Resort

**(L)** Beijing summers can be unbearably hot, even if you're the emperor. The Qing emperors, who were accustomed to the cooler climes of Manchuria, decided it was better to relocate their courts during the sweltering summer heat to higher, cooler ground, choosing a mountain in Chengde, Hebei Province, to serve as their summer capital. Legendary emperors, including Kangxi, Yongzheng, and Qianlong, escaped the heat while continuing to perform their imperial duties. The compound is loosely modeled on the Forbidden City, but its gardens, pagoda, and outlying temples give it a character all its own.

# CHINA TODAY

### Government

Mao Zedong's announcement of the establishment of the People's Republic of China on October 1, 1949, finished one turbulent chapter in Chinese history and began another. The fall of the Qing, growing incursion by foreign countries, and the devastation of World War II sandwiched between two periods of bloody civil war gave way to purges of the country's artists and intellectuals, increasing isolationism, the colossal failure of the Great Leap Forward, and the tragic chaos of the Cultural Revolution.

The last quarter century has been characterized by relative stability and growth. Since the late 1970s the sole power holder in the People's Republic of China, the Chinese Communist Party, has brought hundreds of millions out of poverty and significantly relaxed its iron grip on personal freedoms. Diplomatically, Beijing has also become an increasingly savvy power broker on the global stage, while Western powers have been distracted by war and economic woes.

The party has no shortage of challenges that threaten its mandate to rule, including widespread corruption, an increasingly vocal and media-savvy populace, environmental disasters, and a widening wealth gap.

### Economy

China is undergoing the greatest economic expansion the world has ever seen, with the country now the world's most important producer and consumer of just about everything. Since the launch of Paramount Leader Deng Xiaoping's reform and open policy in 1978, the Middle Kingdom has experienced roughly 10% annual GDP growth and has become the world's sec-

ond-largest economy, trailing only that of the United States (for now).

China's coastal region was the early beneficiary of economic reforms, with cities such as Shanghai, Beijing, Shenzhen, and Guangzhou powering an export-focused economic model. Today the story is the awakening of markets in second- and third-tier cities as the country moves toward a consumption-driven economy.

### Media

The media in China has primarily served as a government mouthpiece since 1949. Since 1999 the Internet has not only provided Chinese people with greater access to information, it has also given rise to "Netizens," Chinese who use the Internet to voice their concerns and displeasures with modern society.

Beijing's attempts to manage the Internet have drawn much criticism beyond China's borders, but that hasn't stopped the Internet from becoming a part of daily life for more and more Chinese. With more than 457 million people regularly going online, China is the world's largest Internet market.

Government attempts to control the Internet have caused some of the world's biggest companies to pull out of the country or be blocked. Google made headlines in 2010, when it shut down its Beijing operations and redirected traffic to its Hong Kong site. Sites including Facebook and Twitter were blocked in 2009, presumably owing to government concerns about the potential for social media to be used in organizing anti-government activities.

### Religion

Officially an atheist country, China is home to large numbers of Buddhists, Muslims, Christians, and Taoists. Until recently, practicing any religion could lead

to detention or worse, but now the country's temples, mosques, and churches are active once more—although the watchful eye of the government is never far away.

Despite its general increasing tolerance toward religion, the Chinese government has taken strong measures against groups that it considers a threat to its rule, most notably the Falun Gong, which it considered a cult and banned in 2000. Buddhists in Tibet and Uighur Muslims in Xinjiang have also clashed with police and soldiers in recent years, leading to heightened tension in those regions.

### Sports

Despite its Olympic success, China has not been able to develop popular homegrown sports leagues. Men's soccer is seen as one of the country's biggest disappointments—China's national team has only once qualified for the World Cup. The national soccer league is riddled with corruption and empty seats, with most Chinese preferring to watch European matches.

Basketball is also extremely popular in China—even remote mountaintop villages have a court or two. In the late 1990s NBA games began to be broadcast on the mainland, to the delight of sports fans. Everyone from kids to grandparents seemed to have a Chicago Bulls cap, and Michael Jordan was as recognizable as Bill Clinton. Today Kobe Bryant and a new generation of stars are being emulated by Chinese streetballers, and many former NBA players are finding second careers in the Chinese Basketball Association.

### Sexual Mores

China is often thought of as a sexually conservative country, but you don't get to be the world's most populous country by being a bunch of prudes. Over the centuries Chinese society has seen it all, from polygamy to prostitutes, from eunuchs to transvestite actors.

Premarital sex in China may be discouraged, but young Chinese all over the country are engaging in sex, whether it be with a steady boyfriend or girlfriend or a drunken one-night stand. Public displays of affection in broad daylight aren't commonplace, but also not unheard-of.

Part and parcel with China's economic development has been the return of prostitution. More often than not, Chinese hotels will have on-site prostitution, and the odd international five-star occasionally gets busted for offering "special services" to guests. Officially discouraged by the government, it is generally understood that prostitution is a major contributor to China's "gray GDP."

Homosexuality was officially considered a mental illness in China until 2001—since then the country has become considerably more accepting of gays, lesbians, and transgendered individuals. These days nearly every major city has a few gay bars, and even straight Chinese take fashion cues from their homosexual "comrades"—a handful of the country's biggest celebrities are effeminate men or boyish women.

Sexual relations between Chinese and foreigners are generally accepted, but there is occasional friction or unpleasantness. On the short end of China's gender-imbalance stick, some Chinese men resent socially active foreign men and the Chinese women who date them. On the flip side of that coin, a Chinese man who is dating a foreign woman is often hailed as a stud.

# FLAVORS OF CHINA

Chinese cuisine spans the entire spectrum of flavors, ingredients, and cooking styles. Almost every city or town is known for at least one or two specialty dishes. Wheat is the staple of choice in China's dry north, but in the wet south rice is favored. Most large Chinese cities offer a bit of everything from around the country, plus lots of local specialties. There's plenty of delicious street food out there—hygiene levels can vary, so look for stalls with a long line of locals and make sure your food is cooked while you're waiting.

## Vegetables and Tofu

Vegetables are usually a part of any Chinese meal, with most varieties common to Western countries available—plus many that aren't, such as bitter melon or morning glory. Cold dishes such as pickled radishes or cucumber chunks in garlic and vinegar are a common way to start off a meal. Hot vegetable dishes can take on all forms. Many, especially leafy greens, are often simply chopped and stir-fried with just a bit of seasoning. Where you are in China often affects the cooking method of your favorite veggie. If you're hungry for potatoes in Harbin, they may be cooked with green pepper and eggplant in a red sauce, whereas in Yunnan, spicy mashed potatoes, crispy hash browns, and even potato and pumpkin soup are more common. Tofu, known in China as *doufu*, is available in a wide variety of shapes, sizes, and colors. Firm white tofu is commonly eaten in the Sichuanese style—bathed in a spicy and numbing sauce—but it is also served in soups with spinach or other greens. More adventurous eaters might try tofu with preserved eggs. Tofu skin (*doufu pi*) is a byproduct of normal tofu production, and contains fewer impurities. It can be stir-fried with peppers or mushrooms, and is a popular

ingredient for cooking in hotpot. Vegetarians traveling in China should keep in mind that many restaurants will add small amounts of pork, ham, oyster sauce, or other non-veggie items to seemingly vegetarian dishes, including tofu. Make sure you emphasize no meat whatsoever when ordering to maximize the chance of getting what you want.

## Meat

Chinese cuisine features nearly every type of meat imaginable—nothing is too strange to consume, and there are no prohibitions on consumption of certain animals. Dog, bullfrog, rabbit, and snake are perfectly ordinary ingredients, as are all varieties of organs, including kidneys, liver, ears, and even penises. Pork and chicken are the most popular meats. Beef is also commonly consumed, but lamb tends to be found mainly only in Muslim dishes. It's difficult to find Western-style large chunks of meat—shredded, sliced, or cubed, it all comes small and chopstick-ready. Chicken is often cooked on the bone. In Beijing, Peking duck is a specialty that can't be missed—wrap it in pancakes with scallions and dip it in tangy sauce. Dishes from the predominantly Muslim northwest feature hearty stews, usually with lamb or chicken. Sichuan cuisine, while too spicy for some, features some great meat dishes, including the accessible kung pao chicken. In Yunnan, the local ham is famous, and works great adding flavor to fried vegetable dishes. Iron plate beef (*tieban niurou*) is a popular fajita-style dish that can be found countrywide, and features strips of beef cooked with onion and green pepper in gravy, served on an iron hot plate. If you're into street snacks, slender kebabs of barbecued meat can be found for sale across the country, usually flavored with chili and cumin.

Yunnan takes this a step further—the province is known for its night stalls selling all manner of skewered treats.

### Seafood

Fish holds a special place in Chinese cuisine—it's both a status dish and an auspicious symbol. Any banquet celebrating a festival or a special occasion will feature a fish. The fish is usually cooked and served whole, swimming in soy sauce with a dressing of scallions. In the seafaring south, superstitious eaters never turn the fish over, but eat "through" it. The quality and variety of seafood is much better on China's coast, but it is consumed countrywide, with farmed fish keeping inland diners happy. Most river or lake fish should be avoided, owing to pollution issues.

Seafood is kept alive as long as possible to preserve freshness, so don't be surprised to find yourself choosing your ingredients from tanks at the front of the restaurant or watching your fish being killed in front of you. Given this extra difficulty when ordering, Hong Kong is a great place to eat seafood. All manner of shellfish are on the menu, from expensive abalone to simple clams. Generally cooking styles are simple, and focus on the flavor of the ingredients. Some diners may find shellfish less well cooked than they are used to. Shrimp is usually served with the shells on.

Shark-fin soup is one of the most expensive delicacies to be found in China, and is often served to esteemed guests or at important business banquets. Many Chinese are unaware of the massive negative impact the harvesting of shark fins is having on the oceanic ecosystem. Prior to an expensive banquet, you may want to tell your host that you do not eat shark-fin soup for environmental reasons—this can save you the social awkwardness of refusing it when it is placed before you.

### Staple foods

As noted earlier, China's staple foods are split along a north-south divide, but that doesn't mean that people in the north don't eat rice and southerners don't enjoy a bowl of wheat noodles.

Wheat is the primary grain grown in China's north, and wheat flour is used in making a wide variety of noodles as well as dumplings, breads, and pancakes. *Lamian*—wheat noodles made fresh by an entertaining process of stretching, swinging, and smacking wheat dough— are one of the most popular noodles in China. Lanzhou-style lamian are available almost anywhere in China, and are typically served in a mutton broth with green onions and sprigs of cilantro. Stir-fried noodles (*chaomian*) are also popular, and can be made with virtually any ingredient. Xinjiang cuisine features some of the most delicious noodles found in China, ranging from chunks of diced noodles to long, flat, wide noodles and everything in between. Dumplings are a popular wheat-based staple, and can be a meal on their own. They can be prepared by boiling, steaming, or boiling and then pan-frying. Steamed buns with filling (*baozi*) or without (*mantou*) are often eaten for breakfast. Steamed rice is most commonly eaten white, with other dishes piled on top of it, but many people enjoy it stir-fried with any imaginable combination of vegetables, egg, meats or seafood. Rice noodles can be found throughout southern China, from fat spaghetti-like *mixian* to fettucine-style *fen*, to *fensi*, a transparent noodle that resembles vermicelli.

# FAQ

### Will I need a visa?
Yes! Most foreign nationals traveling to China must have an entry visa. These visas are not issued upon arrival. Americans are currently charged a flat rate of $140 per visa, regardless of duration. Tourist visas vary in length from 30 days to six months, and allow for one or multiple entries over the course of their validity. The number of entries and length of stay are up to you when you fill out the application. Applications can be completed in person if you live in a city with a Chinese consulate. If not, there are many visa service centers available online that will process your application. Fees may vary, so shop around and check the Better Business Bureau if you have any questions regarding legitimacy.

### What's the best way to get around?
Domestic airline services connecting cities in China have increased greatly in the past decade, and even smaller out-of-the-way cities have small airports. If you have more time, train travel is also an option. The country is crisscrossed by one of the world's most extensive railway systems, and train travel is one way to get a feel for the vastness of China. Often it is also cheaper than flying, and is very dependable. China has converted several lines between major metropolises into high-speed (or bullet) train routes. Bus routes between cities are also well established, and in rural areas are often the only way to travel between small towns. Car rental is becoming more popular, but you must first obtain a Chinese driver's license, a time-consuming and convoluted process, or also hire a driver.

### Should I take a package tour?
If you are traveling to China to see only the major tourist attractions, or are very concerned about the language differences, a package tour is the answer. However, if your travel plans allow for improvisation or you want to stray a bit off the beaten path, skip the tours. Part of the adventure of traveling is exploring the unknown, and with most packages you will be with other tourists and have little say in where you stay or eat, or how long you have to view a specific site. Also, once in China you can find any number of small tours that last from an afternoon to a few days and will help tailor your trip so it is uniquely your own.

### How big is the language barrier?
For the uninitiated, Chinese can be very intimidating. The language is tonal, has no alphabet, and regional dialects vary widely. Learning a few phrases in Mandarin Chinese before you go helps tremendously. Nonetheless, interest in learning English is a national phenomenon in China, and schoolchildren are all taught English from the first grade. Tourist destinations and other places catering to foreigners will usually have at least one designated English speaker. You may even be assisted by random locals who want to practice their language skills.

### Are any subjects off-limits?
As anywhere, be respectful. The Chinese are gregarious and curious, and you may be surprised at what they think about the rest of the world. There is no one subject that is strictly forbidden or generally considered offensive, but you may want to speak cautiously when discussing touchy subjects like religious tolerance, Tibet, or Xinjiang.

### Will my bankcard work at Chinese ATMs?

Banks in China are ubiquitous, and most ATMs accept cards with the Cirrus or Plus logos. Those with Visa or MasterCard logos are also widely accepted. This is true even in rural areas, especially if they are accustomed to foreign travelers passing through. That said, in more remote places the Bank of China is more reliable than smaller local banks. ATMs usually have an option for directions in English. If you encounter a machine with no English or that won't accept your card, chances are the bank around the corner will be more helpful.

### Can I use my credit cards?

Resorts and major hotels accept credit cards, but for daily purchases like food and drink or souvenir shopping, it's best to use cash. Credit-card use is growing in China, but is by no means widespread.

### Can I drink the water?

No. Tap water in China can contain any number of chemicals and/or parasites that can quickly ruin your vacation. In major cities some hotels have begun to install water-filtration systems, but even these are questionable. Although it can be cumbersome to carry with you, bottled water is sold cheaply everywhere and remains the most reliable option. The boiled water or hot tea that is served in restaurants or available in your hotel room is also considered safe.

### Are the toilets as bad as I've heard?

They can be. Bathrooms in hotels generally should be clean and well maintained, and many have Western-style toilets instead of the typical Asian "squat" toilet. Restrooms in restaurants, train stations, and other public places range from clean to abysmal, so be prepared. In rural areas you can often expect the worst. When going out for the day, it is always a good idea to take some toilet paper and perhaps baby wipes or hand sanitizer. Public toilets on the street charge a small admission fee, so keep some small change with you.

### Should I bring any medications?

The Centers for Disease Control recommend updating your usual vaccinations and visiting a doctor or clinic that specializes in travel medicine four to six weeks before traveling to China. Of course, if you have a daily medication regime, plan accordingly. An anti-diarrhea medication may be a lifesaver, especially on long bus rides or train journeys. Also, if you suffer from motion sickness you may want to bring the proper medicine from home.

### Can I trust Chinese hospitals?

For minor injuries, bumps or bruises, and general maladies like colds or flu, Chinese hospitals are reliable, though often not up to Western standards of hygiene. Major cities usually have both Western and traditional Chinese-style hospitals, but rural areas generally have fewer medical options. Travel insurance providing medical evacuation services is highly recommended in case of serious injury or illness, and is both inexpensive and readily available.

### Should I be concerned about crime?

Violent crime against foreigners is almost unheard of in China. However, petty theft can be a worry when traveling on long-distance buses and trains or when staying at small guesthouses. Always keep your money, passport, and anything else you consider vital on your person when traveling, and be vigilant in crowded places.

# GREAT ITINERARIES

## INTRODUCTION

Stretching over 3,100 miles from east to west, China is an enormous country with wildly varied geography, ranging from the mist-wrapped peaks of Huang Shan in the east to the dusty Tarim Basin in the northwest, one of the lowest points on earth. To get around this vast country you'll need plenty of patience and a good sense of humor. With the development of high-speed trains, it's now easy to zip between major cities like Beijing and Shanghai, but travel to more distant destinations is generally slower and more unpredictable. Domestic flights can get you almost anywhere, though they are often more expensive than other options. Whether traveling by plane, train, or bus, it's good to book ahead, especially during Chinese New Year, when you are competing for tickets with 1.3 billion people on the move.

### Lay of the Land
#### Beijing to Shanghai

Once home to emperors, China's capital city of Beijing presides over the heavily industrialized northeast. Hyper-modern Shanghai is halfway down China's prosperous east coast and is iconic for its architecture and fashion. Suzhou lies within an arm's reach from Shanghai and is famous for its classical gardens and unique stone bridges. Upriver from Shanghai on the banks of the Yangtze, you'll find the ancient city of Nanjing, once China's southern capital. The lofty peaks of Huang Shan, only a few hours by train from Nanjing, are a wonderful place to take refuge from the summer heat.

#### East Coast

Zhejiang is China's wealthiest province. Hangzhou, surrounded by forested hills and tea plantations, is most famous for its lovely West Lake and is a wonderful place for a biking excursion. Nestled within the Yangtze Delta, the province also has a number of charming restored waterways and villages waiting to be explored. Rugged, mountainous Fujian boasts verdant tea fields, ancient Hakka roundhouses, and unspoiled beaches. On the coast, prosperous Xiamen is worth exploring for its colonial architecture.

#### Hong Kong and the Pearl River Delta

Guangzhou, in Guangdong province, is a noisy, crowded metropolis and the heart of the Pearl River Delta. Scratch the surface of its frenetic exterior and you'll find a thriving art scene, fabulous food, and a rich cultural history. On the border of Hong Kong, Shenzhen is a young, fast-paced city known as much for shopping as for factories. Colorful, vibrant Hong Kong is a not-to-be-missed hodgepodge of steel and glass skyscrapers, open-air markets, luxury boutiques, and traditional temples.

#### The Southwest

The dramatic karst peaks and winding rivers of Guilin and Yangshuo in Guangxi province grace so many postcards of China. Lush mountains dotted with villages surround Guiyang, Guizhou's capital. Kunming, the capital of Yunnan, is also home to many of China's ethnic groups and boasts some of the most stunning topography in China, ranging from the sweltering jungles of the Mekong Delta in the south to the dramatic snow-capped mountains of the Tibetan Plateau in the west. The province shares road connections with neighboring Myanmar and Laos and is linked by rail to Vietnam.

**1**

### Sichuan and Chongqing

Southwestern Sichuan province, known as the "rice bowl" of China, includes the fertile Sichuan basin and is considered the country's agricultural heartland. Its capital, Chengdu, is the financial hub of the southwest, and its many rail and bus connections link eastern and western China. Outside of Chengdu is the Buddhist holy mountain of Emeishan, famous not only for its temples but also its unruly golden monkeys. In the very center of China sits hilly Chongqing, or "Mountain City," and the best place to hop on a Three Gorges cruise along the Yangtze.

### The Silk Road

In northwest China is Xi'an, long-ago capital of the Tang dynasty. Once the most cosmopolitan city in the world, Xi'an was the terminus of the eastern Silk Road. The emblematic Terracotta Warriors are now its most famous attraction. The Mogao Caves of Gansu offer a glimpse into the most important Buddhist pilgrimage site along the Silk Road. Sweeping deserts and plains make up the Xinjiang Autonomous Region, China's largest province. Xinjiang is home to the Uyghurs, a large Muslim minority. Its capital city, Ürümqi, is an excellent place to launch explorations into the desert or westwards to the ancient Silk Road city of Kashgar.

### Tibet

With its stunning snowcapped peaks, picturesque river valleys, and magnificent palaces and temples, Tibet has long-conjured up romantic visions of a windswept mountain kingdom, pristine and inaccessible. In reality, the Tibetan Autonomous Region is undergoing a massive infrastructure overhaul, and the Lhasa-Beijing railway has made it much easier to reach the Roof of the World. In Lhasa, dramatic Potala

Palace is a central attraction, along with the Bhakor pilgrimage circuit. If you're looking to get off the beaten path, you can arrange for four-wheel-drive vehicles and guides to take trips further afield to Gyantse and onwards to Everest. As this was written, Tibet was largely closed to foreigners because of political unrest.

### Timing

Because China is so vast, the best time to visit depends on where you are traveling. In general, the most comfortable times of year are in spring or fall to avoid extreme temperatures. Summers can be unbearably hot and humid, with drenching rain and flooding. Winters in the north are bitterly cold. Whatever season you go, don't travel during the rush of peak holiday times, especially the first week of October and May and during Chinese New Year.

## BEIJING AND THE SILK ROAD (14 DAYS)

This journey covers the best of ancient China. Visit Beijing's historic sites and climb the Great Wall before embarking along the fabled Silk Road to Xi'an, once the capital of the Tang dynasty, and beyond to the remote desert towns of Dunhuang, Turpan, and Ürümqi.

### Day 1: Welcome to Beijing

Beijing is the cultural heart of China and the nation's top travel destination. Check into the impeccable Kapok Hotel, a short walk from the Forbidden City and close to Tiananmen Square, where you can watch the daily flag-raising ceremony at dawn. After the flag raising, take a stroll around the square and soak in the atmosphere. And of course, a tour of the Forbidden City is an essential Beijing experience. Finish your day with a traditional feast at the

Li Qun Roast Duck Restaurant, Beijing's most popular spot for Peking duck.

### Day 2: The Great Wall
*(Excursion will take approximately 8 hours, either by private car or tour bus)*

When visiting Beijing, a trip to the Great Wall is a must. Most tours run to the more commercial Badaling, but the best places to see the Wall are further afield at Mutianyu, Simatai, or Jinshaling. Tour buses congregate around Tiananmen Square, or you could book a private tour or hire a car and driver.

### Day 3: Jewels of the Empire

Beijing is dotted with numerous imperial palaces and pleasure gardens. Take a taxi to the city's northwestern reaches to visit the lovely Summer Palace, which has come to symbolize the decadence that brought about the fall of the Qing Dynasty. The Temple of Heaven is considered to be the perfect example of Ming Dynasty architecture, and is a great place to take a break from the frenetic pace of the capital. For dinner, try a savory bowl of traditional hand-pulled noodles at Old Beijing Noodle King, a short walk from the Temple of Heaven.

### Day 4: Capital Entertainment

Beijing teems with cultural performances, fabulous restaurants, and sprawling outdoor markets. Spend the day hunting for souvenirs at Beijing Curio City or the Silk Alley Market in the Chaoyang district. In the evening, music enthusiasts will want to take in a glass-shattering performance of Beijing Opera. For dinner, head to elegant Mei Fu, on the south side of Houhai Lake. The restaurant serves delicious set meals in a restored Beijing courtyard.

### Days 5–8: Xi'an, China's Ancient Capital
*(2 hours by plane from Beijing; 12 hours by train from Beijing's West Rail Station)*

For most of China's history, Xi'an was the nation's capital. As the eastern terminus of the Silk Road, the area is packed with historically significant destinations, most of which can be covered in just a few days. For convenience, head to Xi'an's Old City and check yourself into the Ibis Xi'an, which has simple but comfortable rooms. Your first day should be spent visiting Xi'an's most popular attractions, including the Bell Tower and Big Wild Goose Pagoda. Make sure to attend the Tang Dynasty dinner theater, which serves imperial cuisine and acrobatic shows every evening.

Devote your next day to visiting the Terracotta Warriors Museum, east of Xi'an. The famous warriors, built to protect China's first emperor in the afterlife, are part of a huge tomb complex that stretches for miles. If you have the time, we also recommend a day trip to the spectacular peaks of Hua Shan. To get to either of these sites, book a tour or catch a public bus.

### Days 9–10: Dunhuang
*(3 hours by plane from Xi'an; 22 hours by train from Xi'an)*

Once the border between China and the unknown barbarian lands to the west, Dunhuang was also a major stop for merchants and religious pilgrims traveling the Silk Road. Filled with more than 1,000 years of Buddhist carvings, the Mogao Grottoes are widely considered to be the best surviving example of early religious art in China. The Feitian Hotel is the most convenient place to stay in Dunhuang. The night market is packed with stands

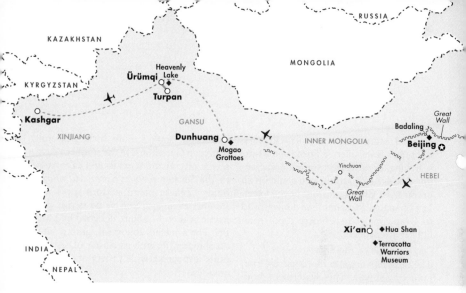

selling grilled kebabs, lamb burgers, and other tasty snacks.

## Days 11–14: Ürümqi and Turpan

*(1 hour by plane from Dunhuang; 15 hours by train from Dunhuang)*

Xinjiang is China's vast western frontier, where the pagodas and temples of the East melt into the bazaars and minarets of Central Asia. The capital city of Ürümqi has enough attractions to keep you occupied for a day or so, but for a real taste of the region you'll want to head out to the countryside. The popular Hoi Tak Hotel near People's Square is an excellent place to plan your excursions into Xinjiang. For Uyghur dishes like pilaf and lamb dumplings, head to the Horma Restaurant in the International Grand Bazaar.

Three hours by bus from Ürümqi is Heavenly Lake, perhaps the most beautiful body of water in the whole country. It's possible to stay in a yurt with a Kazakh family and go horseback riding in the surrounding mountains.

Another three hours by bus from Ürümqi is the small city of Turpan, which provides a fascinating look into the Silk Road history that once defined the area and the Uighur minority way of life that dominates today. The Turpan Hotel has basic rooms and a decent restaurant serving up

noodles and grilled lamb. Make sure to see the ruins of Jiaohe and Gaochang, two ancient desert cities. If you have time, head even farther west to Kashgar, closer to Baghdad than Beijing in both distance and culture.

# SHANGHAI AND THE CHINESE HEARTLAND (11–14 DAYS)

Eastern China is a showcase of China's amazingly diverse topography. Journey from the glittering skyscrapers of Shanghai to the wilds of Huang Shan and the Yangtze River. Because of the distances covered, it's suggested to fly some legs of this trip to save time.

## Day 1: Welcome to Shanghai

Shanghai is all about the country's future, not its past. Catch the ultrafast train from the airport to the city center. The most convenient place for hotels is the neighborhood of Puxi, which includes the Former French Concession, close to most of Shanghai's most popular attractions. Stay in the charming Old House Inn, a small boutique hotel near Jing'an Park. After checking in, explore some of Shanghai's fascinating colonial history by foot or taxi. Walk through Xintiandi, where restored traditional houses mix with bars, boutiques, and galleries. Spend some time searching for the perfect souvenir on Nanjing Road. Alternatively, you could brush up on your Chinese history at the excellent Shanghai Museum. For dinner, head to Grape for great Chinese food in an upbeat atmosphere.

### Day 2: Paris of the East

The next day explore the Bund by foot, taxi, or subway. This waterfront boulevard is the city's best spot for people-watching and culinary exploration. For a bird's-eye view of China's sprawling economic capital, head across the Huangpu River to Pudong, where you can mount the Oriental Pearl Tower, the Jinmao Tower, or the Shanghai World Financial Center, also known as the "Bottle Opener." There's also Yu Garden, where you can relax amid meticulous landscaping and traditional architecture. In the alleys round Yu Garden are many local restaurants serving terrific food in unpretentious surroundings. Within the complex itself is the well-known Lv Bo Lang, a favorite of celebrities and dignitaries. Reservations are necessary.

### Days 3–4: Suzhou and Zhouzhuang

*(Suzhou is 35 minutes by high-speed train from Shanghai; Zhouzhuang is 1½ hours by bus from Suzhou)*

Regarded in ancient times as heaven on earth, Suzhou retains many of its charms despite the encroaching forces of modernization. Stroll through elegant gardens and temples along the gently flowing branches of the Grand Canal.

Suzhou is close enough to work well as a day trip from Shanghai. but it's highly recommended to spend the night and catch a bus the next day to Zhouzhuang, a restored water village. If you're staying

in Suzhou, book a room at the peaceful Nanyuan Guesthouse in the southern part of the city. A quick walk will take you to the Master of Nets Gardens, which holds Chinese opera performances on summer evenings. Not far by taxi is the iconic Suzhou Museum, designed by I.M. Pei. For a memorable meal, grab a bite on Shiquan Jie, with its cluster of restaurants featuring a wide variety of Chinese cuisines.

After two days spent exploring Suzhou and Zhouzhuang, take the train back to Shanghai where you can catch a plane to Huang Shan.

### Days 5–8: Huang Shan

*(1 hour by plane from Shanghai to Tunxi)*

One of China's best-known natural wonders, Huang Shan (Yellow Mountain) is a breathtaking range of 72 jagged peaks punctuated by fantastically twisted pine trees and unusual rock formations. Tunxi, or Huang Shan City, is about 40 miles from Huang Shan. After landing in Tunxi, hire a taxi or take a minibus to Tangkou at the base of the mountain. There are numerous ways to the top, either on foot or by cable car. Spend a night at the Baiyun Hotel, one of the mountaintop guesthouses, before waking at dawn to watch the sun rise over an eerie sea of fog.

After visiting Huang Shan, the quickest way to continue on to the Three Gorges is to return to Shanghai where you can catch a flight onwards to Yichang, in Hubei province.

### Days 9–13: Yichang and The Three Gorges

*(2 hours by plane from Shanghai to Yichang)*

A cruise along the Yangtze River through the Three Gorges is an unforgettable

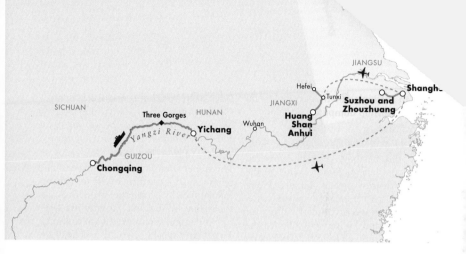

experience. Along the way you'll pass over abandoned metropolises that were humming with life only a few years ago, as well as their modern counterparts that were built on higher ground. One recommended cruise line is Victoria Cruises, which offers a range of excursions up and down the Yangtze.

The town of Yichang sits at the eastern entrance of the Three Gorges. Cruises will sail through the Gezhou Dam and offer excursions to the Three Gorges Dam site, Fengdu, or "Ghost City," and the Little Three Gorges before disembarking at Chongqing.

#### Day 14: Chongqing
*(5 days by boat from Yichang)*

After finishing a cruise along the Yangtze, Chongqing has enough to recommend a day or two of exploration. Built into the side of a hill, the city is a maze of steep stairways, hills and tunnels. Most of the main tourist sites and hotels are located around the Jiefang Bei area. The convenient Howard Johnson ITC Plaza offers plush rooms and an excellent restaurant. After settling in, walk to 18 Steps, one of the most curious attractions in Chongqing. Not to be missed is a ride in a cable car, where you are treated to a bird's-eye view of the Yangtze and the sprawling city

below. For traditional Sichuan cuisine, head to Xiaotian'e Sichuan Restaurant on the banks of the Yangtze to indulge in hotpot and other fiery specialties.

## SOUTHERN CHINA (15–18 DAYS)

With its lush geography, karst limestone peaks, and rich cultures, a visit to southern China offers opportunities to witness the country's incredible natural and ethnic diversity. Begin your trip in fast-paced Hong Kong before heading further south to the gorgeous backcountry of Guangxi, Guizhou, and Yunnan.

#### Day 1: Welcome to Hong Kong

Despite the city's return to Chinese rule in 1997, Hong Kong still feels a world away from the mainland. Get settled in at the Lan Kwai Fong Hotel with its amazing harbor views. When you're rested, take a ride on the Star Ferry connecting Hong Kong Island with Kowloon. Don't miss the smoke-filled Man Mo Temple and Hong Kong's famous assortment of antiques shops and art galleries. Ride the very steep tram to the summit of Victoria Peak, with views of the entire harbor. Try evening dim sum at the legendary Tim

*Yellow Sea*

e coconut cream
ngs are superb.

## Day 2: Get... the City
*(30 minutes by express ferry to Lantau)*

While the business districts clustered around the harbor feature some of the world's densest urban jungle, Hong Kong also has a relaxed natural side. Lantau Island is a favorite of visitors for its beaches and hiking trails. Board the ferry at the Outlying Islands Ferry Pier on Hong Kong Island. Arriving at the town of Mui Wo, you can catch a bus to the island's top two attractions: Po Lin Monastery, featuring the world's tallest outdoor bronze statue of Buddha, and Tai O, an old fishing village dotted with terrific seafood restaurants. For even greater solitude, take the ferry to one of the smaller Outer Islands.

## Day 3: Macau
*(1 hour by TurboJet from Hong Kong)*

Even with a recent push to become Asia's Las Vegas, Macau is still decidedly quieter and more traditional than Hong Kong. The slower pace of development has left much of the city's colonial charm intact. Start with a visit to Largo do Senado (Senate Square), paved with Portuguese-style tiles and surrounded by brightly colored colonial buildings. The city is home to two beautiful churches, São Domingos and São Paulo, the latter featuring exhibits on the early history of Asian Christianity. If you plan to stay overnight, the Altira Macau has breathtaking ocean views. For flavorful Macanese dishes like steamed crab and clams stewed in beer, A Lorcha restaurant is highly recommended.

## Days 4–8: Yangshuo and Longsheng
*(1½ hour flight from Hong Kong to Guilin; 90-minute bus ride or 4-hour boat ride from Guilin to Yangshuo; 3 hours by bus from Guilin to Longsheng)*

The scenery in northern Guangxi is some of the most beautiful in all of China. Enchanted by dramatic groupings of sheer limestone karst mountains, visitors often find themselves loath to leave. To get to Yangshuo, you'll first head to Guilin, where you'll have a choice of taking the bus or the more scenic four-hour Li River Cruise. Once in Yangshuo, the Giggling Tree is an excellent base for exploring natural sites like Green Lotus Peak and Moon Hill. For meals, join the backpackers at Kelly's Place for beer and dumplings. Head back through Guilin to the town of Longsheng, home to the famously photogenic Dragon's Backbone Rice Terraces before returning to Guilin.

## Days 9–14: Northwest Yunnan
*(2–2½ hour flight from Guilin to Dali or Lijiang with connection in Kunming)*

Sandwiched between the Tibetan Plateau and Myanmar, this area has long attracted foreigners with its mix of minority cultures and stunning natural beauty. Dali, beside the waters of Erhai Lake, is home to the Bai people, who settled here 4,000 years ago; the elegant Three Pagodas north of town is one of China's most iconic images. For a unique experience, book a room at the Yunnan Inn, owned by Chinese artist Fang Lijun. Pancakes and decent coffee at Café de Jack will fill you up before heading out to explore Dali's scenic Old Town. A three-hour bus ride north of Dali lies Lijiang, home of the Naxi people. The East River Hotel offers a tranquil location and is close to Mishi for

grilled yak meat and beer. The highlight of the region is Tiger Leaping Gorge, one of the deepest river gorges in the world and a popular two-day hike.

### Day 15–18: Chengdu
*(1½ hour flight from Dali to Chengdu)*

As the capital of Sichuan Province, Chengdu has long been one of China's great cultural centers. Famous for its spicy cuisine, the city also manages to maintain a pleasant atmosphere of yesteryear. Stay at the elegant Minshan Fandian in the center of town near People's Park. A quick taxi ride away is the remarkable Buddhist Wenshu Monastery, known for its peaceful tea gardens. For animal lovers, take a bus 45 minutes out of town to the Giant Panda Breeding Research Base. If you crave authentic Sichuan hotpot, Shijing Shenghuo brings the fire. No matter how little time you have available, make the three-hour bus trip south to Leshan to see the world's largest stone-carved Buddha. With toes the size of a small bus, the seated Grand Buddha is impressive, to say the least.

# PEOPLE OF CHINA

People often think of China as an ancient, monolithic culture comprised of a single, massive group of genetically similar people. In actuality, China contains a rich mosaic of different cultures and ethnicities, and officially recognizes 56 distinct ethnic groups. Ranging from populations of a few thousand to 1.2 billion, each group has made a unique contribution to China's cultural diversity with its language, costume, cuisine, philosophies, and traditions.

The largest of these groups is the Han people, who make up more than 90 percent of China's total population and around one-fifth of all humanity. They trace their origins to the Yellow River region, and take their name from the Han Dynasty, which was established in 206 BC. The Han have had the biggest impact on China's history, and every major dynasty but two—the Yuan and the Qing—has been Han.

Most of Eastern and Central China is dominated by the Han, with the outlying regions a fascinating stir-fry of people and cultures. Mountainous Yunnan Province in the country's southwest is home to the largest variety of ethnic groups, with some like the Jinuo and Pumi found nowhere else. Tibetans, Naxi, Bai, Yi, and Lisu are major ethnic groups found in the highlands of northwest Yunnan. In southern Yunnan, near the borders with Laos and Vietnam, there are ethnic Dai, Hani, and Miao, who have more in common with Southeast Asia than northern China.

The Mongols and Manchus are the two Chinese ethnic groups that can claim to have ruled the Han. Kublai Khan founded the Yuan Dynasty in 1271, but keeping control over China and other territories proved too much for the Mongols, and the dynasty was finished just under a century later. Today Mongols in China are primarily found in Inner Mongolia in the country's north, where many still live nomadic lives on the grasslands.

The Qing Dynasty of the Manchus had more staying power, running from 1644 to 1912 and producing several notable emperors. Under Qing rule Han Chinese adopted some Manchu customs, including the long braids worn by men and the disfigurement and binding of women's feet. Most Manchus in China live in the northeastern provinces of Jilin, Liaoning, and Heilongjiang.

Tibetans—known for their unique brand of Buddhism—are the best-known ethnic group inhabiting China's more rugged geography, but there are plenty of others. The Muslim Uighurs of Xinjiang in northwest China are more numerous than Tibetans, and are related to modern-day Turks—some Uighurs have blonde hair and green eyes.

Outside of China, few people know of the Zhuang people, but they are China's second-largest ethnic group. The Zhuang speak a language related to Thai, and are primarily found in Guangxi, which is officially an "autonomous region" and ruled by the Zhuang, at least in theory.

The Hui are China's largest Muslim group, and are known for being skilled businesspeople—not a big surprise, considering that they are descended from Silk Road traders. Of China's minorities, the Hui are the most widely dispersed—Hui-run Muslim restaurants can be found in virtually every city or large town. The Miao people are spread across Southern China, and are typically found in mountain villages.

Terracotta soldiers

# THE AGE OF EMPIRES

When asked his opinion on the historical impact of the French Revolution, Chairman Mao quipped, "It's too early to tell." Though a bit tongue in cheek, China does measure its history in millennia, and in its grand timeline, interactions with the West have been mere blips.

According to historical records, Chinese civilization stretches back to the 15th century BC—markings found on turtle shells carbon dated to around 1500BC bear some similarity to modern Chinese script. China then resembled city-states rather than a unified nation. Iconic figures such as Lao Tzu (the father of Taoism), Sun Tzu (author of the Art of War), and Confucius lived during this period. Generally, 221BC is accepted as the beginning of Imperial China, when the city-states united under various banners.

Over the next 2,200 years (give or take a few), China alternated between periods of harmony and political upheaval. Its armies conquered new territory and were in turn conquered by external invaders (most of whom wound up themselves being assimilated).

By the early 18th century, the long, slow decline of the Qing—the last of China's Imperial dynasties—was already in progress, making the ancient nation ripe for exploitation by rising European powers. The Imperial era ended with the forced abdication of child Emperor Puyi (whose life is chronicled in Bernardo Bertolucci's The Last Emperor), and it's here that the history of modern China, first with the founding of the republic under Sun Yat-sen and then with the establishment of the People's Republic under Mao Zedong, truly begins.

Writing Appears

1500BC 1200BC 900BC

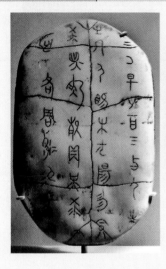

(left) Oracle shell with early Chinese characters. (top, right) The Great Wall stretches 4,163 miles from east to west. (bottom, right) Confucius, Lao-tzu, and a Buddhist Arhat.

## circa 1500 BC — Writing Appears

The earliest accounts of Chinese history are still shrouded in myth and legend, and it wasn't until 1959 that stories were verified by archaeological findings. For millennia, people formed communities in the fertile lands of what is now central China. The first recorded Chinese characters are said to have been developed 3,500 years ago. Though sometimes referred to as the Shang Dynasty, this period was more of a precursor to modern Chinese dynasties than a truly unified kingdom.

## 722–475 BC — The Warring States Period

China was so far from unified that these centuries are collectively remembered as the Warring States Period. As befitting such a contentious time, military science progressed, iron replaced bronze, and weapons material improved. Some of China's greatest luminaries lived during this period, including the father of Taoism, Lao-tzu, Confucius, and Sun-Tzu, one of the greatest military tacticians and the author of the infamous *Art of War*, which is still studied in military academies around the world.

## 221–207 BC — The First Dynasty

The Qin Dynasty eventually defeated all of the other warring factions thanks to their cutting-edge military technology, namely the cavalry. The Qin were also called Ch'in, which may be where the word China first originated. The first Emperor, Qin Shi Huang, unified much of the lands and established a legal code and vast bureaucracy to hold it together. The Qin dynasty also standardized the written and spoken language and introduced a common currency.

IN FOCUS THE AGE OF EMPIRES

(left) Terracotta warrior.
(top right) Temple of Xichan in Fuzhou

In order to protect his newly unified country, Qin Shi Huang ordered the creation of the massive Great Wall of China, which was built and rebuilt over the next 1,000 years. He was also a sculpture enthusiast and commissioned a massive army of stone soldiers to follow him into the afterlife. Buried with him, these terracotta warriors would remain hidden from the eyes of the world for two thousand years, until they were found by a farmer digging in a field just outside of Xian. These warriors are among the most important archaeological finds of the 20th century.

## 265-220 BC Buddhism Arrives

Emperor Qin's dreams of a unified China fell apart, and eventually the kingdom split into three warring factions. But what was bad for stability turned out to be good for literature. The Three Kingdoms Period is still remembered in song and story. *The Romance of the Three Kingdoms* is as popular among Asian book worms as the *Legend of King Arthur* is among Western readers. It's still widely read and has been translated into almost every language. Variations of the story have been adapted for

manga, television series, and video games.

The Three Kingdoms period was filled with court intrigue, murder, and massive battles that, while exciting to read about centuries later, weren't much fun at the time. Armies ravaged the countryside, and most people lived and died in misery. Perhaps it was the carnage and disunity of the time that turned the country into a magnet for forces of harmony; it was during this period that Buddhism was first introduced into China, traveling over the Himalayas from India, via the Silk Road.

Religion Diversifies

600       800       1000

(left) Statue of Genghis Khan. (top right) Donguan Mosque in Xining, Qinghai. (bottom right) Empress Shengshen

## Religion Diversifies

**618-845**

Chinese spiritual life continued to diversify. Nestorian Monks from Asia Minor arrived bearing news of Christianity, and Saad ibn Abi Waqqas (a companion of the Prophet Muhammad) supposedly visited the Middle Kingdom to spread the word of Islam. During this era, Wu Zetian, onetime concubine, seized power from the Tang Dynasty and became the first (and only) woman to assume the title of emperor. She ruled for 25 years through puppet emperors and finally, for 15 years as Emperor Shengshen.

## Ghengis Invades

**1271-1368**

*In Xanadu did Kublai Khan a stately pleasure dome decree . . .*
Or so goes the famed Coleridge poem. But Kublai's grandfather Temujin (better known as Ghengis Khan) had bigger things in mind. One of the greatest war tacticians in history, he united the restive nomads of Mongolia's grassy plains and eventually sacked, looted, and pillaged much of the known west and most of the Chinese landmass. By the time Ghengis died in 1227, his grandson was well-tutored and ready to take on the rest of China.

By 1271, Kublai had established a capital in a land-locked city that would only much later become known as Beijing. This marks the beginning of the first (but not last) non-Han dynasty. Kublai Khan kept fighting southward and by 1279, Guangzhou fell to the Mongols, and Khan became the ultimate monarch of China. Though barbarians at heart, the Mongols must be credited for encouraging the arts and a number of early public works projects, including extending the highways and grand canals.

(left) Emperor Chengzu of the Ming Dynasty. (top right) Forbidden City in Beijing (bottom right) Child emperor Puyi.

## Ming Dynasty
**1368-1644**

Many scholars believe that the Mongols' inability to relate with the Han is what ultimately pushed the Han to rise up and overthrow them. The reign of the Ming Dynasty was the last ethnically Han Dynasty to rule over a unified China. At its apex, the Bright Empire encompassed a landmass easily recognized as China, even by today's mapmakers. The Ming Emperors built a huge army and navy, refurbished the agricultural system, and printed many books using movable type long before Gutenberg. In the 13th century, Emperor Yongle began construction of the famous Forbidden City in Beijing, a veritable icon of China.

Also during the Ming Dynasty, China's best known explorer, Zheng He, plied the seven seas in massive treasure fleets that dwarfed in size and range the ships of Christopher Columbus. A giant both in stature and persona, Admiral Zheng (who was also a eunuch) spent two decades expanding China's knowledge of the world outside of its already impressive borders. He traveled as far as India, Africa, and (some say) even the coast of the New World.

## Qing Dynasty
**1644-1911**

The final dynasty represented a serious case of minority rule. They were Manchus from the northeast. The early Qing dynasty was a brutal period as forces loyal to the new emperor crushed those loyal to the old. The Qing Dynasty peaked in the mid-to-late 18th century but soon after, its military powers began to wane. In the 19th century, Qing control weakened and prosperity diminished. By 1910 China was fractured, a baby sat on the Imperial throne, and the Qing Dynasty was on its deathbed.

(top left) A depiction of the Second Opium War. (bottom left) Chiang Kai-shek (top, right) Mao Zedong on December 6, 1944. (bottom, right) Sun Yat Sen.

## The Opium Wars

**1834-1860**

European powers were hungry to open new territories up for trade, but the Qing weren't buying. The British East India Company, strapped for cash, realized they could sell opium in China at huge profits. The Chinese government quickly banned the nefarious trade and in response, a technologically superior Britain declared war. After a humiliating defeat in the first Opium War, China was forced to cede Hong Kong. Other foreign powers soon followed with territorial demands of their own.

## Republican Era

**1912-1949**

China's Republican period was chaotic and unstable. The revolutionary Dr. Sun Yat-sen —revered by most Chinese as the father of modern China—was unable to build a cohesive government without the aid of regional warlords and urban gangsters. When he died of cancer in 1925, power passed to Chiang Kai-shek, who set about unifying China under the Kuomintang. What began as a unified group of both left- and right-wingers quickly deteriorated, and by the mid-1920s, civil war between the Communists

and Nationalists was brewing.

The '30s and '40s were bleak decades for the Chinese people, caught between a vicious war with Japan and periodic clashes between Kuomintang and Communist forces. After Japan's defeat in 1945, China's civil war kicked into high gear. Though the Kuomintang were armed with superior weapons and backed by American money, the majority of Chinese people rallied behind the Communists. Within four years, the Kuomintang were driven off the mainland to Taiwan, where the Republic of China exists to the present day,

(top left) 1950s
Chinese stamp with
Mao and Stalin.
(top right) Shenzhen
(bottom left) Poster of
Mao's slogans.

1949-Present

## The People's Republic

On October 1, 1949, Mao Zedong declared from atop Beijing's Gate of Heavenly Peace that "The Chinese People have stood up." And so the People's Republic of China was born. The Communist party set out to overhaul China's ancient feudal system, emphasizing class struggle, redistribution of wealth, and elimination of foreign dominance. The next three decades would see a massive, often painful transformation of Chinese society from feudalism into the modern age.

The Great Leap Forward was a disaster—Chinese peasants were encouraged to cram 100 years of industrial development into as many weeks. Untenable decisions led to industrial and agricultural ruin, widespread famine, and an estimated 30 million deaths. The trauma of this period, however, pales in comparison to The Great Proletarian Cultural Revolution. From 1966–1976, fear and zealotry gripped the nation as young revolutionaries heeded Chairman Mao's call to root out class enemies. During this decade, millions died, millions were imprisoned, and much of China's accumulated religious,

historical, and cultural heritage literally went up in smoke.

Like a phoenix rising from its own ashes, China rose from its own self-inflicted destruction. In the early 1980s, Deng Xiao-ping took the first steps in reforming China's stagnant economy. With the maxim "To Get Rich is Glorious," Deng loosened central control on the economy and declared Special Economic Zones where the seeds of capitalism could be incubated. Three decades later, the nation is one of the world's most vibrant economic engines. Though China's history is measured in millennia, her brightest years may well have only just begun.

**DID YOU KNOW?**

*Beijing's Lama Temple (Yonghe Temple) is one of the largest and most important Tibetan Buddhist monasteries in the world. The temple houses a 55-foot-high golden statue of Maitreya Buddha.*

# BEIJING

# WELCOME TO BEIJING

## TOP REASONS TO GO

★ **The Forbidden City:** Built by more than 200,000 workers, it's the largest palace in the world and has the best-preserved and most complete collection of imperial architecture in China.

★ **Tiananmen Square.** The political heart of modern China, the square covers 100 acres, making it the largest public square in the world.

★ **Temple of Heaven:** One of the best examples of religious architecture in China, the sprawling, tree-filled complex is a pleasant place for wandering: watch locals practice martial arts, play traditional instruments, and enjoy ballroom dancing on the grass.

★ **Magnificent Markets:** So much to bargain for, so little time! Visit outdoor Panjiayuan (aka the Dirt Market), the Silk Alley Market, or the Yashow Market.

★ **Summer Palace.** This garden complex dates back eight centuries, to when the first emperor of the Jin Dynasty built the Gold Mountain Palace on Longevity Hill.

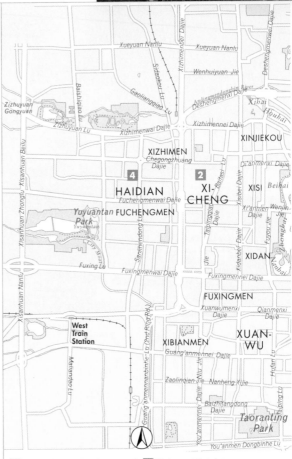

**1 Dongcheng District.** Dongcheng (East District) encompasses the Forbidden City, Tiananmen Square, Wangfujing (a major shopping street), the Lama Temple, and many other historical sights dating back to imperial times.

**2 Xicheng District.** Xicheng (West District), west of Dongcheng, includes Beihai Park, former playground of the imperial family, and a series of connected lakes bordered by willow trees, courtyard-lined *hutong*, and lively bars.

## GETTING ORIENTED

Laid out like a target with ring roads revolving around a bull's-eye, with **Chang'an Jie** (Eternal Peace Street) cutting across the middle, Beijing sprawls outward from the central point of the **Forbidden City.** The ring roads are its main arteries, and, along with Chang'an Jie, you will find yourself traveling them just about anytime you go from one place to another aboveground. As you explore Beijing, you'll find that taxis are often the best way to get around. However, if the recently expanded subway system goes where you're headed, it's often a faster option than dealing with traffic. The city is divided into 18 municipal and suburban districts ($qu$). Only six of these districts are the central stomping grounds for most visitors.

**3 Chaoyang District.** Chaoyang is the biggest and busiest district, occupying the areas north, east, and south of the eastern Second Ring Road. It's home to foreign embassies, multinational companies, the Central Business District, and the Olympic Park.

**4 Haidian District.** Haidian is the technology and university district. It's northwest of the Third Ring Road and packed with shops selling electronics and students cramming for the next exam.

Updated by Sky Canaves, Gareth Clark, Ami Li, and Adrian Sandiford

Beijing is a vibrant jumble of neighborhoods and districts. It's a city that was transformed almost overnight in preparation for the 2008 Olympics, often leveling lively old *hutong* (alleyway neighborhoods) to make way for the glittering towers that are fast dwarfing their surroundings. Still, day-to-day life seems to pulse the lifeblood of a Beijing that once was.

Hidden behind Beijing's pressing search for modernity is an intriguing historic core. Many of the city's ancient sites were built under the Mongols during the Yuan Dynasty (1271–1368). A number of the capital's imperial palaces, halls of power, mansions, and temples were rebuilt and refurbished during the Ming and Qing dynasties. Despite the ravages of time and the Cultural Revolution, most sites are in good shape, from the Niujie Mosque, with Koranic verse curled around its arches, to Tiananmen Square, the bold brainchild of Mao Zedong.

The city is divided into 18 municipal and suburban districts ($q\bar{u}$). Only a handful of these districts are the central stomping grounds for most visitors. **Dongcheng** (East District) encompasses the Forbidden City, Tiananmen Square, Wangfujing (a major shopping street), the Lama Temple, and many other historical sites dating back to imperial times. **Xicheng** (West District), directly west of Dongcheng, is a lovely lake district that includes Beihai Park, former playground of the imperial family, and a series of connected lakes bordered by willow trees, courtyard-lined hutongs, and lively bars. The Chongwen District is also home to some of the city's most famous restaurants, some more than 100 years old. **Chaoyang** is the biggest and busiest district, occupying the areas north, east, and south of the eastern Second Ring Road. As it lies outside the Second Ring Road, which marked the eastern demarcation of the old city wall, there is little of historical interest here. The district is home to foreign embassies, multinational companies, the Central Business District, and the Olympic Park. **Haidian,** the technology and university district, is northwest of the Third Ring Road; it's packed with shops selling electronics and students cramming for the next exam.

### STREET VOCABULARY

Here are some terms you'll see over and over again. These words will appear on maps and street signs, and they are part of the name of just about every place you go:

**Dong** is east, **xi** is west, **nan** is south, **bei** is north, and **zhong** means middle. **Jie** and **lu** mean street and road respectively, and **da** means big.

**Gongyuan** means park. Jingshan Park is also called Jingshan Gongyuan.

**Nei** means inside and **wai** means outside. You will often come across these terms on streets that used to pass through a gate of the old city wall. Andingmen Nei Dajie, for example, is the section of the street located inside the Second Ring Road (where the gate used to be), whereas Andingmen Wai Dajie is the section outside the gate.

**Qiao,** or bridge, is part of the place name at just about every entrance and exit on the ring roads.

**Men,** meaning door or gate, indicates a street that once passed through an entrance in the old wall that surrounded the city until it was mostly torn down in the 1960s. The entrances to parks and some other places are also referred to as *men*.

## PLANNING

### WHEN TO GO

The best time to visit Beijing is spring or early fall, when the weather is pleasant and crowds are a bit smaller. Book at least one month in advance for travel during these two times of year. In winter Beijing's Forbidden City and Summer Palace can look fantastical and majestic, when the traditional tiled roofs are covered with a light dusting of snow and the venues are devoid of tourists.

Avoid the two long national holidays: Chinese New Year, which ranges from mid-January to mid-February; and National Day holiday, the first week of October, when Chinese normally get a lengthy holiday. Millions of Chinese travel during these weeks, making it difficult to book hotels, tours, and transportation.

The weather in Beijing is at its best in September and October, with a good chance of sunny days and mild temperatures. Winters are cold, but it seldom snows. Although hotels are usually well heated, some restaurants may be poorly heated, so be prepared with a warm sweater when dining out. Late April through June is lovely, but come July the days are hot and excruciatingly humid with a greater chance of rain. Spring is also the time of year for Beijing's famous dust storms.

### GETTING AROUND

#### ON FOOT

Though traffic and modernization have put a bit of a cramp in Beijing's walking style, meandering remains one of the best ways to experience the capital—especially the old hutong that are rich with culture and sights.

### BIKE TRAVEL

The proliferation of cars (some 1,000 new automobiles take to the streets of the capital every day, bringing the total to more than 5 million vehicles) has made biking less pleasant and more dangerous here. Fortunately, most streets have wide, well-defined bike lanes often separated from other traffic by an island. If a flat tire or sudden brake failure strikes, seek out the nearest

> **ETIQUETTE**
>
> It is respectful to dress modestly: cover your shoulders and don't wear short skirts or shorts when you're visiting religious buildings. Keep in mind that authorities are very sensitive about public behavior in Tiananmen Square.

street-side mechanic, easily identified by the bike parts and pumps. Bikes can be rented at many hotels and next to some subway stations.

### SUBWAY TRAVEL

The subway is the best way to avoid Beijing's frequent traffic jams. With the opening of new lines, Beijing's subway service is increasingly convenient. The metropolitan area is currently served by 14 lines as well as an express line to the airport. The subway runs from about 5 am to midnight daily, depending on the station. Fares are Y2 per ride for any distance and transfers are free. Stations are marked in both Chinese and English, and stops are also announced in both languages. Subways are best avoided during rush hours, when severe overcrowding is unavoidable.

### TAXI TRAVEL

The taxi experience in Beijing has improved significantly as the city's taxi companies gradually shift to cleaner, more comfortable new cars. In the daytime, flag-fall for taxis is Y10 for the first 3 km (2 miles) and Y2 per kilometer thereafter. The rate rises to Y3 per kilometer on trips over 15 km (8 miles) and after 11 pm, when the flag-fall also increases to Y11. At present, there's also a Y1 gas surcharge for any rides exceeding 3 km (2 miles). ⚠ **Be sure to check that the meter has been engaged to avoid fare negotiations at your destination.** Taxis are easy to hail during the day, but can be difficult during evening rush hour, especially when it's raining. If you're having difficulty, go to the closest hotel and wait in line there. Few taxi drivers speak English, so ask your hotel concierge to write down your destination in Chinese.

### GOOD TOURS

Taking a tour will make it easier to sightsee without the hassle. However, if you're adventurous, you can easily explore the city on your own, even if you don't speak Chinese. You can't rely on taxi drivers to know the English names of the major tourist sites, but armed with the names in Chinese in this guide, you should have few or no problems getting around. If you do opt for an organized tour, keep in mind that a little research pays off.

### GENERAL TOURS

Local guides are often creative when it comes to showing you history and culture, so having an expert with you can make a big difference. WildChina is a local company with unusual trips: one of their

Shoppers enjoy a sunny day in the Xidan neighborhood.

cultural trips explores China's little-known Jewish history. The China Culture Center is a wonderful local resource for tours, classes, lectures, and other events in Beijing. The China Guide is a Beijing-based, American-managed travel agency offering tours that do *not* make shopping detours.

**Contacts**

**China Culture Center** ✉ *Rm 4916, Liangma Antique Market, 27 Liangmaqiao Rd., Chaoyang District* ☎ *010/6432-9341, 010/8420-0671 Weekend number* ⊕ *www.chinaculturecenter.org.* **The China Guide.** This Beijing-based, American-managed travel agency offers tours that do *not* make shopping detours. ✉ *Room 81, 8th Floor, Building 7-1, Jianguomenwai Waijiaogongyu Diplomatic Compound* ☎ *010/8532-1860* ✉ *book@thechinaguide.com* ⊕ *www.thechinaguide. com* ⊙ *Office Mon.–Fri. 10–6.* **WildChina** ✉ *Room 803, Oriental Place, No. 9 Dongfang Donglu, Dongsanhuan Beilu, Chaoyang District* ☎ *888/902-8808 US Toll-Free, 010/6465-6602* ✉ *info@wildchina.com* ⊕ *www.wildchina.com.*

## BIKE TOURS

Pedaling among the city's cyclists isn't as challenging as it looks: copy the locals—keep it slow and ring your bell often. And, of course, be very careful. Punctured tire? Not to worry: curbside repairmen line most streets. Remember to park your bike (and lock it to something stationary, as bike theft is common) only in designated areas. There are designated bike-parking lots throughout the city with attendants charging a nominal fee, usually about 3 mao.

Cycle China offers plenty of cycling trips in and around Beijing and beyond, such as the Great Wall. You can hire bikes from them, or take your own. Bike China Adventures organizes trips of varying length and difficulty all over China.

**Contacts Bike China Adventures** ☎ *800/818–1778* ⊕ *www.bikechina.com.* **Cycle China** ✉ *12 Jingshan Dong Jie, Dongcheng District* ☎ *139/1188–6524, 010/6402 5653* ⊕ *www.cyclechina.com.*

### HIKING TOURS

Beijing Hikers offer multiple hikes and camping stays on and around the Great Wall and always make sure that they leave no rubbish behind, unlike many other companies.

**Contacts Beijing Hikers** ✉ *Suite 4012, Building A, 10 Jiuxianqiao Zhong Lu* ☎ *010/6432–2786* ⊕ *www.beijinghikers.com/.*

### PEDICAB TOURS

Pedicabs (basically large tricycles with room for passengers behind a pedaling driver) were once the vehicles of choice for Beijingers laden with a week's worth of groceries or tourists eager for a street's-eye city tour. Today many residents are wealthy enough to bundle their purchases into taxis or their own cars, and the tourist trade has moved on to the tight schedules of air-conditioned buses. But pedicabs have made a big comeback in Beijing in recent years and can now be hired near major tourist sites. A ride through the hutong near Houhai is the most popular pedicab journey. ■TIP→ **Be absolutely sure to negotiate the fare in advance, clarifying whether the fare is on yuan or dollars, whether the fare is considered a one-way or round-trip, and whether it is for one person or two.** Government-approved pedicab tours are supposed to be fixed at Y35 per hour, though the actual price is often higher. Feel free to tip your driver for good service on longer tours. Independent pedicabs for hutong tours can be found in the small plaza between the Drum Tower and the Bell Tower.

**Beijing Hutong Tourist Agency.** This agency was one of the first to offer guided pedicab tours of Beijing's back alleys, with glimpses of old courtyard houses and daily Beijing life. It offers trips ranging from 40 minutes to two and a half hours priced at Y80–Y220 per person (solo travlers pay extra). The longer tours will take you through what was once Beijing's most prestigious neighborhood (Houhai) and include a stop at the Drum and Bell towers as well as a visit to the home of a local family. ✉ *26 Di'anmen Xidajie, Dongcheng District* ☎ *010/6615–9097.*

### VISITOR CENTERS

For general information, including advice on tours, insurance, and safety, call, or visit China National Tourist Office's website, as well as the website run by the Beijing Tourism Administration (BTA). ■TIP→ **The BTA maintains a 24-hour hotline for tourist inquiries and complaints, with operators fluent in English.** BTA also runs Beijing Tourist Information Centers, whose staff can help you with free maps and directions in Beijing.

**Beijing Tourist Information Beijing Tourism Administration** ✍ *visitbeijingeng@163.com* ⊕ *english.visitbeijing.com.cn.*

# EXPLORING BEIJING

Existing on a seemingly superhuman scale that matches its status as the capital city of the world's most populous nation, Beijing is laid out with vast expanses of wide avenues and roadways organized in an orderly pattern. Though the city's original grid layout has remained the same for many years (as has remnants of its past as the last capital of Imperial China), its infrastructure has undergone numerous transformations, most recently in preparation for the 2008 Summer Olympics. Despite all the changes necessitated by the proliferation of lacquered office towers, high-rise residences, and shopping centers, there are still plenty of world-class historic sites to be discovered, along with tranquil residential oases of a bygone time, most beloved of which are the rapidly disappearing style of alleyway neighborhoods called *hutong*.

Underlying Beijing's thrust toward modernity is an intriguing historic core. Scores of the city's imperial palaces, halls of power, mansions, and temples built under the Mongols during the Yuan Dynasty (1271–1368) were rebuilt during later Ming and Qing dynasties. Despite the ravages of time and the depredations of the Cultural Revolution, many of these refurbished sites are still in excellent condition including, to name a few, the Niujie Mosque, with Koranic verses curling around its arches, and Tiananmen Square, bold brainchild of Mao Zedong.

## DONGCHENG DISTRICT

Dongcheng District, with its idyllic hutong and plethora of historical sites, is one of Beijing's most pleasant areas. It's also one of the smaller districts in the city, which makes it easy to get around. A day exploring Dongcheng will leave you feeling as if you've been introduced to the character of the capital. From the old men playing chess in the hutong to the sleek, chauffeured Audis driving down Chang'an Jie, to the colorful shopping on Wangfujing, Dongcheng offers visitors a thousand little tastes of what makes Beijing a fascinating city. ■ TIP→ **Note that indoor photography in many temples and sites like the Forbidden City is not permitted.**

### GETTING HERE AND AROUND

Dongcheng is easily accessible by subway, with stops along most of its perimeter: Tiananmen East station to Jianguomen on Line 1 forms the south side of this district; Jianguomen to Gulou Dajie on Line 2 forms the district's north and east sides. Line 2 stops at the Lama Temple, the Ancient Observatory, Wangfujing, and Tiananmen Square. Taxi travel during peak hours (7 to 9 am and 5 to 8 pm) is difficult. At other times traveling by taxi is affordable, convenient, and the fastest option (especially at noon, when much of the city is at lunch, and after 10 pm). Renting a bike to see the sites is also a good option. Bus travel within the city is only Y1 for shorter distances and can be very convenient, but requires reading knowledge of Chinese to find the correct bus to take. Once on the bus, stops are announced in Chinese and English.

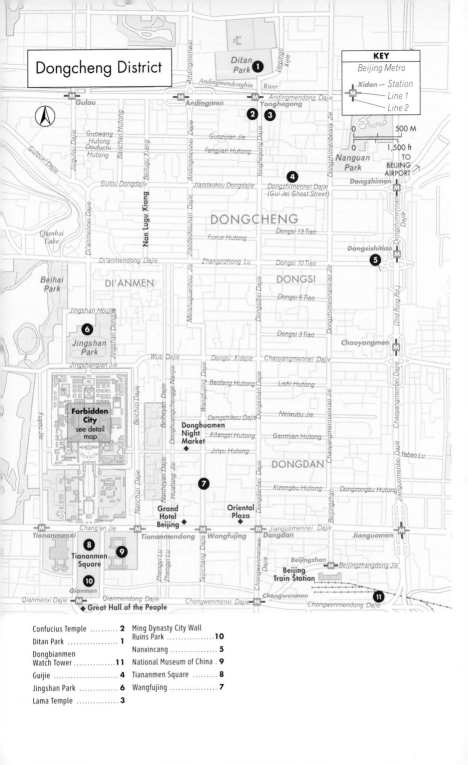

# Dongcheng District

## KEY
**Beijing Metro**

Xidan — Station
Line 1
Line 2

Forbidden City see detail map

DONGCHENG

DI'ANMEN

DONGSI

DONGDAN

Jingshan Park

Tiananmen Square

Confucius Temple .......... **2**
Ditan Park ................. **1**
Dongbianmen Watch Tower ............... **11**
Guijie ....................... **4**
Jingshan Park ............. **6**
Lama Temple ............... **3**

Ming Dynasty City Wall Ruins Park ................. **10**
Nanxincang ................. **5**
National Museum of China . **9**
Tiananmen Square ......... **8**
Wangfujing ................. **7**

**MAKING THE MOST OF YOUR TIME**

Most of Dongcheng can be seen in a day, but it's best to set aside two, because the **Forbidden City** and **Tiananmen Square** will likely take the better part of one day. The climb up Coal Hill (also called Prospect Hill) in **Jingshan Park** will take about 30 minutes for an average walker. From there, hop a taxi to the **Lama Temple**, which is worth a good two hours, then visit the nearby **Confucius Temple.**

**TOP ATTRACTIONS**

Fodor's Choice ★ **Confucius Temple** (孔庙 *Kŏngmiào*). This tranquil temple to China's great sage has endured close to eight centuries of additions and restorations. The Hall of Great Accomplishment in the temple houses Confucius's funeral tablet and shrine, flanked by copper-colored statues depicting China's wisest Confucian scholars. As in Buddhist and Taoist temples, worshippers can offer sacrifices (in this case to a mortal, not a deity). The 198 tablets lining the courtyard outside the Hall of Great Accomplishment contain 51,624 names belonging to advanced Confucian scholars from the Yuan, Ming, and Qing dynasties. Flanking the Gate of Great Accomplishment are two carved stone drums dating to the Qianlong period (1735–96). In the Hall of Great Perfection you'll find the central shrine to Confucius. Check out the huge collection of ancient musical instruments.

In the front and main courtyards of the temple you'll find a cemetery of stone tablets. These tablets, or stelae, stand like rows of creepy crypts. On the front stelae you can barely make out the names of thousands of scholars who passed imperial exams. Another batch of stelae, carved in the mid-1700s to record the *Thirteen Classics,* philosophical works attributed to Confucius, line the west side of the grounds.

■ TIP→ We recommend combining a tour of the Confucius Temple with the nearby Lama Temple. Access to both is convenient from the Yonghegong subway stop at the intersection of Line 2 and Line 5. You can also easily get to the Temple of Heaven by taking Line 5 south to Tiantandongmen.

The complex is now combined with the Imperial Academy next door, once the highest educational institution in the country. Established in 1306 as a rigorous training ground for high-level government officials, the academy was notorious, especially during the early Ming Dynasty era, for the harsh discipline imposed on scholars perfecting their knowledge of the Confucian classics. The Riyong Emperors Lecture Hall is surrounded by a circular moat (although the building is rectangular in shape). Emperors would come here to lecture on the classics. This ancient campus would be a glorious place to study today with its washed red walls, gold-tiled roofs, and towering cypresses (some as old as 700 years). ✉ *13 Guozijian Lu, off Yonghegong Lu near Lama Temple, Dongcheng District* ☎ *010/8401–1977* ⊕ *www.kmgzj.com* ☑ *Y30* ⊙ *Daily 8:30–5* Ⓜ *Yonghegong.*

**MUSLIM QUARTER**

Recent urban renewal has wiped out much of Beijing's old Muslim Quarter, one of the oldest areas in the city dating back to the 10th century. The main survivor is the **Niujie (Ox Street) Mosque,** which was built in 996; it is often

*Continued on page 60*

# THE FORBIDDEN CITY

Undeniably sumptuous, the Forbidden City, once home to a long line of emperors, is Beijing's most enduring emblem. Magnificent halls, winding lanes, and stately courtyards await you—welcome to the world's largest palace complex.

As you gaze up at roofs of glazed-yellow tiles—a symbol of royalty—try to imagine a time when only the emperor ("the son of God") was permitted to enter this palace, accompanied by select family members, concubines, and eunuch-servants. Now, with its doors flung open, the Forbidden City's mysteries beckon.

The sheer grandeur of the site—with 800 buildings and more than 8,000 rooms—conveys the pomp and circumstance of Imperial China. The shady palaces, musty with age, recall life at court, where corrupt eunuchs and palace officials schemed and bored concubines gossiped.

### BUILDING TO GLORY

Under the third Ming emperor, Yongle, 200,000 laborers built this complex over the course of 14 years, finishing in 1420. Yongle relocated the Ming capital to Beijing (from Nanjing in the south) to strengthen China's northern frontier. After Yongle, the palace was home to 23 Ming and Qing emperors, until the dynastic system crumbled in 1911.

In imperial times, no buildings were allowed to exceed the height of the palace. Moats and massive timber doors protected the emperor. Gleaming yellow roof tiles marked the vast complex as the royal court's exclusive dominion. Ornate interiors displayed China's most exquisite artisanship, including ceilings covered with turquoise-and-blue dragons, walls draped with priceless scrolls, intricate cloisonné screens, sandalwood thrones padded in delicate silks, and floors of golden-hued bricks. Miraculously, the palace survived fire, war, and imperial China's collapse.

### MORE THAN FENG SHUI

The Forbidden City embodies Feng Shui, architectural principles used for thousands of years throughout China. Each main hall faces south, opening to a courtyard flanked by lesser buildings. This symmetry repeats itself along a north–south axis that bisects the imperial palace, with a broad walkway paved in marble. This path was reserved exclusively for the emperor's sedan chair.

The entire complex follows the principles of Feng Shui.

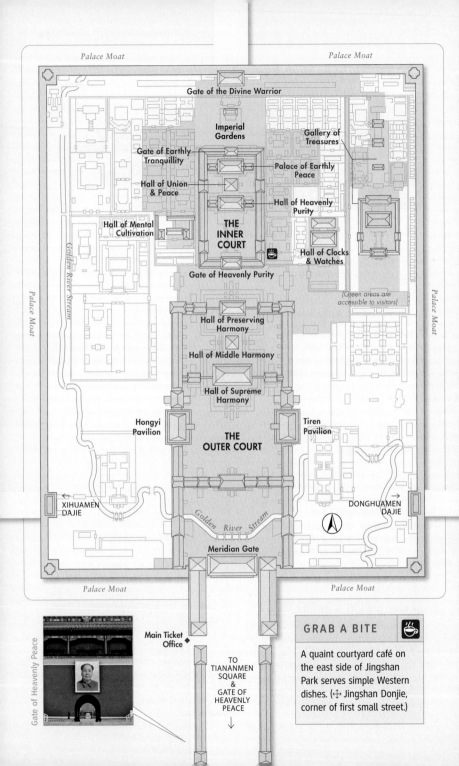

Palace Moat

Palace Moat

Gate of the Divine Warrior

Imperial Gardens

Gallery of Treasures

Gate of Earthly Tranquillity

Palace of Earthly Peace

Hall of Union & Peace

Hall of Heavenly Purity

Hall of Mental Cultivation

THE INNER COURT

Hall of Clocks & Watches

Gate of Heavenly Purity

(Green areas are accessible to visitors)

Golden River Stream

Palace Moat

Palace Moat

Hall of Preserving Harmony

Hall of Middle Harmony

Hall of Supreme Harmony

Hongyi Pavilion

THE OUTER COURT

Tiren Pavilion

← XIHUAMEN DAJIE

DONGHUAMEN DAJIE →

Golden River Stream

Meridian Gate

Palace Moat

Palace Moat

Gate of Heavenly Peace

Main Ticket Office ◆

TO TIANANMEN SQUARE & GATE OF HEAVENLY PEACE ↓

GRAB A BITE

A quaint courtyard café on the east side of Jingshan Park serves simple Western dishes. (⊕ Jingshan Donjie, corner of first small street.)

## WHAT TO SEE

The most impressive way to reach the Forbidden City is through the **Gate of Heavenly Peace** (Tiananmen), connected to Tiananmen Square. The Great Helmsman himself stood here to establish the People's Republic of China on October 1, 1949.

The **Meridian Gate** (Wumen), sometimes called Five Phoenix Tower, is the main southern entrance to the palace. Here, the emperor announced yearly planting schedules according to the lunar calendar; it's also where errant officials were flogged. The main ticket office and audio-guide rentals are just west of this gate.

The central entrance of the Meridian was reserved for the emperor. The one day the empress was allowed to walk through it was her wedding day.

### THE OUTER COURT

The **Hall of Supreme Harmony** (Taihedian) was used for coronations, royal birthdays, and weddings. Bronze vats, once kept brimming with water to fight fires, ring this vast expanse. The hall sits atop three stone tiers with an elaborate drainage system with 1,000 carved dragons. On the top tier, bronze cranes symbolize longevity. Inside, cloisonné cranes flank the imperial throne, above which hangs a heavy bronze ball—placed there to crush any pretender to the throne.

Take a close look at the bronze vats and you'll see the telltale scratch marks of greedy foreign soldiers who scraped the gold with their bayonets.

Emperors greeted audiences in the **Hall of Middle Harmony** (Zhonghedian). It also housed the royal plow, with which the emperor would turn a furrow to commence spring planting.

The highest civil service examinations, which were personally conducted by the emperor, were once administered in the **Hall of Preserving Harmony** (Baohedian). Behind the hall, a 200-ton marble relief of dragons, the palace's most treasured stone carving, adorns the staircase.

The Hall of Supreme Harmony was the site of many imperial weddings.

A short jaunt to the right is **Hall of Clocks and Watches** (Zhongbiaoguan), where you'll find a collection of early timepieces. It's pure opulence: there's a plethora of jeweled, enameled, and lacquered timepieces (some astride elephants, others implanted in ceramic trees). Our favorites? Those crafted from red sandalwood. *(Admission: Y10)*

You'll see that lions in the palace live in pairs. A female lion playing with a cub symbolizes imperial fertility. A male lion, sitting majestically with a sphere beneath his paw, represents power.

Marble dragons will greet you behind the Hall of Preserving Harmony.

## DID YOU KNOW?

■ 24 emperors and two dynasties ruled from within these labyrinthine halls.

■ The emperor was the only non-castrated male allowed in the eastern and western palaces. This served as proof that any pregnant concubine was carrying the royal one's baby.

■ If you prepared for your trip by watching Bertolucci's *The Last Emperor*, you may recognize the passage outside the Hall of Mental Cultivation: this is where young Puyi rode his bike in the film.

■ Women can enter the Forbidden City for half price on March 8, International Women's Day.

■ When it was first built in the 15th century, the palace was called the Purple Forbidden City; today, its official name is the Ancient Palace Museum (Gugong Bowuguan); often it's shortened simply to Gugong.

Emperors Throne in the Palace of Heavenly Purity

### THE INNER COURT

Now you're approaching the very core of the palace. Several emperors chose to live in the Inner Palace with their families. The **Hall of Heavenly Purity** (Qianqinggong) holds another imperial throne; the **Hall of Union and Peace** (Jiaotaidian) was the venue for the empress's annual birthday party; and the **Palace of Earthly Peace** (Kunninggong) was where royal couples consummated their marriages. The banner above the throne bizarrely reads DOING NOTHING.

On either side of the Inner Palace are six western and six eastern palaces—the former living quarters of concubines, eunuchs, and servants. The last building on the western side, the **Hall of Mental Cultivation** (Yangxindian), is the most important of these; starting with Emperor Yongzheng, all Qing Dynasty emperors attended to daily state business in this hall.

# AN EMPEROR CHEAT SHEET

### JIAJING (1507–1567)

Ming Emperor Jiajing was obsessed with Taoism, which he hoped would give him longevity, but which also led him to ignore state affairs for 25 years. His other fixation was the pursuit of girls: his 18 concubines conspired to strangle him in his sleep, but their plot was uncovered. Nearly all of the girls, and their families, were killed.

### YONGZHENG (1678–1735)

The third emperor of the Qing Dynasty, Yongzheng was tyrannical but efficient. He became emperor amid rumors that he had forged his father's will. He appeased his brothers by promoting them, but then proceeded to murder and imprison anyone who posed a challenge, including his own brothers, two of whom died in prison.

Pagoda in the Imperial Garden

**The Gallery of Treasures** (Zhenbaoguan), actually a series of halls, has breathtaking examples of imperial ornamentation. The first room displays candleholders, wine vessels, tea sets, and a golden pagoda commissioned by Qing emperor Qian Long in honor of his mother. A cabinet on one wall contains the 25 imperial seals. Jade bracelets, golden hair pins, and coral fill the second hall; carved jade landscapes a third. *(Admission: Y10)*

**HEAD FOR THE GREEN**

North of the Forbidden City's private palaces, beyond the **Gate of Earthly Tranquillity,** lie the most pleasant parts of the Forbidden City: the **Imperial Gardens** (Yuhuayuan), composed of ancient cypress trees and stone mosaic pathways. During festivals, palace inhabitants climbed the Hill of Accumulated Elegance. You can exit the palace at the back of the gardens through the park's **Gate of the Divine Warrior** (Shenwumen).

**FAST FACTS**

**Address:** The main entrance is just north of the Gate of Heavenly Peace, which faces Tiananmen Square on Chang'an Jie.

**Phone:** 010/8513-2255

**Web site:** www.dpm.org.cn

**Admission:** Y60

**Hours:** Oct. 16–Apr. 15, daily 8:30–4:30; Apr. 16–Oct. 15, daily 8:30–5

**UNESCO Status:** Declared a World Heritage Site in 1987. You must check your bags prior to entry and also pass through a metal detector.

■ The palace is always packed with visitors, but it's impossibly crowded on national holidays.

■ Allow 2–4 hours to explore the palace. There are souvenir shops and restaurants inside.

■ You can hire automated audio guides at the Meridian Gate for Y40 and a Y100 returnable deposit.

**2**

**IN FOCUS THE FORBIDDEN CITY**

**CIXI** (1835–1908)

The Empress Dowager served as de facto ruler of China from 1861 until 1908. She was a concubine at 16 and soon became Emperor Xianfeng's favorite. She gave birth to his only son to survive: the heir apparent. Ruthless and ambitious, she learned the workings of the imperial court and used every means to gain power.

**PUYI** (1906–1967)

Puyi, whose life was depicted in Bertolucci's classic *The Last Emperor,* took the throne at age two. The Qing dynasty's last emperor, he was forced to abdicate after the dynasty fell. During an attempted restoration in 1917, he held the throne for 12 days. Puyi was forced out of the Imperial City in 1924 by a warlord.

crowded with members of Beijing's Muslim community. Like other mosques in China, the Niujie Mosque looks like a traditional Buddhist temple with the addition of inscriptions in Arabic. The Tower for Observing the Moon and the main hall have restricted entry, and women can visit only certain areas. A few Muslim shops—mainly halal restaurants and butchers—remain in the neighborhood, which is now dominated by high-rise apartment buildings.

**Dongbianmen Watch Tower** (东便门角楼 *Dōngbiànmén jiǎolóu*). This is Beijing's last remaining Ming watchtower. Be sure to check out the Red Gate Gallery located inside, which shows works by well-known contemporary Chinese artists. The gallery was set up in 1991 by Brian Wallace, an Australian who studied art history at China's Central Academy of Fine Arts. The second and third floors are devoted to the history of the Chongwen District. ⊠ *Dongbianmen Watchtower, Chongwen District* ☎ *010/6525–1005* ⊕ *www.redgategallery.com* ✉ *Free* ☻ *Daily 9–5.*

**Forbidden City.** ⇨ *See the feature earlier in this chapter.*

**Jingshan Park** (景山公园 *Jǐngshān gōngyuán*). This park, also known as Coal Hill Park, was built around a small peak formed from earth excavated for the Forbidden City's moats. Ming rulers ordered the hill's construction to improve the feng shui of their new palace to the south. You can climb a winding stone staircase past peach and apple trees to Wanchun Pavilion, the park's highest point. On a clear day it offers unparalleled views of the Forbidden City and the Bell and Drum towers. Chongzhen, the last Ming emperor, is said to have hanged himself at the foot of Coal Hill as his dynasty collapsed in 1644. ⊠ *Jingshanqian Dajie, opposite the north gate of the Forbidden City, Xicheng and Dongcheng districts* ☎ *010/6404–4071* ✉ *Y2* ☻ *Daily 6 am–7 pm.*

**Lama Temple** (雍和宫 *Yōnghégōng*). Beijing's most-visited religious site and one of the most important functioning Buddhist temples in Beijing, this Tibetan Buddhist masterpiece has five main halls and numerous galleries hung with finely detailed *thangkhas* (Tibetan religious scroll paintings). The entire temple is decorated with Buddha images—all guarded by somber lamas dressed in brown robes. Originally a palace for Prince Yongzheng, it was transformed into a temple once he became the Qing's third emperor in 1723. The temple flourished under Emperor Qianlong, housing some 500 resident monks. This was once the official "embassy" of Tibetan Buddhism in Beijing but today only about two dozen monks live in this complex.

Don't miss the **The Hall of Heavenly Kings,** with statues of Maitreya, the future Buddha, and Weitou, China's guardian of Buddhism. This hall is worth a slow stroll. In the courtyard beyond, a pond with a bronze mandala represents paradise. The Statues of Buddhas of the Past, Present, and Future hold court in **The Hall of Harmony**. Look on the west wall where an exquisite silk thangkha of White Tara—the embodiment of compassion—hangs. Images of the Medicine and Longevity Buddhas line **The Hall of Eternal Blessing. In The Pavilion of Ten Thousand Fortunes** you see the breathtaking 26-meter (85-foot) Maitreya Buddha carved from a single sandalwood block. ■ **TIP** → **Combine** a visit to the Lama Temple with the Confucius Temple and the Imperial Academy, which are a five-minute walk away, within the hutong neighborhood opposite the main entrance. ⊠ *12 Yonghegong Dajie, Beixingqiao, Dongcheng District* ☎ *010/6404–4499* 🖃 *Y25* ⊙ *Daily 9–4:30* Ⓜ *Yonghegong, Line 2.*

**Ming Dynasty City Wall Ruins Park** (明城墙遗址公园 *Míng chéngqiáng yízhǐ gōngyuán*). The new Ming Dynasty City Wall Ruins Park is a renovated section of Beijing's old inner-city wall. The structure was rebuilt using original bricks that had been snatched decades earlier after the city wall had been torn down. This rebuilt section of the wall is a nicely landscaped area with paths full of Chinese walking their dogs, flying kites, practicing martial arts, and playing with their children. At the eastern end of the park is the grand Dongbianmen Watch Tower, home to the popular Red Gate Gallery. ⊠ *Dongbianmen, Dongdajie Street, Chongwen District* 🖃 *Free* ⊙ *Daily, park open 24 hrs.*

**National Museum of China** (中国国家博物馆 *Zhōngguó guójiā bówùguǎn*). Re-opened in 2011 following a lengthy $400 million renovation, this monumental edifice on the eastern side of Tiananmen Square showcases 5,000 years of history in immaculate surroundings. With 2 million square feet of exhibition space, it's impossible to see everything, though the propaganda-heavy history sections are safely skipped. Focus instead on the ancient China section on the lower level, which houses magnificent displays of bronzes and jade artifacts. The museum also features strong shows of visiting works from abroad, such as Renaissance art from Florence and ceramics from the British Museum and Victoria and Albert Museum. ⊠ *16 Dong Chang An Jie, Dongcheng District* ☎ *010/6511–6400* ⊕ *en.chnmuseum.cn* 🖃 *Free with passport* ⊙ *Tues.–Sun. 9–5, ticket booth closes at 3:30* Ⓜ *Tiananmen East.*

Fodor's Choice ★  **Tiananmen Square** (天安门广场 *Tiānānmén guǎngchǎng*). The world's largest public square, and the very heart of modern China, Tiananmen Square owes little to grand imperial designs and everything to Mao Zedong. At the height of the Cultural Revolution, hundreds of thousands of Red Guards crowded the square; in June 1989 the square was the scene of tragedy when student demonstrators were killed.

Today the square is packed with sightseers, families, and undercover policemen. Although formidable, the square is a little bleak, with no shade, benches, or trees. Come here at night for an eerie experience—it's a little like being on a film set. Beijing's ancient central axis runs right through the center of Mao Zedong's mausoleum, the Forbidden City, the Drum and Bell towers, and the Olympic Green. The square is sandwiched between two grand gates: the Gate of Heavenly Peace (Tiananmen) to the north and the Front Gate (Qianmen) in the south. Along the western edge is the Great Hall of the People. The National Museum of China lies along the eastern side. The 125-foot granite obelisk you see is the Monument to the People's Heroes; it commemorates those who died for the revolutionary cause of the Chinese people. ⊠ *Bounded by Chang'an Jie to the north and Qianmen Dajie to the south, Dongcheng District* 🖃 *Free* ⊙ *5 am–10 pm* Ⓜ *Tiananmen East.*

**DID YOU KNOW?** A network of tunnels lies beneath Tiananmen Square. Mao Zedong is said to have ordered them dug in the late 1960s after Sino-Soviet relations soured. They extend across Beijing.

**Wangfujing** (王府井 *Wángfǔjǐng*). Wangfujing, one of the city's oldest and busiest shopping districts, is still lined with a handful of *laozihao*, or old brand name shops, some dating back a century, and 1950s-era state-run stores. This short walking street is a pleasant place for window-shopping. Also on Wangfujing is the gleaming Oriental Plaza, with its expensive high-end shops (think Tiffany's, Burberry, Ermenegildo Zegna, and Audi), interspersed with Levi Jeans, Esprit, Starbucks, Pizza Hut, KFC, Häagen-Dazs, and a modern cinema multicomplex. ⊠ *Wangfujing, Dongcheng District.*

**WORTH NOTING**

**Ditan Park** (地坛公园 *Dìtán gōngyuán*). In this 16th-century green space, translated as "Temple of Earth Park," are the square altar where emperors once made sacrifices to the earth god and the Hall of Deities. This is a lovely place for a stroll, especially if you're already near the Drum Tower or Lama Temple. ⊠ *Hepingli Xilu, just north of Second Ring Rd., Dongcheng District* ☎ *010/6421–4657* 🎫 *Y2* 🕐 *Daily 6 am–9 pm.*

**Guijie** (簋街 *Guǐjiē*). For a nighttime-munchies cure, head to Guijie, also known as Ghost Street, which is full of restaurants serving up Chinese specialties such as noodles, hotpot, and fried delights. One of the most popular dishes here is *malaxia*, or spicy crawfish. ⊠ *Dongzhimennei Dajie.*

**Nanxincang** (南新仓 *Nánxīncāng*). China's oldest existing granary, dating back to the Yongle period (1403–24), is now Beijing's newest entertainment venue. It's home to three art galleries, a teahouse, and several bars and restaurants, including a branch of the famed Dadong Roast Duck. The structures at Nanxincang—just 10 years younger than those of the Forbidden City—were among the more than 300 granaries that existed in this area during imperial days. Have a glass of wine on the second floor of Yuefu, an audio and book shop, where you can admire the old interior, then have dinner at one of the excellent restaurants in the compound. ⊠ *Dongsi Shitiao, 1 block west of the Second Ring Road, Dongcheng District.*

**NEED A BREAK?** **Donghuamen Night Market** (东华门夜市 *Dōnghuāmén yèshì*). Crunchy deep-fried scorpions and other critters are sold at the Donghuamen Night Market, at the northern end of Wangfujing's wide walking boulevard. We'll admit: this is more of a place to look at and perhaps photograph food rather than devour it. In addition to standard street foods, hawkers here also serve up deep-fried starfish, plus a variety of insects and other hard-to-identify food items. Most street-market food is usually safe to eat as long as it's hot. The row of interesting outdoor evening stalls makes for an intriguing walk with great photo ops. ⊠ *Donganmen Dajie, on the northern side of Wangfujing, Dongcheng District.*

A portrait of the Great Helmsman gazes down on Tiananmen Square.

## XICHENG DISTRICT

Xicheng District is home to an eclectic mix of a few of Beijing's favorite things: delicious food, venerable hutong and old courtyard houses, charming lakes, and engaging nightlife. The lakes at Shichahai are fun for all ages, both day and night. Take a boat ride on the lake in the warmer months, or ice-skate here in the cold winter months when the lakes are crowded with parents taking their children out for a day of fun.

Our top experience? Taking a walk or bicycle tour of the surrounding hutongs: there is no better way to scratch the surface of this sprawling city (before it disappears!) than by exploring the hutongs lined by courtyard houses. Wander in and out of historic sites in the area, such as Prince Gong's palace, the courtyard house of famed opera legend Mei Lanfang, and the Drum and Bell towers (which fall right between Dongcheng and Xicheng). In the evening, find a restaurant or bar with a view of the lake.

### GETTING HERE AND AROUND

The Line 1 subway stops include Tiananmen West, Xidan, and Fuxingmen, while Line 2 makes stops from Fuxingmen to the Drum Tower (Gulou), following Xicheng's perimeter. Xizhimen is a major terminus with access to the northwest via subway. ■ TIP→ Houhai and Beihai Park are more conveniently reached by taxi.

**MAKING THE MOST OF YOUR TIME**

Xicheng's must-see sites are few in number but all special. Walk around **Beihai Park** in the early afternoon. When you get tired, either retire to one of Houhai's many cafés or take a pedicab hutong tour. If you come to Beijing in the winter, **Qianhai** will be frozen and you can rent skates, runner-equipped bicycles to pedal across the ice, or, the local favorite, a chair with runners welded to the bottom and a pair of metal sticks with which to propel yourself—quite a tiring sport. Dinner along the shores of **Houhai** is a great option—stick around into the evening to enjoy the booming bar scene. Plan to spend a few hours shopping at **Xidan** on your last day in Beijing; this is great place to pick up funky, cheap gifts.

## TOP ATTRACTIONS

**Beihai Park** (北海 *Běihǎi*). A white stupa is perched on a small island just north of the south gate. Also at the south entrance is **Round City**, which contains a white-jade Buddha and an enormous jade bowl given to Kublai Khan. Nearby, the well-restored **Temple of Eternal Peace** houses a variety of Buddhas. Climb to the stupa from Yongan Temple. Once there, you can pay an extra Y1 to ascend the Buddha-bedecked **Shanyin Hall**.

The lake is Beijing's largest and most beautiful public waterway. On summer weekends the lake teems with paddleboats. The **Five Dragon Pavilion**, on Beihai's northwest shore, was built in 1602 by a Ming Dynasty emperor who liked to fish under the moon. ⊠ *Weijin Jie, Xicheng District* ☎ *010/6403–3225* ⊕ *www.beihaipark.com.cn* ⊡ *Y5; extra fees for some sites* ⊙ *Apr.–May and Sept.–Oct., daily 6 am–8:30 pm; Nov.–Mar., daily 6 am–8 pm; June–Aug., daily 6 am–10 pm.*

**Capital Museum** (首都博物馆 *Shǒudū bówùguǎn*). Moved to its architecturally striking new home west of Tiananmen Square in 2005, this is one of China's finest cultural museums. Artifacts are housed in the unique multistoried bronze cylinder that dominates the building's facade, while paintings, calligraphy, and photographs of historic Beijing fill the remaining exhibition halls. The museum gets extra points for clear English descriptions and modern, informative displays. Entry is free but foreign tourists must show their passports to get tickets. ⊠ *16 Fuxingmenwai Dajie, Xicheng District* ☎ *010/6337–0491* ⊕ *www. capitalmuseum.org.cn/en/* ⊡ *Free* ⊙ *Tues.–Sun. 9–5.*

**Drum Tower** (鼓楼 *Gǔlóu*). Until the late 1920s, the 24 drums once housed in this tower were Beijing's timepiece. Sadly, all but one of these huge drums have been destroyed and the survivor is in serious need of renovation. Kublai Khan built the first drum tower on this site in 1272. You can climb to the top of the present tower, which dates from the Ming Dynasty. Old photos of hutong neighborhoods line the walls beyond the drum; there's also a scale model of a traditional courtyard house. The nearby **Bell Tower**, renovated after a fire in 1747, offers fabulous views of the hutong from the top of a long, narrow staircase. The huge 63-ton bronze bell, supported by lacquered wood stanchions, is also worth seeing. ⊠ *North end of Dianmen Dajie, Xicheng District* ☎ *010/6404–1710* ⊡ *Drum Tower Y20, Bell Tower Y15* ⊙ *Daily 9–5* Ⓜ *Guloudajie.*

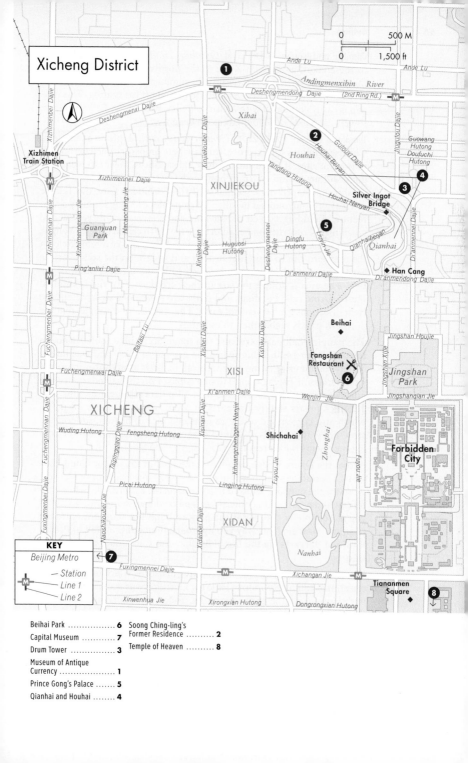

Xicheng District

KEY
Beijing Metro
— Station
Line 1
Line 2

Beihai Park .................. 6
Capital Museum ............ 7
Drum Tower ................. 3
Museum of Antique
Currency ...................... 1
Prince Gong's Palace ....... 5
Qianhai and Houhai ........ 4
Soong Ching-ling's
Former Residence .......... 2
Temple of Heaven .......... 8

**Qianhai and Houhai** (前海后海 *Qiánhǎi, Hòuhǎi*). Most people come to these lakes, along with Xihai to the northwest, to stroll and enjoy the shoreside bars and restaurants. In summer you can boat or fish. In winter, sections of the frozen lakes are fenced off for skating. This daytrip is easily combined with a visit to Beihai Park or the Bell and Drum towers. ⊠ *North of Beihai Lake, Xicheng District.*

Fodor'sChoice ★ **Temple of Heaven** (天坛公元 *Tiāntán gōngyuán*). A prime example of Chinese religious architecture, this is where emperors once performed important rites. It was a site for imperial sacrifices, meant to please the gods so they would generate bumper harvests. Set in a huge, serene, mushroom-shaped park southeast of the Forbidden City, the Temple of Heaven is surrounded by splendid examples of Ming Dynasty architecture, including curved cobalt blue roofs layered with yellow and green tiles. Construction began in the early 15th century under Yongle, whom many call the "architect of Beijing." Shaped like a semicircle on the northern rim to represent heaven and square on the south for the earth, the grounds were once believed to be the meeting point of the two. The area is double the size of the Forbidden City and is still laid out to divine rule: buildings and paths are positioned to represent the right directions for heaven and earth. This means, for example, that the northern part is higher than the south.

The temple's hallmark structure is a magnificent **blue-roofed wooden tower** built in 1420. It burned to the ground in 1889 and was immediately rebuilt using Ming architectural methods (and timber imported from Oregon). The building's design is based on the calendar: 4 center pillars represent the seasons, the next 12 pillars represent months, and 12 outer pillars signify the parts of a day. Together these 28 poles, which also correspond to the 28 constellations of heaven, support the structure without nails. A carved dragon swirling down from the ceiling represents the emperor.

Across the Danbi Bridge, you'll find the **Hall of Prayer for Good Harvests**. The middle section was once reserved for the Emperor of Heaven, who was the only one allowed to set foot on the eastern side, while aristocrats and high-ranking officials walked on the western strip. ■TIP→ If you're coming by taxi, enter the park through the southern entrance (Tiantan Nanmen). This way you approach the beautiful Hall of Prayer for Good Harvests via the Danbi Bridge—the same route the emperor favored.

Directly east of this hall is a long, twisting platform, which once enclosed the animal-killing pavilion. The Long Corridor was traditionally hung with lanterns on the eve of sacrifices. Today it plays host to scores of Beijingers singing opera, playing cards and chess, and fan dancing.

Be sure to whisper into the echo wall encircling the **Imperial Vault of Heaven**. This structure allows anyone to eavesdrop. It takes a minute to get the hang of it, but with a friend on one side and you on the other it's possible to hold a conversation by speaking into the wall. Tilt your head in the direction you want your voice to travel for best results. Just inside the south gate is the **Round Altar**, a three-tiered, white-marble structure where the emperor worshipped the winter solstice; it's based

Playing with ribbons in Beihai Park.

around the divine number nine. Nine was regarded as a symbol of the power of the emperor, as it's the biggest single-digit odd number, and odd numbers are considered masculine and therefore more powerful.

**The Hall of Abstinence,** on the western edge of the grounds, is where the emperor would retreat three days before the ritual sacrifice. To understand the significance of the harvest sacrifice at the Temple of Heaven, it's important to keep in mind that the legitimacy of a Chinese emperor's rule depended on what is known as the *tian ming*, or the mandate of heaven, essentially the emperor's relationship with the gods.

A succession of bad harvests, for example, could be interpreted as the emperor losing the favor of heaven and could be used to justify a change in emperor or even in dynasty. When the emperor came to the Temple of Heaven to pray for good harvests and to pay homage to his ancestors, there may have been a good measure of self-interest to his fervor.

The sacrifices consisted mainly of animals and fruit placed on altars surrounded by candles. Many Chinese still offer sacrifices of fruit and incense on special occasions, such as births, deaths, and weddings.

■ TIP➜ We recommend buying an all-inclusive ticket. If you only buy a ticket into the park, you'll need to pay an additional Y20 to get into each building.

Beijing's new subway Line 5 (purple line) makes getting to the Temple of Heaven easier than ever. Get off at the Tiantan Dongmen (Temple of Heaven East Gate) stop. The line also runs to the Lama Temple (Yonghegong), so combining the two sites in a day makes perfect sense.

Automatic audio guides (Y40) are available at stalls inside all four entrances. ⊠ *Yongdingmen Dajie (South Gate), Xuanwu District* ☎ *010/6702–8866* ⊕ *en.tiantanpark.com* ⊠ *All-inclusive ticket Y35; entrance to park only Y15* ⊙ *Daily 6 am–10 pm; ticket booth closes at 4:30.*

### WORTH NOTING

**Museum of Antique Currency** (北京古代钱币博物馆 *Běijīng gǔdài qiánbì bówùguǎn*). This museum in a tiny courtyard house within the Deshengmen tower complex, showcases a small but impressive selection of rare Chinese coins. Explanations are in Chinese only. Also in the courtyard are coin and curio dealers. ⊠ *Deshengmen Jianlou, Bei'erhuan Zhonglu, Xicheng District* ☎ *010/6602–4178* ⊠ *Y10* ⊙ *Tues.–Sun. 9–4.*

**Prince Gong's Palace** (恭王府 *Gōngwángfǔ*). This grand compound sits in a neighborhood once reserved for imperial relatives. Built in 1777 during the Qing Dynasty, it fell to Prince Gong—brother of Qing emperor Xianfeng and later an adviser to Empress Dowager Cixi—after the original inhabitant was executed for corruption. With nine courtyards joined by covered walkways, it was once one of Beijing's most lavish residences. The museum offers Beijing opera and tea to visitors who pay the higher ticket price. Some literary scholars believe this was the setting for *Dream of the Red Chamber,* one of China's best-known classical novels. ⊠ *17 Qianhai Xijie, Xicheng District* ☎ *010/8328–8149* ⊕ *www.pgm.org.cn* ⊠ *Y40–Y70* ⊙ *Mid-Mar.–mid.-Nov., daily 8–4; mid.-Nov.–mid.-Mar., daily 7:30–4:30.*

**Soong Ching-ling's Former Residence** (宋庆龄故居 *Sòng Qìnglíng gùjū*). Soong Ching-ling (1893–1981) was the youngest daughter of the wealthy, American-educated bible publisher, Charles Soong. At the age of 18, disregarding her family's strong opposition, she eloped to marry the much older Sun Yat-sen. When her husband founded the Republic of China in 1911, Soong Ching-ling became a significant political figure. In 1924 she headed the Women's Department of the Nationalist Party. Then in 1949 she became the vice president of the People's Republic of China. Throughout her career she campaigned tirelessly for the emancipation of women, and she helped lay the foundations for many of the rights that modern-day Chinese women enjoy today. This former palace was her residence and workplace and now houses a small museum, which documents her life and work. ⊠ *46 Houhai Beiyan, Xicheng District* ☎ *010/6404–4205* ⊠ *Y20* ⊙ *Apr.–Oct., daily 9–6; Nov.–Mar., daily 9–4.*

## CHAOYANG DISTRICT

Welcome to the new China. In fact, there's precious little of Beijing's ancient history found in Chaoyang District, where much of the old has been razed to make way for the blingy new. Impeccably dressed Chinese women shop the afternoons away at gleaming new malls, young tycoons and princelings park their Ferraris on the sidewalks, and everyone who's anyone congregates at the booming nightclubs filled with hip-hop music and VIP bottle service.

**DID YOU KNOW?**

The Temple of Heaven's overall layout symbolizes the relationship between Heaven and Earth. Earth is represented by a square and Heaven by a circle. The temple complex is surrounded by two cordons of walls; the taller outer wall is semicircular at the northern end (Heaven) and shorter and rectangular at the southern end (Earth). Both the Hall of Prayer for Good Harvests and the Circular Mound Altar are round structures on a square yard.

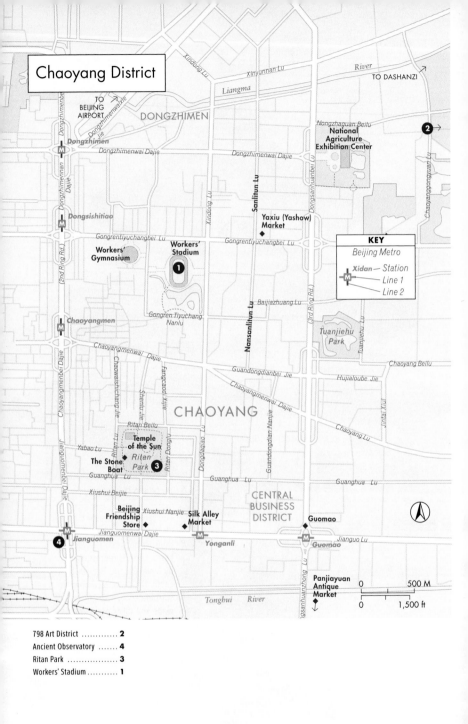

# Chaoyang District

TO BEIJING AIRPORT

DONGZHIMEN

TO DASHANZI

National Agriculture Exhibition Center

Yaxiu (Yashow) Market

Workers' Gymnasium

Workers' Stadium **1**

Tuanjiehu Park

CHAOYANG

CENTRAL BUSINESS DISTRICT

Temple of the Sun

The Stone Boat

Ritan Park **3**

Beijing Friendship Store

Silk Alley Market

Guomao

Panjiayuan Antique Market

Tonghui River

### KEY
*Beijing Metro*

**Xidan** — *Station*
Ⓜ — *Line 1*
— *Line 2*

0 — 500 M
0 — 1,500 ft

798 Art District .......... **2**
Ancient Observatory ....... **4**
Ritan Park .......... **3**
Workers' Stadium .......... **1**

## MAO ZEDONG (1893–1976)

Some three decades after his passing, Mao Zedong continues to evoke radically different feelings. Was he the romantic poet-hero who helped the Chinese stand up against foreign aggression? Or was he a monster whose policies caused the deaths of tens of millions of people? Born into a relatively affluent farming family in Hunan, Mao became active in politics at a young age; he was one of the founding members of the Chinese Communist Party in 1921. When the People's Republic of China was established in 1949, Mao served as chairman. After a good start in improving the economy, he launched radical programs in the mid-1950s. The party's official assessment is that Mao was 70% correct and 30% incorrect. His critics reverse this ratio.

### GETTING HERE AND AROUND

The heart of Chaoyang District is accessible via Lines 1, 2, and 10 on the subway, but the district is huge and the sites are broadly distributed. Taking taxis between sites is usually the easiest way to get around. The 798 Art District is especially far away from central Beijing, and so a taxi is also the best bet (about Y30 from the center of town). Buses go everywhere, but they're slow.

### MAKING THE MOST OF YOUR TIME

You can spend years lost in Chaoyang District and never get bored. There's plenty to do, but very few historical sights. Spend a morning shopping at **Silk Alley Market** or **Panjiayuan Antiques Market** (best on weekend mornings) and the afternoon cooling off at **Ritan Park** or **Chaoyang Park,** the latter a large and pleasant park with a lot of activities for kids. Next, head to one of the numerous bar streets for refreshments. If you like contemporary art, browse the galleries at **798 Art District.**

### TOP ATTRACTIONS

**798 Art District** (798艺术区 *Qījiǔbā yìshù qū*). The Art District, northeast of Beijing, is the site of several state-owned factories, including Factory 798, which originally produced electronics. Beginning in 2002, artists and cultural organizations began to move into the area, gradually developing the old buildings into galleries, art centers, artists' studios, design companies, restaurants, and bars. There are regularly scheduled art exhibits and events; some of the best can be found at the **Ullens Center for Contemporary Art** (ucca.org.cn). ⊠ *Chaoyang District* ⊕ *www.798district.com/.*

**Ancient Observatory** (北京古观象台 *Běijīng gǔguānxiàng tái*). This squat tower of primitive stargazing equipment peeks out next to the elevated highways of the Second Ring Road. It dates to the time of Genghis Khan, who believed that his fortunes could be read in the stars. Many of the bronze devices on display were gifts from Jesuit missionaries who arrived in Beijing and shortly thereafter ensconced themselves as the Ming court's resident stargazers. To China's imperial rulers, interpreting the heavens was key to holding onto power; a ruler knew when, say, an eclipse would occur, or he could predict the best time to plant crops. Celestial phenomena like eclipses and comets were believed to portend change; if left unheeded they might cost an emperor his legitimacy—or mandate of heaven. Records of celestial observations at or near this site go back more than 500 years, making this the longest documented astronomical viewing site in the world.

The main astronomical devices are arranged on the roof. Writhing bronze dragon sculptures adorn some of the astronomy pieces at Jianguo Tower, the main building that houses the observatory. Among the sculptures are an armillary sphere to pinpoint the position of heavenly bodies and a sextant to measure angular distances between stars, along with a celestial globe. Inside, the dusty exhibition rooms shelter ancient star maps with information dating back to the Tang Dynasty. A Ming Dynasty star map and ancient charts are also on display. Most of the ancient instruments were looted by the Allied Forces in 1900, only to be returned to China at the end of World War I. ⊠ *2 Dongbiaobei Hutong, Jianguomenwai Dajie, Chaoyang District* ☎ *010/6524–2202* ✑ *Y10* ☉ *Daily 9–4:30* Ⓜ *Jianguomen.*

### WORTH NOTING

**Ritan Park** (日坛公园 *Rìtán gōngyuán*). A cool oasis of water and trees just west of the Central Business District, Ritan Park (also known as "Temple of the Sun Park") is highly popular. Locals go to stretch their legs, but the embassy crowd is drawn in by the mojitos served at the Stone Boat. ⊠ *Ritan Lu, northeast of Jianguomen, Dongcheng District* ☎ *010/8561–4261* ✑ *Free* ☉ *Daily 6 am–9 pm.*

**Workers' Stadium** (工人体育场 *Gōngrén tǐyùchǎng*). North of Ritan Park is the Workers' Stadium complex, where many of the biggest visiting acts perform. The famous Sanlitun Bar Street is several blocks east of Workers' Stadium and runs north–south; this is the area that's known for its nightlife catering to foreigners, expats, and young Chinese. ⊠ *Gongti Rd, Chaoyang District* ✑ *Varies according to event* ☉ *Varies according to event* Ⓜ *Dongsishitiao.*

## HAIDIAN DISTRICT

In the last decade or so, Haidian has become Beijing's educational and techno mecca. The major IT players are all located here (including offices of Microsoft, Siemens, NEC, and Sun). Here, in the Wudaokou and Zhongguancun neighborhoods, you'll find kids geeking out over the latest gadgets at electronics superstores, studying in one of the many cafés, or blowing off steam at some of the area's dance clubs.

### GETTING HERE AND AROUND

Subway Line 13 stops at Wudaokou, the heart of Haidian. Line 4 stops at both the Beijing Zoo and the Old Summer Palace. Otherwise, the Summer Palace, Old Summer Palace, Fragrant Hills Park, and the Beijing Botanical Garden are all rather far away in the northwest of the city and are best reached by taxi. To save money, take the train to the Xizhimen (or Wudaokou) subway station and take a taxi from there.

**MAKING THE MOST OF YOUR TIME**

Because the **Summer Palace** is so large, with its lovely lakes and ancient pavilions, it makes for an entire morning of great exploring. The **Old Summer Palace** is close by, so visiting the two sites together is ideal if you've got the energy.

**Fragrant Hills Park** is a charming outing, but keep in mind that it takes at least an hour and a half to get there from the city center. The **Beijing Botanical Garden,** with some 2,000 types of orchids, bonsai, and peach and pear blossoms, along with the **Temple of the Reclining Buddha,** is also fun, especially for green thumbs. Plan to spend most of a day if you go to either of these sites.

**TOP ATTRACTIONS**

**Beijing Botanical Garden** (北京植物园 *Běijīng zhíwùyuán*). Sitting at the feet of the Western Hills in Beijing's northwestern suburbs, the Beijing Botanical Garden, opened in 1955, hosts China's largest plant collection: 6,000 different plant species from all over northern China, including 2,000 types of trees and bushes, more than 1,600 species of tropical and subtropical plants, 1,900 kinds of fruit trees, and 500 flower species. With its state-of-the-art greenhouse and a variety of different gardens, this is a pleasant place to explore, especially in spring, when the peach trees burst with pretty blooms. An added feature is the wonderful Temple of the Reclining Buddha, which has an enormous statue that, it's said, took 7,000 slaves to build. ⊠ *Xiangshan Wofosi, Haidian District* ☎ *010/6259–1283* ⊠ *Outdoor garden Y5* ⊗ *7–5 (outdoor garden).*

**Beijing Zoo** (北京动物园 *Běijīng dòngwùyuán*). Though visitors usually go straight to see the giant pandas, don't miss the other interesting animals, like tigers from the northeast, yaks from Tibet, enormous sea turtles from China's seas, and red pandas from Sichuan. The zoo started out as a garden belonging to one of the sons of Shunzhi, the first emperor of the Qing dynasty. In 1747, the Qianlong emperor had it refurbished (along with other imperial properties, including the summer palaces) and turned it into a park in honor of his mother's 60th birthday. In 1901, the Empress Dowager gave it another extensive facelift and used it to house a collection of animals given to her as a gift by a Chinese minister who had bought them during a trip to Germany. By the 1930s, most of the animals had died and were stuffed and put on display in a museum on the grounds. ⊠ *137 Xizhimenwai Dajie, Xicheng District* ☎ *010/6839–0274* ⊠ *Apr.–Oct. Y15; Nov.–Mar. Y10 plus Y5 for panda site* ⊗ *Apr.–Oct. 7:30–6; Nov.–Mar. 7:30–5.*

**Big Bell Temple** (大钟寺 *Dàzhōng sì*). This 18th-century temple shields China's biggest bell and more than 400 smaller bells and gongs from the Ming, Song, and Yuan dynasties. The Buddhist temple—originally used for rain prayers—has been restored after major damage inflicted during the Cultural Revolution. Before it opened as a museum in 1985, the buildings were used as Beijing No. 2 Food Factory. The bells here range from a giant 7 meters (23 feet) high to hand-sized chimes, many of them corroded to a pale green by time.

The giant, two-story bell, inscribed with the texts of more than 100 Buddhist scriptures (230,000 Chinese characters), is also said to be

China's loudest. Believed to have been cast during Emperor Yongle's reign, the sound of this 46-ton relic can carry more than 15 km (10 miles) when struck forcibly. The bell rings 108 times on special occasions like Spring Festival, one strike for each of the 108 personal worries defined in Buddhism. People used to throw coins into a hole in the top of the bell for luck. The money was swept up by the monks and used to buy food. Enough money was collected in a month to buy provisions that would last for a year. ■TIP➔ **You can ride the subway to the temple: transfer from Dongzhimen on Line 2 to the above-ground Line 13 and go one stop north to Dazhong Si station.** ✉ *1A Beisanhuanxi Lu, Haidian District* ☎ *010/8213–2630* 💴 *Y20* ⏱ *Tues.–Sun. 9–4:30* Ⓜ *Dazhong Si.*

Fodor's Choice ★ **Old Summer Palace** (圆明园 *Yuánmíngyuán*). About the size of New York's Central Park, this ruin was once a grand collection of palaces—the emperor's summer retreat from the 15th century to 1860, when it was looted and blown up by British and French soldiers. More than 90% of the original structures were Chinese-style wooden buildings, but only the European-style stone architecture (designed after Versailles by Jesuits and added during the Qing Dynasty) survived the fires. Many of the priceless relics that were looted are still on display in European museums, and China's efforts to recover them have been mostly unsuccessful. Beijing has chosen to preserve the vast ruin as a "monument to China's national humiliation," though the patriotic slogans that were once scrawled on the rubble have now been cleaned off.

The palace is made up of three idyllic parks: Yuanmingyuan (Garden of Perfection and Light) in the west, Wanchunyuan (Garden of 10,000 Springs) in the south, and Changchunyuan (Garden of Everlasting Spring) where the ruins are like a surreal graveyard to European architecture. Here you'll find ornately carved columns, squat lion statues, and crumbling stone blocks that lie like fallen dominoes. An engraved concrete wall maze, known as Huanghuazhen (Yellow Flower), twists and turns around a European-style pavilion. Recently restored and located just to the left of the west gate of Changchunyuan, it was once the site of lantern parties during midautumn festivals. Palace maids would race each other to the pavilion carrying lotus lanterns. The park costs an extra Y15 to enter, but it's well worth it. The park and ruins take on a ghostly beauty if you come after a fresh snowfall. There's also skating on the lake when it's frozen over. ■TIP➔ **It's a long trek to the European ruins from the main gate. Electric carts buzz around the park; hop on one heading to Changchunyuan if you feel tired. Tickets are Y5.**

If you want to save money, take subway Line 13 to Wudaokou and then catch a cab to Yuanmingyuan. The recently opened Line 4 stops at the Old Summer Palace. ✉ *28 Qinghua Xilu, northeast of the Summer Palace, Haidian District* ☎ *010/6262–8501* 💴 *Park Y10; extra Y15 fee for sites* ⏱ *Park, daily 7–7; exhibits 8:30–5.*

Fodor's Choice ★ **Summer Palace** (颐和园 *Yíhéyuán*). Emperor Qianlong commissioned this giant royal retreat for his mother's 60th birthday in 1750. Anglo-French forces plundered, then burned, many of the palaces in 1860, and funds were diverted from China's naval budget for the renovations.

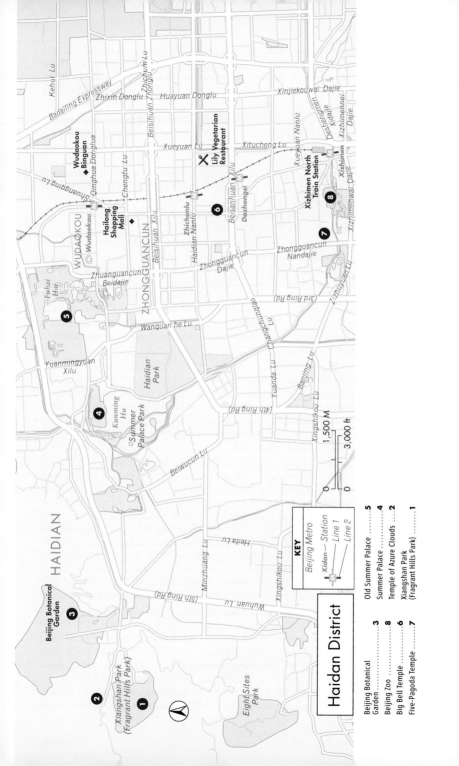

# Haidan District

KEY

Beijing Metro
Xidan — Station
— Line 1
— Line 2

Beijing Botanical Garden ........ **3**
Beijing Zoo ........ **8**
Big Bell Temple ........ **6**
Five-Pagoda Temple ........ **7**

Old Summer Palace ........ **5**
Summer Palace ........ **4**
Temple of Azure Clouds ........ **2**
Xiangshan Park
(Fragrant Hills Park) ........ **1**

Empress Dowager Cixi retired here in 1889. Nine years later it was here that she imprisoned her nephew, Emperor Guangxu, after his reform movement failed. In 1903, she moved the seat of government from the Forbidden City to the Summer Palace, from where she controlled China until her death in 1908.

Nowadays the place is undoubtedly romantic. Pagodas and temples perch on hillsides; rowboats dip under arched stone bridges; and willow branches brush the water. The greenery provides a welcome relief from the loud, bustling city. It also teaches a fabulous history lesson. You can see firsthand the results of corruption: the opulence here was bought with siphoned money as China crumbled, while suffering repeated humiliations at the hands of colonialist powers. The entire gardens were for Empress Dowager's exclusive use. UNESCO placed the Summer Palace on its World Heritage list in 1998.

The **Hall of Benevolent Longevity** is where Cixi held court and received foreign dignitaries. It's said that the first electric lights in China shone here. Just behind the hall and next to the lake is the **Hall of Jade Ripples**, where Cixi kept the hapless Guangxu under guard while she ran China in his name. Strung with pagodas and temples, including the impressive Tower of the Fragrance of Buddha, Glazed Tile Pagoda, and the Hall that Dispels Clouds, **Longevity Hill** is the place where you can escape the hordes of visitors—take your time exploring the lovely northern side of the hill.

Most of this 700-acre park is underwater. **Kunming Lake** makes up around three-fourths of the complex, and is largely man-made. The excavated dirt was used to build Longevity Hill. This giant body of water extends southward for 3 km (2 miles); it's ringed by tree-lined dikes, arched stone bridges, and numerous gazebos. In winter, you can skate on the ice. The less-traveled southern shore near Humpbacked Bridge is an ideal picnic spot.

At the west end of the lake you'll find the **Marble Boat**, which doesn't actually float and was built by Dowager Empress Cixi with money meant for the navy. The **Long Corridor** is a wooden walkway that skirts the northern shoreline of Kunming Lake for about half a mile until it reaches the marble boat. The ceiling and wooden rafters of the Long Corridor are richly painted with thousands of scenes from legends and nature—be on the lookout for Sun Wukong (the Monkey King). Cixi's home, in the Hall of Joyful Longevity, is near the beginning of the Long Corridor. The residence is furnished and decorated as Cixi left it. Her private theater, called the **Grand Theater Building**, just east of the hall, was constructed for her 60th birthday and cost 700,000 taels of silver.

Subway Line 4 stops at the Summer Palace. Get off at Beigongmen and take exit C for the easiest access to the north gate of the park. Otherwise, you'll have to take a taxi. It's best to come early in the morning to get a head start before the busloads of visitors arrive. You'll need the better part of a day to explore the grounds. Automatic audio guides can be rented for Y40 at stalls near the ticket booth. ⊠ *Yiheyuan Lu and Kunminghu Lu, 12 km (7½ miles) northwest of downtown Beijing, Haidian District* ☏ *010/6288–1144* ⊕ *www.summerpalace-china.com*

The marble ruins of the Old Summer Palace can be found in Changchunyuan (Garden of Everlasting Spring).

*Y60 summer all-inclusive, Y50 winter* ⊘ *Apr.–Oct., daily 8:30–5; Nov.–Mar., daily 9–4* Ⓜ *Beigongmen.*

**Xiangshan Park** (香山公园 *Xiāngshān gōngyuán*). This hillside park, also known as Fragrant Hills Park, is northwest of Beijing and was once an imperial retreat. From the eastern gate you can hike to the summit on a trail dotted with small temples. If you're short on time, ride a cable car to the top. Note that the park becomes extremely crowded on pleasant fall weekends, when Beijingers turn out en masse to view the changing colors of the autumn leaves. ⊠ *Haidian District* ☎ *010/6259–1155* *Y10, one-way cable car Y60* ⊘ *Daily 6–6.*

## WORTH NOTING

**Five-Pagoda Temple** (五塔寺 *Wŭtă sì*). Hidden among trees just behind the zoo and set amid carved stones, the temple's five pagodas reveal obvious Indian influences. It was built during the Yongle years of the Ming Dynasty (1403–1424), in honor of an Indian Buddhist who came to China and presented a temple blueprint to the emperor. Elaborate carvings of curvaceous figures, floral patterns, birds, and hundreds of Buddhas decorate the pagodas. Also on the grounds is the **Beijing Art Museum of Stone Carvings,** with its collection of some 1,000 stelae and stone figures. ⊠ *24 Wuta Si, Baishiqiao Lu, Haidian District* ☎ *010/6217–3543* *Y20* ⊘ *Tues.–Sun. 9–4.*

**Temple of Azure Clouds** (碧云寺 *Biyún sì*). Once the home of a Yuan Dynasty official, the site was converted into a Buddhist temple in 1366 and enlarged during the 16th and 17th centuries by imperial eunuchs who hoped to be buried here. The temple's five main courtyards ascend a slope in **Fragrant Hills Park**. Although severely damaged during the Cultural Revolution, the complex has been beautifully restored.

The main attraction is the Indian-influenced **Vajra Throne Pagoda**. Lining its walls and five pagodas are gracefully carved stone-relief Buddhas and bodhisattvas. The pagoda once housed the remains of Nationalist China's founding father, Dr. Sun Yat-sen, who lay in state here between March and May 1925, while his mausoleum was being constructed in Nanjing. A hall in one of the temple's western courtyards houses about 500 life-size wood and gilt arhats (Buddhists who have reached enlightenment)—each displayed in a glass case. ⊠ *Xiangshan Park, Haidian District* ☎ *010/6259–1155* ⊲ *Park Y10, temple Y10* ⊘ *Daily 8–4:30.*

# WHERE TO EAT

China's economic boom has fueled a culinary revolution in Beijing, with just about every kind of food now available in the capital. Today you can eat a wide variety of regional cuisines, including unusual specialties from Yunnan, earthy Hakka cooking from southern China, Tibetan yak and *tsampa* (barley flour), numbingly spicy Sichuan cuisine, and chewy noodles from Shaanxi.

The capital also offers plenty of international cuisines, including French, German, Thai, Japanese, Brazilian, Malaysian, and Italian, among others.

You can spend as little as $5 per person for a decent meal or $100 and up on a lavish banquet. The venues are part of the fun, ranging from swanky restaurants to holes-in-the-wall and refurbished courtyard houses. Reservations are always a good idea, so book as far ahead as you can and reconfirm as soon as you arrive.

People tend to eat around 6 pm and even though the last order is usually taken around 9 pm, some places remain open until the wee morning hours. Tipping can be tricky. Though it isn't required, some of the larger, fancier restaurants will add a 15% service charge to the bill. Be aware before you go out that small and medium venues take only cash payment; more established restaurants usually accept credit cards.

Great local beers and some international brands are available everywhere in Beijing, and many Chinese restaurants now have extensive wine menus.

*Prices in the reviews are the average cost of a main course at dinner or, if dinner is not served, at lunch. Use the coordinate (✛ A1) at the end of each listing to locate a site on the corresponding map.*

## DONGCHENG DISTRICT

$ ✕ **Café de la Poste** (云游驿 *Yúnyóu yì*). In almost every French village,
FRENCH town, or city there's a Café de la Poste, where people go for a cup of coffee, a beer, or a simple family meal. This haunt lives up to its name: It's a steak-lover's paradise, with such favorites as finely sliced marinated beefsteak served with lemon-herb vinaigrette and steak tartare. If the next table orders banana flambé, we promise the warm

## CHINESE CUISINE

To help you navigate China's cuisines, we have used the following terms in our restaurant reviews.

**Beijing:** As the seat of government for several dynasties, Beijing cuisine has melded the culinary traditions of many cultures. Specialties include Peking duck, *ma doufu* (spicy tofu), zhajiang noodles, flash-boiled tripe, and a wide variety of snack food.

**Cantonese:** A diverse cuisine that roasts and fries, braises and steams. Spices are used in moderation. Dishes include steamed fish, sweet-and-sour pork, and roasted goose.

**Chinese:** Catchall term used for restaurants that serve cuisine from multiple regions of China.

**Chinese fusion:** Any Chinese cuisine with international influences.

**Chiu chow:** Known for its vegetarian and seafood dishes, which are mostly poached, steamed, or braised. Specialties include *popiah* (non-fried spring rolls) and fish-ball noodle soup.

**Hunan:** Flavors are spicy, with chili peppers, ginger, garlic, and dried salted black beans and preserved vegetables. Signature dishes are Mao's braised pork, steamed fish head with coarse chopped salted chilies, and cured pork with smoked bean curd.

**Guizhou:** The two most important cooking condiments that are used to prepare Guizhou's fiery hot cuisine are *zao lajiao* (pounded dried peppers brined in salt) and fermented tomatoes. The latter are used to make sour fish soup, the region's hallmark dish.

**Northern Chinese (Dongbei):** Staples are lamb and mutton, preserved vegetables, noodles, steamed breads, pancakes, stuffed buns, and dumplings.

**Sichuan (central province):** Famed for bold flavors and spiciness from chilies and numbing Sichuan peppercorns. Dishes include kong pao chicken, mapo bean curd, "dan dan" spicy noodles, twice-cooked pork, and tea-smoked duck.

**Shanghainese and Jiangzhe:** Cuisine characterized by rich flavors produced by braising and stewing, and the use of rice wine in cooking. Signature dishes are steamed hairy crabs and "drunken chicken."

**Taiwanese:** Diverse cuisine centers on seafood. Specialties include "three cups chicken" with a sauce made of soya, rice wine, and sugar; oyster omelets; cuttlefish soup; and dried tofu.

**Tibetan:** Cuisine reliant on foodstuffs grown at high altitudes including barley flour, yak meat, milk, butter, and cheese.

**Tan Family Cuisine:** Tan family cuisine originated in the home of Tan Zongjun (1846–1888), a native of Guangdong, who secured a high position in the Qing inner court in Beijing. He added other regional influences into his cooking, which resulted in this new cuisine.

**Yunnan (southern province):** This region's cuisine is noted for its use of vegetables, bamboo shoots, and flowers in its spicy preparations. Dishes include rice-noodle soup with chicken, pork, and fish; steamed chicken with ginseng and herbs; and cured Yunnan ham.

2

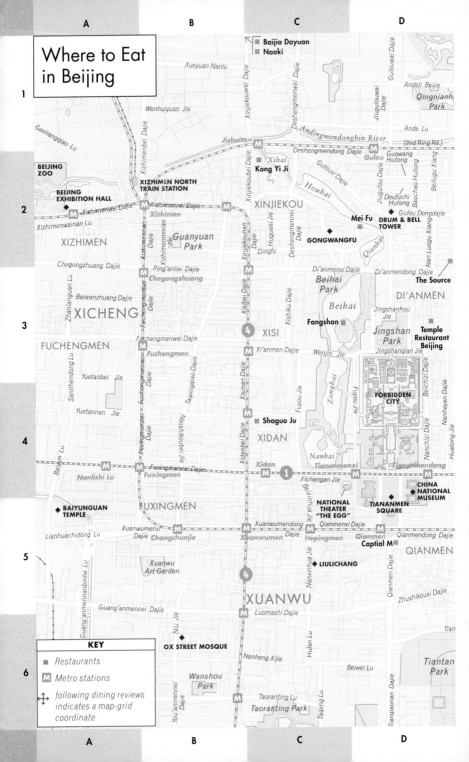

# Where to Eat in Beijing

KEY
- ■ Restaurants
- Ⓜ Metro stations
- ↔ following dining reviews indicates a map-grid coordinate

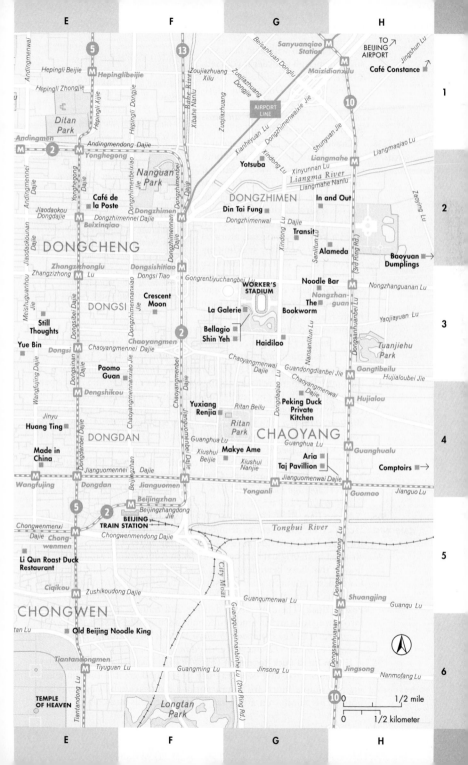

scent of its rum will soon have you smitten enough to order it yourself. $ *Average main: Y100* ✉ *58 Yonghegong Dajie, Dongcheng District* ☎ *010/6402–7047* ⊕ *www.cafedelaposte.net* ▬ *No credit cards* Ⓜ *Yonghegong* ✛ *E1.*

$$$$
ECLECTIC
Fodor'sChoice
★

✕ **Capital M.** This is one of the few restaurants in the capital with both stunning views and food worthy of the divine setting in front of Tiananmen Square. Australian-influenced classics with a Mediterranean twist are the order of the day here, served amid a vibrantly modern, muraled interior. Try the crispy suckling pig or roasted leg of lamb, and save room for the famed pavlova dessert: a heavenly cloud of meringue and whipped cream sprinkled with fresh fruit. On weekends, hearty brunches and afternoon high tea are served. $ *Average main: Y268* ✉ *2 Qianmen Pedestrian Street, Dongcheng District* ☎ *010/6702–2727* ⊕ *www.m-restaurantgroup.com* ⌛ *Reservations essential* ✛ *D5.*

$
ASIAN

✕ **Crescent Moon** (弯弯的月亮 *Wānwānde yuèliàng*). Unlike many of the bigger Xinjiang restaurants in town, there's no song and dance performance at this Uygur family-run spot, and none needed, as the solid cooking stands on its own merits. The heaping platters of grilled lamb skewers, *da pan ji* (chicken, potato, and green pepper stew), homemade yogurt, and freshly baked flatbreads are all terrific, as are the light and dark Xinjiang beers available here. The traditional green-and-white Islamic decor, Uygur CDs playing on the stereo, and clouds of hookah smoke lend an authentic Central Asian vibe to the dining experience. $ *Average main: Y60* ✉ *16 Dongsi Liutiao, Dongcheng District* ☎ *010/6400–5281* ▬ *No credit cards* ✛ *F3.*

$$$
CANTONESE
Fodor'sChoice
★

✕ **Huang Ting** (凰庭 *Huángtíng*). Beijing's traditional courtyard houses, facing extinction as entire neighborhoods are demolished to make way for high-rises, provide an exquisite setting here. The walls are constructed from original hutong bricks taken from centuries-old courtyard houses that have been destroyed. This is arguably one of Beijing's best Cantonese restaurants, serving southern favorites such as braised shark fin with crab meat and seared abalone with seafood, as well as a classic Peking duck. The dim sum is delicate and refined, and the deep-fried taro spring rolls and steamed pork buns are not to be missed. $ *Average main: Y200* ✉ *The Peninsula, 8 Jinyu Hutong, Wangfujing, Dongcheng District* ☎ *010/6512–8899* Ⓜ *Dongdan* ✛ *E4.*

$$
CHINESE
Fodor'sChoice
★

✕ **Li Qun Roast Duck Restaurant** (利群烤鸭店 *Lìqún kǎoyādiàn*). Juicy, whole ducks roasting over fragrant pear wood greet you upon entering this simple courtyard restaurant in a ramshackle hutong neighborhood. This family-run affair, far from the crowds and commercialism

Street food is ubiquitous in Beijing; kebabs, from China's northwest, are local favorites.

of Quanjude, remains a popular choice for the city's signature dish. The spot is a bit tricky to find: It's about a five-minute walk east from Qianmen Donglu, and you may have to stop to ask for directions until you start seeing duck graffiti and arrows pointing the way. Sure, the restrooms and dining room are a bit shabby, but it's hosted everyone from Al Gore to Anthony Bourdain. $ *Average main: Y140* ⊠ *11 Beixiangfeng Hutong, Zhengyi Lu, Dongcheng District* ☎ *010/6705–5578* ⌂ *Reservations essential* ▬ *No credit cards* Ⓜ *Chongwen* ✛ *E5.*

$$$
NORTHERN
CHINESE
Fodor's Choice
★

✕ **Made In China** (长安壹号 *Cháng'ān yīhào*). Discover one of Beijing's most exciting dining rooms at the Grand Hyatt: A glossy, deep cavern dotted with glassed-in kitchens where you can watch the chefs work their magic. From Peking duck to noodles to vegetable dishes, all are meticulously prepared before your eyes. The Peking duck is the standout dish, and some say it's the best to be found in this duck-crazed city. $ *Average main: Y200* ⊠ *Grand Hyatt, 1 Dong Chang An Jie, Dongcheng District* ☎ *010/8518–1234* ⌂ *Reservations essential* ✛ *E4.*

$
NORTHERN
CHINESE

✕ **Old Beijing Noodle King** (老北京炸酱面大王 *Lǎo Běijīng zhájiàngmiàn dàwáng*). This small chain of noodle houses serves hand-pulled noodles and traditional local dishes in a lively old-time atmosphere, with waiters shouting across the room to announce customers arriving. Try the classic *zhajiang* noodle served in a ground meat sauce with accompaniments of celery, bean sprouts, green beans, soybeans, slivers of cucumber, and red radish. $ *Average main: Y30* ⊠ *56 Dong Xinglong Jie, Dongcheng District* ☎ *010/6701–9393* ▬ *No credit cards* ✛ *E6.*

$
NORTHERN
CHINESE

✕ **Paomo Guan** (泡馍馆 *Pàomó guǎn*). The colorful murals decorating the front porch of this adorable spot will immediately catch your eye. Paomo Guan focuses on *paomo*—a Shaanxi trademark dish. Guests break a large piece of hardened flat bread into little pieces and then put them in a bowl. After adding condiments, the waiter takes your bowl to the kitchen where broth—simmered with spices, including star anise, cloves, cardamom, cinnamon sticks, and bay leaves—is poured over the bread bits. It's Chinese comfort food at its best. $ *Average main: Y20* ⊠ *53 Chaoyangmennei Nanxiaojie, Dongcheng District* ☎ *010/6525–4639* ▭ *No credit cards* ✛ *E3.*

$$$
SICHUAN
Fodor'sChoice
★

✕ **The Source** (都江源 *Dōujiāngyuán*). Amid a loft-like courtyard setting, this restaurant serves a set menu of Sichuan specialties that changes every two weeks. The menu includes several appetizers, both hot and mild dishes, and a few surprise concoctions from the chef. On request, the kitchen will tone down the spiciness. The location was once the backyard of a Qing Dynasty general regarded by the Qing court as "The Great Wall of China" for his military exploits. The grounds have been painstakingly restored; an upper level overlooks a small garden filled with pomegranate and date trees. Dining in the central yard is serene and acoustically protected from the hustle and bustle from outside the walls. $ *Average main: Y188* ⊠ *14 Banchang Hutong, Kuanjie, Dongcheng District* ☎ *010/6400–3736* ⌕ *Reservations essential* ✛ *D2.*

$
VEGETARIAN

✕ **Still Thoughts** (静思素食坊 *Jìngsī sùshí fāng*). Soft Buddhist chants hum in this clean, cheerful restaurant. Even though there's no meat on the menu, carnivores may still be happy here as much of the food is prepared to look and taste like meat. Try the crispy Peking "duck," or a "fish" (made of tofu skin) that even has scales carved into it. *Zaisu jinshen,* another favorite, has a filling that looks and tastes like pork. It's wrapped in tofu skin, deep-fried, and coated with a light sauce. $ *Average main: Y50* ⊠ *18A Dafosi Dongjie, Dongcheng District* ☎ *010/6405–2433* ▭ *No credit cards* ✛ *E3.*

$$$$
MODERN
EUROPEAN
Fodor'sChoice
★

✕ **Temple Restaurant Beijing.** Worship at the altar of Epicureanism and surround yourself with serenity at the city's best new restaurant, nestled in the heart of Old Beijing. TRB (as it's also known) serves high-end European cuisine in a spacious, minimalist dining room within a fabulously restored Ming dynasty Buddhist temple complex. The four-course tasting menu offers a selection of dishes such as hamachi carpaccio and broiled pigeon for Y398, or go all out with the Y980 eight-course degustation. The wine list is excellent, with a deep focus on Champagne, Bordeaux, and Burgundy. $ *Average main: Y250* ⊠ *23 Songzhusi, Shatan Beijie, Dongcheng District* ☎ *010/8400–2232* ⊕ *www. temple-restaurant.com* ⌕ *Reservations essential* ✛ *D3.*

$
CHINESE

✕ **Yue Bin** (悦宾饭馆 *Yuèbīn fànguǎn*). Holding the historic distinction of being the first private restaurant to open in Beijing after the Cultural Revolution era, Yue Bin's home-style cooking still attracts neighborhood residents, as well as hungry visitors from the nearby National Museum of Art. The no-frills dining room is just big enough for half a dozen spotless tables, where you'll see families chowing down on local favorites such as *suanni zhouzi,* garlic-marinated braised pork shoulder; *guota doufuhe,* tofu pockets stuffed with minced pork; and *wusitong,* a spring roll filled with duck and vegetables. $ *Average main: Y50* ⊠ *43 Cuihua Hutong, Dongcheng District* ☎ *010/6524–5322* ▭ *No credit cards* ✛ *E3.*

## XICHENG DISTRICT

**$$$$**
CHINESE

✕**Fangshan** (仿膳 *Fǎngshàn*). You can dine in imperial style at this extravagant courtyard villa on the shore of Beihai. Established in 1925 by three palace chefs, Fangshan serves elaborate dishes once prepared for the imperial family, based on recipes gathered across China. The place is best known for its filled pastries and steamed breads—traditional snack foods developed to satisfy Empress Dowager Cixi's sweet tooth. Banquet-style set meals are also available starting at Y228 per person. Be sure to make reservations two or three days in advance. $ *Average main: Y228* ✉ *Beihai Park, northwest of the Forbidden City, Xicheng District* ☎ *010/6401–1879* ⊕ *www.fangshanfanzhuang.com. cn* ⌖ *Reservations essential* Ⓜ *Tiananmen West* ✛ *C3.*

**$**
SHANGHAINESE

✕**Kong Yi Ji** (孔乙己 *Kǒngyǐjǐ*). Named for the down-and-out protagonist of a short story by Lu Xun (one of China's most famous writers), the first thing you'll see upon entering this restaurant is a bust of the author. The old-fashioned menu, which is bound with thread in a traditional fashion, features dishes from Lu's hometown of Shaoxing, near Shanghai. Also served is a wide selection of the region's famed *huangjiu*, sweet rice wine; it comes in heated silver pots and you can sip it from a special ceramic cup. The peaceful lakeside location is a perfect launching point for an after-dinner stroll. $ *Average main: Y80* ✉ *South shore of Shichahai, Deshengmennei Dajie, Xicheng District* ☎ *010/6618–4915* ✛ *C2.*

**$$$$**
CHINESE
Fodor's Choice
★

✕**Mei Fu** (梅府家 *Méifǔjiā*). In a plush courtyard on Houhai's south bank, Mei Fu oozes intimate elegance. The interior is filled with antique furniture and velvet curtains punctuated by pebbled hallways and waterfalls. Black-and-white photos of Mei Lanfang, China's famous opera star, who performed female roles, hang on the walls. Diners choose from set menus, starting at Y500 per person, which feature typical Jiangsu and Zhejiang cuisine, such as stir-fried shrimp, tender leafy greens, and dates filled with glutinous rice. A Y244 (per person) lunch is also available. $ *Average main: Y500* ✉ *24 Daxiangfeng Hutong, south bank of Houhai Lake, Xicheng District* ☎ *010/6612–6845* ⊕ *chinameilanfang. oinsite.cn* ⌖ *Reservations essential* ✛ *D2.*

**$**
CHINESE

✕**Shaguo Ju** (沙锅居 *Shāguō jū*). Established in 1741, Shaguo Ju serves a simple Manchu favorite—*bairou*, or white-meat pork, which first became popular 300 years ago. The first menu pages list all the dishes cooked in the *shaguo* (the Chinese term for a casserole pot). The classic shaguo bairou consists of strips of pork neatly lined up, concealing bok choy and glass noodles below. Shaguo Ju emerged as a result of ceremonies held by imperial officials and wealthy Manchus in the Qing Dynasty, which included sacrificial offerings of whole pigs. The meat offerings were later given away to the nightwatch guards, who shared the "gifts" with friends and relatives. Such gatherings gradually turned into a small business, and white meat became very popular. $ *Average main: Y60* ✉ *60 Xisi Nan Dajie, Xicheng District* ☎ *010/6602–1126* ▭ *No credit cards* Ⓜ *Xidan* ✛ *C4.*

2

## CHAOYANG DISTRICT

$$ BRAZILIAN 🍴 **Alameda.** Specializing in Brazilian fare, Alameda serves simple but delicious dishes in a funky outdoor mall tucked behind the hubbub of Sanlitun's bar street. The weekday lunch specials, at Y78–Y98, are one of the best deals in town. Their menu is light yet satisfying, with plenty of Latin influences. Crowds seek out the *feijoada*—Brazil's national dish—a hearty black-bean stew with pork and rice, served only on Saturdays. The glass walls and ceiling make it a bright, pleasant place to dine but magnify the din of the crowded room. [$] *Average main: Y120* ✉ *Nali Mall, Sanlitun Lu, Chaoyang District* ☎ *010/6417–8084* ✣ *H2.*

$$$$ INTERNATIONAL Fodor's Choice ★ 🍴 **Aria** (阿郦雅 *Ālìyǎ*). Enjoy deluxe hotel dining amid murals and paintings of cheerful Italian Renaissance characters at Aria. Choose from three settings: the posh dining and bar area on the first floor, intimate private rooms upstairs, or alfresco on a terrace, protected by the din of downtown by neatly manicured bushes and roses. A perfectly decadent meal would include foie gras and seafood bisque, followed by one of the excellent steaks, with the playful deconstructed cheesecake for dessert. The best deal at this elegant restaurant is the three-course weekday business lunch for just Y198. [$] *Average main: Y300* ✉ *China World Hotel, 1 Jianguomenwai Dajie, Chaoyang District* ☎ *010/6505–2266* [M] *Guomao* ✣ *H4.*

$ NORTHERN CHINESE 🍴 **Baoyuan Dumpling** (宝源饺子屋 *Bǎoyuán jiǎozi wū*). There's so much more to dumplings than standard pork and veggie fillings at this cheerfully homey joint. The photo-filled menu here offers dozens of creative filling options, many wrapped in bright skins of purple, green, and orange, thanks to the addition of vegetable juice to the dough. The options are mind-boggling, but feel free to mix and match: the minimum order for any kind of dumpling is 100 grams, or about 6 dumplings. If you can manage not to completely stuff yourself on dumplings, there's a separate menu with a solid selection of classic Chinese dishes—you'll see the popular *mapo doufu* on many tables. [$] *Average main: Y40* ✉ *North of 6 Maizidian Jie, Chaoyang District* ☎ *010/6586–4967* ▭ *No credit cards* ✣ *H3.*

$ TAIWANESE 🍴 **Bellagio** (鹿港小镇 *Lùgǎng xiǎozhèn*). This popular chain of bright, trendy-but-comfortable restaurants dishes up Taiwanese favorites to a largely young and upwardly mobile clientele. A delicious choice is their "three-cup chicken" *(sanbeiji)*, served in a fragrantly sizzling pot with ginger, garlic, and basil. You can finish your meal with a Taiwan-style mountain of crushed ice topped with condensed milk and beans, mangoes, strawberries, or peanuts. This branch is open until 4 am, making it a favorite with Beijing's clubbing set. The smartly dressed all-female staff—clad in black and white—have identical short haircuts. [$] *Average main: Y60* ✉ *6 Gongti Xilu, Chaoyang District* ☎ *010/6551–3533* ✍ *Reservations essential* ✣ *G3.*

$ CAFÉ 🍴 **The Bookworm** (书虫 *Shūchóng*). We love this Beijing spot when we're craving a double-dose of intellectual stimulation and decent café food. Thousands of English-language books fill the shelves and may be borrowed for a fee or read inside. New books and magazines are also for sale. This is a popular venue for guest speakers, poetry readings, film screenings, and live-music performances. The French chef offers a three-course set lunch and dinner. For a nibble, rather than a full meal, sandwiches, salads, and a cheese platter are also available. $ *Average main: Y80* ⊠ *Building 4, Nan Sanlitun Lu, Chaoyang District* ☎ *010/6586–9507* ⊕ *www.beijingbookworm.com* ▭ *No credit cards* ⊕ *G3.*

**$**
GERMAN
✕ **Café Constance.** Teutonic timbers frame the facade of this two-story restaurant and bakery offering specialities from southern Germany. Downstairs, find excellent breads, pastries, prepared sandwiches, and a fantastic Sacher torte, for take away or eating in at one of the café's tables. For more filling fare, head upstairs, where a hearty menu of sausages, schnitzels, and dumplings awaits, along with a selection of imported beers. $ *Average main: Y90* ⊠ *No. 27 Lucky St., Zaoying Lu, Chaoyang District* ☎ *010/5867–0201* ⊕ *www.germanbakery.com.cn* ⊕ *H1.*

**$**
FRENCH
✕ **Comptoirs de France Bakery** (法派 *Fǎpài*). This small chain of contemporary French-managed patisseries is the go-to shop in Beijing for fine cakes and pies, and makes an especially decadent chocolate tart. A variety of other goodies are on offer: airy macaroons, flaky croissants, savory croquettes and quiches, as well as hot beverages. Beside the standard coffee options of Americano, cappuccino, and latte, Comptoirs has a choice of unusual hot chocolate flavors. In the Sichuan pepper–infused chocolate drink, peppercorns float in the brew, giving it a pleasantly spicy aroma. $ *Average main: Y50* ⊠ *China Central Place, Building 15, N 102, 89 Jianguo Rd.(just northeast of Xiandai Soho), Chaoyang District* ☎ *010/6530–5480* ⊕ *www.comptoirsdefrance.com* ▭ *No credit cards* ⊕ *H4.*

**$$**
TAIWANESE
Fodor's Choice
★
✕ **Din Tai Fung** (鼎泰丰 *Dīngtàifēng*). Taipei's best known restaurant is this high-quality chainlet, now with several branches in Beijing, specializing in *xiaolongbao*—steamed dumplings with piping hot soup inside. Din Tai Fung offers several variations on the standard pork xiaolongbao, such as crab, chicken, or shrimp, and a luxurious pork and black truffle soup dumpling. At the risk of getting completely stuffed on carbs, the dandan noodles, fried rice, and sweet dessert dumplings are also worth a try. $ *Average main: Y120* ⊠ *24 Xinyuan Xili Zhongjie, Chaoyang District* ☎ *010/6462–4502* ⊕ *G2.*

**$**
CHINESE
✕ **Haidilao** (海底捞 *Hǎidǐlāo huǒguō*). There's often a wait for a table at this upscale hotpot haven, but don't despair, because there's plenty to do in the meantime. Enjoy a complimentary manicure or shoeshine while you munch on crunchy snacks to whet your appetite for the main draw: bubbling pots of broth (spices optional), a variety of fresh ingredients for dipping, and a DIY sauce bar with loads of choices. Order the Kungfu Noodles, and you'll get a show as a young waiter hand-pulls the noodles table-side. More than a dozen locations can be found around town. $ *Average main: Y90* ⊠ *2A Baijiazhuang Lu, Chaoyang District* ☎ *010/6595–2982* ⊕ *G3.*

**$**
NORTHERN
CHINESE
✕ **Hai Wan Ju** (海碗居 *Hǎiwǎnjū*). Haiwan means "a bowl as deep as the sea," fitting for this eatery that specializes in crockery filled with hand-pulled noodles. The interior is simple, with traditional wooden tables and benches. A *xiao'er* (a "young brother" in a white mandarin-collar shirt and black pants) greets you with a shout, which is then echoed in a thundering chorus by the rest of the staff. The clanking dishes and constant greetings re-create the busy atmosphere of an old teahouse.

There are two types of noodles here: *guoshui,* noodles that have been rinsed and cooled; and *guotiao,* meaning "straight out of the pot," ideal for winter days. Vegetables, including diced celery, radish, green beans, bean sprouts, cucumber, and scallions, are placed on individual small dishes. Nothing tastes as good as a hand-pulled noodle: it's doughy and chewy, a texture that can only be achieved by strong hands repeatedly stretching the dough. [$] *Average main: Y50* ✉ *36 Songyu Nanlu, Chaoyang District* ☎ *010/8731–3518* ✣ *G4.*

$ YUNNAN 🍴 **In and Out** (一坐一忘 *Yīzuò yīwàng*). In a loft-like setting, the atmosphere here is as light and fresh as the Yunnan cuisine on offer. Sink into a sofa by the big windows that look out onto a tree-lined street and enjoy some of the delightful treats: a soul-warming bowl of steamed chicken in broth, crispy potato pancakes, or eggs scrambled with fragrant jasmine flowers. [$] *Average main: Y60* ✉ *1 Sanlitun Beixiaojie, Chaoyang District* ☎ *010/8454–0086* ✣ *G2.*

$ CANTONESE 🍴 **La Galerie** (中国艺苑 *Zhōngguó yìyuàn*). Choose between two outdoor dining areas: one a wooden platform facing bustling Guanghua Road; the other well hidden in the back, overlooking the greenery of Ritan Park. Inspired Cantonese food and dim sum fill the menu. *Changfen* (steamed rice noodles) are rolled and cut into small pieces then stir-fried with crunchy shrimp, strips of lotus root, and baby bok choy, accompanied by sweet soybean, peanut, and sesame pastes. *Xiajiao* (steamed shrimp dumplings) envelop juicy shrimp and water chestnuts. [$] *Average main: Y90* ✉ *South gate of Ritan Park, Guanghua Lu, Chaoyang District* ☎ *010/8562–8698* [M] *Jianguomen* ✣ *G3.*

$ TIBETAN 🍴 **Makye Ame** (玛吉阿米 *Mǎjíāmǐ*). Prayer flags lead you to the second floor entrance of this Tibetan restaurant, where a pile of mani stones and a large prayer wheel greet you. Long Tibetan Buddhist trumpets, lanterns, and handicrafts decorate the walls, and the kitchen serves a range of hearty dishes that run well beyond the staples of yak-butter tea and *tsampa* (roasted barley flour). Try the vegetable *pakoda* (a deep-fried dough pocket filled with vegetables), curry potatoes, or roasted lamb spareribs. Heavy wooden tables with brass corners, soft lighting, and Tibetan textiles make this an especially soothing choice. [$] *Average main: Y70* ✉ *11 Xiushui Nanjie, 2nd floor, Chaoyang District* ☎ *010/6506–9616* [M] *Jianguomen* ✣ *G4.*

$ CANTONESE 🍴 **Noodle Bar** (面吧 *Miàn bā*). With a dozen seats surrounding the open kitchen, this petite dining room lives large when it comes to flavor. The brief menu lists little more than beef brisket, tendon, and tripe, which are stewed to chewy perfection and complemented with noodles hand-pulled right before your eyes. For those seeking a moment of respite in Beijing's busy Sanlitun district, this is the place for a light lunch and a quick noodle-making show. The service is efficient and friendly. [$] *Average main: Y70* ✉ *1949 The Hidden City, Gongti Beilu, Behind Pacific Century Place, Chaoyang District* ☎ *010/6501–1949* ✣ *G3.*

$ NORTHERN CHINESE Fodor's Choice ★ 🍴 **Peking Duck, Private Kitchen** (私房烤鸭 *Guǒguǒ sīfáng kǎoyā*). Delicious duck in comfortable surroundings, what more could one ask for? Doing away with the formal, banquet-style scene that accompanies most places serving roast duck, diners here lounge on comfortable sofas in a moderately sized, warmly lit dining room where the signature dish is made to perfection. The set menus, all including succulent Peking duck, are a terrific value and include other northern-style dishes such as kung pao shrimp and green beans in sesame sauce. Despite the name, this restaurant is very much open to the public, and it's quite popular so it's best to book ahead. $ *Average main: Y80* ⊠ *Vantone Center, 6A Chaowai Dajie, FS2015, Chaoyang District* ☎ *010/5907–1920* ✛ *G4.*

$

TAIWANESE

✕ **Shin Yeh** (欣叶 *Xīnyè*). The focus here is on Taiwanese flavors and freshness. *Caipudan* is a scrumptious turnip omelet and *fotiaoqiang* ("Buddha jumping over the wall") is a delicate soup with medicinal herbs and seafood. Last but definitely not least, try the *mashu*, a glutinous rice cake rolled in ground peanuts. Service is friendly and very attentive. $ *Average main: Y100* ⊠ *Xin Zhongguancun Shopping Center, 19 Zhongguancun Dajie, 4th Floor, Chaoyang District* ☎ *010/8248–6288* ✛ *G3.*

$

INDIAN

✕ **Taj Pavilion** (泰姬楼 *Tàijī lóu*). Beijing's best Indian restaurant, Taj Pavilion has been serving up all the classics since 1998, including chicken tikka masala, *palak panir* (creamy spinach with cheese), and *rogan josh* (tender lamb in curry sauce). Consistently good service and an informal atmosphere make this a well-loved neighborhood haunt. Newer branches have opened in Lido and Shunyi. $ *Average main: Y75* ⊠ *China Overseas Plaza North Tower, No 8 Guanghua Dong Li, Jianguomenwai Ave., 2nd floor, F2-03, Chaoyang District* ☎ *010/6505–5866* ⊕ *www.thetajpavilion.com* Ⓜ *Guomao* ✛ *H4.*

$

CHINESE

✕ **Three Guizhou Men** (三个贵州人 *Sānge Guìzhōurén*). The popularity of this cuisine prompted three Guizhou artist friends to set up shop in Beijing. There are many dishes here to recommend, but among the best are "beef on fire" (pieces of beef placed on a bed of chives over burning charcoal) accompanied by ground chilies; pork ribs; spicy lamb with mint leaves; and *mi doufu*, a rice-flour cake in spicy sauce. $ *Average main: Y70* ⊠ *Jianwai SOHO, Bldg. 7, 39 Dong Sanhuan Zhonglu, Chaoyang District* ☎ *010/5869–0598* Ⓜ *Guomao* ✛ *G5.*

$

SICHUAN

Fodor's Choice

★

✕ **Transit** (渡金湖 *Dùjīnhú*). This is one of Beijing's hottest restaurants, and we're not just talking about the chilies at the this glam Sichuan establishment. Located in the upscale Sanlitun Village North, Transit holds its own amid the surrounding luxury retailers, with designer interiors as sleek as a chic boutique. The region's fiery classics are stunningly prepared, with cold chicken in chili oil and dandan noodles garnering some of the ravest reviews. $ *Average main: Y100* ⊠ *Sanlitun Village North, N4-36, Chaoyang District* ☎ *010/6417–9090* ⌲ *Reservations essential* ☾ *Dinner only* ✛ *G2.*

$$$

JAPANESE

Fodor's Choice

★

✕ **Yotsuba** (四叶 *Sìyè*). This tiny, unassuming restaurant is arguably the best Japanese restaurant in town. It consists of a sushi counter—manned by a Japanese master working continuously and silently—and two small tatami-style dining areas, evoking an old-time Tokyo restaurant. The seafood is flown in from Tokyo's Tsukiji fish market. Reservations are a must for this dinner-only Chaoyang gem. A second location has opened nearby at Sanlitun Beixiaojie. $ *Average main: Y200* ⊠ *2 Xinyuan Xili Zhongjie, Building 2, Chaoyang District* ☎ *010/6464–2365* ⌲ *Reservations essential* ☾ *No lunch* ✛ *G2.*

**DID YOU KNOW?**

The Sanlitun became a favorite destination soon after the economic reforms of the late 1970s and early 1980s, when bars serving expatriates began to open. Today, the area is lined with bars, dance clubs, top-notch restaurants, and big-name shops, including the world's largest Adidas store.

**$** ✕ **Yuxiang Renjia** (渝乡人家 *Yúxiāng rénjiā*). Of the many Sichuan
SICHUAN restaurants in Beijing, the Yuxiang Renjia chain is the top choice for
many Sichuan natives living in the capital. Huge earthen vats filled
with pickled vegetables, hanging bunches of dried peppers and garlic,
and simply dressed servers evoke the Sichuan countryside. The restaurant does an excellent job of preparing provincial classics such as
*gongbao jiding* (diced chicken stir-fried with peanuts and dried peppers) and *ganbian sijidou* (green beans stir-fried with olive leaves and
minced pork). Thirty different Sichuan snacks are served for lunch on
weekends, all at very reasonable prices. There are now more than a
dozen locations around the city. $ *Average main: Y50* ✉ *Lianhe Dasha,
101 Chaowai Dajie, 5th Floor, Chaoyang District* ☎ *010/6588–3841*
⊕ *www.yuxiangrenjia.com* Ⓜ *Chaoyangmen* ✛ *F4.*

## HAIDIAN DISTRICT

**$$$$** ✕ **Baijia Dayuan** (白家大宅门 *Báijiā dà zháimén*). Staff dressed in rich-
CHINESE hued, Qing-dynasty attire welcome you at this grand courtyard house.
Bowing slightly, they'll say *"Nin jixiang"* ("May you have good fortune"). The mansion's spectacular setting was once the garden of Prince
Li, son of the first Qing emperor. Cao Xueqin, the author of the Chinese
classic *Dream of the Red Chamber,* is said to have lived here as a boy.
Featured delicacies include bird's-nest soup, braised sea cucumber, abalone, and authentic imperial snacks. On weekends, diners are treated
to short, live performances of Beijing opera. $ *Average main: Y250*
✉ *15 Suzhou St., Haidian District* ☎ *010/6265–4186* ⌔ *Reservations
essential* ✛ *C1.*

**$$$** ✕ **Naoki** (直树怀石料理餐厅 *Zhíshùhuáishí liàolǐcāntīng*). Modern
JAPANESE Beijing doesn't lack for fancy restaurants, but few are able to approach
FUSION the level of refinement found at this Japanese haven, set in the ultra-
luxe, restored imperial grounds of the Aman Resort at the Summer
Palace. The multi-course set menu introduces diners to chef Naoki Oku-
mura's selection of small dishes that marries French cooking techniques
to Japanese traditions, such as seared foie gras served on steamed egg
custard. If the weather is fine, sit outside by the reflecting pool for
a transcendent experience. $ *Average main: Y180* ✉ *Aman at Sum-
mer Palace, 1 Gongmenqian Jie, Summer Palace, Haidian District*
☎ *010/5987–9999* ⌔ *Reservations essential* ✛ *C1.*

# WHERE TO STAY

The hotel scene in Beijing today is defined by a multitude of polished
palaces. You can look forward to attentive service, improved ameni-
ties—such as conference centers, health clubs, and nightclubs—and, of
course, rising prices. "Western-style" comfort, rather than history and
character, is the main selling point for Beijing's hotels. Gone forever is
the lack of high-quality hotels that distinguished Beijing in the '70s.

If you're looking for something more intimate and historical, check out
the traditional courtyard houses that have been converted into small
hotels—they offer a quiet alternative to the fancier establishments.

There are a few things you should know before you book. Beijing's busiest seasons are spring and fall, with summer following closely behind. Special rates can be had during the low season, so make sure to ask about deals involving weekends or longer stays. If you are staying more than one night, you can often get some free perks—ask about free laundry service or free airport transfers.

The local rating system does not correspond to those of any other country. What is called a five-star hotel here might only warrant three or four elsewhere. This is especially true of the state-run hotels, which often seem to be rated higher than they deserve. And lastly, children 16 and under can normally share a room with their parents at no extra charge—although there may be a modest fee for adding an extra bed. Ask about this when making your reservation.

*Prices in the reviews are the lowest cost of a standard double room in high season. Use the coordinate (⊕ A1) at the end of each listing to locate a site on the corresponding map.*

## DONGCHENG DISTRICT

**$$**
HOTEL
Fodor'sChoice
★

**3+1 Bedrooms.** Modern, minimalist design—pure white interiors, freestanding bathtubs, individual courtyards—meets old Beijing at this intimate four-bedroom boutique hidden away within the quaint alleyways (*hutong*) near the historic Drum and Bell towers. **Pros:** spacious rooms; free in-room Wi-Fi and minibar; private terraces. **Cons:** no health club; no restaurants; some staff struggle with English. $ *Rooms from: Y1360* ✉ *17 Zhangwang Hutong, Jiu Gulou Dajie, Drum Tower, Dongcheng District* ☎ *010/6404–7030* ⊕ *www.3plus1bedrooms.com* ⟳ *3 rooms, 1 suite* ❤️❤️ *Breakfast* Ⓜ *Gulou Dajie* ⊕ *C2.*

**$$$**
HOTEL

**The Emperor** (皇家驿栈 *Huángjiā yìzhàn*). Though fronted by a boring brick facade, this hotel features a "cutting-edge" interior created by a team of international designers: guest rooms, replete with tube pillows, built-in sofas, angled desks, and color schemes bold enough to rely on bright yellows, rich reds, or sleek grays, can perhaps best be described as minimalist sci-fi chic (look for the wall-mounted flatscreen TVs and Wi-Fi)—whether or not you'll spend most of your time at the rooftop terrace and bar (with great Forbidden City views) remains to be seen. **Pros:** best rooftop terrace in the city; unbeatable views of the Forbidden City; unique, modern room design. **Cons:** no elevator; limited gym facilities; far from the subway. $ *Rooms from: Y1800* ✉ *33 Qihelou Jie, Dongcheng District* ⊕ *www.theemperor.com.cn* ⟳ *46 rooms, 9 suites* ❤️❤️ *No meals* Ⓜ *Dengshikou* ⊕ *D4.*

**$$$$**
HOTEL
Fodor'sChoice
★

**Grand Hyatt Beijing** (北京东方君悦酒店 *Běijīng Dōngfāngjūnyuè jiǔdiàn*). The wow factor at the Grand Hyatt Beijing—located close to Tiananmen Square and the Forbidden City—comes via its huge glass facade and even more extraordinary Olympic-size swimming pool: surrounded by lush vegetation, waterfalls, and statues, it has a "virtual sky" ceiling that imitates different weather patterns. **Pros:** great dining; plenty of shopping; very impressive pool and gym. **Cons:** dull rooms; overpriced bar; Internet is extra. $ *Rooms from: Y2500* ✉ *1 Dongchang'an Jie, corner of Wangfujing, Dongcheng District*

☎ *010/8518–1234* ⊕ *www.beijing.grand.hyatt.com* ⤢ *825 rooms, 155 suites* ⏹ *No meals* Ⓜ *Wangfujing* ✛ *D5.*

$
HOTEL
FAMILY
Fodor's Choice
★

🖼 **Holiday Inn Express Beijing Dongzhimen** (*Běijīng dōngzhīmén zhìxu*). Cheap and cheerful does it at this budget hotel close to Sanlitun (Beijing's lively nightlife center)—yes, it lacks the facilities you'd expect in pricier establishments (such as a pool and gym), and the guest rooms are somewhat small, but everything here is super spick-and-span, from the gleaming lobby to the surprisingly comfortable beds, while touches such as six shiny Apple Macs next to the front desk (free for use), plus a games area complete with Xbox, Wii, and foosball table add a little something extra; book yourself here for great value from a Holiday Inn that goes beyond brand expectations. **Pros:** cheap yet extremely modern and clean; tour operator next door; close to some great nightlife. **Cons:** breakfast can be crowded (and no lunch or dinner options); small rooms; subway is a long walk away. Ⓢ *Rooms from: Y558* ✉ *1 Chunxiu Road, Dongcheng District* ☎ *010/6416–9999* ⊕ *www.holidayinnexpress.com* ⤢ *350 rooms* ⏹ *Breakfast* Ⓜ *Dongzhimen* ✛ *G3.*

$
HOTEL

🖼 **Hotel Kapok** (木棉花酒店 *Mùmiánhuā jiǔdiàn*). Designed by Studio Pei Zhu (who also worked on the Olympics), this minimalist-style offering helped kick-start the boutique hotel movement in Beijing. **Pros:** comfortable rooms; near top sites; friendly staff. **Cons:** no pool; not everyone will like the glass-walled bathrooms; refurbishment needed. Ⓢ *Rooms from: Y800* ✉ *16 Donghuamen, Dongcheng District* ☎ *010/6525–9988* ⊕ *www.kapokhotelbeijing.com* ⤢ *89 rooms* ⏹ *Breakfast* Ⓜ *Tiananmen East* ✛ *D5.*

$$$$
HOTEL
Fodor's Choice
★

🖼 **Legendale** (励骏酒店 *Lìjùn jiǔdiàn*). Those fond of a classic European ambience will be drawn to the old-world spectacle that is the Legendale, a gigantic "château" from the outside, while inside a breathtaking gilded staircase winds upward to the towering atrium—a veritable "theater" with gilt balconies and a domelike atrium—with plenty of sparkling chandeliers and an antique Parisian fireplace at the center of it all. **Pros:** plenty of pampering; in a great neighborhood; luxurious rooms. **Cons:** high prices; vast size can make it feel empty; the faux European style will put off those in search of a more traditional Chinese experience. Ⓢ *Rooms from: Y2100* ✉ *90-92 Jinbao Street, Dongcheng District* ☎ *010/8511–3388* ⊕ *www.legendalehotel.com* ⤢ *390 rooms, 81 suites* ⏹ *Breakfast* Ⓜ *Dengshikou* ✛ *E5.*

$
HOTEL
Fodor's Choice
★

🖼 **LüSongyuan** (侣松园宾馆 *Lǚsōngyuán bīnguǎn*). The traditional wooden entrance to this delightful courtyard hotel, on the site of an old Mandarin's residence, is guarded by two *menshi* (stone lions)—this is a classic old-Beijing experience, turned over to tourism, with no attempts at modern updates or fancy design, but, rather, just a good choice for cheap, traditional living. **Pros:** convenient location; near restaurants; unfussy courtyard conversion. **Cons:** a lack of luxury; can be hard to find; carpets are in need of a clean. Ⓢ *Rooms from: Y850* ✉ *22 Banchang Hutong, Kuanjie, Dongcheng District* ☎ *010/6401–1116* ⤢ *55 rooms* ⏹ *No meals* Ⓜ *Zhangzizhonglu* ✛ *D3.*

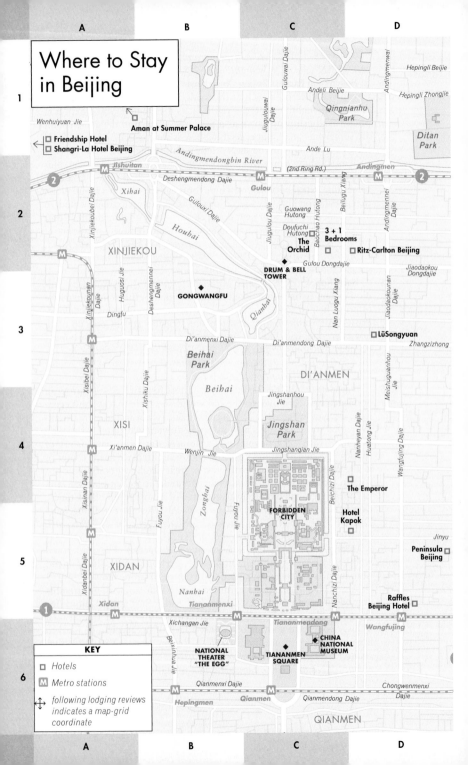

# Where to Stay in Beijing

**KEY**

- ☐ Hotels
- Ⓜ Metro stations
- ↔ following lodging reviews indicates a map-grid coordinate

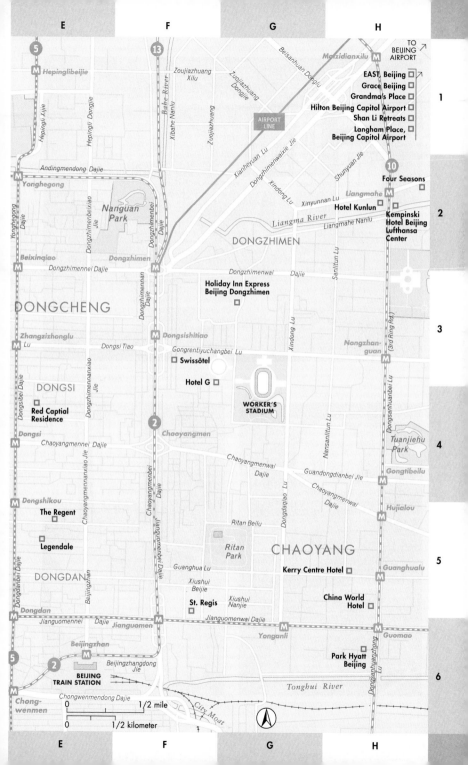

Fodor'sChoice ★

Red Capital Residence

Hotel G

Hotel Kapok

$ HOTEL Fodor's Choice ★ **The Orchid.** A smash hit in recent years, and a firm favorite among cool, independent travellers after somewhere trendy, and yet down-to-earth, the Orchid may be located in the middle of the action but is actually hidden away in an old network of hutong alleyways, rewarding guests after their search with its beautiful internal courtyard and rooftop terraces (with great views), its simple yet cozy and modern rooms; and hugely knowledgeable staff. *Rooms from: Y735 ✉ 65 Baochao Hutong, Gulou Dong Dajie, Gulou, Dongcheng District ☎ 010/8404–4818 www.theorchidbeijing.com 10 rooms Breakfast Ⓜ Guloudajie ✣ C2.*

WORD OF MOUTH

"I stayed at the Peninsula and it's in a great area—walkable to Tiananmen Square and the Forbidden City. St. Regis, Raffles and the Grand Hyatt were also nearby. However, this Peninsula was not as impressive as the Bangkok hotel." —moremiles

$$$ HOTEL Fodor's Choice ★ **Peninsula Beijing** (王府半岛酒店 *Wángfǔ bàndǎo jiǔdiàn*). Guests at the Peninsula Beijing enjoy an impressive combination of modern facilities and traditional luxury—guest rooms are a little small for this sort of hotel, but are superlatively well-appointed, with teak and rosewood flooring, colorful rugs, and high-tech touches like custom bedside control panels that let you adjust lighting, temperature, and the flat-screen TVs; the service is excellent, as is the spa. **Pros:** close to sightseeing, restaurants, and shopping; rooms are impeccable; near the Forbidden City. **Cons:** lobby is squeezed by the surrounding luxury shopping mall; hectic atmosphere; rooms could be bigger. *Rooms from: Y1800 ✉ 8 Jinyu Hutong, Wangfujing, Dongcheng District ☎ 010/8516–2888 www.peninsula.com 525 rooms, 59 suites No meals Ⓜ Dengshikou ✣ D5.*

$$$$ HOTEL Fodor's Choice ★ **Raffles Beijing Hotel** (北京饭店莱佛士 *Běijīng fàndiàn láifóshì*). Raffles is an iconic brand in Asia and this property certainly doesn't disappoint; in 2006, Singaporean designer Grace Soh transformed half of what used to be the Beijing Hotel into a vivid, modern space (crystal chandeliers in the lobby; a grand white staircase enveloped in a royal-blue carpet) while retaining its history—service is excellent, and the location, for tourism purposes, is flawless. **Pros:** within easy walking distance of the Forbidden City; nifty location for sightseeing; switched-on staff; spacious rooms. **Cons:** pricey restaurants; not in the right part of town for business travellers; occasional problems with the pool. *Rooms from: Y2500 ✉ 33 Dongchang'an Jie, off Wangfujing Dajie, Dongcheng District ☎ 010/6526–3388 www.raffles.com/beijing 171 rooms, 24 suites No meals Ⓜ Wangfujing ✣ D5.*

$ HOTEL Fodor's Choice ★ **Red Capital Residence** (新红资客栈 *Xīnhóngzī kèzhàn*). Each of the four rooms at this boutique courtyard hotel—located in a carefully restored home in Dongsi Hutong—are decorated with antiques and according to different themes, such as the Chairman's Suite, in playful homage to Mao, and the two Author's Suites (one inspired by Edgar Snow, a 1930s US journalist who lived in Beijing, and the other by Han Suyin, the Japanese novelist who wrote *Love is a Many-Splendored Thing,* among others); there is a cigar lounge where you can sit on original furnishings used by China's early revolutionary leaders, as well as a wine bar in a Cultural Revolution–era bomb shelter. **Pros:** Fodorites rave about the friendly service, unique atmosphere, and intimate feel. **Cons:** small rooms; limited facilities; quaint more than comfortable; dysfunctional web-

**WORD OF MOUTH**

"Really enjoyed our stay at the Ritz-Carlton Beijing. We were at the Ritz Financial Street, about a 10-minute walk from the subway. First class all the way." —Shar

site. $ *Rooms from: Y1050* ✉ *9 Dongsi Liutiao, Dongcheng District* ☎ *010/6402–7150* ⊕ *www.redcapitalclub.com.cn* ☞ *4 rooms* ⦿ *Breakfast* Ⓜ *Zhangzizhonglu* ✛ *E4.*

$$$$ 🛏 **The Regent** (北京丽晶酒店 *Běijīng lìjīng jiǔdiàn*). Some of the most
HOTEL suavely elegant guest rooms in the city, an excellent location—a block
Fodor's Choice from the Wangfujing shopping district—and an imposing, soaring glass-
★ walled lobby are just some reasons why the Regent is a top choice for the rich and famous (and those getting there). **Pros:** convenient location; close to the subway; spacious rooms. **Cons:** unimpressive breakfast; occasional blemishes in some rooms; check-in can be slow. $ *Rooms from: Y2250* ✉ *99 Jinbao Street, Dongcheng District* ☎ *010/8522–1888* ⊕ *www.regenthotels.com* ☞ *500 rooms, 25 suites* ⦿ *No meals* Ⓜ *Dengshikou* ✛ *E5.*

$ 🛏 **Zhuyuan Hotel** (竹园宾馆 *Zhúyuán bīnguǎn*). The charming "Bam-
HOTEL boo Garden" was actually once the residence of Kang Sheng, a sinister
FAMILY character responsible for "public security" during the Cultural Revolution, who nevertheless had fine taste in Chinese art and antiques (some which are still on display) but, as the hotel's English name suggests, the beautiful and peaceful grounds are the real highlight here. **Pros:** traditional feel; interesting *hutong* neighborhood; free Wi-Fi. **Cons:** room quality is variable; pricey for what you get; not that close to the big-name sights. $ *Rooms from: Y880* ✉ *24 Xiaoshiqiao Hutong, Jiugulou Dajie, Dongcheng District* ☎ *010/5852–0088* ⊕ *www.bbgh.com.cn* ☞ *40 rooms, 4 suites* ⦿ *No meals* Ⓜ *Gulou Dajie* ✛ *H3.*

## XICHENG DISTRICT

$$$$ 🛏 **Ritz-Carlton Beijing, Financial Street** (北京金融街丽思卡尔顿酒店
HOTEL *Běijīng lìsīkǎ'ěrdùn jiǔdiàn*). With ample amounts of glass and chrome, the Ritz-Carlton could be mistaken for one of the many sleek financial buildings that crowd its business-like Financial Street area; the interior is equally swish and contemporary, with crystal mythological animals in place for good luck and smart East-meets-West decors that match the Ritz standard—its location, excellent amenities, and eager-to-please staff make it popular with tour groups and business folk. **Pros:** impeccable service; luxurious atmosphere; incredible Italian dining. **Cons:** far from the city's attractions; expensive; lobby lacks pizzazz. $ *Rooms from: Y3500* ✉ *18 Financial Street, Xicheng District* ☎ *010/6601–6666* ⊕ *www.ritzcarlton.com* ☞ *253 rooms, 33 suites* ⦿ *No meals* Ⓜ *Fuchengmen* ✛ *D2.*

## CHAOYANG DISTRICT

**$$$$** **China World Hotel** (中国大饭店 *Zhōngguó dàfàndiàn*). Once placing
HOTEL high on lists of top Beijing hotels, this place now does opulence in a
rather unsubtle way—gold highlights in the lobby; marble tubs in the
luxe rooms; high-priced fine dining—but it more than lives up to its
look: the service is top rate, the restaurants are excellent (Aria, serving contemporary European cuisine, is particularly special), and the
attached mall/cinema offers a welcome escape. **Pros:** convenient location for business travelers; some superb restaurants; close to both the
subway and shopping. **Cons:** the bustle here can overwhelm; big and
impersonal; rooms are small for the price. $ *Rooms from: Y2800* ⊠ *1
Jianguomenwai Dajie, Chaoyang District* ☎ *010/6505–2266* ⊕ *www.
shangri-la.com* ⇆ *716 rooms, 26 suites* M *Guomao* ✛ *H5.*

**$$** **EAST, Beijing** (*Běijīng dōngyú*). Launched in 2012, EAST is the lat-
HOTEL est attempt by the people behind the Opposite House (a luxurious
Fodor's Choice boutique wonder) to create a business hotel with style, a place to do
★ business without the stiffness—note the communal networking space in
the cafe-inspired lounge. **Pros:** a business hotel with style; impeccable
service; great in-house dining and drinking. **Cons:** far from the main
tourist sights (other than 798); nearby subway yet to open; adjacent
park area still in development. $ *Rooms from: Y1250* ⊠ *22 Jiuxianqiao
Lu, Jiangtai, Chaoyang District* ☎ *010/8426–0888* ⊕ *www.east-beijing.
com* ⇆ *346 rooms, 23 suites* ⦿ *No meals* ✛ *H1.*

**$$$$** **Four Seasons Hotel Beijing** (*Běijīng sìjì jiǔdiàn*). When it comes to hospi-
HOTEL tality it's fair to say that the Four Seasons has become synonymous with
Fodor's Choice service of a level that still somehow manages to exceed expectations.
★ **Pros:** some of the best service in the city; elegant rooms; impeccable
attention to detail. **Cons:** extraordinarily expensive; not particularly
close to key tourist hubs; lobby feels a little cramped. $ *Rooms from:
Y3200* ⊠ *48 Liangmaqiao Road, Chaoyang District* ☎ *010/5695–8888*
⊕ *www.fourseasons.com/beijing* ⇆ *247 rooms, 66 suites* ⦿ *No meals*
M *Liangmaqiao* ✛ *H2.*

**$** **Grace Beijing** (一驿 Yì).Formerly known as Yi House, this unique
HOTEL concept hotel was once home to a crystal factory; today, however, the
Fodor's Choice red-brick Bauhaus structure has been transformed into a stylish bou-
★ tique hotel. **Pros:** unique art-themed hotel; onsite restaurant is excellent;
perfect for visiting 798. **Cons:** far from everything else; no subway; no
pool. $ *Rooms from: Y850* ⊠ *D-Park, Jiuxianqiao Lu 2 Hao Yuan, 798
Art District, Chaoyang District* ☎ *010/6436–1818* ⊕ *www.gracebeijing.
com* ⇆ *30 rooms* ⦿ *Breakfast* ✛ *H1.*

**$$$** **Hotel G** (北京极栈 *Běijīng jízhàn*). Vibrant, stylish, and next to the
HOTEL Gongti nightclub strip, this trendy boutique hotel has a multi-colored
Fodor's Choice facade that masks a slick interior, where Mid-Century modern design
★ uses subtle Chinese accents to add an understated glamor. **Pros:** adjacent
to one of the hottest nightlife areas; chic design; good restaurants. **Cons:**
too colorful for some; can be noisy; no pool. $ *Rooms from: Y1520*
⊠ *7 Gongti Xilu, Chaoyang District* ☎ *010/6552–3600* ⊕ *www.hotel-g.
com* ⇆ *110 rooms* ⦿ *No meals* ✛ *F3.*

$ HOTEL Fodor's Choice ★ **Hotel Kunlun** (北京昆仑饭店 *Běijīng Kūnlún fàndiàn*). With a magnificently spectacular series of restaurants, bars, and lounges, this hotel nearly trumps the Forbidden City for sheer magic and splendor. **Pros:** gorgeous decors throughout; well-finished, restful rooms; a good choice of dining. **Cons:** staff can be a little slow; not a top choice for sightseeing; quite business-orientated. [$] *Rooms from: Y980* ✉ *2 Xinyuan Nanlu, Sanlitun, Chaoyang District* ☎ *010/6590–3388* 🌐 *www.hotelkunlun.com* 🛏 *600 rooms, 50 suites* 🍴 *Breakfast* ✥ *H2.*

$$ HOTEL **Kempinski Hotel Beijing Lufthansa Center** (凯宾斯基饭店 *Kǎibīnsījī fàndiàn*). At around 20 years old, if the Kempinski were a man, it would just be starting out in the world. **Pros:** excellent service; a good bar; easy access to the airport. **Cons:** some areas are in need of renovation; far from the big tourist spots. [$] *Rooms from: Y1290* ✉ *50 Liangmaqiao Lu, Chaoyang District* ☎ *010/6465–3388* 🌐 *www.kempinski.com* 🛏 *526 rooms, 114 suites* 🍴 *No meals* [M] *Liangmaqiao* ✥ *H2.*

$$$ HOTEL FAMILY **Kerry Centre Hotel** (北京嘉里中心饭店 *Běijīng jiālǐ zhōngxīn fàndiàn*). An ongoing renovation has seen this Shangri-La-owned hotel get a new lease of life. **Pros:** reasonably priced luxury; great location; nearby shopping. **Cons:** smallish rooms; congested area; ridiculously expensive bar. [$] *Rooms from: Y1403* ✉ *1 Guang Hua Lu, Chaoyang District* ☎ *010/6561–8833* 🌐 *www.shangri-la.com/beijing/kerry* 🛏 *487 rooms, 23 suites* 🍴 *No meals* [M] *Guomao* ✥ *H5.*

$$$ HOTEL Fodor's Choice ★ **The Opposite House** (瑜舍 *Yúshě*). If you want a taste of 21st-century China then look no further than this place (located in the heart of the Sanlitun nightlife district), a prime contender for being Beijing's best boutique hotel: designed by award-winning Kengo Kuma, the look and feel of this place is unlike anywhere else, featuring a huge atrium and contemporary art in the stunning lobby, plus spacious and warm guest rooms kitted out with natural wood and Scandi-Asian minimalist chic along with a bevy of splendid restaurants and bars abuzz with the city's cool kids. **Pros:** a design addict's dream; fantastic food and drink options (both within and around); unique experience. **Cons:** too trendy for those who thrive on formality; not super close to the tourist trail; beyond awful traffic. [$] *Rooms from: Y1725* ✉ *11 Sanlitun Lu, Chaoyang District* ☎ *010/6417–6688* 🌐 *www.theoppositehouse.com* 🛏 *98 studios, 1 penthouse* 🍴 *No meals* [M] *None* ✥ *H3.*

$$$$ HOTEL Fodor's Choice ★ **Park Hyatt Beijing** (北京柏悦酒店 *Běijīng bòyuè jiǔdiàn*). An easy-to-like (if costly) slice of luxury, this 63-store tower hotel offers plenty of pampering (just imagine your own spa-inspired bathroom with over-sized rain shower, deep-soak tub and heated floors), with large guest rooms that are a tad functional but packed with the obligatory mod cons. **Pros:** spectacular views of the city; the hotel's buzzing Xue bar has a fab rooftop terrace; centrally located. **Cons:** pricey; lacks intimacy; hard area to walk around. [$] *Rooms from: Y2000* ✉ *2 Jianguomenwai Dajie., Chaoyang District* ☎ *010/8567–1234* 🌐 *beijing.park.hyatt.com* 🛏 *237 rooms, 18 suites.* 🍴 *No meals* [M] *Guomao* ✥ *H6.*

$$$ HOTEL Fodor's Choice ★ **St. Regis** (北京国际俱乐部饭店 *Běijīng guójì jùlèbù fàndiàn*). A favorite of business travelers and dignitaries alike, the luxurious interiors here combine classic Chinese elegance with modern furnishings, but it's the facilities that really stand out: the fine health club is

Fodor'sChoice ★

Park Hyatt Beijing

St. Regis

equipped with a Jacuzzi that gets its water direct from a natural hot spring deep beneath the hotel, the glass-atrium swimming pool offers a sun-drenched backstroke, and the smart, wood-panelled Press Club Bar has the air of a private club. **Pros:** nice location; fantastic facilities; good Asian and European dining options. **Cons:** the little extras really add up; may look too formal for some; lack of local atmosphere. $ *Rooms from: Y1742* ✉ *21 Jianguomenwai Dajie, Chaoyang District* ☎ *010/6460–6688* ⊕ *www.stregis.com/beijing* ↗ *156 rooms, 102 suites* Ⓜ *Jianguomen* ✛ *F5.*

$ 
HOTEL
🖼 **Swissôtel Beijing** (港澳中心瑞士酒店 *Găngào zhōngxīn ruìshì jiŭdiàn*). With easy access to the Second Ring Road and Line 2 of the subway, this well-run hotel provides something of a welcome hub for tourists: the marble lobby is impressive, guest rooms are of a high quality (decked out in a recognizably European style), and the health club has a large pool and tennis courts: while it'll never be one of the city's more glamourous hotels, it's a solid fit. **Pros:** regular jazz nights in the lobby; great amenities; easy access to the city. **Cons:** can be noisy; generally mediocre food; not next to the sites. $ *Rooms from: Y750* ✉ *2 Chaoyangmennei Dajie, Dongsishiqiao Flyover Junction (Second Ring Rd.), Chaoyang District* ☎ *010/6553–2288* ⊕ *www.swissotel-beijing. com* ↗ *430 rooms, 50 suites* ⦿ *No meals* Ⓜ *Dongsishitiao* ✛ *F3.*

## HAIDIAN DISTRICT

$$$$
HOTEL
Fodor's Choice
★
🖼 **Aman at Summer Palace** (北京颐和安缦 *Běijīng yíhé ānmàn*). The epitome of blissful indulgence, this luxury hotel belonging to the famed Aman chain is spread out across a series of carefully renovated ancient Qing Dynasty courtyards—it even has its own private entrance to the Summer Palace—with guest rooms decorated in restful earth tones (lovely traditional wooden screens and bamboo blinds) and grounds that are positively stunning. **Pros:** right next to the Summer Palace; restaurant Naoki serves fine *kaiseki* (Japanese) cuisine; beautiful setting. **Cons:** very pricey; extremely far from downtown; too isolated for some. $ *Rooms from: Y3820* ✉ *1 Gongmen Qian Street, Summer Palace, Haidian District* ☎ *010/5987–9999* ⊕ *www.amanresorts.com* ↗ *51 rooms, 33 suites* ⦿ *Breakfast* Ⓜ *Yiheyuan* ✛ *B1.*

$
HOTEL
🖼 **Friendship Hotel** (友谊宾馆 *Yŏuyì bīnguăn*). The name is telling, as the hotel was built in 1954 to house foreigners, mostly Soviets, who had come to help rebuild the nation; these days, it relies more on tour groups and those who need to be close to the university area, since it remains far removed from most sights; still, this place retains a certain glory as one of the largest garden-style hotels in Asia, even if many of its rooms could do with the gentle caress of modernity. **Pros:** a bit of history; inexpensive; gardens are attractive. **Cons:** far from the city center; needs updating; not much to do nearby (unless you're a student in search of cheap drinks). $ *Rooms from: Y538* ✉ *1 Zhongguancun Nan Dajie, Haidian District* ☎ *010/6849–8888* ⊕ *www.bjfriendshiphotel.com* ↗ *1,700 rooms, 200 suites* ⦿ *No meals* Ⓜ *Renmin University* ✛ *A1.*

$$
HOTEL
🖼 **Shangri-La Hotel, Beijing** (北京香格里拉饭店 *Běijīng xiānggélĭlā fàndiàn*). With its landscaped gardens, luxury mall and the addition of a more modern wing, the Shangri-La is a slice of charm for

business travelers and those who don't mind being far from the city center; the service is spot-on throughout, from the pristine rooms to the efficient check-in, while the dining options are excellent (the pick of the bunch being the superb, if rather expensive, S.T.A.Y, a French restaurant from the brain of Michelin-loved, three-starred chef Yannick Alléno). **Pros:** nice gardens; excellent amenities; great restaurants. **Cons:** far from the city center; no subway; older wing not as good as the newer one. $ *Rooms from: Y1180* ✉ *29 Zizhuyuan Lu, Haidian District* ☎ *010/6841–2211* ⊕ *www.shangri-la.com* ⤳ *670 rooms, 32 suites* ⊚ *Breakfast* ✛ *A1.*

## BEIJING AIRPORT AREA

**$$$$**  ⌂ **Grandma's Place (Schoolhouse Hotels)** (奶奶家 *Nǎinaijiā*). This two-
RENTAL  bedroom rental cottage is part of a project by Jim Spears, a long-term
FAMILY  resident of Mutianyu, called Schoolhouse Hotels, which offers gorgeous self-catering stays in remote villages around the Great Wall; Grandma's Place is the pick of the bunch, created using stones salvaged from Ming and Qing Dynasty structures, as well as massive beams from an old village house, featuring a cosy, traditional *kang*—a brick bed heated from beneath—and a very private fruit garden and terrace that provides jaw-dropping views of the Great Wall. **Pros:** a wonderfully rustic getaway with modern comforts; views of the Great Wall; The Schoolhouse restaurant is nearby. **Cons:** guests need a car to reach the property; no hotel services; outside of Beijing. $ *Rooms from: Y2600* ✉ *The Schoolhouse, 12 Mutianyu Village, Huairou District* ☎ *010/6162–6282* ⊕ *www.grandmasplaceatmutianyu.com* ⤳ *2 rooms (8 homes available)* ▭ *No credit cards* ⊚ *Breakfast* ✛ *H1.*

**$$**  ⌂ **Hilton Beijing Capital Airport.** The number of worthwhile options next
HOTEL  to Beijing's airport has flourished in recent years, and the arrival of the Hilton, in particular, has added that brand's usual five-star standards to the mix. **Pros:** easy access to the airport; good choice of restaurants; slick rooms. **Cons:** far from Beijing sights; a pain to get a taxi from; not really geared towards tourism. $ *Rooms from: Y1398* ✉ *1 San Jing Road, Beijing Capital International Airport (Terminal 3)* ☎ *010/6458–8888* ⊕ *beijingairport.hilton.com* ⤳ *265 rooms, 57 suites* ⊚ *No meals* Ⓜ *Airport Express* ✛ *H1.*

**$$$**  ⌂ **Langham Place, Beijing Capital Airport.** Airport hotels have a reputation
HOTEL  for being boring—not so with Langham Place, a fun and funky spot
Fodor'sChoice  next to Terminal 3 that screams style while whispering quiet comfort.
★  **Pros:** airport hotels are rarely this stylish; fantastic service; good facilities. **Cons:** far from the city center; overly long corridors; can feel too quiet at times. $ *Rooms from: Y1608* ✉ *1 Er Jing Road, Beijing Capital International Airport (Terminal 3)* ☎ *010/6457–5555* ⊕ *beijingairport. langhamplacehotels.com* ⤳ *372 rooms, 67 suites* ⊚ *No meals* Ⓜ *Airport Express* ✛ *H1.*

**$**  ⌂ **Shan Li Retreats.** Sometimes you need to get out of the city, and that's
RENTAL  especially true for those living in China's capital, constantly crowded by
FAMILY  20 million other such souls. **Pros:** a truly bucolic escape from the city;
Fodor'sChoice  good hikes nearby; beautifully restored village homes. **Cons:** a car is
★  required to get there; guests need to take their own food; not open all

year round. $ *Rooms from: Y900* ✉ *Huangyankou Cun, Beizhuang, Miyun County* ☎ *138/1171–6326* ⊕ *www.shanliretreats.com* ⟳ *Five homes* ☾ *Closed Nov.–Mar.* ⦿ *No meals* ✛ *H1.*

# ARTS AND NIGHTLIFE

No longer Shanghai's staid sister, Beijing is reinventing herself as a party town with just a smattering of the pretensions of her southern sibling. There's now a venue for every breed of boozer, from beer-stained pub to designer cocktail lounge and everything in between. There are also more dance clubs than you can count. An emerging middle class means that you'll find most bars have a mixed crowd and aren't just swamps of expatriates, but there will be spots where one or the other set will dominate.

Bars aside, Beijing has an active, if not international-standard, stage scene. There's not much to see in English, although the opening of the Egg, properly known as the National Center for the Performing Arts, has changed that somewhat. Music and dance transcend language boundaries, and Beijing attracts some fine international composers and ballet troupes for the crowds. For a fun night on the town that you can enjoy in no other place in the world, Beijing opera, acrobatics, and kung fu performances remain the best bets.

# THE ARTS

The arts in China took a long time to recover from the Cultural Revolution (1966–76), and political works are still generally avoided. Film and theater reflect an interesting mix of modern and avant-garde Chinese and Western influences. On any given night in Beijing, you can see a drama by the revered playwright Lao She, a satire by a contemporary Taiwanese playwright, or a stage version of *Animal Farm*.

As most of the stage is inaccessible to non-Chinese speakers, visitors to Beijing are more likely to hunt out the big visual spectacles, such as Beijing opera or kung fu displays. These long-running shows are tailored for travelers: your hotel will be able to recommend performances and venues and will likely be able to help you book tickets.

### ACROBATICS AND KUNG FU

**Chaoyang Theater** (朝阳剧场 *Cháoyáng jùchǎng*). This space is the queen bee of acrobatics venues, especially designed to unleash oohs and ahhs. Spectacular individual and team acrobatic displays involving bicycles, seesaws, catapults, swings, and barrels are performed here nightly. It's touristy but fun. ✉ *36 Dongsanhuan Beilu, Chaoyang District* ☎ *010/6507–2421* Ⓜ *Hujialou.*

Fodor'sChoice ★ **The Red Theatre** (红剧场 *Hóng jùchǎng*). If it's Vegas-style stage antics you're after, the *Legend of Kung Fu* show is what you want. Extravagant martial arts—performed by dancers, not martial artists—are complemented by neon, fog, and heavy-handed sound effects. Shows are garish but also sometimes glorious. ✉ *44 Xingfu Dajie, Chongwen District* ☎ *010/5165–1914* ⊕ *www.redtheatre.cn* Ⓜ *Tiantan Dong Men.*

**Tianqiao Acrobatic Theater** (天桥杂技剧场 *Tiānqiáo zájì jùcháng*). The Beijing Acrobatics Troupe of China is famous for weird, wonderful shows. Content includes a flashy show of offbeat contortions and tricks, with a lot of high-wire action. There are two shows per night, at 5:30 and 7:15 pm. ⊠ *30 Beiwei Lu, Xuanwu District* ☎ *010/6303–7449.*

### ART GALLERIES

**Chambers Fine Art.** Named after noted British architect Sir William Chambers, Chambers Fine Art Beijing opened in 2007 in the art village of Caochangdi. Situated in a red-brick gallery complex designed by Chinese contemporary artist Ai Weiwei, Chambers consistently puts on exhibitions of young native Chinese artists. ⊠ *Red No. 1-D, Caochangdi, Chaoyang District* ☎ *010/5127–3298* ⊕ *www.chambersfineart. com.*

**Pace Beijing** (佩斯北京 *Pèisībĕijīng*). This Beijing branch of the famed Pace Gallery operates with an independent program focusing on Chinese contemporary artists. ⊠ *No. 2 Jiuxianqiao Lu, 798 Art District, Chaoyang District* ☎ *010/5978–9781.*

**Pékin Fine Arts.** Founded by expatriate Bostonian Meg Maggio, who has lived in Beijing for 20 years, Pékin Fine Arts focuses on contemporary artists from around Asia, emphasizing individuals working across different media and with both international and domestic exhibition experience. ⊠ *No. 241 Caochangdi, Cuigezhuang Village, Chaoyang District* ☎ *010/5127–3220* ⊕ *pekinfinearts.com.*

**Red Gate Gallery.** This gallery, one of the first to open in Beijing, displays and sells contemporary Chinese art in the extraordinary location of the old Dongbianmen Watchtower, which dates back to the 16th century. The venue is worth a visit even if you're not interested in the art. Be aware that the subway stop listed here is about a 25-minute walk from the gallery. ⊠ *1/F & 4/F, Dongbianmen Watchtower, Chongwenmen Dongdajie, Chongwen District* ☎ *010/6525–1005* ⊕ *www. redgategallery.com* Ⓜ *Jianguomen.*

### BEIJING OPERA

**Chang'an Grand Theater** (长安大戏院 *Cháng'ān dàxìyuàn*). In this new theater specializing in Chinese opera, spectators can choose to sit either in the traditional seats or at cabaret-style tables. Besides Peking-style opera, the theater also puts on performances of other regional styles, such as *yueju* (from Guangdong) and *chuanju* (from Sichuan). ⊠ *7 Jianguomennei Dajie, Dongcheng District* ☎ *010/6510–1309* ⊕ *www. changantheater.com.*

**Huguang Guild Hall** (湖广会馆 *Húguǎng huìguǎn*). Built in 1807, the Huguang Guild Hall was at its height one of Beijing's "Four Great" theaters. In 1925, the Guild Hall hosted Dr. Sun Yat-sen at the founding of the Chinese Nationalist Party (KMT). Today, the Guild Hall has been restored to its former glory and hosts regular opera performances. The venue also hosts a small museum of Peking opera artifacts. ⊠ *3 Hufangqiao, Xuanwu District* ☎ *010/6351–8284.*

**Lao She Teahouse** (老舍茶馆 *Lǎoshě cháguǎn*). Named for famed Beijing author Lao She, this teahouse in the pedestrianized Qianmen area plays host to a variety of traditional performances including acrobatics, opera, and vaudeville shows. Dinner is served on the premises and reservations are required one day in advance for the shows, which occur at 7:15 pm nightly. ⊠ *Building 3, 3 Qianmenxi Dajie, Xuanwu District* ☎ *010/6303–6830.*

**Fodor's Choice** ★ **Liyuan Theater** (梨园剧场 *Líyuán jùcháng*). Unabashedly touristy, it's still a great time. You can watch performers put on makeup before the show (come early) and then graze on snacks and sip tea while watching English-subtitled shows. Glossy brochures complement the crooning. ⊠ *1/F, Qianmen Hotel, 175 Yong'an Lu, Xuanwu District* ☎ *010/6301–6688* ⊕ *www.qianmenhotel.com/en/liyuan.html.*

**Tianqiao Theater** (天桥剧场 *Tiānqiáo jùcháng*). A traditional theater that hosts everything from contemporary dance performances to ballet, folk music, and cross-talk revues. ⊠ *30 Beiwei Rd., Xuanwu District* ☎ *010/8315–6300.*

### MUSIC

**Beijing Concert Hall** (北京音乐厅 *Běijīng yīnyuètīng*). Beijing's main venue for Chinese and Western classical-music concerts also hosts folk dancing and singing, and many celebratory events throughout the year. The 1,000-seat venue is the home of the China National Symphony Orchestra. ⊠ *1 Bei Xinhua Jie, Xicheng District* ☎ *010/6605–7006* Ⓜ *Tiananmen West.*

**Fodor's Choice** ★ **Forbidden City Concert Hall** (北京中山公园音乐堂 *Běijīng Zhōngshān gōngyuán yīnyuètáng*). One of the nicest venues in Beijing, the 1,400-seat Forbidden City Concert Hall plays host to a variety of classical, chamber, and traditional music performances in plush surroundings and world-class acoustics. Though the facilities are completely modern, concertgoers are treated to a moonlit walk through Zhongshan Park, a former imperial garden dotted with historical landmarks. ⊠ *In Zhongshan Park, Xichang'an Jie, Xicheng District* ☎ *010/6559–8285* ⊕ *www.fcchbj.com* Ⓜ *Tiananmen West.*

**MAO Live House.** With the finest acoustics in the city and live music almost every night of the week, this is the place to experience the vibrant local music scene. ⊠ *111 Gulou Dongdajie, Dongcheng District* ☎ *010/6402–5080* ⊕ *www.maolive.com* Ⓜ *Gulou Dajie.*

**Poly Plaza International Theater** (保利剧院 *Bǎolì jùyuàn*). This is a modern shopping-center-like complex on top of Dongsishitiao subway station. One of Beijing's better-known theaters, the Poly hosts Chinese and international concerts, ballets, and musicals. ■TIP→ **If you're seeking a performance in English, this is your best bet.** ⊠ *1/F Poly Plaza, 14 Dongzhimen Nandajie, Dongcheng District* ☎ *010/6408–2666* Ⓜ *Dongsishitiao.*

### THEATER

**Beijing Exhibition Theater** (北京展览馆剧场 *Běijīng zhǎnlǎnguǎn jùchǎng*). Chinese plays, Western and Chinese operas, and ballet performances are staged in this Soviet-style building that's part of the exhibition center complex. Talk about a wide range of shows: In 2010 the Michael Jackson musical *Thriller* was staged here, followed closely

**DID YOU KNOW?**

Chinese acrobatics has existed for more than two thousand years. Like vaudeville in the West, acrobatic performances in old China were considered low class; they were even banned from theaters. Many of the acts used props such as chairs, tables, and plates. Today you'll see amazing feats like traditional group gymnastics, springboard stunts, and gymnastics on double-fixed poles.

**CLOSE UP**

# Fringe Art: The Dashanzi 798 Art District

**798 Art District.** Chinese contemporary art has exploded in the past decade, and to see some of the finest examples of the scene look no further than 798 Art District, located in the northeast corner of the city. Experimenting with classical mediums such as paint and printmaking as well as forays into new and digital media, installation, and performance art, young Chinese artists are caught between old and new, Communism and capitalism, urban and rural, rich and poor, and East and West. These contrasts inform their artistic output, with varying results. Although more and more Chinese artists are achieving international recognition, 798 still abounds with cheap knockoffs of bad Western art and tacky Socialist Realist portraits. Yet the area remains the hub of contemporary creative arts in Beijing and is worth a visit.

Built in the 1950s, this factory district was a major industrial project by East German architects backed by Soviet aid. All but abandoned by the 1980s, the complex was rediscovered in the late 1990s by a small group of Beijing artists who had just been evicted from their previous haunts and were looking for a new place to set up working and living spaces. Initially a completely DIY affair similar to the squats of the East Village in the 1980s and East Berlin of the 1990s, the quality of art produced and international media attention starting from the early 2000s meant that the district government took notice. Eventually the area was declared a protected arts district, paving the way for commercial galleries, cafés, and souvenir shops. Priced out of their original studios, many working artists have decamped further afield to the Caochangdi and Songzhuang neighborhoods. Both of these smaller areas are worth visiting, though neither is easily accessible except via taxi. Ask your hotel concierge for a detailed map or better yet, call ahead to the galleries you're interested in visiting and get driving instructions.

798 is more accessible, however, and eminently walkable. Keep in mind that cabs are prohibited from driving into the complex and much of the area is pedestrianized. Though it's open on weekdays (except for Monday), most people visit on the weekend, when throngs of locals and foreigners congregate to see what's on display.

Many of the galleries there now are hit or miss, but establishments such as the Ullens Center for Contemporary Arts (UCCA) and Galleria Continua always put on informative, challenging exhibitions. If you need to refuel, stop by At Cafe, billed as the first café in 798 and still co-owned by Huang Rui, one of the district's cofounders. ✉ *2–4 Jiuxianqiao Rd., Dashanzi, Chaoyang District.*

by some traditional folk art performances. ✉ *135 Xizhimenwai Dajie, Xicheng District* ☎ *010/6835–4455* Ⓜ *Xizhimen.*

FAMILY **China National Puppet Theater** (中国木偶剧院 *Zhōngguó guójiā mùǒujùyuàn*). The shadow and hand-puppet shows at this theater convey traditional stories—it's lively entertainment for children and adults alike. This venue also attracts overseas performers, including the Moscow Puppet Theater. ☒ *1 Anhuaxili, Chaoyang District* ☎ *010/ 6424–7888.*

Fodor's Choice ★ **National Centre for Performing Arts** (国家大剧院. *Guójiā dàjùyuàn*). Architecturally, the giant silver dome of this performing arts complex is stunning, and its interior holds a state-of-the-art opera house, a music hall, and a theater. The "Egg" offers a world-class stage for national and international performers. If you don't wish to see a show, you can tour the inside of the building by paying for an entrance ticket. ☒ *2 Xi Chang'an Jie, Xicheng District* ☎ *010/6655–0000* ⊕ *www.chncpa.org* Ⓜ *Tiananmen West.*

## NIGHTLIFE

Now quite the international nightlife destination, there's something for everyone in Beijing. From intimate bars and world-class cocktail lounges to pumping dance halls, sports bars, and proper English-style pubs, Beijing (almost) has it all. Establishments seemingly rise up overnight, and can disappear just as quickly in the breakneck pace of development that Beijingers have become used to ever since the Olympics.

Sanlitun—the heart of Beijing's nightlife—has spread its party presence around Gongti. Sanlitun Jiuba Jie, or "Bar Street," offers mainly crass live-music pubs; it's quite popular with locals. On Gongti West Gate, a stream of pumping dance clubs have attracted some big-name DJs—Tiesto, Felix Da Housecat, and Paul Oakenfold, among others. The city's main gay club, Destination, is also here.

Houhai, once a quiet lakeside neighborhood home to Beijing's *laobaixing* (ordinary folk), has exploded into a bumping bar scene. This is a great place to come for a drink at dusk: park yourself on an outdoor seat and enjoy. There are a few hidden gems here, but most of the bars are bland and expensive, with disappointingly weak drinks. Stick to the bottled beer to get your money's worth. The hutong, or mazelike neighborhoods, around the lake also hide some cute courtyard bars.

**OFF THE BEATEN PATH**

There are a couple of smaller pockets with notable watering holes, such as Chaoyang West Gate, which has a predominately expat feel; Dashanzi 798, an artsy warehouse area with wine bars; and Wudaokou, a student district in Haidian with cheap drinks aplenty.

### BARS

#### DONGCHENG AND XICHENG DISTRICTS

Fodor's Choice ★ **Amilal** (按一拉尔 *Àn yī lā'ěr*). If you have the patience to track this cozy courtyard bar down a tiny alley, you'll be rewarded with one of the city's hidden gems. Grab a seat at one of the rough wooden tables, listen to the low-key live music that's often playing, and enjoy the laid-back hutong vibe that's so unique to Beijing. ☒ *48 Shoubi Hutong, off Gulou Dongdajie, Dongcheng District.*

**Cu Ju** (蹴鞠 *Cùjú*). Cu Ju is Beijing's first hutong sports bar cum rum-tasting room. Proprietor Badr is a Moroccan expat who's lived in the city for many years and the bar is the culmination of all his many passions, such as rum, Moroccan food, and sporting events. ☒ *28 Xiguan Hutong, Dongcheng District* ☎ *010/6407–9782* ⊕ *www.cujubeijing.com.*

**DID YOU KNOW?**

There are more than 1,000 different kinds of makeup patterns used in the Beijing opera. Colors symbolize character traits. Red conveys bravery or loyalty, white signifies treachery, yellow suggests brutality, black stands for integrity or fierceness, and purple expresses wisdom. Bandits often have blue faces; gods and spirits are marked with gold and silver.

**East Shore Live Jazz Café** (东岸咖啡 *Dōng'àn kāfēi*). There's no competition: This place has the most fabulous views of Houhai lake, hands-down, and authentic jazz on stage every night. ✉ *2nd Floor, 2 Qianhai Nanyanlu, west of the Post Office on Di'anmen Waidajie, Xicheng District* ☏ *010/8403–2131.*

**Great Leap Brewing** (大跃啤酒 *Dàyuèpíjiǔ*). Beijing's first microbrewery, Great Leap Brewing's beers utilize unique ingredients such as tea and Sichuan peppercorns. The courtyard operation also hosts weekly movie screenings and the odd special event. Don't miss the bar peanuts—spicy and salty, they'll keep you going back to the bar for just one more brew. ✉ *No. 6 Doujiao Hutong, Dongcheng District* ☏ *010/5717–1399* ⊕ *www.greatleapbrewing.com* ⊘ *Closed Mondays.*

**Mao Mao Chong** (毛毛虫 *Máomáochóng*). This bar is known for infused cocktails, including a chili-infused vodka Bloody Mary and Sichuan peppercorn Moscow Mule. ✉ *No. 12 Banchang Hutong, Dongcheng District* ☏ *159/9264–6024* ⊕ *www.maomaochongbeijing.com.*

**Slow Boat Brewery Taproom.** A sleek yet cozy taproom nestled in the hutong, the Slow Boat is another addition to the rapidly growing number of microbreweries in the capital city. There are at least a dozen beers on tap at any given moment, from all-weather tipples such as pale ales and IPAs, to seasonal specialities including warming stouts in the winter and refreshing citrusy brews come summertime. ✉ *56–2 Dongsi Batiao, Dongsi Beidajie, Dongcheng District* ☏ *010/6538–5537* ⊕ *www.slowboatbrewery.com* ⊘ *Closed Mondays* Ⓜ *Zhangzizhong Lu (Line 5).*

### CHAOYANG DISTRICT

**Apothecary** (药剂员 *Yào jì yuán*). Like an old-fashioned pharmacist doling out carefully concocted medicinals, the mixologists at this low-key venue artfully blend all of your favorite ingredients into cocktails that will soothe the soul. Mixologist-in-chief Leon Lee is something of a local celebrity for good reason. The location, in the trendy Nali Patio complex, and the New Orleans–style bar food are bonuses. ✉ *3/F, Nali Patio, 81 Sanlitun Beilu, Chaoyang District* ☏ *010/5208–6040* Ⓜ *Tuanjiehu.*

**The Den.** This old-school dive's attraction is sports on wide-screen TVs. The owner runs the city's amateur rugby club, so you'll find players and their supporters drinking rowdily. Open 24 hours a day, it's guaranteed to be buzzing every night, especially during happy hour, when you can grab half-price drinks and pizza until 10 pm. ✉ *4 Gongti Donglu, next to the City Hotel, Chaoyang District* ☏ *010/6592–6290* Ⓜ *Tuanjie Hu.*

**D.Lounge.** Raising the bar for bars in Beijing, this New York–style lounge is swank, spacious, and has an innovative drink list. At the moment, it's the place to rub elbows with the city's *it* crowd, and occasionally the doormen restrict entry to the more dapperly dressed. It's a bit tricky to find: Walk behind Salsa Caribe and head south. ✉ *Courtyard 4, Gongti Beilu, behind the Bookworm, Chaoyang District* ☏ *010/6593–7710.*

**Face** (飞色 *Fēi sè*). Stylish without being pretentious, Face is justifiably popular, especially with the mature, well-heeled crowd. The complex has a multitude of restaurants, but the real gem is the bar. Grab a lounge bed surrounded by silky drapes, take advantage of the happy-hour drink specials, and enjoy some premier people-watching. ✉ *26 Dongcaoyuan, Gongti Nanlu, Chaoyang District* ☎ *010/6551–6788* ⊕ *www.facebars.com.*

**Mokihi.** Tucked behind an Italian-fusion restaurant with a Japanese chef on an unassuming strip mall of establishments near Chaoyang Park, Mokihi is a perfect oasis from the hustle and bustle of everyday Beijing. Have the Japanese-trained

**WHEN TO HAGGLE**

Bargaining is acceptable, and expected, in markets and mom-and-pop shops, though not in department stores and malls. Also, an increasing number of higher-end local boutiques follow the lead of their Western peers in not allowing bargaining. The bottom line is to pay what you think is fair.

bartenders mix up one of their signature cocktails and nibble on exquisite hors d'oeuvres while engaging in quiet conversation with your drinking companions. ✉ *C12, Haoyun Jie (Lucky Street), 3rd Floor, Chaoyang District* ☎ *010/5867–0244.*

Fodor's Choice
★
**Q Bar.** Echo's cocktails—strong, authentic, and not superexpensive—are a small legend here in Beijing. This tucked-away lounge off the main Sanlitun drag is an unpretentious option for an evening out. Don't be put off by the fact that it's in a bland, 1980s-styled motel; in the summer the terrace more than makes up for that. ✉ *Top floor of Eastern Inn Hotel, 6 Baijiazhuang Lu, Chaoyang District* ☎ *010/6595–9239* Ⓜ *Tuanjie Hu.*

**The Tree.** For years now, expats have crowded this bar for its Belgian beer, wood-fired pizza, and quiet murmurs of conversation. It does, however, get a bit smoky; if you're sensitive you may want to give this venue a pass. For pasta instead of pizza, its sister restaurant Nearby the Tree is, well, nearby, at 100 meters to the southeast. ✉ *43 Sanlitun Beijie, Chaoyang District* ☎ *010/6415–1954* Ⓜ *Tuanjie Hu.*

### HAIDIAN DISTRICT

**Lush.** The go-to hangout in the university district of Wudaokou, Lush is a home-away-from-home for many a homesick exchange student. With weekly pub quizzes, open-mic nights, and large, strong drinks, Lush is an excellent place to start the night. ✉ *2nd Floor, Bldg. 1, Huaqing Jiayuan, across the street from the Wudakou light-rail station, Haidian District* ☎ *010/8286–3566* ⊕ *www.lushbeijing.com.*

# SHOPPING

Large markets and malls in Beijing are generally open from 9 am to 9 pm, though some shops close as early as 7 pm or as late as 10 pm. Weekdays are always less crowded. During rush hour, avoid taking taxis. If a shop looks closed (the lights are out or the owner is resting), don't give up. Many merchants conserve electricity or take catnaps if the store is free of customers. Just knock or offer the greeting "*ni hao.*" More likely than not, the lights will flip on and you'll be invited to come

**DID YOU KNOW?**

In a country increasingly filled with cars, shopping malls and pedestrian-only streets are becoming all the rage—and for good reason. Not only are the air and noise pollution less oppressive when there are no cars around, but dodging taxis tends to detract from one's shopping enjoyment.

in and take a look. Shops in malls have regular hours and will only be closed on a few occasions throughout the year, like Chinese New Year. Major credit cards are accepted in pricier venues. Cash is the driving force here, and ATMs abound. Before accepting those Mao-faced Y100 notes, most vendors will hold them up to the light, tug at the corners, and rub their fingers along the surface. Counterfeiting is becoming increasingly more difficult, but no one, including you, wants to be cheated. In some department stores, you must settle your bill at a central payment counter.

Shops frequented by foreigners sometimes have an employee with some fluency in English. But money remains the international language. In many cases, whether or not there is a common language—the shop assistant will still whip out a calculator, look at you to see what they think you'll cough up, then type in a starting price. You're expected to counter with your offer. Punch in your dream price. The clerk will come down Y10 or Y20 and so on and so on. Remember that the terms *yuan*, *kuai*, and *RMB* are often used interchangeably.

## DONGCHENG DISTRICT

### MALLS AND DEPARTMENT STORES

FAMILY **Hongqiao Market** (红桥市场 *Hóngqiaó shìchǎng*). Hongqiao, or Pearl Market, is full of tourist goods, knockoff handbags, and cheap watches, but it's best known for its three stories of pearls. Freshwater, seawater, black, pink, white: The quantity is overwhelming and quality varies by stall. Prices also range wildly, though the cheapest items are often fakes. Fanghua Pearls (No. 4318), on the fourth floor, displays quality necklaces and earrings, with photos of Hillary Clinton and Margaret Thatcher shopping there to prove it. Fanghua has a second store devoted to fine jade and precious stones. Stallholders here can be pushy, but accept their haggling in the gamelike spirit it's intended. Or wear headphones to drown them out. ✉ *9 Tiantan Lu, east of the northern entrance to Temple of Heaven, Dongcheng District* ☎ *010/6711–7630* ⊙ *Daily 9:30–7* Ⓜ *Tiantan Dongmen.*

**Malls at Oriental Plaza** (东方广场购物中心 *Dōngfāng guǎngchǎng*). This enormous shopping complex originates at the southern end of Wangfujing where it meets Chang'an Jie and stretches a city block east to Dongdan Dajie. It's a true city within a city and certainly geared toward higher budgets. Some of the more upscale shops include Kenzo and Armani Exchange, while ladies should check out the boutique from iconic Chinese-American designer Anna Sui for clothes, accessories, and make-up. ✉ *1 Dongchang'an Jie, Dongcheng District* ☎ *010/8518–6363* ⊙ *Daily 10–10* Ⓜ *Wangfujing.*

### CHINESE MEDICINE

**Tongrentang** (同仁堂 *Tóngréntáng*). A first-time consultation with a Chinese doctor can feel a bit like a reading with a fortune-teller. With one test of the pulse, many traditional Chinese doctors can describe the patient's medical history and diagnose current maladies. China's most famous traditional Chinese medicine shop, Tongrentang, is one of the oldest establishments on Dashilan Street. Hushed and dimly illuminated, this 300-year-old shop even smells healthy. Browse the glass displays of deer antlers and pickled snakes, dried seahorses and frogs, and delicate tangles of roots with precious price tags of Y48,000. If you don't speak Chinese and wish to have a consultation with a doctor, consider bringing along a translator. ⊠ *24 Dashilan, Qianmen, Exit C, Xicheng District* ☎ *010/6701–5895* ☉ *Daily 8:30–5* Ⓜ *Qianmen.*

> **EARLY-BIRD CATCHES**
>
> A common superstition in Chinese markets is that if you don't make a sale with your very first customer of the day, the rest of the day will go badly. So set out early, and if you know you're the first customer of the day, bargain relentlessly.

### CLOTHING

**Plastered T-Shirts.** Now over 15 years old, this store—originally called Plastered 8—has weathered well, with a second branch now open in 798 Art District. Stop here for T-shirt designs that capture the nostalgic days of Old Peking, as well as posters, notebooks, and traditional thermoses. Fun and kitschy, everything costs around Y100. This is a must-visit for anyone in search of that rarest of all things: a souvenir you'd actually use when home. ⊠ *61 Nanluoguxiang Hutong, Dongcheng District* ☎ *010/6407–8425* ⊕ *www.plasteredtshirts.com* ☉ *Daily 9:30 am–11 pm* Ⓜ *Zhangzizhonglu* ⊠ *798 Art Zone, 4 Jiuxianqiao Lu, Chaoyang District* ☎ *136/7137–9896* ⊕ *www.plasteredtshirts.com* ☉ *Daily 9:30 am–11 pm.*

**Wuhao Curated Shop** (五号 *Wǔhào*). Part fashion gallery, part shop, all chic! Seasonal new designs are scattered in eccentric installations throughout this beautifully converted *siheyuan* (courtyard). Browsing is a pleasure, with international designers across the fields of art, fashion, jewelry, and ceramics on display. Thankfully, guests are encouraged to explore, although be warned: The prices are quite steep. ⊠ *35 Mao'er Hutong, Dongcheng District* ☎ *189/1135–5035* ⊕ *www.wuhaoonline. com* ☉ *Wed.–Sun. 2–8* Ⓜ *Zhangzizhonglu.*

**Zi'an Print & Graphics** (子安版画 *Zí ān Bǎnhuà*). Exquisite Chinese and European prints (from Y50) decorate the shelves of this adorable little store on Fangjia Hutong. Owner Zi'an is an avid collector of graphic art, engravings, and *ex libris* (the small prints traditionally pasted into the front of books). Many of the works on display here date from the 19th century onwards and nearly all have links to China's past, depicting everything from life during the Three Kingdoms period to the Opium Wars. ⊠ *30 Fangjia Hutong, Dongcheng District* ☎ *131/4649–3917* ☉ *Daily noon–6* Ⓜ *Beixinqiao.*

### SILK AND FABRICS

**Daxin Textiles Co.** (大新纺织 *Dàxīn fǎngzhī*). For a wide selection of all types of fabrics, from worsted wools to sensuous silks, head to this shop. It's best to buy the material here and find a tailor elsewhere, as sewing standards can be shoddy. ⊠ *Northeast corner of Dongsi, Dongcheng District* ☎ *010/6403–2378* ☉ *9–7:30* Ⓜ *Dongsi.*

## XICHENG DISTRICT 西城区

### MALLS AND DEPARTMENT STORES

**Seasons Place** (金融街购物中心 *Jīnróngjiē gòuwù zhōngxīn*). This ritzy mall is further west in Beijing's Financial Street area. If you're staying at one of the business hotels nearby, Seasons Place will fulfill your shopping needs—as long as you're not on a budget. Designer labels like Louis Vuitton, Gucci, and Versace are here, as well as the Beijing branch of Hong Kong's fab department store, Lane Crawford. ⊠ *2 Jinrong Jie, Xicheng District* ☎ *010/6622–0088* ⊕ *www.seasonsplace.com* ⊗ *Daily 11–8:30* Ⓜ *Fuxingmen.*

### SILK AND FABRICS

**Beijing Silk Shop** (北京谦祥益丝绸商店 *Běijīng qiānxiángyì sīchóu shāngdiàn*). Since 1830, the Beijing Silk Shop has been supplying the city with quality bolts of silks and fabrics. There are tailors on-site to whip up something special and the second floor has ready-to-wear clothing. To reach the shop, walk all the way down Dashilan then head directly onto Dashilan West Street. ⊠ *50 Dashilan Xi Jie, Xicheng District* ☎ *010/6301–6658* ⊗ *Daily 9–7:30* Ⓜ *Qianmen.*

### TOYS

**Three Stones Kite Store** (三石斋风筝店 *Sān dàn zhāifēng zhēngdiàn*). For something more traditional, go fly a kite. But not the run-of-the-mill type you see anywhere. Here, for three generations, the same family has hand-painted butterflies and birds onto bamboo frames to delight adults and children alike. ⊠ *25 Di'anmen Xidajie, Xicheng District* ☎ *010/8404–4505* ⊗ *Daily 10–5* Ⓜ *Zhangzizhonglu.*

## CHAOYANG DISTRICT

### BOOKS

**The Bookworm** (书虫 *Shūchóng*). Book lovers, hipsters, and aspiring poets take note: This lending library and bookstore offers a spacious second-story reading room with a full café and bar. All are welcome to browse: the magazine and new-books section are a stupendous sight for English-starved travelers. The store frequently hosts poetry readings and lectures, as well as an annual literary festival in March. ⊠ *4 Sanlitun Nan lu, set back slightly in an alley 50 meters south of the Gongti Beilu junction, Chaoyang District* ☎ *010/6586–9507* ⊕ *www.beijingbookworm.com* ⊗ *Daily 9 am–midnight* Ⓜ *Tuanjiehu.*

**Timezone 8** (东八时区 *Dōngbā shíqū*). This bookstore-café is a welcome pit stop for those with brows higher than the average. A nice selection of Belgian brews and a recently added sushi bar makes it a lunchtime gem, but literati should flock here for its overflowing collection of up-to-date local art and fashion books, as well as magazines and monographs in both English and Mandarin. ⊠ *798 Art District, 4 Jiuxianqiao Lu, Chaoyang District* ☎ *010/5978–9917* ⊕ *www.timezone8.com.cn* ⊗ *Daily 8:30 am–2 am.*

### CLOTHING

**Dong Liang Studio** (栋梁工作室 *Dòngliáng gōngzuòshì*). Prices begin at steep and climb to positively perpendicular at this boutique. A visit here is key for anyone wanting to get under the skin of the local fashion scene. Its stock reads like a who's who of rising Chinese designers, including clothes by Vega Wang, He Yan, Manchit Au, and more. ✉ *Shop 102, Building 2, Central Park, 6 Chaoyangmenwai Dajie, Chaoyang District* ☎ *010/8404–7648* ⊙ *Daily 11–9* Ⓜ *Yong'anli.*

**Heyan'er** (何燕服装店 *Héyán fúzhuāng diàn*). He Yan's design philosophy is stated in her label: "*bu yan bu yu*" or "no talking." Her linen and cotton tunics and collarless jackets speak for themselves. From earth tones to aubergine hues and peacock patterns, He Yan's designs echo traditional Tibetan styles. ✉ *15–2 Gongti Beilu, Chaoyang District* ☎ *010/6415–9442* ⊙ *Daily 9:30–9:30* Ⓜ *Dongsishitiao* ✉ *Holiday Inn Lido, 6 Fangyuan Xilu* ☎ *010/6437–6854* ⊙ *Daily 9:30–9:30* Ⓜ *Sanyuanqiao.*

**UCCA Design Store** (东八时区 *UCCA shèjì shāngdiàn*). The 798 Art District is home to a burgeoning collection of housewares, fashion, and design shops. The most innovative of these, however, is an offshoot of the Ullens Center for Contemporary Art (UCCA), located just one door down from the gallery. Clothes, posters, ingenious knickknacks, and artist Sui Jianguo's iconic (if pricey) "Made in China" plastic dinosaurs make it a must-visit for anyone in the area. ✉ *798 Art District, 4 Jiuxianqiao Lu, Chaoyang District* ☎ *010/5780–0228* ⊕ *ucca.org.cn/en/uccastore* ⊙ *Daily 10–6:30.*

### ELECTRONICS

**Buy Now Computer Shopping Mall** (百脑会电脑广场 *Bǎinǎohuì diànnǎo guǎngchǎng*). Buy Now (or Bainaohui) is home to hundreds of stalls shilling laptops, PCs, iPods, speakers, phones, and just about any electrical malarkey you can imagine. However, both real and knockoff goods tend to be mixed in with each other, so choose wisely. Some stall owners will bargain, others won't, but it's always worth a try. ✉ *10 Chaoyangmenwai Dajie, Chaoyang District* ☎ *010/6599–5912* ⊙ *Daily 9–8* Ⓜ *Hujialou.*

### JEWELRY

**Shard Box Store** (慎 德阁 *Shèndégé*). The signature collection here includes small to midsize jewelry boxes fashioned from the broken shards of antique porcelain. Supposedly the shards were collected during the Cultural Revolution, when scores of antique porcelain pieces were smashed in accordance with the law. Birds, trees, pining lovers, and dragons decorate these affordable ceramic-and-metal containers, which range from Y20 to Y200. ✉ *1 Ritan Beilu, Chaoyang District* ☎ *010/8561–3712* ⊙ *Daily 10–10* Ⓜ *Yong'anli* ✉ *2 Jiangtai Lu, near the Holiday Inn Lido* ☎ *010/5135–7638* ⊙ *Daily 10–10* Ⓜ *Sanyuanqiao.*

### MARKETS

**Beijing Curio City** (北京古玩城 *Běijīng gǔwán chéng*). This complex has four stories of kitsch and curio shops and a few furniture vendors, some of whom may be selling authentic antiques. Prices are high (driven up by free-spending tour groups), so don't be afraid to lowball your offer. Ignore the overpriced duty-free shop at the entrance. ⊠ *21 Dongsanhuan Nan Lu, Chaoyang District* ☎ *010/6774–7711* ⊙ *Daily 10–6* Ⓜ *Jinsong.*

Fodor's Choice
★

**Panjiayuan Antiques Market** (潘家园市场 *Pānjiāyuán shìchǎng*). Every day the sun rises over thousands of pilgrims rummaging in search of antiques and the most curious of curios, though the biggest numbers of buyers and sellers is at the weekends. With over 3,000 vendors crowding an area of 48,500 square meters, not every jade bracelet, oracle bone, porcelain vase, and ancient screen is authentic, but most people are here for the reproductions anyway. Behold the bounty: watercolors, scrolls, calligraphy, Buddhist statues, opera costumes, old Russian SLR cameras, curio cabinets, Tibetan jewelry, tiny satin lotus-flower shoes, rotary telephones, jade dragons, antique mirrors, and infinite displays of "Maomorabilia." If you're buying jade, first observe the Chinese customers, how they hold a flashlight to the milky-green stone to test its authenticity. As with all Chinese markets, bargain with a vengeance, as many vendors inflate their prices astronomically for *waiguoren* ("outside country people"). A strip of enclosed stores forms a perimeter around the surprisingly orderly rows of open-air stalls. Check out photographer Xuesong Kang and his **Da Kang** store (No. 63-B) for some fascinating black-and-white snaps of Beijing city life dating from the start of the 20th century up to the present day. Also be sure to stop by the **Bei Zhong Bao Pearl Shop** (No. 7-A) for medium-quality freshwater pearls cultivated by the Hu family. Also here are a sculpture zoo, a book bazaar, reproduction-furniture shops, and an area stashing propaganda posters and Communist literature. ⊠ *18 Huaweili, Panjiayuan Lu, Chaoyang District* ☎ *010/6774–1869* ⊙ *Weekdays 8:30–6; weekends 6–6* Ⓜ *Jinsong.*

**Ritan Office Building Market** (日坛商务楼 *Rìtán shāngwù lóu*). Don't let the gray-brick and red-trim exterior fool you: The three stories of offices inside the Ritan Building are strung with racks of brand-name dresses and funky-fab accessories. Unlike the tacky variations made on knockoff labels and sold in less expensive markets, the collections here, for the most part, retain their integrity—perhaps because many of these dresses are actually designer labels. They're also more expensive and bargaining is discouraged. The **Ruby Cashmere Shop** (No. 1009) sells genuine cashmere sweaters and scarves at reduced prices, while **Fandini** (No. 1011) serves up a modern selection of typically "street" womenswear. ⊠ *15A Guanghua Lu, just east of the south entrance to Ritan Park, opposite the Vietnam Embassy, Chaoyang District* ☎ *010/6502–1528* ⊙ *Daily 10–7* Ⓜ *Yong'anli.*

Fodor's Choice
★

**Silk Alley Market** (秀水市场 *Xiùshuǐ shìchǎng*). Once a delightfully chaotic sprawl of hundreds of outdoor stalls, the Silk Alley Market is now corralled inside a huge shopping center. The government has been cracking down on an increasing number of certain copycat items, so if you don't see that knockoff Louis Vuitton purse or Chanel jacket, just ask; it might magically appear from a stack of plastic storage bins. You'll face no dearth, however, of knockoff Pumas and Nikes or Paul Smith polos. Chinese handicrafts and children's clothes are on the top floors. Bargain relentlessly, check carefully the quality of each intended purchase, and guard your wallet against pickpockets. ⊠ *8 Xiushui Dong Jie, Chaoyang District* ☎ *010/5169–9003* ⊕ *www.xiushui.com.cn* ⊙ *Daily 9:30–9* Ⓜ *Yong'anli.*

**Yashow/Yaxiu Market** (雅秀市场 *Yǎxiù shìchǎng*). Especially popular among younger Western shoppers, Yashow is yet another indoor arena stuffed to the gills with low-quality knockoff clothing and shoes. Prices are slightly cheaper than Silk Alley, but the haggling no less cruel— don't pay any more than Y50 for a pair of "Converse" sneakers. Also, don't be alarmed if you see someone sniffing the shoes or suede jackets: they're simply testing if the leather is real. On the third floor, **Wendy Ya Shi** (No. 3066) is the best of the many tailors on offer, with a basic suit usually starting out at around Y1,500 (including fabric) after a good haggle. ■TIP→ **The Lily Nails salon on the first floor offers inexpensive manicures and foot rubs if you need a break.** ⊠ *58 Gongti Beilu, Chaoyang District* ☎ *010/6416–8699* ⊙ *Daily 9:30–9* Ⓜ *Tuanjiehu.*

**Zhaojia Chaowai Market** (朝外市场 *Zhàojiā cháowài gǔdiǎnjiāju shìchǎng*). Beijing's best-known venue for affordable antiques and reproduction furniture houses scores of independent vendors who sell everything from authentic Qing Dynasty-era chests to traditional baskets, ceramics, carpets, and curios. Be sure to bargain; vendors routinely sell items for less than half their starting price. ⊠ *43 Huawei Bei Li, Chaoyang District* ☎ *010/6776–5318* ⊙ *Daily 9:30–7* Ⓜ *Jinsong.*

## HAIDIAN DISTRICT

Travelers usually frequent the northwestern quadrant of Beijing to visit the Summer Palace or the Beijing Zoo, though because Haidian has several universities, cheap and cheerful boutiques aimed at students are commonplace.

**Ai Jia Gu Dong Market** (镌爱家红木大楼 *Aìjiā hóngmù dàlóu*). For something more refined, collectors of antiques can spend hours perusing the quiet halls of Ai Jia Gu Dong Market, a large antiques and jade market, hidden just under the South Fourth Ring Road beside the Big Bell Museum. It's open daily, but shops close early on weekdays. ⊠ *Chengshousi Lu, Beisanhuan Xilu, Haidian District* Ⓜ *Zhichunlu.*

# SIDE TRIPS FROM BEIJING

Beijing a fascinating city to visit, but its outskirts are also packed with history- and culture-laden sites for the admirer of early empires and their antiquities. First and foremost, a trip to the Great Wall is a must— you simply can't miss it!

After the Great Wall, there are a variety of wonderful things to do and see: you can go horseback riding at Yesanpo, or take a dip at the beach and gorge yourself with fresh seafood in Beidaihe.

Buddhist temples and ancient tombs, as well as historical bridges and anthropological digs, are all located within a few hours of Beijing. For all these sites, getting there is half the fun—traveling through rural China, even for a day trip, is always something of an adventure.

Inspecting the goods at the Panjiayuan Antiques Market.

## THIRTEEN MING TOMBS

*48 km (30 miles) north of Beijing.*

**Thirteen Ming Tombs** (明十三陵 *Míng shísānlíng*). A narrow valley just north of Changping is the final resting place for 13 of the Ming Dynasty's 16 emperors (the first Ming emperor was buried in Nanjing; the burial site of the second one is unknown; and the seventh Ming emperor was dethroned and buried in an ordinary tomb in northwestern Beijing). Ming monarchs once journeyed here each year to kowtow before their clan forefathers and make offerings to their memory. These days, few visitors can claim royal descent, but the area's vast scale and imperial grandeur do convey the importance attached to ancestor worship in ancient China.

The road to the Thirteen Ming Tombs begins beneath an imposing stone portico that stands at the valley entrance. Allow ample time for a hike or drive northwest from Changling to the six fenced-off **unrestored tombs,** a short distance farther up the valley. Here, crumbling walls conceal vast courtyards shaded by pine trees. At each tomb, a stone altar rests beneath a stele tower and burial mound. In some cases the wall that circles the burial chamber is accessible on steep stone stairways that ascend from either side of the altar. At the valley's terminus (about 5 km [3 miles] northwest of Changling), the **Zhaoling Tomb** rests beside a traditional walled village that's well worth exploring.

Picnics amid the ruins have been a favorite weekend activity among Beijingers for nearly a century; if you picnic here, be sure to carry out all trash. ⊠ *Changping County* ☎ *010/6076–1888, 010/6076–1424* ☜ *Y30 (for Zhaoling tomb)* ☼ *Zhaoling tomb Apr.–Oct., daily 8–5:30; Nov.–Mar., daily 8:30–5.*

**Shendao.** Beyond the entrance, the Shendao (or Sacred Way) passes through an outer pavilion and between rows of stone sculptures depicting elephants, camels, lions, and mythical beasts that scatter the length of its 7-km (4½-miles) journey to the burial sites. This walk is not to be missed and is a route that was once reserved only for imperial travel. ☎ *Y30 (Y20 Nov.–Mar.)* ☼ *Apr.–Oct., daily 8–5:30; Nov.–Mar., daily 8–5*

**Changling (长陵** *Chánglíng*). The spirit way leads to Changling, the head tomb built for Emperor Yongle in 1427. The designs of Yongle's great masterpiece, the Forbidden City, are echoed in this structure. ☎ *010/6076–1888, 010/6076–1424* ☎ *Y45 (Y40 Nov.–Mar.)* ☼ *Apr.–Oct., daily 8–5; Nov.–Mar., daily 8:30–4:30*

**Dingling (定陵** *Dìnglíng*). Changling and a second tomb, Dingling, were rebuilt in the 1980s and opened to the public. Both complexes suffer from over-restoration and overcrowding, but they're worth visiting if only for the tomb relics on display in the small museums at each site. Dingling is particularly worth seeing because this tomb of Emperor Wanli is the only Ming Dynasty tomb that has been excavated. Unfortunately, this was done in 1956 when China's archaeological skills were sadly lacking, resulting in irrecoverable losses. Nonetheless, it's interesting to compare this underground vault with the tomb of Emperor Qianlong at Qingdongling. ☎ *010/6076–1888, 010/6076–1424* ☎ *Y60 (Y40 Nov.–Mar.)* ☼ *Apr.–Oct., daily 8–5; Nov.–Mar., daily 8:30–5*

## FAHAI TEMPLE

*20 km (12 miles) west of Beijing.*

**Fahai Temple (法海寺** *Fǎhǎi sì*). The stunning works of Buddhist mural art at Fahai Temple, which underwent extensive renovation and reopened in 2008, are among the most underappreciated sights in Beijing. Li Tong, a favored eunuch in the court of Emperor Zhengtong (1436–49), donated funds to construct Fahai Temple in 1443. The project was highly ambitious: Li Tong invited only celebrated imperial and court painters to decorate the temple. As a result, the murals in the only surviving chamber of that period, Daxiongbaodian (the Mahavira Hall), are considered the finest examples of Buddhist mural art from the Ming Dynasty. Sadly, statues of various Buddhas and one of Li Tong himself were destroyed during China's Cultural Revolution.

The most famous of the nine murals in Mahavira Hall is a large-scale triptych featuring Guanyin (the Bodhisattva of Compassion) and Wenshu (the Bodhisattva of Marvelous Virtue and Gentle Majesty) in the center, and Poxian (the Buddha of Universal Virtue) on either side. The depiction of Guanyin follows the theme of "moon in water," which compares the Buddhist belief in the illusoriness of the material world to the reflection of the moon in the water. Typically painted with Guanyin are her legendary mount Jin Sun and her assistant Shancai Tongzi. Wenshu is often presented with a lion, symbolic of the bodhisattva's wisdom and strength of will, while Poxian is shown near a six-tusked elephant, each tusk representing one of the qualities that leads to enlightenment. On the opposite wall is the *Sovereign Sakra and Brahma* mural, with a panoply of characters from the Buddhist canon.

The murals were painted during the time of the European Renaissance, and though the subject matter is traditional, there are comparable experiments in perspective taking place in the depiction of the figures, as compared with examples from earlier dynasties. Also of note is a highly unusual decorative technique; many contours in the hall's murals, particularly on jewelry, armor, and weapons, have been set in bold relief by the application of fine gold threads.

The temple grounds are also beautiful, but of overriding interest are the murals themselves. Visitors stumble through the dark temple with rented flashlights (free with your ticket). Viewing the murals in this way, it's easy to imagine oneself as a sort of modern-day Indiana Jones unraveling a story of the Buddha as depicted in ancient murals of unrivaled beauty. Fahai Temple is only a short taxi ride from Beijing's Pingguoyuan subway station. ⌧ *Moshikou Lu, Shijingshan District* ⊹ *Take an approximate Y12 taxi ride from Pinguoyuan subway station directly to the temple* ☎ *010/8871–5776* ⌦ *Y20* ☾ *Daily 9–4.*

**Tian Yi Mu** (北京宦官文化陈列馆(田义幕) *Tiányì mù*). Eunuchs have played a vital role throughout Chinese history, frequently holding great sway over the affairs of state. Their importance, however, has often been overlooked; a reality which the **Beijing Eunuch Culture Exhibition Hall** and the tomb of the most powerful eunuch of all, **Tian Yi** (1534–1605), shows to be false. Tian Yi was only nine when he was voluntarily castrated and sent into the service of the Ming emperor Jiajing. During the next 63 years of his life, he served three rulers and rose to one of the highest ranks in the land. By the time he died, there were over 20,000 eunuchs in imperial service. Thanks to their access to private areas of the palace, they became invaluable as go-betweens for senior officials seeking gossip or the royal ear, and such was Tian Yi's influence. It's said that upon his death The Forbidden City fell silent for three days.

Though not as magnificent as the Thirteen Ming Tombs, the final resting place of Tian Yi befits a man of high social status. Of special note are the intricate stone carvings around the base of the central burial mound. The four smaller tombs on either side belong to other eunuchs who wished to pay tribute to Tian Yi by being buried in the same compound as him. Elsewhere, the small exhibition hall at the front of the tomb complex contains the world's only "eunuch museum" and offers some interesting background (albeit mostly in Mandarin), particularly on China's last eunuch, Sun Yaoting (1902–96). It's worth visiting, if only to see the rather gruesome mummified remains of one unlucky castrati that holds center stage—you can still make out the hairs on his chin. Another equally squirm-inducing sight is the eye-watering collection of castration equipment; plus keep a look out for the ancient Chinese character meaning "to castrate," which resembles two knives, one inverted, side by side. The hall and tomb are a five-minute walk from Fahai Temple; just ask people the way to Tian Yi Mu. ⌧ *80 Moshikou Lu, Shijingshan District* ☎ *010/8872–4148* ⌦ *Y8* ☾ *Daily 9–4:30.*

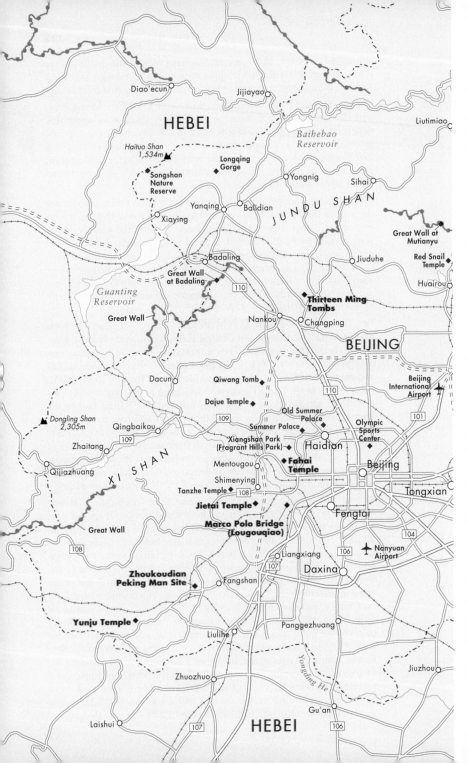

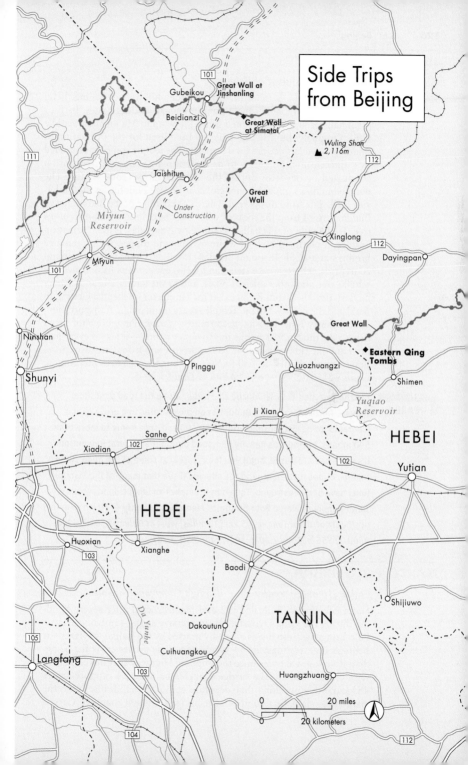

Side Trips from Beijing

## JIETAI TEMPLE

*35 km (22 miles) west of Beijing.*

**Jietai Temple** (戒台寺 *Jiètái sì*). On a wooded hill west of Beijing, Jietai Temple is one of China's most famous ancient Buddhist sites. Its four main halls occupy terraces on a gentle slope up to Ma'an Shan (Saddle Hill). Originally built in AD 622, it's been used for the ordination of Buddhist novices since the Liao Dynasty. The temple complex expanded over the centuries and grew to its current scale in a major renovation conducted by devotees during the Qing Dynasty (1644–1912). The temple buildings, plus three magnificent bronze Buddhas in the Mahavira Hall, date from this period. There's also a huge potbellied Maitreya Buddha carved from the roots of what must have been a truly enormous tree. To the right of this hall, just above twin pagodas, is the Ordination Terrace, a platform built of white marble and topped with a massive bronze statue of Shakyamuni Buddha seated on a lotus flower. Tranquil courtyards, where ornate stelae and well-kept gardens bask beneath a scholar tree and other ancient pines, add to the temple's beauty. Many modern devotees from Beijing visit the temple on weekends. Getting to Jietai and the nearby Tanzhe Temple is easy using public transportation. Take subway Line 1 to its westernmost station, Pingguoyuan. From there, take the No.931 public bus to either temple—it leaves every half hour and the ride takes about 70 minutes. A taxi from Pingguoyuan to Jietai Temple should be Y50 to Y60; the bus fare is Y6. ✉ *Mentougou County* ☎ *010/6980–6611* 🎫 *Y45* 🕒 *Daily 8:30–5.*

**NEARBY**

**Tanzhe Temple** (潭柘寺 *Tánzhè sì*). Farther along the road past Jietai Temple, Tanzhe Temple is a Buddhist complex nestled in a grove of *zhe* (cudrania) trees. Established around AD 400 and once home to more than 500 monks, Tanzhe was heavily damaged during the Cultural Revolution. It's since been restored, but if you look closely at some of the huge stone tablets, or *bei*, littered around the site you'll see that many of the inscriptions have been destroyed. The complex makes an ideal side trip from Jietai Temple or Marco Polo Bridge. ✉ *Mentougou County* ✛ *10 km (6 miles) northeast of Jietai Temple, 45 km (28 miles) west of Beijing* ☎ *010/6086–2500* 🎫 *Y55* 🕒 *Daily 7:30–5:30 (winter 8:30–4:30).*

## MARCO POLO BRIDGE

*16 km (10 miles) southwest of Beijing's Guanganmen Gate.*

**Marco Polo Bridge.** Built in 1192 and reconstructed after severe flooding during the Qing Dynasty, this impressive span—known as Marco Polo Bridge because it was allegedly praised by the Italian wayfarer—is Beijing's oldest bridge. Its 11 segmented-stone arches cross the Yongding River on what was once the Imperial Highway that linked Beijing with central China. The bridge's marble balustrades support nearly 485 carved-stone lions that decorate elaborate handrails. Note the giant stone slabs that comprise the bridge's original roadbed. Carved

## YESANPO AND BEIDAIHE

**Beidaihe** (北戴河 *Běidàihé*). Chairman Mao and the party's favorite spot for sand, sun, and seafood, Beidaihe, (250 km [170 miles] northeast of Beijing) is one of China's few beach resorts (though it's definitely no Bali). This crowded spot is just 2½ hours by train from Beijing Station. Nearly every building in town has been converted to a hotel, and every restaurant has tanks of pick-your-own seafood lining the street. ⊠ *West of Beidaihe District, Qinhuangdao.*

**Yesanpo** (野三坡 *Yěsān pō*). Yesanpo (150 km [90 miles] northeast of Beijing) is a sleepy village between Beijing and neighboring Hebei province. Go here if you're craving a slower-paced scene and some outdoor fun. The accommodations aren't first class, but there are plenty of great things to do. Leave Beijing from Beijing West Station for the two-hour ride. Traditionally, locals have houses with extra rooms for guests, and owners will strive to make your stay as comfortable as possible. A clean room with two beds and an air conditioner should run you no more than Y150. There are also a few hotels on the main street by the train station with rooms running approximately Y200. This scenic town is nestled in a valley. The area is best toured on horseback, and horses are available for rent for Y300 per day (with a guide), or Y100 for an hour or so. Yesanpo is also known for its whole barbecued lamb. Train No. 6437 leaves Beijing West Station at 8:29 pm and arrives at 8:29 pm. Return train 6438 leaves at 9:35 am daily.

imperial stelae at either end of the span commemorate the bridge and surrounding scenery.

The Marco Polo Bridge is best remembered in modern times as the spot where invading Japanese armies clashed with Chinese soldiers on June 7, 1937. The assault began Japan's brutal eight-year occupation of eastern China, which ended with Tokyo's surrender at the end of World War II. The bridge has become a popular field-trip destination for Beijing students. On the Beijing side of the span is the **Memorial Hall of the War of Resistance Against Japan.** Below the bridge on the opposite shore, local entrepreneurs rent horses (the asking price is Y120 per hour, but you should bargain) and lead tours of the often-dry grassy riverbed. ⊠ *Near Xidaokou, Fengtai District* ☎ *010/8389–4614* 🎫 *Y20* 🕐 *Daily 7 am–8 pm.*

## ZHOUKOUDIAN PEKING MAN SITE

*48 km (30 miles) southwest of Beijing.*

**Zhoukoudian Peking Man Site** (周口店北京人现场 *Zhōukǒudiàn Běijīngrén xiànchǎng*). This area of lime mines and craggy foothills ranks among the world's great paleontological sites (and served as the setting for Amy Tan's *The Bonesetter's Daughter*). In 1929, anthropologists, drawn to Zhoukoudian by apparently human "dragon bones" found in a Beijing apothecary, unearthed a complete cranium and other

*Continued on page 138*

**DID YOU KNOW**

The Great Wall is the longest man-made structure on earth. It was designated a UNESCO World Heritage Site in 1987. Sections were built from the 5th Century BC to the 17th Century AD.

# THE GREAT WALL

For some people, the Great Wall is the main reason for a trip to China; for any visitor to Beijing, it's a must-see. Originally intended to keep foreigners out, the world's most famous wall has become the icon of an increasingly open nation. One of the country's most accessible attractions, the Great Wall promises both breathtaking scenery and cultural illumination.

Built by successive dynasties over two millennia, the Great Wall isn't one structure built at one time, but a series of defensive installations that shrank and grew. Especially vulnerable spots were more heavily fortified, while some mountainous regions were left un-walled altogether. The actual length of the wall remains a topic of considerable debate: at its longest, some estimates say the protective cordon spans 6,437 km (4,000 mi)—a distance wider than the United States. Although attacks, age, and pillaging (not to mention today's tourist invasion) have caused the crumbling of up to two-thirds of its length, new sections are being uncovered even today.

As kingdoms scrambled to protect themselves from marauding nomads, portions of wall cropped up, leading to a motley collection of northern borders. It was the first emperor of a unified China, Qin Shi-huang (circa 259–210 BC), founder of the Qin Dynasty, who linked these fortifications into a single network. By some accounts, Qin mustered nearly a million people, or one-fifth of China's workforce, to build this massive barricade, a mobilization that claimed countless lives and gave rise to many tragic folktales.

The Ming Dynasty fortified the wall like never before: for an estimated 5,000 km (3,107 mi), it stood 26 feet tall and 30 feet wide at its base. However, the wall failed to prevent the Manchu invasion that toppled the Ming in 1644. That historical failure hasn't tarnished the Great Wall's image, however. Although China once viewed it as a model of feudal oppression, the Great Wall is now touted as the national symbol. "Love China, Restore the Great Wall," declared Deng Xiaoping in 1984. Since then large sections have been repaired and opened to visitors, turning it also into a symbol of the tension between preservation and restoration in China.

## AN ETERNAL WAIT

One legend concerns Lady Meng, whose husband was kidnapped on their wedding night and forced to work on the Great Wall. She traveled to the work site to await his return, believing her determination would bring him back. She waited so long that, in the end, she turned into a rock, which to this day stands at the head of the Great Wall in the beautiful seaside town of Qinhuangdao.

## MATERIALS & TECHNIQUES

■ During the 2nd century BC, the wall was largely composed of packed earth and piled stone.

■ Some sections, like those in the Taklimakan Desert, were fortified with twigs, sand, and even rice (the jury's still out on whether workers' remains were used as well).

■ The more substantial brick-and-mortar ruins that wind across the mountains north of Beijing date from the Ming Dynasty (14th–17th centuries). Some Ming mortar kilns still exist in valleys around Beijing.

# YOUR GUIDE TO THE GREAT WALL

As a visitor to Beijing, you simply must set aside a day to visit one of the glorious Great Wall sites just outside the capital. The closest, Badaling, is just an hour from the city's center—in general, the farther you go, the more rugged the terrain. So choose your adventure wisely!

**BADALING**, the most accessible section of the Great Wall, is where most tours go. This location is rife with Disneylike commercialism, though: from the cable car you'll see both the heavily reconstructed portions of wall and crowds of souvenir stalls.

If you seek the wall less traveled, book a trip to fantastic **MUTIANYU**, which is about the same distance as Badaling from Beijing. You can enjoy much more solitude here, as well as amazing views from the towers and walls.

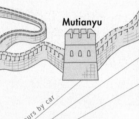

Mutianyu

Badaling

70 km; 1 hour by car

90 km; 1.25 hours by car

✪ BEIJING

## TRANSPORTATION

**CARS:** The easiest and most comfortable way to visit the wall is by private car. Though taxis are occasionally willing to make the trip to more accessible sections like Badaling and Mutianyu, most hotels can arrange a four-passenger car and an English-speaking driver for 8 hours at around Y400–Y600. Settle details in advance, and remember that it's polite to invite your driver to eat meals with you. To ensure your driver doesn't return to Beijing without you, pay after the trip is over.

**TOURS:** In addition to the tour buses that gather around Tiananmen Square, most hotels and tour companies offer trips (in comfortable, air-conditioned buses or vans) to Badaling, Mutianyu, Simatai, and Jinshanling. ■TIP→ Smaller, private tours are generally more rewarding than large bus trips. Trips will run between Y100 and Y500 per person, but costs vary depending on the group size, and can sometimes be negotiated. Wherever you're headed, book in advance.

## TOUR OPERATORS

OUR TOP PICKS

■ **CITS (China International Tour Service)** runs bus tours to Badaling and private tours to Badaling, Mutianyu, and Simatai. (Y400, Y500, Y600 per person) ✉ 1 Dongdan Bei DAJIE, Dongcheng District ☎ 010/6522–2991 ⊕ www.cits.net

■ **Beijing Service** leads private guided tours by car to Badaling, Mutianyu, and Simatai (Y420–Y560 per person for small groups of 3-4 people). ☎ 010/5166–7026 ✉ travel@beijingservice.com ⊕ www.beijingservice.com

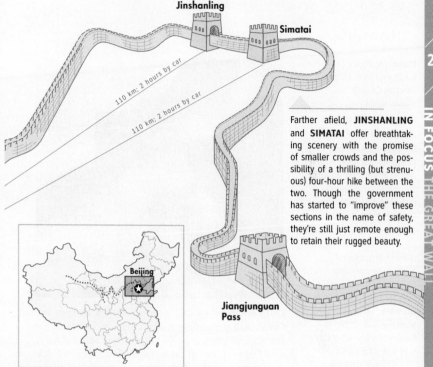

Jinshanling

Simatai

110 km; 2 hours by car

110 km; 2 hours by car

Farther afield, **JINSHANLING** and **SIMATAI** offer breathtaking scenery with the promise of smaller crowds and the possibility of a thrilling (but strenuous) four-hour hike between the two. Though the government has started to "improve" these sections in the name of safety, they're still just remote enough to retain their rugged beauty.

Beijing

Jiangjunguan Pass

■ **Great Wall Adventure Club** organizes private bus and car trips to Jinshanling–Simatai (Y380–Y650) and Mutianyu (Y160–Y350). ☎138/1154–5162 ✐ great-wall@greatwalladventure.com ⊕ www.greatwalladventure.com

ADDITIONAL TOURS

■ **Abercrombie & Kent** also offers pricey personalized group tours to the wall. Call for prices. ☎010/6507–7125 ⊕ www.abercrombiekent.com

■ **Cycle China** runs good guided hiking tours of the unrestored Wall at Jiankou, as well as personalized tours to Simatai and Mutianyu. (Y550–Y750 for minimum of 5 people). ☎010/6402–5653, ⊕ www.cyclechina.com

■ **David Spindler,** a Great Wall expert, runs private tours to various sites. Contact him for prices, schedules, and details through Wild China ☎010/6465–6602 Ext. 314 ✐ info@wildchina.com ⊕ www.wildchina.com

■ **Dragon Bus Tours,** which picks up at major hotels, has tours to Badaling (with Ming Tombs), Mutianyu, and a bus to Simatai—with an occasional stop at a souvenir factory. (Y280–350; Y350-Y500 for Simatai) ☎010/6515–8565 ✐ service@beijinghighlights.com

■ **Gray Line/Panda Tours,** with branches in a dozen high-end hotels in Beijing, runs bus tours to Badaling (and Ming Tombs), Mutianyu, and Simatai—but beware of stops at souvenir factories. (Y280 per person) ✉4 fl., Shuang'an Dashi, 421 Beisanhuan, haidian ☎010/6525–8372 ⊕ www.pandatourchina.cn

# GREAT WALL AT BADALING

## GETTING THERE

**Distance:** 70 km (43 mi) northwest of Beijing, in Yanqing County

**Tours:** Beijing Service, CITS, Dragon Bus Tours, Gray Line/Panda Tours

**By Car:** A car for four people to Badaling should run no more than Y600 for five hours, sometimes including a stop at the Thirteen Ming Tombs.

**By Bus:** It's hard to wander south of Tiananmen Square without encountering the many buses going to Badaling. Choose wisely: look for the 1 or 5 bus at Qianmen, across from the southeastern corner of Tiananmen Square (departs 6:30 am–11:30 am for Y12–Y18 per person).

## FAST FACTS

**Phone:** 010/6912–1383
**Hours:** Daily 6:30 am–7 pm
**Admission:** Y40 Apr.–Nov.; cable car is an additional Y35 one-way, Y50 round-trip
**Web Site:** www.badaling.gov.cn

Only one hour by car from downtown Beijing, the Great Wall at Badaling is where visiting dignitaries go for a quick photo-op. Postcard views abound here, with large sections of the restored Ming Dynasty brick wall rising majestically to either side of the fort. In the distance, portions of the early-16th-century Great Wall disintegrate into more romantic but inaccessible ruins.

Badaling is convenient to the Thirteen Ming Tombs and outfitted with tourist-friendly facilities, so it's popular with tour groups and is thus often crowded, especially on weekends. ■TIP→ People with disabilities find access to the wall at Badaling better than elsewhere in the Beijing area. You can either take the cable car to the top, or you can walk up the gently sloping steps, relying on handrails if necessary. On a clear day you can see for miles across leafy, undulating terrain from atop the battlements. The admission price also includes access to the China Great Wall Museum and the Great Wall Circle Vision Theater.

■TIP→ Most tours to Badaling will take you to the Thirteen Ming Tombs, as well. If you don't want a stop at the tombs—or at a tourist-trapping jade factory or herbal medicine center along the way—be sure to confirm the itinerary before booking.

# GREAT WALL AT MUTIANYU

## GETTING THERE

**Distance:** 90 km (56 mi) northeast of Beijing, in Huairou County

**Tours:** CITS, Gray Line/Panda Tours, Great Wall Adventure Tour

**By Car:** A car to Mutianyu should cost no more than Y600 for the day—it takes about an hour to get there.

**By Bus:** Take Bus 916/936 from Dongzhimen to Huairou (Y5). From there take a minibus to Mutianyu (Y25–Y30) or hire a taxi to take you there and back to the bus station (about Y50 each way, Y100–Y150 round-trip after bargaining). On weekends and national holidays, the tourist Bus 6 from outside the South Cathedral at Xuanwumen goes directly to Mutianyu (Y50, leaves 6:30–8:30 am).

## FAST FACTS

**Phone:** 010/6162–6873 or 010/6162–6022

**Hours:** Daily 7:30 am– 5:30 pm

**Admission:** Y45 (students half-price); chairlift, Y35; cable car, Y45 one-way, Y65 round trip with toboggan descent

**Fodor's Choice** Slightly farther from downtown Beijing than Badaling, the Great Wall at Mutianyu is more spectacular and, despite the occasional annoyances of souvenir stands, significantly less crowded. This long section of wall, first built during the Northern Qi Dynasty (6th century) and restored and rebuilt throughout history, can offer a solitary Great Wall experience, with unforgettable views of towers winding across mountains and woodlands. On a clear day, you'll swear you can see the deserts of Mongolia in the distance.

The lowest point on the wall is a strenuous one-hour climb above the parking lot. As an alternative, you can take a cable car on a breathtaking ride to the highest restored section (this is how President Bill Clinton ascended in 1998), from which several hiking trails descend. Take a gorgeous 1½-hour walk east to reach another cable car that returns to the same parking lot. Mutianyu is also known for its toboggan run.

■ TIP→ For those taking a car, the road from Huairou, a suburb of Beijing, to Mutianyu follows a river upstream and is lined with restaurants selling fresh trout. In addition, Hongluo Temple is a short drive from the bottom of the mountain.

# GREAT WALL AT SIMATAI

## GETTING THERE

**Distance:** At around 110 km (68 mi) northeast of Beijing, Simatai is farther than Badaling and Mutianyu, but is well worth the trip—the road runs through lovely farmland, and few visitors make the trek.

**Tours:** Most hotels offer tours here, as do CITS, Gray Line/Panda Tours, and Great Wall Adventure Tour.

**By Car:** A car to Simatai should be no more than Y800 for the day. If you plan to hike from Jinshanling to Simatai, or vice versa, have your car drop you off at one and pick you up at the other.

**By Bus:** Take the early-morning Bus 916 from the bus station at Dongzhimen (Y20), starting at 6 am. On weekends and holidays, a luxury bus leaves Qianmen at 8:30 am (Y85 round-trip) and leaves Simatai at 3 pm.

## FAST FACTS

**Phone:** 010/6903–5025 or 010/6903–1051

**Hours:** Daily 8 am–5 pm

**Admission:** Y40; cable car, Y30 one-way, Y50 round-trip. If you hike to Jinshanling, you will have to buy another Y5 ticket at the border.

★ Remote and largely unrestored, the Great Wall at Simatai is ideal if you're seeking adventure. Near the frontier garrison at Gubeikou, the wall traverses towering peaks and hangs precariously above cliffs. Be prepared for no-handrails hiking, tough climbs, and unparalleled vistas. Several trails lead to the wall from the parking lot.

In summer, a cable car takes you two-thirds of the way up; from there it's a steep 40-minute climb to the summit. Heading east from the Miyun reservoir at a moderate pace will take you to Wangjing Ta, the 12th watchtower, after about 3 hours. For a longer hike, head west over the bridge toward the restored Jinshanling section.

The hike to Jinshanling is a strenuous 9 km (5.6 mi), usually taking around 4 hours up and down sublime sections of the wall. Be aware that crossing to Jinshanling costs Y5. People who wish to hike from one to the other often ask their driver to wait for them at their destination. (Note that hikers usually go from Jinshanling to Simatai, where buses back to Beijing are easier to find.)

# GREAT WALL AT JINSHANLING

## GETTING THERE

**Distance:** 110 km (68 mi) northeast from Beijing

**Tours:** CITS, Cycle China, Gray Line/Panda Tours, Great Wall Adventure Tour

**By Car:** A car should be no more than Y800; the ride is about two hours. If you plan to hike from Jinshanling to Simatai, as many do, it makes sense to be dropped off at Jinshanling and have your car pick you up at Simatai.

**By Train:** Take train L671, which departs at 7:25 am from Beijing North Railway Station, to Gubeikou; there switch to a local minibus or taxi to Jinshanling.

**By Bus:** Take a minibus from Dongzhimen long-distance bus station to Miyun (Y8) and then change to a local bus or taxi. Or take a Chengde-bound bus from Dongzhimen and get off at Jinshanling; a cab can bring you to the entrance for Y10.

★ Though it lacks the rugged adventure of Simatai, Jinshanling is perhaps the least restored of the major Great Wall sections near Beijing, as well as the least visited. Besides being the starting point for a fantastic four-hour hike to Simatai, Jinshanling also serves as one of the few sections of the Great Wall on which you can camp overnight.

A starry night here is gorgeous and unforgettable—go with a tour group such as Cycle China. Don't forget to pack a piece of charcoal and paper to make rubbings of bricks that still bear the stamp of the date they were made.

## FAST FACTS

**Phone:** 031/4883–0222 or 138/3144–8986

**Hours:** Daily 8 am–5 pm

**Admission:** Y50; Y398, Y498, Y598 for overnight stays. If you hike to Simatai, you will have to buy another Y5 ticket at the border

## GREAT WALL MARATHON

Not for the faint of heart, the Great Wall Marathon (and half marathon) takes place each May. The marathon covers approximately 6.5 km (4 mi) of the Great Wall, with the rest of the course running through lovely valleys in rural Tianjin.

⊕ www.great-wall-marathon.com

The Eastern Qing Tombs are the most expansive burial grounds in China.

fossils dubbed *Homo erectus pekinensis*, or Peking Man. These early remains, believed to be nearly 700,000 years old, suggest (as do similar *Homo erectus* discoveries in Indonesia) that humankind's most recent ancestor originated in Asia, not Europe (though today some scientists posit that humans evolved in Africa first and migrated to Asia). A large-scale excavation in the early 1930s further unearthed six skullcaps and other hominid remains, stone tools, evidence of fire, plus a multitude of animal bones, many at the bottom of a large sinkhole believed to be a trap for woolly rhinos and other large game. Sadly, the Peking Man fossils disappeared under mysterious circumstances during World War II, leaving researchers only plaster casts to contemplate. Subsequent digs at Zhoukoudian have yielded nothing equivalent to Peking Man, although archaeologists haven't yet abandoned the search. Trails lead to several hillside excavation sites. A small museum showcases a few (dusty) Peking Man statues, a collection of Paleolithic artifacts, two mummies, and some fine animal fossils, including a bear skeleton and a saber-toothed tiger skull. Because of the importance of Peking Man and the potential for other finds in the area, Zhoukoudian is a UNESCO World Heritage Site, but it may not be of much interest to those without a particular inclination for the subject. If you should find yourself here with little to do after your museum visit and the few dig locations, consider a little hike into the surrounding hills, which are named the Dragon Bone Mountains. ✉ *Zhoukoudian* ☎ *010/6930–1278* 🎫 *Y30* 🕐 *Daily 8:30–4:30.*

## YUNJU TEMPLE

*75 km (47 miles) southwest of Beijing.*

**Yunju Temple** (云居寺 *Yúnjū sì*). Yunju Temple is best known for its mind-boggling collection of 14,278 minutely carved Buddhist tablets. To protect the Buddhist canon from destruction by Taoist emperors, the devout Tang-era monk Jing Wan carved Buddhist scriptures into stone slabs that he hid in sealed caves in the cliffs of a mountain. Jing Wan spent 30 years creating these tablets until his death in AD 637; his disciples continued his work for the next millennium into the 17th century, thereby compiling one of the most extensive Buddhist libraries in the world. A small pagoda at the center of the temple complex commemorates the remarkable monk. Although the tablets were originally stored inside Shijing Mountain behind the temple, they're now housed in rooms built along the temple's southern perimeter.

Four central prayer halls, arranged along the hillside above the main gate, contain impressive Ming-era bronze Buddhas. The last in this row, the Dabei Hall, displays the spectacular *Thousand-Armed Avalokiteshvara*. This 13-foot-tall bronze sculpture—which actually has 24 arms and five heads and stands in a giant lotus flower—is believed to embody boundless compassion. A group of pagodas, led by the 98-foot-tall Northern Pagoda, is all that remains of the original Tang complex. These pagodas are remarkable for their Buddhist reliefs and ornamental patterns. Heavily damaged during the Japanese occupation and again by Maoist radicals in the 1960s, the temple complex remains under renovation. ⊠ *Off Fangshan Lu, Nanshangle Xiang, Fangshan County* ☎ *010/6138–9612* 💲 *Y40* ☻ *Daily 8:30–5 (winter 8:30–4:30).*

## EASTERN QING TOMBS

*125 km (78 miles) east of Beijing.*

Fodor's Choice
★   **Eastern Qing Tombs** (清东陵 *Qīngdōnglíng*). Modeled on the Thirteen Ming Tombs, the Eastern Qing Tombs replicate the Ming spirit ways, walled tomb complexes, and subterranean burial chambers. But they're even more extravagant in their scale and grandeur, and far less touristy. The ruins contain the remains of five emperors, 14 empresses, and 136 imperial concubines, all laid to rest in a broad valley chosen by Emperor Shunzhi (1638–61) while on a hunting expedition. By the Qing's collapse in 1911, the tomb complex covered some 18 square miles (46 square km) of farmland and forested hillside, making it the most expansive burial ground in all China.

The Eastern Qing Tombs are in much better repair than their older Ming counterparts—and considerably less crowded. Although several of the tomb complexes have undergone extensive renovation, none is overdone. Peeling paint, grassy courtyards, and numerous stone bridges and pathways convey a sense of the area's original grandeur. Often visitors are so few that you may feel as if you've stumbled upon an ancient ruin unknown beyond the valley's farming villages.

Of the nine tombs open to the public, two are not to be missed. The first is **Yuling,** the resting place of the Qing Dynasty's most powerful sovereign, Emperor Qianlong (1711–99), who ruled China for 59 years. Beyond the outer courtyards, Qianlong's burial chamber is accessible from inside Stela Hall, where an entry tunnel descends some 65 feet (20 meters) into the ground and ends at the first of three elaborately carved marble gates. Beyond, exquisite carvings of Buddhist images and sutras rendered in Tibetan adorn the tomb's walls and ceiling. Qianlong was laid to rest, along with his empress and two concubines, in the third and final marble vault, amid priceless offerings looted by warlords early in the 20th century.

**Dingdongling** was built for the infamous Empress Dowager Cixi (1835–1908). Known for her failure to halt Western-imperialist encroachment, Cixi once spent funds allotted to strengthen China's navy on a traditional stone boat for the lake at the Summer Palace. Her burial compound, reputed to have cost 72 tons of silver, is the most elaborate (if not the largest) at the Eastern Qing Tombs. Many of its stone carvings are considered significant because the phoenix, which symbolizes the female, is level with, or even above, the imperial (male) dragon—a feature, ordered, no doubt, by the empress herself. A peripheral hall paneled in gold leaf displays some of the luxuries amassed by Cixi and her entourage, including embroidered gowns, jewelry, imported cigarettes, and even a coat for one of her dogs. In a bow to tourist kitsch, the compound's main hall contains a wax statue of Cixi sitting Buddha-like on a lotus petal flanked by a chambermaid and an eunuch.

The Eastern Qing Tombs are a two- to three-hour drive from the capital. The rural scenery is dramatic, and the trip is one of the best full-day excursions outside Beijing. Consider bringing a bed sheet, a bottle of wine, and boxed lunches, as the grounds are ideal for a picnic. ⊠ *Near Malanguan, Hebei province, Zunhua County* ☎ *0315/694–4467* ✉ *Y120* ☉ *Daily 8–5.*

3

# BEIJING TO SHANGHAI

Hebei, Shandong, Jiangsu, and Anhui

# WELCOME TO BEIJING TO SHANGHAI

## TOP REASONS TO GO

★ **Qingdao:** Hit the beach or explore the historic corners of the Bavarian-styled Old City, with its mansions, churches, and burgeoning café culture.

★ **Huangshan:** Framed in spectral mist, Yellow Mountain's towering granite peaks have inspired artists and poets for centuries.

★ **Chengde:** Originally an Imperial summer retreat, this town's magnificent temples, palaces and deer-filled parks now attract weekenders hunting for culture.

★ **Suzhou:** Discover flower-filled classical gardens in a town still threaded with ancient waterways.

★ **Qufu:** Visit the birthplace of China's foremost philosopher and spiritual thinker, the "Great Sage" Confucius.

**1** Anhui. It may be one of China's poorest provinces, but Anhui's wealth lies in its immaculately preserved villages and the sublime mountain scenery at Huangshan.

**2** Hebei. Wrapped around the nation's capital, Hebei's attractions are definitely worth a side trip. The Manchu summer retreat of Chengde puts on an almighty show of pomp and splendor, and in Shanhaiguan the Great Wall finally comes to an end at the ocean.

**3** Jiangsu. A witness to turbulent historic events, Jiangsu abounds with mausoleums and memorials, ancient temples and palaces, and the region's finest cuisine. Nanjing was the country's capital for six dynastic periods. Nearby Suzhou and Yangzhou are renowned for their splendid gardens.

**4** Shandong. Follow in the footsteps of emperors with a pilgrimage to Taishan, the most revered of all China's sacred mountains. For the more earthly pleasures of sun, seafood, and suds, don't miss the seaside city of Qingdao, China's water sports (and drinking) capital.

## GETTING ORIENTED

Stretching from Hebei, which is culturally and geographically Northern China, to the more refined province of Jiangsu, this region is accessible thanks to a well-developed tourist infrastructure. All four provinces have convenient air and rail links to the major transport hubs of Beijing and Shanghai. As you travel from north to south, you can judge for yourself whether Chinese stereotypes are accurate: Northerners are viewed as typically taller and lighter skinned, raised on wheat-based foods like noodles and bread that thrive in the cool, dry climate. Southerners, on the other hand, are thought of as shorter and darker, with rice their staple of choice. The mighty Yangtze River that flows past Nanjing is sometimes taken to represent this vague cultural border.

Updated by Tom O'Malley

Tombs, temples, elegant gardens, and historic water towns are just the beginning of what this extraordinary region has to offer. This is where Confucius was born, where China's two great rivers and the Great Wall meet the sea, and where some of the country's most celebrated mountain landscapes have inspired pilgrimages for millennia.

Despite phenomenal development across Eastern China over the past decade, it's still possible to lose yourself in the canal-side walkways and idyllic gardens of Suzhou, the "Venice of the East," or pick a path through the cobbled streets of old Yangzhou. Eight of China's 43 UNESCO World Heritage Sites dot this region, with Anhui's villages of Xidi and Hongcun and Shandong's Qufu, Confucius's ancestral birthplace, managing to retain their historic and artistic character. Buy Suzhou's famous silk from the owners of the silk-spinning worms, Tsingtao beer straight from the source in Qingdao, and sample the dim-sum delights of Huaiyang cuisine at its most authentic in Yangzhou.

Everyone from Emperor Qin to Chairman Mao has tackled the trail to the summit of Tai Shan, China's most sacred Taoist mountain. And they didn't have a cable car to help them. To the south, Huangshan's mysterious peaks, fringed with spindly pines and swathed in clouds, have inspired whole schools of Chinese painting.

Travel here has never been easier. Increasingly comfortable and internationally minded lodgings are springing up everywhere. Bullet trains have slashed journey times, whisking you from one destination to the next. Remember that the pedestrian in no way has the right of way in China, and take a business card with your hotel's address in Chinese to show a taxi when you've had enough noise, excitement, and pandemonium for one day.

## PLANNING

### WHEN TO GO

Spring and summer is the best time to head to the coast at Qingdao and, farther north, Beidaihe and Shanhaiguan. Save the arduous ascents of Huangshan and Taishan for autumn, when the crowds and temperatures have died down.

The eastern region of China is heavily populated, and sometimes it seems like everyone takes to the road (or train, or plane). Avoid traveling during the Chinese New Year, which is based on the lunar calendar and usually falls at the end of January. The weeklong National Day holiday at the start of October can easily be avoided with a bit of planning.

### GETTING HERE AND AROUND

With the exception of Huangshan, Chengde, and Yangzhou, every destination in this chapter is now connected by the China Highspeed Rail network, by far the most convenient and comfortable way to get around. Buses are very efficient, and tickets can usually be bought the same day. Airline tickets can be purchased close to the departure date and prices are fairly consistent, assuming you avoid traveling during a Chinese holiday, when prices skyrocket.

#### AIR TRAVEL

Besides the major international airports in Beijing and Shanghai, other domestic air hubs include Nanjing, Qingdao, and Shijiazhuang (the capital of Hebei Province). Unlike other areas of the country, distances between sights in this region aren't great. The main operators are Air China and China Eastern Airlines, though there are several regional carriers like Shandong Airlines and Hebei Airlines.

#### BUS TRAVEL

With many thousands of destinations and departures, buses can be handy for short trips, especially to destinations outside the rail network. Buses are usually in reasonable condition and have air-conditioning, assigned seating, and reliably punctual service. Remember to bring a pair of headphones, as you can usually expect a noisy kung-fu movie playing on the video monitor. Never patronize the army of touts who work at the main bus stations; always buy your tickets from the official counters or through your hotel.

#### CAR TRAVEL

Hiring a car and driver gives you the freedom to explore the region at your own leisure, but it can be costly. Expect prices of at least $150 a day if you book through an international hotel, and substantially more if you want an English-speaking guide.

#### TRAIN TRAVEL

China's excellent high-speed rail system has made Shandong and Jiangsu more accessible than ever before, with many trains whizzing along at over 300 kph (186 mph). Tickets can be purchased either through your hotel (strongly recommended) or at the station, although the lines are long and vendors can be curt with non-Chinese speakers. Buy tickets at least 24 hours ahead of when you intend to travel, or longer during peak periods.

### HEALTH AND SAFETY

Take all prescription medicine with you. For minor ailments, such as headaches and stomachaches, Chinese pharmacies are widespread and stocked with both Chinese and Western medicine. Antibiotics can be purchased easily and cheaply over the counter. Carry waterless hand sanitizer and toilet paper. Safe bottled water is widely available.

### RESTAURANTS

Every locality has its own specialties—wild game in Hebei, braised chicken in Shandong, duck cooked myriad ways in Jiangsu. Try Qingdao's famous chili-fried clams, or Suzhou's sweet-and-sour river fish. Jiangsu cuisine, called Huaiyang, is considered one of China's four great cooking styles, and is light, fresh, and sweet (though not as sweet as in Shanghai). As you travel inland to Anhui, the food is famously salty, relying heavily on preserved ham and soy sauce to enhance flavors. Anhui chefs make good use of mountain-grown mushrooms and bamboo shoots. Vegetarian options, often available in or near Buddhist temples, showcase chefs who manipulate tofu, wheat gluten, and vegetables to create "mock" meat that even carnivores will appreciate.

*Prices in the reviews are the average cost of a main course at dinner or, if dinner is not served, at lunch.*

### HOTELS

Hotels in this region are improving every year, and most major cities now have a range of international luxury brands. Don't expect to find such creature comforts in such smaller cities, but you will discover comfortable midrange lodgings. You probably won't find an English-speaking staff at cheaper hotels. Most places these days accept credit cards, and you'll get better rates if you book in advance. Chinese hotels are easy to book, often without prepaying, through English-language Chinese websites like ⊕ *www.ctrip.com* or ⊕ *www.elong.com*.

Prices in the reviews are the lowest cost of a standard double room in high season.

### VISITOR INFORMATION

In the bigger cities you'll find storefronts and street kiosks with signs reading "Tourist Information." However, finding someone who speaks enough English to be helpful might be difficult, as these booths cater to domestic tourists. Your best bets for in-depth assistance are larger hotels. Be polite and persistent. Write dates clearly when inquiring about tickets, speak slowly, and inspect any tickets given to you thoroughly before leaving. Look for copies of the English-language *Redstar* (Qingdao), *Map Magazine* or *The Nanjinger* (Nanjing), and *More Suzhou* in hotels, restaurants, and at Starbucks.

### TOURS

Group tours are always an option, but often feature unwelcome shopping stops, leaving less time to enjoy the sights. Do your research, ask questions, and if the package price seems too high or low, be skeptical. The best source of information is on Fodor's forums (⊕ *www.fodors. com*), where many travelers share the good, the bad, and the ugly, like pressured tipping, frequent shopping stops, and low-quality food.

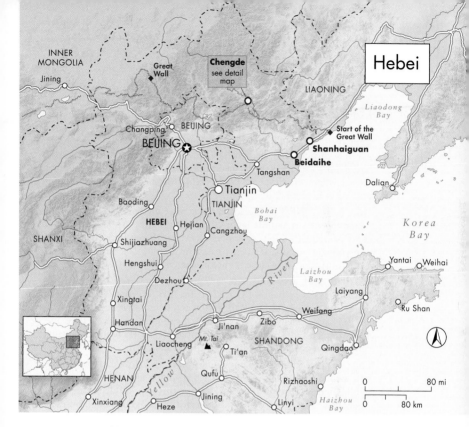

**Beijing Discovery Tours.** Beijing Discovery Tours, an American-Chinese company, can arrange private tours countrywide. The company is not cheap, but is extremely reliable and thorough. ☎ *800/306–1264* ⊕ *www.beijingdiscoverytours.com.*

## HEBEI

Many visitors travel through Hebei without a backward glance on the way to and from the capital, but the province has several sites worth a detour. Chengde is a must for history buffs and fans of the great outdoors. The town's glory days were during the 18th century, when the Emperor Kangxi made it his summer retreat and hunting ground, filling the place with the country's largest royal garden and a bevy of opulent Buddhist temples. The emperors may be long gone, but the town still serves as a holiday destination, now for busloads of Beijing residents. Farther south, at the seaside resorts of Beidaihe and Shanhaiguan, where the Great Wall meets the sea, foreign visitors can experience a singularly Chinese take on the seaside vacation.

# CHENGDE

*4 hrs (230 km [140 miles]) by train northeast of Beijing; 7 hrs (470 km [291 miles]) by train southwest of Shenyang.*

An increasingly common stop on the China tour circuit, some visitors regard Chengde as one of the highlights of their trip. It had been just another village until the 18th century, when Qing Dynasty Emperor Kangxi stumbled upon it during a hunting trip. With the Wulie River gurgling through and the Yanshan Mountains providing an impressive backdrop, Chengde was deemed an ideal spot to establish a summer retreat where the Emperor could escape the heat of the capital and indulge in hunting and fishing.

Now it is a UNESCO World Heritage Site, home to the magnificent Mountain Resort and the Eight Outer Monasteries. Although children enjoy romping through the imperial gardens, there's little else to entertain younger visitors. It's best to visit in summer or early autumn, as some tourist facilities close in the off-season.

### GETTING HERE AND AROUND

TRAIN TRAVEL Most travelers arrive on the K7711 direct train from Beijing, which departs from Beijing Main Rail Station at 8:05 am, arriving in Chengde at 12:31 pm. Chengde is on a northern rail line between Beijing and Shenyang, and the journey from the capital takes 4½ hours. No trains run between Chengde and Beidaihe or Shanhaiguan.

BUS TRAVEL Long-distance buses can be uncomfortable and slow, but they're the only transport linking Chengde with Beidaihe and Shanhaiguan via Qinhuangdao. Several daily buses make this trip, all departing from Chengde's long-distance bus station near the Shenghua Hotel. Buses to Beijing also depart from this station.

TAXI TRAVEL Chengde is a small city, so you shouldn't have to pay more than Y15 to get from the city center out to the temples.

### SAFETY AND PRECAUTIONS

Like most Chinese cities, Chengde is a very safe place to explore. Violent crime is extremely rare, but petty theft can be a problem. Keep a close eye on your personal belongings in crowded places.

### TIMING

Chengde is a small city, and most of the main attractions are bunched northeast of the Mountain Resort, so one or two full days should be enough time to see the sights. That said, the Mountain Resort is huge, and could easily take up a full day. If you want to do any hiking in the surrounding countryside, plan on three full days.

### TOURS

All hotels in Chengde run tours covering the main sights, at least during the high season. An English-speaking guide costs around Y100.

### ESSENTIALS

**Bus Contact Chengde Long-Distance Station** ⊠ *Wulie Lu at Xinhua Lu* ☎ *0314/212–3588.*

**Medical Assistance Chengde Chinese-Western Hospital** ⊠ *12 Xi Da Jie* ☎ *0314/202–2222.*

## EIGHT OUTER MONASTERIES

On the eastern and northern slopes of the Mountain Resort, this collection of temples offers a powerful insight into Chengde's role as not just a royal getaway, but as a political arena. Each temple was built to reflect the architectural style of a different minority, so when meetings with rival border groups took place, they provided handy diplomatic currency (the large Tibetan influence was for the benefit of the Mongols, who were devout Lamaists).

However, of the dozen monasteries originally built during the Qing Dynasty, only eight survive today in good condition (two were destroyed, two are now dilapidated). Just a few are open to the public. Buses No. 6 and 10 take visitors from the Mountain Resort to the eastern and northern temples respectively. If you're strapped for time, though, it's worth prioritizing the Temple of Potaraka Doctrine, which is a stunning replica of Tibet's Potala Palace, and the Temple of Universal Peace, which is still in use by monks today.

**Train Contact Chengde Train Station** ✉ *Chezhan Lu* ☎ *0314/762–2602.*

**Visitor and Tour Info Chengde CITS** ✉ *11 Zhonghua Lu* ☎ *0314/202–7483* ⊕ *www.cits.net.*

### EXPLORING

Don't waste your energy wandering around the city itself. The massive scale of the Mountain Resort, twice as large as Beijing's Summer Palace, means you will be doing plenty of walking. The other monasteries are close to the city.

### TOP ATTRACTIONS

Fodor's Choice ★ **Mountain Resort** (避暑山庄 *Bìshǔ shānzhuāng*). Moved by Chengde's lush mountains, cool weather, and plentiful game—not to mention a desire to enjoy the former while shooting arrows at the latter—Emperor Kangxi ordered construction of the first palaces of the Mountain Resort in 1703. Within a decade, what was previously just a simple village had dozens of ornate temples, pagodas, and spectacular gardens spread out across 1,500 acres. By the end of the 18th century nearly 100 imperial structures filled the town.

The result was more than just a smaller version of the Summer Palace, however. Besides luxurious quarters for the emperor and his court, great palaces and temples were completed to house visiting dignitaries and to impress them with the grandeur of the Chinese empire. Its location was useful, as it lay far enough away from Beijing to host talks with rivals groups who wouldn't otherwise set foot in the capital. From its interconnected palaces, each built in different architectural styles, to its replicas of famous temples representing different Chinese religions, everything about the resort was designed to reflect China's diversity. In retrospect, it was as much a Qing statement of intent as it was a holiday home.

Today, the palace (a UNESCO World Heritage Site) and the surrounding landscape of lakes, meadows, and forests makes for an engaging stroll.

The mountains in the northern half of the park and giant pagoda in the center afford panoramas unmatched elsewhere in the city. It is also home to the largest imperial garden in China. Even during peak season (April to October) it rarely feels crowded. ✉ *Center of town* ☎ *0314/2029771* 🎟 *Apr.–Oct. Y120; Nov.–Mar. Y90* ⏲ *Daily 8 am–5:30 pm.*

**WORD OF MOUTH**

"I particularly enjoyed an exhibit in which mannequins were dressed as the emperors who had spent time at the Mountain Resort. Their costumes were beautiful, and I found it interesting to see how the style of dress changed over time." —kja

**WORTH NOTING**

**Club Rock** (棒槌峰 Bàngchuí fēng). A cable car ride and a 30-minute hike leads from Pule Temple up to Club Rock, a phallic protrusion that spawned a local legend: if the rock should fall, so will the virility of local men. 🎟 *Y50* ⏲ *Daily 8–6.*

## WHERE TO EAT

Given Chengde's role as a royal hunting ground, it's no surprise that the local specialty is wild game. Spiced deer meat sold in clusters for Y5 and pheasant-and-mushroom–stuffed dumplings can be sampled at the visitor-friendly shops on the street south of the Summer Resort.

$$ CHINESE 🍴 **Da Qinghua.** Overlooking Lizheng Gate, this cheerful place with a rustic wooden exterior is a good choice if you want to sample local dishes. Try the specialty: homemade dumplings filled with pheasant and local mushrooms. The picture menu helps, as the staff does not speak English. To find it, look for the dragons on the building's exterior. [$] *Average main: Y80* ✉ *19 Lizhengmen Da Jie* ☎ *0314/2036–2222* 💳 *No credit cards.*

$$ SICHUAN 🍴 **Dongpo Restaurant** (东坡饭庄 *Dōngpō fànzhuāng*). With one branch near Dehui Gate (east of Lizheng Gate) and two others around town, Dongpo serves hearty Sichuan fare. There's no English menu, but classics like *gongbao jiding* (chicken with peanuts) and *niurou chao tudou* (beef and potatoes) are available. [$] *Average main: Y80* ✉ *Shanzhuang Dong Lu* ☎ *0314/505–7766* 💳 *No credit cards.*

## WHERE TO STAY

$ HOTEL 🏨 **Bifeng Hotel.** Although not fit for an emperor, this is as good as it gets in Chengde. **Pros:** central location; decent home-cooking in the restaurant. **Cons:** a bit scruffy; no Western breakfast. [$] *Rooms from: Y170* ✉ *Dehui Building, 9 Huoshenmiao, Tower B* ☎ *0314/205–0668* 🛏 *71 rooms* 🍽 *No meals.*

$ HOTEL 🏨 **Puning Hotel.** Location is everything, as they say: this hotel's historic setting, adjoining Puning Temple, and a pleasant courtyard places it high above the other options in the center of the city. **Pros:** convenient location; easy access to sights; vegetarian dining options. **Cons:** indifferent service; small rooms. [$] *Rooms from: Y320* ✉ *West Courtyard of Puning Temple, Puning Lu* ☎ *0314/205–8888* 🛏 *100 rooms* 🍽 *Breakfast.*

$ HOTEL 🏨 **Shenghua Hotel** (盛华大酒店 *Chénghuá dàjiǔdiàn*). At 14 stories tall, this silver tower of glass and steel soars above the city. **Pros:** tasty

**DID YOU KNOW?**

The 72 scenic spots that you'll see at Chengde's Mountain Resort are copies of famous Chinese gardens, grassy Mongolian plains, and forested mountains and valleys. Renowned structures have also been replicated. The main building on Green Lotus Island, the Tower of Mist and Rain, is a copy of a tower in Nanhu Lake at Jiaxing in Zhejiang Province.

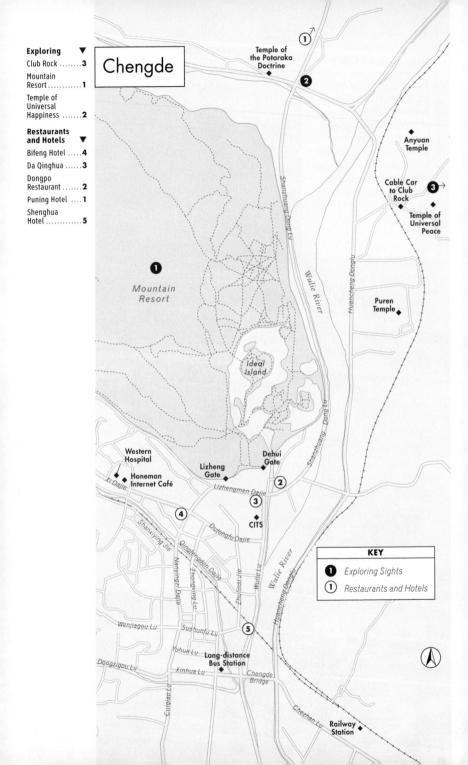

# Chengde

**Exploring** ▼
Club Rock ........3
Mountain Resort ............1
Temple of Universal Happiness .......2

**Restaurants and Hotels** ▼
Bifeng Hotel .....4
Da Qinghua ......3
Dongpo Restaurant .......2
Puning Hotel ....1
Shenghua Hotel .............5

Temple of the Potaraka Doctrine

Anyuan Temple

Cable Car to Club Rock

Temple of Universal Peace

Mountain Resort

Puren Temple

Shanzhuang Dong Lu

Wulie River

Huancheng Donglu

Ideal Island

Shanzhuang Dong Lu

Western Hospital

Honeman Internet Café

Lizheng Gate

Dehui Gate

Xi Dajie

Lizhengmen Dajie

CITS

Dufongfu Dajie

Shanxiying Jie

Qingfengdon Dajie

Nanyingzi Dajie

Zhonging Lu

Zhulinsi Jie

Wulie Lu

Wulie River

Huancheng Donglu

**KEY**
❶ Exploring Sights
① Restaurants and Hotels

Wenjiagou Lu

Sushuntu Lu

Yuhua Lu

Dongzigou Lu

Xinhua Lu

Long-distance Bus Station

Chengde Bridge

Chezhan Lu

Railway Station

restaurant; reliable service; near bus and train stations. **Cons:** a bit far from the main sights. [$] *Rooms from: Y430* ✉ *22 Wulie Lu* ☎ *0314/227–1000* 🌐 *www.shenghuahotel.com* 🛏 *111 rooms* 🍴 *Breakfast.*

### NIGHTLIFE AND THE ARTS

The main shopping street, Nanyingzi Dajie (parallel to Wuli River), is a good place to stroll in the evening, when a night market stretches all the way down the street. Many of the vendors sell antiques and fun knickknacks.

**Puning Song and Dance** (普宁寺 *Pùníng sì*). These performances are a bit touristy, but they're also a great way to see the Temple of Universal Peace illuminated at night. The Y150 admission includes transport to and from your hotel. ✉ *Temple of Universal Peace, Puning Si Lu* ☎ *0314/216–2007.*

## BEIDAIHE

*2 hrs (260 km [160 miles]) by express train east of Beijing; 3 hrs (395 km [245 miles]) by train southwest of Shenyang; 1 hr (35 km [22 miles]) by minibus southwest of Shanhaiguan.*

English railway engineers came across this small fishing village in the 1890s. Not long after, wealthy Chinese and foreign diplomats were visiting in droves. After Mao Zedong came to power, the new rulers developed a taste for sea air. Today the seaside retreat has an interesting mix of beach kitsch and political posturing, with Communist party members past and present owning villas here. Beidaihe is terrifyingly crowded during the summer and practically empty the rest of the year.

### GETTING HERE AND AROUND

Most visitors come directly from Beijing, and the train is the most convenient option. The train station in Beidaihe is about a 15-minute taxi ride to the beachfront.

AIR TRAVEL At time of writing, Qinhuangdao Beidaihe Airport, 34 km (23 miles) from Beidaihe, is under construction.

BOAT AND FERRY TRAVEL Qinhuangdao is one of the biggest harbors in China. Destinations include Dalian (14 hours), Shanghai (28 hours), Qingdao (12 hours), and Tianjin (18 hours). CITS in Qinhuangdao has prices and schedules.

BUS TRAVEL An excellent minibus service links Beidaihe, Qinhuangdao, and Shanhaiguan. Buses leave every 30 minutes. The bus station in Beidaihe is at the intersection of Heishi Lu and Haining Lu. Buy tickets on the bus.

TRAIN TRAVEL Trains traveling up the coast from Beijing all pass through Beidaihe, Shanhaiguan, and Qinhuangdao.

### SAFETY AND PRECAUTIONS

The area's street food is generally safe if cooked at a high heat and not left out in the sun. Be especially careful with seafood, and only dine at crowded places where the food cannot sit for too long.

### TIMING

A half day is sufficient to see what the village has to offer. Most tourists see Baidaihe while on a Great Wall tour. If the weather allows, it can be a great place to bicycle ride and linger for a bit longer.

The rugged landscape around Shanhaiguan

**ESSENTIALS**

**Boat and Ferry Contacts Qinhuangdao CITS.** Qinhuangdao CITS ⊠ *100 Heping Dajie, Qinhuangdao* ☎ *0335/323–1117.***Qinhuangdao CITS** ⊠ *100 Heping Dajie, Qinhuangdao* ☎ *0335/323–1117* ⊕ *www.cits.net.*

**Bus Contact Beidaihe Bus Station** ⊠ *Beining Lu and Haining Lu.*

**Medical Assistance Beidaihe Hospital** ⊠ *200 Lianfeng Lu* ☎ *0335/404–1624.*

**Train Contact Beidaihe Train Station** ⊠ *Zhannan Da Jie.*

**Visitor and Tour Info Beidaihe CITS** ⊠ *Jinshan Hotel, 4 Dongsan Lu* ☎ *0335/428–6891* ⊕ *www.cits.net.*

## EXPLORING

The best way to get around on a sunny day is to rent a bicycle and cruise up and down the seafront. The southern end of Haining Lu leading down to Middle Beach is the liveliest spot, with faux-European buildings delivering a healthy dose of seaside kitsch.

**Lianfeng Hill Park** (联峰山公园 *Liánfēngshān gōngyuán*). North of Middle Beach you'll find this lovely park, where quiet paths through a pine forest lead to the **Guanyin Temple** (Guanyin Si). Look for the aviary, known as the Birds Singing Forest. There are also good views of the sea from the top of Lianfeng Hill. ⊠ *Jianqui Lu* ☎ *0335/404–1591* 🚋 *Y30* ☾ *Daily 8–5.*

## WHERE TO EAT AND STAY

In summer, seafood restaurants line the beach, and you only need to point at the most appetizing thing squirming in red buckets for the waiter to serve up a delicious fresh meal. A plateful of fresh mussels should cost about Y15, fresh crabs a little more. More good seafood restaurants are clustered on Haining Lu near the beach.

$$$ BAKERY 🍴 **Kiesslings** (起士林餐厅 *Qǐshìlín cāntīng*). Originally opened by Austrians, this popular place is actually three restaurants in one: a petite stone lodge serving Russian and Bavarian fare, an expansive dining room serving Chinese dishes, and a European-style café and bakery doing a brisk business selling freshly baked walnut cakes. The first two are situated on the grounds of the attractive Kiessling Beidaihe Hotel; the café-bakery is on the main street. Unlike most places in Beidaihe, it's open all year. [$] *Average main: Y120* ✉ *Kiessling Beidaihe Hotel, 95 Dongjing Lu* ☎ *0335/468–0000.*

$ HOTEL 🏨 **Beidaihe Guesthouse for Diplomatic Missions** (北戴河外交人员宾馆 *Běidàihé wàijiāo rényuán bīnguǎn*). Catering mostly to Russian travelers, this attractive complex is made up of low-slung buildings set among cypresses and pines in a quiet spot close to its own beach. **Pros:** a classic experience; near the ocean. **Cons:** older buildings could use renovation. [$] *Rooms from: Y550* ✉ *1 Baosan Lu* ☎ *0335/428–0600* 🌐 *www.bsbdm.com.cn* 🛏 *165 rooms* 🕒 *Closed Nov.–Mar.*

$ HOTEL 🏨 **Jinshan Hotel** (金山大酒店 *Jīnshān dàiiǔdiàn*). On a quiet stretch of sand, this clean and comfortable hotel is made up of five two-story buildings linked by tree-lined paths. **Pros:** on the beach. **Cons:** some rooms are worn. [$] *Rooms from: Y400* ✉ *4 Dongsan Lu* ☎ *0335/404–1338* 🛏 *267 rooms* 🕒 *Closed Nov.–Mar.* 🍽 *Breakfast.*

## SHANHAIGUAN

*2½ hours (280 km [174 miles]) by train east of Beijing, 1 hr (35 km [22 mi]) by minibus northeast of Beidaihe; 2½ hrs (360 km [223 mi]) southwest of Shenyang.*

On the northern tip of the Bohai Coast, Shanhaiguan is the end of the road for the Great Wall. After 8,850 km (5,500 miles), the massive structure plunges into the sea. During the Ming Dynasty, Shanhaiguan was fortified to prevent hordes of mounted Manchurian warriors from pushing to the south. Now local tourists swarm the town during the summer. An impressive wall still surrounds what was the old town, sadly razed in 2007 and rebuilt as a "historic" tourist area.

### GETTING HERE AND AROUND

Shanhaiguan-bound express trains depart from Beijing several times daily, but it's also possible to take a train to Qinhuangdao and catch a taxi for the 20-minute drive to Shanhaiguan.

AIR TRAVEL Until Qinhuangdao Beidaihe Airport is up and running, air travel is not an option.

BUS TRAVEL A minibus service runs from Beidaihe to Shanhaiguan, with departures every 30 minutes.

TAXI TRAVEL The half-hour taxi ride between Beidaihe and Shanhaiguan costs about Y80.

TRAIN TRAVEL Shanhaiguan has limited train service; it might be necessary to take a train to Qinhuangdao and transfer to a bus or taxi to Shanhaiguan.

**TIMING**

Shanhaiguan has enough to keep you occupied for one day, perhaps two if you plan on doing some serious Great Wall hiking. Shanhaiguan comes alive in the summer, and many restaurants and tourist facilities completely shut down for the season in late October.

**ESSENTIALS**

Bus Contact **Shanhaiguan Bus Station** ⊠ *Nanguan Dajie, west side of the railway station* ☎ *0335/502–3879.*

Medical Assistance **Qinhuangdao Friendship Hospital** ⊠ *28 Jianguo Lu, Qinhuangdao* ☎ *0335/303–1222.*

Train Contact **Shanhaiguan Train Station** ⊠ *Off Nanguan Da Jie.*

**EXPLORING**

**TOP ATTRACTIONS**

**First Gate Under Heaven** (天下第一关 *Tiānxià dìyīguān*). The first heavily fortified pass along the Great Wall as it runs inland from the ocean, this mighty four-sided citadel is an impressive. Patrolling the battlements you can glimpse the Great Wall snaking up the sides of nearby mountains and grasp just how intimidating a barrier this must have presented to potential invaders. Not that it worked—the Manchus overran it in 1644, ultimately bringing down the Ming Dynasty. ⊠ *Diyiguan Lu* ☎ *0335/505–1106* 🎫 *Y50, includes admission to Great Wall Museum* ⊙ *Daily 7:30–6:30.*

**Great Wall Museum** (长城 博物馆 *Chángchéng bówùguǎn*). Housed in a Qing Dynasty–style building past the First Gate Under Heaven, the Great Wall Museum has a diverting collection of historic photographs and cases full of military artifacts, including the fierce-looking weaponry used by attackers and defenders. There are some English captions. ⊠ *South of First Gate Under Heaven, Diyiguan Lu* 🎫 *Y50, includes admission to First Gate Under Heaven* ⊙ *Daily 7:30–4:30.*

**Jiaoshan Great Wall** (角山长城 *Jiāoshān chángchéng*). One way to leave behind the crowds at the First Gate Under Heaven is to scale the wall as it climbs Jiao Mountain, about 3 km (2 miles) from the city. The first part has been fitted with handrails and ladders up the sides of the watchtowers, but you can keep climbing until you reach the "real" wall. After that you can take a path through trees that leads to the Qixian Monastery. A chairlift operates in high season. Jiaoshan is a 10-minute taxi ride from Shanhaiguan. ⊠ *Jiaoshan Lu* ☎ *0335/505–2884* 🎫 *Y30* ⊙ *Daily 7:30–5.*

**Jiumenkou Great Wall** (九门口长城 *Jiǔménkǒu chángchéng*). Further from town than the Jiaoshan Great Wall, Jiumenkou is notable as the only section the Great Wall to ford a river. Clamber up the battlements for dramatic views over the countryside. Jiumenkou is about 15 km (9 miles) north of Shanhaiguan; ask your taxi driver to wait for you for the return trip (a total of about Y80). ⊠ *Zhijiu Xian* 🎫 *Y30* ⊙ *Daily 8–5.*

**Old Dragon Head** (老龙头 *Lǎolóngtóu*). Legend has it that the Great Wall once extended into the Bohai Sea, ending with a giant carved dragon's head. Although the structure you see today was rebuilt in the 1980s, witnessing the waves smash against the massive base is a stirring sight. The admission price gets you into several rebuilt Ming Dynasty naval barracks, but you can just skip it altogether and head on to the beach for the best photo ops. ✉ *1 Laolongtou Lu* ☎ *0335/515–2996* 🎟 *Y50* ⏲ *Daily 8–5.*

### WORTH NOTING

**Mengjiangnu Miao** (孟姜女庙 *Mèngjiāngnǚ miào*). About 8 km (5 miles) up the coast from Old Dragon Head is this shrine commemorating a local legend. As the story goes, a woman's husband died while building the Great Wall. She wept as she searched for his body, and in sympathy the wall split open before her, revealing the bones of her husband and others buried within. Overcome with grief, she threw herself into the sea. The shrine is a 10-minute taxi ride northeast of town. ☎ *0335/505–3159* 🎟 *Y30* ⏲ *Daily 7–5.*

3

### WHERE TO EAT AND STAY

$$ SEAFOOD 🍴 **Wang Yang Lou** (望洋楼饭店 *Wàngyánglóu fàndiàn*). Probably the city's most upmarket option, Wang Yang Lou serves tasty local seafood and an array of family-style Chinese dishes. There's no menu—order at the open kitchen to the left of the entrance by pointing at things swimming in the tanks, or at the photos of dishes themselves. The dining room itself is large but lacks much in the way of character. [$] *Average main: Y70* ✉ *51 Nanhai Xi Lu* ☎ *0335/515–5666* 💳 *No credit cards.*

$ HOTEL 🏨 **Shanhai Holiday Hotel** (山海假日 *Shānhǎi jiàrì jiǔdiàn*). One of the few lodgings inside the walls of the recently rebuilt "ancient city," this Qing Dynasty-styled complex offers simply furnished rooms set around a series of courtyards. **Pros:** close to the First Gate Under Heaven. **Cons:** "ancient city" dead in the evenings. [$] *Rooms from: Y300* ✉ *Beima Lu, beside the west gate* ☎ *0335/535–2800* 🛏 *277 rooms* 🍽 *Breakfast.*

$ HOTEL 🏨 **Wanghai Vacational Village** (望海假村 *Wànghǎi jiàcūn*). A short march from Old Dragon Head, this resort-style hotel is centered around a restaurant that's nestled, rather unexpectedly, in a greenhouse filled with tropical flora. **Pros:** lovely restaurant; on the beach; near the Great Wall. **Cons:** outside of town. [$] *Rooms from: Y300* ✉ *1 Wanghai Lu* ☎ *0335/535–0777* 🛏 *44 rooms* 🍽 *No meals.*

# SHANDONG

Around 100 million people call the Shandong region home, and an annual influx of domestic tourists considerably adds to that number. Most flock to this region for Qingdao, China's most attractive coastal city and best known for its beaches, beer (sold as "Tsingtao" in the West) and Bavarian architecture, the walled town of Qufu, home of the philosopher Confucius, and Mount Tai, the most revered of all China's sacred mountains.

## JI'NAN

*1½ hours (500 km [220 miles]) by bullet train south of Beijing; 2½ hours (395 km [245 miles]) by bullet train west of Qingdao.*

Known for its 70 or so active springs, Ji'nan has earned the nickname "City of Springs." Ji'nan's three main sights are Thousand Buddha

Shandong

Mountain, Daming Lake, and Baotu Spring Park. These and a handful of other attractions easily occupy visitors for a day or so.

Ji'nan may be Shandong's provincial capital, but Ji'nan is overshadowed in almost every way by its coastal rival, Qingdao. However, this modern and easygoing metropolis is a good place to stay if you are visiting nearby Qufu, Taishan, or Qingdao.

In 1901, Ji'nan was hauled into the 20th century by the construction of a railway linking it to Qingdao. European and Japanese companies found Ji'nan to be a convenient place to do business. A few buildings from this era remain in the downtown area, although they are increasingly overshadowed by new shopping centers and hotels

**GETTING HERE AND AROUND**
Far and away the best way to get here from Beijing is to catch one of the many daily bullet trains, which stop at Jinan Station or the newer Jinan West Station. The trip takes between 1½ and 2 hours.

AIR TRAVEL  Regular flights link Ji'nan Yaoqiang Airport with Beijing, Shanghai, Hong Kong, and other major Chinese cities. The airport is 40 km (25 miles) northeast of downtown Ji'nan. The journey takes 45 minutes in a taxi and costs around Y100.

BUS TRAVEL  Regular buses link Ji'nan with Tai'an (one hour) and Qufu (three hours).

TRAIN TRAVEL Ji'nan is connected to Qufu, Tai'an, and Qingdao, and accessible from Shanghai, stopping at both Suzhou and Nanjing on route. There is no shortage of fast trains, and it's possible to buy your tickets mere minutes before getting on board, though during busy periods it pays to purchase in advance.

### SAFETY AND PRECAUTIONS

As in most inland Shandong cities, air pollution can be a problem, especially in hot weather.

### TIMING

Jinan's sights are relatively close together, making one day enough time to comfortably visit them as well as walk around the city.

### ESSENTIALS

**Air Contact Ji'nan Yaoqiang Airport** ✉ *Jichang Lu, Yaoqiang* ☎ *0531/96888.*

**Bus Contacts Ji'nan Long-Distance Bus Station** ✉ *131 Jiluo Lu* ☎ *0531/96369.* **Tai'an Bus Station** ✉ *139 Dongyue Dajie, opposite the train station, Tai'an* ☎ *0538/833–2938.* **Qufu Bus Station** ✉ *Yulong Lu, Qufu* ☎ *0537/441–2554.*

**Medical Assistance Shandong Shengli Hospital** ✉ *324 Jingwu Lu* ☎ *0531/8793–8911.*

**Train Contacts Ji'nan Train Station** ✉ *19 Chezhan Jie* ☎ *0531/8601–2520.* **Ji'nan West Train Station** ✉ *Weihai Lu, Huayin District, Ji'nan.* **Tai'an Train Station** ✉ *Dongyue Dajie, Tai'an* ☎ *0538/9510–5688.*

**Visitor and Tour Info Ji'nan CITS** ✉ *Building 30, 1 Jiefang Lu, 6th fl.* ⊕ *www. cits.net.* **Ji'nan Tourist Service** ✉ *86 Jingshi Lu* ☎ *800/420–8858* ⊕ *www. travelshandong.us.*

### EXPLORING

Ji'nan's downtown area is relatively compact. A meandering ring-shaped canal connects Baotu Spring Park with other tourist spots, eventually spilling out into Daming Lake. Tourist boats ply the waterways; an all-day pass costs Y100. The grid of streets south of the main railway station, which bear the most European influence, are well worth exploring on foot.

**Baotu Spring Park** (趵突泉 *Bàotūquán*). Qing Dynasty Emperor Qianlong proclaimed this the finest of Ji'nan's many natural springs gurgling north from the foothills of Mount Tai. The spring is most active after the summer rains, when crowds gather under pavilions to watch it frothing and gushing. The water is said to be ideal for making tea; try it out at the Wangheting Teahouse, just east of the spring. A small museum in the park recounts the life of Jinan's most prized poetess Li Qingzhao, who lived near here in the 11th century. ✉ *Baotuquan Nan Lu* 🎫 *Y40* ⊙ *Daily 7–9.*

**Daming Lake** (大明湖 *Dàmíng hú*). Fed by artesian springs and garlanded by vivid banks of willows, Daming Lake has been inspiring Chinese poets and writers for 1,500 years. Surrounded by temples, pavilions, and leafy walkways, it's a pleasant spot for a stroll. There's a teahouse on top of the 50-meter tall pagoda on the island in the east of the lake. You're treated to views of Thousand Buddha Hill clear days. ✉ *Daming Hu Lu* 🎟 *Y30* ⏲ *Daily 6:30–6.*

**Ji'nan Protestant Church** (济南市经四路教堂 *Jīngsìlù jiàotáng*). One interesting architectural legacy of the foreign occupation is an imposing brick Protestant Church, with its landmark twin towers. Built in 1927, it is still in use. ✉ *425 Jing Si Lu* ☎ *0531/8793–6327.*

**Nanjing Sifang Art Museum** (南京四方当代美术馆 *Nánjīng sìfāng dāngdài měishùguǎn*). This museum explores Chinese art and architecture, but its main draw could be the stunningly angular design of its buildings, set in Laoshan National Park. Designed by American architect Steven Holl, it includes a gallery seemingly suspended in midair and a courtyard paved with bricks from destroyed houses in central Nanjing. ✉ *178 Zhenzhu Lu, Nanjing* ☎ *025/6819–0789* 🌐 *www.sifangartmuseum.org.*

NEED A BREAK?

**Shandong Elite Teahouse** (山东名人茶馆 *Shāndōng míngrén cháguǎn*). This teahouse makes for a lovely break after climbing Thousand Buddha Mountain. The exquisite room is decorated with lattice paneling, ornate vases, and musical instruments. Serving many varieties of tea, the staff is friendly and does its best. ✉ *9 Qianfoshan Lu* ☎ *0531/8296–0376.*

**Thousand Buddha Mountain** (千佛山 *Qiānfóshān*). On the southern outskirts of the city is Thousand Buddha Mountain, which gets its name from the multitude of Buddha images chiseled into the cliffs since the early Sui Dynasty. It is still the focus of religious festivals, although many of the original statues have been lost to history, replaced by modern reconstructions. Getting to the top of the hill requires a 30-minute walk or a cable car ride (Y25 round-trip). Either way you'll be rewarded with a good view of Ji'nan—air quality permitting. For kids, there's an excellent slide to whiz back down to the bottom. ✉ *18 Jingshiyi Lu* ☎ *0531/8266–2321* 🎟 *Y30* ⏲ *Daily 6–6.*

## WHERE TO EAT

$$ VEGETARIAN

🍴 **Foshan Yuan** (佛山院素食店 *Fóshānyuàn sùshídiàn*). This comfy vegetarian restaurant specializes in dishes that look and taste remarkably like meat or fish. If sea cucumbers made from textured soy protein sounds like a gastronomic step too far, fear not: the delicious vegetable dumplings, braised mushrooms, and hearty tofu dishes are sure to satisfy. This place is a little tricky to find; locals should be able to point you in the right direction. [$] *Average main: Y95* ✉ *Foshan Yuan Xiao Qu, near Chaoshan Jie* ☎ *0531/8602–7566* 💳 *No credit cards.*

$$ INTERNATIONAL

🍴 **Jenny's Café** (西餐厅 (美食) *Xīcài cāntīng měishí*).Recognizable by its bright pink sign, this centrally located eatery turns out passable

### HIT THE STREET

Escape the city's hubbub by exploring the warren of cobblestone alleyways around Lotus Street (Furong Jie), close to the Confucian Temple. A 19th-century wooden church at the corner of Houzaimen Jie is surrounded by vendors hawking crispy pastry spirals called *youxuan*. Further along Lotus Street you'll find restaurants, cafés, and quirky gift shops.

Burning incense at the Thousand Buddha Mountain

salads, soups and other light fare, but its tasty selection of cakes and coffees makes it a better bet for a mid-afternoon break. There's a fully stocked bar if you need something stronger. Locals love the daintily laid tables and shabby-chic European touches. $\boxed{S}$ *Average main: Y90* $\boxtimes$ *2 Wenhua Xi Lu* ☎ *0531/8260–0214* ▭ *No credit cards.*

$ ✕ **Jiu Wan Ban** (九碗伴 *Jiǔwǎnbàn*). On a street filled with 24-hour
SHANGHAINESE joints, this cheerful place is where in-the-know locals return to again and again. You can choose from platters of fresh local fish or a range of family-style Chinese dishes. Try the seafood version of *xiaolongbao,* the dainty soup dumplings that are a specialty of Shanghai. $\boxed{S}$ *Average main: Y50* $\boxtimes$ *18 Chaoshan Jie* ☎ *0531/8612–7228* ▭ *No credit cards.*

## WHERE TO STAY

$ ⌂ **C.Sohoh Business Hotel** (舜和商誉酒店 *Shùnhé shāngyù jiǔdiàn*). A
HOTEL short walk from the main sights, this affordable business hotel is small enough to feel intimate and welcoming. **Pros:** personalized service; great location; reasonable rates. **Cons:** small rooms. $\boxed{S}$ *Rooms from: Y280* $\boxtimes$ *53 Luoyang Lu* ☎ *0531/8615-1388* ⊕ *www.csohoh.com* ⤶ *125 rooms* ❙❍❙ *Breakfast.*

$$ ⌂ **Sheraton Ji'nan** (济南喜来登 *Jǐnán xǐláidéng jiǔdiàn*). This impos-
HOTEL ing structure overlooks the massive, lotus-shaped sports venue built to host the 11th Chinese National Games. **Pros:** excellent facilities; great Japanese restaurant. **Cons:** isolated location. $\boxed{S}$ *Rooms from: Y1100* $\boxtimes$ *8 Long Ao Bei Lu* ☎ *0531/8162–9999* ⊕ *www.starwoodhotels.com* ⤶ *410 rooms* ❙❍❙ *No meals.*

$$$ ⌂ **Sofitel Ji'nan Silver Plaza** (苏菲特银座大酒店 *Sūfēité yínzuò*
HOTEL *dǎjiǔdiàn*). Looking somewhat like a tube of lipstick, this 49-story

cylinder sits right in the center of town. **Pros:** excellent location; eye-catching design; very good restaurant. **Cons:** small bathrooms. $ *Rooms from: Y1100* ✉ *66 Luoyuan Dajie* ☎ *0531/8606–8888* ⊕ *www.sofitel.com* ⌑ *426 rooms* ⦿ *No meals.*

### NIGHTLIFE
**Banjo** (班卓音乐酒吧 *Bānzhuó yīnlè jiŭbā*). This funky, eclectic bar has live music every evening. It's set among a row of Chinese, Japanese, and Korean restaurants that are very lively at night. ✉ *51 Foshan Jie* ☎ *0531/8685–8585.*

### SHOPPING
**Shandong Curios City** (山东古玩城 *Shāndōng gŭwán chéng*). This cluster of small antiques shops is huddled around an attractive courtyard. Jade, jewelry, and regional antiques are beautifully displayed. ✉ *283 Quancheng Lu.*

## SIDE TRIP TO LINGYAN TEMPLE

Shandong played a vital role in the spread of Buddhism in China. In the 4th century AD the Chinese Buddhist monk Faxian landed on the coast near present day Qingdao to decode scriptures he'd gathered on travels to India, Sri Lanka, and Nepal. Ji'nan became the center of Buddhist culture for the whole province. During the Tang and Song Dynasties, the Lingyan Temple was one of the most important Buddhist Temples in China.

### GETTING HERE AND AROUND
Lingyan Temple is about 76 km (46 miles) south of the city. The best way to get here is to arrange a car and driver through your hotel or a travel agency.

**Lingyan Temple** (灵岩寺 *Língyán sì*). In a dramatic mountain setting, the 1,600-year-old Lingyan Temple is most famous for its Thousand Buddha Hall, with its cast of 40 hand-carved and painted figures seated around the chamber. Unerringly lifelike, each one is distinct, from facial features to the folds of their robes. Dating back to the Song Dynasty, these are some of the finest religious sculptures in China. Several years ago, researchers cracked one of the life-sized statues open and found a full set of internal organs inside, made out of stuffed silk. In the temple grounds, the Pagoda Forest (da lin) is a totemic graveyard of sculpted towers, each marking the passing of a prominent monk. The size and artistry of each tower points not to the status of the deceased, but the prosperity of the temple at the time. Boom and bust, it would appear, is eternal. ✉ *Changqing District, Wande* ☎ *0531/8746–8099* ⌑ *Y40* ⊗ *8–5.*

## SIDE TRIP TO MOUNT TAI

A destination for pilgrims for 3,000 years, the mountain was named a UNESCO World Heritage Site in 1987. Confucius is said to have climbed it, scanned the horizon and observed: "The world is very small." Much later, Mao Zedong reached the top and even more famously proclaimed: "The East is red."

**GETTING HERE AND AROUND**

Mount Tai is near the town of Tai'an, a major stop on the Shanghai–Beijing railway. Dozens of trains travel through Tai'an daily. By road, Tai'an is about 50 km (30 miles) south of Ji'nan. Buses to Tai'an leave Ji'nan's main bus station every 25 minutes between 5 am and 6 pm. From any spot in Tai'an, a taxi to Taishan takes less than 15 minutes and costs about Y10.

**Mount Tai** (泰山 *Tàishān*). Reaching 5,067 feet above sea level, Mount Tai is the most venerated of the five sacred mountains of China. If you are keen to reach a ripe old age, legend has it that climbing Mount Tai means you'll live to 100. It is possible to climb the steps to the summit and back down in a day, but spending the night on the mountain is also an option. The classic photo—sunrise over the cloud-hugged peaks—is actually a rare sight because of the mist. ⌧ *Dec. 1–Jan. 31, Y100; Feb. 1–Nov. 30, Y125.*

**WHERE TO STAY**

$ ⌧ **Ramada Plaza Tai'an** (东尊华美达大酒店 *Dōngzūn huáměidá*
HOTEL *dàjiǔdiàn*). Make sure to ask for a mountain-view room in this resort in the quiet foothills of Mount Tai. **Pros:** lovely setting; great facilities; **Cons:** not on the summit; buffet breakfast just average. $ *Rooms from: Y550* ⌧ *16 Yinhsheng Donglu, Tai'an* ☎ *0538/836–8888* ⬏ *328 rooms* ⦿| *Breakfast.*

$$$ ⌧ **Shenqi Hotel** (泰山神憩宾馆 *Tàishān shénqì bīnguǎn*). This is the
HOTEL only real hotel on the summit, but it's overpriced considering its barely adequate rooms. **Pros:** perfect place to watch the sunrise. **Cons:** expensive for what you get; very basic rooms. $ *Rooms from: Y600* ⌧ *10 Tian Jie, Tai'an* ☎ *0538/822–3866* ⬏ *62 rooms* ⦿| *No meals.*

## SIDE TRIP TO QUFU

This sleepy provincial town is the birthplace of the country's foremost spiritual teacher and philosopher, Kong Fu Zi, known to the West as Confucius. His impact was immense in China, and his code of conduct was a part of daily life here until it fell out of favor two millennia later during the Cultural Revolution. His teachings—that son must respect father, wife must respect husband, citizens must respect officials—were swept away by Mao Zedong because of their associations with the past. Qufu suffered greatly during the Cultural Revolution, with the Red Guards smashing statues and burning buildings. But the pendulum has swung back, and Confucius's teachings are back in vogue. Encircled by a Ming Dynasty wall, Qufu certainly has character, though there's little to do once the tourist sights close for the day.

**GETTING THERE AND AROUND**

A handful of Qufu-bound bullet trains leave Beijing each day, passing through Jinan and Tai'an on route. The trip takes about 2½ hours. Regular buses also run trips from Ji'nan to Qufu. The Qufu bus station is south of the town center at the intersection of Shen Dao and Jingxuan Lu.

The Confucius Temple on top of the beautiful Mt. Tai

### EXPLORING QUFU

**Confucius Temple** (孔庙 *Kǒngmiào*). Within Qufu's restored city walls, the sprawling Confucius Temple comprises 66 buildings spread across more than 50 acres, making this one of the largest palace complexes from Imperial China. Like the Forbidden City, built 80 years earlier, its colonnaded halls and courtyards flow symmetrically along a central axis. The Hall of Great Achievements features mighty pillars entwined with dragons. Seek out the Apricot Platform in front, where it's said Confucius once preached beneath the shade of an apricot tree. September 28, the date of the Great Sage's birthday, is quite the party here. ✉ *Banbi Jie, Qufu* 🔳 *Y90* ⊙ *Daily 8–5*.

**Confucius Family Mansion** (孔府 *Kǒngfǔ*). Beside the east wall of the Confucius Temple is the Confucius Family Mansion. An impressive collection of stately abodes and gardens, it dates from the 16th century and illustrates the wealth and glory once enjoyed by Confucius's descendants. ✉ *Banbi Jie, Qufu* 🔳 *Y60* ⊙ *Daily 8–5*.

**Confucian Forest** (孔林 *Kǒnglín*). Confucius and his descendants have been buried in this tree-shaded cemetery for the past 2,000 years. Surrounded by a 10-km (6-mile) wall, Confucian Forest has more than 100,000 pine and cypress trees, jostling for space with burial

> ### CONFUSING CONFUCIUS
>
> Many locals claim to be direct descendants of Confucius, and they take great pride in their heritage. Although the philosopher would have raised an eyebrow, the townspeople do a good line in Confucius-brand cookies, wine, and many other items.

mounds, grave stones, and statues commemorating generations of the Kong family. ⊠ *Lindao Lu, Qufu* 🎫 *Y40* 🕙 *Daily 8–5.*

### WHERE TO STAY

$ 🏨 **Queli Hotel** (阙里宾馆 *Quēlǐ*
HOTEL *bīnguǎn*). In a small town lacking lodging options, this well-run hotel, a short stroll from the Confucius Temple and the Confucius Family Mansion, is your best bet. **Pros:** prime location for attrac-

> **WISEMAN PASS**
>
> If you want to soak up as much Confucianism as possible during your visit to Qufu, get a ticket that grants access to all three sites. That's Y185 for a ticket that covers the Confucius Temple, Confucius Family Mansion, and the Confucian Forest.

tions. **Cons:** showing its age; unispiring rooms; hard beds. $ *Rooms from: Y500* ⊠ *1 Queli Lu, Qufu* ☎ *0537/486–6818* 🛏 *150 rooms* 🍴 *Breakfast.*

## QINGDAO

*4½ hrs (540 km [335 miles]) by bullet train southeast of Beijing; 2½ hrs by train (390 km [242 miles]) east of Ji'nan.*

Qingdao has had a turbulent century, but it's emerged as one of China's most charming cities. It was a sleepy fishing village until the end of the 19th century, when Germany, using the killing of two German missionaries as a pretext, set up another European concession to take advantage of Qingdao's coastal position. The German presence lasted only until 1914, but locals continued to build Bavarian-style houses, and today a walk around the Old Town can feel like you've stumbled into a town in the Black Forest. Unlike many cities that had foreign concessions, Qingdao has recognized the historical value of these buildings and is now enthusiastic about preserving them. With its seafront promenades, winding colonial streets, and pretty parks, Qingdao is probably China's best city for strolling.

Home to the country's best-known beer, Tsingtao, Qingdao is very accommodating when it comes to alcohol consumption. (Look for beer being sold on the streets in plastic bags.) But wine drinkers should take heart, as the region is also developing a much-talked-about wine industry.

The city is a destination for golfers, having many of the country's best courses.

### GETTING HERE AND AROUND

A comfortable way to get to Qingdao is aboard one of the several daily bullet trains that link Qingdao to Beijing (4½ hours). Buy tickets from travel agents or through your hotel, as lines are long and there are few English speakers at the station.

The long-distance bus terminal is opposite the train station. Taxis are a cheap way to get around. Getting anywhere in town will generally cost less than Y30.

Under construction at time of writing, Line 1 of the new Qingdao Metro underground network should be up and running at some point in 2014.

AIR TRAVEL Qingdao Liuting Airport is 30 km (19 miles) north of the city. In a taxi, the journey takes 40 minutes and costs around Y80. Direct flights link Qingdao with Osaka and Seoul, as well as Hong Kong and other major Chinese cities.

BUS TRAVEL Buses travel between Ji'nan and Qingdao every 20 minutes; the trip is four to five hours.

TRAIN TRAVEL Direct trains link Qingdao with Ji'nan (three hours), Beijing (4½ hours), and Shanghai (6½ hours).

**WORD OF MOUTH**

"Drinking beer out of a plastic bag through a straw in front of a Gothic church in Qingdao, China, had to be one of the most hysterical moments on my two week tour." —Jilly

### TIMING
Qingdao is a very pleasant seaside city. Two full days is just about enough to cram in all the sights, but the city has enough attractions and nightlife to keep you happily occupied for longer.

### ESSENTIALS
**Air Contact Qingdao Liuting Airport** ⊠ *Liuting* ☎ *0532/96567.*

**Boat and Ferry Contact Qingdao Ferry Terminal** ⊠ *6 Xinjiang Lu, 2 km (1 mile) north of the train station* ☎ *0532/8282–5001.*

**Bus Contact Qingdao Long-Distance Bus Station** ⊠ *2 Wenzhou Lu* ☎ *0532/8371–8060.*

**Medical Assistance International Clinic of Qingdao Municipal Hospital** ⊠ *5 DongHai Zhong Lu* ☎ *0532/8593–7690.*

**Train Contact Qingdao Train Station** ⊠ *2 Tai'an Lu* ☎ *0532/12306.*

**Visitor and Tour Info Qingdao CITS** ⊠ *73 Xianggang Zhong Lu* ☎ *0532/8386–3960* ⊕ *www.cits.net.* **Qingdao Tourism Administration** ⊠ *7 Minjiang Lu* ☎ *0532/8591–2029.*

## EXPLORING
### TOP ATTRACTIONS
**German Governor's Residence** (青岛迎宾馆 *Qīngdǎo yíngbīnguǎn*). The cookie dough–colored German Governor's Residence, transformed into a museum in 1996, was where the mustachioed governor and his aristocratic entourage wined, dined, and held sway over Qingdao for their short but influential tenure. Built in 1906 on a commanding perch over the Old City, the interior resembles a Bavarian hunting lodge, with wood paneling, glazed tile fireplaces, colored glass chandeliers and quirky grandfather clocks. Notable Chinese guests since include Mao Zedong, Zhou Enlai, and Deng Xiaoping. English audio guides are available. ⊠ *26 Longshan Lu, below Xinhao Hill Park* ☎ *0532/8288–9888* ⊠ *Y20* ☉ *Daily 8:30–4:30.*

**Granite Mansion** (花石楼 *Huāshí lóu*). After the German Governor's Residence, the 1903 Granite Mansion is Qingdao's most famous example of traditional German architecture. This miniature castle was built as a villa for a Russian aristocrat, but soon became a fishing retreat for the governor. ⊠ *18 Huanghai Lu* ⊠ *Y7* ☉ *Daily 8–5.*

Qingdao

Eight Passes ............... 2
German Governor's
Residence .................... 8
Granite Mansion ......... 1
Lu Xun Park ................ 5
Navy Museum .............. 6
Protestant Church ......... 7
St. Michael's Cathedral ... 10
Sun Yat-sen Park .......... 3
Tsingtao Beer Museum ... 9
Underwater World ......... 4

**Protestant Church** (基督教堂 *Jīdū jiàotáng*). Qingdao's charming Protestant Church is easy to spot: look for the ostentatious green spire resembling a medieval castle. It was built in 1910 at the southwest entrance of Xinhao Hill Park. Puff up the steps to the bell tower for sea views and to marvel at the German-engineered clock mechanism. ⊠ *15 Jiangsu Lu* 🖾 *Free* ☉ *Daily 8:30–4:30.*

**St. Michael's Cathedral** (青岛天主教堂 *Qīngdǎo tiānzhǔ jiàotáng*). This Qingdao landmark has towering 200-foot twin steeples and red-tile roof. The classic Gothic Revival structure was built by the Germans in 1934 but was badly damaged during the Cultural Revolution. The surrounding area is a great place to explore, with venerable German buildings contrasting with uninspired modern architecture. Street vendors hawk grilled kebabs on the cobbled streets leading to the church. ⊠ *15 Zhejiang Lu* 🖾 *Y8* ☉ *Mon.–Sat. 8–5, Sun. 10–5.*

FAMILY **Sun Yat-sen Park** (中山公园 *Zhōngshān gōngyuán*). The largest of the city's parks, Sun Yat-sen Park is inland from Huiquan Bay and has a number of attractions, including a small zoo, a botanical garden, and the Zhanshan Buddhist Temple. Qingdao's TV tower, a city landmark, offers striking views from its observation deck. Originally planted by the Japanese in 1915, the park contains some 20,000 cherry trees. The annual Cherry Blossom Festival is held at the end of May. ⊠ *28 Wendeng Lu* 🕾 *0532/8287–0564* 🖾 *Y12* ☉ *Daily 5 am–9 pm.*

**Tsingtao Beer Museum** (青啤博物馆 *Qīngpí bówùguǎn*). Beer fans should make a pilgrimage to the Tsingtao Beer Museum on Dengzhou Lu, also known as *Pijiu Jie* (Beer Street). The area is lined with bottle-shaped benches where weary revelers can rest. The Germans established the brewery more than a century ago, and a few original brick buildings remain. The old photographs, beer labels, and dioramas are of middling interest; best of all are the beer samples you can enjoy along the way. ⊠ *56 Dengzhou Lu* 🕾 *0532/8383–3437* 🖾 *Y60* ☉ *Daily 8:30–4:30.*

### WORTH NOTING

**Eight Passes** (八大关 *Bādàguān*). Named after the Great Wall's eight strategic passes, this scenic area lies in between Taiping and the Huiquan Cape. Sometimes referred to as "Little Switzerland," the grounds of more than 200 European-style villas are landscaped with pine, ginkgo, and peach trees.

**Lu Xun Park** (*Lǔxùn gōngyuán*). Built in 1929, this park named for the distinguished Chinese writer and revolutionary sits on the rocky coastline of Huiquan Bay. It's a lovely park, with tree-shaded paths, elegant pavillions, and rugged reefs, making for attractive sea vistas. ⊠ *1 Qinyu Lu* 🖾 *Free* ☉ *Daily 7:30–6:30.*

NEED A BREAK?

**Café Roland** (朗园酒吧 *Lǎngyuán jiǔbā*). In a German-style building dating from the 1930s, Café Roland has a lovely wooden interior and a view of No. 3 Beach. Try the excellent, homemade rum-raisin ice cream. ⊠ *9 Taiping Jiao Er Lu* 🕾 *0532/8387–5734.*

**Navy Museum** (海军博物馆 *Hǎijūn bówùguǎn*). A short walk from the west entrance of Lu Xun Park is the Navy Museum, with an arsenal of archaic weaponary, Russian-made fighter planes, and several rusting naval vessels moored in the harbor. You can see much of it—and skip the entrance fee—by walking along the seawall to the Little Qingdao Isle with its charming lighthouse and excellent café. ⊠ *8 Lai Yang Lu* ☏ *0532/286–6784* ✆ *Y50* ⊗ *Daily 8:30–5.*

FAMILY **Underwater World** (青岛海底世界 *Qīngdǎo hǎidǐshijiè*). Located near No. 1 Beach, this family-friendly attraction features a moving platform with 360-degree views of the surrounding marine life. Four underground levels, interactive

> **GANBEI!**
>
> **Qingdao International Beer Festival.** The Qingdao International Beer Festival, China's biggest, has been held since 1991. The state-sponsored fun begins in mid-August, lasts for two weeks, and causes hotel prices to skyrocket. The focus is mostly on big-name brews from around the world, and you won't see any lederhosen, but it's still great fun.

video displays, and tacky marine shows entertain the kids for hours. ⊠ *1 Laiyang Lu* ☏ *0532/8289–2187* ✆ *Y120* ⊗ *Daily 8–5:30.*

### WHERE TO EAT

Clams, crabs, crayfish, shrimp, oysters—it's no surprise that Qingdao's specialty is seafood. A shoal of excellent seafood restaurants can be found in or around Minjiang Lu and Yunxiao Lu, where the time between choosing your catch and having it arrive steaming on your plate is about three minutes. For seafood with sea views, there are some cheap and cheerful lunch spots on Qinyu Lu just west of Lu Xun Park.

In Qingdao's seafood restaurants you're usually expected to order on entry at the row of tanks, and tell whoever's assisting you how you'd like your food cooked. Here's a quick guide: *qing zheng* means simply to steam; *xiang la* means to stir-fry with chillis, garlic and ginger; *zha de* is deep-fried; and *hong shao* is braised in soy sauce, rice wine and a little sugar.

$$ ✕ **Chuan Ge Fish Dumplings** (船歌鱼水饺 *Chuángē yú shuǐjiǎo*). A market-fresh spread of seafood, meats, and vegetables greets you at the entrance of this excellent eatery, a hit with well-heeled locals. Browse the live seafood (a small-sized lobster, freshly steamed, will set you back about Y200), point at the dishes you want to try, and take your seat. Don't miss the signature cuttlefish dumplings (*moyu jiaozi*) wrapped in dough dyed black from the cuttlefish ink. Ⓢ *Average main: Y80* ⊠ *33 Qutangxia Lu* ☏ *0532/8267–0026.*

MANDARIN

$$ ✕ **Din Tai Fung** (鼎泰丰 *Dǐngtàifēng*). Inside the posh Marina City Mall, Din Tai Fung serves up its brand of precisely pleated dumplings. Each dumpling is stuffed with delicate fillings ranging from green melon to juicy pork. Enjoy them as you gaze out at the ocean. Ⓢ *Average main: Y100* ⊠ *Marina City Mall, 86 Ao'men Lu* ⊕ *www.dintaifungusa.com.*

SHANGHAINESE

$$ ✕ **Sitting Bull** (毅牛烤排馆 *Yiniú kǎopái guǎn*). Embracing the mantra of simplicity, Sitting Bull wows with its slow-cooked ribs with a sticky glaze, pulled pork sandwiches, homemade bratwursts, and freshly baked cornbread. Everything here is washed down with Californian wines and beers courtesy of the local craft brewery Strong Ale Works. A diamond in a rough retail area, the exposed-brick dining room has communal

AMERICAN

bench tables and a contemporary, laid-back vibe. $ *Average main: Y80* ⊠ *Tai Gu Square, 138 Zhangzhou Lu* ☎ *0532/8571–7103.*

**$$**
**SEAFOOD**
✕ **Yumatou Seafood Restaurant** (渔码头海鲜舫 *Yúmǎtóu hǎixiānfǎng*). Size up your dinner at this quintessential seafood place, one of many on or around Minjiang Lu. Rows of tanks swarm with live sea creatures, with prices marked per *jin* (about 500 grams). For shellfish, this is enough for two to share. Order a round of clams fried

> **IN THE NEWS**
>
> Qingdao also has a lively foreign-restaurant scene, with new venues opening up all the time. Get a copy of the local expat magazine *Redstar* from your hotel for the latest information, or check out their website (⊕ *www.myredstar.com*) for reviews, recommendations, and happenings around town.

with chilis and garlic (*gala* in the local dialect), which pairs perfectly with a jug of fresh Tsingtao beer. Point at the scallops and ask for them to be served *suanrong fensi*, meaning steamed with garlic and vermicelli noodles. $ *Average main: Y60* ⊠ *24 Yunxiao Lu* ☎ *0532/8577–9999.*

## WHERE TO STAY

**$**
**HOTEL**
**Fodor's Choice**
★
⌂ **The Castle** (怡堡酒店 *Yíbǎo jiǔdiàn*). Sharing the same historic gardens as the German Governer's Residence, this lovely boutique hotel belies its mock-Bavarian exterior with artsy (sometimes over-designed) guest rooms. **Pros:** in the heart of the Old City; excellent service; great value. **Cons:** you might have to wait for taxis in the evening. $ *Rooms from: Y550* ⊠ *26 Longshan Lu, grounds of the German Governer's Residence* ☎ *0532/8869–1111* ⊕ *www.thecastle-hotel.com* ⇥ *50 rooms* ❍*| Breakfast.*

**$**
**HOTEL**
⌂ **Huiquan Dynasty Hotel** (汇泉王朝大店 *Huìquán wángcháo dàjiǔdiàn*). Looming over the city's most popular beach, this long-established hotel capitalizes on its enviable location with rooms that underwhelm for the price. **Pros:** great ocean views from some rooms; convenient beach access; English-speaking staff. **Cons:** rooms don't justify price. $ *Rooms from: Y800* ⊠ *6 Nanhai Lu* ☎ *0532/8287–1122* ⇥ *405 rooms* ❍*| No meals.*

**$$$**
**HOTEL**
⌂ **InterContinental Qingdao** (青岛海尔洲际酒店 *Hǎiěr zhōujì jiǔdiàn*). Adjacent to the Olympic Sailing Center and a short walk from the Marina City shopping complex, this ultramodern hotel boasts contemporary rooms with dark wood paneling, built-in mood lighting, massive LCD TVs, and stand-alone bath tubs. **Pros:** Qingdao's most luxurious lodging; marina location; gorgeous rooms. **Cons:** among the city's priciest hotels. $ *Rooms from: Y1200* ⊠ *98 Ao Men Lu* ☎ *0532/665–6666* ⇥ *422 rooms* ❍*| No meals.*

**$$**
**HOTEL**
⌂ **Shangri-La** (香格里拉大酒店 *Xiānggélǐlā dàjiǔdiàn*). Only a block from the scenic coastline, the Shangri-La is also close to some of the best shopping and dining in town. **Pros:** convenient to beach; comfortable rooms; cozy bar. **Cons:** immediate area difficult to navigate on foot. $ *Rooms from: Y1100* ⊠ *9 Xiang Gang Zhong Lu* ☎ *0532/8388–3838* ⇥ *696 rooms* ❍*| No meals.*

Qingdao has lovely seafront promenades, winding colonial streets, and pretty parks.

## NIGHTLIFE AND THE ARTS

Most of the action takes place in the eastern part of the city. Jiangxi Lu and Minjiang Lu are two lively streets east of Zhongshan Park with a smattering of decent nightlife options.

**Charlie's Bar** (查理斯酒吧 *Chálǐsī jiǔbā*). A convenient base camp in Qingdao's party zone, Charlie's Bar is a laid-back establishment with a sports-pub atmosphere, a long wooden bar, and Guinness on draft. ✉ *167 Jiangxi Lu* ☎ *532/8575–8560.*

**Room Lounge** (入目有你 *Rùmù yǒunǐ*). Opened by a local whiskey aficionado, Room Lounge has Qingdao's best collection of single malts, as well as expertly mixed cocktails and musical menu favoring reggae and electronic beats. The cozy, smoke-filled space attracts a discerning local crowd. Well-kept secrets aren't always easy to find—this one is on the ground floor of an apartment building. ✉ *Haihua Building, 1 Shandong Lu* ☎ *0532/8666–3559.*

**Tsingtao Brewery Bar** (青岛啤酒厂 *Qīngdǎo píjiǔchǎng jiǔbā*). At the Tsingtao Brewery Bar you can drink from the source. In front of the Tsingtao Brewery Museum, it's cavernous, brightly lit, and packed in high season with convivial gangs of beer-swilling Chinese tourists. ✉ *56 Dengzhou Lu* ☎ *0532/8383–3437.*

## SPORTS AND THE OUTDOORS

Chinese visitors come to Qingdao by the tens of thousands for the beaches. Each of the seven sandy beaches that run along the coast for more than 10 km (6 miles) has a variety of facilities ranging from changing rooms to kiosks renting inflatable toys.

### BEACHES

**No. 1 Beach** is the busiest, and in summer it can be difficult to find a place for your towel. If your goal is peace and quiet, head to **No. 2 Beach,** as fewer Chinese tourists venture out that way. In the summer, look out for the armies of brides and bridegrooms using the beaches for their wedding photos.

### GOLF

**Qingdao International Golf Club.** The 18-hole Qingdao International Golf Club is 20 minutes from downtown. It has driving ranges and a fine-dining restaurant. Booking ahead, especially on weekends, is recommended. ⊠ *Songling Lu* ☎ *0532/8896–0001.*

### WATER SPORTS

The waterfront at Fushan Bay has been completely transformed with the construction of the Olympic Sailing Center. Several other places will also help you get on or in the water.

**Qingdao Qinhai Scuba Diving Club.** Near No. 1 Beach, the Qingdao Qinhai Scuba Diving Club is one of the few government-approved diving clubs in northern China. All equipment is provided for PADI certification courses or guided recreational dives. ⊠ *5 Huiquan Lu* ☎ *0532/8387–7977.*

**Yinhai International Yacht Club.** One of the country's largest yacht clubs, Yinhai International Yacht Club has more than 30 yachts for rent, and offers lessons to beginners and more experienced sailors. The club is in the east of town, near the Olympic Sailing Center. ⊠ *30 Donghai Zhong Lu* ☎ *0532/8588–6666* ⊕ *www.yinhai.com.cn.*

## SHOPPING

The north end of Zhongshan Lu has a cluster of antiques and cultural artifacts shops.

**Cultural Relics Store.** Established in the 1960s, the Cultural Relics Store is worth a look for its collection of antiques and curios. ⊠ *40 Zhongshan Lu* ☎ *0532/8285–4435.*

**Michael's.** Very near St Michael's Cathedral is Michael's, a gallery specializing in calligraphy. ⊠ *15 Zhejiang Lu* ☎ *0532/8286–6790.*

**Qingdao Arts and Crafts Store** (青岛 *Qīngdǎo*). The city's largest antiques shop is the Qingdao Arts and Crafts Store, with four floors of porcelain, scroll paintings, silk, gold, jade, and other stones. ⊠ *212 Zhongshan Lu* ☎ *0532/8281–7948.*

## SIDE TRIPS FROM QINGDAO

**Mount Lao** (崂山 *Láoshān*). Rising to a height of more than 3,280 feet, Mount Lao is just as scenic—though not quite as famous—as Mount Tai. A place of pilgrimage for centuries, Laoshan once had nine palaces, eight temples, and 72 convents. Most have been lost over the years, but those remaining are worth seeking out for their elegant architecture and stirring sea views. With sheer cliffs and cascading waterfalls, Laoshan is the source of the country's best-known mineral water (a vital ingredient in the local brew, Tsingtao). It's possible to see the mountain's sights in less than a day. Tourist buses to Laoshan leave from the main pier in

Qingdao, or hop on to public bus 304. Mount Lao is 40 km (25 miles) east of Qingdao. ⌔ *Y80* ⊙ *Daily 7–5.*

**Huadong Winery** (华东百利酒庄 *Huádōng bǎilì jiǔzhuāng*). Near Laoshan is Huadong Winery, Shandong's premier vinous brand. Although not as famous as the province's brewery, it's already won a string of prizes. The vines were imported from France in the 1980s. Both the grapes and wines are available for tasting. The beautiful scenery alone makes this a worthwhile side trip from Qingdao. ⊠ *Nanlong Kou* ☎ *0532/8881–7878.*

# JIANGSU

Coastal Jiangsu is defined by water. This eastern province is crossed by one of the world's great rivers, the mystical Yangtze, and has a coastline stretching hundreds of miles along the Yellow Sea. Jiangsu is also home to the Grand Canal, an ancient feat of engineering. This massive waterway, the longest ancient canal in the world, with some parts dating from the 5th century BC, allowed merchants to ship the province's plentiful rice, vegetables, and tea to the north. Within the cities, daily life was historically tied to the water, and many old neighborhoods are still crisscrossed by countless small canals.

As a result of its trading position, Jiangsu has long been an economic and political center of China. The founder of the Ming Dynasty established the capital in Nanjing, and it remained there until his son moved it back north to Beijing. Even after the move, Nanjing and Jiangsu retained their nationwide importance. After the 1911 revolution, the province once again hosted the nation's capital in Nanjing.

Planning a trip in the province is remarkably easy. The cities are close together and connected by many buses and trains. Autumn tends to be warm and dry, with ideal walking temperatures. Spring can be rainy and windy, but the hills burst with blooms. Summers are infamously oppressive, hot, and humid. The winter is mild, but January and February are often rainy.

## REGIONAL TOURS

Jiangsu Huate International Travel Service has a number of guides who speak English. Jinling Business International Travel Service offers a range of options for travelers. The company has its own fleet of comfortable cars with knowledgeable drivers. It can arrange trips throughout the region.

**Tour Contacts Jiangsu Huate International Travel Service** ⊠ *33 Jinxiang He Lu, Nanjing* ☎ *025/8337–8695.* **Jinling Business International Travel Service** ⊠ *Junling Guoji Building, 5 Guangzhou Lu, Nanjing* ☎ *025/5186–0969.*

## NANJING

*1½ hrs (309 km [192 miles]) by bullet train west of Shanghai, 3½ hrs (1,039 km [646 miles]) by bullet train southeast of Beijing.*

The name *Nanjing* means Southern Capital, and for six dynastic periods, as well as during the country's brief tenure as the Republic of

China, the city was China's administrative capital. It was never as successful a capital as Beijing, and the locals chalk up the failures of several dynasties here to bad timing, but it could be that the laid-back atmosphere of the Yangtze Delta just isn't as suited to political intrigue as the north.

Nanjing offers travelers significantly more sites of historical importance than Shanghai. Among the most impressive are the remnants of the colossal Ming Dynasty city wall, built by 200,000 laborers to protect the new capital in the 14th century. A number of important monuments, tombs, and gates reflect the glory and instability of Nanjing's incumbency.

The city lies on the Yangtze, and the Yangtze River Bridge or the more subdued park at Swallow Rock are great places for viewing the river. The sheer amount of activity on the water is testimony to its continued importance as a corridor for shipping and trade. Downtown, the streets are choked with traffic, but the chaotic scene is easily avoided with a visit to any of the large parks. You can also take a short taxi ride to Zijin (Purple) Mountain, where quiet trails lead between Ming Tombs and the grand mausoleum of Sun Yat-sen.

### GETTING HERE AND AROUND

Regular daily flights connect Nanjing with all other major Chinese cities. The airport is located just 36 km (22 miles) from the city center.

Nanjing's position on the Beijing-Shanghai high-speed railway line makes train travel a great option. Bus travel in this area of China is considerably more comfortable than elsewhere, thanks to a network of highways linking the cities and a fleet of air-conditioned luxury coaches with comfortable seats.

The Nanjing subway is quick, comfortable, and extremely inexpensive, with distance-based fares starting at Y2. Getting around Nanjing by taxi is both fast and inexpensive, though taxi drivers generally cannot speak any English, so be prepared with the address of your destination written in Chinese. For the more adventurous, bicycles can be rented from some small hotels and tourist agencies; the city is very bicycle-friendly, with mostly flat roads and many dedicated bicycle lanes.

The best way to explore some of Nanjing's tourist destinations, once you're on Purple Mountain, is aboard the tourist buses (Y1, Y2, Y3) that runs from the train station to Ming Tomb, Sun Yat-sen Botanical Gardens, Sun Yat-sen Mausoleum, and Spirit Valley Pagoda. The fare is Y3.

AIR TRAVEL  Most flights from Europe or North America go through Shanghai or Beijing before continuing on to Nanjing's Lukou Airport, but there are direct flights from Asian hubs like Seoul, Singapore, Nagoya, and Bangkok. From Nanjing several flights leave daily for Shanghai, Beijing, Guangzhou, Xiamen, Wuhan, and Hong Kong; flights leave daily for Xi'an, Chengdu, and Zhengzhou.

Taxis from Nanjing Lukou Airport, 36 km (22 miles) southwest of the city, should take between 20 and 30 minutes. The fare should be between Y90 and Y120.

BUS TRAVEL  Buses are the best way to reach Yangzhou, and they leave frequently from the main long-distance bus station and take about an hour. The trip to Shanghai takes between three and four hours, and the trip to Suzhou can take as little as two hours; buses to both cities depart from the Zhongshan Nan Road Bus Station.

TRAIN TRAVEL  There are many bullet trains daily, arriving at either Nanjing Railway Station or the newer Nanjing South Railway station. Trains to Suzhou take about 90 minutes. The train to Yangzhou also takes 90 minutes, but it's a pleasant trip with the bonus of crossing the Yangtze via the Yangtze River Bridge.

### SAFETY AND PRECAUTIONS

Nanjing is a huge, crowded city, but is safe to explore day or night. Use common sense in crowded places such as the metro and train stations, where petty theft is a possibility.

### TIMING

Considering the massive size of the city and the sheer number of attractions, try to devote at least two to three full days exploring.

### TOURS

Major hotels will often arrange a tour guide for a group. Nanjing China Travel Service can arrange almost any type of tour of the city.

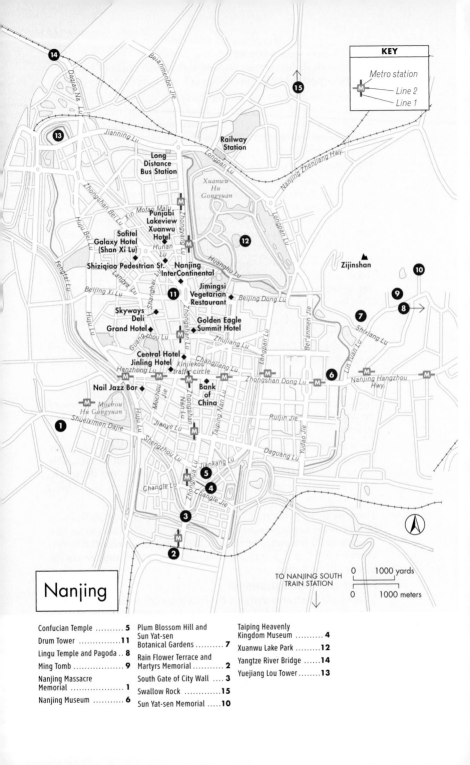

# Nanjing

**KEY**
Metro station
Line 2
Line 1

Confucian Temple .......... **5**
Drum Tower .............. **11**
Lingu Temple and Pagoda .. **8**
Ming Tomb ................ **9**
Nanjing Massacre Memorial ................... **1**
Nanjing Museum .......... **6**

Plum Blossom Hill and Sun Yat-sen Botanical Gardens ......... **7**
Rain Flower Terrace and Martyrs Memorial .......... **2**
South Gate of City Wall .... **3**
Swallow Rock ............. **15**
Sun Yat-sen Memorial ..... **10**

Taiping Heavenly Kingdom Museum .......... **4**
Xuanwu Lake Park ........ **12**
Yangtze River Bridge .... **14**
Yuejiang Lou Tower ........ **13**

**ESSENTIALS**

**Air Contacts Air China** ☎ 025/8449–9378 ⊕ www.airchina.com.cn/en.
**anjing Lukou Airport** ⊠ Lukou Jie, Jiangning District ☎ 025/968–890 ⊕ www.njiairport.com.

**Bus Contact Nanjing Long Distance Bus Station** ⊠ 1 Jianning Lu
☎ 025/8553–1299.

**Medical Assistance International SOS Clinic** ⊠ Grand Metro Park Hotel, 319 Zhongshan Dong Lu ☎ 025/8480–2842 ⊕ www.internationalsos.com.

**Train Contact Nanjing Train Station** ⊠ 264 Long Pan Lu ☎ 025/8582–2222.
**Nanjing South Train Station** ⊠ Yuxie Jie, Yuhuatai District.

**Visitor and Tour Info Nanjing China Travel Service** ⊠ 12 Baixin Building, Baizi Ting, south of the Drum Tower ☎ 025/8336–6582. **Nanjing CITS** ⊠ 313 Zhongshan Bei Lu ☎ 025/8343–9898 ⊕ www.cits.net.

## EXPLORING

### TOP ATTRACTIONS

**Confucian Temple** (夫子庙 *Fūzǐmiào*). Overlooking the Qinhuai River, a tributary of the Yangtze, a Confucian Temple has stood on this spot for 1,000 years, give or take. The present incarnation dates back to the 1980s, rebuilt a few decades after it was destroyed by the Japanese in 1937. The surrounding area is the city's busiest shopping and entertainment district, festooned with neon at night and packed with tourists. The alleys behind the temple, once home to China's most famous district of courtesans, now house a market and curio shops. Boat tours of the Qinhuai River leave from in front of the temple every evening. ⊠ Zhongshan Lu and Jiankang Lu, on the Qinhuai River ⊕ www.njfzm. com ☎ Y25 ☉ Daily 9–8.

Fodor's Choice ★ **Ming Tomb** (明孝陵 *Míngxiàolíng*). One of the largest and most important burial mounds in China, this is the final resting place of Emperor Hong Wu, the founder of the Ming Dynasty. Born a peasant and orphaned at a young age, he became a monk and eventually led the army that overthrew the Yuan Dynasty, making Nanjing his capital in 1368 and building its mighty walls. You approach the tomb along the Spirit Way, flanked by auspicious stone lions, elephants, camels, and mythical beasts. Winding paths make the area around the tomb perfect for strolling. ⊠ Mingling Lu, on Purple Mountain ☎ Y70 (includes Plum Blossom Hill and Sun Yat-sen Botanical Park) ☉ Daily 8–6.

**Nanjing Massacre Memorial** (大屠杀纪念馆 *Dàtúshā jìniànguǎn*). In the winter of 1937, Japanese forces occupied Nanjing. In the space of a few days, thousands of Chinese were killed in the chaos, which became known as the "Rape of Nanjing." This monument commemorates the victims, many of whom were buried in mass graves. Be advised, this is not for the squeamish. Skeletons have been exhumed from the "Grave of Ten Thousand" and are displayed with gruesomely frank explanations as to how each lost his or her life. The memorial also displays artifacts from the Sino-Japanese reconciliation after World War II, which ended the conflict between the two countries on a less strident, more hopeful note. To get here, take the subway to Yunjinlu (Line 2). ⊠ 418

A happy visitor at the Ming Tombs

*Shui Ximen Da Jie, west of Mouchou Lake Park* ☎ *025/8661–2230* ⊕ *www.nj1937.org* ✉ *Free* ⏱ *Tues.–Sun. 8:30–4:30.*

**Nanjing Museum** (南京博物馆 *Nánjīng bówùguǎn*). Extensive renovations are underway to provide a more contemporary setting for the museum's many thousands of artifacts, including bronze tools, lacquer items, jade, silks, calligraphy, and folk art. The Ming and Qing Imperial porcelain collection is one of the world's largest. ✉ *Zhongshan Dong Lu, inside Zhongshan Gate* ☎ *025/8480–2119* ⊕ *www.njmm.cn* ✉ *Y20* ⏱ *Daily 9–4:30.*

FAMILY **South Gate of City Wall** (中华门 *Zhōnghuámén*). Built as the linchpin of the city's defenses, this is less a gate than a complete fortress, with multiple courtyards and tunnels where several thousand soldiers could withstand a siege. It was rarely attacked; armies wisely avoided it in favor of the less heavily fortified areas to the north. Today, bonsai enthusiasts maintain displays in several of the courtyards. ✉ *Southern end of Zhonghua Lu, south side of city wall* ✉ *Y25* ⏱ *Daily 8–6.*

**Taiping Heavenly Kingdom Museum** (太平天国历史博物馆 *Tàipíngtiānguó lìshǐ bówùguǎn*). Commemorating a fascinating period of Chinese history, this museum follows the life of Hong Xiuquan, a Christian who led a peasant revolt in 1859. He ultimately captured Nanjing and ruled for 11 years. Hong, who set himself up as emperor, claimed to be the younger brother of Jesus. On display are artifacts from the period. After browsing through the museum, stroll through the grounds of the surrounding Ming Dynasty garden compound, once the home of high-ranking Taiping officials. In the evening there are performances of opera and storytelling. ✉ *128 Zhanyuan Lu, beside the Confucian*

Temple ☎ 025/8662–3024 🎫 Y30 ⏱ Daily 8:30–5.

**Xuanwu Lake Park** (玄武湖公园 *Xuánwǔhú gōngyuán*). More lake than park, this pleasant garden is bounded by one of the longer sections of the monumental city wall, which you can climb for a good view of the water. Purple Mountain rises in the east, and the glittering skyscrapers of modern Nanjing are reflected on the calm water. Causeways lined with trees and benches connect several large islands in the lake. Pedal-powered boats cost Y60 an hour. ✉ *Off Hunan Lu, outside the city wall* 🎫 *Y30* ⏱ *Daily 9–9.*

**WORTH NOTING**

**Drum Tower** (鼓楼 *Gǔlóu*). First built in 1382, the Drum Tower gives the central city district of Gulou its name. In ancient times, drums housed inside were used to signal important events, from the changing of the watch to an enemy attack to a fire. Today just one drum remains. ✉ *1 Dafang Xiang, beside Gulou People's Square* ☎ 025/8663–1059 🎫 *Y5* ⏱ *8:30 –5.*

**Shou Jia Massage** (手佳盲人按摩保健中心 *Shǒujiāmángrén ànmó bǎojiàn zhōngxīn*). This health center is serious about traditional Chinese medicine. The center trains and employs the visually impaired for therapeutic massage treatments, and the friendly staff brings you endless cups of medicinal tea. ✉ *136 Chang Jiang Lu* ☎ *025/8470–2129.*

**Lingu Temple and Pagoda** (灵谷寺,灵谷塔 *Línggǔsì and Línggǔtǎ*). Close to the Sun Yat-sen Memorial, this temple commemorates Xuan Zang, the roving monk who brought Buddhist scriptures back to China from India. Seek out the Beamless Hall, a magnificent 14th-century structure, today given over to propagandistic "historical" reenactments. Farther up the hill is a nine-story granite pagoda built in 1929 as a memorial to fallen revolutionaries. Vendors sell balloons to toss from the upper balcony. ✉ *Ta Lu, southeast of Sun Yat-sen Memorial* ☎ 025/8444–6443 🎫 *Y80 (includes Sun Yat-sen Mausoleum)* ⏱ *8–5.*

**Plum Blossom Hill and Sun Yat-sen Botanical Gardens** (梅花山, 中山植物园 *Méihuāshān and Zhōngshān zhíwùyuán*). March and April are the best months to visit Plum Blossom Hill, when peach, pear, plum, and cherry trees explode with color and fragrance. The rest of the year it's probably not worth a special trip. The exhibits at the botanical gardens, established in 1929, are a rewarding experience year-round for those interested in the country's flora. ✉ *1 Shixiang Lu, northeast of Nanjing Museum* 🎫 *Y70 (includes Ming Tomb)* ⏱ *Daily 7–6:30.*

**Rain Flower Terrace and Martyrs Memorial** (雨花台,烈士陵园 *Yǔhuātái, Lièshì língyuán*). This scenic area gets its name from the legend of

**GOING UNDERGROUND**

Getting around a city the size of Nanjing can be a daunting task, but the easy-to-use subway system has made navigating safer and easier. Useful stops for travelers on its two lines include Sanshan Jie (Confucius Temple area), Xuanwu Gate (Xuanwu Lake and Hunan Road area), and Yunjinlu (Nanjing Massacre Memorial). Fares are inexpensive, only Y2 to Y6, depending on how many stations you travel.

NEED A MAS-SAGE?

3

Yunzhang, a 15th-century Buddhist monk who supposedly pleased the gods so much with his recitation of a sutra that they showered flowers on this spot. It was put to a grim purpose in the 1930s, when the Nationalists executed thousands of their left-wing political enemies here. In 1950, after the founding of the People's Republic of China, it was transformed into a memorial park furnished with statues of heroic martyrs, soaring obelisks, and a museum. ⊠ *215 Yuhua Lu, outside Zhonghua Gate* ⊞ *Free* ☾ *Daily 8–5.*

**Swallow Rock** (燕子矶 *Yànzijī*). North of the city, this small park overlooking the Yangtze River is worth the trip for stirring views of Asia's longest waterway. The

**PEDESTRIAN STREETS**

**Confucius Temple Area** (*Fūzǐmiào*). In the Confucius Temple Area are souvenir and shopping streets around the Qinhuai River. ⊠ *Zhongshan Lu and Jiankang Lu.*

**Hunan Road.** These streets are filled with snacks, shops, and restaurants. ⊠ *Hunan Lu, west of Zhongshan North Rd. and east of Zhongyang Lu.*

**Xinjiekou City Center.** Around the big malls and shopping centers are several bustling pedestrian streets. ⊠ *Xinjiekou, between Huaihai Lu and Zhongshan Lu.*

"rock" refers to a huge boulder jutting out into the water, a spot where Tang Dynasty poet Li Bai found inspiration. To get here, take Bus 8 to the last stop. ⊠ *Northeast of Mount Mufu, on the Yangtze River* ⊞ *Y10* ☾ *Daily 7:30–6.*

**Sun Yat-sen Mausoleum** (中山陵 *Zhōngshān líng*). Acknowledged by both the Nationalist and Communist governments as the father of modern China, Sun Yat-sen lies buried in a delicately carved marble sarcophagus, reached by a wide staircase. His final resting place is the center of a solemn and imposing monument to the ideas that overthrew the imperial system. Steep trails wind up the pine-covered hillside, which feels a world away from the Nanjing's hyperkinetic buzz. ▪TIP→ **The mausoleum gets crowded on weekends, so try to come during the week.** ⊠ *Lingyuan Lu, east of the Ming Tomb* ⊞ *Y80 (includes Linggu Temple and Pagoda)* ☾ *8–5.*

**Yangtze River Bridge** (长江大桥 *Chángjiāng dàqiáo*). Completed in 1968 at the height of the Cultural Revolution, this bridge was touted as a defining symbol of the spirit and ingenuity of the Chinese. Decorated in stirring Socialist-Realist style, huge stylized flags sculpted from red glass rise from the bridge's piers, and groups of giant-size peasants, workers, and soldiers stride forward heroically. The Great Bridge Park lies on the southern side; from here you can take an elevator up to the top or browse a gallery of old photographs. Bus No. 1 from the Confucian Temple takes you to the bridge. ⊠ *End of Daqiao Nan* ⊞ *Y15* ☾ *Daily 7:30–5.*

**Yuejiang Lou** (阅江楼 *Yuèjiāng lóu*). Ming Dynasty founding emperor Hongwu wrote a poem describing his plans to have a tower built on top of Lion Mountain, from where he could gaze out at the Yangtze River. Other imperial business got in the way, and for several centuries the building remained on paper. In 2001, his dreams were realised; a gargantuan, historically accurate, and slightly sterile tower arose. The views are great. ✉ *202 Jianning Lu* ☎ *025/5880–3977* 🎟 *Y40* 🕐 *Daily 7–5.*

### WHERE TO EAT

For more information on bars and restaurants in Nanjing, pick up a copy of the local bilingual *Map Magazine* or *The Nanjinger* at your hotel. Printed monthly, it has the latest listings and reviews of many popular spots in the city, as well as upcoming cultural events.

3

$$ MANDARIN Fodor's Choice ★ 🍴 **Da Pai Dang** (南京大牌档 *Nánjīng dàpáidàng*). Lined with street-food-style stalls, this wildly popular dining hall offers a delicious initiation to the specialties of the Yangtze wetlands. Waterfowl is the big draw; try Nanjing's famous salted duck, served sliced on the bone, or a steamer full of duck dumplings. Appetizers and soups focusing on the area's vegetables offer light relief from the more starchy offerings. Order from the picture menu (with tiny English translations) or get up and browse, pointing to what you want and giving your table number to one of the costumed attendants. There are five locations around town, but this is the original and the best. [$] *Average main: Y60* ✉ *Hunan Lu* ☎ *025/8330–5777.*

$ FAST FOOD 🍴 **Hui Wei** (回味 *Huí wèi*). Beloved by locals, Nanjing's very own fast-food chain makes for a convenient pit stop to try two regional specialties: *xiaolongbao* (soup-filled pork dumplings) and *maoxue fensi tang* (rice noodle soup with duck blood cubes). The original branch is located on Hunan Lu, but the nicest location is on the causeway crossing Xuanwu Lake, where you'll find tables at the water's edge. [$] *Average main: Y20* ✉ *Along the causeway crossing Xuanwu Lake.*

$$ VEGETARIAN 🍴 **Jimingsi Vegetarian Restaurant** (鸡鸣寺百味斋茶社 *Jīmíngsì báiwèi zhāicháshè*). Inside the Jiming Temple, this establishment uses wheat gluten and other ingredients to create mock pork, fish, chicken, and goose dishes. An English menu features a selection of the best offerings. Tofu threads and the Sichuan-style "fish" are recommended. This restaurant is noteworthy more for its view of the temple grounds than its food, but overall it's worth a lunch stop. [$] *Average main: Y60* ✉ *Jiming Temple, off Beijing Dong Lu, south of Xuanwu Lake Park* ☎ *025/8771–3690* 💳 *No credit cards* 🕐 *No dinner.*

$$$ INDIAN 🍴 **Punjabi** (本杰比印度料理 *Běnjiébǐ Yìndù liàolǐ*). Indian chefs slap naan dough to the sides of roaring *tandor* ovens in the open kitchen of this popular North Indian restaurant. Typically rich Punjabi dishes like butter chicken make up most of the menu, with *biryanis* (spiced rice dishes) and southern-style *dosas* (savory pancakes) toward the back. Look for the large red and blue sign halfway down Hunan Pedestrian Street pointing you down the alley. [$] *Average main: Y100* ✉ *2 Hunan Lu* ☎ *025/832–45421* 💳 *No credit cards.*

$$ CHINESE 🍴 **Shizi Lou** (狮子楼大酒店 *Shīzilóu dàjiǔdiàn*). Near the Shanzi Road Market, this bustling restaurant is a great introduction to Huaiyang fare, one of the "four great traditions" of Chinese cuisine. Try the signature "lion's head" meatballs (*shizitou*), large and succulent orbs of pork stewed with vegetables in a clear soup, or the gut-bustingly oversized potstickers (*guotie*). If you're feeling brave, opt for a round of stinky

tofu, malodorous for the uninitiated but mouthwateringly tasty. $ *Average main: Y80 ⊠ 29 Hunan Lu, near Shizi Bridge ☎ 025/8360–7888 ▭ No credit cards.*

**$$** ✕ **Skyways Deli** (云中食品店 *Yúnzhōng shípǐndiàn*). Popular with over-
**CAFÉ** seas students studying at Nanjing University, Skyways is the perfect antidote to oily Chinese food. Clean and sterile, this user-friendly deli offers a list of sandwiches and salads that lets youchoose, check, and chow in a matter of minutes. Most impressive are the bakery items, especially the chocolate-dipped coconut macaroons and the Swedish Napoleon cookies. A small grocery area offers pricy imported meats and cheeses. The owners also manage Swede and Kraut, a restaurant serving German fare, just up the road. $ *Average main: Y60 ⊠ 160 Shanghai Lu ☎ 025/8331–7103 ▭ No credit cards.*

## WHERE TO STAY

**$** ⊞ **Central Hotel** (中心大酒店 *Zhōngxīn dàjiǔdiàn*). Steps from the heart
**HOTEL** of the city, this well-run hotel has an offbeat charm. **Pros:** good value; convenient location; nice decor. **Cons:** some rooms better than others. $ *Rooms from: Y600 ⊠ 75 Zhongshan Lu ☎ 025/8473–3888 ⊕ www. njcentralhotel.com ⇱ 339 rooms ⦿ No meals.*

**$** ⊞ **Golden Eagle Summit** (南京金鹰国际酒店管 *Jīnyīngguójì*
**HOTEL** *jiǔdiànguǎn*). Connected to an upscale shopping mall, the Golden Eagle Summit offers services and amenities a step above most other five-star domestically owned hotels. **Pros:** good location; nice rooms; bang for your buck. **Cons:** staff speaks spotty English. $ *Rooms from: Y700 ⊠ 1 Zhujiang Lu ☎ 025/8321–8888 ⊕ www.gesummithotel.com ⇱ 280 rooms ⦿ No meals.*

**$** ⊞ **Grand Hotel** (南京古南都饭店 *Nánjīng gǔnándōu fàndiàn*). Over-
**HOTEL** looking the busy shopping centers in Nanjing's commercial center, the Grand Hotel is an affordable and reliable base for seeing the sights. **Pros:** good for families with kids; central location; helpful staff. **Cons:** some rooms need renovations. $ *Rooms from: Y500 ⊠ 208 Guangzhou Lu ☎ 025/8331–1999 ⊕ www.njgrandhotel.com ⇱ 305 rooms, 11 suites ⦿ No meals.*

**$$$** ⊞ **InterContinental Nanjing** (南京绿地洲际酒店 *Nánjīng lùdìzhōujì*
**HOTEL** *jiǔdiàn*). The loftiest five-star pile in town, this hotel towers above its rivals in height and price, although its decor and fittings—all blacks, creams and chromes—is geared more to the Chinese businessman than foreign tourists. **Pros:** international luxury and service; location. **Cons:** expensive; very businesslike. $ *Rooms from: Y1400 ⊠ 1 Zhongyang Lu, Gulou District ☎ 025/8353-8888 ⇱ 433 rooms, 37 suites ⦿ Breakfast.*

**$$** ⊞ **Jinling Hotel** (金陵饭店 *Jīnlíng fàndiàn*). Something of an institution,
**HOTEL** Nanjing's first modern five-star hotel is worth a look for its great location in the center of town, solicitous service, and recently renovated rooms. **Pros:** luxurious accommodations; attentive service; wide array of shopping opportunities. **Cons:** expensive rates; not a great breakfast. $ *Rooms from: Y1100 ⊠ 2 Xinjiekou ☎ 025/8471–1888, 025/8472–2888 ⊕ www.jinlinghotel.com/en ⇱ 592 rooms, 33 suites ⦿ No meals.*

$ **Lakeview Xuanwu Hotel** (南京玄武饭店 *Nánjīng xuánwǔ fàndiàn*).
HOTEL Ask for an east-facing room at this welcoming hotel and you'll be
Fodor's Choice treated to rousing views of Xuanwu Lake and the wall surrounding
★ Nanjing's old city. **Pros:** good views; luxe rooms; great value. **Cons:**
some outdated facilities. $ *Rooms from: Y600* ⊠ *193 Zhongyang Lu*
☎ *025/8335–8888* ⊕ *www.xuanwu.com.cn* ⤳ *258 rooms, 47 suites*
❡❶ *No meals.*

$$ **Sofitel Galaxy Hotel** (苏菲特银河 *Sūfēitèyínhé dàjiǔdiàn*). If you're
HOTEL looking for luxury, this 48-story tower remains the city's best option
Fodor's Choice despite all the recent competition. **Pros:** premium facilities; great loca-
★ tion; lovely views. **Cons:** cigarette smoke in public areas. $ *Rooms from:*
*Y1100* ⊠ *9 Shanxi Lu* ☎ *025/8371–8888* ⤳ *278 rooms* ❡❶ *No meals.*

### NIGHTLIFE

Nanjing's nightlife centers on the 1912 neighborhood, named for the
year the Republic of China was founded. A few dozen restaurants, bars,
and clubs are packed into several pedestrian-only blocks at the inter-
section of Taiping Lu and Changjiang Lu, a 15-minute walk northeast
of the city center. For something a little more bohemian, a burgeoning
café and restaurant scene can be found along Shanghai Lu, close to
Nanjing University.

**Blue Marlin** (蓝枪鱼 *Lánqiāngyú*). Sandwiched between glitzy night-
clubs, Blue Marlin is the place to kick off a night out. Big, brash, and
commercial, it caters to all tastes with imported beers, decent cocktails,
and finger food. Evenings bring televised sports and live music from
a house band. ⊠ *8 Changjiang Hou Jie* ☎ *025/8453–7376* ⊕ *www.
bluemarlin.cn/en.*

**Finnegan's Wake** (芬尼根酒吧 *Fēnnígēn jiǔbā*). Expect a proper Irish (or
Scottish) welcome at this beautifully designed pub, depending on which
of the two owners pours your pint of Guinness or Kilkenny. Get chat-
ting and you may well move on to one of the 70 whiskies, best enjoyed
by the fireplace in the upstairs lounge. An extensive menu includes Irish
stew and the "ultimate" Dublin fried breakfast. There's live Celtic music
most nights. ⊠ *Off Zhongshan Nan Lu* ☎ *025/5220–7362* ⊕ *www.
finneganswake.com.cn.*

**Myth Bar** (谜酒吧 *Mǐjiǔbā*). A step above the other Nanjing watering
holes, this hacienda-themed bar (less tacky than it sounds) draws a
smart crowd of locals and expats who imbibe draft beers and potent
cocktails while kicking back on communal sofas. Listen to the pop-
skewed house band, or shoot a few rounds of pool. Italian DJs host
occasional parties. ⊠ *60-6 Jiangsu Lu* ☎ *025/8330–7877.*

**Nail Jazz Bar** (钉子酒吧 *Dīngzi jiǔbā*). This cozy bar has the look and
feel of a neighborhood jazz joint—sadly, it lacks a jazz band, opting
for a bored-looking singer who warbles along to a backing track.
It has a friendly atmosphere and the city's most eclectic selection of
bottled beers. ⊠ *10 Luolang Xiang, south of the Sheraton Nanjing*
☎ *025/8653–2244* ⊕ *www.nailbar.cn.*

Fodor's Choice **Prime** (南京绿地洲际酒店 *Nánjīng lǜdì zhōujì jiǔdiàn*). Jiangsu's high-
★ flyers toast their bottom line over classy cocktails on the 78th floor
of the Zifeng Tower, China's third-tallest building. Nestled atop the

InterContinental Nanjing, the bar boasts the city's best wine selection, with a good number available by the glass. Smog permitting, there are stunning city views across Xuanwu Lake to the leafy mound of Zhongshan Park. ⊠ *InterContinental Nanjing, 1 Zhongyang Lu, 78th fl.* ☎ *025/8353–8888.*

### SHOPPING

The best place to buy traditional crafts, art, and souvenirs is the warren of small shops in the center of the city. Nanjing is a convenient place to pick up many of the traditional crafts of Jiangsu—purple sand teapots, flowing silks, interesting carvings, and folk paper cuttings.

**Brocade Research Institute** (南京云锦研究所有限公司 *Nánjīngyún jǐnyán jiūsuǒ yǒuxiàn gōngsī*). These lavishly embroidered robes once worn by emperors were produced in Nanjing. The Brocade Research Institute has a fascinating museum and workshop where the brocades are still made today using huge, old-fashioned looms. The gift shop sells beautiful examples of the fabric. ⊠ *240 Chating Dong Jie, behind Nanjing Massacre Memorial* ☎ *025/8651–8580.*

**Chaotian Gong Antique Market** (朝天宫古玩市场 *Cháotiān gōng gǔwán shìchǎng*). In the courtyard of the Confucian Temple, the Chaotian Gong Antique Market has an array of curios, from genuine antiques to fakes of varying quality. A vendor's opening price can border on the ludicrous, especially with foreign customers, but some good-natured bargaining can yield success. The market is liveliest on weekend mornings. ⊠ *Zhongshan Lu and Jiankang Lu.*

**Fabric Market.** Northwest of the Drum Tower, the Fabric Market sells silks, linen, and traditional cotton fabrics. Bargaining is necessary, but the prices are reasonable. Expect to pay Y50 to Y60 per meter of silk. Many vendors can also arrange tailoring. ⊠ *215 Zhongshan Bei Lu.*

**Nanjing Arts & Crafts Company.** This place stocks a range of locally created items, from jade and lacquerware to tapestries. Prices are high, but you get what you pay for. ⊠ *31 Beijing Dong Lu* ☎ *025/5771–1189.*

## YANGZHOU

*1 hr (106 km [66 miles]) by bus northeast of Nanjing, 3½ hrs (300 km [185 miles]) by bus from Shanghai.*

Despite rapid outward expansion, the historic center of Yangzhou has retained a laid-back feel not often found in Eastern China. Small enough to be seen in a day, its charm may encourage you to linger.

Due to its fortuitous position on the Grand Canal, Yangzhou has flourished since the Tang Dynasty. Drawing on thousands of years as a trade center for salt and silk, Yangzhou maintains a cosmopolitan feel. Indeed, some of the most interesting sites demonstrate a blending of cultures: Japanese relations are evidenced in the monument to Jian Zhen, a monk who helped spread Buddhist teachings to Japan. European influence is seen in the Sino-Victorian gardens of He Yuan, and Persian contact is preserved in the tomb of Puddahidin, a 13th-century trader and descendant of Mohammed.

**DID YOU KNOW?**

The Sun Yat-sen Memorial honors the father of modern China. He inspired the overthrow of the Qing Dynasty and was the first provisional president of the newly founded Republic of China in 1912. However, his real fame lies in his political philosophy, the Three Principles of the People: nationalism, democracy, and the people's livelihood.

## GETTING HERE AND AROUND

The best way to get to Yangzhou is by bus. It lies on the Beijing–Shanghai and Nanjing–Nantong highways. Yangzhou's West Bus Station is the fastest way to get to Nanjing, while Yangzhou East Bus Station serves Suzhou and Shanghai.

> **IN THE NEWS**
>
> Nanjing is a dynamic metropolis with thousands of foreign students and a dynamic bar scene. Get the latest updates on the ever-changing nightlife from *Map Magazine* or *The Nanjinger.*

AIR TRAVEL Yangzhou Taizhou Airport, which opened in 2012, is located 30 km (21 miles) northeast of the city. It has daily flights from Beijing, Chengdu, and Guangzhou.

BUS TRAVEL Frequent bus service runs between Yangzhou and Nanjing and Suzhou, and on to Shanghai. Most routes have air-conditioned buses. Yangzhou West Bus Station is about 6 km (4 miles) west of the city on Jiangyang Xi Lu. Yangzhou East Bus Station is east of the city along Yunhe Xi Lu.

TRAIN TRAVEL Yangzhou has a recently built train station in the western outskirts beside the Shangri-La Hotel that's only practical if you are coming from nearby Nanjing.

## TOURS

Hotels are the chief source of tourist information in Yangzhou. Not only for the young, China Youth Travel in Yangzhou can put together any kind of trip, from morning boat rides around Slender West Lake to evening cruises down the Great Canal. The staff speaks English and has the most experience working with foreign travelers.

## TIMING

Many travelers explore Yangzhou as a day trip from Nanjing, which is perfectly possible, but to get the most out of the city we recommend staying at least one night.

## ESSENTIALS

**Bus Contact Yangzhou West Bus Station** ✉ *Jiangyang Xi Lu* ☎ *0514/8786–1812.*

**Medical Assistance Yangzhou No. 1 People's Hospital** ✉ *45 Taizhou Lu* ☎ *0514/8790–7353.*

**Train Contact Yangzhou Train Station** ✉ *Wenchang Xi Lu* ☎ *0514/8554–6222.*

**Visitor and Tour Info Yangzhou China Youth Travel Agency** ✉ *6 Siwangting Lu* ☎ *0514/8793–3876.*

## EXPLORING
### TOP ATTRACTIONS

**Da Ming Temple** (大明寺 *Dàmíng sì*). Built 1,600 years ago, the Da Ming Temple is one of the more interesting Buddhist shrines in Eastern China. The main attraction is a memorial to Tang Dynasty monk Jian Zhen, who traveled to Japan to spread the teachings of Buddha. It took the determined missionary six attempts to cross the East China Sea, and cost him his eyesight. For refreshment, seek out the still flowing Fifth Spring Under Heaven in the temple grounds. The water's high mineral content means it's great for tea, which you can sip in a small teahouse.

✉ *8 Pingshan Tang Lu, next to Slender West Lake* ☏ *0514/8734–0720* ✆ *Y45* ⏰ *Daily 7:45–5.*

**Ge Garden** (个园 *Gè yuán*). With more than 60 varieties of bamboo, this garden is so named because the trio of leaves on a bamboo plant look like the Chinese character *ge* (个). There are yellow stalks, striped stalks, huge treelike stands, and dwarf bamboo with delicate leaves. The place was built by a wealthy salt merchant named Huang Zhiyun, who believed bamboo represented the loyalty of a good man. As you wander the quiet paths, note the loose bricks in the path arranged to clack under your footsteps. The garden is also accessible from an entrance on Dongguan Jie. ✉ *10 Yangfu Dong Lu, east of Yangzhou Hotel* ☏ *0514/8793–5233* ⊕ *www.ge-garden.net/en_about.htm* ✆ *Y40* ⏰ *Daily 7:15–6.*

**Slender West Lake** (瘦西湖 *Shòu xīhú*). Originally part of a river, Slender West Lake was created during the Qing Dynasty by wealthy salt merchants hoping to impress Emperor Qianlong on his many visits to Yangzhou. The park, laced with willows and dotted with pavilions, bridges, and tearooms, can be seen in an hour or savored for a half-day. The **Fishing Terrace** is where the emperor decided he'd try his hand at angling; the merchants reportedly had their servants wade into the lake and hook a fish on each line he cast. Another mark left by the emperor is the **White Pagoda**, a dome-shaped Buddhist stupa. The emperor casually remarked that Slender West Lake only lacked a stupa to resemble Beijing's Beihai Park. By the time the sun shone through the morning mist, there was the emperor's stupa, hastily carved out of salt and convincing from a distance. A permanent structure was completed much later. It seems all the flattery had the desired effect; Yangzhou prospered as a trading center right up until the 20th century. ✉ *28 Da Hongqiao Lu, in the northern part of the city* ☏ *0514/8733–0189* ✆ *Y90* ⏰ *Daily 7–6.*

Fodor's Choice ★ **Wang's Residence** (汪氏小苑 *Wāngshì xiǎoyuàn*). This was once one among dozens of private mansions belonging to Yangzhou's prosperous merchant class, but it alone survived the ravages of the Cultural Revolution, thanks to its conversion into a factory. Keep an eye out for the exquisite wood carving, especially the crisscrossing bamboo design carved in layers out of *nanmu*, a glimmering wood now extinct in this area of China. There's even a bomb shelter in the small inner garden—a reminder of the Japanese invasion. ✉ *14 Di Gong Di, between Taizhou Lu and Guoqing Lu* ☏ *0514/8732–8869* ✆ *Y25* ⏰ *Daily 8–5:30.*

**Yangzhou Museum** (扬州博物馆 *Yángzhōu bówùguǎn*). Housed in an impressive building in the town's western suburbs, this museum has a lovely location on Mingyue Lake. It has seven exhibition halls packed with Chinese jade, earthenware, bronze vessels, porcelain, and paper-cutting. It shares space with the neighboring China Block Printing Museum. ✉ *Wenchang Xi Lu, Bowuguan Lu* ☏ *0514/8522-8018* ✆ *Free* ⏰ *8:30–4:30.*

The Wang Residence was spared during the Cultural Revolution because it had been converted into a factory.

**WORTH NOTING**

**Garden Tomb of Puhaddin** (普哈丁墓 *Pǔhādīngmù*). The Garden Tomb of Puhaddin faces the Grand Canal, from where you climb a stairway to a graveyard of marble-slab headstones. Towards the back a garden with a charming pavilion reveals both Persian and Chinese design elements. Largely ignored by local tourists, a visit to the garden tomb is a reminder of the city's Islamic influence. ⊠ *Laopai Lu at Quanfu Lu, near Jiefang Bridge* ☞ *Y10* ☉ *Daily 7:30–4:30.*

**He Garden** (何园 *Hé yuán*). In the southeast part of the old town, the Victorian-influenced He Garden is notable for its melding of European and Chinese architecture and landscape design. Dating from the 1880s, it differs from a traditional Chinese garden partly because of the wooden pathway linking the buildings. Other East-meets-West aspects include Victorian-style fireplaces inside the residence. ⊠ *66 Xuning Men Dalu, southeast corner of the city* ☎ *0514/8723–2360* ☞ *Y40* ☉ *Daily 7:30–5:30.*

**WHERE TO EAT**

$ ✕ **Fu Chun Teahouse** (富春茶社
CHINESE *Fùchūn cháshè*). Busiest at breakfast, this venerable institution steams all sorts of delicious buns and dumplings that are hungrily wolfed down by locals and tourists along with cups of kui dragon tea,

**REPLANTING GARDENS**

Many of the country's historic gardens have been recently pieced back together. Most were ravaged during the Cultural Revolution, when for years Red Guard troops were encouraged to smash China's heritage to pieces. To this day, China is still replanting gardens, repairing temples, and restoring historic architecture.

CLOSE UP

## Adopting in China

For some, the gardens, the architecture, the history, and the scenery are all secondary reasons to visit Yangzhou. Theirs is a more personal and momentous trip. On the outskirts of town there is a white-tiled compound called the Yangzhou Social Welfare Institute. This is where American parents and Chinese children come together to form families. Since Chinese law began promoting foreign adoption in 1991, there has been a huge surge in the number of families adopting from China. More than 60,000 children have been brought to the United States from China over the past 20 years, although numbers have declined in recent years due to a tightening of restrictions and an increase in domestic adoption.

Around 95% of children in orphanages are female. There persists a strong preference for boys, especially in rural areas. This is largely due to a combination of bias and traditional social structures whereby girls marry out and males help provide for the family. An unintended consequence of the One Child Policy exacerbates prejudices against women. Some Chinese parents, desperate to have a male child, take drastic measures like gender-selective abortion and even abandon their girls on the steps of orphanages.

The first wave of American-adopted Chinese girls are already teens. As they come of age, their transracial families face unique challenges as they grapple with questions of racial and cultural identity. Support groups, social organizations, and even specialized heritage tour groups address these questions and assist children in learning more about their places of birth.



a light and fragrant green tea known colloquially as "Monkey King." Try the *xièfěn tāngbāo*, oversized crabmeat dumplings from which you slurp out the rich soup through a straw. Served in bamboo steamers, the jade dumplings are filled with a local leafy vegetable. Fu Chun is also a good place to sample the dish Yangzhou gave to the world: fried rice. [$] *Average main: Y40* ✉ *35 Desheng Qiao Lu* ☎ *0514/8723–3326* 💳 *No credit cards* 🕒 *No dinner.*

$$$ EUROPEAN 🍴 **The Old Brewery** (**老啤酒厂** *Lǎo píjiǔ chǎng*). With an affable Chinese-American owner, this riverside brewery and restaurant offers three varieties of home-brewed beer—note the stainless-steel tanks by the entrance. The ambitious menu has everything from pan-seared foie-gras to squid-ink risotto, but the crisp-crusted, generously-topped pizzas are a safe bet. Live music plays nightly. The canal-side location is ideal for an after dinner stroll. [$] *Average main: Y110* ✉ *128 Nantong Donglu, Guangling district* ☎ *0514/8721–5225* 💳 *No credit cards.*

### WHERE TO STAY

$ HOTEL Fodor's Choice ★ 🏨 **Changle Inn** (**长乐客栈** *Chánglè kèzhàn*). It's worth dragging your suitcase along the cobblestones of historic Donguang Street to reach this atmospheric guesthouse in the heart of old Yangzhou. **Pros:** directly opposite Ge Garden; gorgeous setting; smart rooms. **Cons:** difficult to get taxis here. [$] *Rooms from: Y600* ✉ *357 Dongguan Jie, Opposite*

*Ge Garden* ☎ *0514/8799–3333* 🌐 *www.yangzhoucentre-residence.com* 🛏 *80 rooms* 🍴 *Breakfast.*

$ HOTEL 🏨 **Ramada Plaza Yangzhou Casa** (华美达凯莎酒店 *Huáměidá kǎishā jiǔdiàn*). Overlooking the Grand Canal in an enviable city-center location, the Ramada Plaza Yangzhou Casa sits within striking distance of Slender West Lake and Ge Garden. **Pros:** great location; modern rooms; efficient facilities. **Cons:** lengthy check-in times. [$] *Rooms from: Y600* ✉ *318 Wen Chang Zhong Lu* ☎ *0514/8780–0000* 🌐 *www.ramada.com* 🛏 *204 rooms* 🍴 *No meals.*

$$ HOTEL 🏨 **Shangri-La Yangzhou** (扬州香格里拉酒店 *Yángzhōu Xiānggélǐlā jiǔdiàn*). Yangzhou's first international luxury lodging, the Shangri-La makes up for its out-of-center location with the city's must sumptuously appointed rooms and suites. **Pros:** excellent service; modern facilities; chic rooms. **Cons:** hidden among office buildings; a 15-minute taxi ride from the center. [$] *Rooms from: Y1200* ✉ *472 Wenchang Xi Lu* ☎ *0514/8512–8888* 🌐 *www.shangri-la.com/yangzhou/shangrila* 🛏 *369 rooms* 🍴 *No meals.*

### NIGHTLIFE

Similar to the 1912 area in Nanjing and opposite the Old Brewery, Yangzhou's 1912 area is a collection of glitzy Chinese restaurants, bars, and karaoke dives.

## SUZHOU

*Approximately 60 minutes (84 km [52 miles]) by bullet train west of Shanghai, 90 minutes (217 km [135 miles]) by bullet train southeast of Nanjing, or 5 hrs (1,146 km [712 miles]) by bullet train south of Beijing.*

Suzhou has long been known as a center of culture, beauty, and sophistication. The "Venice of the East" produced scores of artists, writers, and politicians over the centuries, developing a local culture based on refinement and taste. Famous around the world for its meticulously landscaped classical gardens and crisscrossing waterways, Suzhou's elegance extends even to its local dialect—a Chinese saying purports that two people arguing in the Suzhou dialect sound more pleasant than lovers talking in standard Chinese.

Unlike in other cities in Eastern China, glass-and-steel office parks have been barred from the Old City, and this preservation makes Suzhou a pleasant place to explore. There is excellent English signage on the roads, and the local tourism board has even set up a convenient information center to get you on the right track.

Only an hour outside of Shanghai, the tourist trail here is well worn, and during the high season you will find yourself sharing Suzhou's gardens with packs of foreign and domestic tour groups. It's worth getting up early to hit the most popular places before the crowds descend.

### GETTING HERE AND AROUND

Buses and trains to Shanghai take about an hour. Buses bound for Nanjing (two hours) and Yangzhou (three hours) depart from the North Bus Station. Frequent trains to Nanjing take 90 minutes. It's a popular route, so be sure to buy tickets in advance.

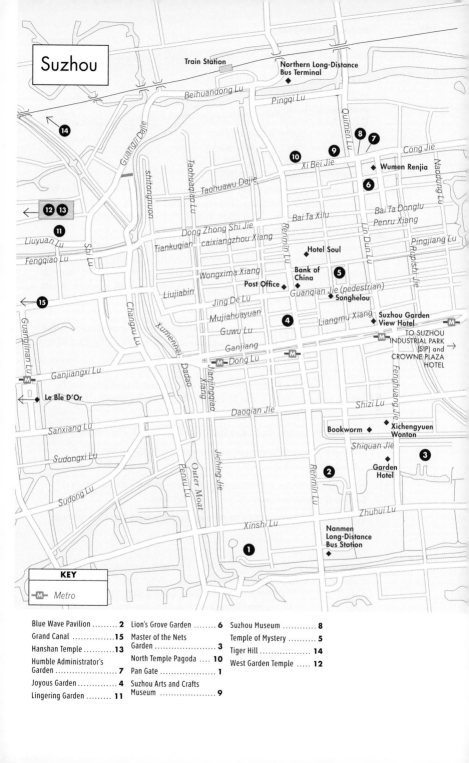

# Suzhou

KEY

Ⓜ Metro

Blue Wave Pavilion ........ 2
Grand Canal ..............15
Hanshan Temple ..........13
Humble Administrator's Garden ......................7
Joyous Garden ............. 4
Lingering Garden ......... 11

Lion's Grove Garden ........ 6
Master of the Nets Garden ........................ 3
North Temple Pagoda ..... 10
Pan Gate ..................... 1
Suzhou Arts and Crafts Museum ..................... 9

Suzhou Museum ........... 8
Temple of Mystery ......... 5
Tiger Hill .................. 14
West Garden Temple ..... 12

AIR TRAVEL Suzhou is served by Shanghai's international airports, Hongqiao and Pudong. Hongqiao Airport is about 86 km (53 miles) from Suzhou, and shuttle buses run throughout the day. The trip takes less than two hours. If you are coming into Pudong, buses that make the 120-km (65-mile) trip from the airport leave about once an hour.

> **WORD OF MOUTH**
>
> "Go to Suzhou and spend a few days there, explore the gardens and perhaps make day trips to the water towns, e.g. Tongli."
> —Nywoman

BUS TRAVEL Bus service between Suzhou and Nanjing is frequent. Suzhou has two long-distance bus stations. The North Bus Station is beside Suzhou Railway Station; the South Bus Station is located on the South Ring Road where it meets Yingchun Lu.

TRAIN TRAVEL Trains arriving from Shanghai, Nanjing, and Beijing stop at Suzhou Railway Station or the newer Suzhou North Railway Station, a 25-minute taxi ride from the Old City. Tickets can be purchased through your hotel or at the station, though lines are long and vendors can be curt with non-Chinese speakers.

### TIMING
Suzhou has more than enough attractions to merit at least two full days. Gardens are spread throughout the city so traveling to and fro takes a bit of time.

### ESSENTIALS
**Air Contacts China Eastern Airlines** ✉ *115 Ganjiang Xi Lu* ☎ *0512/6522–2788* ⊕ *www.ce-air.com.* **China Southern Airlines** ✉ *943 Renmin Lu* ⊕ *www.flychinasouthern.com.*

**Bus Contact Suzhou North Bus Station** ✉ *29 Xihui Lu* ☎ *0512/6753–0686.*

**Medical Assistance Suzhou Municipal Hospital** ✉ *26 Daoqian Jie* ☎ *0512/6900–9090.*

**Train Contact Suzhou Train Station** ✉ *Beihuan Xi Lu* ☎ *0512/6753–2831.* **Suzhou North Train Station** ✉ *Fulin Lu, Xiangcheng.*

**Visitor and Tour Info CITS** ✉ *18 Da Jing Xiang* ☎ *0512/6511–7505* ⊕ *www.cits.net.*

### EXPLORING
**Grand Canal** (京杭大运河 *Jīngháng dàyùnhé*). Suzhou is threaded by a network of narrow waterways, with an outer moat surrounding its ancient center. The canals that now seem quaint were once choked with countless small boats ferrying goods between the city's merchants. All of these channels connect eventually to imperial China's main conduit of trade and travel, the **Grand Canal**, which passes through the town's southern outskirts.

### TOP ATTRACTIONS
**Blue Wave Pavilion** (沧浪亭 *Cānglàng tíng*). The oldest existing garden in Suzhou, the Blue Wave Pavilion dates back more than 900 years to the Song Dynasty. With a rambling, maze-like design, the grounds feel a little wild. The central pond is surrounded by a wooden walkway and

The Humble Administrator's Garden is the largest garden in Suzhou.

reflects the upturned eaves of the surrounding buildings. More than 100 different latticework motifs in the windows provide visual variety as you saunter along the corridor that winds through the grounds. The **Pure Fragrance Pavilion** showcases Qing Dynasty furniture at its most extreme; the entire suite is created from gnarled banyan root. ⊠ *3 Canlanting Jie, between Shiquan Jie and Xinshi Lu* ☎ *0512/6519–4375* ✉ *Mid-Apr.–Oct., Y20; Nov.–mid-Apr., Y15* ☉ *Daily 7:30–5.*

Fodor's Choice **Humble Administrator's Garden** (拙政园 *Zhuōzhèng yuán*). More than ★ half of Suzhou's largest garden is occupied by ponds and lakes. The garden was built in 1509 by Wang Xianjun, an official dismissed from the imperial court. He chose the garden's name from a Tang Dynasty line of poetry reading "humble people govern," perhaps a bit of sarcasm considering the grand scale of his private residence. In the warmer months the pond overflows with fragrant lotuses and the garden fills with tourists. Seek out the tiny museum for an informative display on the aesthetics of Chinese gardens. ⊠ *178 Dongbei Jie, 1 block east of Lindun Lu* ☎ *0512/6751–0286* ⊕ *www.szzzy.cn* ✉ *Mid-Apr.–Oct., Y70; Nov.–mid-Apr., Y50* ☉ *Daily 7:30–5:30.*

**Lingering Garden** (留园 *Liú yuán*). Windows frame other windows, undulating rooflines recall waves, and a closed corridor transforms into a room open to the pond at this interesting garden. The compound provides an endless array of architectural surprises: in a corner an unexpected skylight illuminates a planted nook; windows are placed to frame bamboos as perfectly as if they were painted. The **Mandarin Duck Hall** is particularly impressive, with a lovely moon gate engraved with vines and flowers. In the back of the garden stands a 70-foot-tall rock moved here from Lake Taihu. Occasional solo musical performances on erhu and zither enliven the halls. ⊠ *338 Liuyuan Lu, west of the moat* ☎ *0512/6557–9466* ⊕ *www.gardenly.com* ⊠ *Mid-Apr.–Oct., Y40; Nov.–mid-Apr., Y30* ⏱ *Daily 7:30–5.*

FAMILY **Lion's Grove Garden** (狮子林 *Shīzilín*). This garden employs countless craggy rock formations from nearby Lake Taihu to create a surreal moonscape. A labyrinth of caves surrounds a small lake; they're great fun for kids to explore, but watch for sharp edges. There's a popular local saying that if you talk to rocks, you won't need a psychologist, making this garden a good place to spend a 50-minute hour. A tearoom on the second floor of the main pavilion overlooks the lake. ⊠ *23 Yuanlin Lu, 3 blocks south of the Humble Administrator's Garden* ☎ *0512/6727–8316* ⊕ *www.szszzl.com* ⊠ *Y30* ⏱ *Daily 8:15–5:30.*

Fodor'sChoice **Master of the Nets Garden** (网师园 *Wǎngshī yuán*). All elements of
★ Suzhou style are here in precise balance: rocky hillscapes, layered planting, undulating walkways, and charming pavilions overlooking a central pond. Representing mountains, rivers, and the four seasons, it's a theme park of sorts, centuries before Walt Disney. It's also a fine example of how Chinese garden design creates the illusion of space. To avoid the crowds, visit in the evening, when you can saunter from room to room enjoying traditional opera, flute, and dulcimer performances—as the master himself might have done. Evening performances are held from mid-March to mid-November. ⊠ *11 Kuo Jia Tou Gang, south of Shiquan Lu, east of Daichengqiao Lu* ☎ *0512/6529–3190* ⊕ *www.szwsy.com* ⊠ *Mid-Apr.–Oct, Y30; Nov.–mid-Apr., Y20* ⏱ *Daily 7:30–5.*

**Temple of Mystery** (玄妙观 *Xuánmiàoguān*). One of the best-preserved Taoist compounds, the Temple of Mystery backs a large square that is now a touristy market. Founded in the 3rd century, the temple is a rare example of a wooden structure that has stood the test of time, with parts from the 12th century. Fortunately, it suffered little damage in the Cultural Revolution, and retains a splendid ceiling of carefully arranged beams and braces painted in their original colors. ⊠ *Guanqian Jie* ☎ *0512/6777–5479* ⊠ *Y10* ⏱ *Daily 8:30–5.*

**Tiger Hill** (回球 *Hǔqiū*). This hill is the burial place of the king of the State of Wu, who founded the city in 514 BC. At the top of the approach is a huge sheet of stone called **Thousand Man Rock,** where legend has it that the workers who built the tomb were thanked for their labors with an elaborate banquet. The wine, alas, was drugged, so they perished to keep the tomb's entrance a secret. Modern archaeologists think they have discovered it hidden under the artificial lake. The secret may be out, but the king's wish to rest in peace is ensured by the fact that excavating the tomb would bring down the fragile Song Dynasty pagoda that stands above. The **Leaning Pagoda** is one of the most impressive monuments in Suzhou, with Persian influence evident in the arches and other architectural elements. A helpful audio guide explains many of the park's legends. ⊠ *Huqiu Lu, northwest of the city* ☎ *0512/6532–3488* 🖃 *Mid-Apr.–Oct., Y60; Nov.–mid-Apr., Y40* ⊗ *Daily 7:30–5.*

**WORTH NOTING**

**Hanshan Temple** (寒山寺 *Hánshān sì*). Best known as a subject of one of the Tang Dynasty's most famous poems, which described the sound of its massive bell at midnight, this large, pristinely painted temple may leave those unfamiliar with the ancient poetry feeling a little underwhelmed. The place has the frenetic feel of a tourist attraction rather than the serenity of a temple. Literary pilgrims can line up to ring the temple bell themselves for an extra charge. ⊠ *24 Hanshan Si Nong* ☎ *0512/6533–6634* 🖃 *Mid-Apr.–Oct, Y20; Nov.–mid-Apr., Y15* ⊗ *Daily 8–5.*

**Joyous Garden** (怡园 *Yí yuán*). The youngest garden in Suzhou, Joyous Garden was built in 1874. It borrows elements from Suzhou's other famous gardens: rooms from the Humble Administrator's, a pond from the Master of the Nets. The most unusual feature is an oversize mirror, inspired by the founder of Zen Buddhism, who stared at a wall for years to find enlightenment. The garden's designer hung the mirror opposite a pavilion, to let the building contemplate its own reflection. From April to October the garden doubles as a popular teahouse in the evening. ⊠ *343 Renmin Lu* ☎ *0512/6524–9317* 🖃 *Y15* ⊗ *Daily 7:30–5.*

**North Temple Pagoda** (北寺塔 *Běisìtǎ*). One of the symbols of ancient Suzhou, this temple towers over the Old City. The complex has a 1,700-year history, dating to the Three Kingdoms Period. The wooden pagoda has nine levels; you can climb as high as the eighth level for what might be the best view of Suzhou. Within the grounds are the Copper Buddha Hall and Plum Garden, which, built in 1985, lacks the history and complexity of Suzhou's other gardens. ⊠ *Xibei Jie and Renmin Lu, 2 blocks west of Humble Administrator's Garden* ☎ *0512/6753–1197* 🖃 *Y25* ⊗ *Mar.–Oct., Daily 7:45–6.*

**Pan Gate** (盘门 *Pánmén*). Traffic into Old Suzhou came both by road and canals, so the city's gates were designed to control access by both land and water. This gate—more of a small fortress—is the only one that remains. In addition to the imposing wooden gates on land, a double sluice gate can be used to seal off the canal and prevent boats from entering. A park is filled with colorful flowers, in contrast to the subdued hues in the city's traditional gardens. You can climb the **Ruiguang Pagoda,** a tall, slender spire originally built more than 1,000 years ago. ⊠ *1 Dong Dajie, southwest corner of the Old City* ☎ *0512/6526–0004* 🖃 *Panmen Gate Y40; Ruigang Pagoda Y6* ⊗ *Daily 8–4:45.*

**Suzhou Arts and Crafts Museum** (工艺美术博物馆 *Gōngyì měishù bówùguǎn*). This impressive collection of contemporary art is proof that Suzhou craftsmanship remains very healthy. It's just a shame that, all too often, ivory seems to be the material of choice. A highlight here is watching artists in action during high season, carving jade, cutting latticework fans from thin sheets of sandalwood, and fashioning traditional calligraphy brushes. Perhaps most amazing is the careful attention to detail of the women embroidering silk. The museum is

**CLOSE UP**

# Exploring the Water Villages

Centuries-old villages, preserved almost in their original state, are scattered around Suzhou. Bowed bridges span narrow canals, as traditional oared boats paddle by, creating an almost picture-perfect scene of life long past. A trip to one of these villages could well be the photographic highlight of your trip to Eastern China.

Be careful which village you choose, though. The tourist dollars that flow in may have saved these villages from the wrecking ball, but they have also changed their character to differing degrees. Those closest to the larger cities are the most swamped by tour groups. Trekking to an out-of-the-way destination can pay off by letting you find a village that, outside of high season, you might have mostly to yourself.

**Zhouzhuang** (周庄 *Zhōuzhuāng*). The most famous of the water villages is undoubtedly Zhouzhuang. Its fame is partly due to its proximity from Suzhou and Shanghai, just 45 minutes and an hour away, respectively. As a result, more than 2.5 million visitors head here each year to catch a glimpse of Old China. Its charm is reduced by the sheer number of tourists who elbow their way through the streets. Next to the "ancient memorial archway," which isn't ancient at all, is a ticket window. The entrance fee of Y100 gets you into the water-village-turned-gift shop.

Crowds aside, Zhouzhuang is fun for families. Several residences, some 500 years old, let you see what life was like in the Ming and Qing dynasties. There are several storefronts where you can see brick making, bamboo carving, and basket weaving—traditional crafts that up until recently

were in widespread use throughout the countryside. The food is typical country fare, making it a nice break from the fancier cuisine of Suzhou and Shanghai. Braised pork belly, crunchy stir-fried water chestnuts, pickled vegetables, and wild greens abound. For crafts, skip the snuff bottles and teapots and opt for something you probably won't find elsewhere: homemade rice wine, rough-hewn ox-horn combs, and bamboo rice baskets.

Buses bound for Zhouzhuang depart from Suzhou's North Bus Station every 20 minutes between 7 and 5. The 90-minute trip costs Y25.

**Tongli** (同里 *Tóngli*). The pick of the water villages is Tongli, 30 minutes from Zhouzhuang and 90 minutes from Suzhou. A number of locals still live and work here, lending this village a more authentic atmosphere than Zhouzhuang. The streets are cobbled, and the complete absence of cars makes Tongli feel like it's from a different era, provided you can get away from the crowds. You can still find yourself wandering on quaint side streets or creeping down impossibly narrow alleyways that open onto canals and bridges. Tongli is the largest of the water villages, imminently photographable, and a pleasure to explore. Near the entrance gate are several private homes offering beds, and throughout the village are tea shops and small tables set out in front of the canals. Hiring a boat (Y100 for up to six people) to be punted along the waterways gives a different perspective on the town. The admission fee is Y100.

The fastest buses to Tongli leave from Suzhou South Bus Station every 20 minutes between 7 and 5. The journey

The canals of Tongli.

costs Y12. Most taxis in town will also take you; when you negotiable a fee, aim for about Y150. This is by far the fastest way to get there, and you can take the bus back.

**Ancient Chinese Sexual Culture Museum** (古代性文化展示 *Gǔdài xìngwénhuà zhǎnshì*). A favorite spot in Tongli is Tuisi Garden, a slightly smaller version of the private courtyard parks found in Suzhou. Tongli is also home to the Ancient Chinese Sexual Culture Museum, housed in a former girl's school. The controversial exhibition of ancient erotic toys and artworks is the project of a retired university professor. ⌧ *Entrance to town* ☎ *0512/6332–2973* ✆ *Y20* ⊙ *8–4:30.*

**Luzhi** (角直 *Lùzhí*). Even farther off the beaten path than Zhouzhuang or Tongli is the water village Luzhi, roughly half an hour from Suzhou. Though it's a popular tourist destination, it remains one of the more peaceful communities in the area. Described as a "museum of bridges,"

the village has more than 40 in all shapes and styles. Many of the older women in the village preserve traditional customs, wearing folk headdresses and skirts.

Luzhi-bound buses leave from Suzhou's North Bus Station every 30 minutes between 6:30 am and 6:30 pm. The 40-minute ride costs Y10. ✆ *Y100.*

**Baosheng Temple** (保圣寺 *Bǎoshèng sì*). Luzhi is notable for the spectacular Baosheng Temple, a yellow-walled compound built in 503 that is famous for its breathtaking collection of Buddhist arhats. Arranged on a wall of stone, these clay sculptures are the work of Yang Huizhi, a famous Tang Dynasty sculptor. Made more than 1,000 years ago, they depict Buddhist disciples who have gained enlightenment. The temple also features a well-preserved bell from the end of the Ming Dynasty. ⌧ *Luzhi* ☎ *0512/6501–0011* ✆ *Free* ⊙ *8–4:30*

set within attractive gardens and traditional buildings. ✉ *58 Xibei Jie, between Humble Administrator's Garden and the North Pagoda* ☎ *0512/6753–4874* 🌐 *www.szgmb.cn* 🎫 *Y15* 🕒 *Daily 9–5.*

> **WORD OF MOUTH**
>
> "Once you get inside the old town, there are no motorized vehicles, just bikes and pedestrian traffic. Nothing really seems to be rebuilt here, so you can get a feel for the old ways of living, people still doing their laundry and washing vegetables in the canal. Stopped and had tea at a cute tea shop. Good local art here in Tongli, as well as inexpensive embroidered wall art." —quimbymoy

**Suzhou Museum** (苏州博物馆 *Sūzhōu bówùguǎn*). This is the most modern building to emerge amid a neighborhood of traditional architecture. The museum is the valedictory work for 90-year-old modernist master I.M. Pei. A controversy erupted over whether to allow Pei to construct the glass-and-steel structure in historical Suzhou. Like his crystal pyramid in the courtyard of the Louvre, this building thrives on juxtapositions of old and new. The museum houses historical objects from Suzhou's ancient past and an impressive collection of Ming and Qing Dynasty paintings and calligraphy. English language docent tours cost Y100. ✉ *204 Dongbei Jie, next to Humble Administrator's Garden* ☎ *0512/6757–5666* 🌐 *www.szmuseum.com* 🎫 *Free* 🕒 *Tues.–Sun. 9–5.*

**West Garden Temple** (西园寺 *Xīyuán sì*). This temple is most notable for the **Hall of 500 Arhats** (*wǔbǎi luóhàn táng*), which houses 500 gold-painted statues of these Buddhist guides. They are humorous carvings: one struggling with dragons, another cradling a cat. ✉ *8 Xiwan Lu, across from Lingering Garden* 🎫 *Y25* 🕒 *Daily 7–5.*

## WHERE TO EAT

Shiquan Jie is quickly becoming one of the city's restaurant hubs, with both Suzhou-style restaurants and Chinese regional cuisine from Xinjiang to Yunnan. Many offer English menus.

$$$$ CHINESE 🍴 **Songhelou** (松鹤楼 *Sònghèlóu fàndiàn*). Ever since Emperor Qianlong, the Qing Dynasty's most famous tourist, declared the fish here a triumph, Songhelou has ridden on his yellow coattails. The most famous eatery in town, the pricey "Pine and Crane" is overhyped, but that doesn't stop tourists coming in droves to chow on braised tofu with crabmeat, pork belly with cherry sauce, and other local specialties. If folks are queuing out the door, try the similarly venerable Deyuelou, selling much the same Suzhou fare, just across the street. [$] *Average main: Y200* ✉ *72 Taijian Nong, south of the Temple of Mystery* ☎ *0512/6770–0688.*

$$$ CHINESE Fodor's Choice ★ 🍴 **Wumen Renjia** (吴门人家 *Wúmén rénjiā*). Shelled river shrimp (*wumen xiaren*) are a light and delicate signature dish at this lovely restaurant accessed via a narrow alley north of Lion's Grove Garden. The busy kitchen also pulls off a satisfactorily crisp rendition of the region's famous *songshu guiyu* (squirrel fish), scored and fried so that the white meat fans outwards in chopstick-friendly mouthfuls. Sweet and sour sauce completes the experience. The traditional setting means

Wumen Renjia is popular with Chinese travelers. $ *Average main: Y120* ⊠ *31 Panru Xiang, north of Lion's Grove Garden* ☎ *0512/6728–8041.*

$ ✕ **Xichengyuan Wonton** (熙盛源馄饨 *Xīchéngyuán húntun*). Locals

SHANGHAINESE  squeeze around tables at this simple eatery, a quick hop from the Master

Fodor's Choice  of the Nets Garden, to lunch on mouthwateringly zingy wonton soup

★  and *xiaolongbao* (freshly steamed, soup-filled pork dumplings). There is no menu—order at the entrance, take a number, and find a seat. Try the pork wontons in spicy soup or go for the wontons filled with *jiecai*, a local green vegetable, and served in a fragrant clear broth. $ *Average main: Y30* ⊠ *43 Fenghuang Jie* ☎ *0512/6512–8707.*

## WHERE TO STAY

$$  🛏 **Crowne Plaza Hotel Suzhou** (中茵皇冠假日酒店 *Zhōngyín xīngguān*

HOTEL  *jiàrì jiǔdiàn*). This ship-shaped luxury hotel on Jinji Lake is so convincing that you might feel like waving to passersby from the deck. **Pros:** whimsical design; light-filled rooms; lovely pool. **Cons:** pricey in-room Internet access; outside the city center. $ *Rooms from: Y1100* ⊠ *68 Xinggang Lu* ☎ *512/6761–6688* ⊕ *www.crowneplaza.com* ➟ *344 rooms* ⍾ *No meals.*

$  🛏 **Garden Hotel** (南园 *Nányuán bīnguǎn*). After a day exploring Suzhou's

HOTEL  many gardens, return to one of your own—10 acres, to be precise, complete with flowering trees, tranquil ponds, and colorful pagodas. **Pros:** pleasant grounds, peaceful atmosphere; great service. **Cons:** interior a little sterile; some rooms overdue for renovations. $ *Rooms from: Y700* ⊠ *249 Shiquan Jie* ☎ *0512/6778–6778* ➟ *104 rooms* ⍾ *No meals.*

$  🛏 **Hotel Soul** (苏哥利酒店 *Sūgēlì jiǔdiàn*). This centrally located design

HOTEL  hotel is by no means the quintessential Suzhou experience, but the comfortable beds, international cable channels, and a bistro-style restaurant could be just the ticket after a long day of wandering around the city's classical gardens. **Pros:** great value; friendly service; central location. **Cons:** no historic value; gym very basic. $ *Rooms from: Y500* ⊠ *27-33 Qiaosikong Xiang, east of Pingan Fang* ☎ *0512/6777–0777* ⊕ *www.hotelsoul.com.cn* ➟ *225 rooms* ⍾ *No meals.*

$  🛏 **Pan Pacific Suzhou** (吴宫泛太平洋酒店 *Súzhōu wúgōng táipǐngyáng*

HOTEL  *dájiǔdiàn*). One of the city's more unique luxury hotels, the Pan Pacific

Fodor's Choice  Suzhou has a two-story stone entrance topped by a pagoda that's mod-

★  elled after the Pan Gate. **Pros:** beautiful architecture; peaceful gardens; pretty pool. **Cons:** in an older part of town. $ *Rooms from: Y800* ⊠ *259 Xinshi Lu* ☎ *0512/6510–3388* ⊕ *www.panpacific.com/suzhou* ➟ *481 rooms* ⍾ *No meals.*

$  🛏 **Pingjiang Lodge** (平江客栈 *Píngjiāng kèzhàn*). This grand old man-

B&B/INN  sion offers a delightful balance of historic atmosphere and affordable

Fodor's Choice  comfort. **Pros:** quaint style; great location; affordable rates. **Cons:** ser-

★  vice can be a little frosty; some rooms a bit dark. $ *Rooms from: Y500* ⊠ *32 Niu Jia Xiang, southern end of Pingjiang Jie* ☎ *0512/6523–3888* ➟ *50 rooms* ⍾ *No meals.*

$  🛏 **Suzhou Garden View Hotel** (苏州人家 *Súzhōu rěnjià dájiǔdiàn*). Beside

HOTEL  a canal, this peaceful hotel wraps around an expansive courtyard and Suzhou-style garden. **Pros:** great value; distinctive touches **Cons:** difficult to find taxi; small bathrooms; poor amenities. $ *Rooms from: Y500* ⊠ *66 Luo Guaqia, Lindun Lu* ☎ *0512/6777–8888* ⊕ *www.szrj-h.com* ➟ *188 rooms* ⍾ *No meals.*

## NIGHTLIFE AND THE ARTS

### NIGHTLIFE

At night, the stretch of Shiquan Jie between Renmin Lu and Fenghuang Lu, is home to a cluster of Irish pubs, small hole-in-the wall Chinese bars, and karaoke clubs. Storefronts change quickly, but you are guaranteed to find something lively and fun. A newer nightlife area has developed on the west shore of Jinji Lake, a stroll south of the Dongfangzhimen Subway Station.

**The Bookworm** (老书虫 *Lǎoshūchóng*). Visit this canal-side town house to peruse a wide selection of English-language books and magazines while sipping imported wines and beers. At night there's regular live music. ✉ *77 Gunxi Fang, off Shiquan Jie* ☎ *0512/6581–6752* ⊕ *www. suzhoubookworm.com.*

**Le Ble D'or** (金色三麥 *Jīnsè sānmài*). This enormous place has servers garbed in Bavarian dirndls, a jarringly French name, and a self-described "American style." Occupying the entire fourth floor of a high-rise building, it's the local outpost of a popular Taiwanese chain of brewpubs. Three types of beer are brewed on the premises, and the menu includes sticky barbecue pork ribs, fried chicken, and truffle fries in portions meant for sharing. The Munich-inspired *bierkeller* interior can seat a staggering 900 people at its long tables. ✉ *Jinhe Guoji Dasha Building, 34 Shishan Lu, 4th fl., East New Town* ☎ *0521/6665–5909* ⊕ *www.lebledor.com.*

**OFF THE BEATEN PATH**

Pingjiang Lu is an ancient, well-preserved cobbled street in the center of the Old City, following the course of a narrow canal. Dating back 800 years, this north-to-south lane and its side streets feature bygone scenes of daily life. Quaint whitewashed canal-side houses with overhanging balconies and black-tiled roofs cluster under weeping willows and jasmine trees. Arched bridges reflected in the canals are picture-perfect. The area has become trendy in recent years, drawing new bars, restaurants, and art galleries, but for now the old and new coexist in relative harmony. Moreover, it's possible to duck into one of the alleyways and discover locals clinging to a way of life relatively unchanged for hundreds of years.

### THE ARTS

**Le Pont des Arts.** This French-owned contemporary art and photography studio has rotating exhibits of both Chinese and foreign artists. ✉ *112–115 Pingjiang Lu* ☎ *0512/6581–3330.*

## SHOPPING

Districts around the major gardens and temples teem with silk shops and outdoor markets. The city's long history of wealth and culture has encouraged a tradition of elegant and finely worked craft objects. One of the best-known is double-sided embroidery, where two designs are carefully stitched on both sides of a sheet of silk. The city is also famous for its finely latticed sandalwood fans. Both are available at the Suzhou Arts and Crafts Museum. The area outside the west gate of the Master of the Nets Garden has dozens of small stalls selling curios and inexpensive but interesting souvenirs.

**Suzhou Cultural Relics Store** (苏州文物商店 Sūzhōu wénwù shāngdiàn). Since 1956, the Suzhou Cultural Relics Store has been selling antiques, calligraphy, jades, and other items. ⊠ *1208 Renmin Lu* ☎ *0512/ 6523–3851.*

**Suzhou Jade Carving Factory.** You can get certified jewelry and carvings at the Suzhou Jade Carving Factory. ⊠ *33 Baita Xi Lu* ☎ *0512/6727–1224.*

**Suzhou Silk Museum Shop.** (苏州丝绸博物馆商店 Sūzhōu sīchóu bówùguǎn shàngdiàn). Near the North Pagoda, the Suzhou Silk Museum Shop is the main reason to come to the Silk Museum. ⊠ *661 Renmin Lu* ☎ *0512/6753–4941.*

# ANHUI

Eastern China's most rural province, Anhui has a rugged terrain that forces families to fight their hardscrabble farmland for every acre of harvest. Today it remains significantly poorer than its neighbors, with an average income half that of neighboring Zhejiang, a successful manufacturing hub. But what Anhui lacks in material wealth it makes up for in splendid natural landscape. Travelers here enjoy countryside largely untouched by the last century. Near Huangshan (Yellow Mountain), towering granite peaks loom over green fields, and round-shouldered water buffalo plow the flooded rice paddies.

The foothills of Huangshan have a remarkable wealth of historical architecture. Tiny communities dot the landscape in Shexian and Yixian counties. Many of these villages were far enough out of the way that even the Cultural Revolution's zealous Red Guards left them alone. Today, though increasingly visited by tourists, whole villages retain their original architecture, and in some cases, generations of inhabitants.

Anhui boasts significant contributions to Chinese civilization. The province produces both the paper and ink most favored for Chinese calligraphy. Hui opera, an ancient musical form developed in the province, was a major influence on Beijing Opera. Hui cuisine is included among China's great culinary traditions, making use of mountain vegetables and herbs, with many stewed and braised dishes.

Most of the province's highlights lie in the south, accessible from Shanghai, Hangzhou, and Nanjing.

## REGIONAL TOURS

Nearby Nanjing is a good place in which to make arrangements for your travels in Anhui, particularly around Huangshan.

**Jiangsu Huate International Travel Service.** For organized tours, flights, and other arrangements, contact Jiangsu Huate International Travel Service. ⊠ *33 Jinxiang He Lu, Nanjing* ☎ *025/8337–8598* ⊕ *www. hitravels.com.*

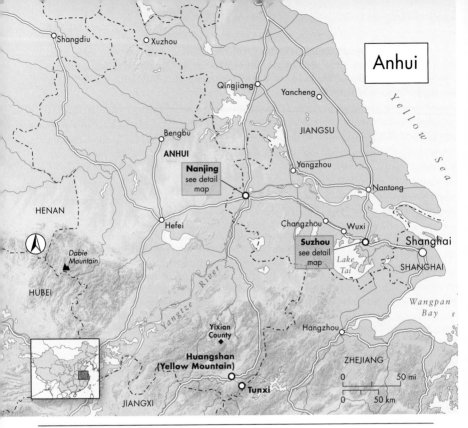

## HUANGSHAN

*5½ hrs (250 km [155 miles]) by train west of Nanjing; 3½ hrs by long-distance bus.*

Fodor's Choice ★ **Huangshan** (黄山 *Huángshān*). Eastern China's most impressive natural landscape, Yellow Mountain's peaks thrust upward through rolling seas of clouds, spindly pines clinging precipitously to their sides. A favorite retreat of emperors and poets past, its vistas have inspired some of China's most outstanding artworks and literary endeavors. So beguiling were they that centuries of labor went into constructing the paths and stone stairways, some ascending gently through virgin forest, others sharp and steep. Since 1990, the area has been designated a UNESCO World Heritage Site.

The common English translation—Yellow Mountain—is misleading. Huangshan is not a single mountain but a range of peaks stretching across four counties. To complicate matters, the name is not a reference to color. The region was originally called the "Black Mountains," but a Tang Dynasty emperor renamed it to honor Huangdi, the Yellow Emperor. And according to legend, it was from these slopes that he rode off to heaven on the back of a dragon.

The mountain is renowned for its gnarled stone formations, many sporting fanciful names to describe their shape. Some will require a stretch of the imagination, while others will leap out at you on first glance. Generations of Chinese poets and travelers have humanized these peaks and forests in this way, and left their mark on the area.

■ TIP→ **Be forewarned: Huangshan has its own weather.** More than 200 days a year, precipitation obscures the famous views. It can be sunny below, but in the mountains it's damp and chilly. That said, even on the foggiest of days the wind is likely to part the mist long enough to offer a satisfactory glimpse of the famous peaks. ✉ *Mar.–Nov., Y300; Dec.–Feb., Y150* ☉ *Open 24 hrs.*

### GETTING HERE AND AROUND

Most long-distance transportation, including trains and airplanes, arrives in Tunxi, the largest city near Yellow Mountain. Be aware, however, that Tunxi is still about an hour from Yellow Mountain. Minibuses to Tangkou and other destinations around the base of the mountain leave from the plaza in front of Tunxi's Huangshan Railway Station. The cost should be Y15 to Y30. There are also plenty of taxi drivers who are happy to offer their services, usually for around Y70 per carload.

Some buses from Nanjing, Hangzhou, and Shanghai go directly to Tangkou, the entrance at the base of the mountain. The airport is close to Tunxi, about a Y15 to Y20 cab ride from the center of town.

AIR TRAVEL If you plan to fly to Yellow Mountain, you'll land at the Huangshan City Airport near Tunxi, about 60 to 90 minutes from the mountain. There are direct flights from Beijing, Guangzhou, Shanghai, and Ji'nan.

TAXI AND MINIBUS TRAVEL In Tunxi, minibuses and taxis that congregate around the train station will take you to Yellow Mountain. For about Y20 they will drop you at the main gate at the bottom of the mountain or at the beginning of the climbing section.

TRAIN TRAVEL There is one overnight train from Shanghai to Huangshan Railway Station, arriving at about 9 am. From the station you can catch a minivan or taxi to Yellow Mountain.

### SAFETY AND PRECAUTIONS

The roads leading to Huangshan can be dangerous in heavy rain or during the winter months. Check the local weather forecast, as good weather is essential. Minibuses and taxis are known to drive too fast on the approach.

### TIMING

Allow at least two days for a visit to Huangshan, and another day or so to see the villages around Tunxi. Thanks to the cable cars on the mountain, it is possible to take in a lot of scenery in one full day.

### TOURS

Tours up the mountain are unnecessary. A better bet is to buy a good map from one of the local vendors and chart the path you want to take. Some Tunxi companies offer trips that include accommodations for little more than the cost of the admission price to the park. And there's no need to spend the day with strangers—you can hike on your own, joining the rest of the group in time to catch the bus back.

The Tunxi branch of China Travel Service (CTS) can arrange transportation and book a place to stay on the mountain. It also has info on exploring the surrounding countryside. The best place for current information about the region is the English-language Huangshan Travel Net, run in conjunction with CTS.

**ESSENTIALS**

Nearly all services are 90 minutes away in Tunxi.

**Medical Assistance Beihai Medical Center** ⊠ *Huangshan Scenic Area, across from Beihai Hotel, Huangshan Scenic Area* ☎ *0559/558–2555.* **Jade Screen Tower First-Aid Station** ⊠ *Jade Screen Tower Hotel, Huangshan Summit, Huangshan* ☎ *0559/558–2288.*

**Visitor and Tour Info uangshan Travel Net** ⊠ *27 Xin'an North Rd., Tunxi* ☎ *0559/251–2155, 0559/251–2133* ⊕ *www.uhuangshan.com.*

**EXPLORING**

There are two primary hiking routes up the mountain. The Eastern Steps, a straightforward path through forests, is both the shortest and the easiest. The Southern Steps (some guidebooks call these the Western Steps, which causes confusion with another set of steps used primarily by porters) require more effort, but they pay off with remarkable scenery. The steep, winding path reveals sheer peaks and precipitous lookouts over mist-enshrouded valleys.

Climbing up is physically taxing, but climbing down is mentally exhausting, requiring far more concentration. If you have the time and the leg muscles, it's nice to ascend the South Steps, where the scenery stretches before you. The views are a good excuse to stop and catch your breath.

**EASTERN STEPS**

The Eastern Steps are quicker than the Southern Steps, but the scenery isn't as rewarding and there are fewer scenic side routes. Along the way is a building called **Fascinating Pavilion,** most notable as a rest stop along the way. There's a short half-hour side hike to **Pipeng,** with a good view out over a number of the smaller eastern peaks. By the time you reach **Cloud Valley,** the landscape that makes Huangshan famous begins to come into view. **Beginning to Believe Peak** is the start of the awe-inspiring landscape, and the first true majestic vista on this path.

**Cloud Valley Temple Cable Car Station** (云谷寺索道 *Yúngǔsì suǒdào*). The Eastern Steps begin at the Cloud Valley Temple Cable Car Station. The cable car takes eight minutes to traverse what takes hikers three or more hours. Large windows provide an aerial view of the mountain and bamboo forests below. This area was once home to several monasteries, nunneries, and temples. By the beginning of the 20th century they had been abandoned, but the name Cloud Valley Temple Area remains. ☏ *Y80* ☉ *Weekdays 6:30–4:30, weekends 6:30–5.*

**SOUTHERN STEPS**

The steep Southern Steps are by far the tougher path. However, the climb pays off with great views and some beautiful side trails. Although the Eastern Steps feel like a walk through the woods, the Southern Steps truly feel like an ascent into the clouds. The steps begin around the Hot Springs, at the **Mercy Light Temple** area. **Midway Mountain Temple** has facilities to rest, eat, and even stay overnight, but no temple. It's here that the splendor of Huangshan comes into full view. At the **Three Islands at Penglai,** a trio of peaks emerge from a sea of mist. If you're feeling energetic, a side tour of **Heavenly Capital Peak** affords spectacular views out over the rest of the range. The effort is worth a try even if it looks cloudy, because the mist can sometimes clear by the time you get to the top. This may not be the highest peak in the range, but it is one of the steepest.

**Jade Screen Cable Car** (玉屏 *Yùpíng suǒdào*). The Jade Screen Cable Car runs parallel to the Southern Steps, leaving riders close to the Welcoming Guests Pine. It can close unexpectedly in inclement weather. ✉ *Huangshan* 🎫 *Y80* 🕐 *Weekdays 6:30–4:30, weekends 6:30–5.*

**THE SUMMIT**

The entrance to the summit area is announced by the **Welcoming Guest Pine,** a lone pine clinging to the edge of a cliff, one branch outstretched. Behind it a sheer stone slope rises out of the clouds. Continuing onward, you can climb **Lotus Peak,** the tallest in the province. A walk through **Turtle Cave,** an arched pathway straight through the hillside, brings the weary traveler to **Bright Top Peak,** slightly lower than Lotus, and an easier climb.

The recently opened **Xihai Grand Canyon** loop starts at the Cloud Dispelling Pavilion and ends at the Haixin Ting Pavilion. Rock formations called "Upside Down Boot" and "Lady Playing Piano" may be clumsily translated, but they are stunning. The farther along you walk, the fewer travelers you'll come across. At the southern end of the loop, near Haixin, the trail reaches the **Immortal's Walk Bridge,** a dizzying arch over the misty abyss that leads to a terrace on one of the mountain's spires. A huge landscape spreads out beneath, without a single tour group in sight.

A highlight of any trip is sunrise, visible from several places on the mountain. Most hikers arrive well after dawn, but you'll be rewarded with the spectacle of Huangshan materializing from the shadows if you arrive just before first light. A popular spot near the Beihai Hotel is the **Dawn Pavilion.** There are several less crowded peaks with equally good views a little farther from the hotels. **Refreshing Terrace, Lion Peak,** and **Red Cloud Peak** all provide unobstructed views of the rising sun.

Compared to the ascent, the summit area is relatively level, but there is still a good amount of stair climbing. It takes about three to four hours to walk the full summit circle, and considerably more if you take side trails.

**DID YOU KNOW?**

Climbing the rough-hewn steps of Huangshan is not something you'll quickly forget. More than 60,000 steps have been carved into the side of the mountains, some as far back as 1,500 years ago.

### WHERE TO EAT

Tangkou, a village that has sprung up to serve mountain climbers, has the most for travelers, including hotels, restaurants, grocery stores, and shops to gear up for the long climb ahead. Tangkou sits near the front gate of the park, and buses run regularly to the trailheads for both the Southern and Eastern steps. If you want to take the shorter route up the Eastern Steps, the Cloud Valley Temple Area is a convenient option. The Hot Springs area is also a much more pleasant option than Tangkou.

> **BE PREPARED**
>
> Most paths are well maintained with good steps and sturdy handrails, but Huangshan still has sheer drop-offs and steep, uneven, rain-slicked steps. A walking stick (sturdy wooden dragon-head staffs are on sale around the mountain) will help steady your ascent. It can get very cold on the peaks, and rain can come unexpectedly. Dress in layers, and consider bringing a hooded sweatshirt to stay warm.

$$ CHINESE **Celebrity's Banquet** (喜来大酒店 *Xǐlái dàjiǔdiàn*). The best restaurant on the summit, Celebrity's Banquet inside the Xihai Hotel celebrates local culture with a range of traditional Hui dishes. Soups of dried vegetables, jellied tofu, braised pork, and a delicately flavored pumpkin soup shouldn't be missed. *Average main: Y80 ✉ Xihai Hotel, Grand Canyon Loop, Summit Area, Huangshan ☎ 0559/558–8888.*

$$ CHINESE **Tangzhen Hotel Restaurant** (汤镇大酒店 *Tāngzhèn dàjiǔdiàn*). This hotel is nothing to write home about, but the Hui cuisine here is especially good, attracting locals from around the area. Specialties include cured mandarin fish, home-cured pork with bamboo, and stewed dishes served in clay pots. *Average main: Y80 ✉ Tangzhen Hotel, at the main entrance to Huangshan, Tangkou ☎ 0559/556–2665 ⊕ www.tangzhenhotel.com ▭ No credit cards.*

### WHERE TO STAY

Several small, basic huts can be found along the Southern Steps, but it would be better to push on to the hotels in the Summit Area. They are your only option if you want to catch the sunrise. As a bonus, you'll have the dew-drenched forests to yourself for a few hours before the latecomers arrive. Reservations are strongly recommended, especially for weekends; this is a popular destination for Chinese travelers, as well as tourists from Japan and Korea.

$ HOTEL **Baiyun Hotel** (白云宾馆 *Báiyún bìnguǎn*). This hotel offers comfortable rooms and a good location on the summit—a short walk away from Bright Top Peak. **Pros:** good location; great restaurant. **Cons:** few amenities. *Rooms from: Y950 ✉ Summit Area, Huangshan ☎ 0559/558–2708 ⇆ 80 rooms, 1 suite No meals.*

$ HOTEL **Beihai Hotel** (北海 *Běihǎi bìnguǎn*). With rooms set among flowering rhododendrons and azaleas, the Beihai Hotel is one of the nicest places to stay on the mountain. **Pros:** ideal location; soothing sauna. **Cons:** some rooms face away from the views you came here for. *Rooms from: Y750 ✉ Huangshan Scenic Area, Huangshan ☎ 0559/556–2555 📠 0559/556–2996 ⇆ 137 rooms, 2 suites No meals.*

$ HOTEL **Huangshan Xingang Hotel** (黄山新港 *Huángshān xīngǎng jiǔdiàn*). Because practically every guest is coming up or down the mountain, the staff at this comfortable hotel is a great repository of knowledge of what to see, how to climb, and the best routes to take. **Pros:** a comfortable stop before your climb. **Cons:** basic amenities. [$] *Rooms from: Y200* ✉ *At the main entrance to Huangshan, Tangkou* ☎ *0559/556–1048* 🛏 *115 rooms, 2 suites* 🍴 *No meals.*

$ HOTEL **Jade Screen Tower Hotel** (玉屏楼宾馆 *Yùbǐng lóu bīnguǎn*). The views from this hotel are unmatched, although like most of its neighbors it has small and fairly basic rooms. **Pros:** great place to catch the sunrise; welcome sight after a long climb. **Cons:** limited facilities. [$] *Rooms from: Y650* ✉ *Summit Area, past Welcoming Guest Pine, Huangshan* ☎ *0559/558–2288* 🌐 *www.hsyplhotel.com* 🛏 *29 rooms, 1 suite.*

## TUNXI

*5½ hrs (250 km [155 miles]) by train west of Nanjing; 3½ hrs by long-distance bus.*

This is the gateway to the Yellow Mountain area. Apart from being a transportation hub, Tunxi also has a charming strip of shops and restaurants and is a convenient place from which to take trips to Shexian and Yixian counties, famous for their historical architecture.

### GETTING HERE AND AROUND

Unless you arrive on a long-distance bus bound for Tangkou, your bus or train is probably bound for Tunxi, around 65 km (40 miles) from the mountain.

AIR TRAVEL Huangshan Tunxi International Airport, located near Tunxi, welcomes flights from Beijing, Guangzhou, Chengdu, Xian, and Shanghai. There are also roughly two flights a week from Hong Kong. Taxis to Tunxi cost Y15 to Y20.

BUS TRAVEL Buses are a convenient way of getting to Tunxi from Zhejiang, Jiangsu, and even Shanghai. Buses that run hourly from Hangzhou take 3½ hours and cost Y65. The route takes you through some gorgeous scenery. Buses from Nanjing take around five hours and cost Y80. From Shanghai, buses take eight to nine hours and cost Y120.

TRAIN TRAVEL Several trains depart daily for Nanjing (6 hours, Y60), and there are two trains each day for Shanghai (12–13 hours, Y160).

### TIMING

Tunxi is mostly a place to spend a night before your Huangshan trek. It can also be a good place to arrange tours of the area.

### TOURS

Guides are a good idea if you are exploring the countryside around Huangshan. CTS has private village tours in Yixian county and architecture tours in Shexian county.

### ESSENTIALS

**Air Contacts Air China** ✉ *23 Huashan Lu* ☎ *0559/953–4111* 🌐 *www.airchina.com.cn/en/index.jsp* ✉ *49 Huangshan Donglu* ☎ *0559/254–1222.* **Huangshan Tunxi International Airport** ✉ *Yingbin Dadao, west of the city* ☎ *0559/293–4111* 🌐 *www.hsairport.com.*

**Bus Contact Tunxi Bus Station** ⌧ *95 Huangshan Dong Lu* ☎ *0559/256–6666.*

**Medical Assistance People's Hospital of Huangshan City** ⌧ *4 Liyuan Lu, Huangshan* ☎ *0559/251–7036.*

**Train Contact Huangshan Train Station** ⌧ *Northern end of Qianyuan Beilu* ☎ *0559/211–6222.*

**Visitor and Tour Info TS** ⌧ *12 Qianyuan Bei Lu* ☎ *0130/1312–1152 English-language hotline* ⊕ *www.chinatravelservice.com* ⌧ *1Binjiang Xi Lu* ☎ *0559/251–5303* ⊕ *www.huangshanguide.com.*

## EXPLORING

**Tunxi Old Street** (屯溪老街 *Túnxī lǎojiē*). In Tunxi, the best place to stroll is along Old Street. The avenue is quiet during the day, but comes alive in the early evening. Shops along the way stay open until about 10 or 11. Wade through the junk and you may find some treasures.

## WHERE TO EAT AND STAY

**$$**
**CHINESE**
✕ **Diyilou** (老街第一楼 *Lǎojiē dìyīlóu*). At this lively restaurant in a traditional house, the local specialties include tender bamboo shoots, four-mushroom soup, braised tofu, and a mushroom-wrapped meatball that is not to be missed. Order by pointing to plated sample dishes. $ *Average main: Y70* ⌧ *247 Tunxi Lao Jie, at Lao Jie* ☎ *0559/253–9797.*

**$$**
**HOTEL**
🏨 **Crowne Plaza Huangshan Yucheng** (昱城皇冠假日酒店 *Yùchéng huángguān jiàrì jiǔdiàn*). Huangshan's first international five-star hotel, it's nevertheless great value for the quality, especially by local standards. $ *Rooms from: Y550* ⌧ *1 Huizhou Lu* ☎ *0800/830-1275* 🛏 *485 rooms.*

**$**
**HOTEL**
🏨 **Huashan Hotel** (華山賓館 *Huàshān bīnguǎn*). A block away from the city's main shopping district, this ideally located hotel has enormous guest rooms that come as a pleasant surprise. **Pros:** great access to shopping; plenty of room to spread out. **Cons:** so-so restaurant. $ *Rooms from: Y300* ⌧ *3 Yanan Lu* ☎ *0559/232–2888* 🛏 *186 rooms, 14 suites* 🍴 *No meals.*

**$**
**B&B/INN**
**Fodor's Choice**
★
🏨 **Pig's Heaven Inn** (猪栏酒吧 *Zhūlán jiǔbā*). Wake to the crowing of roosters in this 400-year-old stone house on the fringes of Xidi, a village an hour's drive from Tunxi. **Pros:** traditional lodging; beautiful surroundings; drivers at the ready. **Cons:** a bit far from Huangshan; staff knows very little English. $ *Rooms from: Y800* ⌧ *Renrang Li, Xidi* ☎ *0559/515–4555* 🛏 *5 rooms* 🍴 *No meals.*

## SHOPPING

**Sanbai Yanzhai.** When shopping along Lao Jie, the best offerings are traditional calligraphy ink and paper. The best ink stones are sold at Sanbai Yanzhai. ⌧ *173 Lao Jie* ☎ *0559/253–5538.*

**Stone and Bamboo Shop.** The Stone and Bamboo Shop sells exquisite examples of traditional bamboo carving. ⌧ *122 Lao Jie* ☎ *0559/751–5042.*

## SIDE TRIP TO SHEXIAN COUNTY

Shexian County has been called a living architectural art museum because of its natural beauty and array of historic buildings. Over the centuries, it has inspired philosophers, poets, and painters. Today, there is no lack of tourists, but it's a pleasant day trip from Tunxi.

The shops and restaurants on Old Street in Tunxi

**GETTING HERE AND AROUND**

Buses run throughout the day from the Tunxi long-distance bus station. The trip should take about 45 minutes and costs approximately Y10. Once you get to Shexian Bus Station in Huizhou Old City, you can board a minibus or take a taxi to outlying scenic spots. However, if you are traveling with several people, it's best to hire a car and driver for the day, as many of these places are quite remote and spread out.

**EXPLORING SHEXIAN COUNTY**

**Huashan Mysterious Grottoes** (华山谜窟 *Huàshān míkū*). The Huashan Mysterious Grottoes are a combination of natural caves and rooms carved into the rock. No one is quite certain when or why they were built, but they are impressive and illuminated with colored lights. ⊠ *Between Xiongcun and Tunxi* ☎ *0559/235–9888* ⌕ *Y70* ⊙ *Daily 7:30–6:30.*

**Huizhou Old Town** (惠州老城 *Huìzhōu lǎochéng*). This place boasts a centuries-old city wall and a magnificent four-sided memorial gate guarded by sculptures of frolicking lions. ⊠ *Huizhou* ☎ *0559/653–1586* ⌕ *Y80* ⊙ *Daily 7:30–6:30.*

**Memorial Arches** (堂樾牌楼群 *Tángyuè páilouqún*). Dating from the Ming and Qing dynasties, these archways represent traditional values like morality, piety, and female chastity. ⊠ *5 km (3 miles) west of Huizhou Old Town, Tangyue* ⌕ *Y80* ⊙ *Daily 8–5:30.*

**Yuliang Village** (渔梁古镇 *Yúliáng gǔzhèn*). Near Huizhou Old Town, Yuliang Village overlooks a Tang Dynasty dam with water gurgling over its sloped sides. Fishermen in wooden skiffs still make their living here. A narrow street parallel to the river is a pleasant spot for a stroll.

Most families leave their doors open, allowing a peak into simple homes where pages from magazines are often used as wallpaper. Inexpensive pedicabs travel here from the Shexian Bus Station in Huizhou Old City, or you can catch Bus 1 from the train station. ⊠ *Changxi Xian, Yuliang* ⊞ *Y30* ⊙ *Daily 7:30–6:30.*

## SIDE TRIP TO YIXIAN COUNTY

A pleasant day trip from Tunxi, Yixian County is the site of some beautiful and ancient rural architecture set in bucolic surroundings. Yixian County receives nearly 2.5 million visits per year, but don't let that deter you, as the UNESCO World Heritage sites in the area are eminently photogenic.

### GETTING HERE AND AROUND

To reach Yixian County, take the buses that leave from in front of Tunxi's train station. They cost about Y10 and depart every 20 minutes. Because of a nearby military base, police-issued travel permits costing Y50 are required for travel in Yixian County. The ticket offices at the gates of Xidi Village and Hongcun Village can take care of this for you. A passport is necessary to register for the permits.

### EXPLORING YIXIAN COUNTY

**Hongcun Village** (宏村 *Hóngcūn*). An arched bridge leads to Hongcun Village. From above, the village is said to resemble a buffalo. Two 600-year-old trees mark its horns, a lake its belly, and streams diverted for irrigation are its intestines. In recent years a number of films have been partially shot here, including *Crouching Tiger, Hidden Dragon.* Several large halls and old houses are open to tour. The Salt Merchant's House is especially well preserved, with intricate decorations and carvings that were unharmed during the Cultural Revolution. ⊠ *Yi Xian, Hongcun* ☎ *0559/251–7464* ⊞ *Y80* ⊙ *Daily 6:30–6:30.*

**Xidi Village** (西递村 *Xīdìcūn*). A UNESCO World Heritage Site, Xidi Village is known for its exquisite memorial gate. There were once a dozen gates, but they were destroyed during the Cultural Revolution. The existing gate was left standing as a "bad example" to be criticized. There are several houses with excellent examples of brick carving and an impressive Clan Temple with massive ginkgo columns and beams. ⊠ *Off Taohuayuan Lu, Xidi* ☎ *0559/515–4030* ⊞ *Y80* ⊙ *Daily 6:30–6:30.*

# SHANGHAI

# WELCOME TO SHANGHAI

## TOP REASONS TO GO

★ **Skyline Views:** Head to the top of the *Shanghai World Financial Center,* known to locals as the "bottle opener," or the pagoda-inspired Jin Mao and look straight into the clouds.

★ **Shanghai Museum:** The far-flung Power Station of Art is a contemporary hub worth the trek down to the former World Expo site.

★ **Shopping Overload:** For a break from Shanghai's conspicuous consumption, head west from Xintiandi to Fuxing Park, where couples ballroom dance all afternoon long.

★ **Yu Garden:** When not too crowded, the garden offers a few minutes of peace and beauty amid the clamor of the city, with rocks, trees, and walls curved to resemble dragons, bridges, and pavilions.

**1 The Bund.** Shanghai's famous waterfront boulevard is lined on one side with Art Deco, renaissance, and neoclassical buildings and on the other with souvenir stands. It's great for people-watching, shopping for increasingly chic clothes, and sampling some of Shanghai's best restaurants. It's also where you'll get that postcard view of Pudong's futuristic skyline.

**2 Xintiandi.** Shopping, bars, restaurants, and the odd museum mix together in restored *shikumen* (stone gate) houses. Especially in nice weather, Xintiandi is an enormously popular location for hanging out and people-watching, and there are a few cute boutiques. The small museums have interesting exhibits related to Shanghai's and the Communist Party's history.

**3 Former French Concession.** Whether you're an architecture fanatic, a photographer, a romantic, or just plain curious, a wander through these streets is always a wonderful way to pass an afternoon. Fuxing Lu is a good long walk, and the streets around Sinan Lu and Fuxing Park have some real architectural treats. Take your time, and allow for breaks at cafés or in small boutiques.

Luxun Museum ◆

People's Park

Shanghai Museum ◆

1 THE BUND

Oriental Pearl Tower ◆

Minzhu Park

PUDONG

Jin Mao Tower

Fuxing Park

XINTIANDI 2

Yu Garden ◆

OLD CITY

Penglai Park

## GETTING ORIENTED

Shanghai is fast and tough, so bring good shoes and a lot of patience. Don't expect the grandeur of ancient sights, but rather relish the small details like exquisitely designed Art Deco buildings or laid-back cafés. Shanghai hides her gems well, so it's important to be observant and look up and around. The crowds of people and the constant change can make travelers weary, so take advantage of the wide range of eateries and convenient benches.

4 Nanjing Dong Lu. People come from all over China to shop on what was once China's premier shopping street—and it sometimes feels as though they're all here at the same time. The pre-1960s department stores have all but been replaced by modern chain stores, but the pedestrian-only street, which teems with people all day, every day, is still a sight to be seen.

Updated by Sophie Friedman

Until 1842, the "City Above the Sea" was a small fishing village. After the first Opium War, the village was carved up into autonomous concessions administered concurrently by the British, French, and Americans. As the most Westernized city in China after Hong Kong, Shanghai is at the forefront of China's modernization. Nearly a quarter of the world's construction cranes stand in this city. Still, architectural remnants of a colonial past survive along the winding, bustling streets.

In its heyday, Shanghai had the best art, the greatest architecture, and the strongest business in Asia. With dance halls, glitzy restaurants, international clubs, brothels, and a racetrack, it catered to the rich. The Paris of the East was known as a place of vice and indulgence. Amid this glamour and degradation the Communist Party held its first meeting in 1921.

In the '30s and '40s the city suffered raids, invasions, and occupation by the Japanese. After the war's end, Nationalists and Communists fought a three-year civil war for control of China. The Communists declared victory in 1949 and established the People's Republic of China. Between 1950 and 1980, Shanghai's industries soldiered on through periods of extreme famine and drought, reform, and suppression. Politically, the city was central to the Cultural Revolution and the Gang of Four's base. The January Storm of 1967 purged many of Shanghai's leaders, and Red Guards set out to destroy the "Four Olds": old ways of ideas, living, traditions, and thought.

In 1972, with the Cultural Revolution still going, Shanghai hosted the historic meeting between Premier Zhou Enlai and U.S. President Richard Nixon. In 1990 China's leader, Deng Xiaoping, chose Shanghai as the center of the country's commercial renaissance, and it has again become a testament to hedonism and capitalism, one of China's most ideologically, socially, culturally, and economically open cities.

■TIP→ Shanghai is a sprawling city with large districts, but the downtown area is fairly compact, and the subway reaches many place you'll want to visit.

## PLANNING

### WHEN TO GO

The best time to visit Shanghai is early spring or early fall, when the weather is good and crowds diminish. Although temperatures are scorching and the humidity can be unbearable, summer is the peak tourist season, and hotels and transportation can get very crowded.

Avoid the two main national holidays, Chinese New Year (which ranges from mid-January to mid-February) and the National Day holiday (always the first week of October), when a billion people are on the move.

### GETTING HERE AND AROUND

#### TO AND FROM THE AIRPORT

Shanghai has two major airports: most international flights go through Pudong International Airport (PVG), which is 45 km (30 miles) east of the city, whereas many domestic routes operate out of the older Hongqiao International Airport (SHA), 15 km (9 miles) west of the city center.

Taking a taxi is the most comfortable way into town from Pudong International Airport. Expect to pay around Y180 to Y220 for the 45-minute trip to Puxi; getting to the closer Pudong area takes 25 minutes and should cost no more than Y100. At rush hour, these times can easily double.

Speed demons may wish to catch the Maglev train, which tops out at 431 km/h (268 mph). At the Longyang Lu metro station in Pudong it connects to lines 2 and 7, which can get you downtown in about 25 minutes. It costs Y50 for a single trip (Y40 if you present your ticket from a same-day flight) and Y80 per round-trip. For a mere Y7 you can hop on metro line 2 at Pudong International Airport, cross the platform at Guanlan Road Station, and be downtown in just under an hour. Note that the Maglev train runs 6:30 am–9:30 pm and the metro 9:30 am–9:15 pm.

From Hongqiao Airport, a taxi to Puxi will cost you Y45–Y75 and takes 30 to 40 minutes; it takes about an hour to reach Pudong. You can take metro lines 2 and 10 from Hongqiao for Y5. A taxi from one airport to the other takes about an hour and costs upwards of Y250. Metro Line 2 also connects Hongqiao Airport and Pudong Airport, making trips between the two significantly cheaper.

Many hotels offer free airport transfers to their guests. Otherwise, shuttle buses link Pudong Airport with a number of hotels (routes starting with a letter) and transport hubs (routes starting with a number) in the city center. Most shuttle buses depart every 10 to 20 minutes between roughly 7 am and midnight. Trips to Puxi take about 90 minutes and cost between Y25 and Y40. From Hongqiao Airport, Bus 925 runs to People's Square, but there's little room for luggage. It costs Y4.

### AIR TRAVEL

Shanghai's two major airports make it easy to get here from the rest of the world. United Airlines runs daily direct flights from Newark to Pudong; Delta flies direct from Pudong to Tokyo and Detroit, and Virgin to Heathrow. Loads of budget airlines also service both Pudong Airport and Hongqiao Airport, so you can hop Air Asia to Kuala Lumpur, China Southern to Seoul, or Thai Airways to Bangkok.

### BIKE TRAVEL

Few hotels rent bikes, but you can inquire at bike shops like Giant, where the rate is around Y50 a day, plus a large refundable deposit. Note that for about Y200 you can buy your own basic bike at Tesco or Carrefour. Shanghai's frenzied traffic is not for the faint of heart, though most secondary streets have wide, well-defined bike lanes.

### BUS TRAVEL

Taking buses is possible—the stops are called out in English—but as they are often crowded, slow, and the maps are only in Chinese, it is easier to stick to the metro.

### FERRY TRAVEL

Ferries run around the clock every 10 minutes between the Bund and Pudong's terminal just south of the Riverside Promenade. The per-person fare is Y2 each way.

### SUBWAY TRAVEL

Shanghai's quick and efficient subway system—called the Shanghai metro—is an excellent way to get around town, and the network is growing exponentially every year. English maps and exit signs abound, and the single-ticket machines have an English option, too. In-car announcements for each station are given in both Chinese and English. Keep your ticket handy: you'll need to insert it into a second turnstile as you exit at your destination.

■TIP➜ Transport cards costing Y30 are available from metro stations. Add as much money as you like, and use them to pay for taxi, metro, ferry, and bus rides. The transport cards aren't discounted, but they'll save you time you would have spent joining queues and fumbling for cash. To purchase, say, *Wo yao yi zhang ka* (which means "I want a card").

### TAXI TRAVEL

Taxis are plentiful, cheap, and easy to spot. Your hotel concierge can call for one by phone or you can hail one on the street. The available ones have a small lighted sign on the passenger side. If you're choosing a cab from a line, peek at the driver's license on the dashboard. The lower the license number, the more experienced the driver. Drivers with a number below 200,000 can usually get you where you're going. Few speak English, so it's best to give them a piece of paper with your destination written in Chinese. (Keep a card with the name of your hotel on it handy for the return trip.) Taxis start at Y14 for the first 2.40 km; after 11 pm this jumps to Y18.

## HEALTH AND SAFETY

Tap water in Shanghai is safe for brushing teeth. However, it contains a high concentration of metals, so you should buy bottled water to drink. It is available at every corner store—look for FamilyMart, Kedi, AllDays, and Watsons—and will cost you between Y1.50 and Y3. Make sure that food has been thoroughly cooked and is served to you fresh and hot; avoid vegetables and fruits that you haven't washed (in bottled or purified water) or peeled yourself. Shanghai's polluted air can bring on, or aggravate, respiratory problems. If you're a sufferer, take the cue from locals, who wear surgical masks or a scarf or bandanna as protection. Masks can be purchased at convenience stores.

The most reliable places to buy prescription medication is the 24-hour pharmacy at the ParkwayHealth Medical Center or the Shanghai United Family Health Center. During the day, the Watson's chain is good for over-the-counter medication, but has limited selection; there are dozens of branches around over town. Chinese pharmacies offer a fuller range of over-the-counter drugs and are usually open later; look for the green cross on a white sign. Pantomiming works well for things like band-aids, ace bandages, and cough medicine, so do not feel embarrassed to use hand gestures.

There is almost no violent crime against tourists in China, partly because the penalties are severe for those who are caught—China's yearly death-sentence tolls run into the thousands. Single women can move about Shanghai with little to no hassle, though as in all major cities, handbag-snatching and pickpocketing do happen in markets and on crowded buses or trains.

Shanghai is full of people looking to make a quick buck. The most common scam involves people persuading you to go with them for a tea ceremony, which is often so pleasant that you don't smell a rat until several hundred dollars appear on your credit-card bill. "Art students" who pressure you into buying work is another common scam. Avoiding such scams is as easy as refusing *all* unsolicited services—be it from taxi or pedicab drivers, tour guides, or potential "friends." Simply put: if someone is offering you something, you don't want it. It is not considered rude to ignore them.

Shanghai traffic is as manic as it looks, and survival of the fittest (or the biggest) is the main rule. Do not be afraid to cross when the light is red, as you may not have a chance once it's green. Beware of buses, which make wide turns and regularly ignore pedestrians' rights.

## HOURS OF OPERATION

Almost all businesses close for Chinese New Year and other major holidays.

**Shops:** Stores are generally open daily 10 to 9; some stores stay open as late as 10 pm.

**Temples and Museums:** Most temples are open daily 8 to 5. Museums and most other sights are generally open 9 to 4, six days a week, with Monday being the most common closed day. Parks are usually open round the clock, and entering after dark is perfectly safe; in fact, you may be treated to the sight of a dozen seniors ballroom dancing.

**CLOSE UP**

# Tips to Unlocking the City

## NAVIGATING THE STREETS

The Huangpu River divides Shanghai into east and west sides. The metro area is huge, but the city center is a relatively small district in Puxi, west of the river. On the east side lies Pudong, which has undergone massive urbanization in the past decade. The city is loosely laid out on a grid, and most neighborhoods are easily explored on foot. Massive construction in many neighborhoods makes pavements uneven and the air dusty, but if you can put up with this, walking is the best way to really get a feel for the city and its people. Taxis are readily available and good for traveling longer distances, and the subway network covers almost all of downtown and many far-flung areas.

Major east–west roads are named for Chinese cities and divide the city into *dong* (east), *zhong* (middle), and *xi* (west) sections. North–south roads divide the city into *bei* (north) and *nan* (south) segments. The heart of the city is found on its chief east–west streets—Nanjing Lu, Huaihai Lu, and Yan'an Lu overpass.

■ TIP→ Street signs in Shanghai are written in Chinese and English, not in pinyin, the transliteration of Chinese. When asking for directions, pinyin will guide your pronunciation; for this reason we have written all our street names as Nanjing Xi Lu or Shiji Dadao, not West Nanjing Road or Century Avenue.

## NAVIGATING VOCABULARY

Below are some terms you'll see on maps and street signs and in the names of most places you'll go:

**Dong** is east, **xi** is west, **nan** is south, **bei** is north, and **zhong** means middle. **Jie** and **lu** mean street and road, respectively, **da dao** means avenue, **da** means big, and **xiao** means small.

**Qiao,** or bridge, is part of the place name at just about every entrance and exit on the ring roads.

**Men,** meaning door or gate, indicates a street that passed through an entrance in the fortification wall that surrounded the city hundreds of years ago. The entrances to parks and some other places are also referred to as *men.* For example, Xizhimen literally means Western Straight Gate.

**Banks and Offices:** Government offices are open weekdays 9 to 5, but some close for lunch between noon and 2. Most banks are open seven days a week from 9 to 6. Bank branches and CITS tour desks in hotels offer 24 hour ATMs. Many hotel currency-exchange desks stay open 24 hours.

## VISITOR INFORMATION

The best thing to hit Shanghai since an extended metro system is the Shanghai Call Centre (☎ 962288), where a host of English-speaking operators answer any question you have, help you communicate with taxi drivers, and provide restaurant, bar, and shopping recommendations. There are also a number of French-, German-, and Spanish-speaking operators. Though you'll see what appear to be information

## BEST CITY TOURS

These day tours are a nice way to unwind post-flight, and can help you get your bearings on that stressful first afternoon.

### BOAT TOURS

Huangpu River boat tours afford a great view of Pudong and the Bund, but after that it's mostly ports and cranes.

**Huangpu River Cruises.** This company launches several small boats for one-hour daytime or nighttime cruises. The company also runs a 3½-hour trip up and down the Huangpu River to Wusong, where the Huangpu meets the Yangtze. You'll see barges, bridges, and factories, but not much scenery. Tickets are Y50 to Y150. ⊠ *239 Zhongshan Dong Lu(the Bund), Huangpu* ☎ *021/6374–4461.*

**Cruises from Oriental Pearl Tower.** Forty-minute boat tours run along the Bund from the Pearl Tower's cruise dock in Pudong. Tickets are Y180 and can be purchased at the gate to the Pearl Tower. Follow the brown signs to the dock and, if you can't find it, ask a Pearl Tower staffer to help you. ⊠ *Oriental Pearl Cruise Dock, 1 Shiji Dadao(Century Avenue), Pudong* ☎ *021/5879–1888.*

### BUS TOURS

**Gray Line Tours.** Escorted half- and full-day coach tours of Shanghai as well as one-day trips to Suzhou, Hangzhou, and other nearby waterside towns are offered by Gray Line Tours. Prices range from Y350 to Y3,000. ⊠ *A19, 2F Youth Centre Plaza, 1888 Hanzhong Lu, Putuo* ☎ *021/6150–8061* ⊕ *www.grayline. com/shanghai.*

**Jinjiang Tours.** This company runs a full-day bus tour of Shanghai that includes the French Concession, People's Square, Jade Buddha Temple, Yu Garden, the Bund, and Xintiandi. Tickets cost Y580, lunch included. ⊠ *161 Changle Lu, Xuhui* ☎ *021/6415–1188* ⊕ *www.jjtravel.com.*

### HERITAGE TOURS

**Shanghai Jews.** This half-day tour, available daily in Hebrew or English, takes you to the sites of Shanghai's Jewish history, such as the 1920 Ohel Rachel Synagogue. The cost is Y400 per person. ⊕ *www.shanghai-jews.com.*

kiosks on the street, bypass these; they're staffed by well-meaning college students who rarely offer valuable information.

### ESSENTIALS

**Airport Information Hongqiao International Airport** ☎ *021/6268–8918* ⊕ *www.shanghaiairport.com.* **Pudong International Airport** ☎ *021/9608–1388* ⊕ *www.shanghaiairport.com.*

**Bike Rental Bohdi Bikes** ☎ *021/5266–9013, 139/1875–3119* ⊕ *www.bohdi. com.cn.* **Giant Bikes** ⊠ *743 Jianguo Xi Lu, Xuhui* ☎ *021/6437–5041.*

**Bus Contact Shanghai Central Long Distance Bus Station** ⊠ *1662 Zhongxing Lu, near Shanghai Railway Station, Zhabei* ☎ *021/6605–0000.*

**Consulate United States Consulate** ⊠ *American Citizen Services, Westgate Mall, 1038 West Nanjing Rd., 8th fl., Jing'an* ☎ *021/6433–6880, 021/6433–*

*3936 after-hours emergencies, 021/3217–4650 citizen services ⊕ shanghai. usembassy-china.org.cn.*

**Emergency Contacts Fire** ☎ *119.* **Police** ☎ *110, 021/6357–6666 in English.* **Shanghai Ambulance Service** ☎ *120.*

**Ferry Contacts China-Japan International Ferry Company** ✉ *908 Dong-daming Lu, Hongkou* ☎ *021/6325–7642.* **Pudong–Puxi Ferry** ✉ *Puxi dock, Jinling Lu, Huangpu* ✉ *Pudong dock, 1 Dongchang Lu, south of Binjiang Dadao, Pudong.* **Shanghai Ferry Company** ☎ *021/6537–5111, 021/5393–1185* ⊕ *www.shanghai-ferry.co.jp.*

**Medical Services Huashan Hospital** ✉ *Foreigners' Clinic, 15F, 12 Wulu-muqi Zhong Lu, Jing'an* ☎ *021/6248–9999 for 24-hour hotline.* **Parkway-Health** ✉ *Shanghai Center West Tower, 1376 Nanjing Xi Lu, Room 203, Jing'an* ☎ *021/6445–5999.* **Hongqiao Clinic** ✉ *Mandarine City, 1F, Unit 30, 788 Hon-gxu Lu, Hongqiao.* **Jinqiao Clinic** ✉ *51 Hongfeng Lu, Pudong* ☎ *021/6445–5999.* **Shanghai East International Medical Center** ✉ *150 Jimo Lu, near Pudong Da Dao, Pudong* ☎ *021/5879–9999* ⊕ *www.seimc.com.cn.* **Shanghai United Family Hospital and Clinics** ✉ *1139 Xianxia Lu, Changning* ☎ *021/5133–1900, 021/5133–1999 emergencies* ⊕ *www.unitedfamilyhospitals.com.*

**Postal Services Post Office** ✉ *276 Suzhou Bei Lu, Hongkou* ✉ *Shanghai Center, 1376 Nanjing Xi Lu, Jing'an* ✉ *133 Huaihai Lu, Xuhui* ✉ *105 Tianping Lu, Xuhui.*

**Subway Contacts Maglev Train** ☎ *021/2890–7777* ⊕ *www.smtdc.com.* **Shanghai Metro Passenger Information** ☎ *021/6318–9000* ⊕ *www.shmetro. com.*

**Train Contacts Hongqiao Railway Station** ✉ *Hongyu Elevated Road Exit, just west of Hongqiao Airport, Minhang* ☎ *021/12306.* **Shanghai Railway Station** ✉ *303 Moling Lu, Zhabei* ☎ *021/6317–9090.* **Shanghai South Railway Station** ✉ *289 Humin Lu, at Liuzhou Lu, Xuihui* ☎ *021/5436–9511.*

**Visitor Info Shanghai Tourist Information Services** ✉ *Yu Garden, 149 Jiujia-ochang Lu, Huangpu* ☎ *021/6355–5032.*

# EXPLORING SHANGHAI

Today beauty and charm coexist with kitsch and commercialism. From the colonial architecture of the Former French Concession to the forest of cranes and the neon-lit high-rises of Pudong, Shanghai is a city of paradox and change.

## OLD CITY

Tucked away in the east of Puxi are the remnants of Shanghai's Old City. Once encircled by a thick wall, a fragment of which still remains, the Old City has a sense of history among its fast disappearing old *shikumen* (stone gatehouses), temples, and markets; it wasn't until 1854 that Chinese were allowed to move out of the so-called "Chinese City" and into the foreign concessions. Delve into narrow alleyways where residents still hang their washing out on bamboo poles and chamber

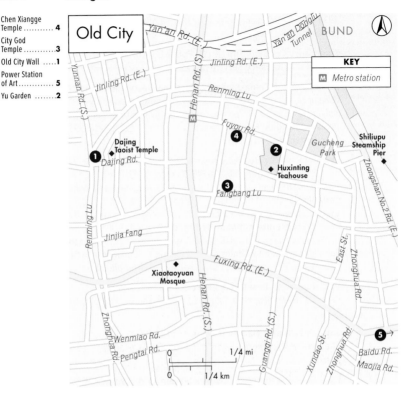

pots remain in use. Burn incense with the locals in small temples, sip tea in a teahouse, or get a taste of Chinese snacks and street food. This is the place to get a feeling for Shanghai's past, but you'd better get there soon, as the wrecker's ball knows no mercy.

**GETTING AROUND**

This area could take a very long afternoon or morning, as it's a good one to do on foot. Browsing the shops in and around the Yu Garden might add a couple of hours. Metro line 10 has a Yu Garden station, and it's walkable from Nanjing Dong Lu station on lines 2 and 10.

**EXPLORING**

**Chen Xiangge Temple** (陈向阁寺 *Chénxiànggé sì*). If you find yourself passing by this tiny temple on your exploration of the Old City, you can make an offering to Buddha with the free incense sticks that accompany your admission. Built in 1600 by the same man who built Yu Garden, it was destroyed during the Cultural Revolution and rebuilt in the 1990s. The temple is now a nunnery, and you can often hear the women's chants rising from the halls beyond the main courtyard. ⊠ *29 Chenxiangge Lu, Huangpu* ☎ *021/6320–0400* ☞ *Y5* ⊙ *Daily 7–4.*

**City God Temple** (城隍庙 *Chénghuángmiào*). At the southeast end of the Yu Gardens bazaar stands this Taoist temple, built during the early part of the Ming Dynasty and destroyed by fire in 1924. The main hall was rebuilt in 1926, and has been renovated many times over the years. Inside are gleaming gold figures, and atop the roof you'll see statues of crusading warriors—flags raised, arrows drawn. ⊠ *249 Fangbang Zhong Lu, Huangpu* ☎ *021/6386–8649* 🎟 *Y10* 🕙 *Daily 8:30–4:30.*

**Old City Wall** (上海古城墙大 *Shànghǎi gǔ chéngqiáng dà*). The Old City used to be completely surrounded by a wall, built in 1553 as a defense against Japanese pirates. Most of it was torn down in 1912, except for one 50-yard-long (40-meter-long) piece that still stands at Dajing Lu and Renmin Lu. You can walk through the remnants and check out the rather simple museum nearby, which is dedicated to the history of the Old City (signs are in Chinese). Stroll through the tiny neighboring alley of Dajing Lu for a lively panorama of crowded market life in the Old City. ⊠ *269 Dajing Lu, at Renmin Lu, Huangpu* 🎟 *Y5* 🕙 *Daily 9–4:30.*

FAMILY
Fodor's Choice
★
**Power Station of Art** (上海当代艺术博物馆 *Shànghǎi dāngdài yìshù bówùguǎn*). The site of the Shanghai World Expo was a barren wasteland until this massive contemporary art museum opened in late 2012. It did so with a bang, opening the ninth Shanghai Biennale and simultaenously hosting an exhibition from the Centre Pompidou in Paris. Rather than a permanent collection, the museum hosts one large-scale exhibition after another and is the city's new home for major touring exhibitions, like an Andy Warhol retrospective. Housed in a former power plant that's undergone serious renovation, this is a proper world-class museum with architectural cred to boot. It can be reached by a 15-minute walk from Xizang Nan Lu metro station. ⊠ *200 Huayu-angang Lu, near Miaojiang Lu, Huangpu* ☎ *021/3127–8535* 🌐 *www.powerstationofart.org/en* 🎟 *Free; special exhibits Y20.*

Fodor's Choice
★
**Yu Garden** (豫园 *Yùyuán*). Since the 18th century, this complex, with its traditional red walls and upturned tile roofs, has been a marketplace and social center where local residents gather, shop, and practice *qi gong* in the evenings. Although overrun by tourists and not as impressive as the ancient palace gardens of Beijing, Yu Garden is a piece of Shanghai's past, and one of the few old sights left in the city.

To get to the garden itself, you must wind your way through the bazaar. The garden was commissioned by the Ming Dynasty official Pan Yunduan in 1559 and built by the renowned architect Zhang Nanyang over 19 years. When it was finally finished it won international praise as "the best garden in southeastern China." In the mid-1800s, the Society of Small Swords used the garden as a gathering place for meetings. It was here that they planned their uprising with the Taiping rebels against the French colonists. The French destroyed the garden during the first Opium War, but the area was later rebuilt.

Winding walkways and corridors bring you over stone bridges and carp-filled ponds and through bamboo stands and rock gardens. Within the park are an **old opera stage,** a **museum** dedicated to the Society of Small Swords rebellion, and an **exhibition hall** of Chinese calligraphy and paintings. ⊠ *218 Anren Lu, bordered by Fuyou Lu, Jiujia-ochang Lu, Fangbang Lu, and Anren Lu, Huangpu* ☎ *021/6326–0830, 021/6328–3251* 🌐 *www.yugarden.com.cn* 🎟 *Y40* 🕙 *Daily 8:30–5.*

A nighttime view of a teahouse in Yu Garden

## XINTIANDI AND CITY CENTER

Xintiandi is Shanghai's showpiece restoration project. Reproduction *shikumen* (stone gate houses) contain expensive bars, restaurants, and chic boutiques. It's at its most magical on a warm night, when locals, expats, and visitors alike pull up a chair at one of the open-air restaurants and watch the world go by.

Another good people-watching spot is the area around People's Square, which has some magnificent examples of modern and historical architecture and a smattering of museums. The adjoining People's Park is a pleasant green space where it's possible to escape the clamor of the city for a while.

### GETTING AROUND

People's Square metro station is the point of convergence for Shanghai's metro lines 1, 2, and 8. The often-packed underground passageways can be confusing, so it's best to take the first exit and then find your way aboveground. Xintiandi can be reached by taking line 10 to the Xintiandi stop or line 1 to the Huangpi Nan Lu station, which is a block or two north of Xintiandi.

The sights in this area are divided into two neat clusters—those around People's Square and those

### DRAGON BOAT DAY

About 2,000 years ago, a poet named Qu Yuan threw himself into the river in protest against the emperor. To commemorate him, people now race dragon boats and eat *zongzi* (sticky rice dumplings). The date of the Dragon Boat Festival varies, but is often in late May or early June.

around Xintiandi. You can easily walk between the two in 20 minutes. Visiting all the museums in the People's Square area could take a good half day. Xintiandi's sights don't take very long at all, so you could go in the afternoon, check out the museums, and then settle down for a pre-dinner drink.

### TOP ATTRACTIONS

Fodor's Choice
★ **Dongtai Lu Antiques Market** (东台路 *Dōngtái lù*). Here you'll find porcelain, jade, and anything else worth buying or selling. The same bowls and vases pop up in multiple stalls,

> ### WORD OF MOUTH
>
> "The matchmaking market at People's Park is a unique weekly event which should not be missed by tourists. The place is crowded with parents mingling with each other eagerly looking for their future son- or daughter-in-law. It is interesting to see the details of their children plastered all over a portion of People's Park."
> —curli_topz

so if your first bargaining attempt isn't successful, you'll likely have another opportunity a few stores down. The authenticity of everything is questionable, so in deciding what you'll pay, assume nothing is a true antique. ⊠ *Enter on Xizang Lu, Huangpu* ☽ *Daily 10–6.*

Fodor's Choice
★ **People's Square** (人民广场 *Rénmín guǎngchǎng*). Home of the Shanghai Museum, the city's main square has become a social and cultural center. During the day, visitors and residents stroll, fly kites, and take their children to feed the pigeons. In the evening, kids roller-skate, ballroom dancers hold group lessons, and families relax together. Weekends here are especially busy. ⊠ *Enter at Xizang Lu, Huangpu.*

Fodor's Choice
★ **Shanghai Museum** (上海博物馆 *Shànghǎi bówùguǎn*). Look past the eyesore of an exterior—this museum holds the country's premier collection of relics and artifacts. Eleven galleries exhibit Chinese artistry in all its forms: paintings, bronzes, sculpture, ceramics, calligraphy, jade, Ming and Qing dynasties furniture, coins, seals, and art by indigenous populations. Its bronze collection is one of the best in the world, and its dress and costume gallery showcases intricate handiwork from several of China's 55 ethnic minority groups. Even if you opt not to rent the audio guide, you'll find signs in English. You can relax in the museum's pleasant tearoom or head to the shop for postcards, crafts, and reproductions of the artwork. ⊠ *201 Renmin Dadao, Huangpu* ☎ *021/6372–3500* ⊕ *www.shanghaimuseum.net/en/index.jsp* ⌧ *Free, Y40 for English-language audio guide* ☽ *Daily 9–5.*

Fodor's Choice
★ **Xintiandi** (新天地 *Xīntiāndì*). By World War II, more than two-thirds of Shanghai's residents lived in a *shikumen*, or "stone gate house." Most have been razed in the name of progress, but this 8-acre collection of stone gate houses has been transformed into an upscale shopping-and-dining complex called Xintiandi, or "New Heaven on Earth." The restaurants are busy from lunch until past midnight, especially those with patios for watching the passing parade of shoppers. ⊠ *181 Taicang Lu, Bordered by Madang Lu, Zizhong Lu, and Huangpi Nan Lu, Huangpu* ☎ *021/6311–2288* ⊕ *www.xintiandi.com.*

**Shikumen Museum** (石库门博物馆 *Shí kù mén bówùguǎn*). Just off Xintiandi's main thoroughfare is the Shikumen Museum, a beautifully restored stone gate house filled with furniture and artifacts collected from others nearby. Exhibits explain the European influence on shikumen design, the history of the neighborhood's renovation, and future plans for the entire 128-acre project. ⊠ *House 25, Xintiandi North Block, 123 Xingye Lu, Huangpu* ☏ *021/6281–6408* ⊕ *www.xintiandi. com* ✉ *Y20* ⊙ *Daily 10:30–10:30*

**WORTH NOTING**

**Grand Theater** (上海大劇院 *Shànghǎi dàjùyuàn*). The spectacular front wall of glass shines as brightly as the star power in this magnificent theater. Its three stages present the best domestic and international performances. The dramatic curved roof atop a square base is meant to invoke the Chinese traditional saying, "the earth is square and the sky is round." ■TIP→ **The best time to see it is at night.** ⊠ *300 Renmin Dadao, Huangpu* ☏ *021/6386–8686* ⊕ *www.shgtheatre.com.*

**Park Hotel** (国际饭店 *Guójì fàndiàn*). This Art Deco structure overlooking People's Park was once the tallest hotel in Shanghai. Completed in 1934, it was known for its luxurious rooms, fabulous nightclub, and chic restaurants. Today the lobby is the most vivid reminder of its glorious past. It was an early inspiration for architect I.M. Pei (creator of the glass pyramids at the Louvre). ⊠ *170 Nanjing Xi Lu, Huangpu* ☏ *021/6327–5225.*

**People's Park** (人民公园 *rénmín gōngyuán*). In colonial days this park was the northern half of the city's racetrack. Today the 30 acres of flower beds, lotus ponds, and trees are crisscrossed by a large number of paved paths. It's also home to the **Museum of Contemporary Art.** ⊠ *231 Nanjing Xi Lu, Huangpu* ☏ *021/6327–1333* ✉ *Free.*

**Shanghai Urban Planning Center** (上海城市规划中心 *Shànghǎi chéngshí guīhuà*). To understand the true scale of Shanghai and its ongoing building boom, visit the Master Plan Hall of this museum. Sprawled out on the third floor is a 6,400-square-foot planning model of Shanghai—the largest of its kind in the world—showing the metropolis as city planners expect it to look in 2020. You'll find familiar existing landmarks like the Pearl Tower and Shanghai Center as well as a detailed model of the Shanghai Expo, complete with miniature pavilions. ⊠ *100 Renmin Dadao(People's Avenue), Huangpu* ☏ *021/6372–2077* ⊕ *www.supec. org* ✉ *Y30* ⊙ *Mon.–Thurs. 9–5, Fri.–Sun. 9–6, last ticket sold 1 hr before closing.*

**Site of the First National Congress of the Communist Party** (共产党第一次全国代表大会 *Gòngchǎndǎng dì yī cì quánguó dàibiǎo dàhuì*). The secret meeting on July 31, 1921 that marked the first National Congress was held at the Bo Wen Girls' School, where 13 delegates from Marxist, Communist, and Socialist groups gathered from around the country. The upstairs of this restored shikumen is a well-curated museum detailing the rise of communism in China. Downstairs lies the very room where the first delegates worked. It remains frozen in time, the table set with matches and teacups. Ironically, the site today is surrounded by Xintiandi, Shanghai's center of capitalist conspicuous consumption. ⊠ *374 Huangpi Nan Lu, Huangpu* ☏ *021/5383–2171* ✉ *Free, audio tour Y10* ⊙ *Daily 9–4.*

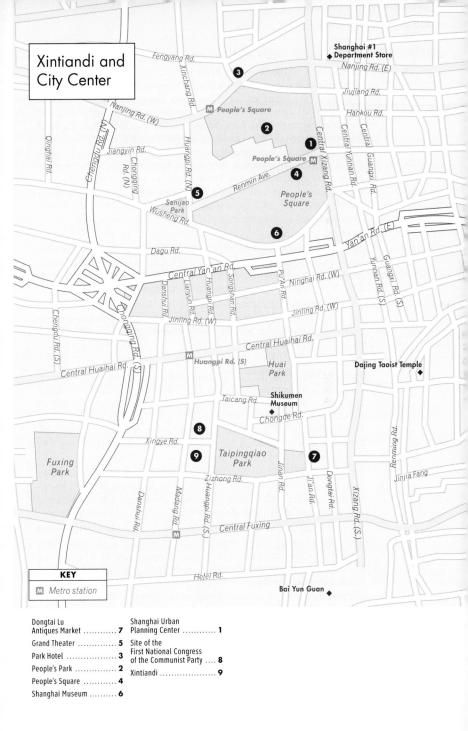

# Xintiandi and City Center

**KEY**

Ⓜ Metro station

Dongtai Lu Antiques Market ........... 7

Grand Theater .............. 5

Park Hotel .................. 3

People's Park .............. 2

People's Square ........... 4

Shanghai Museum .......... 6

Shanghai Urban Planning Center ............ 1

Site of the First National Congress of the Communist Party .... 8

Xintiandi ................... 9

## THE BUND AND NANJING DONG LU

On the bank of the Huangpu River is the Bund, Shanghai's most recognizable sightseeing spot, lined with massive foreign buildings that predate 1949. Some of these buildings have been developed into hip "lifestyle" complexes with spas, restaurants, bars, galleries, and designer boutiques. The Bund is also an ideal spot for that photo of Pudong's famous skyline. Leading away from the Bund, pedestrian-only Nanjing Dong Lu is returning to being the stylish street it once was, and it's a popular shopping spot for locals who flock to massive the outposts of American chains. Some of the adjacent streets still have a faded glamour, and some—lined with shops selling hardware or those bicycle parts—are great for a peek at local life. The best time to visit Nanjing Dong Lu is at night.

### GETTING AROUND

The simplest way to get here is to take metro Line 2 or 10 to Nanjing Dong Lu station, and then head east for the Bund or west for the main shopping area of Nanjing Dong Lu. Alternatively, you can take Line 1, 2, or 8 to People's Square station and walk east for about 30 minutes.

### SAFETY AND PRECAUTIONS

As in any tourist area, there are pickpockets. Not so much a safety issue as an annoyance are the "art students" who press you to buy their overpriced work.

### EXPLORING

**Bank of China** (中国银行 *Zhōngguó yínháng*). British Art Deco and Chinese elements combine in this 1937 building, which was designed to be the tallest in the city. However, opium magnate Victor Sassoon insisted that no building surpass his Cathay Hotel (now the Peace Hotel). Were it not for the Cathay Hotel's copper-faced pyramid roof, the bank would indeed be taller. ⊠ *23 Zhongshan Dong Yi Lu, The Bund* ☏ *021/6329–1979.*

Fodor's Choice  ★ **The Bund** (外滩 *Wàitān*). Shanghai's waterfront boulevard best shows both the city's pre-1949 past and its focus on the future. Both the northern and southern ends of Bund are constantly changing, with hotels and restaurants popping up amid scooter repair shops and hardware stores.

On the riverfront side of the Bund, Shanghai's street life is in full force. The city has rebuilt the promenade, making it an ideal gathering place for both tourists and residents. In the morning, just after dawn, the Bund is full of people ballroom dancing, doing aerobics, and practicing kung fu, qi gong, and tai chi. The rest of the day, people walk the embankment, snapping photos of the Oriental Pearl Tower, the Huangpu River, and each other. In the evenings, lovers come out for romantic walks amid the floodlit buildings and tower. ▪TIP➔ Be prepared for the aggressive souvenir hawkers; while you can't completely avoid them, just ignore them. ⊠ *Zhongshan Dong Yi Lu, between Jinling Lu and Suzhou Creek, Huangpu.*

**Former Hong Kong and Shanghai Bank Building** (浦东发展银行 *Pǔdōng fāzhǎn yínháng*). When this beautiful neoclassical structure was built by the British in 1923, it was the second-largest bank building in the world.

One of the many cafés on the Bund overlooking Pudong

After the building was turned into offices for the Communist Party in 1949, the beautiful 1920s Italian-tile mosaic in the building's dome was deemed too extravagant and covered by white paint. Ironically enough, this protected it from being destroyd by the Red Guards during the Cultural Revolution. The mural was then forgotten until 1997, when the Pudong Development Bank renovated the building. If you walk in and look up, you'll see the circular mosaic in the dome—an outer circle portraying the cities where the bank had branches at the time: London, Paris, New York, Bangkok, Tokyo, Calcutta, Hong Kong, and Shanghai; a middle circle made up of the 12 signs of the zodiac; and the center painted with a large sun and Ceres, the Roman goddess of abundance. ⊠ *12 Zhongshan Dong Yi Lu, Huangpu* ☎ *021/6161–6188* ⌁ *Free* ☉ *Weekdays 9–5:30, weekends 9–5.*

**Peace Hotel** (和平饭店 *Hépíng fàndiàn*). This hotel at the corner of the Bund and Nanjing Dong Lu is among Shanghai's most treasured buildings. If any establishment will give you a sense of Shanghai's past, it's this one. Its high ceilings, ornate woodwork, and streamlined fixtures are still intact. Following a renovation in 2010, the jazz bar, tea lounge, restaurant, shopping arcade, and ballroom have all been restored to their original glory, evoking old Shanghai cabarets and gala parties.

The south building, formerly the Palace Hotel, was built in 1906. The north building, once the Cathay Hotel, built in 1929, is more famous. It was known as the private playroom of its owner, Victor Sassoon, a wealthy landowner who invested in the opium trade. Sassoon lived and entertained his guests in the copper penthouse. The hotel was rated on a par with the likes of Raffles in Singapore and the Peninsula in Hong

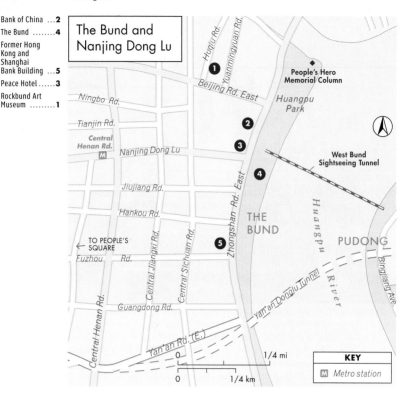

The Bund and Nanjing Dong Lu

Kong. It was *the* place to stay in old Shanghai; Noël Coward wrote *Private Lives* here. ✉ *20 Nanjing Dong Lu, Huangpu.*

FAMILY **Rockbund Art Museum** (上海外滩美术馆 *Shànghǎi wàitān měishù* Fodor's Choice *guǎn*). The detailing on this 1932 Art Deco building is as enticing as ★ the artwork inside. Rockbund has no permanent collection, which keeps things exciting. Exhibits come from both Chinese and international artists, and some include interactive elements. Lectures and film screenings are well worth the trip; many are in English, and some are family friendly. The cherry on the sundae is the museum's roof deck. ✉ *20 Huqiu Lu, just off Beijing Dong Lu, Hongkou* ☏ *021/3310–9985* ⊕ *www.rockbundartmuseum.org* 🎫 *Y15* ⊙ *Tues.–Sun. 10–6.*

## FORMER FRENCH CONCESSION

With its tree-lined streets and crumbling old villas, the Former French Concession is Shanghai's most visitor-friendly area, with ample shade and sidewalks meant to be pounded. It's a wonderful place to go wandering and make serendipitous discoveries of stately architecture, groovy boutiques and galleries, or cozy cafés. Much of Shanghai's past beauty remains, although many of the old buildings are in desperate state of disrepair. One of the major roads through this area, Huaihai Lu, is a popular shopping location, with all the big foreign chains and an

## A BRIEF HISTORY

The district's name is derived from the Anglo-Indian, and literally means "muddy embankment." In the early 1920s, the Bund became the city's foreign street: Americans, British, Japanese, French, Russians, Germans, and other Europeans built banks, trading houses, clubs, consulates, and hotels in styles from neoclassical to Art Deco.

As Shanghai grew to be a bustling trading center in the Yangtze Delta, the Bund's warehouses and ports became the heart of the action. With the Communist victory, the foreigners left Shanghai, and the Chinese government moved its own banks and offices here.

assortment of local brands. Julu Lu, Fumin Lu, Fuxing Xi Lu, Yongfu Lu, and Yongkang Lu are where many of Shanghai's restaurants, bars, and clubs are located, so if you are looking for an evening out, head to this area.

**GETTING AROUND**

This is a lovely area to walk around, so it's best to leave cabs behind and go on foot. The only site that is at a distance is Soong Qingling's Former Residence, which is a bit farther down Huaihai Lu. Access it via metro Line 1 at Hengshan Lu if you don't want to walk. Any of the three line 1 metro stops (Shaanxi Nan Lu, Changshu Lu, or Hengshan Lu) will land you somewhere in the French Concession area. Line 7 also connects at Changshu Lu.

**EXPLORING**

**Cathay Theatre** (国泰电影院 *Guótài diànyǐngyuàn*). The Art Deco–style Cathay Cinema was one of the first movie theaters in Shanghai. The building still serves as a theater, showing a mix of Chinese and Western films. The theater was a favorite of Shanghainese author Eileen Chang, of *Lust, Caution* fame. ⊠ *870 Huaihai Zhong Lu, at Maoming Nan Lu, Xuhui* ☎ *021/5404–0415* ⊕ *www.guotaifilm.com.*

**Former Residence of Dr. Sun Yat-sen** (故居的孫逸仙 *Gùjū de sūnyìxian*). Sun Yat-sen, the father of the Republic of China, lived in this two-story house for five years, from 1919 to 1924. His wife, Soong Qingling, continued to live here until 1937. Today it's been turned into a museum, and tours are conducted in Chinese and English. ⊠ *7 Xiangshan Lu, Xuihui* ☎ *021/6437–2954* ⊠ *Y8* ☺ *Daily 9–4:30.*

**Fuxing Park** (复兴公园 *Fùxīng gōngyuán*). This European-style park, once open only to Shanghai's French residents, is one of the city's most tranquil spots. Here you'll find people strolling hand and hand, practicing tai chi, and playing cards and mah-jongg. The open spaces double as dance floors, with elderly couples dancing away the day. Tourists are welcome to join in. ⊠ *105 Fuxing Zhong Lu, enter on Sinan Lu, Xuhui* ☎ *021/5386–1069* ⊠ *Free* ☺ *Daily 6–6.*

**Lyceum Theatre** (兰新大戏院 *Lánxīn dàxìyuàn*). In the days of Old Shanghai, the Lyceum Theatre was the home of the British Amateur

**DID YOU KNOW?**

On one short stretch of the famous Bund, there are 52 buildings in architectural styles, including Romanesque, Gothic, Renaissance, Baroque, Neo-classical, Beaux-Arts, and, of course, Art Deco. In fact, Shanghai features some of the finest Art Deco architecture in the world.

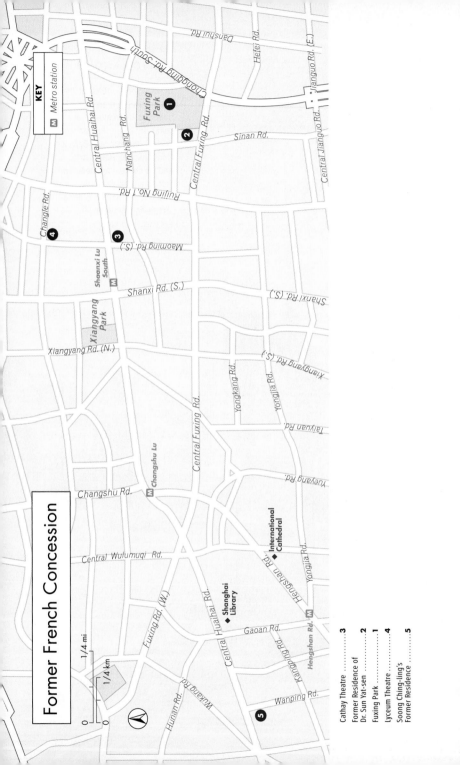

Former French Concession

KEY
Ⓜ Metro station

Cathay Theatre .............**3**
Former Residence of
Dr. Sun Yat-sen .............**2**
Fuxing Park .............**1**
Lyceum Theatre .............**4**
Soong Ching-ling's
Former Residence .............**5**

Drama Club. The old stage is still in use as a concert hall. ⊠ *57 Maoming Nan Lu, Xuhui* ☎ *021/6217–8530.*

**Soong Qing-ling's Former Residence** (故居的宋庆龄 *Gùjū de sòngqìnglíng*). A daughter of the prominent Soong family, Soong Qing-ling (also known as Madame Sun Yat-sen) was first a Nationalist and then a Communist. Her sister Mei-ling married Chiang Kai-shek, who was the head of the Nationalist government from 1927 to 1949. This three-story house, built in 1920 by a German ship owner, was Soong's primary residence from 1948 to 1963. It has been preserved as it was during her lifetime, and includes her 4,000 books in the study and furniture in the bedroom that her parents gave as her dowry. The small museum next door has some nice displays from Soong Qingling and Sun Yat-sen's life, including pictures from their 1915 wedding in Tokyo. ⊠ *1843 Huaihai Zhong Lu, Xuhui* ☎ *021/6437–6268* ⊕ *www.shsoong-chingling.com* ☞ *Y20* ◷ *Daily 9–4:30.*

## NANJING XI LU AND JING'AN

Shanghai's glitziest malls are on or near the main street in this area, Nanjing Xi Lu. If you're into designer threads, luxury spas, or expensive brunches, you can satisfy your spending urges and max out your credit here. For those of a more spiritual bent, Jing'an Temple, whose reconstruction is ongoing, is one of Shanghai's largest temples and stands in sharp contrast to its materialistic surroundings. The small Jing'an Park across the street is popular with couples. Behind the temple is an interesting network of back streets.

### GETTING AROUND

Sights are thin in this area, but if you like international designer labels, this is where you can work the plastic. Metro line 2 takes you to the Nanjing Xi Lu stations, and line 2 and 7 take you to **Jing'an Temple.** To wander the small streets behind Jing'an Temple, take line 7 to Changshou Lu station and walk south. If you want to take a taxi afterward, joining the line at the Shanghai Centre/Portman Ritz-Carlton is a good idea, especially when it's raining.

### EXPLORING

**Jing'an Temple** (静安寺 *Jìng'ān Sì*). Originally built about AD 300, this temple has been rebuilt and renovated numerous times. The temple's main draw is its copper Hongwu bell, cast in 1183 and weighing 3.5 tons. Much of the temple today looks very new, but it's still an interesting contrast with the surrounding skyscrapers, shopping malls, and luxury boutiques. ⊠ *1686 Nanjing Xi Lu, next to the Jing'an Si subway entrance, Jing'an* ☎ *021/6256–6366* ☞ *Y30* ◷ *Daily 7:30–5.*

**Moller Villa** (马勒别墅饭店 *Mǎ lēi biéshù*). Built by Swedish shipping magnate Eric Moller in 1936, this massive villa resembles a fairy-tale castle. It's a surprising sight when you come down from the pedestrian bridge that leads from Jing'an into the French Concession. Inside is a rather gaudy hotel. ⊠ *30 Shaanxi Nan Lu, Jing'an* ☎ *021/6247–8881* ⊕ *www.mollervilla.com.*

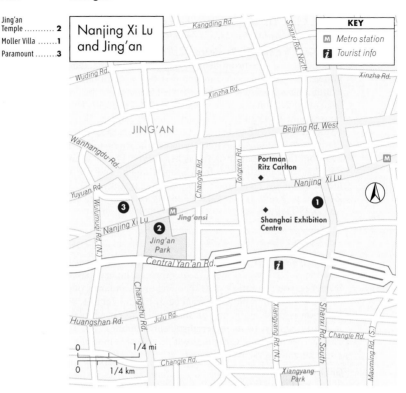

**Paramount.** Built in 1933, the Paramount was considered the finest dance hall in Asia. Until 1949, the so-called "Gate of 100 Pleasures" was the place for very late, very wild nights. You'll still find ballroom dancers here, but it's a much more chaste affair. Come nightfall, the domed roof glows blue. ⊠ *218 Yuyuan Lu, Jing'an* ☎ *021/6249–8866.*

## PUDONG

Shanghai residents used to say that it was better to have a bed in Puxi than an apartment in Pudong, but the neighborhood has come a long way in recent years. It's now a futuristic city of wide boulevards and towering skyscrapers topped by the Shanghai World Financial Center, fondly referred to as "the bottle-opener." Apartments here are some of the most expensive in Shanghai. Although a little on the bland side, it is home to expat compounds designed in a bizarre medley of architectural styles, international schools, and malls. However, there are quite a few sites here worth visiting, particularly if you have children.

### GETTING AROUND
The Bund Tourist Tunnel is a strange and rather garish way of making the journey under the Huangpu River to Pudong. You might get a few laughs from the light displays. Otherwise, you can take the metro on line 2 to Lujiazui, or catch the ferry from the Bund.

Outside of the Lujiazui metro stop and Century Park, Pudong is not a pedestrian-friendly area, as there are large, rather featureless distances between the sights. You can either take the metro to get around or jump in a cab. If you visit all the sights, you could easily spend a day out here.

## TOP ATTRACTIONS

**Jin Mao Tower** (金茂大厦 *Jīn Mào Dàshà*). Rising 88 floors—eight being the Chinese number implying wealth and prosperity—this tower combines the classic 13-tier Buddhist pagoda design with postmodern steel and glass. It houses one of the highest hotels in the world—the Grand Hyatt Shanghai occupies the 53rd to 87th floors. The 88th-floor observation deck, reached in 45 seconds by two high-speed elevators, offers 360-degree views of the city. ∎TIP→ **Your admission ticket is good for a drink at the hotel's 87th-floor Cloud 9 bar.** ⊠ *88 Shiji Dadao, Pudong* ☎ *021/5047–0088* 🎫 *Observation deck Y100* ⊙ *Daily 8 am–10 pm.*

**Oriental Pearl Tower** (东方明珠塔 *Dōngfāng Míngzhūtǎ*). Looking like a futuristic Eiffel Tower, this was the country's tallest structure until 1997. It's especially kitschy at night when it flashes with colored lights. A museum in the base recalls Shanghai's pre-1949 history. Each with its own observation deck, the three spheres are supposed to represent pearls (as in the city's nickname, the "Pearl of the Orient"). Go to the top sphere for a 360-degree bird's-eye view of the city, or grab a drink in the tower's revolving restaurant (skip the food). ⊠ *1 Shiji Dadao, Pudong* ☎ *021/5879–1888* 🎫 *Y100–Y150* ⊙ *Daily 8 am–9:30 pm.*

**Shanghai World Financial Center** (上海环球金融中心 *Shànghǎi huánqiú jīnróng zhōngxīn*). China's tallest building, the "bottle opener" has three observation decks, the highest of which is on the 100th floor. The Park Hyatt is housed on floors 79 to 93, giving it a loftier perch than its older sibling, the neighboring Grand Hyatt. The view from up here is knockout; on a clear day, you can see far and wide; on an overcast day, you'll feel as though you're floating in the clouds. ∎TIP→ **Consider skipping the observation decks in favor of the hotel. Afternoon tea at the 87th-floor Living Room is a treat.** ⊠ *100 Shiji Dadao, Pudong* ☎ *021/5878–0101* ⊕ *www.swfc-observatory.com* 🎫 *Y120–Y150* ⊙ *Daily 8 am–11 pm.*

## WORTH NOTING

FAMILY **Century Park** (世纪公园 *Shìjì gōngyuán*). This giant swath of green is a great place to take kids, as it has a variety of bicycles for hire, good flat paths for rollerblading, and pleasure boats. On a fine day, pack a lunch and head to the designated picnic areas, fly a kite in the open areas, or take a walk among the trees. ⊠ *Huamu Lu, near Fangdian Lu, Pudong* ☎ *021/3876–0588* ⊕ *www.centurypark.com.cn* 🎫 *Y10* ⊙ *Daily 7–6 pm.*

Fodor's Choice **China Art Palace** (中华艺术宫 *Zhōnghuá yìshù gōng*). Housed inside the
★ China Pavilion at the Shanghai World Expo site, this gleaming homage to contemporary art has a whopping 27 exhibition halls. Much of the work is underwhelming, but be sure to stop by the animation hall, where you can catch shorts and feature-length films from the '50s to the '90s. The touring exhibits are often a real treat; besides a huge Picasso retrospective, the museum has hosted works from New York's

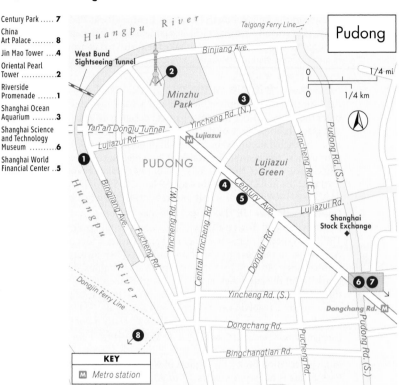

Whitney Museum, London's British Museum, and Paris's Maisons de Victor Hugo. Look for works from David Hockney, Jasper Johns, and Rodin. Reservations are required, and your hotel should be able to help. ⊠ *161 Shangnan Lu, Pudong* ☎ *021/6222–8822* ⊕ *artshow.eastday. com/zhysg* ☐ *Free* ☉ *Tues.–Sun. 9–5; last entry at 4.*

**Riverside Promenade** (滨江大道 *Bīnjiāng dàdào*). Although this park along the Huangpu River has a sterile atmosphere, it offers the most beautiful views of the Bund. As you stroll on the grass and concrete you get a perspective of Puxi unavailable from the west side. If you're here in the summer, you can "enjoy wading," as a sign indicates, in the chocolate-brown Huangpu River from the park's wave platform. ⊠ *Bingjiang Dadao, Pudong* ☐ *Free.*

FAMILY **Shanghai Ocean Aquarium** (上海海洋水族馆 *Sh̆nghǎi hǎiyáng shuǐzúguǎn*). As you stroll through the aquarium's 120-meter (394-foot) glass viewing tunnel, you may feel like you're walking your way through the seven seas—or at least five of them. The aquarium's 10,000 fish represent 300 species, five oceans, and four continents. You'll also find penguins and species representing all 12 of the Chinese zodiac symbols, such as the tiger barb, sea dragon, and seahorse. ■TIP→ To avoid crushing crowds, never, ever plan on a weekend visit. ⊠ *1388*

*Lujiazui Ring Road, Pudong* ☎ *021/5877–9988* ⊕ *www.sh-soa.com* 🎫 *Y160* ⏱ *Daily 9–6 pm.*

FAMILY **Shanghai Science and Technology Museum (上海科技馆** *Shànghǎi kējì guǎn*). This family favorite has more than 100 hands-on exhibits in its sprawling galleries. Earth Exploration takes you through fossil layers to the earth's core for a lesson in plate tectonics. Spectrum of Life introduces you to the animal and plant kingdoms in a simulated rain forest. Light of Wisdom explains basic principles of light and sound through interactive exhibits, and simulators in AV Paradise put you in a plane's cockpit and on television. Children's Technoland has a voice-activated fountain and a miniature construction site. Two IMAX theaters and a "4-D" IWERKS theater screen larger-than-life movies, though some are in Chinese. All signs are in English. ■TIP➔ **The best times to visit are weekday afternoons.** ✉ *2000 Shiji Dadao, Pudong* ☎ *021/6854–2000* ⊕ *www.sstm.org.cn* 🎫 *Y60* ⏱ *Tues.–Sun. 9–5:15.*

## NORTH SHANGHAI

Although often neglected in favor of more glamorous neighborhoods, the northern Shanghai districts of Putuo, Hongkou, and Zhabei still offer some interesting sights. Hongkou District is relatively undeveloped and unchanged, and buildings from the past are visible behind cheap clothing stores. Shanghai's old Jewish Quarter is here, too. An area with an interesting history, Hongkou has the most sights worth seeing, as well as the lush green sweep of Lu Xun Park. The old buildings and warehouses around Suzhou Creek, which feeds into the Huangpu, are slowly being turned into a hip and happening arty area, particularly the M50 development. Also in Putuo District is another one of Shanghai's main temples, the Jade Buddha Temple.

### GETTING AROUND

For the Jade Buddha Temple and M50, you can hop off the metro Line 3 or 4 at Zhongtan Lu, and then it's a short walk to M50 and a longer one to Jade Buddha. You can take line 3 to Baoxing Dong Lu and Hongkou Stadium for Lu Xun Park and Duolun Lu. The easiest way to get around is by taxi.

The galleries at M50 open later in the morning, so it may be best to head to some other sites first. Many galleries are closed on Monday. Qipu Lu gets very busy as the day goes on, and is unbearable on weekends.

### EXPLORING

**Duolun Lu (多伦文化街** *Duō lún wénhuà jiē*). Although Duolun Lu has been neatly restored, its architecture and general ambiance takes you back in time to the 1930s, when the 1-km (½-mile) lane was a favorite haunt of writer Lu Xun and fellow social activists. Bronze statues of those literary luminaries dot the lawns between the villas and row houses whose ground floors are now home to cafés, antiques shops, and art galleries. As the street takes a 90-degree turn, its architecture shifts 180 degrees with the seven-story stark gray **Shanghai Duolun Museum of Modern Art.** ✉ *Off Sichuan Bei Lu, Hongkou.*

**Jade Buddha Temple** (玉佛寺 *Yù fósì*). Completed in 1918, this temple is fairly new by Chinese standards. During the Cultural Revolution, the monks pasted portraits of Mao Zedong on the outside walls so that the Red Guards couldn't tear them down without destroying Mao's face as well. The temple is built in the style of the Song Dynasty, with symmetrical halls and courtyards, upturned eaves, and bright yellow walls. The temple's great treasure is its 2-meter (6½-foot) seated Buddha made of white jade with a robe of precious gems, originally brought to Shanghai from Burma. Frightening guardian gods of the temple populate the halls, home to a collection of Buddhist scriptures and paintings. The temple is madness at festival times. ■TIP→ There's a simple vegetarian restaurant serving inexpensive noodle dishes. ⊠ *170 Anyuan Lu, Putuo* ☎ *021/6266–3668* ⊕ *www.yufotemple.com* 🖭 *Y30* ⊙ *Daily 8–4:30.*

**M50** (莫干山路 *Mò gàn shān lù*). This cluster of art galleries and artist studios sits beside Suzhou Creek. The galleries are filled almost exclusively with work by Chinese artists, but a few, like the m97 Gallery, showcase foreign work. There are also a few shops selling music and art supplies and a couple coffee shops. Don't be shy about nosing around—occasionally artists will be up for a chat. ■TIP→ Mind the weather, as some of galleries lack heating and cooling systems. ⊠ *50 Moganshan Lu, Putuo* 🖭 *Free* ⊙ *Most galleries are closed on Mon. Opening times vary.*

**Ohel Moishe Synagogue and Huoshan Park** (摩西会堂 *Mó xī huì táng*). Built in 1927, this synagogue, the spiritual center of Shanghai's Jewish ghetto in the '30s and '40s, now houses the Jewish Refugee Memorial Hall of Shanghai. More than 20,000 Central European refugees fled to Shanghai during World War II, and the museum has a good selection of photos and newspaper clippings. Around the corner is Huoshan Park, where a memorial tablet erected in honor of Israeli prime minister Yitzhak Rabin's 1993 visit. ⊠ *62 Changyang Lu, Hongkou* ☎ *021/6541–5008* 🖭 *Y50* ⊙ *Mon.–Sat. 9–5.*

**Shanghai Duolun Museum of Modern Art** (上海多伦现代美术馆 *Shànghǎi duō lún xiàndài měishù guǎn*). Covering more than 14,400 square feet, Shanghai's first state-owned modern art gallery wraps around a metal spiral staircase that's a work of art in itself. The frequently changing exhibits are cutting-edge for Shanghai. They've showcased electronic art from American artists, examined gender issues among the Chinese people, and featured musical performances ranging from Chinese electronica to the *dombra*, a traditional Kazak stringed instrument. A tiny shop sells art books. ⊠ *27 Duolun Lu, Hongkou* ☎ *021/6587–2530* 🖭 *Y20* ⊙ *Sun.–Tues. 10–5.*

## XUJIAHUI AND SOUTH, HONGQIAO AND GUBEI

Buyers throng the large malls in the shopping precinct at Xujiahui, which shines with neon and giant billboards. To the west are the districts of Hongqiao and Gubei, where expats live in high-walled compounds and drive huge SUVs. If you're feeling homesick, a visit to Hongmei Lu and its string of Western restaurants will do the trick.

**DID YOU KNOW?**

Different Buddhist sects wear different colors, and there are many theories on the significance of color. This is one of our favorites: Buddhist monks and nuns wear yellow because when one looks at a tree, it's easy to tell which leaves will fall based on the yellow, orange, or brown color. Yellow is a constant reminder of the importance of letting go.

**North Shanghai**

### GETTING AROUND

Metro line 1 takes you right into the depths of the Grand Gateway Mall at Xujiahui. The other sights are fairly far-flung, so a taxi is a good idea. If you are going to places like the Shanghai Botanical Gardens, be prepared for a hefty fare. Otherwise, you can get off at Shanghai South Railway Station.

### EXPLORING

**Longhua Martyrs Cemetery** (龙华烈士陵园 *Lónghuá lièshì língyuán*). It may seem tranquil now, but Longhua Martyrs Cemetery has had a bloody history. It has been the execution site of many Communists, particularly during the Guomingdang crackdown in 1927. Nowadays, it's full of large Soviet-style sculpture and immaculate lawns. The most chilling is the small, unkempt, grassy execution area accessed by a tunnel. In the 1950s, the remains of murdered Communists were found here still wearing leg irons. ⊠ *180 Longhua Lu, Xuihui* ☎ *021/6468–5995* ⊕ *www.slmmm.cn* ☞ *Park Y1, museum Y5* ⊗ *Daily 6–5; museum 9–3:30.*

**Longhua Temple** (龙华寺 *Lónghúa Sì*). Shanghai's largest and most active temple has as its centerpiece a seven-story, eight-sided pagoda. While the temple, which made a cameo in Spielberg's *Empire of the Sun*, is thought to have been built in the 3rd century, the pagoda dates from the

## TEE OFF

Some 20 golf clubs dot the countryside within two hours of downtown Shanghai. Some run buses, so call to inquire; some are on metro lines, and others suggest that you take a taxi. All run on a membership basis, but most allow nonmembers to play when accompanied by a member.

**Grand Shanghai International Golf and Country Club.** This club has a Ronald Fream–designed 18-hole championship course and driving range. ⊠ *18 Yangcheng Zhonglu, Yangcheng Lake Holiday Zone, Kunshan City* ☎ *0512/5789-1999* ⊕ *www.grandshanghaigolf. com.cn.*

**Shanghai Binhai Golf Club.** Peter Thomson designed the Scottish links–style, 54-hole course at this club far out in Pudong. ⊠ *Binhai Resort, Baiyulan Dadao, Nanhui County* ☎ *021/3800-1888 reservation hotline* ⊕ *www.binhaigolf.com.*

**Shanghai International Golf and Country Club.** This 18-hole course designed by Robert Trent Jones Jr. is Shanghai's most difficult. There are water hazards at almost every hole. ⊠ *961 Yinzhu Lu, Zhujiajiao, Qingpu District* ☎ *021/5972-8111.*

**Shanghai Links Golf and Country Club.** This Jack Nicklaus–designed 18-hole course is about a 45-minute drive east of downtown. ⊠ *1600 Lingbai Lu, Tianxu Township, Pudong* ☎ *021/5897-3068* ⊕ *www. shanghailinks.com.cn.*

**Shanghai Silport Golf Club.** This 27-hole course on Dianshan Lake was designed by Bobby J. Martin. ⊠ *1 Xubao Lu, Dianshan Lake Town, Kunshan City* ☎ *0512/5748-1111* ⊕ *www.silport.com.cn.*

**Shanghai Sun Island International Club.** You'll find a 27-hole course designed by Nelson & Haworth at the Shanghai Sun Island International Club, as well as an excellent driving range. ⊠ *2588 Shantai Lu, Zhu Jia Jiao, Qingpu District* ☎ *021/6983-3001* ⊕ *www. sunislandclub.com.*

**Tianma Country Club.** Tianma is the most accessible course to the public. Its 18 holes have views of Sheshan, a 328-foot-tall hill atop which sits an observatory and a basilica. ⊠ *3958 Zhaokun Lu, Songjiang District* ☎ *021/5766-1666* ⊕ *www.tianmacc.com.*

10th century; it's not open to visitors. Near the front entrance stands a three-story bell tower, where a 3.3-ton bronze bell is rung at midnight every Lunar New Year's Eve. Along the side corridors you'll find a room filled seven rows deep with small golden statues. The third hall is the most impressive. Its three giant Buddhas sit beneath a swirled red and gold dome. ⊠ *2853 Longhua Lu, Xuhui* ☎ *021/6456–6085, 021/6457–6327* 🖃 *Y10* ⏱ *Daily 7–4:30.*

# WHERE TO EAT

You'll notice that most Chinese restaurants in Shanghai have large, round tables. The reason becomes clear the first time you eat a late dinner at a local restaurant and are surrounded by jovial, laughing

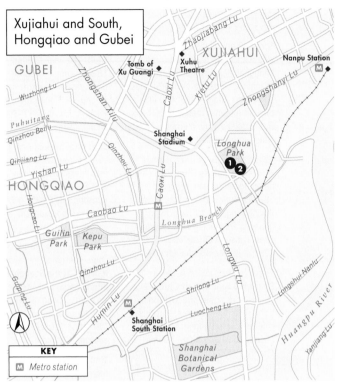

Longhua Martyrs Cemetery ........**1**

Longhua Temple ...........**2**

Xujiahui and South, Hongqiao and Gubei

**KEY**

Ⓜ Metro station

groups of people toasting and topping off from communal bottles of beer, sharing cigarettes, and spinning the lazy Susan loaded with food. Whether feting guests or demonstrating their wealth, hosts will order massive, showy spreads.

Shanghai's standing as China's most international city is reflected in its dining scene. You can enjoy *jiaozi* (dumplings) for breakfast, foie gras for lunch, and Korean beef for dinner. It's traditional to order several dishes to share among your party. Tipping is not expected, but sophistication comes at a price. Although you can eat at Chinese restaurants for less than Y30 per person, Western meals go for Western prices.

Most restaurants in Shanghai offer set lunches—multicourse feasts—at a fraction of the dinner price. Also, check out the dining section of *City Weekend, That's Shanghai, Time Out Shanghai,* or Smartshanghai.com, all of which list dining discounts and promotions around town.

*Prices in the reviews are the average cost of a main course at dinner or, if dinner is not served, at lunch. Use the coordinate (✛ B2) at the end of each listing to locate a site on the Where to Eat in Shanghai map.*

**ON THE MENU**

Shanghainese food is fairly typical Chinese, with dark, sweet, and oily dishes served in great abundance. The plates can be quite small—it's not unusual for two diners to polish off six different dishes. The drink of choice is *huangjiu,* or yellow wine. It's a mild-tasting sweetish rice wine that pairs well with the local cuisine.

Sometimes the finest dining experience in the city can be had with a steamer tray of *xiaolongbao*—Shanghai's signature dumplings, which are small steamed buns filled with pork and crab meat in broth. They're best eaten by poking a hole in the top with a chopstick—watch out, they're hot!—and sucking out the innards. Match dumplings with a cold beer. River fish is often the highlight (and most expensive part) of the meal, and hairy crab is a seasonal delicacy.

### MEAL TIMES

Dinner hours in restaurants begin at around 5 pm, but often carry on late into the night. Many of the classic restaurants popular with the Shanghainese only close after the last diners have left, which sometimes keeps them open until the wee hours of the morning. Generally, though, dinner is eaten between 6 and 11 pm.

### PRICES

Even in the fanciest restaurants, main courses are unlikely to cost more than US$50. However, famous restaurants charge as much as the international market will bear—prices that often don't reflect the quality of the dining experience. If you're looking for an excellent meal and you don't care about the restaurateur's name, then exceptional dining experiences can be had for half the price.

Great local food can be found for supremely cheap prices (starting at 20 cents per dish), both on the street and in sit-down restaurants. The experience of eating at a small, unknown restaurant is pure China.



## OLD CITY

Narrow and crowded, the Old City is all that's left of Old China in Shanghai. The area is home to the impressive Yu Garden, and is a good place to find traditional food in an authentic environment. Adventurous diners should explore the side streets around Fangbang Lu in search of authentic Chinese snacks. **TIP→ At this neighborhood's eateries, always inquire about the price first—with no English menu, many sellers aren't above raising the price after your first bite. To do so, ask "duo shao tian?"**

$$ TAIWANESE FAMILY 🍴 **Din Tai Fung** (鼎泰豐 *Dǐng tài fēng*). The delicate, impeccably folded *xiaolongbao* (soup dumplings) are the star attraction at Din Tai Fung, and the pork and black truffle version is especially delectable. The atmosphere at this Taiwanese chain is far less chaotic than at its neighbors in and around Yu Garden, and it also has better food. The service is very good, especially for those with children; the staff will fawn over your offspring and immediately bring over a high chair and kid-sized tableware. [$] *Average main: Y100* ✉ *168 Fangbang Zhong Lu, Huangpu* ☎ *021/6334–1008* ✥ *F3.*

$$ CHINESE 🍴 **Lv Bo Lang** (绿波廊 *Lǜ bō láng*). A popular stop for visiting dignitaries, Lv Bo Lang is a perfect photo op of a restaurant. The traditional three-story Chinese pavilion with upturned eaves sits next to the Bridge of Nine Turnings in Yu Garden. The food is good but not great, with

many expensive fish choices on the menu. Among the best dishes are the crab meat with bean curd, the braised eggplant with chili sauce, and the sweet *osmanthus* cake, made with the sweetly fragrant flower of the same name. $ *Average main: Y150* ⊠ *115 Yuyuan Lu, Huangpu* ☎ *021/6328–0602* ⌕ *Reservations essential* ✛ *F3.*

## XINTIANDI AND CITY CENTER

$$$

EUROPEAN

✕ **The 5 Tables Bistro** (5桌餐厅 *5 Zhuō cāntīng*). This restaurant is diminutive in size but packs in plenty of personality. The friendly Singaporean owner is the sole waiter, yet no water glass goes unfilled; the service here puts fully staffed restaurants to shame. The menu is just one sheet of paper and on offer are one soup, one starter, a few mains, and two desserts. Dishes change frequently, so one week, if you're lucky, you'll be slurping up bacon potato soup; another will find you tucking eagerly into seared scallops paired with caper sauce and a vegetable puree. $ *Average main: Y150* ⊠ *210 Danshui Lu, Huangpu* ☎ *021/3304–1205* ⌕ *Reservations essential* ✛ *D4.*

$

CHINESE

FAMILY

✕ **Jia Jia Tang Bao** (佳家汤包 *Jiā jiā tāng bāo*). It would be a shame to leave Shanghai without trying *xiaolongbao* (soup dumplings), and locals flock here in droves for what are said to be the best in town. They are the only thing on the menu, and once the kitchen runs out the restaurant shuts down for the day. It's a proper local hole-in-the-wall, with orange plastic chairs and grimy tabletops and floors, but eating here is an authentic and delicious experience not to be missed. $ *Average main: Y20* ⊠ *90 Huanghe Lu, Huangpu* ☎ *021/6327–6878* ⊟ *No credit cards* ✛ *E3.*

$$

AMERICAN

✕ **Kabb.** Serving burgers, salads, and other standard American fare, this café in Xintiandi is best known for its outdoor seating. The food is good but without distinction, though the portions are massive. The service is slightly indifferent, and the prices are rather high. However, it does fill the bill for lunch in the sun. $ *Average main: Y85* ⊠ *Xintiandi, 181 Taicang Lu, Huangpu* ☎ *021/3307–0798* ✛ *D3.*

$$$

INTERNATIONAL

Fodor'sChoice

★

✕ **T8** (T 八 *T bā*). A veteran of the Shanghai fine dining scene, T8 has garnered its share of headlines for its impressive interior and inspired contemporary cuisine. The restaurant occupies a traditional shikumen house in Xintiandi and has modernized the space with raw stone floors, carved-wood screens, and imaginative lighting that transforms shelves full of glasses into a modern-art sculpture. The kitchen turns out exciting fusion dishes from fresh seasonal ingredients, so the menu changes with the seasons. $ *Average main: Y250* ⊠ *Xintiandi, 181 Taicang Lu, Huangpu* ☎ *021/6355–8999* ⊕ *www.t8shanghai.com* ⌕ *Reservations essential* ✛ *D4.*

$$

JAPANESE

✕ **Tairyo.** At Y200 for all you can eat and drink, the appeal of this Japanese barbecue restaurant is obvious. Just walk in, take a seat at the grill, and indulge while the chef prepares your dinner as you watch. We recommend the Mongolian beef, but feel free to pick and choose from the English menu. There's sushi and sashimi for those who abstain from beef. $ *Average main: Y200* ⊠ *15 Dongping Lu, Luwan* ☎ *021/6445–4734.* ✛ *A4*

Cheap snacks can be found on the streets around the Old City.

**$$$**
CANTONESE
✕**Wan Hao** (万豪 *Wànháo*). Overlooking People's Square, this elegant restaurant on the 38th floor of the JW Marriott Shanghai at Tomorrow Square specializes in Cantonese dishes, though the menu contains other popular options like Peking duck. The food is good without being exceptional, and the ambience is pleasant. Look to the seasonal dishes for the freshest options; the chef is always updating the menu. Servings tend to be on the small side—Chinese-style—despite the Western place settings, so expect to order several dishes per person. If you're unsure about your order, the staff is happy to help. $ *Average main: Y250* ✉ *JW Marriott Shanghai at Tomorrow Square, 399 Nanjing Xi Lu, 38th fl., Luwan* ☎ *021/5359–4969* ⊕ *www.marriott.com* ✛ *D2.*

**$**
SICHUAN
Fodor'sChoice
★
✕**Yu Xin Chuan Cai** (渝信川菜 *Yú xìn chuāncài*). This place offers fantastic Sichuan food that is extremely popular with the locals. Try the tea-smoked duck, and whatever you order, be sure to get rice, too. Book ahead, or be prepared to wait around 30 to 60 minutes for a table. $ *Average main: Y90* ✉ *333 Chengdu Bei Lu, 3rd fl., Huangpu* ☎ *021/5298–0438, 021/5298–0439* ⌾ *Reservations essential* ▭ *No credit cards* ✛ *D3.*

## NANJING DONG LU AND THE BUND

The Bund is the heart of modern Shanghai, with the colonial history of Puxi facing the towering steel and glass of Pudong. The stellar view of the river and Pudong has attracted some of the finest restaurant development in town. The Bund has been expanding to the south, with the opening of a handful of restaurants. Bund-side eateries are, on the

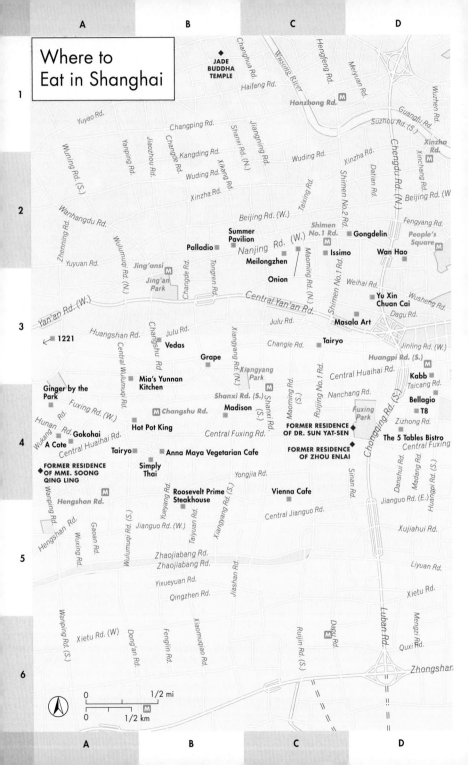

# Where to Eat in Shanghai

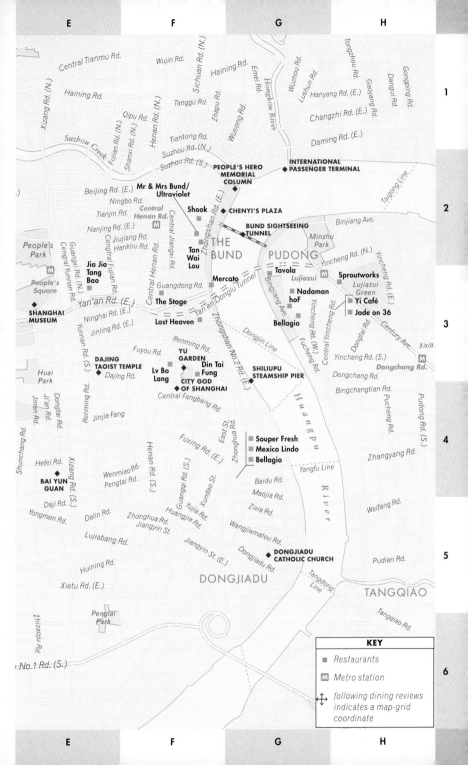

KEY

■ Restaurants

Ⓜ Metro station

↔ following dining reviews indicates a map-grid coordinate

Xintiandi is a great place to hang out and watch the crowds pass by.

whole, expensive; we've listed places where you're paying not just for the view.

$ VEGETARIAN Fodor's Choice ★ 🍴 **Gongdelin.** A two-story engraving of a golden Buddha pays tribute to the origins of the inventive vegetarian dishes this restaurant has served since 1922. The chefs transform tofu into such surprising and tasty creations as mock duck, eel, and pork. The interior is just as inspired, with Ming-style wood-and-marble tables, metal latticework, and a soothing fountain. The tables fill up quickly, so either arrive before 6 pm or buy some goodies to go at the take-out counter. There's another branch on 97 Wukang Lu in Xuhui. [$] *Average main: Y45* ✉ *445 Nanjing Xi Lu, Huangpu* ☎ *021/6327–0218.* ✥ *D2*

$$$ ITALIAN Fodor's Choice ★ 🍴 **Mercato.** Prolific restaurateur Jean Georges Vongerichten's namesake restaurant has delighted Shanghai for quite a few years now, but Mercato is a whole different animal, erring on the chic side of industrial chic. There's heavy use of iron, steel, and reclaimed wood, and the black leather and wooden chairs celebrate form and function. Chef Sandy Koon, who came from Spice Market in New York, has clearly passed her expertise on to her sous chefs. The pasta dishes are good, but the smaller plates are where the kitchen really shines: the octopus is so tender it is gobbled up in seconds, the ricotta and seasonal fruit compote reached for immediately by the entire table. [$] *Average main: Y200* ✉ *Three on the Bund, 17 Guangdong Lu, 6th fl., Huangpu* ☎ *021/6321–9922* ⏲ *No lunch* ✥ *F3.*

$$$ FRENCH 🍴 **Mr & Mrs Bund** (先生和小姐外滩的 *Xiānshēng hé xiǎojiě wàitāndé*). This is the place for a late-night bite: Shanghai-famous French chef Paul Pairet's Bund-side eatery is open until 2 am Tuesday to Thursday and

4 am Friday and Saturday. With 32 wines by the glass and inventive dishes like foie-gras crumble, a giant french fry, and lip-smacking lemon tart, you'll leave here more than satisfied. This is a popular spot for proposals. $\boxed{S}$ *Average main: Y250* ⊠ *18 Zhongshan Dong Yi Lu, 6th fl., Huangpu* ☎ *021/6323–9898* ⊕ *www.mmbund.com* ✛ *F2.*

**$$$**
ECLECTIC
✕ **Shook!** This Kuala Lumpur import is housed in the plush confines of the Swatch Art Peace Hotel.

> **WORD OF MOUTH**
>
> "Walked to JiaJia Dumpling. Unfortunately, most dumplings on the menu were sold out already before noon, but the one I wanted was still available—crab and pork. The order found its way to me and I got the most delicious, delicate dumpling I've had in my life."
> —mmyk72

The cuisine is Pan-Asian accompanied by a few Western dishes, so you might see the staff delivering to a neighboring table hand rolls and sashimi alongside a Wagyu beef burger stuffed with foie gras and served with truffle fries. The wine selection is impressive and expensive. The decor is sleek and luxurious—leather banquettes, modern lights above the bar, and a catwalk-like hallway lined in transparent wine coolers. Book early to get a window seat or take advantage of pleasant weather and while away the afternoon on the roof deck. $\boxed{S}$ *Average main: Y185* ⊠ *Swatch Art Peace Hotel, 23 Nanjing Dong Lu, 5th and 6th fls., Huangpu* ☎ *021/2329–8522* ⊕ *www.shookrestaurantshanghai. com* ✛ *F2.*

**$$$$**
ECLECTIC
FAMILY
✕ **The Stage** (舞台餐厅 *Wǔtái cān tīng*). Although lunch and dinner buffet is fairly standard stuff, this eatery is home to Shanghai's most popular Sunday champagne brunch. Costing Y538 and booked two to three weeks in advance, the meal has become an institution. Check it out if you feel the need for some decadent indulgence, as you'll feast on crab legs, charcuterie, and loads of champagne. It runs from 11:30 to 2:30. $\boxed{S}$ *Average main: Y538* ⊠ *The Westin Shanghai Bund Center, 88 Henan Zhong Lu, Huangpu* ☎ *021/6335–0577* ⊕ *www.starwoodhotels.com* ⌕ *Reservations essential* ✛ *F3.*

**$$$$**
ECLECTIC
✕ **Ultraviolet.** The location of this "experimental restaurant" by Paul Pairet (of Mr & Mrs Bund fame) is a secret. You meet at Mr & Mrs Bund and board a minibus bound for a location somewhere near Suzhou Creek. The 10-seat dining room at Ultraviolet is a world unto itself. Each course is paired with wraparound video projections, an appropriate song (The Beatles' "Ob-La-Di, Ob-La-Da," for example, when Pairet serves his take on fish-and-chips), and even customized scents. A place at the table will cost you a cool Y2,500. Bookings are accepted three months in advance, and you'll need to put down a deposit. $\boxed{S}$ *Average main: Y2500* ⊠ *Mr & Mrs Bund, 18 Zhongshan Dong Yi Lu, 6th fl., Huangpu* ☎ *021/6142–5198* ⊕ *www.uvbypp.cc/ bookings* ⌕ *Reservations essential* ⊘ *No lunch. Closed Mon.* ✛ *F2*

## FORMER FRENCH CONCESSION

**$$**
PIZZA
FAMILY
✕ **A Cote.** After opening Franck and then Le Petite Franck over the past several years, Franck Pecol has turned to pizza with A Cote, which translates as (and literally is) "next door." Pecol is very, very French,

and so is his pizza—it's not New York–style, not Neapolitan, and for that it makes no apologies. Quality ingredients are used, and the pies are fired in a wood oven that's just behind the wooden communal table. The diminutive menu offers 10 pies dressed with toppings like salty anchovies, ham, and olives. The outdoor seating fills up quickly on Shanghai's rare blue-sky days. The restaurant is at the edge of Shanghai's gay neighborhood, so it's a popular spot for those who want to fill up before going out. $ *Average main: Y85* ⊠ *376 Wukang Lu, Xuhui* ☎ *021/3368–8757* ▭ *No credit cards* ☉ *Closed Mon.* ✛ *A4*

$$ ✕ **Ginger by the Park** (金各咖啡 *Jīngé kā fēi*). Tucked away in the Former French Concession, Ginger is a café with a strong European flavor. Small and intimate, this is a place for quiet conversations over lunch or a relaxing afternoon coffee. For a rare tranquil Shanghai moment, we recommend having your drinks on the patio. Located in the triangle that forms what many Shanghai denizens refer to as the gay neighborhood, this is a welcoming spot for all. $ *Average main: Y75* ⊠ *91 Xingguo Lu, near Hunan Lu, Xuhui* ☎ *021/3406–0599* ⊕ *www.gingerfoods. com* ✛ *A4.*
CAFÉ
FAMILY

$$ ✕ **Gokohai** (钰香海 *Yùxiānghǎi*). Possibly the best Japanese hotpot restaurant in Shanghai, Gokohai gives each diner a selection of meats (served in enormous, sombrero-shaped piles) and vegetables to cook in a pot full of steaming broth. Ask for the all-you-can-eat-deal for Y88, and wash it down with an Asahi beer. Meat plays the starring role here; vegetarians will likely leave a little hungry. $ *Average main: Y88* ⊠ *1720 Huaihai Lu, near Wuxing Lu, Xuihui* ☎ *021/6471–7657* ⌂ *Reservations essential* ▭ *No credit cards* ✛ *A4.*
JAPANESE

$$ ✕ **Grape** (葡萄园 *Pútáoyuán*). This cheerful restaurant's name gives no hint of what it serves—entry-level Shanghainese food that's been a favorite for decades among expatriates and travelers wandering the Former French Concession. The English menu, complete with photos, includes such recognizable fare as sweet-and-sour pork and lemon chicken, as well as delicious dishes like garlic shrimp and *jiachang doufu* (home-style bean curd), all of which are served with a smile. $ *Average main: Y50* ⊠ *55 Xinle Lu, Xuhui* ☎ *021/5404–0486* ▭ *No credit cards* ✛ *B3.*
CHINESE

$$ ✕ **Hot Pot King.** The popular *huo guo*, or hotpot, is an at-the-table cooking method in which you simmer fresh ingredients in a broth. Hot Pot King continues to reign over the hotpot scene in Shanghai because of its extensive menu and refined setting. The most popular of the 17 broths is the yin-yang, half spicy red, half basic white pork-bone broth. Add in a mixture of seafood, meat, vegetables, and dumplings for a well-rounded pot, then dip each morsel in the sauces mixed tableside by your waiter. The minimalist white-and-gray interior has glass-enclosed booths and well-spaced tables, a nice change from the usual crowded, noisy joints. ■TIP➔ **Strict vegetarians won't find much on the menu.** $ *Average main: Y160* ⊠ *1416 Huaihai Lu, 2nd fl., Xuhui* ☎ *021/6473–6380.* ✛ *A4*
CHINESE

$$ ✕ **Lost Heaven** (话马天堂 *Huāmǎtiāntáng*). This place serves Yunnan cuisine—Southern Chinese from the borders of Myanmar and Cambodia. The well-prepared food is reminiscent of Thai cuisine, and the
YUNNAN

dining room evokes the grace of traditional Yunnan architecture. The service is acceptable, without being polished. There's another location in the middle of the Former French Concession. $ *Average main: Y100* ⊠ *17 Yan'an Dong Lu, The Bund* ☎ *021/6330–0967* ⊕ *www. lostheaven.com.cn.* $ *Average main: Y100* ⊠ *38 Gaoyou Lu, Xuhui* ☎ *086/6433–5126* ✛ *B4*

$$$
MODERN
AMERICAN
FAMILY

✕ **Madison.** After a globetrotting childhood and a stint at New York's Gramercy Tavern, Austin Hu returned to Shanghai and opened Madison. There's a heavy emphasis on carbs and butter, and every weekend the light-filled space is packed with equal parts locals and foreigners, all hungrily digging into banana-stuffed French toast. Dinner at the Nouveau American eatery is more refined, and includes such favorites as bone marrow crostini and a refreshing salad with blue cheese from Beijing. $ *Average main: Y100* ⊠ *3 Fenyang Lu, Xuhui* ☎ *021/6437–0136* ⌂ *Reservations essential* ✛ *B4.*

$
YUNNAN

✕ **Mia's Yunnan Kitchen** (香所 *Xiāng suǒ*). A wall of picture windows looks out onto leafy Anfu Lu, so you can watch passersby from this simply furnished dining room. Tuck into such homestyle dishes as pickled mashed potatoes and *ru bing* (rectangles of pan-fried goat milk cheese). Wash everything down with a Belgian beer or one of house juices. Several staff members speak English and are happy to make recommendations. $ *Average main: Y80* ⊠ *45 Anfu Lu, Xuhui* ☎ *021/5403–5266* ▭ *No credit cards* ✛ *A3.*

$$$
STEAKHOUSE
Fodor's Choice
★

✕ **Roosevelt Prime Steakhouse** (罗斯福顶级牛排馆 *Luósīfú dǐngjí niúpáiguǎn*). Located in the historic Marshall Mansion—which was built in 1920 and takes its name from one-time Secretary of State George Marshall—Roosevelt offers excellent cuts of meat in a clubby steakhouse ambience. The meat is USDA Prime, cooked to your specification in an imported stone oven. These steaks are not cheap, ranging in price from Y300 up to Y1,200, though regular main dishes are more reasonable. Try the mac and cheese with black truffles or the excellent Caesar salad. $ *Average main: Y500* ⊠ *160 Taiyuan Lu, Xuhui* ☎ *021/6433–8240* ⊕ *www.rooseveltsteakhouse.com* ☾ *No lunch* ✛ *B5.*

$$
THAI
Fodor's Choice
★

✕ **Simply Thai** (天泰餐厅 *Tiāntài cāntīng*). Unpretentious Thai fare at moderate prices has earned this restaurant a loyal expat clientele. Customers flock to the tree-shaded patio to savor such favorites as green and red curries (on the spicy side) and stir-fried rice noodles with chicken (for tamer tastes). The appetizers are all first-rate, especially the crispy spring rolls and samosas. The wine list includes a few bottles under Y200, a rarity in Shanghai. The branch in Xintiandi is a bit noisier, but features the same great food and prices. $ *Average main: Y120* ⊠ *5C Dongping Lu, Xuhui* ☎ *021/6445–9551* ⌂ *Reservations essential* ✛ *B4.*

$$
INDIAN

✕ **Vedas** (度餐厅 *Dù cāntīng*). The far-too-bright lobby belies the more flatteringly lighted Vedas, where the traditional decor is dark and comfortable. The menu focuses on northern Indian cuisine, and the handpulled naan bread, thick and succulent curries, fiery vindaloos, and house-made chutneys are excellent. Vedas is extremely popular, and always bustling. You won't have an intimate, tranquil dining experience, but do expect spectacular food and great service. $ *Average main:*

4

*Y100* ⊠ *83 Changshu Lu, 3rd fl., Xuhui* ☎ *021/6445–8100* ⊕ *www. vedascuisine.com* ⌂ *Reservations essential* ✛ *B3.*

**$$**
GERMAN
Fodor'sChoice
★

✕ **Vienna Café** (维也纳咖啡 *Weíyěnà kā fēi*). Serving up cakes, pastries, and excellent breakfasts, the Vienna Café is a Shanghai institution for those in the know. This place is definitely not trendy, nor is it trying to be anything other than an Austrian coffeehouse. With a wood-paneled main dining room and a tiny solarium, this is the perfect setting for a weekend breakfast or an afternoon coffee break. Indulge yourself with the Sachertorte, and never mind the effects on your waistline. Ⓢ *Average main: Y80* ⊠ *25 Shaoxing Lu, near Ruijin Er Lu, Xuhui* ☎ *021/6445–2131* ▭ *No credit cards* ✛ *C4.*

## NANJING XI LU AND JING'AN

**$$**
SHANGHAINESE

✕ **1221** (1221餐厅 *Yīèrèryī cāntīng*). This stylish but casual eatery is a favorite with expatriates. The streamlined dining room is very chic, its crisp white tablecloths contrasting with the warm golden walls. Shanghainese food is the mainstay, with a few Sichuan dishes thrown in for good measure. From the extensive 26-page menu (in English, pinyin, and Chinese), you can order dishes like sliced *you tiao* (fried bread sticks) with shredded beef, a whole chicken in a green-onion soy sauce, and *shaguo shizi tou* (pork meatballs). Ⓢ *Average main: Y130* ⊠ *1221 Yanan Xi Lu, Changning* ☎ *021/6213–6585, 021/6213–2441* ⌂ *Reservations essential* ✛ *A3.*

**$**
ECLECTIC

✕ **Anna Maya Vegetarian Cafe** (尔苑咖啡厅 *Ěr yuàn kāfēi tīng*). Tucked away in the Former French Concession, this quaint café has a bohemian vibe that might remind you of New York City's East Village. With comfy furniture and Wi-Fi connections, it's a good place to kick back. Snack on freshly squeezed juices, quiches, salads, and soups, as well as a great veggie burger. The vegan chocolate tofu cheesecake will satisfy even the most die-hard carnivore. Ⓢ *Average main: Y75* ⊠ *3 Taojiang Lu, Xuhui* ☎ *21/6433–4602* ✛ *B4.*

**$$**
ITALIAN

✕ **Issimo.** The Italian fare here is well prepared and plentiful (all the pasta dishes are more than enough for two), and the ambience is as exquisite as a designer boutique venue should be. The menu is small and focused on seasonal offerings, and the wine list is excellent. Lunch sets are well priced, and you'll notice plenty of business meetings taking place. Reservations are recommended. Ⓢ *Average main: Y275* ⊠ *JIA Shanghai, 931 West Nanjing Lu, 2nd fl., Jing'an* ☎ *021/3302–4997* ✛ *C2.*

**$$**
INDIAN

✕ **Masala Art** (香料艺术 *Xiāngliàoyìshù*). A stalwart of the Shanghai dining scene, Masala Art serves excellent breads, sublime curries, and delicious tandoor dishes in an understated dining area. The place wins praise for fine food at reasonable prices. Ⓢ *Average main: Y85* ⊠ *397 Dagu Lu, Jing'an* ☎ *021/6327–3571* ⌂ *Reservations essential* ✛ *D3.*

**$$$**
SHANGHAINESE
Fodor'sChoice
★

✕ **Meilongzhen** (梅龙镇 *Méilóngzhèn*). Probably Shanghai's most famous restaurant, the venerable Meilongzhen first opened its doors in 1938. The building served as headquarters for the Communist Party in the 1930s, and the traditional Chinese dining rooms retain their intricate woodwork and mahogany and marble furniture. The exhaustive menu has more than 80 seafood options, including such traditional

Hotpot can be found in almost every city in China.

Shanghainese fare as Mandarin fish; some dishes have a more Sichuan flair, like shredded spicy eel and prawns in chili sauce. Since this is a stop for many tour buses, expect a wait if you haven't booked ahead. $ *Average main: Y150 ⊠ 1081 Nanjing Xi Lu, Jing'an ☎ 021/6253–5353 ⌛ Reservations essential ✛ C2.*

$ ✕ **Onion** (洋葱餐厅 *Yángcōng cāntīng*). On a bustling section of Nan-
CANTONESE jing Xi Lu, the Onion is a simple Cantonese restaurant serving quality Cantonese dishes at reasonable prices. The decor is light and airy, with well-spaced tables and efficient service. This is a very low-stress restau-rant, and a great destination for a simple and satisfying meal. The menu is extensive, and there are also lunch specials and dim sum. $ *Average main: Y60 ⊠ 881 Nanjing Xi Lu, 3rd fl., Jing'an ☎ 021/6267–5477 ▭ No credit cards ✛ C2.*

$$$$ ✕ **Palladio** (帕兰朵 *Pàlánduǒ*). As befits any restaurant operating
ITALIAN under the Ritz-Carlton's banner, the award-winning Palladio is sim-ply excellent. The menu here broadly encompasses dishes from across Italy. Stand-out plates include beef tartar and lobster capelletti. With a seasonal menu and positively obsequious service, this restaurant will always satisfy your senses—though it might also deplete your wallet. Set lunches begin at Y280, and dinners soar into the heady heights. $ *Average main: Y250 ⊠ Portman Ritz-Carlton, 1376 Nanjing Xi Lu, Jing'an ☎ 021/6279–7188 ⌛ Reservations essential ✛ B2.*

## PUDONG

$ ECLECTIC FAMILY
🍴 **hoF** (巧薈 *Qiǎo huì*). It's a mystery how owner Brian Tan stays so slim with all this tempting chocolate. Desserts are, perhaps literally, to die for; our pick of the dizzying lot is the orange chocolate mud cake with caramel and sea salt. There are savories on the menu, too, including duck confit and superb salmon rilettes. Ogle the neighboring Oriental Pearl Tower and toast to your fantastic trip with glasses of the well-priced port. There's another branch at 30 Sinan Lu in Xuhui. [$] *Average main: Y65* ✉ *DBS Tower, 1318 Lujiazui Huan Lu, B1, Pudong* ☎ *021/5010–0800* ⏲ *Closed Sun.* ✥ *G3.*

$$$$ INTERNATIONAL Fodor's Choice ★
🍴 **Jade on 36** (翡翠36 *Fěicuìsānshíliù*). This is a restaurant that must be experienced to be believed. Perched on the 36th floor of the Shangri-La, it offers great views of Pudong. There is no à la carte menu; instead, you choose from a selection of set menus named simply by colors and sizes. The cuisine is innovative and extremely fresh, the service impeccable, and the view pleasant. Menus vary from five to eight courses, with an emphasis on fresh seafood and tender meats. It's an expensive indulgence, but worth every penny. [$] *Average main: Y600* ✉ *Pudong Shangri-La, 33 Fucheng Lu, 36th fl., Pudong* ☎ *021/6882–8888* ✍ *Reservations essential* ✥ *G3.*

$$$$ JAPANESE
🍴 **Nadaman.** Sleekly elegant and stylized, Nadaman is modern Japanese dining taken to its extreme. The accents of raw granite merged into a formalized designer interior reflect the restaurant's origins in modern Tokyo. With a focus on freshness and presentation, Nadaman gives diners superb cuisine at a price tag to match. The sushi is some of the finest in the city. [$] *Average main: Y450* ✉ *Pudong Shangri-La, 33 Fucheng Lu, 2nd fl., Pudong* ☎ *021/6882–8888* ✍ *Reservations essential* ✥ *G2.*

$$ DELI FAMILY Fodor's Choice ★
🍴 **Sproutworks** (豆苗工坊 *Dòu miáo gōng fang*). From two American-born Chinese comes mana from heaven for Shanghai residents starving for ruffage. In the West, the concept is far from groundbreaking—a menu of affordable, rotating salads, sandwiches, and sides—but there's not yet a single other place like it in Shanghai. It's easy to stay healthy tucking into sides like shredded Brussels sprouts with hazelnuts and Parmesan, but dieters will find it hard to pass up buttery chocolate-chip cookies, baked by one owner's lovely wife and placed tauntingly next to the register. [$] *Average main: Y65* ✉ *Super Brand Mall, 168 Lujiazui Lu, Pudong* 🌐 *www.sproutworks.com.cn* ✥ *H3.*

$$ ITALIAN FAMILY
🍴 **Tavola.** Time was the riverside promenade on the Pudong side, known as Binjiang Da Dao, was completely devoid of restaurants. Tavola's not the first to move in, but it's one of the best, a serene place to kick back after a long stroll and refeul with Neapolitan-style pizza and a smattering of pasta, meat, and fish dishes. The lunch sets, served 11:30 to 2:30, are the best deal. [$] *Average main: Y150* ✉ *2500 Binjiang Da Dao, Pudong* ☎ *021/2022–8288* ✥ *G3.*

$$$$ ECLECTIC FAMILY
🍴 **Yi Café** (怡咖啡 *Yí kāfēi*). Serving a world of cuisines, this open-kitchen eatery is very popular with the Lujiazui business set, as well as local diners, for the quality and variety of the food. It's a great place to people-watch over a selection of the finest dishes Asia has to offer. The amount of food here is copious, and you will leave stuffed. This experience doesn't come cheap, at Y368 for dinner, but if you've got a

big appetite, it's worth it, especially with the make-your-own sundae bar. $ *Average main: Y368* ✉ *Pudong Shangri-La, 33 Fucheng Lu, 2nd fl., Pudong* ☎ *021/6882–8888* ✢ *H3.*

## HONGQIAO AND GUBEI

$$ ✕**Bellagio** (百乐宫 *Bǎi lè gōng*). Taiwanese expats pack the dining room

TAIWANESE of Bellagio, so you know this is an authentic taste of Taiwan. Red fab-

FAMILY ric–covered chairs and black streamlined tables contrast with the white walls and decorative moldings. Waitresses with short, chic hairstyles move efficiently between the closely spaced tables. The menu includes such traditional entrées as three-cup chicken, as well as 25 noodle dishes spanning all of Southeast Asia. Save room for dessert: shaved-ice snacks are obligatory Taiwanese treats, and come in 14 varieties. The Gubei and Hongqiao branches tend to be filled with Asian expats, while the downtown outlets see more Westerners. $ *Average main: Y90* ✉ *778 Huangjin Cheng Dao, by Gubei Lu, Gubei* ☎ *021/6278–0722* ⟐ *Reservations not accepted.* ✢ *G4.*

$$ ✕**Mexico Lindo** (灵得墨西哥餐厅 *Língdé Mòxīgē cāntīng*). Fiery fare in

MEXICAN a south-of-the-border setting has made this Tex-Mex cantina a stalwart

FAMILY in Shanghai. In addition to tacos, fajitas, and quesadillas, the menu includes a few healthier options like grilled salmon. A stairway mural depicts farm workers as well as fiesta revelers, whose ranks you can join with the many, many margaritas and tequilas on the drinks menu. Round out the meal with banana chimichangas with vanilla ice cream. $ *Average main: Y120* ✉ *3338 Hongmei Lu, Gubei* ☎ *021/6262–2797* ⟐ *Reservations essential* ✢ *G4.*

$ ✕**Souper Fresh.** When boiled and blanched vegetables and heavy meat

AMERICAN dishes become too much, take respite at Souper Fresh, where the prices

FAMILY are extremely reasonable, the salad bar is simple but well stocked, and the desserts are worth saving room for. The atmosphere is eminently casual, and the magazine rack is packed with American and British tabloid magazines. $ *Average main: Y58* ✉ *3213 Hongmei Lu, Hongqiao* ☎ *021/3415–1677* ✢ *G4.*

# WHERE TO STAY

Shanghai's stature as China's business capital hasn't stopped it from catering both to business and leisure travelers, especially the handful of boutique hotels. Business hotels can be divided into two categories: modern Western-style hotels with all the latest amenities and older hotels built during the city's glory days. The latter may lack great service, modern fixtures, and convenient facilities, but they often make up for it in charm, tradition, and history.

Judging by the number of international chain hotels in Shanghai, the city has proven just how much it has opened to the outside world. Many aren't merely hotels; they're landmarks on the Shanghai skyline. Even the historic properties that make up the other half of Shanghai's hotel market feel the pressure to update their rooms and facilities.

*Prices in the reviews are the lowest cost of a standard double room in high season. Use the coordinate (✛ B2) at the end of each listing to locate a site on the Where to Stay in Shanghai map.*

**RESERVATIONS AND RATES**

Increasing competition means there are bargains to be had, especially during the low season from November through March. Avoid traveling during the Golden Week (always the first week of October), when the city is packed and rooms and prices are at a premium. During Chinese New Year (mid-January to mid-February) there are excellent deals to be had and the city is astoundingly quiet; the downside is that *everything* is closed.

Rates are generally quoted for the room alone; breakfast, whether Continental or full, is usually extra. All hotel prices listed here are based on high-season rates.

## XINTIANDI AND CITY CENTER

**$$$$** **88 Xintiandi** (88 新天地酒店 *88 Xîntiândì jiŭdiàn*). Although it tar-
**HOTEL** gets business travelers, this groundbreaking boutique hotel is a shopper's delight. **Pros:** prime location in Xintiandi; interesting traditional Chinese decor. **Cons:** can feel a little dated; some street noise. $ *Rooms from: Y1800* ✉ *380 Huangpi Nan Lu, Huangpu* ☎ *021/5383–8833* ⊕ *www.88xintiandi.com* ⤳ *12 suites, 41 rooms* ⦿❘ *No meals* ✛ *D4.*

**$$$** **JW Marriott** (JW 万豪酒店 *JW wànháo jiŭdiàn*). For the best views in
**HOTEL** Puxi, look no further. **Pros:** fantastic location; great views; unbeatable rooftop pool. **Cons:** exterior is far more contemporary than interiors. $ *Rooms from: Y1680* ✉ *399 Nanjing Xi Lu, Huangpu* ☎ *021/5359– 4969, 888/236-2427* ⊕ *www.jwmarriottshanghai.com* ⤳ *305 rooms, 37 suites* ⦿❘ *No meals* ✛ *D3.*

**$$$$** **The Langham Xintiandi.** Since it opened, The Langham Xintiandi has
**HOTEL** been receiving nothing but praise for service that's impeccable without being intrusive and rooms that are big and plush. **Pros:** unbeatable service and location; well-kept pool; modern gym. **Cons:** light sleepers may find street-facing rooms a tad noisy; staff answering the phone often seem a bit confused. $ *Rooms from: Y2000* ✉ *99 Madang Lu, Huangpu* ☎ *021/2330–2288* ⊕ *www.xintiandi.langhamhotels.com/ info/hotels_in_xintiandi.htm* ⤳ *316 rooms, 41 suites* ⦿❘ *No meals* ✛ *D4.*

**$** **Pacific Hotel** (金门大酒店 *Jinmen dàjiŭdiàn*). This 1926 property has
**HOTEL** done an admirable job of preserving its charm: the marble lobby and the downstairs bar, with leather chairs and photos from 1920s Shanghai, sweep you back to the city's glory days. **Pros:** near People's Park; lots of lovely details; great views. **Cons:** erratic service; institutional bathrooms; aging property. $ *Rooms from: Y600* ✉ *108 Nanjing Xi Lu, Huangpu* ☎ *021/6327–6226* ▤ *021/6372–3634* ⤳ *177 rooms, 5 suites* ✛ *E2.*

**$** **Park Hotel** (国际饭店 *Guoji Fandian*). Once Shanghai's tallest build-
**HOTEL** ing, the 20-story Park Hotel has long since been eclipsed by other hotels whose glory days are present instead of past. **Pros:** central location; historic property; grand lobby. **Cons:** aging rooms; inadequate service;

not many amenities. $\boxed{\$}$ *Rooms from: Y858* ⊠ *170 Nanjing Xi Lu, Huangpu* ☏ *021/6327–5225* 📠 *021/6327–6958* ⤳ *225 rooms, 25 suites* ⦿ *No meals* ✛ *E2.*

$$

HOTEL **Radisson Blu Hotel Shanghai New World** (新世界丽笙大酒店 *Xînshìjiè Lìshçng dàjiǔdiàn*). A prominent landmark not only on People's Square, but also on the Shanghai skyline, the Radisson Blu is topped by what looks for all the world like a flying saucer. **Pros:** prime location; city views; distinctive architecture. **Cons:** somewhat dated decor; taxis not readily available. $\boxed{\$}$ *Rooms from: Y1200* ⊠ *88 Nanjing Xi Lu, Huangpu* ☏ *021/6359–9999* ⊕ *www.radisson.com/shanghaicn_newworld* ⤳ *429 rooms, 91 suites* ⦿ *No meals* ✛ *E2.*

## THE BUND AND NANJING DONG LU

$$$

HOTEL **Hyatt on the Bund.** Near the banks of Suzhou Creek, the Hyatt on the Bund offers beautifully appointed rooms in an airy and modern building. **Pros:** gorgeous facilities; views are hard to beat; short walk from the Bund. **Cons:** rather bland neighborhood; the food underwhelms; can be difficult to get taxis. $\boxed{\$}$ *Rooms from: Y1550* ⊠ *199 Huangpu Lu, near Wuchang Lu, Huangpu* ☏ *021/6393–1234* ⊕ *www.shanghai. bund.hyatt.com* ⤳ *600 rooms, 31 suites* ⦿ *No meals* ✛ *G2.*

$$

HOTEL

Fodor's Choice
★

**Le Royal Meridien.** (上海世茂皇家艾美酒店 *Shìmào huángjia àiměi jiǔdiàn*). Dominating the foot of the Nanjing Pedestrian Street, Le Royal Meridien has changed the face of Puxi hospitality. **Pros:** central location; excellent facilities; elegant rooms. **Cons:** service hiccups; annoying elevator system. $\boxed{\$}$ *Rooms from: Y1219* ⊠ *505 Nanjing Dong Lu, Huangpu* ☏ *021/3318–9999* ⊕ *www.lemeridien.com.cn* ⤳ *646 rooms, 115 suites* ⦿ *No meals* ✛ *E2.*

$$$$

HOTEL **Les Suites Orient.** This Taiwanese-owned hotel is a favorite of ours, and not just because of its excellent location on the Bund. **Pros:** homey feeling; excellent service. **Cons:** far from the subway. $\boxed{\$}$ *Rooms from: Y1900* ⊠ *1 Jinling Dong Lu, Huangpu* ☏ *021/6320–0088* ⤳ *43 suites* ⦿ *Breakfast* ✛ *F3.*

$$$

HOTEL **Shanghai Marriott City Centre** (上海雅居乐万豪酒店 *Shànghǎi yǎjūlè wànháo jiǔdiàn*). This hotel caters to business travelers, but its location two blocks north of People's Square and Nanjing Dong Lu makes it great for tourists. **Pros:** solid service; central location; reasonable rates. **Cons:** rather bland decor. $\boxed{\$}$ *Rooms from: Y1600* ⊠ *555 Xizang Zhong Lu, Huangpu* ☏ *021/2312–9888* ⊕ *www.marriott.com* ⤳ *664 rooms, 54 suites* ⦿ *No meals* ✛ *E2.*

$$$

HOTEL **Sofitel Hyland.** Facing the pedestrian-only Nanjing Road, the Sofitel Hyland is a convenient base for shopping and exploring the city center. **Pros:** handy location; close to shopping; rooms with some nice details.

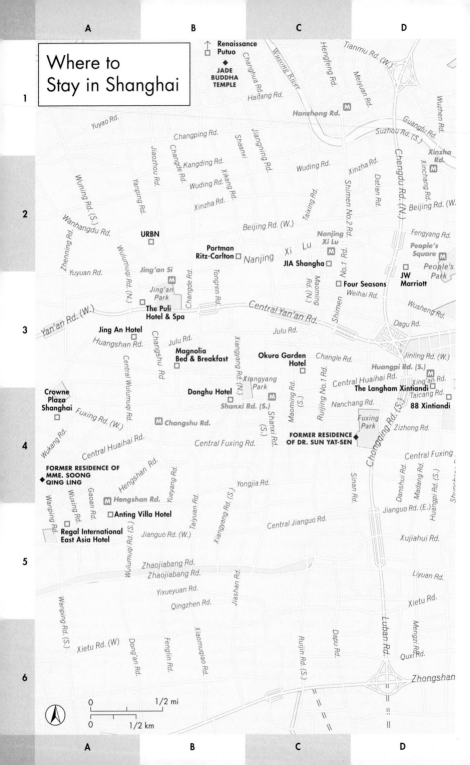

# Where to Stay in Shanghai

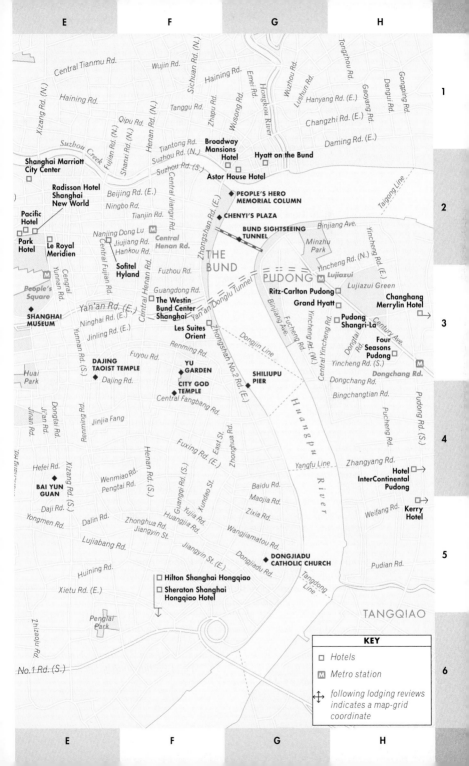

## WHICH NEIGHBORHOOD?

Shanghai may have an excellent subway system and cheap, plentiful taxis, but if you want to take full advantage of Shanghai's popular tourist sights, restaurants, and nightlife, opt to stay in downtown Puxi, incorporating the quiet, leafy green Former French Concession, the historic promenade of the Bund, and the bustling shopping street of Nanjing Dong Lu. From these neighborhoods you'll have easy access to the rest of Shanghai.

### FORMER FRENCH CONCESSION

Sneak away from the city's frenetic energy in one of the historic hotels lining the Former French Concession's tree-lined streets. Excellent restaurants and shopping abound, and the neighborhood's relaxing atmosphere can be a nice break after a hectic day of sightseeing. A short cab or metro ride takes you straight to any of the city's sights on the Bund and Nanjing Dong Lu.

### HONGQIAO DEVELOPMENT ZONE

Hongqiao is not a destination for leisure travelers. A combination of residential complexes and business offices, the western stretch of Hongqiao lacks many sights or restaurants. Unless business brings

you here or you have an early flight from the Hongqiao airport, there aren't many reasons to stay so far from the action.

### THE BUND AND NANJING DONG LU

Breathtaking views of the Pudong skyline, skyscrapers juxtaposed with Victorian architecture, and easy access to great shopping and some of the city's best restaurants are just a few reasons to stay here. Best of all, most major sites, from the Bund to the Shanghai Museum, are all within comfortable walking distance. If you want to see Shanghai old and new, this is the place to be.

### PUDONG

Although Pudong—with its shiny new skyscrapers and wide boulevards—can feel impersonal, and it's too far from downtown Puxi for some, it has some superb hotels that are closer to Pudong International Airport. Phenomenal views of the Bund are a major bonus. But if you stay here, be prepared to spend at least 30 minutes shuttling back and forth to Puxi (and it could take even longer during rush hour, as millions of locals compete to flag down taxis or squeeze into subway cars).

**Cons:** small rooms; poor frontage. $ *Rooms from: Y1470* ⊠ *505 Nanjing Dong Lu, Huangpu* ☎ *021/6351–5888* ⊕ *www.accorhotels-asia. com* ⌨ *299 rooms, 73 suites* ⎢◯⎢ *No meals* ✛ *E2.*

$$ ⎢⎽⎢ **The Westin Bund Center Shanghai.** With its distinctive room layouts,
HOTEL glittering glass staircase, and 90-plus works of art on display, the Westin
FAMILY Shanghai is a masterpiece near the majestic Bund. **Pros:** very attentive service. **Cons:** expensive for what you get; far from most shopping. $ *Rooms from: Y1250* ⊠ *Bund Center, 88 Henan Zhong Lu, Huangpu* ☎ *021/6335–1888, 888/625–5144* ⊕ *www.westin.com/shanghai* ⌨ *570 rooms, 24 suites* ⎢◯⎢ *No meals* ✛ *F3.*

## FORMER FRENCH CONCESSION

$ HOTEL **Anting Villa Hotel** (安亭别墅花园酒店 *Antíng biéshù huayuán jiǔdiàn*). Although it's just two blocks from the Hengshan Road nightlife district, the Anting Villa Hotel is a convenient and surprisingly quiet retreat tucked away down a small side street. **Pros:** central location; well-priced for the neighborhood; **Cons:** a little faded; can be hard to communicate. [$] *Rooms from: Y660* ✉ *46 Anting Lu, Xuhui* ☎ *021/6433–1188* 🌐 *www.antingvillahotel-shanghai.com* 🛏 *135 rooms, 11 suites* 🍴 *No meals* ⊕ *A5.*

$$ HOTEL **Crowne Plaza Shanghai** (银星皇冠假日酒店 *Yínxīng Huángguān Jiàrì jiǔdiàn*). On the far western side of the Former French Concession, this hotel makes up for its out-of-the-way location with great service. **Pros:** good service; lots of amenities; pretty pool. **Cons:** you'll need taxis to get to and from the hotel; spaces feel dated. [$] *Rooms from: Y1100* ✉ *400 Panyu Lu, Xuhui* ☎ *021/6280–8888, 800/227–6963* 🌐 *www.ihg.com* 🛏 *488 rooms, 12 suites* 🍴 *No meals* ⊕ *A4.*

$ HOTEL **Donghu Hotel** (東湖賓館 *Dōnghú bīnguǎn*). Just off the frenzied shopping street of Huaihai Lu, the Donghu Hotel remains one of Shanghai's best-preserved hotels from the city's heyday in the 1920s. **Pros:** traditional and elegant; indoor pool; great for window-shoppers. **Cons:** poor service; could be better maintained. [$] *Rooms from: Y400* ✉ *70 Donghu Lu, Xuhui* ☎ *021/6415–8158* 🌐 *www.donghuhotel.com* 🛏 *240 rooms, 30 suites* 🍴 *No meals* ⊕ *B4.*

$ HOTEL **Jing An Hotel** (静安宾馆 *Jìng'ān bīnguǎn*). The weekly chamber-music concert in its lobby is just one example of how the Jing An Hotel has retained its elegance and charm. **Pros:** elegantly appointed; near the subway station; beautiful surroundings. **Cons:** poorly maintained facilities; inconsistent service. [$] *Rooms from: Y590* ✉ *370 Huashan Lu, Xuhui* ☎ *021/6248–0088* 🌐 *shanghai.jinjianghotels.com/ja/en_index.asp* 🛏 *210 rooms, 17 suites* 🍴 *No meals* ⊕ *A3.*

$ B&B/INN **Magnolia Bed & Breakfast** (白玉兰 *Bái yùlán*). At the intersection of five tree-lined streets in the Former French Concession, the Magnolia is a charming little B&B that's perfect if you want to be in the center of the action. **Pros:** great location; rich in character; a taste of local culture. **Pros:** it can be loud; there's no 24-hour service. [$] *Rooms from: Y650* ✉ *36 Yanqing Lu, Xuhui* ☎ *021/5403–5306* 🌐 *www.magnoliabnbshanghai.com* 🛏 *4 rooms, 1 suite* 🍴 *Breakfast* ⊕ *B3.*

$$ HOTEL **Okura Garden Hotel** (花园饭店 *Huāyuán fàndiàn*). A parklike setting in the heart of the Former French Concession makes this 33-story tower a favorite retreat, especially among Japanese travelers familiar with the Okura name. **Pros:** gorgeous surroundings; historic building; convenient to Former French Concession. **Cons:** you're paying more for beauty and location than service. [$] *Rooms from: Y1100* ✉ *58 Maoming Nan Lu, Luwan* ☎ *021/6415–1111* 🌐 *www.gardenhotelshanghai.com* 🛏 *478 rooms, 22 suites* 🍴 *No meals* ⊕ *C3.*

### DRINK AND A VIEW

Check out the spectacular Vue bar at the Hyatt on the Bund and enjoy expansive vistas and a rooftop hot tub.

Fodor'sChoice ★

Le Royal Meridien

JIA Shanghai

$ **Regal International East Asia Hotel**
HOTEL (富豪环球东亚酒店 *Fùháo huánqiú dōngyà jiǔdiàn*). Its exclusive Shanghai International Tennis Center is the Regal International's trump card among the other big hotels. **Pros:** easy access to public transportation; top-notch fitness center; lots of activities for nights you want to stay in. **Cons:** on a high-traffic street. $ *Rooms from: Y600* ✉ *516 Hengshan Lu, Xuhui* ☎ *021/6415–5588* ⊕ *www.regal-eastasia.com* ⚲ *278 rooms, 22 suites* ⦿ *No meals* ✛ *A5.*

> **UNIQUE SPOT**
>
> Magnolia B&B is one of Shanghai's most charming budget boutique hotels and a must if you're looking for a personalized experience that the larger hotels just can't offer.

## NANJING XI LU AND JING'AN

$$$$ **The Four Seasons** (四季酒店 *Sìjì jiǔdiàn*). With palm trees, babbling
HOTEL fountains, and golden-hued marble as warm as sunshine, the lobby of the Four Seasons is an elegant oasis in bustling downtown Puxi. **Pros:** impeccable service; convenient location; indulgent spa with Balinese treatments. **Cons:** ongoing construction from the metro is loud and dusty. $ *Rooms from: Y2100* ✉ *500 Weihai Lu, Jing'an* ☎ *021/6256–8888, 800/819–5053* ⊕ *www.fourseasons.com* ⚲ *360 rooms, 79 suites* ⦿ *No meals* ✛ *C3.*

$$ **JIA Shanghai** (家上海 *Jiā shànghǎi*). In a handsome 1920s build-
HOTEL ing on Nanjing Xi Lu, JIA Shanghai's unprepossessing exterior masks
Fodor'sChoice its elegantly styled interior. **Pros:** exquisite design and unique setting;
★ kitchenettes; privacy. **Cons:** no pool; no business center. $ *Rooms from: Y1280* ✉ *931 Nanjing Xi Lu, near Taixing Lu, Jing'an* ☎ *021/6217–9000* ⊕ *www.jiashanghai.com* ⚲ *47 rooms* ⦿ *No meals* ✛ *C2.*

$$$ **Kerry Hotel** (嘉里大酒店 *Jiā lǐ dà jiǔdiàn*). This hotel within easy
HOTEL driving distance of Pudong International Airport is great if you're
FAMILY traveling with a brood—across the street is Century Park, where tandem bikes and pleasure boats are available. **Pros:** great for kids; easy access to greenery. **Cons:** far from downtown. $ *Rooms from: Y1500* ✉ *1388 Huamu Lu, Pudong* ☎ *021/6169–8800* ⊕ *www.shangri-la.com/shanghai/kerryhotelpudong* ⚲ *843 rooms, 31 suites* ⦿ *No meals* ✛ *H5.*

$$$$ **The Portman Ritz-Carlton** (波特曼丽嘉酒店 *Bō tè màn lì jiā jiǔdiàn*).
HOTEL Outstanding facilities and a prime location in the Shanghai Centre have made the Portman Ritz-Carlton one of the city's most desirable destinations for more than a decade. **Pros:** superb location; rooftop pool; well-stocked fitness room. **Cons:** staying here can feel like you're in a bubble. $ *Rooms from: Y2250* ✉ *1376 Nanjing Xi Lu, Jing'an* ☎ *021/6279–8888, 800/241–3333* ⊕ *www.ritzcarlton.com* ⚲ *510 rooms, 68 suites* ⦿ *No meals* ✛ *B2.*

$$$$ **The PuLi Hotel & Spa.** An oasis of calm in the center of bustling Shang-
RESORT hai, the PuLi Hotel & Spa is billed as an urban resort with an emphasis
Fodor'sChoice on soothing decor and relaxing amenities. **Pros:** long list of complimen-
★ tary amenities; great location; quiet; popular Sunday brunch. **Cons:** service can be hit or miss. $ *Rooms from: Y3920* ✉ *1 Changde Lu, Jing'an* ☎ *021/3203–9999* ⊕ *www.thepuli.com/en* ⚲ *193 rooms, 36 suites* ⦿ *Breakfast* ✛ *A3.*

4

$$$ HOTEL Fodor's Choice ★ **URBN** (雅悦酒店 *Yǎ yuè jiǔdiàn*). Innovatively designed and environmentally friendly, this is Shanghai's first carbon-neutral hotel. **Pros:** eco-friendly vibe; luxe setting; quiet location. **Cons:** not terribly suitable for mobility-impaired guests. [$] *Rooms from: Y1500* ✉ *183 Jiaozhou Lu, near Beijing Xi Lu, Jing'an* ☎ *021/5153–4600* 🌐 *www.urbnhotels.com* 🛏 *24 rooms, 2 suites* ✥ *B2.*

## PUDONG

$ HOTEL **Changhang Merrylin Hotel** (长航美林阁大酒店 *Zhăng háng měi lín gé dà jiǔdiàn*). Merrylin is better known throughout China for its restaurants, and the Changhang Merrylin Hotel's lively eatery overshadows its fair-size, inexpensive rooms. **Pros:** reasonable rates; convenient to shopping and public transportation; decent food in the restaurant. **Cons:** poor service. [$] *Rooms from: Y350* ✉ *818 Zhangyang Lu, Pudong* ☎ *021/5835–5555* 📠 *021/5835–7799* 🛏 *192 rooms, 32 suites* 🍴 *No meals* ✥ *H3.*

$$$$ HOTEL **Four Seasons Pudong** (浦东四季酒店 *Pǔdōng sìjì jiǔdiàn*). While its older sister is more posh, the Pudong outpost of the Four Seasons is flashy and hip. **Pros:** sleek design; prompt service; nice little terrace. **Cons:** it's a long walk to restaurants; no nearby nightlife. [$] *Rooms from: Y2300* ✉ *210 Shiji Da Dao, Pudong* ☎ *021/2036–8888* 🛏 *187 rooms, 15 suites* 🍴 *No meals* ✥ *H3.*

$$$$ HOTEL **Grand Hyatt** (上海金茂君悦大酒店 *Shànghǎi jīnmàojūn yuè dà jiǔdiàn*). Views, views, views are what this hotel is all about—occupying floors 53 through 87 of the spectacular Jin Mao Tower, the Grand Hyatt's interior is defined by contemporary lines juxtaposed with Space Age grillwork and sleek furnishings and textures. **Pros:** beautiful rooms; high-tech amenities; fantastic city views. **Cons:** pricey rates; no guarantee of clear views. [$] *Rooms from: Y1760* ✉ *Jin Mao Tower, 88 Shiji Dadao(Century Avenue), Pudong* ☎ *021/5049–1234, 800/233–1234* 🌐 *www.shanghai.grand.hyatt.com* 🛏 *510 rooms, 45 suites* 🍴 *No meals* ✥ *H3.*

$$$ HOTEL **Hotel InterContinental Pudong** (锦江汤臣洲际大酒店 *Jǐnjiāng tāng chén zhōujì dà jiǔdiàn*). The pièce de résistance of the 24-story Hotel InterContinental Pudong is a nearly 200-foot-high Italian Renaissance–inspired atrium, decorated with red Chinese lanterns, that shines natural light onto the 19 guest floors. **Pros:** well priced for its amenities. **Cons:** not the best location for exploration on foot. [$] *Rooms from: Y1680* ✉ *777 Zhangyang Lu, Pudong* ☎ *021/5831–8888, 800/327–0200* 🌐 *www.intercontinental.com* 🛏 *317 rooms, 78 suites* 🍴 *No meals* ✥ *H4.*

$$$$ HOTEL Fodor's Choice ★ **Pudong Shangri-La** (浦东香格里拉酒店 *Pǔdōng xiānggélǐlā jiǔdiàn*). The Shangri-La occupies one of the most prized spots in Shanghai: overlooking the Huangpu River, opposite the Bund, and near the Pearl Tower. **Pros:** fantastic location; good restaurants; glorious views. **Cons:** expensive rates; nearby restaurants are in shopping malls. [$] *Rooms from: Y2050* ✉ *33 Fucheng Lu, Pudong* ☎ *021/6882–8888, 800/942–5050* 🌐 *www.shangri-la.com* 🛏 *916 rooms, 65 suites* 🍴 *No meals* ✥ *H3.*

URBN

Pudong Shangri-La

St. Regis

**$$$$** 🏨 **Ritz-Carlton Pudong** (上海浦东丽思卡尔顿上海世茂皇家艾美酒店
HOTEL *Shànghǎi pǔdōng lì sī kǎ'ěr dùn shànghǎi shìmào huángjiā ài měi*
FAMILY *jiǔdiàn*). The Ritz-Carlton Pudong boasts a 55th-floor spa with staggering views of the Huangpu River and the entire downtown skyline, an impressive Italian restaurant, and a rooftop bar that's such a good lookout point you may never want to leave. **Pros:** near upscale shopping; easy access to financial center; great views. **Cons:** the only nearby restaurants are in shopping malls. $ *Rooms from: Y2800* ✉ *8 Shiji Dadao(Century Avenue), Lujiazui* ☎ *021/2020–1888* ⊕ *www. ritzcarlton.com* ➵ *285 rooms* ⦿ *No meals* ✛ *H3.*

**$$** 🏨 **Renaissance Putuo** (上海明捷万丽酒店 *Shànghǎi míng jié wàn lì*
HOTEL *jiǔdiàn*). Though it's outside the downtown district, this reasonably priced hotel is adjacent to a station on metro line 7, putting you four stops from the Jing'an Temple and five from the Former French Concession. **Pros:** good value; well-appointed rooms; nice pool. **Cons:** far from the action. $ *Rooms from: Y988* ✉ *50 Tongchuan Lu, Hongkou* ☎ *021/2219–5888* ⊕ *www.marriott.com* ➵ *315 rooms, 15 suites* ⦿ *No meals* ✛ *B1.*

## NORTH SHANGHAI

**$$** 🏨 **Astor House Hotel** (浦江饭店 *Pǔjiāng fàndiàn*). The oldest Western
HOTEL hotel in China, the Astor House does an admirable job of capturing the ambience of Victorian Shanghai. **Pros:** gorgeous building; historic atmosphere; good price. **Cons:** confused service; Spartan furnishings. $ *Rooms from: Y1280* ✉ *15 Huangpu Lu, Hongkou* ☎ *021/6324–6388* ⊕ *www.pujianghotel.com/index.htm* ➵ *127 rooms, 3 suites* ⦿ *No meals* ✛ *G2.*

**$** 🏨 **Broadway Mansions Hotel** (百老汇大厦酒店 *Bǎilǎohuì dàshà jiǔdiàn*).
HOTEL One of Shanghai's most revered buildings, the Broadway Mansions Hotel has anchored the northern end of the Bund since 1934. **Pros:** Hongkou location; a sense of Shanghai history. **Cons:** service irregular; rooms worn; some street noise. $ *Rooms from: Y937* ✉ *20 Suzhou Bei Lu, Hongkou* ☎ *021/6324–6260* ⊕ *www.broadwaymansions.com* ➵ *161 rooms, 72 suites* ⦿ *No meals* ✛ *G2.*

## HONGQIAO AND GUBEI

**$$$** 🏨 **Hilton Shanghai Hongqiao** (上海虹桥希尔顿酒店 *Shànghǎi hóngqiáo*
HOTEL *xī'ěrdùn jiǔdiàn*). A 20-minute drive from Hongqiao Airport, this behemoth is ideal for business travelers catching a flights to Hong Kong or elsewhere in China. **Pros:** very close to the airport; good value; good restaurants nearby. **Cons:** more geared toward business travelers. $ *Rooms from: Y1500* ✉ *1116 Hongsong Dong Lu, Hongqiao* ☎ *021/3323– 6666* ⊕ *www3.hilton.com* ➵ *623 rooms, 51 suites* ⦿ *No meals* ✛ *F5.*

**$** 🏨 **Sheraton Shanghai Hongqiao Hotel** (虹桥喜来登上海太平洋大饭店
HOTEL *Hóngqiáo xǐláidēng shànghǎi tàipíngyáng dà fàndiàn*). Still the go-to
FAMILY hotel for savvy business travelers staying in Hongqiao, this Japanese-
Fodor's Choice managed property has four club floors, an indoor swimming pool, and
★ golf privileges at Shanghai International Golf Club. **Pros:** beautifully decorated; reasonable rates; great for business travelers. **Cons:** far

CLOSE UP

## Spa Treatments

Around Shanghai are hundreds of blind massage parlors, inexpensive no-frills salons whose blind masseurs are closely attuned to the body's soft and sore spots. At the other end of the spectrum lie the hotel spas, luxurious retreats where pampering is at a premium.

**Banyan Tree Spa.** The Banyan Tree Spa, the first China outpost of this ultraluxurious spa chain, occupies the third floor of the Westin Shanghai. The spa's 13 chambers as well as its treatments are designed to reflect *wu sing,* the five elemental energies of Chinese philosophy: earth, gold, water, wood, and fire. Relax and choose from a menu of massages, facials, body scrubs, or indulgent packages that combine all three. ⊠ *Westin Shanghai, 88 Henan Zhong Lu, 3rd fl., Huangpu* ☎ *021/6335–1888* ⊕ *www. banyantreespa.com.*

**Double Rainbow Massage House** (双彩虹按摩 *Shuangcaihong ànmúo).* With instructions clearly spelled out in English, Double Rainbow Massage House provides an inexpensive, nonthreatening introduction to traditional Chinese massage. Choose a masseur, state your preference for soft, medium, or hard pressure, then keep your clothes on for a 45- to 90-minute massage. There's no ambience, just a clean room with nine massage tables. ⊠ *47 Yongjia Lu, Xuhui* ☎ *021/6473–4000.*

**Dragonfly** (悠亭保健会所 *Youting baojian huìsuǒ).* Dragonfly is one in a chain of therapeutic retreat centers that has claimed the middle ground between expensive hotel spas and workmanlike blind-man massage parlors. Don the suede-soft treatment robes for traditional Chinese massage

or take them off for an aromatic oil massage. Dragonfly also has waxing and nail services. ⊠ *206 Xinle Lu, Xuhui* ☎ *021/5403–9982.*

**Evian Spa** (依云水疗 *Yiyun shuǐliáo).* The first Evian Spa outside of France, this palace of pampering has 14 theme rooms that offer head-to-toe treatments. There are nine different massages and a detox package will ease the effects of pollution and late-night partying. ⊠ *Three on the Bund, 17 Guangdong Lu, 2nd fl., Huangpu* ☎ *021/6321–6622* ⊕ *www. threeonthebund.com.*

**Mandara Spa** ( 蔓达梦水疗 *Màndámèng shuǐliáo).* With its exposed wood beams, unpolished bricks, and soothing fountains, the Mandara Spa in the JW Marriott resembles a traditional Chinese water town. Face and body treatments include the spa's signature massage, a 75-minute rubdown in which two therapists administer a blend of five massage styles: Shiatsu, Thai, Lomi Lomi, Swedish, and Balinese. ⊠ *JW Marriott, 399 Nanjing Xi Lu, Huangpu 200003* ☎ *021/5359–4969* ⊕ *www. mandaraspa.com.*

**Ming Massage** (*Míngyi ànmó).* This Japanese-style salon caters to women. Cross the footbridge to one of five small treatment rooms for a foot, body, or combination massage. ⊠ *298 Wulumuqi Nan Lu, Xuhui* ☎ *021/5465–2501.*

4

from downtown. [$] *Rooms from: Y772* ✉ *5 Zunyi Nan Lu, Hongqiao* ☎ *021/6275–8888, 888/625–5144* 🌐 *www.sheratongrand-shanghai.com* 🛏 *474 rooms, 22 suites* 🍴 *No meals* ✥ *F5.*

# ARTS AND NIGHTLIFE

Fueled equally by expatriates and an increasingly adventurous population of locals, Shanghai boasts an active and diverse nightlife. Shanghai lacks the sort of performing-arts scene you'd expect from a city its size, but it's getting there. Chinese opera remains popular with an older crowd and is even enjoying resurgence with a younger audience.

## THE ARTS

For modern culture more in tune with Shanghai's vibe head to the Shanghai Dramatic Arts Center, which balances sumptuous historical epics with small, provocative plays examining burning social issues like infidelity, divorce, and AIDS. Plucky modern-dance troupes perform at private venues like the Downstream Warehouse.

### ACROBATICS

**Shanghai Acrobatics Troupe** (上海杂技团 *Shànghǎi aájìtuán*). This troupe performs remarkable gravity-defying stunts at both the Shanghai Centre Theater, inside the Portman Ritz-Carlton and at Shanghai Circus World, a glittering, gold, 1,600-seat dome, which is north of the city center, in Zhabei. There are also performances at the Shanghai Circus World at 2266 Gonghe Xin Lu in Zhabei. ✉ *Shanghai Centre Theater, 1376 Nanjing Xi Lu, Jing'an* ☎ *021/6279–8945 Shanghai Centre, 021/5665–3646 Circus World* 🎟 *Y150–Y280* 🕒 *Daily at 7:30 pm.*

### CHINESE OPERA

**Kunju Opera Troupe** (上海昆剧团 *Shànghǎi kûnjùtuán*). Kun opera, or Kunju, originated in Jiangsu Province more than 400 years ago. Because of the profound influence it exerted on other Chinese opera styles, it's often called the mother of Chinese opera. Its troupe and theater are located in the lower part of the Former French Concession. ✉ *9 Shaoxing Lu, Luwan* ☎ *021/6437–1012* 🎟 *Y30–Y280* 🕒 *Sat. at 7:15.*

**Yifu Theatre** (逸夫舞台 *Yífû wûtái*). Not only Beijing Opera but also China's other regional operas, such as Huju, Kunju, and Yueju, are performed regularly at this theater in the heart of the city center. Considered the marquee theater for opera in Shanghai, it's just a block off People's Square. ✉ *701 Fuzhou Lu, Huangpu* ☎ *021/6351–4668.*

### DANCE AND CLASSICAL MUSIC

**Downstream Garage** (下河米仓 *Xiàhémicâng*). This small underground space hosts everything from experimental dance to performances of Joe Orton's edgy *What the Butler Saw*. Occasional film screenings or literary events (usually in Chinese) are also popular. ✉ *No. 100, 200 Longcao Lu, 3rd fl., Xujiahui* ☎ *021/6408–9520.*

**Shanghai Centre Theater** (上海商城剧院 *Shànghǎi shāngchéng jùyuàn*). This stage serves as a home to tourist favorites like the Shanghai Acrobatic Troupe and has hosted such performers as the Israel Contemporary

Dance Group and Wynton Marsalis. The building's distinct bowed front was designed to resemble the Marriott Marquis Theater in New York's Times Square. ✉ *Shanghai Center, 1376 Nanjing Xi Lu, Jing'an* ☎ *021/6279–8663.*

**Shanghai Concert Hall** (上海音乐厅 *Shànghǎi yīnyuètīng*). More than a decade ago, city officials spent $6 million to move this venerable concert hall two blocks to avoid the rumble from the nearby highway. Only then did they discover that it now sat over an even more rumbling subway line. Oops. It's the home of the Shanghai Symphony Orchestra, and hosts top-level classical musicians from around China and the world. ✉ *523 Yan'an Dong Lu, Huangpu* ☎ *021/6386–9153.*

**THEATER**

**Lyceum Theatre** (兰馨大戏院 *Lánxīn dàxìyuàn*). Although the renovation of Shanghai's oldest theater sadly replaced the richly stained wood with glaring marble and glass, the design of the space makes for an intimate theater experience. The Lyceum regularly hosts drama and music from around China as well as smaller local plays and Chinese opera performances. ✉ *57 Maoming Nan Lu, Xuhui* ☎ *021/6217–8539.*

Fodor's Choice ★ **Shanghai Dramatic Arts Center** (上海话剧艺术中心 *Shànghǎi huàjù yìshù zhōngxīn*). The city's premier theater venue and troupe, the Shanghai Dramatic Arts Center presents an award-winning lineup of its own original pieces, plus those of other cutting-edge groups around China. It also stages Chinese-language adaptations, sometimes very inventive, of Western works, such as a festival of Samuel Beckett works reinterpreted through Chinese opera. ✉ *288 Anfu Lu, Xuhui* ☎ *021/6473–4567* ⊕ *www.china-drama.com.*

**Shanghai Oriental Art Center** (上海东方艺术中心 *Shànghǎi dōngfāng yìshù zhōngxīn*). This cultural powerhouse present traditional Chinese works as well as a superb selection of Western shows. The Royal New Zealand Ballet, Munich Philharmonic Orchestra, and Netherlands Symphony Orchestra are just three among a slew of groups that have performed here. ✉ *425 Dingxiang Lu, Pudong* ☎ *021/6854–1234* ⊕ *en.shoac.com.cn.*

# NIGHTLIFE

## BARS

### XINTIANDI AND CITY CENTER

**Barbarossa** (爸爸露沙 *Bābālùshā*). Barbarossa is a popular evening destination, especially with nearby office workers who pack in for happy hour. The interior is straight out of *Arabian Nights*, albeit possibly flammable, with billowing draperies swathing the space. Usually quiet and classy, it switches to hot, hip, and hopping on weekend nights, especially in summer. ✉ *231 Nanjing Xi Lu, next to Shanghai Art Museum, Huangpu* ☎ *021/6318–0220.*

**TMSK** (透明思考酒吧 *Tòumíngsīkǎo jiǔba*). Short for Tou Ming Si Kao, this exquisitely designed little bar is an aesthete's dream. Glisteningly modern, TMSK is stunning—as are the prices of its drinks.

TMSK Bar in Xintiandi is a designer's dream.

✉ *Xintiandi North Block, Unit 2, House 11, 181 Taicang Lu, Luwan* ☎ *021/6326–2227.*

### THE BUND AND NANJING DONG LU

**Mokkos Jiao.** For a laid-back night out near the Bund, Mokkos Jiao is your best (and only) bet. The music, when it's playing at all, is very low, so you can focus on the drinks, snacks, and conversation. Choose from a huge selection of *shochus*—Japanese liquor made with barley or rice—and order a few rounds of edamame. ✉ *68 Jinling Dong Lu, Huangpu* ☎ *021/3331–6559.*

**Muse on the Bund.** Loud and crowded, Muse on the Bund is where people end up after hitting a few other drinking establishments. It plays hip-hop, house, and electro music and throws themed parties. When you need to chill out, there's a huge rooftop with a wading pool. Weekends see the club absolutely teeming with monied locals (and a smattering of expats) ordering up bottle after bottle from the top shelf. This is the flagship club of a chain that includes M2 at 283 Huaihai Zhong Lu in the City Center and Muse at Park 97 at 2A Gaolan Lu in the Former French Concession. ✉ *Yi Feng Galleria, 77 Beijing Dong Lu, 5th fl., Huangpu* ☎ *021/5213–5228.*

**Unico** (惟壹 *Wéi yī*). A Latin-inspired lounge where you can kick off your night before you go clubbing, Unico offers a dizzying array of cocktails, divided up by compass coordinates. From the Carribean, there's the El Presidente, made with rum, sweet vermouth (made in-house), and grapefruit bitters, topped with an orange twist. The music is loud enough that you can dance, but if you're not standing next to the band you can still have a conversation. Skip the lackluster food.

## LOCAL BREWS

Northern Chinese swear by their *baijiu*, a strong, usually sweet, clear liquor, but Shanghainese opt for milder poison. Most beloved is *huangjiu*, a brown brew from Shaoxing with a mild taste that resembles whiskey, which may explain why the latter is the most popular foreign liquor among locals. Huangjiu's quality is determined by whether it was brewed 2, 5, or 10 years ago. It is usually served warm, sometimes with ginger or dried plum added for kick.

Beer is also widely consumed; although there is a Shanghai beer brand, it is cheap, very bitter, and mostly found in the suburbs. Stores stock brands like Suntory, Reeb (yes, it's "beer" spelled backward), and Li Bo; of the three, Suntory is by far the best. Bars serve Tsingtao and imports like Tiger, Heineken, and Budweiser, which are more expensive. You'll find Sinkiang Black at Xinjiang restaurants. Craft beer can be had at Shanghai's small but strong homegrown breweries.

✉ *Three on the Bund, 3 Zhongshan Dong Yi Lu, 2nd fl., Huangpu* ☎ *021/5308–5399.*

### FORMER FRENCH CONCESSION

Fodor'sChoice ★ **Cotton's** (棉花酒吧 *Miánhuā jiŭbā*). This friendly, laid-back favorite moved many times before settling into the current old garden house. Busy without being loud, Cotton's is a rare place where you can have a conversation with friends—or make some new ones. The patio here is one of Shanghai's loveliest. ✉ *132 Anting Lu, Xuhui* ☎ *021/6433–7995.*

Fodor'sChoice ★ **Salute.** The hottest wine bar in Shanghai, Salute has three ramshackle rooms and a courtyard that are positively teeming all weekend and on spring, summer, and fall evenings. It's bottles only here, but for China, they're reasonably priced. The charcuterie and cheese platters are good, but the teeny kitchen really shines with its delicious panini. ✉ *59 Fuxing Xi Lu, Xuhui* ☎ *021/3461–9828.*

**Senator Saloon.** On a quiet street in the Former French Concession, a few blocks from the bars along Yongfu Lu, is Senator Saloon. The unmarked entrance is easy to miss, and you'd never guess there was a swinging speakeasy within. Cocktails include classics as well as contemporary concoctions. Big band music on the stereo, velvet wallpaper, and a pressed-tin ceiling all lend to the feeling that you've traveled back in time. ✉ *98 Wuyuan Lu, Xuhui* ☎ *021/5423–1330.*

**Time Passage** (昨天今天明天酒吧 *Zuotianjintianmingtian jiŭbā*). Shanghai favors slick nightclubs and posh wine bars, but Time Passage has always been the exception. Cheap beers, friendly service, and a cool, if grungy, atmosphere makes it the best way to start—or end—a night on the town. ✉ *183 Caojiayan Lu, near Huashan Lu, Changning* ☎ *021/6240–2588.*

### NANJING XI LU AND JING'AN

**Kaiba** (开巴 *Kāi ba*). Unpretentious and free of frills, Kaiba is the ideal neighborhood bar. It's been around for a while, serving Belgian brews and a few other imports. ✉ *479 Wuding Lu, Jing'an* ☎ *021/6288–9676.*

**UVA.** Its name means "grape" in Italian, so it's no surprise that UVA is a little wine bar. Run by a pair of Italians, it offers quite good value wine by the glass and bottle. The bar is popular with couples as well as office workers who turn out for happy hour. From the kitchen come some of Shanghai's better pizzas. ⊠ *819 Shaanxi Bei Lu, Jing'an* ☎ *021/5228–0320.*

### PUDONG

**The Brew** (嘉里大酒店 *Jiā lǐ dà jiǔdiàn*). The Kerry Hotel's microbrewery is tightly run by Kiwi brewmaster Leon Mickelson. The crisp cider is very good for those who don't love beer, while the Pilsner and IPA are the most popular among brew-heads. Shooting pool, tossing back peanuts from a tin pail, and sipping brewskies, you may well forget you're in China. ⊠ *The Kerry Hotel, 1388 Huamu Lu, Pudong* ☎ *021/6169–8888.*

**Cloud 9** (九重天). Perched on the 87th floor of the Grand Hyatt, Cloud 9 is among the city's loftiest bars. It has unparalleled views of Shanghai from among—and often above—the clouds. The sky-high views come with sky-high prices: after 7 pm, there's a Y100 entrance fee (even if all you want is a bottle of beer or a glass of house wine). Kick back while nibbling the tasty Asian-inspired tapas. ⊠ *Grand Hyatt, 88 Shiji Dadao, Pudong* ☎ *021/5049–1234* ⊕ *Jiǔ chòngtiān.*

**Jade on 36** (翡翠36酒吧 *Fěicuì 36 jiǔbā*). This swanky spot in the newer tower of the Pudong Shangri-La is the place for creative cocktails. Exquisite design and corresponding views (when Shanghai's pollution levels cooperate) have made Jade popular with locals. ⊠ *Pudong Shangri-La, 33 Fucheng, 36th fl., Pudong* ☎ *021/6882–3636.*

### HONGQIAO AND GUBEI

FAMILY **Shanghai Brewery** (上海啤酒坊 *Shànghǎi píjiǔ fang*). It's a family affair at Shanghai Brewery, where you're equally likely to find a group of sports-loving parents with toddlers in tow. There are seven house-made brews here, including a Black-Eyed Pear Stout and the sweet, summery peach beer. The food menu is all over the place, with both Western dishes and a handful of Asian options, but it's all quite solid. ⊠ *3338 Hongmei Lu, Hongqiao* ☎ *021/6406–5919.*

## CLUBS

### THE BUND AND NANJING DONG LU

**Bar Rouge.** In the trendy Bund 18 complex, Bar Rouge is the destination du jour of Shanghai's beautiful people. Pouting models and visiting celebrities are among the regular clientele. Views of Pudong are knockout, and so are drink prices. ⊠ *Bund 18, 18 Zhongshan Dong Lu, 7th fl., Huangpu* ☎ *021/6339–1199* ⊕ *www.bar-rouge-shanghai.com.*

### FORMER FRENCH CONCESSION

**The Apartment** (汉俱 *Hàn jù*). This bumping club is packed to the gills every weekend night with throngs of sweaty young dancers grinding up against one another to Top-40 hits. The rooftop, with its own bar, is a far better option. ⊠ *47 Yongfu Lu, Xuhui* ☎ *021/6437–9478.*

**The Shelter** (庇护所 *Bìhù suǒ*). Opened by a collective of Shanghai's leading DJs, this former bomb shelter is not for the claustrophobic but is a favorite with Shanghai scenesters for its cheap drinks and reasonable

## NIGHTLIFE LOWDOWN

Offerings range from world-class swank to dark and dingy dens or from young Shanghainese kids screaming experimental punk to Filipino cover bands singing "Hotel California" in a hotel basement. Prices, scenes, crowds, and ambience range just as wildly.

For an array of pleasant but pricey bars, head to **Xintiandi** or further east to **The Bund**, which every year sees swank new destinations debuting in its historic halls.

**Yongfu Lu,** near Fuxing Lu, once the top destination for the city's expats, is still lined with bars, including the excellent el Coctel, but now

**Yongkang Lu** is also packed at night. A dozen blocks to the east, the tiny watering holes along **Yongkang Lu** are most popular in the summer, when the street becomes so thronged with revelers that no vehicles can pass.

Shanghai's seedy bar strips are going the way of dial-up Internet connections. **Tongren Lu** and **Huashan Lu** still have a few bars for those who like their nightlife more on the wild side. They feature "fishing girls" who ask gents to give them money to buy drinks in exchange for their company (or something more). They either pocket the money or take a cut from the bar.

cover charge. It's a bit musty and damp down in the basement, but that doesn't stop revelers from packing in whenever there are big-name shows. ✉ *47 Yongfu Lu, by Fuxing Lu, Luwan* ☎ *021/6437–0400.*

### NANJING XI LU AND JING'AN

**Judy's** (杰迪 *Jié dí*). A veteran on the club scene, Judy's is infamous for its hard-partying crowd. The den of iniquity was memorialized in Wei Hui's racy novel *Shanghai Baby.* ✉ *142-146 Tongren Lu, Jing'an* ☎ *021/6289–3715.*

### GAY-LESBIAN BARS AND CLUBS

**390 Bar** (酒吧 *390 Jiǔbā*). Shanghai's only gay live music venue, 390 bar is also popular with Shanghai's straight club-goers. The decor is outrageous and flaming, perfect for the space. The drinks are proper cocktails, so before you try the A Clockwork Orange (made with gin and orange liqueur), fill up on a sausage and chutney made by a local British jam merchant. ✉ *390 Panyu Lu, Changning* ☎ *021/186–2124–9854.*

**Eddy's** (嘉侬咖啡厅 *Jiā nóng kāfēi tīng*). Flamboyant drag queen Eddy has had to move this gay bar around the city over the years, but it has found a more permanent home on this stretch of Huaihai Zhong Lu, from which the "gayborhood" spreads out. ✉ *1877 Huaihai Zhong Lu, Xuhui* ☎ *021/6282–0521.*

**Shanghai Studio.** At the heart of Shanghai's "alternative"—that is, gay—scene, Studio is the place to see and be seen, pick up, drop off, dance, sing, and remove one's shirt. ✉ *1950 Huaihai Zhong Lu, Xuhui* ☎ *021/6283–1043.*

### KARAOKE

Karaoke is ubiquitous in Shanghai; most nights the private rooms at KTV (Karaoke TV) establishments are packed with Shanghainese crooning away with their friends. Many bars employ "KTV girls" who sing along with male patrons and serve cognac and expensive snacks. (At some establishments, KTV girls are also prostitutes.)

**Cashbox Party World** (钱柜KTV *Qiánguì KTV*). This giant establishment is one of Shanghai's most popular KTV bars, and among the few that are dedicated to the KTV instead of the KTV girls. There's another location at 139 Xinhui Lu in Putuo. ⊠ *109 Yandan Lu, inside Fuxing Park, Huangpu* ☎ *021/5306–3888.*

**Haoledi** (好乐迪KTV *Hāolèdī KTV*). Crowded at all hours with locals of all ages crooning pop favorites, the popular Haoledi chain has branches virtually everywhere. A few of the outlets in downtown are at 180 Xizang Zhong Lu in Huang Pu and 1111 Zhaojiabang Lu in Xuhui. ⊠ *438 Huaihai Zhong Lu, Huangpu* ☎ *021/6311–5858.* ⊠ *438 Huaihai Zhong Lu, Luwan* ☎ *021/6311–5858*

## LIVE MUSIC

### XINTIANDI AND CITY CENTER

**288/The Melting Pot** (688阳光小筑 *688 Yángguāng xiǎo zhù*). With live performers of varying styles nightly, and up-and-coming rockers on the weekend, this laid-back bar is a favorite with music lovers, locals, and foreigners alike. ⊠ *288 Taikang Lu, Huangpu* ☎ *021/6467–9900.*

**Brown Sugar.** In addition to all manner of jazz, this lounge hosts weekly soul and world music nights, often to a packed house. Loud, dark, and smokey, this is the place to cut a rug, snap your fingers, and bop your head. ⊠ *Xintiandi North Block, 181 Taicang Lu, Huangpu* ☎ *021/5382–8998* ⊕ *www.brownsugarlive.com.*

**MAO Livehouse** (光芒 *Guāngmáng*). To the west and south of Xintiandi is Shanghai's most active large-scale concert venue. Past performers include Thee Oh Sees, Grimes, and Gang of Four. Up and coming local and foreign bands regularly take to the stage, and the acts vary from heavy metal to folk. ⊠ *308 Chongqing Nan Lu, 3rd fl., Huangpu* ☎ *021/6445–0086.*

### FORMER FRENCH CONCESSION

**Cotton Club** (棉花俱乐部 *Miánhuā jùlèbù*). A dark and smoky jazz and blues club, the Cotton Club is an institution in Shanghai, and still one of the best places to catch live music. It's in a great neighborhood for barhopping, so head here for the 9 pm set and get your night rolling. ⊠ *8 Fuxing Xi Lu, Xuhui* ☎ *021/6437–7110.*

**JZ Club** (爵士酒吧 *Juéshì jiǔbā*). This place is the king of Shanghai's jazz offerings. Various house bands and stellar guest performers mix it up nightly. Look for plush seating and drink prices to match. When you need a break from the noise and crowds, cool off on the roof deck. ⊠ *46 Fuxing Xi Lu, Xuhui* ☎ *021/6431–0269.*

Hang out with the beautiful people at Rouge Bar on the Bund.

### NANJING XI LU AND JING'AN
**House of Blues and Jazz** (布鲁斯与爵士之屋 *Bùlǔsī yǔ juéshì zhīwu*). Decked out in memorabilia from Shanghai's jazz era of the 1930s, the House of Blues and Jazz would be a great bar even without the music, but the several nightly sets make it a must-visit, and the dark-wood paneling and low lighting, plus the requisite smoke, all add to the ambience. ⊠ *60 Fuzhou Lu, Huangpu* ☎ *021/6437–5280.*

**Wooden Box Cafe** (木盒咖啡馆 *Mù hé kāfēi guǎn*). On a quiet lane off busy Nanjing Xi Lu, this café and bar mimics the inside of a tree house, with high ceilings and wood paneling on the rounded walls. The performers here play a variety of jazz and acoustic music, which you can listen to while sipping wine and beer. ⊠ *9 Qinghai Lu, Jing'an* ☎ *021/5213–2965.*

### NORTH SHANGHAI
**Bandu Music** (半度音乐 *Bàndù yīnyuè*). An unpretentious café and bar in the M50 art compound, Bandu sells hard-to-find CDs and occasionally holds concerts of traditional Chinese folk music. ⊠ *50 Moganshan Lu, Unit 11, 1F, Putuo* ☎ *021/6431–0269.*

### XUJIAHUI AND SOUTH SHANGHAI
Fodor's Choice
★
**Yuyintang** (育音堂 *Yùyīntáng*). No one has done as much to bring Shanghai rock out from the underground and into the open as has this collective. Headed by sound engineer and former musician Zhang Haisheng, the group started hosting regular concerts around town and eventually opened its own space. Shows, usually on Friday and Saturday nights or Sunday afternoons, spotlight the latest in young Chi-

nese music. ⊠ *851 Kaixuan Lu, enter behind metro station, Changning* ☎ *021/5237–8662* ⊕ *www.yuyintang.org.*

# SHOPPING

Malls usually don't open until 10 and boutiques at 11. The upside is that stores tend to stay open later, with many closing at 10 pm. Markets generally start earlier, at around 7:30 or 8, and close at around 6. Most stores are open seven days a week.

## XINTIANDI AND CITY CENTER

### CLOTHING AND SHOES

**Raffles Privato.** The sketches of Raffles Design Institute grads come to life at this boutique, where the well-curated selection highlights Shanghai's rising design talents. Graduates apply for six-month showcases and, during their residency, must produce two more collections. Its mostly women's clothing and certainly not cheap. Jersey tops start from around Y600, while jackets and the like hover around Y2,000. ⊠ *Xintiandi Style, 245 Madang Lu, Huangpu* ☎ *021/3304–1108.*

### GIFTS

**Shanghai Museum Shop** (上海博物馆商店 *Shànghài bÛwˇguan shāngdiàn*). This selection of books on China and Chinese culture is impressive, and there are also some interesting children's books. Expensive reproduction ceramics are available, as are more affordable gifts like magnets, scarves, and notebooks. ⊠ *Shanghai Museum, 201 Renmin Dadao (People's Avenue), Huangpu* ☎ *021/6372–3500.*

**Zen Lifestore** (钲艺廊 *Zhēng yì láng*). The porcelain goods here are truly lovely, available in an eye-popping array of colors. Designs range from delicate Chinese landscapes to modern geometric prints. You'll also find here equally pretty candles, incense holders, and pipe-and-water-spigot candlabras (which are very cool, but a bit large to carry home). There's a second location on Dongping Lu in Xuhui. ⊠ *118 Xingye Lu, Huangpu* ☎ *02/5382–2070.*

### JEWELRY

**Amy Lin's Pearls and Jewelry** (艾敏林氏珠宝 *Imǐnlínshì zhubǎo*). Friendly owner Amy Lin has sold pearls to European first ladies and American presidents, but treats all her customers like royalty. Her shop offers inexpensive trinket bracelets, strings of seed pearls, and stunning Australian seawater pearl necklaces. ⊠ *Han City, 580 Nanjing Xi Lu, 3rd fl., Huangpu* ☎ *021/5228–2372* ⊕ *www.amy-pearl.com.*

## NANJING DONG LU AND THE BUND

### ANTIQUES

**Shanghai Antique and Curio Store** (上海文物商店 *Shànghǎi wénwù shāngdiàn*). A pleasant departure from the touristy shops in the area, this government-owned store is an excellent place to gauge whether you are being taken for a ride elsewhere. Goods range from small pieces of embroidery to wedding baskets (traditionally used to hold part of the bride's dowry). A sign warns that some pieces may not be taken out of the country, and we don't recommend you try and find out. ✉ *192–246 Guangdong Lu, Huangpu* ☎ *021/6321–5868.*

### BOOKS AND ART SUPPLIES

**Yangzhenhua Pen Store** (杨振华笔庄 *Yángzhènhuá bǐ zhuāng*). Calligraphy supplies at excellent prices—fine brushes start at just Y4—can be purchased at this long-established shop. It still has the original glass counters and dark-wood shelves and a staff that relaxes at the back with tea and pumpkin seeds. ✉ *290 Fuzhou Lu, Huangpu* ☎ *021/6322–3117.*

### CERAMICS

**Blue Shanghai White** (海上青花 *Hǎishàngqīnghuā*). The eponymous colored ceramics here are designed and hand-painted by the owner and are made in Jingdezhen, once home to China's imperial kilns. Some larger pieces are made with wood salvaged from demolition sites around Shanghai. Prices start at Y70 for a cup to Y30,000 for a screen with ceramic panels. ✉ *17 Fuzhou Lu, Room 103, Huangpu* ☎ *021/6323–0856* ⊕ *www.blueshanghaiwhite.com.*

### CLOTHING AND SHOES

**Suzhou Cobblers** (苏州臭皮匠 *Sūzhōu chòu píjiang*). Beautifully embroidered handmade shoes and slippers with quirky designs such as cabbages are sold alongside funky bags made from rice sacks. Also sold here are sweet knitted toys and children's shoes and sweaters. ✉ *17 Fuzhou Lu, Room 101, Huangpu* ☎ *021/6321–7087* ⊕ *www.suzhoucobblers.com.*

### JEWELRY

**Ling Ling Pearls and Jewelry** (玲玲珠宝 *Inglíng zhubǎo*). Traditional pearl necklaces and inexpensive fashion jewelry that is hipper than the competition's stand out here. Pearl and stone combinations are priced high, but large discounts are often available. The shop is in Pearl City (not to be confused with Hongqiao Pearl Market), among the other pearl and jewelry sellers. ✉ *Pearl City, 558 Nanjing Dong Lu, 2nd fl., Huangpu* ☎ *021/6322–9299.*

## FORMER FRENCH CONCESSION

### CARPETS

**Carpetstan** (手工羊毛地毯 *Carpetstan Shǒugōng yángmáo dìtǎn*). The Kashgari owner here brings in all his rugs from artistans in Kashbar, Afghanistan, Samarkand, and Isfahan. The shop occasionally hosts lectures on carpets and other woven goods. ✉ *570 Yongjia Lu, Room 313, Xuhui* ☎ *021/6082–3065.*

### CLOTHING AND SHOES

**Boutique Cashmere Lover.** The small collection of wickedly soft cashmere and blends is contemporary in design; some have Chinese details. ✉ *248 Taikang Lu, No. 31, Luwan* ☎ *021/6473–7829.*

**Culture Matters** (飞跃回力国货专售 *Fēiyuè huílì guóhuò zhuān shòu*). Feiyue sneakers are sold in Paris for €50, but in Shanghai, where

## TOP SHOPPING STOPS

**Duolun Lu** is a pedestrian street in Shanghai's historic Hongkou. Not only is it lined with examples of old architecture and home to a contemporary art gallery, its stalls and curio stores are ripe for browsing.

**Moganshan Lu** once housed poor artists but has been been developed and repackaged as M50, with galleries and cafés making this a worthy place to while away an afternoon.

**Tianzifang**, often referred to as Taikang Lu, after the street on which it's on, is a former residential area whose redbrick lane houses are now home to quaint boutiques, cafés, restaurants, and bars.

In **Xintiandi**, exclusive and expensive stores are housed in reproduction traditional shikumen—stone gate houses. Your plastic will get plenty of work here, but step outside Xintiandi proper and you'll find charming streets upon which pajama clad citizens still do their marketing.

**Xujiahui,** where six major shopping malls and giant electronics complexes converge, looks like it's straight out of mid-'90s Tokyo. Shop 'til you drop, or play with the gadgets and compare prices at the electronics shops.

**Yu Garden,** a major tourist haunt in the Old Town area of Shanghai, can be overwhelming, but if you're looking for tchotchkes, hard bargaining brings rewards. Here is where you'll find imitation jade, tiny Buddha statues, jewelry and jewelry boxes, scarves, and the like.

Also check out these streets that specialize in specific traditional products: **Fenyang Lu** and **Jinling Lu** for musical instruments; **Changle Lu** and **Maoming Lu** for *qipao* (Chinese-style dresses); and **Fuzhou Lu** for books and art supplies, including calligraphy supplies.

they're made, you can get them starting from just Y50. Most are canvas with rubber soles, although there are a few stylish felt models and a couple in rubber that are great for rainy weather. There's another location at 47 Changle Lu in Xuhui. ⊠ *15 Dongping Lu, Xuhui* 🕾 *021/136–7188–2040.*

**Feel** (金粉世家 *Jīnfěnshìjiā*). The *qipao* may be a traditional Chinese dress, but Feel makes it a style for modern times as well with daring cutouts and thigh-skimming designs. ⊠ *Tianzifang, Lane 210, No. 3, Room 110, 110 Taikang Lu, Huangpu* 🕾 *021/5465–4519, 021/6466–8065.*

**insh** (莺裳工贸 *Yīngshàng gongmào*). A local designer sells cheeky clothes that are not for the fainthearted. Skirts barely cover bottoms, but there are cute takes on traditional *qipao*, as well as a more lifestyle-oriented range in the streetside store. It's a good place for T-shirts featuring stylish Chinese-inspired designs. ⊠ *200 Taikang Lu, Luwan* 🕾 *021/6466–5249.*

**L'Atelier Mandarine.** Clothing and accessories here focus on lounging. The French designer uses natural fabrics such as silk, cotton, and cashmere for her own designs, and stocks other local labels. The simple and chic designs let the quality of the fabric speak for itself. ⊠ *210 Taikang*

*Lu, Studio No. 318, Huangpu* ☎ *021/6473–5381.*

**Shanghai Tang** (上海滩 *Shànghǎitān*). This is one of China's leading fashion brands, with distinctive acid-bright silks, soft-as-a-baby's-bottom cashmere, and funky housewares. Sigh at the beautiful fabrics and designs and gasp at the inflated prices. There are other branches at the Jinjiang Hotel, 59 Maoming Nan Lum in Xuhui, and the Shangri-La Hotel, 33 Fucheng Lu in Pudong. ✉ *181 Taicang Lu, Huangpu* ☎ *021/6384–1601* ⊕ *www.shanghaitang.com.*

**Shanghai Trio** (上海组合 *Shànghǎizuhé*). Chinese fabrics mixed with French flair, irresistible children's clothes and sweet little kimonos in bright colors, great utilitarian satchels that scream urban chic, and crafty necklaces are the stars of this range. This is the shop to come to when you want to spoil your precious nieces and nephews. ✉ *Xintiandi, 181 Taicang Lu, Huangpu* ☎ *021/6355–2974* ⊕ *www. shanghaitrio.com.cn.*

> ### WHO ARE THE MIAO?
>
> Famous for their intricate embroidery work, the Miao are one of the oldest ethnic-minority groups in China and one of the largest groups still in Southwest China. The Miao may have existed as early as 200 BC, in the Han Dynasty. It's not only the Miao, however, who are accomplished embroidery artists. Many ethnic-minority groups in southwestern China make pieces of similar quality.

## GIFTS AND HOUSEWARES

**Brocade Country** (锦绣纺 *Jǐnxiufǎng*). The English-speaking owner, Liu Xiao Lan, has a Miao mother and a broad knowledge of her pieces. The Miao sew their history into the cloth, and she knows the meaning behind each one. Some pieces are collector's items, and Ms. Liu has also started designing more wearable items. Antique embroidery can cost an arm and a leg, but smaller embroidery pieces are affordable and easy to slip into a suitcase. ✉ *616 Julu Lu, Jing'an* ☎ *021/6279–2677.*

Fodor's Choice ★ **BrutCake** (創意製作社 *BrutCake chuàngyì zhìzuò shè*). Taiwanese designer Nicole Teng's showroom is at once welcoming, with comfy oversized chairs (for sale), reclaimed wood, and quirky ceramic pieces on every surface. In addition to dinnerware and ceramic lampshades, BrutCake sells beautiful hand-woven and dyed fabrics. ✉ *232 Anfu Lu, Xuhui* ☎ *021/5448–8159* ⊕ *brutcake.com* ☽ *Closed Mon.*

**Jooi** (瑞逸 *Ruìyì*). This Danish-owned design studio focuses on bags and accessories in fabrics ranging from industrial felt to shiny patent leather. The small home decor collection features a handful of pillows—convenient souvenirs as they double as plane accessories. Jooi employs local artistans, so you can feel good about what you're buying. ✉ *International Artist Factory, 210 Taikang Lu, Studio 201, Huangpu* ☎ *021/6473–6193* ⊕ *www.jooi.com.*

**Madame Mao's Dowry** (毛太设计 *Máotài shèjì*). This shop claims its covetable collection of mostly propaganda items from the '50s, '60s, and '70s is sourced from the countryside and areas in Sichuan Province and around Beijing and Tianjin. Whether they're authentic is up for debate. Mixed in with the older pieces are hip designs from local and international designers. Although this could be your one-stop shopping experience, remember this is communism at capitalist prices: expect to pay around Y100 for a small Revolution-era teapot and nearly Y2,000 for a mirror from the same period. ⊠ *207 Fumin Lu, Luwan* ☎ *021/5403–3551.*

### TEA

**Shanghai Huangshan Tea Company** (上海黄山茶叶有限公司 *Shànghǎi huángshān cháyè yǒuxiàn gōngsī*). This tea shop sells traditional Yixing teapots as well as a huge selection of China's best teas. The higher the price, the better the tea. ⊠ *605 Huaihai Zhong Lu, Huangpu* ☎ *021/5306–2974.*

**Song Fang Maison de Thé.** Parisian Florence Samson, who has lived in Shanghai for more than a decade, sells both Chinese and French tea at inflated prices, but the location in a 1930s lane house and the second-floor café, up a winding narrow staircase, make it quite charming. If you decide to purchase one of the cornflower-blue tea canisters as a souvenir, we recommend filling it up at a local shop. ⊠ *227 Yongjia Lu, Xuhui* ☎ *021/6433-8283* ⊕ *www.songfangtea.com.*

## PUDONG

### MALLS

**Super Brand Mall** (正大广场 *Zhèngdà guāngchǎng*). One of Asia's largest malls, this 10-story behemoth has a mind-boggling array of international shops and food stops, as well as a cineplex. It can be overwhelming if you don't love to shop. The basement food court has several good restaurants, including salad spot called Sproutworks and pizza joint known as Matto. ⊠ *168 Lujiazui Lu, Pudong* ☎ *021/6887–7888* ⊕ *www.superbrandmall.com.*

**ifc.** Like its Hong Kong sister, this shiny mall is packed with luxury goods stores. The basement food court has everything from octopus balls to Japanese-style crepes, as well as very expensive imported groceries. The upper levels are dotted with restaurants serving varying fare, high in quality and in price. ■TIP→ **The Lujiazui station of metro line 2 is inside the mall.** ⊠ *8 Shiji Da Dao(Century Avenue), Pudong* ☎ *021/2020–7070.*

## NORTH SHANGHAI

### GIFTS AND HOUSEWARES

**Spin** (旋 *Xuán*). Halfway between a gallery and a shop, Spin sells contemporary Chinese pottery handmade in Jingdezhen, China's pottery capital. We love the chopstick rests shaped like bone fragments and the too-cute dim sum paperweights in a little bamboo steamer. The second level has dinnerware, tea sets, and—the perfect gift for Canadians—beautifully cast maple leaves that are just the right size for change or keys. ⊠ *360 Kangding Lu, Jing'an* ☎ *021/6279–2545.*

Shanghai is known for high-end shopping.

### TEA

**Tianshan Tea City** (大不同天山茶城 *Dàbùtóng tiānshān cháchéng*). This place stocks all the tea in China, and then some. More than 300 vendors occupy three floors, making the whole experience so very China. You can buy such famous teas as West Lake dragon well tea, from nearby Hangzhou, and Wuyi red-robe tea, as well as the tea sets to serve them in. ✉ *520 Zhongshan Xi Lu, Changning* ☎ *021/6259–9999.*

## XUJIAHUI AND SOUTH SHANGHAI

### ANTIQUES

**Henry Antique Warehouse** (汉瑞古典家俱 *Hànruì gǔdiǎn jiājù*). This showroom sometimes serves as an exhibition hall for modern designs created jointly by students at Tongji University and a team of 50 craftsmen. Wandering through the pieces on display is a trek through Chinese history, from intricately carved traditional altar tables to streamlined contemporary pieces. ✉ *Building 2, 361 Hongzhong Lu, 3rd fl., Minhang* ☎ *021/6401–0831* ⊕ *www.h-antique.com.*

**Hu & Hu Antiques** (古悦家俱 *Uyuè jiājù*). Co-owner Marybelle Hu worked at Taipei's National Palace Museum as well as Sotheby's in Los Angeles before opening this shop with sister-in-law Lin in 1998. The bright, airy showroom contains Tibetan chests and other rich furniture as well as a large selection of accessories, from lanterns to mooncake molds. The prices are higher than their competitors', but so is their standard of service. ✉ *Alley 1885, 8 Caobao Lu, Minhang* ☎ *021/3431–1212* ⊕ *www.hu-hu.com.*

# EASTERN CHINA

Zhejiang and Fujian

# WELCOME TO EASTERN CHINA

## TOP REASONS TO GO

★ **Hangzhou Teatime:** Sip sublime Longjing tea and buy silk in the footsteps of Marco Polo at Hangzhou's romantic West Lake.

★ **Qiantian Tidal Bore:** Marvel at one of nature's most enthralling spectacles: the mighty tidal bore at the mouth of Zhejiang's Qiantian River.

★ **Gulangyu:** Wander through narrow alleyways filled with a fascinating blend of Chinese and European architecture, and recharge in seaside garden pavilions without dodging traffic on this historic, car-free island.

★ **Shaoxing Wine:** Dramatized by one of China's most famous writers, Lu Xun, Shaoxing wine is celebrated throughout the region. Potent for sure, Shaoxing wine is de rigueur for local dining.

★ **Hakka Roundhouses:** The founder of modern China, Dr. Sun Yat-sen, came from China's proud Hakka minority people, whose ancient tradition of rounded-home architecture is now treasured.

**1 Hangzhou.** Described by Marco Polo as the finest and noblest city in the world, Hangzhou is famous for the beautiful West Lake. In recent years Hangzhou has also emerged as one of China's most vibrant cities. Visit the plantations that produce the area's famous Longjing tea, or stroll in forested hills to take in the views of the surrounding area.

**2 Shaoxing.** Shaoxing is famed for its historic homes and many traditional bridges. This small, well-preserved town is perhaps the best place to experience the historic atmosphere of a traditional Yangze Delta town. Visit the stunning Figure 8 Bridge, which is indeed shaped like a figure eight and was erected more than 800 years ago.

**3 Ningbo.** A perfect blend of old and new, this bustling seaside metropolis is the ideal place to comfortably veer off the standard tourist trail. Climb the ancient Tianfeng Pagoda to survey the busy masses, and as night falls, head over to Laowaitan, the city's entertainment district complete with a centuries-old Portuguese church and dozens of international bars and restaurants.

**4 Xiamen.** With a bird's-eye view of the Taiwan Straight, Xiamen is poised to profit from the windfall of increased economic activity between Taiwan and the mainland. Famous for its party atmosphere and popular with young expats, Xiamen's trendy clubs and upscale restaurants are becoming as popular as the city's famous beaches and botanical gardens.

JIANGXI

Wuyi Mountain Natural Reserve

Shaowu

Sanming

Changting

Longyan

Hakka Settlements of Yongding

GUANGDONG

## GETTING ORIENTED

With thousands of miles of coastline, the provinces of Zhejiang and Fujian are the rounded belly section of China's east coast. Indeed, their shores front the East China Sea and the South China Sea. Zhejiang Province's primary ports of call are the cities of Ningbo and Hangzhou, both of which are within two hours of Shanghai by bus. Hangzhou is also famous as the southernmost city of the Grand Canal. Directly south of Zhejiang is the lush and mountainous province of Fujian. With its proximity to the Taiwan Straight, the wealthy coastal cities of Fujian are convenient to each other, but the province's mountainous interior make them a long train trip away from the rest of the region.

5

0       75 mi

0       75 km

Updated by
Kate Springer

In Eastern China, the past's rich legacy and the challenges and aspirations for China's future combine in a present that is dizzying in its variety and speed of transformation. Zhejiang and Fujian, often overlooked on the standard Beijing–Shanghai–Hong Kong tourist trail, offer some of the country's most verdant scenery and a plethora of diversions, like hiking through ancient villages, bicycling along lush tea fields, and lounging on lively beaches.

Zhejiang has always been a hub of culture, learning, and commerce. The cities, with their elegant gardens, elaborate temples, and fine crafts, evoke the sophisticated and refined world of classical China's literati. Since the Southern Song Dynasty (1127–79), large numbers of Fujianese have emigrated around Southeast Asia. As a result, Fujian Province has strong ties to overseas Chinese. In 1979 Fujian was allowed to form the first Special Economic Zone (SEZ)—a testing ground for capitalist market economy—at Xiamen. Today, although Xiamen is a wealthy place with a vibrant economy, the city has managed to retain its Old World charm.

## PLANNING

### WHEN TO GO

Fall and spring are the ideal times to visit the region. Spring, especially April and May, has very comfortable temperatures, and the trees and flowers are in full bloom. Hangzhou's spectacular cherry blossoms bloom in spring, dotting the gardens surrounding the West Lake. Summers are hot and muggy, and winters are short (the temperature rarely dips below zero) but miserably wet, windy, and chilly. Typhoons can strike any time from late summer through autumn. The region has a long and very pleasant fall season—moderate weather and clear skies lasting into early December. Chinese tourists flood in during the two "Golden Week" holidays at the start of May and October and during the Lunar New Year (late January to mid-February), so avoid traveling during these times.

## GETTING HERE AND AROUND

Shanghai is generally the best place to begin exploring Eastern China. It has good amenities, and with two airports and train stations it offers myriad connections across the country. Most major travel agents in Shanghai speak English. If you want to make Hangzhou your base, many cheap flights are available, although choice of destinations is more limited.

### AIR TRAVEL

Air travel in Eastern China is very straightforward and simple. Hangzhou's Xiaoshan International Airport is modern and well connected, and domestic flights are abundant. Hangzhou is increasingly adding more international routes, already including Amsterdam (KLM), Kuala Lumpur (Dragonair), Tokyo (Air Nippon), Seoul (Asiana Airlines), Bangkok (Hainan Airlines), Chicago (Delta), Los Angeles (United), Malé (China Southern Airlines), Hong Kong (Hong Kong Airlines) and Paris (Lufthansa). Ningbo offers direct flights to Taipei (Hainan Air), Hong Kong (Dragonair), Beijing (China Southern Airlines) and Xiamen is well connected to Jakarta (Air China), Singapore (Cathay Pacific), and Manila (Air China).

### BUS TRAVEL

Traveling by bus in Eastern China is a great way to get around, as even tiny cities and villages will have a station. Large cities such as Hangzhou will have several stations. Buses in Eastern China will usually be relatively new, air-conditioned vehicles, and almost always leave on time. The biggest headache you'll likely encounter is trying to navigate through the masses at the stations to buy your tickets. Ask your hotel to purchase tickets in advance, as line etiquette in China is nonexistent and can be frustrating, especially for non-Mandarin speakers. If traveling between major cities, such as between Hangzhou and Ningbo, buses leave frequently, so just show up and get on the next available departure.

### CAR TRAVEL

Hiring a driver is possible, but unreasonably expensive. Plan on paying at least $200 for an eight-hour day. Hangzhou Car Service operates an impressive fleet of Japanese, German, and American vehicles, and can arrange city tours, intercity transport, and airport pickup. Since taxis are cheap and plentiful, navigating the cities is fairly easy.

**Contact Info Hangzhou Car Service.** Hangzhou Car Service ☏ *0755/2594–1385* ⊕ *www.hangzhoucarservice.com.*

### TRAIN TRAVEL

Bullet trains are the easiest, quickest, and most comfortable option. For the shortest journeys, look for G-coded trains, or the letters CHR (China High-Speed Rail). Shanghai to Hangzhou, for example, takes approximately an hour, and there are roughly 30 daily departures. D-coded trains take 1 hour and 40 minutes. Slower trains are uncomfortable for long distances and best avoided.

### HEALTH AND SAFETY

Many big cities have foreign doctors and clinics catering to the expatriate community. These clinics charge exponentially more than Chinese hospitals, but hygiene standards are comparable to those of North America and Western Europe. Chinese hospitals, crowded and grimy, should be used as a last resort.

Petty crime is common, especially in crowded places such as train and bus stations. Use common sense and keep an eye on your valuables. Violent crime targeting foreigners is practically nonexistent, and most visitors feel comfortable walking around any time of day.

### MONEY MATTERS

Prices are negotiable everywhere except supermarkets. Do not accept prices quoted in foreign currency, and never pay more than you think the article is really worth. Tourist markups can hit 1,000% in major attractions. Don't be afraid to say *"Tai gui le!"* ("too expensive") and walk away. He or she will probably call you back with a better price.

China is not a tipping country; however, tips constitute the majority of a tour guide's income.

### RESTAURANTS

Zhejiang cuisine is often steamed or roasted, and has a subtler, salty flavor; specialties include yellow croaker with Chinese cabbage, sea eel, drunken chicken, and stewed chicken. In Shaoxing locals traditionally start the day by downing a bowl or two of *huang jiu* (rice wine), the true breakfast of champions. Shaoxing's most famous dish is its deep-fried *chou dofu,* or stinky tofu. Try it with a touch of the local chili sauce.

The cuisine of Fujian has its own characteristics. Spareribs are a specialty, as are soups and stews using a soy and rice-wine stock. The coastal cities of Fujian offer a wonderful range of seafood, including river eel with leeks, fried jumbo prawns, and steamed crab.

*Prices in the reviews are the average cost of a main course at dinner or, if dinner is not served, at lunch.*

### HOTELS

Hotels in this region cater to all budgets, all the way up to luxurious resorts and international chains offering every creature comfort. Besides a general lack of amenities, cheaper options may not be able to accept foreign credit cards. Family-run guesthouses are rare, as are boutique hotels. Consider a domestic chain called the Orange Hotel, with dozens of locations in Hangzhou, Ningbo, and Nanjing. Comfortable and imaginative rooms are available from US$70 to $85 a night.

*Prices in the reviews are the lowest cost of a standard double room in high season.*

### VISITOR INFORMATION

Tourist kiosks are ubiquitous in major cities and tourist destinations, but mostly cater to domestic travelers. The best sources for visitor information are the English-language city magazines like *More Hangzhou* (⊕ *www.morehangzhou.com*), Nanjing's *Map* (⊕ *www.myq.com.cn*), and *What's On Xiamen* (⊕ *www.whatsonxiamen.com*) can be found at international hotels and restaurants.

Zheijang

## TOURS

Countless pricey tour operators serve Eastern China, but it's easy to get around on your own. Taking the subway or a long walk to just one attraction can be more fascinating than a whole day's worth of attractions with a large group of strangers.

Tea lovers should consider Seven Cups, which offers 12- to 15-day visits to tea gardens and hands-on experience with harvest and production methods of the country's finest teas. Experience the Tulou Hakka Roundhouse with Discover Fujian. The reasonably priced company leads day trips, as well as four- to five-day journeys, to these ancient, circular structures.

**Tour Info Seven Cups** ☎ 520/628–2952 ⊕ www.sevencups.com. **Discover Fujian** ✉ 1118 Xiahe Lu, 10th fl., Xiamen ☎ 592/398–9901 ⊕ www. discoverfujian.com.

# ZHEJIANG

The province of Zhejiang showcases the region's agricultural prowess and dedication to nature, even as it is one of China's most populous urban regions. The capital city of Hangzhou is famous for West Lake, which is visited by millions of tourists annually. A center of culture and trade, Zhejiang is also one of China's wealthiest provinces. Hangzhou served as one of the country's eight ancient capital cities, after the Song Dynasty rulers fled Jurchen invaders. Throughout history, the city also benefited from its position as the last stop on the Grand Canal, the conduit for supplying goods to the imperial north.

Shaoxing showcases another aspect of Zhejiang life. The small-town flavor of this city-on-canals survives, despite a growing population. Several high-profile figures helped put Shaoxing on the map, including former Premier Zhou Enlai and novelist Lu Xun.

Geographically, the river basin's plains in the north near Shanghai give way to mountains in the south of the province. Besides grain, the province also is recognized in China for its tea, crafts, silk production, and long tradition of sculpture and carving.

## HANGZHOU

*Approximately an hour (202 km, 126 miles) southwest of Shanghai by train.*

Residents of Hangzhou are immensely proud of their city, and will often point to a classical saying that identifies it as an "earthly paradise." Indeed, Hangzhou is one of the country's most enjoyable cities. The green spaces and hilly landscape that surround the city make Hangzhou unique in Eastern China. Add to the experience a thriving arts scene, sophisticated restaurants, and vibrant nightlife, and Hangzhou vies with nearby Shanghai as the hippest city in the East.

### GETTING HERE AND AROUND

Hangzhou is best accessed by train; the tourist express takes around an hour from Shanghai. Buses will get you here from Shanghai in three hours or from Suzhou in 2½ hours.

AIR TRAVEL Hangzhou Xiaoshan International Airport, about 27 km (17 miles) southeast of the city, has frequent flights to Hong Kong, Guangzhou, and Beijing, which are all about two hours away. There are also flights from other major cities around the region.

Major hotels offer limousine service to the airport. Taxis to the airport cost around Y100. A bus (Y20 per person) leaves from the CAAC office on Tiyuchang Lu every 30 minutes between 5:30 am and 9 pm.

BUS TRAVEL Hangzhou is the bus hub for the province and has several stations. The Hangzhou Passenger Transport Station (Jiubao) is the city's biggest, with several hundred departures per day to destinations like Shaoxing (1 hour), Suzhou (2½ hours), and Shanghai (3 hours). The West Bus Station (Xi Zhan) has several buses daily to the Yellow Mountain, as well as to Yushan, and the South Bus Station has buses to Xiamen. About 9 km (5 miles) north of the city is the North Bus Station (Bei Zhan), where there are buses to Beijing (6 to 6½ hours).

In addition to Hangzhou's regular city buses, a series of modern, air-conditioned buses connect most major tourist sights. Bus Y1 links Baidi Causeway, Solitary Hill Island, Yue Fei Mausoleum, the Temple of the Soul's Retreat, and Orioles Singing in the Willows. Bus Y3 runs to

Diamond Hill, the China National Silk Museum, and the China Tea Museum.

TAXI TRAVEL  Hangzhou's clean, reliable taxi fleet makes it easy to get from West Lake to far-flung sights like the Temple of the Soul's Retreat and the China Tea Museum. Fares usually run Y30 to Y45. You can also book cabs by the hour (Y100) or half-day (Y400). ■ TIP➔ Avoid looking for a taxi between 4 and 5 pm, as virtually all drivers are finishing their shifts and refuse to pick anyone up.

TRAIN TRAVEL  Travel between Shanghai and Hangzhou is very efficient. Fast trains take about an hour, while local trains take two or more. The train station can be chaotic, but hotel travel desks will often book advance tickets for a small fee. Trains also run to Suzhou (1½ hours), Nanjing (2½ hours), and most cities in Fujian.

### RENT A BIKE

Shaded by willow trees, West Lake is one of the country's most pleasant places for bicycling. This path, away from car traffic, is also a quick way to move between the area's major sights. Numerous public bike-rental agencies are scattered around the lake, especially near Orioles Singing in the Willows. Rentals are free for the first hour, maxing out at Y3 per hour after three hours. A Y200 deposit and some form of identification are required.

### SAFETY AND PRECAUTIONS
Hangzhou is a very safe city. To be on the safe side, be cautious in crowded places, such as the train station, and keep a close eye on valuables.

### TIMING
More than any other city in China, Hangzhou shouldn't be rushed. Give yourself at least two full days to explore the city. The West Lake and the pagodas and gardens that dot its periphery will occupy at least a full day. Hefang Pedestrian Street, Lingyin Temple, and a variety of museums will fill another day. It's easy to spend four to five days exploring the tea fields and surrounding villages.

### TOURS
Hotels can set up tours of the city's sights. You can also hire a car, driver, and translator through CITS, which has an office east of West Lake in the Zhejiang Tourism Board building. It's relatively inexpensive, and you'll get discounts you wouldn't be able to negotiate for yourself. Smaller agencies tend to be less experienced with the needs of foreign travelers.

Taxi drivers often offer tours. Although these can be as good as official ones, your driver's knowledge of English may be minimal.

### ESSENTIALS
**Air Contacts CAAC** ✉ 390 Tiyuchang Lu ☎ 0571/8515–4259. **Dragonair** ✉ Radisson Plaza Hotel Hangzhou, 333 Tiyuchang Lu, 5th fl. ☎ 0571/8506–8388 ⊕ www.dragonair.com. **Hangzhou Xiaoshan International Airport** ☎ 0571/8666–1234 ⊕ www.hzairport.com.

**Bank Bank of China** ✉ 321 Feng Qi Lu ☎ 0571/8501–1888.

**Boat and Ferry Contact CITS** ✉ Huancheng Bei Lu ☎ 0571/8515–3360.

**Bus Contacts Passenger Transport Station** ⊠ *71 Genshan Xi Lu*
☎ *0571/8519–1122.* **North Bus Station** ⊠ *766 Moganshan Lu* ☎ *0571/8809–3099.* **West Bus Station** ⊠ *357 Tianmushan Lu* ☎ *0571/8522–2237.*

**Medical Assistance Sir Run Run Shaw Hospital International Service Clinic** ⊠ *3 East Qingchun Lu, Tower 3, 5th fl.* ☎ *0571/8600–6118.*

**Train Information Hangzhou Train Station** ⊠ *1 Huan Cheng Dong Lu, near intersection of Jiang Cheng Lu and Xihu Da Dao* ☎ *0571/9510–5105.*

**Visitor and Tour Info Hangzhou Tourism Commission** ⊠ *228 Yan'an Lu*
☎ *0571/8792–5073.* **China International Travel Service Zhejiang** ⊠ *1 Shihan Lu, next to the Hangzhou Tourism Bureau* ☎ *0571/8515–3301* ⊕ *www.cits.net.*

## EXPLORING HANGZHOU

### AROUND WEST LAKE

**West Lake** (西湖 *Xīhú*). With arched bridges stretching over the water, West Lake is the heart of Hangzhou. Originally a bay, the whole area was built up gradually throughout the years, a combination of natural changes and human shaping of the land. The shores are idyllic and imminently photographable, enhanced by meandering paths, artificial islands, and countless pavilions with upturned roofs. Two pedestrian causeways cross the lake: **Bai** in the north and **Su** in the west. They are named for two poet–governors from different eras who invested in landscaping and developing the lake. Ideal for strolling or biking, both walkways are lined with willow and peach trees, crossed by bridges, and dotted with benches where you can pause to admire the views. ⊠ *Along Nanshan Lu.*

**Diamond Hill (Precious Stone Hill)** (宝石山 *Bǎoshíshān*). The slender spire of Baochu Pagoda rises atop Diamond Hill. The brick and stone pagoda is visible from about anywhere on the lake. From the hilltop you can see across the lake to Hangzhou City. Numerous paths from the lakeside lead up the hill, which is dotted with Buddhist and Taoist shrines. Several caves provide shade from the hot summer sun. ⊠ *North of West Lake.*

Fodor's Choice ★   **Evening Sunlight at Thunder Peak Pagoda** (雷锋夕照 *Léifēng xīzhào*). On the southeastern shore of West Lake is the Evening Sunlight at Thunder Peak Pagoda. Local legend says that the original Thunder Peak Pagoda was constructed to imprison a snake-turned-human who lost her mortal love on West Lake. The pagoda collapsed in 1924, perhaps finally freeing the White Snake. A new tower, completed in 2002, sits beside the remains of its predecessor. There's a sculpture on each level, including one that depicts the tragic story of the White Snake. The foundation dates to AD 976 and is an active archaeological site, where scientists uncovered a miniature silver pagoda containing what is said to be a lock of the Buddha's hair; it's on display in a separate hall. The view of the lake is breathtaking, particularly at sunset. ⊠ *15 Nanshan Lu* ☎ *0571/8798-2111* 🎫 *Y40* ⊙ *Daily 8 am–8:30 pm.*

**Orioles Singing in the Willows** (柳浪闻莺 *Liǔlàng wényíng*). Along the eastern bank of West Lake is Orioles Singing in the Willows, a nice place to watch boats on the water. This park comes alive during the Lantern Festival, held in the winter. Paper lanterns are set to float on the river,

A picture-perfect sunset over West Lake

under the willow boughs. ⊠ *11 Nanshan Lu, near intersection of Hefang Jie and Nanshan Lu.*

**Solitary Hill Island** (孤山岛 *Gūshāndǎo*). A palace for the exclusive use of the emperor during his visits to Hangzhou once stood on Solitary Hill Island, the largest island in West Lake. On its southern side is a small, carefully composed park with several pavilions and a pond. A path leads up the hill to the Xiling Seal Engraver's Society, where professional carvers design and create seals. The society's garden has one of the best views of the lake. ⊠ *Bai Causeway* ☑ *Free* ☉ *Daily 8–dusk.*

**NEED A BREAK?**

**Cathay View Foot Massage.** Reward yourself with a heavenly foot or full-body massage at Cathay View Foot Massage. We recommend the 90-minute (Y228) body massage package, which includes a 30-minute foot bath and massage and endless tea, fruit, and snacks in a cozy, dimly lit private room (up to four people). This spot is just off Nanshan Lu, down a small street near the Crystal Orange Hotel. ⊠ *7 Qingbo Jie, off Nanshan Lu* ☎ *0571/8768-0118.*

**Three Pools Reflecting the Moon** (三潭印月 *Sāntán yínyuè*). Here you'll find walkways surrounding several large ponds, all connected by zig-zagging bridges. Off the island's southern shore are three stone Ming Dynasty pagodas. During the Mid-Autumn Moon Festival, held in the middle of September, lanterns are lit in the pagodas, creating the three golden disks that give the island its name. Boats costing between Y35 and Y45 run between here and Solitary Hill Island. ⊠ *Southern side of West Lake* ☑ *Y45, includes boat ride* ☉ *Daily 7–5:30.*

## WEST LAKE IS THE BEST

A famous poem says, "Of all the lakes, north, south, east and west, the one at West Lake is the best." Start exploring where Pinghai Road meets Harbin Road in the northeastern part of the lake. There's a fabulous boardwalk with weeping willows, restaurants, and a lakeside teahouse.

Wending north, you can cross the street to ascend a small hill capped with the Baochu Pagoda. Here the views of West Lake are some of the best in the city. Once you climb down, you can venture to the Baidi and Sudi causeways through the middle of the lake. Don't miss the classical Lingyin Temple, nestled in the nearby hills.

Take a guided boat from the southern shore by night, when the Three Pools Mirroring the Moon pagoda is alight. This stone pagoda has six incised circles. When candles are set inside them, the light appears as romantic moons.

**Zhejiang Provincial Museum** (浙江省博物馆 *Zhéjiāngshěng bówùguǎn*). Solitary Hill Island is home to the Zhejiang Provincial Museum, which has a good collection of archaeological finds, as well as bronzes and paintings. ⊠ *25 Gushan Lu* ☎ *0571/8798–0281* ⊕ *www. zhejiangmuseum.com* ⊡ *Free* ⊙ *Weekdays 8:30–4:30.*

**TOP ATTRACTIONS**

**China National Silk Museum** (中国丝绸博物馆 *Zhōngguó sīchóu bówùguǎn*). From worm to weave, the China National Silk Museum explores traditional silk production, illustrating every step of the process. By the end, you'll comprehend the cost of this fine fiber made from cocoons of mulberry-munching larvae. On display are looms, brocades, and a rotating exhibit of historic robes from different Chinese dynasties. The first-floor shop has the city's largest selection of silk, and sells it by the meter. The museum is south of West Lake, on the road to Jade Emperor Hill. ⊠ *73–1 Yuhuangshan Lu* ☎ *0571/8703–5150* ⊕ *www. chinasilkmuseum.com* ⊡ *Free* ⊙ *Daily 9–4:45.*

Fodor's Choice ★ **China Tea Museum** (中国茶叶博物馆 *Zhōngguó cháyé bówùguǎn*). The fascinating China Tea Museum explores all facets of China's tea culture, such as the utensils used in the traditional ceremony. Galleries contain fascinating information about the varieties and quality of leaves, brewing techniques, and gathering methods, all with good English explanations. A shop offers a wide range of teas, without the bargaining you'll encounter at Dragon Well Tea Park. ⊠ *88 Longjing Lu, north of Dragon Well Tea Park* ☎ *0571/8796–4221* ⊕ *www.teamuseum.cn* ⊡ *Free* ⊙ *Tues.–Sun., 8:30–4:30.*

**Dragon Well Tea Park** (龙井闻茶 *Lóngjǐng wénchá*). This park is named for an ancient well whose water is considered ideal for brewing the famous local Longjing tea. Distinguishing between varieties and grades of tea can be confusing for novices, especially under the high pressure of the eager hawkers. It is worth a preliminary trip to the nearby tea museum to bone up first. The highest quality varieties are very expensive, but once you take a sip you will taste the difference. Prices are intentionally high, so be sure to bargain. ⊠ *Longjing Lu, next to Dragon Well Temple.*

Fodor's Choice
★ **Temple of the Soul's Retreat** (灵隐寺 *Língyǐn sí*). One of the major Zen Buddhist shrines in China, the Temple of the Soul's Retreat was founded in 326 by Hui Li, a Buddhist monk from India. He looked at the surrounding mountains and exclaimed, "This is the place where the souls of immortals retreat," hence the name. This site is especially notable for religious carvings on the nearby **Peak That Flew from Afar** (Fēilái fēng). From the 10th to the 14th century, monks and artists sculpted more than 300 images on the mountain's face and inside caves. Over the centuries this shrine has changed due to wars and revolution. The main temple was restored in 1974 following the end of the Cultural Revolution. About 3 km (2 miles) southwest of West Lake, the temple and carvings are among the most popular spots in Hangzhou. ■TIP→ To avoid crowds, visit on weekdays. ⊠ *End of Lingyin Lu* ☎ *0571/8796–8665* ✆ *Carvings Y45, temple Y30* ⊙ *Park daily 5:30 am–5:30 pm, temple daily 7–5:30.*

**WORD OF MOUTH**

"About touring Hangzhou—this last time I finally succumbed to paying for a ride in those open, golf-cart-like vehicles. It was wonderful. I wish I had done this on my very first trip to Hangzhou. The motorized carts—with a fringe on the top—circle completely around West Lake. One entire circle costs 40 Yuan (slightly less than $5) per person." —easytraveler

**WORTH NOTING**

**Pagoda of Six Harmonies** (六和塔 *Liùhétǎ*). Atop Moon Mountain stands the impressive Pagoda of Six Harmonies. Those who climb to the top of the seven-story pagoda are rewarded with great views across the Qiantang River. Originally lanterns were lighted in its windows, and the pagoda served as a lighthouse for ships navigating the river. On the 18th day of the eighth lunar month, the pagoda is packed with people wanting the best seat for Qiantang Reversal. On this day the flow of the river reverses itself, creating large waves that for centuries have delighted observers. Behind the pagoda in an extensive park is an exhibit of 100 or so miniature pagodas, representing every Chinese style. The pagoda is 2½ km (1½ miles) south of West Lake. ⊠ *Fuxing Jie, on the Qiantang River* ✆ *Y20* ⊙ *Daily 6:30 am–5:30 pm.*

**Running Tiger Spring** (虎跑梦泉 *Hǔpáo mèngquán*). According to legend, a traveling monk decided this setting would be perfect for a temple, but was disappointed to discover that there was no source of water. That night he dreamed of two tigers that ripped up the earth around him. When he awoke he was lying next to a spring. On the grounds is an intriguing "dripping wall" cut out of the mountain. Locals line up with jugs to collect the water that pours from its surface, believing that the water has special qualities—and it does. Ask someone in the temple's souvenir shop to float a coin on the surface of the water to prove it. ⊠ *Hupao Lu, near the Pagoda of Six Harmonies* ✆ *Y15* ⊙ *Daily 6–6.*

Buddha sculptures on the face of the Peak That Flew from Afar

**Tomb of Yue Fei** (岳飞墓 *Yuéfēimù*). Near Solitary Hill Island stands the Tomb of Yue Fei, a shrine to honor General Yue Fei (1103–42), who led Song armies against foreign invaders. When he was a young man, his mother tattooed his back with the commandment to "Repay the nation with loyalty." This made Yue Fei a hero of both patriotic loyalty and filial piety. At the height of his success, a jealous rival convinced the emperor to have Yue Fei executed. A subsequent leader pardoned the warrior and enshrined him as a national hero. Statues of Yue Fei's accusers kneel in shame nearby. Traditionally, visitors would spit on statues of the traitors, but a recent sign near the statue asks them to glare instead. ⊠ *80 Beishan Lu, sest of Solitary Hill Island* ☎ *0571/8798–6653* ☞ *Y25* ⏲ *Daily 7:30–6.*

**Yellow Dragon Cave** (黄龙洞 *Huánglóngdòng*). At the foot of Gem Hill is Yellow Dragon Cave, famous for a never-ending stream of water spurting from the head of a yellow dragon. Nearby are a garden and a stage for traditional Yue opera performances. In a nearby grove you'll see examples of rare "square bamboo." ⊠ *69 Shuguang Lu* ☎ *0571/8797–2468* ☞ *Y15* ⏲ *Daily 7:30–6.*

### WHERE TO EAT

For traditional Hangzhou food, check out Gaoyin Street (Gāoyín Jiē). It's a lively strip of restaurants, snack stalls, and teahouses. Expect touts, English menus, and blazing neon signs.

$
MIDDLE EASTERN
✕ **Dong Yi Shun** (东伊顺 *Dōng yī shùn*). Lines form all day at the take-out window for the sesame-coated naan breads and plump, well-seasoned lamb skewers. Sit inside for a large picture menu of Western Chinese and Middle Eastern dishes. The lamb and cheese pancake

with a side order of yogurt comes highly recommended. It's a great alternative to oily Chinese dishes. Walk off the calories afterwards on neon-lit Gaoyin Street. $ *Average main: Y40* ⊠ *99 Gaoyin Jie* ☎ *0571/8780–5163* ▭ *No credit cards.*

$ ✕ **Hanyan Coffee House** (寒烟咖啡馆
INTERNATIONAL  *Hányān kāfēiguǎn*). On a quiet street just east of West Lake, this Himalayan cafe brews some of the city's best java. It's nearly impossible to pass by the curious streetside seating—picture a colorful wooden bench surrounded by potted plants, a vintage TV, and two golden Buddhas—without taking a peek inside.

> **FOR THE KIDS**
>
> **Pagoda of Six Harmonies Garden** (六和塔公园 *Liùhétǎ gōngyuán*). One of our favorite child-friendly places is the garden behind the Pagoda of Six Harmonies in Hangzhou. Climb the stairs of the seven-story pagoda, picnic among the flowerbeds, and play among the miniature versions of China's most famous pagodas and temples. The pagoda is 2½ km (1½ miles) south of West Lake. ⊠ *Fuxing Jie, on the Qiantang River* ☎ *Y20* ⊙ *Daily 6:30 am–5:30 pm.*

Guests are greeted with a welcoming smile, plaid tablecloths, comfy sofas, knit blankets and walls stacked with books and knickknacks. Aside from a room exploding with character, you can also expect freshly brewed coffees, steamy teas, tasty set menus, and a well-stocked bar. $ *Average main: Y50* ⊠ *128 Laodong Lu* ☎ *0571/8160–6978.*

$ ✕ **Honeymoon Dessert.** Originally from Hong Kong, this popular dessert
CAFÉ  spot is rapidly expanding all over the mainland. Occupying a prime piece of real estate along the main drag of the West Lake area, this bright place is sleek and spotless. Trendy Hangzhou locals pack this place at all hours for the inventive and exotic creations. The mango or durian pancake filled with fresh whipped cream is yummy, and the almond and walnut soup is creamy and refreshing. An English picture menu will help guide you. $ *Average main: Y25* ⊠ *98 You Dian Rd.* ☎ *0571/8706–7050* ⊕ *www.honeymoon-dessert.com* ▭ *No credit cards.*

$ ✕ **Lingyin Si Vegetarian Restaurant** (灵隐寺素斋 *Língyǐn sí sùzhāi*). Inside
VEGETARIAN  the Temple of the Soul's Retreat, this restaurant has turned the Buddhist restriction against eating meat into an opportunity to invent a range of delicious vegetarian dishes. Soy replaces chicken and beef, meaning your meal is as benevolent to your health as to the animal world. $ *Average main: Y45* ⊠ *End of Lingyin Si Lu, western shore of West Lake* ☎ *0571/8796–9691* ▭ *No credit cards* ⊙ *No dinner.*

$$$ ✕ **Louwailou Restaurant** (楼外楼 *Lóuwàilóu*). Back in 1848, this place
CHINESE FUSION  opened as a fish shack on West Lake. Business boomed and it became
Fodor's Choice  the most famous restaurant in the province. Specializing in Zhejiang
★  cuisine, Lou Wai Lou specializes in lake perch, which is steamed and served with vinegar sauce. Another highlight is the classic *su dongpo*, pork slow cooked in yellow-rice wine and tender enough to cut with chopsticks. Hangzhou's most famous dish, beggar's chicken, is wrapped in lotus leaves and baked in a clay shell. It's as good as it sounds. $ *Average main: Y130* ⊠ *30 Gushan Lu, southern tip of Solitary Hill Island* ☎ *0571/8796–9023.*

5

## WHERE TO STAY

$ HOTEL Fodor's Choice ★ 🏨 **Crystal Orange Hotel** (桔子水晶酒店 *Júzi shuǐjīng jiǔdiàn*). Travelers love this quirky boutique hotel so much that branches are popping up in other Chinese cities, but the Hangzhou location is a step up from the rest (hence the glittering name). **Pros:** excellent location near West Lake; bicycle rental; free Wi-Fi. **Cons:** bad breakfast; limited amenities; public spaces allow smoking. [$] *Rooms from: Y400* ✉ *122 Qingbo Jie* ☎ *0571/2887–8988* 🌐 *www.orangehotel.com.cn* 🛏 *113 rooms* 🍴 *No meals.*

$$ HOTEL 🏨 **Dragon Hotel** (黄龙饭店 *Huánglóng fàndiàn*). Within walking distance of Diamond Hill and the Yellow Dragon Cave, this hotel stands in quiet and attractive surroundings. **Pros:** good location; reasonable rates; Wi-Fi. **Cons:** indifferent service; lacks atmosphere; staff doesn't speak English. [$] *Rooms from: Y900* ✉ *120 Shuguang Lu, at Hangda Lu* ☎ *0571/8799–8833* 🌐 *www.dragon-hotel.com* 🛏 *529 rooms, 28 suites* 🍴 *No meals.*

$$$$ HOTEL 🏨 **Four Seasons Hotel Hangzhou at West Lake** (杭州西子湖四季酒店 *Hángzhōu xīzǐhú sìlǐ jiǔdiàn*). Combining contemporary Chinese decor, modern amenities, and superlative service, the Four Seasons Hotel Hangzhou at West Lake may be the city's most luxurious retreat. **Pros:** great location; spacious rooms; English-speaking staff. **Cons:** outdoor pool lacks privacy; added cost for Wi-Fi; heavy traffic to and from the hotel. [$] *Rooms from: Y3000* ✉ *5 Lingyin Lu* ☎ *0571/8829–8888* 🌐 *www.fourseasons.com* 🛏 *73 rooms, 5 suites, 3 villas* 🍴 *No meals.*

$$ HOTEL Fodor's Choice ★ 🏨 **Hyatt Regency Hangzhou** (杭州凯悦酒店 *Hángzhōu kǎiyué jiǔdiàn*). Hangzhou's most recognizable and centrally located hotel, the Hyatt Regency combines careful service, comfortable rooms, and a great location. **Pros:** gorgeous views; good service; excellent pool. **Cons:** long check-in time; beginning to show its age; Wi-Fi costs extra. [$] *Rooms from: Y1200* ✉ *28 Hu Bin Lu* ☎ *0571/8779–1234* 🌐 *www.hyatt.com* 🛏 *390 rooms, 22 suites* 🍴 *No meals.*

$$ HOTEL Fodor's Choice ★ 🏨 **Shangri-La Hotel Hangzhou** (杭州香格里拉饭店 *Hángzhōu xiānggélǐlā fàndiàn*). On the site of an ancient temple, the picturesque Shangri-La is an historic landmark. **Pros:** excellent location; staff speaks fluent English; free Wi-Fi. **Cons:** starting to show its age; crowded restaurants; winter fog can ruin views. [$] *Rooms from: Y1216* ✉ *78 Beishan Lu* ☎ *0571/8797–7951* 🌐 *www.shangri-la.com* 🛏 *344 rooms, 39 suites* 🍴 *No meals.*

$$ HOTEL 🏨 **Sofitel Westlake Hangzhou** (杭州索菲特西湖大酒店 *Hángzhōu suǒfēitéxīhú dàjiǔdiàn*). A stone's throw from West Lake, this high-end hotel sits in a lively neighborhood of restaurants, bars, and shops. **Pros:** good location; helpful staff; comfortable beds. **Cons:** small rooms; no Wi-Fi in rooms; some mediocre views. [$] *Rooms from: Y1100* ✉ *333 Xihu Dadao* ☎ *0571/8707–5858* 🌐 *www.sofitel.com* 🛏 *200 rooms, 15 suites* 🍴 *No meals.*

**WORD OF MOUTH**

"We took a fancy pleasure boat out to an island with lots of inlets and flowering plants like rhododendrons and azaleas. The air actually smelled sweet."

—Magster2005

CLOSE UP

# The Qiantang Tidal Bore

During the autumnal equinox, when the moon's gravitational pull is at its peak, huge waves crash up the Qiantang River. Every year at this time, crowds gather at a safe distance to watch what begins as a distant line of white waves approaching. As it nears, it becomes a towering, thundering wall of water.

The phenomenon, known as a tidal bore, occurs when strong tides surge against the current of the river. The Qiantang Tidal Bore is the largest in the world, with speeds recorded up to 25 mi an hour and heights of 30 feet. The Qiantang has the best conditions in the world to produce these tidal waves. Incoming tides are funneled into the shallow riverbed from the Gulf of Hangzhou. The bell shape narrows and concentrates the wave. People have been swept away in the past, so police now enforce a strict viewing distance.

**$$** **☆ Wyndham Grand Plaza Royale Hangzhou** (温德姆大酒店 *Wēndémǔ*
HOTEL *dàjiǔdiàn*). With West Lake only a few steps away, this space-ship–shaped international hotel combines excellent customer service with flawless mountain, lake, and garden views. **Pros:** free Wi-Fi; great location; excellent customer service. **Cons:** locker rooms need renovation; too-firm mattresses; inconsistent restaurant service. $ *Rooms from: Y1120* ⊠ *555 Fengqi Lu* ☎ *0571/8761–6888* ⊕ *www.wyndham.com* ⤴ *283 rooms* ⊙ *No meals.*

## NIGHTLIFE AND THE ARTS

**Eudora Station** (亿多瑞站 *Yìduōruì zhàn*). A more recent addition to Nanshan Road's ever-expanding foreign bar and restaurant scene, Eudora Station fills up on the weekend thanks to live music and cheap drink specials. If you're craving something familiar, the pizzas and salads are decent. ⊠ *101–7 Nanshan Lu* ☎ *0571/8791–4760.*

**JZ Club** (黄楼 *Huáng lóu*). For a refined night out, head to the southeastern edge of the West Lake and visit this well-established jazz club with a cultured clientele. ⊠ *6 Liuying Lu, at the intersection of Nanshan Lu* ☎ *0571/8702–8298* ⊕ *www.jzclub.cc.*

**Maya Bar** (玛雅酒吧 *Mǎyǎ jiǔbā*). Maya Bar is known for its generous pours and a consistent Tex-Mex menu, and occasional live music has made this place popular with expats and locals for years. ⊠ *94 Baisha Quan Lu, Shuguang Lu* ☎ *0571/8999–7628* ⊙ *Daily 12 pm–2 am.*

## SHOPPING

The best souvenirs to buy in Hangzhou are green tea and silk, but all sorts of wooden crafts, silk fans and umbrellas, and antiques are sold in small shops sprinkled around town. For the best Longjing tea, head to Dragon Well Tea Park or the China Tea Museum.

**China Silk Town** (中国丝绸城 *Zhōngguó sīchóu chéng*). Lining a nearly 4,000-foot-long pedestrian street, the stalls and shops of China Silk Town sell silk ties, pajamas, and shirts, plus silk straight off the bolt. ✉ *217 Xinhua Lu, between Fengqi Lu and Tiyuchang Lu* ☎ *0571/8510–0192.*

Fodor's Choice ★ **Hefang Street** (河坊街 *Héfāng jiē*). Also known as Qinghefang Historic Block, Hefang Street is a lively, crowded pedestrian street and not to be missed on a visit to Hangzhou. Restored old buildings are beautifully illuminated at night and house tea shops, traditional apothecaries, clothing boutiques selling *qipaos* (traditional silk Chinese dresses), scrolls, calligraphy, and wooden fans. Artists draw caricatures, candy makers sculpt sugar into art, blind masseurs alleviate tension, and storytellers re-create ancient Chinese legends. Start at Wushan Square and walk west. At night the glowing Chenghuang Pavilion, perched on a mountain top next to the square, is enchanting.

**Wushan Night Market.** The Wushan Night Market has Hangzhou's best late-night snacks, and you'll find accessories of every kind—ties, scarves, pillow covers—as well as knockoff designer goods and fake antiques. It's open nightly. ✉ *Renhe Lu, east of Huansha Lu.*

**Xihu Longjing Tea Company** (西湖龙井茶叶公司 *Xīhú lóngjǐng cháyè gongsī*). About three blocks north of the China Tea Museum, the Xihu Longjing Tea Company has a nice selection of Longjing tea. ✉ *108 Longjing Lu* ☎ *0571/8796–2219.*

# SHAOXING

*68 km (42 miles) east of Hangzhou.*

Shaoxing is alive in the Chinese imagination thanks to the famous writer Lu Xun, who set many of his classic works in this sleepy southern town. A literary revolutionary, Lu Xun broke tradition by writing in the vernacular of everyday Chinese, instead of the stiff, scholarly prose previously held as the only appropriate language for literature.

Today much of the city's charm is in exploring its narrow cobbled streets. The older sections of the city are made up of low stone houses connected by canals crisscrossed by arched bridges. East Lake is no match for the grandeur of Hangzhou's West Lake, but its bizarre rock formations and caves make for interesting tours. Shaoxing is also famous for its celebrated yellow-rice wine, used by cooks everywhere.

**GETTING HERE AND AROUND**

The most reliable and comfortable way to travel to Shaoxing is by train. Regular train and luxury bus services run to Shaoxing from Hangzhou and Shanghai a few times a day.

BUS TRAVEL  Hangzhou's East Bus Station has dozens of buses each day to Shaoxing. In Shaoxing, buses to Hangzhou leave from the main bus station in the north of town. Luxury buses take about an hour.

TAXI TRAVEL  Although Shaoxing is small enough that walking is the best way to get between many sights, the city's small red taxis are relatively inexpensive. Most trips are Y15.

TRAIN TRAVEL  Trains between Hangzhou and Shaoxing take about an hour, but do not leave as frequently as buses. Shaoxing Train Station is 2½ km (1½ mi) north of the city, near the main bus station.

After dark on Hefang Street

### TIMING
Shaoxing's major attractions can be seen in a day trip from Hangzhou.

### ESSENTIALS
**Bank Bank of China** ⊠ *201 Renmin Middle Lu* ☏ *0575/8858–8858.*

**Bus Contact Shaoxing North Bus Station** ⊠ *2 Jiefang Bei Lu, at Huan Cheng Bei Lu* ☏ *0571/8526–0207.*

**Medical Assistance Shaoxing People's Hospital** ⊠ *61 Shaoxing Dongjie* ☏ *0575/8822–8888.*

**Train Contact Shaoxing Train Station** ⊠ *18 Xianqian Jie, off Chezhan Lu* ☏ *0575/8802–2584.*

## EXPLORING SHAOXING
### TOP ATTRACTIONS
**Cai Yuanpei's House** (蔡元培故居 *Càiyuánpéi gùjūn*). The city's quiet northern neighborhoods are great places to wander, with several historic homes and temples that are now preserved as museums. The largest is the Cai Yuanpei's House. The owner was a famous educator during the republic, and his family's large compound is decorated with period furniture. ⊠ *13 Bifei, off Xiaoshan Lu* ☏ *0575/8511–0652* 🚍 *Y8* ⊙ *Daily 8–5.*

**Figure 8 Bridge** (八字桥 *Bāzíqiáo*). In a city of bridges, the Figure 8 is the city's finest and best known. Its long, sloping sides rise to a flat crest that looks like the character for eight, an auspicious number. The bridge is over 800 years old, and is draped with a thick beard of ivy and vines. It sits in a quiet area of old stone houses with canal-side terraces where

**DID YOU KNOW?**

More than 4.2 million metric tons of tea are produced worldwide each year; after water, tea is the world's favorite drink. In China, tea is usually grown on large plantations and is always picked by hand.

CLOSE UP

## What's Cooking

Shaoxing secured its place in the Chinese culinary pantheon with Shaoxing wine, the best yellow-rice wine in the country. Although cooks around the world know the nutty-flavored wine as a marinade and seasoning, in Shaoxing the fermented brew of glutinous rice is put to a variety of uses, from drinking straight up (as early as breakfast) to sipping as a medicine (infused with traditional herbs and remedies). Like grape wines, Shaoxing mellows and improves with age, as its color deepens to a reddish brown. It is local custom to bury a cask when a daughter is born and serve it when she marries.

The wine is an excellent accompaniment to Shaoxing snacks such as pickled greens and the city's most popular street food, *chou doufu,* which means "stinky tofu." The golden-fried squares of tender tofu have a pleasant flavor, if you can get past the pungent odor. Also, look for dishes made with another Shaoxing product, fermented bean curd. With a flavor not unlike an aged cheese, it's rarely eaten by itself, but complements fish and sharpens the flavor of meat dishes.

people wash clothes and chat with neighbors. ⊠ *Baziqiao Zhi Jie, off Renmin Zhong Lu.*

**Lu Xun Family Home** (鲁迅故居 *Lǔxùn gùjūn*). The Lu Xun Family Home was once the stomping ground of literary giant and social critic Lu Xun. His extended family lived around him in a series of courtyards. Nearby is the local school where Lu honed his writing skills. Explore a traditional Shaoxing home and see some beautiful antique furniture. This is a popular destination, so it's wise to book a tour in high season. ⊠ *398 Lu Xun Zhong Lu, 1 block east of Xianhen Hotel* ☎ *0575/8513–2080* ⊠ *Free* ⊙ *Daily 8:30–5.*

**WORTH NOTING**

**Catholic Church of St. Joseph** (天主教堂 *Tiānzhǔjiào táng*). Near the Figure 8 Bridge is the bright pink Catholic Church of St. Joseph, dating from the turn of the 20th century. A hybrid of styles, the Italian-inspired interior is decorated with passages from the Bible in Chinese calligraphy. ⊠ *Bazi Qiao Zhi Jie, off Renmin Zhong Lu.*

**East Lake** (东湖 *Dōnghú*). The narrow East Lake runs along the base of a rocky bluff rising up from the rice paddies of Zhejiang. The crazily shaped cliffs were used as a rock quarry over the centuries, and today their sheer gray faces jut out in sheets of rock. You can hire a local boatman to take you along the base of the cliffs in a traditional black awning boat for around Y40. ⊠ *Yundong Lu, 5 km (4 miles) east of the city center* ⊙ *Daily 7:30–5:30.*

**Zhou Enlai Family Home** (周恩来故居 *Zhōuēnlái gùjūn*). The Zhou Enlai Family Home belonged to the first premier of Communist China, who came from a family of prosperous Shaoxing merchants. Zhou is credited with saving some of China's most important historic monuments from destruction at the hands of the Red Guards during the Cultural Revolution. The compound, a showcase of traditional architecture, houses exhibits on Zhou's life, ranging from his high-school essays to vacation snapshots with his wife. ⊠ *369 Laodong Lu* ☎ *0575/8513–3368* ✆ *Y18* ⊙ *Daily 8–5.*

### WHERE TO EAT

**$** ✗ **Sanwei Jiulou** (三味酒楼 *Sānwéi jiǔlóu*). This restaurant serves up
**CHINESE** local specialties, including warm rice wine served in Shaoxing's distinctive tin kettles. Relaxed and distinctive, it's in an old restored building and appointed with traditional wood furniture. The second story looks out over the street below. ⓈAverage main: Y40 ⊠ 2 Lu Xun Lu ☎ 0575/8896–8777 ▭ No credit cards.

**$$$** ✗ **Xianheng Winehouse** (咸亨酒店 *Xiánhēng jiǔdiàn*). Shaoxing's most
**CHINESE** famous fictional character, the small-town scholar Kong Yiji, would sit on a bench here, dining on wine and boiled beans. Forgo the beans, but the fermented bean curd is good, especially with a bowl of local wine. ⓈAverage main: Y100 ⊠ 179 Lu Xun Zhong Lu, 1 block east of the Sanwei Jiulou ☎ 0575/8511–6666 ▭ No credit cards.

### WHERE TO STAY

**$** ⊡ **New Century Grand Hotel Shaoxing** (紹興開元名都大酒店 *Shàoxīng*
**HOTEL** *kāiyuán míngdū dàjiǔdiàn*). One of the most modern lodging options in Shaoxing, the New Century has wood-paneled rooms decorated in muted shaded with pops of bright orange. **Pros:** relatively new building; free Wi-Fi; good location. **Cons:** indifferent service; limited English; smoking allowed in public areas. ⓈRooms from: Y538 ⊠ 278 Remin Dong Lu ☎ 0575/8809–8888 ⊕ www.kaiyuanhotels.com ⤵ 355 rooms ⦵Breakfast.

**$** ⊡ **Xianheng Hotel** (绍兴咸亨大酒店 *Shàoxíng xiánhēng dàjiǔdiàn*).
**HOTEL** Conveniently located near many of the city's restaurants and a short walk from the Lu Xun Memorial, the Xianheng claims to be the only eco-friendly hotel in the province (though this is difficult to prove). **Pros:** centrally located; good value; free Wi-Fi. **Cons:** spotty English; some rooms need updating; can be noisy at night. ⓈRooms from: Y598 ⊠ 680 Jiefang Nan Lu ☎ 0575/8806–8688 ⊕ www.xianhengchina.com ⤵ 221 rooms ⦵Breakfast.

### SHOPPING

**Lu Xun Zhong Lu.** In addition to calligraphy brushes, and fans, scrolls, and other items decorated with calligraphy, this street has several shops selling the local tin wine pots. In the traditional way of serving yellow-rice wine, the pots are placed on the stove to heat up wine for a cold winter night. Also popular are traditional boatmen's hats, made of thick waterproof black felt.

## NINGBO

*216 km (134 miles) southeast of Hangzhou, 362 km (225 miles) south of Shanghai.*

One of the country's biggest ports and most prosperous cities, Ningbo is an easy place to explore on foot. Rivers and canals flow through a city that is generously sprinkled with tranquil gardens and parks. Colonial architecture and centuries-old pagodas and temples are mixed (rather

One of Shaoxing's famous Waterways

unfortunately) with featureless, communist-style apartment blocks and hideous glass and steel towers. Unlike Shanghai, Hangzhou, and Suzhou, Ningbo is not set up for tourism. This makes it a relaxing and authentic place to explore. Join the locals for bottomless cups of tea and mah-jongg in one of the many parks, or burn through some cash in the city's lively markets, ritzy shopping malls, and trendy nightclubs.

Ningbo, translated as "tranquil waves," sits at the confluence of three rivers (the Yuyao, Fenghua, and Yongjiang) that eventually snake their way to the nearby sea. Ningbo's history stretches back thousands of years. In the 7th century, the Tang Dynasty developed a complicated system of canals, and trade with Japan and Korea boomed. The Portuguese, with their keen eye for location, settled in as early as the 16th century, and left behind a fair number of churches that are still in use today. More recently, during the Second World War the Japanese bombed the city with fleas carrying the bubonic plague.

### GETTING HERE AND AROUND
It's best to travel here by bus, though the express train does connect it with both Hangzhou and Shanghai. The South Bus Station (across the street from the Asia Garden Hotel) has a steady stream of buses leaving every 10–15 minutes from 6 am to 8 pm for Hangzhou, Shanghai, and other destinations.

AIR TRAVEL A 25-minute drive from downtown is Ningbo's Lishe International Airport. There are connections to all major Chinese cities, as well as Hong Kong and Seoul. Major hotels offer free airport shuttle buses. An airport-bound bus (Y10) leaves from the CAAC office every hour from 7:20 am to 6:20 pm.

BUS TRAVEL Ningbo has five long-distance bus stations. The Ningbo Long-Distance Passenger Transport Center and the South Bus Station are the most useful for travelers. The former serves Nanjing, Suzhou, and Yangzhou, as well as Fujian and Anhui provinces, while the latter serves Hangzhou, Shanghai, and Wenzhou. The North Bus Station serves counties around Ningbo, Jiangbei District, and Putuo Mountain. Buses from the West Bus Station head to many scenic areas in and around Ningbo.

TAXI TRAVEL Taxis are cheap and plentiful. Areas of interest are not far apart and should cost no more than Y15, with about Y45 to the airport.

TRAIN TRAVEL Ningbo's East Railway Station serves express trains, including those that get you to Xiamen in about five hours. The station is a Y30 taxi ride from city center. Taking the bus to Hangzhou and Suzhou is more convenient.

### TIMING

Ningbo has enough to occupy you for two full days, but the major attractions can be seen in one day. The city center is compact, and can be explored on foot.

### TOURS

The centrally located Ningbo Tourist Board is an excellent place to grab city maps, find the free English magazine called *Ningbo Guide*, and get advice on attractions outside the city. The magazine is a must for foreigners, and has a perfect map clearly labeling all the hot spots.

### ESSENTIALS

**Air Contact Ningbo Lishe International Airport** ⊠ *Yinzhou District* ☎ *0574/8742–7888* ⊕ *www.ningboairport.com.*

**Bank Bank of China** ⊠ *139 Yao Hang Jie* ☎ *0574/8719–6666.*

**Bus Contacts South Bus Station** ⊠ *6 Nanshan Lu* ☎ *0574/8709–1212.* **East Bus Station** ⊠ *707 Ningchuan Lu* ☎ *0574/8792–4570.* **Ningbo Passenger Transportation Center** ⊠ *181 Tongda Lu* ☎ *0574/8709–1212.* **North Bus Station** ⊠ *100 Taodu Lu* ☎ *0574/8735–5321.*

**Medical Assistance Yinzhou No. 2 Hospital** ⊠ *1 Qianhe Lu* ☎ *0574/8303–9999* ⊕ *www.yz2y.com.*

**Train Information East Railway Station** ⊠ *Fuming Lu and Xingning Lu* ☎ *0574/8787–4214.*

**Visitor and Tour Info Ningbo Tourist Board** ⊠ *90 Dashani Jie* ☎ *0574/8727–6116.* **CAAC.** CAAC ⊠ *91 Xingning Lu* ☎ *0574/8742–7888* ⊕ *www.caac.gov.cn.*

### EXPLORING

**Drum Tower** (鼓楼 *Gǔ lóu*). This huge yellow pavilion, complete with a medieval clock tower, was built in AD 821. Climb to the top for a birds'-eye view of the entire city. The tower marks the entrance to an interesting pedestrian street lined with restored Ming Dynasty–style buildings. Here you'll find tiny shops, makeshift stalls, and every kind of local snack imaginable. It's an ideal spot for people-watching. ⊠ *Gongyuan Lu and Zhongshan Xi Lu* 🆓 *Free* ☉ *Daily 8–4.*

**Jiangbei Catholic Church** (江北天主教堂 *Jiāngběi tiānzhǔ jiàotáng*). Home to China's highest percentage of Christians, Ningbo is also home to several active churches. Marking the beginning of the Laowaitan district, this church was built by the Portuguese in 1872 and is considered to be the best preserved in Zhejiang Province. On any given day Chinese couples can be found taking their wedding photos. ⊠ *2 Zhong Ma Lu, Laowaitan* ☎ *0574/8735–5903* ⊡ *Free.*

**Moon Lake** (月湖 *Yuè hú*). The lovely park that surrounds this 1,400-year-old lake is dotted with quaint teahouses and pavilions with up-turned eaves. Weeping willows line crooked paths that wrap around bamboo groves. In addition to being a peaceful place for a leisurely stroll, the park is centrally located in the city center and a useful point of reference. ⊠ *Liuting Lu.*

> ### SWEET DUMPLINGS
>
> **Gang Ya Gou** (缸鸭狗 *Gāng yā gǒu*). Be sure to try the city's famous *tangyuan*, multicolored sugar dumplings served in a bowl of syrup and eaten like soup. There's no better place to sample this specialty than Gang Ya Gou, an inexpensive spot near Tianyi Square. Also worth a try are the tofu pancakes and crab meat dumplings. Look for the hard-to-miss logo depicting a dog and a duck fighting over a pot of rice, or simply follow the crowds. ⊠ *Kaiming Jie, Shop 68* ☎ *0571/8732–0228* ☉ *Daily 10:30 am–10 pm.*

**Tianfeng Pagoda** (天封塔 *Tiānfēng tǎ*). Seven stories high, this ancient hexagonal structure was first built in AD 695, then destroyed and rebuilt several times over. The current building was completed in the 14th century and is surrounded by a tiny garden complete with gigantic rocks and several inviting stone benches. For a great view of the pagoda, walk directly across the street from the main entrance, enter the market, and walk up to the second floor. Continue climbing to the top for only Y5 and you'll be rewarded with panoramic cityscapes. ⊠ *Near intersection of Jiefang Nanlu and Kaiming Jie* ⊡ *Y5 to climb* ☉ *Daily 8:30–4:30.*

Fodor's Choice ★ **Tianyi Pavilion** (天一阁 *Tiānyī gé*). Down a peaceful alley off Changchun Road, the Tianyi Pavilion is the oldest private library in China. Built in 1596 and founded by Fan Qin, this spiritual place features gold-plated, wood-paneled buildings, bamboo groves, pools, and a rockery. The scholarly setting, worth a visit for the architecture alone, preserves an atmosphere of seclusion and contemplation. ⊠ *5 Tianyi Lu, west of Moon Lake* ☎ *0574/8729–3856* ⊡ *Y30* ☉ *Daily 8–5.*

**Zhongshan Park** (中山公园 *Zhōngshān gōngyuán*). In one of Ningbo's most delightful parks you'll find winding stone-lined paths that snake over arched bridges and slender canals flowing past pavilions and teahouses. During the humid summer months the city's seniors fan themselves with oversized paper fans, crack sunflower seeds, gossip, and drink tea. Impromptu groups of musicians huddle together; old men play traditional Chinese instruments as women belt out ear-piercing renditions of Chinese opera. This is a wonderful place to relax and soak up the atmosphere. ⊠ *Gongyuan Lu, end of the Drum Tower pedestrian street* ⊡ *Free* ☉ *Daily sunrise–sunset.*

## WHERE TO EAT

$$
MIDDLE EASTERN
Fodor's Choice
★

✕ **Lebanese Restaurant** (黎巴嫩餐厅 *Líbānèn cāntīng*). On the eastern edge of Moon Lake, this Middle Eastern restaurant has consistently excellent food. One bite of the olive-oil-and-pine-nut drizzled hummus and you'll immediately forgive the rather bland interior. A long-standing favorite with the city's Islamic community, the restaurant serves a variety of lamb kebabs, eggplant-based dips, and fresh mint yogurt that are all delicious. An English-language picture menu will help guide you. Ⓢ *Average main: Y55* ✉ *320 Zhenming Lu* ☎ *0574/8731–5861.*

$$
THAI
Fodor's Choice
★

✕ **Nancy's Thai** (南茜泰菜馆 *Nánxī tài càiguǎn*). A Ningbo landmark, this authentic Thai restaurant has an enormous neon sign that make it easy to spot. The first level has a well-stocked bar with a decent selection of reasonably priced wines by the bottle. The second floor contains the dining room, where private tables are perfect for romantic meals. Recommended dishes include the *tom kha gai* (coconut and chicken soup), *tom sum* (spicy papaya salad), and expertly seasoned curries. Ⓢ *Average main: Y80* ✉ *103 Zhenming Lu* ☎ *0574/8731–8266* ⊕ *www.nancysthai.com.*

$
VEGETARIAN

✕ **Vegetarian Life Style** (枣子树净素餐厅 *Zǎozi shùjìng sùcāntīng*). This outpost of one of Shanghai's most famous vegetarian restaurants makes ordering a breeze, thanks to an English-language picture menu. The nourishing and delicious spinach dumplings, fresh juices, and mock-meat dishes are consistently delicious. The restaurant enforces a no-smoking policy, which is highly unusual in China. Ⓢ *Average main: Y45* ✉ *16 Liuting Jie, 2nd fl.* ☎ *0574/8730–1333* ▭ *No credit cards.*

$$$$
CHINESE

✕ **Zhuangyuanlou Restaurant** (状元楼酒店 *Zhuàngyuánlóu jiǔdiàn*). Serving traditional Ningbo cuisine in an opulent setting on the Yu Yao River, Zhuangyuanlou has a stellar reputation for quality and freshness. In the city's most exclusive mall, the restaurant has gigantic red-and-gold doors and intricately carved antique furniture. Hostesses are decked out in elaborate silk dresses. If you're feeling bold, try the exotic and expensive local specialties. The steamed turtle, fried yellow-fish with fresh blueberries, and the pork ribs come highly recommended. Ⓢ *Average main: Y200* ✉ *He Yi Shopping Center, He Yi Lu* ☎ *0574/2796–6666* ▭ *No credit cards.*

## WHERE TO STAY

$
HOTEL

🛏 **Asia Garden Hotel** (亚洲华园宾馆 *Yàzhōu huāyuán bīnguǎn*). With a convenient location next to the South Bus Station, this expansive hotel is a short walk from Ningbo's main attractions. **Pros:** near all the main sights; cable channels in the rooms; free Wi-Fi. **Cons:** could use some renovations; bland breakfasts; staff speak limited English. Ⓢ *Rooms from: Y290* ✉ *271 Ma Yuan Lu* ☎ *0574/8711–6888* ⊕ *www.asiagardenhotel.com* ⤢ *142 rooms* ▭ *No credit cards* 🍽 *Breakfast.*

$
HOTEL

🛏 **Miryam Boutique Hotel** (老别墅旅馆 *Miryam lǎobiéshù lǚguǎn*). The Victorian-era decor at this boutique hotel doesn't exactly blend in with the neighborhood, but it's hard to argue with four-poster beds, elaborate fireplaces, breezy balconies, and sculpted gardens. **Pros:** overlooks the ocean; close to main attractions; free Wi-Fi. **Cons:** some rooms are a bit dark; little English is spoken; far from pier. Ⓢ *Rooms from: Y688*

✉ *70 Huangyan Lu* ☎ *0592/206–2505* 🌐 *www.miryamhotel.com* 🛏 *15 rooms* 🍴 *No meals.*

$$ HOTEL — **Shangri-La Ningbo** (香格里拉酒店 *Xiānggélǐlā jiǔdiàn*). Overlooking the confluence of three rivers, Ningbo's most opulent international hotel offers personalized service, first-rate facilities, and panoramic views of the city. **Pros:** sleek indoor lap pool; outdoor tennis courts; free Wi-Fi. **Cons:** mandatory bathing cap in the pool; loud lobby area; tour groups can flood the facilities. [$] *Rooms from: Y1218* ✉ *88 Yuyuan Lu, 315040* ☎ *0574/8799–8888* 🌐 *www.shangri-la.com* 🛏 *505 rooms, 58 suites* 🍴 *No meals.*

Fodor's Choice ★

$$ HOTEL — **Sheraton Ningbo** (喜来登酒店 *Xǐláidèng jiǔdiàn*). Excellent customer service and a convenient location make this an ideal base from which to explore the city. **Pros:** impressive breakfast buffet; free Wi-Fi access; free transportation to Shanghai. **Cons:** busy lobby; aging facilities; smoking allowed in public areas. [$] *Rooms from: Y1128* ✉ *50 Caihong Lu* ☎ *0574/8768–8688* 🌐 *www.starwoodhotels.com* 🛏 *349 rooms, 31 suites* 🍴 *No meals.*

5

### NIGHTLIFE

If you're looking for a fun night out, head over to Laowaitan, the city's premier entertainment district and Ningbo's answer to Shanghai's Bund. It's designed to look like a mini European city, complete with cobblestone streets. Hundreds of local couples come here to take their wedding photos in the exotic setting.

**O'Reilly's Pub.** For a low-key evening, head to the warm and welcoming O'Reilly's Pub, which has Guinness and Strongbow Cider on tap, a hodgepodge of Irish paraphernalia on the walls, and tasty Western bar grub. There's often live Celtic, folk, and pop music. ✉ *46–9 Caihong Bei Lu* ☎ *0574/8770–4282* 🕒 *Daily 10 am–2 am.*

### SHOPPING

**Antiques Market Curio Bazaar** (范宅古玩集市 *Fànzhái gǔwán jíshì*). At the Antiques Market Curio Bazaar you'll find small clusters of galleries and stalls that sell a variety of jade pieces and antique bric-a-brac of varying levels of authenticity. We like the beautiful Chinese scrolls with traditional watercolor paintings and the kitschy Mao-era memorabilia. Bargain hard, as prices are inflated for tourists. ✉ *85–97 Zhongshan Xi Lu.*

**Gulou Pedestrian Street.** Head east down Zhongshan Xi Lu to Gulou Pedestrian Street, where restored buildings are stuffed to capacity with every type of cheaply made product. This a great place to wander and soak up modern Chinese culture. ✉ *Gu Lou Bu Xing Jie.*

**He Yi Avenue.** The city's newest shopping area is He Yi Avenue, where you'll find high-end luxury chains like Gucci, Dior, Armani, Mont Blanc, and Swarovski. There's plenty of riverfront shopping, dining, and nightlife. This is where Ningbo's créme de la créme comes to spend money on Japanese *mochi* balls (sticky rice filled with ice cream) and other delicacies. ✉ *66 He Yi Lu.*

**Tianyi Square.** Just east of the Tianfeng Pagoda is Tianyi Square, Ningbo's most famous shopping and entertainment complex. Look for the enormous Yaohang Street Catholic Church just outside the square if you need to take a break. ⊠ *88 Zhongshan Dong Lu.*

**OFF THE BEATEN PATH**

**Mount Putuo.** On this tiny island, only 12.5 square km (8 miles), you'll find Putuoshan, one of China's four sacred Buddhist mountains. Legend has it that a ninth-century Japanese monk got caught in a storm, and Guanyin, the Buddhist goddess of mercy, miraculously appeared and guided him safely to the mountain. In thanks, he erected Puji Si, the area's most famous temple. The island can easily be explored on foot and completely circumnavigated in a day. Take time to lounge on Thousand Step Beach, photograph the enormous 108-feet-high bronze Guanyin Statue, eat fresh seafood, and climb Mount Putuo (or take the cable car) for fabulous island vistas. The population is only 3,000, of whom 1,000 are monks and nuns. Getting to the island is fairly easy, with frequent boats leaving from Ningbo's wharf. The island can get crowded, so avoid weekends and holidays.

# FUJIAN

One of China's most beautiful provinces, Fujian has escaped the notice of most visitors. This is because the region, though not too far off the beaten path, is usually passed over in favor of more glamorous destinations like Hong Kong or Shanghai. The city of Xiamen is beautiful, and the surrounding area has some of the best beaches north of Hainan. Gulangyu is a rarity in modern China: a tree-filled island with undisturbed colonial architecture and absolutely no cars.

## XIAMEN

*266 km (165 miles) southwest of Fuzhou; 632 km (393 miles) northeast of Hong Kong.*

By Chinese standards, Xiamen is a new city: it dates back only to the late 12th century. Xiamen was a stronghold for Ming loyalist Zheng Chenggong (better known as Koxinga), who later fled to Taiwan after China was overrun by the Qing. Xiamen's place as a dynasty-straddling city continues to this day due to its proximity to Taiwan. Some see Xiamen as a natural meeting point between the two sides in the decades-long separation. Only a few miles out to sea are islands that still technically belong to the Republic of China, as Taiwan is still officially known.

Xiamen is today one of the most prosperous cities in China, with beautiful parks, amazing temples, and waterfront promenades that neatly complement the port city's historic architecture.

### GETTING HERE AND AROUND

The best way to reach Xiamen is by plane. The city is accessible by long-distance trains and buses, but these entail much longer travel times.

AIR TRAVEL     Xiamen Gaoqi International Airport, one of the largest and busiest in China, lies about 12 km (7 miles) northeast of the city. A taxi from downtown should cost no more than Y40. Most carriers service Xiamen, which has connections to many cities in China and international

destinations like Jakarta, Manila, Penang, and Singapore. A popular regional carrier is Xiamen Airlines.

BUS TRAVEL Xiamen has luxury bus service to all the main cities along the coast as far as Guangzhou and Shanghai. The Xiamen Long-Distance Bus Station is on Hubin Nan Lu, just south of Yuandang Lake.

TAXI TRAVEL In Xiamen taxis can be found around hotels or on the streets; they're a convenient way to visit the sights on the edge of town. Most taxi drivers do not speak English, so make sure that all your addresses are written in Chinese.

TRAIN TRAVEL Rail travel to Xiamen isn't as convenient as in many other cities. Aside from bullet trains from Shanghai and Hangzhou, most journeys involve changing trains at least once. The main railway station is about 5 km (3 miles) northeast of the port; bus service between the station and port is frequent.

### TIMING

Xiamen is a very pleasant city, well worth a few days of exploring and hiking. Much cleaner than other Chinese cities, it's a great place to recharge and take in some fresh air.

**ESSENTIALS**

**Air Contacts Xiamen Airlines** ✉ *22 Dailiao Lu* ☎ *0592/222–6666* ⊕ *www. xiamenair.com.cn.* **Xiamen Gaoqi International Airport** ☎ *0592/95557.*

**Banks Bank of China** ✉ *40 Hu Bin Bei Lu* ☎ *0592/531–7830.* **HSBC** ✉ *189 Xiahe Lu* ☎ *0592/239–7799.*

**Bus Contact Xiamen Long-Distance Bus Station** ✉ *56 Hubin Nan Lu* ☎ *0592/220–1246.*

**Medical Assistance Xiamen Changgung Hospital** ✉ *123 Zhenfei Lu, Xinjang Industrial Area* ☎ *0592/620–3456.*

**Train Contact Xiamen North Train Station** ✉ *Yantong Lu* ☎ *0592/9510–5105.* **Xiamen Train Station** ✉ *Xiahe Lu* ☎ *0592/203–8888.*

**Visitor and Tour Info CTS** ✉ *143 Houdaixi Lu* ☎ *0592/223–1259* ⊕ *www. citsxm.com.*

## EXPLORING XIAMEN

### TOP ATTRACTIONS

**10,000 Rock Botanical Garden** (万石植物园 *Wànshí zhíwùyuán*). Surrounding a pretty lake, the 10,000 Rock Botanical Garden has a fine collection of more than 5,300 species of tropical and subtropical flora, ranging from eucalyptus and bamboo trees to orchids and ferns. There are several pavilions, of which the most interesting are those forming the Temple of the Kingdom of Heaven. ✉ *Huyuan Lu, off Wenyuan Lu* 🎫 *Y40* ⏲ *Daily 5:30 am–6:30 pm.*

**Hongshan Park** (鸿山公园 *Hóngshān gōngyuán*). The rather hilly Hongshan Park has a small Buddhist temple, a lovely waterfall, and beautiful views of the city and the harbor. There's also a teashop serving Iron Buddha tea, a Fujian specialty. ✉ *Siming Nan Lu, near Nanputuo Temple* 🎫 *Free.*

**Nanputuo Temple** (南普陀寺 *Nánpǔtuó sí*). Dating from the Tang Dynasty, Nanputuo Temple has roofs decorated with brightly painted clustered flowers, sinewy serpents, and mythical beasts. It has been restored many times, most recently in the 1980s, following the Cultural Revolution. Pavilions on either side of the main hall contain tablets commemorating the suppression of secret societies by the Qing emperors. As the most important of Xiamen's temples, it is nearly always the center of a great deal of activity as monks and worshippers mix with tour groups. To get here, take Bus 1 or 2 from the port. ✉ *Siming Nan Lu, next to Xiamen University* 🎫 *Y3* ⏲ *Daily 5:40 am–6 pm.*

**NEED A BREAK?** **Coffee Map.** Coffee Map is an unassuming Taiwanese-owned tea and coffee stand. The huge menu offers lots of delicious caffeinated drinks, and the tiny, air-conditioned seating area is a pleasant escape from Xiamen's oppressive summer humidity. It's down a small alley just opposite Xiamen University's main gate and near Nanputuo Temple. ✉ *Laohu Cheng Dian, off Siming Nan Lu* ☎ *0592/256–6388* ⏲ *Daily 8 am–10 pm.*

**Xiamen University** (厦门大学 *Xiàmén dàxué*). Housed in a fascinating mix of traditional and colonial buildings near Nanputuo Temple

The Hakka Roundhouses were added to the UNESCO World Heritage List in 2008.

is Xiamen University. It was founded in the 1920s with the help of Chinese people living abroad. The **Museum of Anthropology** *(Rénlèi bówùguǎn)*, dedicated to the study of the Neolithic era, has a very good collection of fossils, ceramics, paintings, and ornaments. It's open daily 8:30 to 11 and 3 to 5. ⊠ *End of Siming Nan Lu* ⊕ *www.xmu.edu.cn.*

**WORTH NOTING**

**Hakka Roundhouses** (客家土楼 *Ké jiā tǔ lóu*). Legend has it that when these four-story-tall structures were first spotted by the American military, fear spread that they were silos for some unknown gigantic missile. They were created centuries before by the Hakka, or Guest People, an offshoot of the Han Chinese who settled all over southeastern China. Made of raw earth, glutinous rice, and brown sugar and reinforced with bamboo and wood, they are the most beautiful example of Hakka architecture. The roundhouses are in Yong Ding, 210 km (130 miles) northwest of Xiamen. Joining a tour group or hiring a private car is your best option for getting here. ⊠ *Yong Ding.*

**Overseas Chinese Museum** (华侨博物馆 *Huáqiáo bówùguǎn*). In the southern part of the city, the Overseas Chinese Museum was founded by the wealthy industrialist Tan Kah-kee. Three halls exhibit, with the help of pictures and documents, personal items, and relics associated with the great waves of emigration from southeastern China during the 19th century. ⊠ *493 Siming Nan Lu* ☎ *0592/208–4028* 💲 *Free* ☉ *Tues.–Sun. 9–4:30.*

**Zhongshan Park** (中山公园 *Zhōngshān gōngyuán*). Commemorating Dr. Sun Yat-sen, Zhongshan Park is centered around a statue to the great

Continued on page 324

**DID YOU KNOW**

In China, there are three major schools of Buddhism: the Chinese school, embraced mainly by Han Chinese; the Tibetan school (or Lamaism) as practiced by Tibetans and Mongolians; and Theravada, practiced by the Dai and other ethnic minority groups in the southwest of the country.

# SPIRITUALITY IN CHINA

Even though it's officially an atheist nation, China has a vibrant religious life. What are the differences between China's big three faiths of Buddhism, Taoism, and Confucianism? Like much else in the Middle Kingdom, the lines are often blurred.

Walking around the streets of any city in China in the early 21st century, it's hard to believe that only three decades ago the bulk of the Middle Kingdom's centuries-old religious culture was destroyed by revolutionary zealots, and that the few temples, mosques, monasteries, and churches that escaped outright destruction were desecrated and turned into warehouses and factories, or put to other ignoble uses. Those days are long over, and religion in China has sprung back to life. Even though the official line of the Chinese Communist Party is that the nation is atheist, China is rife with religious diversity.

Perhaps the faith most commonly associated with China is Confucianism, an ethical and philosophical system developed from the teachings of the sage Confucius. Confucianism stresses the importance of relationships in society and of maintaining proper etiquette. These aspects of Confucian thought are associated not merely with China (where its modern-day influence is dubious at best, especially in a crowded subway car), but also with East Asian culture as a whole. Confucianism also places great emphasis on filial piety, the respect that a child should show an elder (or subjects to their ruler). This may account for Confucianism's status as the most officially tolerated of modern China's faiths.

Taoism is based on the teachings of the *Tao Te Ching*, a treatise written in the 6th century BC, and blends an emphasis on spiritual harmony with that of the individual's duty to society. Taoism and Confucianism are complementary, though to the outsider, the former might seem more steeped in ritual and mysticism. Think of it this way: Taoism is to Confucianism as Catholicism is to Protestantism. Taoism's mystic quality may be why so many westerners come to China to study "the way," as Taoism is sometimes called.

Buddhism came to China from India in the first century AD and quickly became a major force in the Middle Kingdom. The faith is so ingrained here that many Chinese openly scoff at the idea that the Buddha wasn't Chinese.

Buddhism teaches that the best way to alleviate suffering is to purify one's mind.

# TEMPLE FAUX PAS

The Wenshu Monastery is a top sight in Chengdu.

■ Chinese worshippers are easygoing. Even at the smallest temple or shrine, they understand that some people will be visitors and not devotees. Temples in China have relaxed dress codes, but you should follow certain rules of decorum.

■ You're welcome to burn incense, but it's not required. If you do decide to burn a few joss sticks, take them from the communal pile and be sure to make a small donation. This usually goes to temple upkeep or local charities.

■ Respect signs reading no photo in front of altars and statues. Taoist temples seem particularly sensitive about photo taking. When in doubt, ask.

■ Avoid stepping in front of a worshipper at an altar or censer (where incense is burned).

■ Speak quietly and silence mobile phones inside of temple grounds.

■ Don't touch Buddhist monks of the opposite sex.

■ Avoid entering a temple during a ceremony.

# TEMPLE OBJECTS

For many, temple visits are among the most culturally edifying parts of a China trip. Large or small, Chinese temples incorporate a variety of objects significant to religious practice.

## INCENSE

Incense is the most common item in any Chinese temple. In antiquity, Chinese people burned sacrifices both as an offering and as a way of communicating with spirits through the smoke. This later evolved into a way of showing respect for one's ancestors by burning fragrances that the dearly departed might find particularly pleasing.

## CENSER

Every Chinese temple will have a censer in which to place joss sticks, either inside the hall or out front. Larger temples often have a number of them. These large stone or bronze bowls are filled with incense ash from hundreds of joss sticks placed by worshippers. Some censers are ornate, with sculpted bronze rising above the bowls.

## BAGUA

Taoist temples will have a bagua: an octagonal diagram pointing toward the eight cardinal directions, each representing different points on the compass, elements in nature, family members, and more esoteric meanings. The bagua is often used in conjunction with a compass to make placement decisions in architectural design and in fortune telling.

## STATUES

Chinese temples are known for being flexible, and statues of various deities and mythical figures. Confucius is usually rendered as a wizened man with a long beard, and Taoist temples have an array of demon deities.

## PRAYER WHEEL

Used primarily by Tibetan Buddhists, the prayer wheel is a beautifully embossed hollow metal cylinder mounted on a wooden handle. Inside the cylinder is a tightly wound scroll printed with a mantra. Devotees believe that the spinning of a prayer wheel is a form of prayer that's just as effective as reciting the sacred texts aloud.

## "GHOST MONEY"

Sometimes the spirits need more than sweet-smelling smoke, and this is why many Taoists burn "ghost money" (also known as "hell money"), a scented paper resembling cash. Though once more popular in Taiwan and Hong Kong (and looked upon as a particularly capitalist superstition on the mainland), the burning of ghost money is now gaining ground throughout the country.

5

IN FOCUS SPIRITUALITY IN CHINA

# CHINESE ASTROLOGY

According to legend, the King of Jade invited 12 animals to visit him in heaven. As the animals rushed to be the first to arrive, the rat snuck a ride on the ox's back. Just as the ox was about to cross the threshold, the rat jumped past him and arrived first. This is why the rat was given first place in the astrological chart. Find the year you were born to determine what your astrological animal is.

### RAT
1936 · 1948 · 1960 · 1972 · 1984 · 1996 · 2008 · 2020

Charming and hardworking, Rats are goal setters and perfectionists. Rats are quick to anger, ambitious, and lovers of gossip.

### OX
1937 · 1949 · 1961 · 1973 · 1985 · 1997 · 2009 · 2021

Patient and soft-spoken, Oxen inspire confidence in others. Generally easygoing, they can be remarkably stubborn, and they hate to fail or be opposed.

### TIGER
1938 · 1950 · 1962 · 1974 · 1986 · 1998 · 2010 · 2022

Sensitive, and thoughtful, Tigers are capable of great sympathy. Tigers can be short-tempered, and are prone to conflict and indecisiveness.

### RABBIT
1939 · 1951 · 1963 · 1975 · 1987 · 1999 · 2011 · 2023

Talented and articulate, Rabbits are virtuous, reserved, and have excellent taste. Though fond of gossip, Rabbits tend to be generally kind and even-tempered.

### DRAGON
1940 · 1952 · 1964 · 1976 · 1988 · 2000 · 2012 · 2024

Energetic and excitable, short-tempered and stubborn, Dragons are known for their honesty, bravery, and ability to inspire confidence and trust.

## SNAKE

**1941 · 1953 · 1965 · 1977 · 1989 · 2001 · 2013 · 2025**

Snakes are deep, possessing great wisdom and saying little. Snakes are considered the most beautiful and philosiphical of all the signs.

## HORSE

**1942 · 1954 · 1966 · 1978 · 1990 · 2002 · 2014 · 2026**

Horses are thought to be cheerful and perceptive, impatient and hot-blooded. Horses are independent and rarely listen to advice.

## GOAT

**1943 · 1955 · 1967 · 1979 · 1991 · 2003 · 2015 · 2027**

Wise, gentle, and compassionate, Goats are elegant and highly accomplished in the arts. Goats can also be shy and pessimistic, and often tend toward timidity.

## MONKEY

**1944 · 1956 · 1968 · 1980 · 1992 · 2004 · 2016 · 2028**

Clever, skillful, and flexible, Monkeys are thought to be erratic geniuses, able to solve problems with ease. Monkeys are also thought of as impatient and easily discouraged.

## ROOSTER

**1945 · 1957 · 1969 · 1981 · 1993 · 2005 · 2017 · 2029**

Roosters are capable and talented, and tend to like to keep busy. Roosters are known as overachievers, and are frequently loners.

## DOG

**1946 · 1958 · 1970 · 1982 · 1994 · 2006 · 2018 · 2030**

Dogs are loyal and honest and know how to keep secrets. They can also be selfish and stubborn.

## PIG

**1947 · 1959 · 1971 · 1983 · 1995 · 2007 · 2031**

Gallant and energetic, Pigs have a tendency to be single-minded and determined. Pigs have great fortitude and honesty, and tend to make friends for life.

man. It has a small zoo, pretty lakes, and canals you can explore by paddleboat. The annual Lantern Festival is held here. ⊠ *Zhong Shan Lu and Zhenhai Lu* 🖾 *Free.*

**WHERE TO EAT**

Although Xiamen is known for its excellent seafood, the city's Buddhist population means it has excellent vegetarian cuisine. Xiamen is probably the best place outside of Taiwan to experience Taiwanese cuisine, and many restaurants advertise their *Taiwan Wei Kou* and *Taiwan Xiao Chi,* meaning "Taiwanese flavor" and "Taiwanese snacks."

**$$$**
SEAFOOD
✕**Chinese Restaurant** (观海餐厅 *Guān hǎi cān tīng*). On the rooftop of the waterfront Lujiang Harbourview Hotel, this terrace restaurant has beautiful views over the bay. The Cantonese chef prepares delicious seafood dishes and dim-sum specialties like sweet pork buns and shrimp dumplings. Ⓢ *Average main: Y150* ⊠ *Lujiang Harbourview Hotel, 54 Lujiang Lu, 7th fl.* ☎ *0592/266–1398* ⊕ *www.lujiang-hotel. com* ⌕ *Reservations essential.*

**$$**
MEXICAN
✕**Coyote Café and Cantina** (墨西哥餐厅 *Mòxīgē cāntīng*). With lakeside views that make the jaunt worthwhile, Xiamen's most beloved Mexican restaurant serves steak fajitas and other favorites. Don't expect generous sides of sour cream or guacamole, but after a few well-poured margaritas it won't matter. The service is a bit slow, but the staff is friendly. Ⓢ *Average main: Y80* ⊠ *58–2 Yuandang Lu* ☎ *0592/508–0737* ⊕ *www. coyotecafe.asia* ⊟ *No credit cards.*

**$**
VEGETARIAN
✕**Dafang Vegetarian Restaurant** (大方素菜馆 *Dàfāng sùcàiguǎn*). Across from Nanputuo Temple, this reasonably priced restaurant is popular with students. But don't just come for the low prices—it also has excellent food. Try the sweet-and-sour soup or the mock duck. English menus are available. Ⓢ *Average main: Y45* ⊠ *3 Nanhua Lu* ☎ *0592/209–3236* ⊟ *No credit cards.*

**$$**
VEGETARIAN
✕**Puzhaolou Vegetarian Restaurant** (普照楼素菜馆 *Pǔzhàolóu sùcàiguǎn*). The comings and goings of monks add to the atmosphere at this restaurant next to the Nanputuo Temple. Popular dishes include black-mushroom soup with tofu and stewed yams with seaweed. You won't find any English translations, so point or ask for one of the picture menus. Ⓢ *Average main: Y75* ⊠ *Nanputuo Temple, 515 Siming Nan Lu* ☎ *0592/208–5908* ⊟ *No credit cards.*

**$$$**
SEAFOOD
Fodor's Choice
★
✕**Shuyou Seafood Restaurant** (舒友海鲜大酒楼 *Shūyǒu hǎixiān dàjiǔlóu*). Shuyou means "close friend," and that's how you're treated at this upscale establishment. Considered one of the best seafood restaurants in Xiamen, if not the whole of China, Shuyou serves freshly caught fish in an opulent setting. Downstairs, the tanks are filled with lobster, prawns, and crabs, and upstairs diners feast on dishes cooked in Cantonese and Fujian styles. If you're in the mood for other fare, the restaurant is also known for its excellent Peking duck and goose liver. Ⓢ *Average main: Y100* ⊠ *Hubin Bei Lu, near Marco Polo Xiamen* ☎ *0592/509–8888* ⌕ *Reservations essential.*

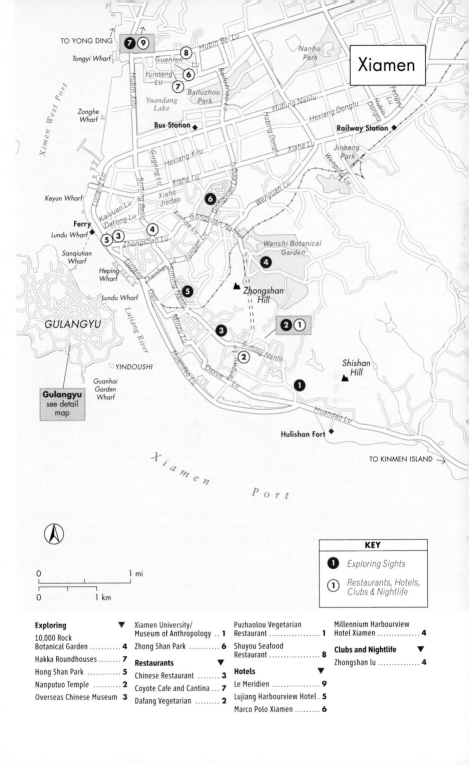

# Xiamen

**KEY**

① Exploring Sights

① Restaurants, Hotels, Clubs & Nightlife

**Exploring** ▼

10,000 Rock Botanical Garden .......... **4**

Hakka Roundhouses ........ **7**

Hong Shan Park ............ **5**

Nanputuo Temple .......... **2**

Overseas Chinese Museum **3**

Xiamen University/ Museum of Anthropology .. **1**

Zhong Shan Park .......... **6**

**Restaurants** ▼

Chinese Restaurant ........ **3**

Coyote Cafe and Cantina ... **7**

Dafang Vegetarian ......... **2**

Puzhaolou Vegetarian Restaurant ................. **1**

Shuyou Seafood Restaurant ................. **8**

**Hotels** ▼

Le Meridien ................. **9**

Lujiang Harbourview Hotel . **5**

Marco Polo Xiamen ......... **6**

Millennium Harbourview Hotel Xiamen .............. **4**

**Clubs and Nightlife** ▼

Zhongshan lu .............. **4**

## WHERE TO STAY

**$$**
**HOTEL**
**Fodor's Choice**
**★**

**Le Meridien** (艾美酒店 *Àimèi jiǔdiàn*). With sweeping views of Xiamen Bay, this stunning property feels more like a high-end Southeast-Asian resort than a crowded Chinese metropolitan lodging. **Pros:** tropical setting; reasonable prices; attentive staff. **Cons:** outside the city center; Wi-Fi costs extra. ⓢ *Rooms from: Y860* ⊠ *7 Guanjun Lu* ☎ *0592/770–9999* ⊕ *www.lemeridien.com* ↘ *314 rooms, 28 suites* ⊚ *No meals.*

**$**
**HOTEL**

**Lujiang Harbourview Hotel** (鹭江宾馆 *Lùjiāng bīnguǎn*). In a nicely renovated colonial building, this hotel has an ideal location opposite the ferry pier and the waterfront boulevard. **Pros:** phenomenal location; good prices; complimentary Wi-Fi. **Cons:** limited English is spoken here; great location; rooms on the small side. ⓢ *Rooms from: Y780* ⊠ *54 Lujiang Lu* ☎ *0592/202–2922* ⊕ *www.lujiang-hotel.com* ↘ *145 rooms, 9 suites* ⊚ *No meals.*

**$$**
**HOTEL**

**Marco Polo Xiamen** (马可波罗大酒店 *Mǎkěbōluó dàjiǔdiàn*). Standing between the historic sights and the commercial district, the Marco Polo has an excellent location for both business and leisure travelers. **Pros:** good location; helpful staff; free Wi-Fi. **Cons:** poor reservation service; basic facilities. ⓢ *Rooms from: Y858* ⊠ *8 Jianye Lu* ☎ *0592/509–1888* ⊕ *www.marcopolohotels.com* ↘ *236 rooms, 64 suites* ⊚ *No meals.*

**$$**
**HOTEL**
**Fodor's Choice**
**★**

**Millenium Harbourview Hotel Xiamen** (厦门海景千禧大酒店 *Xiamen hǎijǐng qiānxī dàjiǔdiàn*). With an excellent location overlooking the harbor, this hotel is among the best in the city. **Pros:** excellent service; travel agents on staff; free Wi-Fi. **Cons:** can be noisy; some rooms very dark. ⓢ *Rooms from: Y1100* ⊠ *12-8 Zhenhai Lu* ☎ *0592/202–3333* ⊕ *www.millenniumhotels.com/cn/millenniumxiamen/index.html* ↘ *329 rooms, 23 suites* ⊚ *Breakfast.*

## NIGHTLIFE AND THE ARTS

The Zhongshan Lu pedestrian street near the ferry pier is charming in the evening, when the colonial-style buildings are lighted with gentle neon. This waterfront promenade is a popular spot for young couples walking arm in arm.

## SPORTS AND THE OUTDOORS

Xiamen offers some excellent hiking opportunities. Most notable of these are the hills behind the Nanputuo Temple, where winding paths and stone steps carved into the sheer rock face make for a fairly strenuous climb. For a real challenge, hike from Nanputuo Temple to 10,000 Rock Garden. If you're still in the mood for a climb after spending a few hours enjoying the garden's beautiful landscape, another more serpentine trail (a relic of the Japanese occupation) leads to Xiamen University. The hike takes the better part of an afternoon.

The area around Xiamen has fine public beaches. Sunbathers abound nearly anywhere along Huandao Lu, the road that circles the island, which is also referred to as Island Ring Road.

## GULANGYU

*5 minutes by boat from Xiamen.*

The best way to experience Gulangyu's charm is to explore its meandering streets, stumbling across a particularly distinctive old mansion or the weathered graves of missionaries and merchants. These quiet back alleys are fascinating to wander in, with the atmosphere of a quiet Mediterranean city punctuated by touches of calligraphy or the click of mah-jongg tiles to remind you where you really are. And unlike most Chinese communities, Gulangyu does not permit cars, so you won't take your life in your hands when crossing the street. This island is easy to reach by ferry from Xiamen.

### GETTING HERE AND AROUND

Boats to the island run from early in the morning until midnight, and depart from the ferry terminal across from the Lujiang. Electric buses are available on the island.

BOAT AND FERRY TRAVEL  Ferry service from the Xiamen Ferry dock starts at 5:45 am, with departures every 10 to 15 minutes. The trip there is free, but it costs Y8 to return to Xiamen. The ferry does not run after midnight, so check the last departure time before you leave Xiamen to avoid getting stranded.

### TIMING

Gulangyu is small enough to be explored on a day trip from Xiamen, but a night here would be well spent.

### TOURS

The best—and really, the only—way to see Gulangyu is on foot. Take a morning or afternoon to climb up the narrow, winding streets to see the hundreds of colonial-era mansions (ranging from restored to ramshackle) that are the heart of this fabulous trove of late-19th- and early-20th-century architecture.

### ESSENTIALS

Many sights on Gulangyu charge admission fees, but a tour aboard the island's electric bus includes admission to all sites included on the tour. Island ATMs are available near major tourist sites, but it is best to do your banking before heading out.

### EXPLORING GULANGYU

**Bright Moon Garden** (皓月园 *Haoyue Yuan*). This garden is a fitting seaside memorial to Koxinga, a famous Ming general. A massive stone statue of him stares eastward from a perch hanging over the sea. ⊠ *Tianwei Lu* 🚋 *Y15* ⊙ *Daily 8–7.*

**Piano Museum** (钢琴博物馆 *Gāngqín bówùguǎn*). Gulangyu holds a special place in the country's musical history, thanks to the large number of Christian missionaries who called the island home in the late 19th and early 20th centuries. Gulangyu has more pianos per capita than anyplace else in China. "Chopsticks" to Chopin—and everything

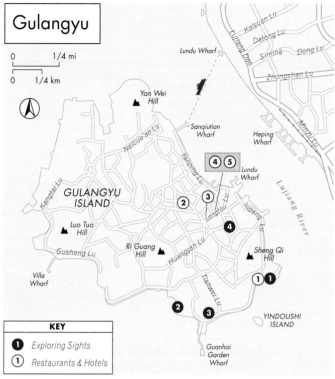

in between—can be heard being played by the next generation's prodigies. The Piano Museum (Island of Drumming Waves) is a must for any music lover. ✉ *45 Huangyan Lu* ☎ *0592/206–0238* 🔗 *Y30* 🕐 *Daily 8:15–5:45.*

**Shuzhuang Garden** (菽庄花园 *Shūzhuāng huāyuán*). This lovely garden is immaculately kept and dotted with pavilions and bridges, some extending out to rocks just offshore. ✉ *Tianwei Lu* 🔗 *Y30* 🕐 *Daily 8–7.*

**Zhen Qi Shi Jie** (珍奇世界 *Zhēnqí shíjié*). Skillfully mixing history and oddities, Zhen Qi Shi Jie is one of the country's odder museums. Part of the museum displays the usual historical information about Fujian and Taiwan. The other part is a veritable museum of oddities, offering pickled genetic mutations like two-headed snakes, conjoined twin sheep, and a few live exhibits like gigantic tortoises. The room of ancient Chinese sex toys will amuse some and mystify others. ✉ *38 Huangyan Lu* ☎ *0592/206–9933* 🔗 *Y60* 🕐 *Daily 8–6.*

**WHERE TO EAT**

$ ✕ **Fu Lin Chun Canting** (福林春餐厅 *Fúlínchūn cāntīng*). Serving home-
SEAFOOD style seafood cooked to order, this closet-size restaurant is almost always packed with locals during peak hours. If it comes from the sea, you'll find it here, with steamed crab, deep-fried shrimp, and whole fish

No cars are allowed on Gulangyu Island.

served in a variety of tantalizing styles. $ *Average main: Y45* ✉ *109 Long Tou Lu* ☎ *0592/206–2847* ▭ *No credit cards.*

**$$$**
**SEAFOOD**

✕**Long Wen Canting** (龙文餐厅 *Lóngwén cāntīng*). Serving fresh seafood dishes, this expansive restaurant near the ferry terminal is popular with tourists from Taiwan. The chef unabashedly admits to being an enthusiastic consumer of his own cuisine—never a bad sign. Specialties include whole steamed fish, oyster soup, and a wide variety of seafood dishes. The decor is traditional Chinese. $ *Average main: Y125* ✉ *21 Long Tou Lu* ☎ *0592/206–6369.*

**$**
**CAFÉ**

✕**Pan Xiaolian Yogurt Shop** (潘小莲 *Pānxiǎolián*). This lovely little shop is easy to spot, thanks to its large orange awning and Thai-inspired exterior. It's reputed to serve the best yogurt in Xiamen. A small English menu offers a few choices, including plain homemade yogurt or yogurt topped with fresh, sweet mangoes. Walls in soothing shades of green and yellow serve as a canvas for massive jungle paintings. Grab a seat by the window, enjoy the world music soundtrack, and watch the tourists go by. $ *Average main: Y20* ✉ *8 Long Tou Lu* ▭ *No credit cards.*

## WHERE TO STAY

**$**
**HOTEL**

☗**Bright Moon Leisure and Holiday Club** (皓月休闲度假俱乐部 *Héo yué xiu xién du jiéju lé bu*). Located in Bright Moon Garden, this lovely little hotel consists of nine wooden houses perched on seaside cliffs. **Pros:** quiet atmosphere; fantastic views. **Cons:** few amenities; limited English. $ *Rooms from: Y400* ✉ *3 Zhangzhou Lu* ☎ *0592/206–9730* ⬙ *9 rooms* ⫲ *No meals.*

**$**
**B&B/INN**

☗**Nana Inn Gulangyu Coast** (娜娜鼓浪屿海岸旅馆 *Nànà Gǔlàngyǔ hǎi'àn lǚguǎn*). Just down the street from the ferry terminal, this quirky inn has the friendly atmosphere of a hostel without the cramped quarters. **Pros:** convenient location; self-service kitchen and laundry; free Wi-Fi. **Cons:** basic facilities; limited English; confusing website. $ *Rooms from:* Y360 ⊠ *8 Longtou Lu* ☎ *0592/206–6396* ⊕ *www. naya-hotel.com* ⤴ *25 rooms* ⵏⵔ *No meals.*

# HONG KONG

# WELCOME TO HONG KONG

## TOP REASONS TO GO

★ **Harbor views:** The skyline that launched a thousand postcards . . . See it on a stroll along the Tsim Sha Tsui waterfront, from a Star Ferry crossing the harbor, or from the top of Victoria Peak.

★ **Dim sum:** As you bite into a moist *siu mai* it dawns on you why everyone says you haven't done dim sum until you've done it in Hong Kong.

★ **Cultural immersion:** The Hong Kong Heritage Museum chronicles the city's history. On a Lantau Island hill, see the 242-ton Tian Tan Buddha statue sits in the lotus position beside the Po Lin Buddhist Monastery.

★ **Shopping as religion:** At Kowloon's street markets, clothes, electronics, and souvenirs compete for space with food carts. Antiques fill windows along Hollywood Road.

★ **Horsing around:** Every year, Hong Kongers gamble billions of dollars, and the Happy Valley Racetrack is one of their favorite places to do it.

**1 Hong Kong Island.** It's only 78 square km (30 square miles), but it's where the action is, from high finance to nightlife to luxury shopping. The commercial districts—Western, Central, and Wan Chai—are on the north coast. Southside is home to small towns, quiet coves, and reserve areas. A 20-minute taxi ride from Central can have you breathing fresh air and seeing only greenery.

**2 Kowloon.** This peninsula on the Chinese mainland is just across from Central and bounded in the north by the string of mountains that give it its poetic name: *gau lung,* "nine dragons" (there are eight mountains, the ninth dragon was the emperor who named them).

**3 New Territories.** The expanse between Kowloon and the Chinese border feels far removed from urban congestion and rigor. Nature reserves (many with great trails), temples, and traditional Hakka villages fill its 200 square miles. Conversely public housing projects have led to the creation of new towns like Sha Tin and Tsuen Mun, some of which are now home to a half million people.

**4 Outer Islands.** Off the west coast of Hong Kong Island lie Lamma, Cheung Chau, and Lantau islands. Lantau, which is home to the Tian Tau Buddha, is connected by ferries to Hong Kong Island and by a suspension bridge to west Kowloon.

## GETTING ORIENTED

Hong Kong Island and the Kowloon Peninsula are divided by Victoria Harbour. On Hong Kong Island, the central city stretches only a few kilometers south before mountains rise up. But the city really also continues several more kilometers north into Kowloon. In the main districts, luxury boutiques are a stone's throw from old hawker stalls, and a modern, high-tech horseracing track isn't far from a temple housing more than 10,000 Buddha statues.

**6**

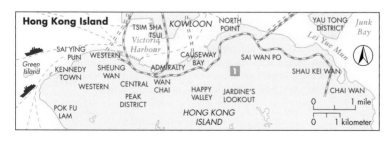

Updated by Doretta Lau, Samantha Leese, Maloy Luakian, Dorothy So, Jason Spotts, and Kate Springer

The Hong Kong Island skyline, with its ever-growing number of skyscrapers, speaks to the triumph of ambition over fate. Whereas it took Paris and London 10 to 20 generations and New York six to build the spectacular cities seen today, in Hong Kong almost everything you see has been built in the time since today's young investment bankers were born.

On Hong Kong Island the central city goes only a few kilometers south into the island before mountains rise up. In the main districts and neighborhoods luxury boutiques are a stone's throw from old hawker stalls.

When you're on Hong Kong Island and feeling disoriented, remember that the water is always north. Central, Admiralty, and Wan Chai, the island's main business districts, are opposite Tsim Sha Tsui on the Kowloon Peninsula. West of Central are Sheung Wan and the other (mainly residential) neighborhoods that make up Western. Central backs onto the slopes of Victoria Peak, so the districts south of it—the Midlevels and the Peak—look down on it. Causeway Bay, North Point, Quarry Bay, Shau Kei Wan, and Chai Wan East run east along the shore after Wan Chai. Developments on the south side of Hong Kong Island are scattered: the beach towns of Shek O and Stanley sit on two peninsulas on the southeast; high-tech Cyberport, industrial Aberdeen, and Ap Lei Chau are to the west.

West of Hong Kong Island lie Lamma, Cheung Chau, and Lantau islands. Lantau is connected by a suspension bridge to west Kowloon. More than 200 other islands also belong to Hong Kong.

Hong Kong's older areas—the southern side of Central, for example—show erratic street planning, but the newer developments and reclamations follow something closer to a grid system. Streets are usually numbered odd on one side, even on the other. There's no baseline for street numbers and no block-based numbering system.

# HONG KONG PLANNER

## WHEN TO GO

Hong Kong's high season, from September through late December, sees sunny, dry days and cool, comfortable nights. January and February are mostly cool and dank, with long periods of overcast skies. March and April are fairly pleasant, and by May the temperature is consistently warm and comfortable.

June through August are the cheapest months for one reason: they coincide with the hot, sticky, and very rainy typhoon (hurricane) season. Hong Kong is prepared for blustery assaults; if a big storm approaches, the airwaves crackle with information, and your hotel will post the appropriate signals (a No. 10 signal indicates the worst winds, and a black warning means a rainstorm is brewing). This is serious business—bamboo scaffolding and metal signs can come hurtling through the streets like spears, trees can break or fall, and large areas of the territory can flood. Museums, shops, restaurants, and transport shut down at signal No. 8, but 7-Elevens and cinemas typically stay open.

## GETTING HERE AND AROUND

### AIR TRAVEL

Modern, easy to navigate, and full of amenities, Hong Kong International Airport (HKG)—also known as Chek Lap Kok, after its location—is a traveler's dream. Terminal 1, the third-largest terminal in the world, services the departures for most major airlines, as well as all arriving flights. The newer but smaller Terminal 2 handles all other airlines, including budget carriers.

The Airport Express train service is the quickest and most convenient way to and from the airport. Citybus runs five buses ("A" precedes the bus number) from the airport to popular destinations. Taxis from the airport are reliable and plentiful. Trips to Hong Kong Island destinations cost around HK$280, while those to Kowloon are around HK$230.

### BUS TRAVEL

An efficient network of double-decker buses covers most of Hong Kong. Double-decker bus fares range from HK$2.50 to HK$48; minibus fares from HK$2 to HK$20.

### FERRY TRAVEL

With fabulous views of both sides of Victoria Harbour, the Star Ferry is so much more than just a boat. It's an iconic Hong Kong landmark in its own right, and has been running across the harbor since 1888. Double-bowed, green-and-white vessels connect Central and Wan Chai with Kowloon in less than 10 minutes, daily from 6:30 am to 11:30 pm.

### SUBWAY TRAVEL

By far the best way to get around Hong Kong is on the Mass Transit Railway (MTR). Entrances, platforms, and exits are clearly marked and signposted, and all MTR areas are air-conditioned and Wi-Fi enabled. Most stations have wheelchair access, and all have convenience stores and other shops or services. The 14 MTR stations have free Wi-Fi, as well as computer terminals with free Internet access.

## THE OCTOPUS

Public transportation options are many and varied—all are good, too. The first step is to get an Octopus (☎ 2266-2222 ⊕ www.octopus.com. hk) stored-value card, which can be used on all public transportation. The initial cost of an Octopus Card is HK$150, and you will have HK$100 available for your use right away. The remaining HK$50 is a refundable deposit that provides a buffer in case you go beyond the card's value. You can top up the card at ticket counters or Add Value machines at any MTR station, or at convenience stores, supermarkets, or fast-food chains. These retail outlets also accept the card as a mode of payment, as do many other places, including coffee chains, clothing stores, and vending machines.

You can buy tickets from ticket machines (using coins or notes) or from English-speaking staff behind glass-windowed customer-service counters near the turnstile entrances. Fares range from HK$3.70 to HK$42.50, depending how far you travel.

### TRAM TRAVEL

Old-fashioned double-decker trams have been running along the northern shore of Hong Kong Island since 1904. Most routes start in Kennedy Town or Western Market, and go eastward all the way through Central, Wan Chai, Causeway Bay, North Point, and Quarry Bay to Shau Kei Wan. A branch line turns off in Wan Chai toward Happy Valley, where horse races are held in season.

Destinations are marked on the front of each tram and route maps are displayed at the stops; you board at the back and get off at the front, paying HK$2.30 regardless of distance as you leave.

### TAXI TRAVEL

While there are some 18,000 taxis in Hong Kong, heavy daytime traffic in Central, Causeway Bay, and Tsim Sha Tsui means they aren't the best option for getting around the city quickly. They're more useful outside these areas, or after dark, especially after the MTR closes.

### HEALTH AND SAFETY

Hong Kong is an incredibly safe place—day and night. The police maintain law and order, but a few pickpockets are still about, especially in Tsim Sha Tsui. So avoid carrying large amounts of cash or valuables with you, and you should have no problems.

### PASSPORTS AND VISAS

Citizens of the United States need only a valid passport to enter Hong Kong for stays up to three months. You need at least six months' validity on your passport before traveling to Asia. Upon arrival, officials at passport control will give you a Hong Kong entry slip. Keep this slip safe; you must present it with your passport for your return trip home. If you're planning to pop over the border into mainland China, you must first get a visa.

**VISITOR INFORMATION**

For a guide to what's happening in Hong Kong, check out the Hong Kong Tourist Board's excellent website.

**ESSENTIALS**

**Airport Information Hong Kong International Airport** ☎ *2181-8888* ⊕ *www. hongkongairport.com.*

**Consulate U.S. Consulate General** ✉ *26 Garden Rd., Central* ☎ *2523-9011* ⊕ *hongkong.usconsulate.gov.*

**Ferry Information Star Ferry** ☎ *2367-7065* ⊕ *www.starferry.com.hk.*

**Hospitals and Clinics**

**Caritas Medical Centre** ✉ *111 Wing Hong St., Sham Shui Po, Kowloon* ☎ *3408-7911* ⊕ *www.ha.org.hk.* **Pamela Youde Nethersole Eastern Hospital** ✉ *3 Lok Man Rd., Chai Wan* ☎ *2595-6111* ⊕ *www.ha.org.hk.* **Prince of Wales Hospital** ✉ *30-32 Ngan Shing St., Sha Tin, New Territories* ☎ *2632-2211* ⊕ *www.ha.org.hk/pwh.* **Queen Elizabeth Hospital** ✉ *30 Gascoigne Rd., Yau Ma Tei, Kowloon* ☎ *2958-8888* ⊕ *www.ha.org.hk/qeh.* **Queen Mary Hospital** ✉ *102 Pok Fu Lam Rd., Pok Fu Lam, Western* ☎ *2855-3838* ⊕ *www.ha.org.hk/qmh.*

**Postal Services**

**General Post Office** ✉ *2 Connaught Rd., Central* ☎ *2921-2222* ⊕ *www. hongkongpost.com.* **Kowloon Central Post Office** ✉ *405 Nathan Rd., Yau Ma Tei, Kowloon* ☎ *2928-6247.*

**Subway and Train Information MTR** ☎ *2881-8888* ⊕ *www.mtr.com.hk.*

**Tram Information Hong Kong Tramways** ☎ *2548-7102* ⊕ *www.hktramways. com.*

**Taxi Information Hong Kong Kowloon Taxi & Lorry Owners Association Ltd.** ☎ *2572-0097.*

# EXPLORING HONG KONG

## WESTERN

Western has been called Hong Kong's Chinatown, and though it's a strange-sounding epithet, there's a reason for it. The area is light-years from the dazzle of Central, despite being just down the road. And although developers are making short work of the traditional architecture, Western's colonial buildings, rattling trams, Old World medicine shops, and lively markets still recall bygone times.

The Midlevels Escalator forms a handy boundary between Western and Central. Several main thoroughfares run parallel to the shore, each farther up the slope: Des Voeux Road (where the trams run), Queen's Road, Hollywood Road (where SoHo starts), and Caine Road (where the Midlevels begin).

Shopping at the Western Market.

As to how far west Western goes, it technically reaches all the way to Kennedy Town, where the tram lines end, but there isn't much worth noting beyond Sheung Wan.

**GETTING AROUND**

The most scenic way to Sheung Wan is on a tram along Des Voeux Road. From Central or Admiralty it's probably the quickest, too: no traffic, no subway lines, or endless underground walks. There are stops every two or three blocks. The Sheung Wan MTR station brings you within spitting distance of Western Market.

**TOP ATTRACTIONS**

**Hong Kong Museum of Medical Sciences.** You can find out all about medical practices, disease outbreaks, and breakthroughs at this private museum, which is housed in a redbrick building at the top of Ladder Street that references Edwardian style architecture. The 11 exhibition galleries cover 10,000 square feet, and present information on both Western and Chinese medical practices. ⊠ *2 Caine Lane, Midlevels, Western* ☎ *2549–5123* ⊕ *www.hkmms.org.hk* ✉ *HK$10* ⊘ *Tues.–Sat. 10–5, Sun. and holidays 1–5* Ⓜ *Sheung Wan, Exit A2.*

**Man Mo Temple.** No one knows exactly when Hong Kong Island's oldest temple was built—the consensus is sometime around the arrival of the British in 1841. The temple is dedicated to the Taoist gods of literature and of war: Man, who wears green, and Mo, dressed in red. The temple bell, cast in Canton in 1847, and the drum next to it are sounded to attract the gods' attention when a prayer is being offered. ⊠ *Hollywood Rd. at Ladder St., Sheung Wan, Western* ⊘ *Daily 8–6* Ⓜ *Sheung Wan, Exit A2.*

Fodor's Choice ★ **University Museum and Art Gallery, The University of Hong Kong.** Chinese harp music and a faint smell of incense float through peaceful rooms filled with a small but excellent collection of Chinese antiquities. On view are ceramics and bronzes, some dating from 3,000 BC; fine paintings; lacquerware; and carvings in jade, stone, and wood. Some superb ancient pieces include ritual vessels, decorative mirrors, and painted pottery. The museum has the world's largest collection of Nestorian crosses, dating from the Mongol Period (1280–1368). These belonged to a heretical Christian sect who came to China from the Middle East during the Tang Dynasty (618–907).

There are usually two or three well-curated temporary exhibitions on view; contemporary artists who work in traditional mediums are often featured. ■TIP→ **Don't miss part of the museum: the collection is spread between the T.T. Tsui Building and the Fung Ping Shan Building, which you access via a first-floor footbridge.** The museum is a bit out of the way—20 minutes from Central via Buses 3B, 23, 40, 40 M, or 103, or a 15-minute uphill walk from Sheung Wan MTR—but it's a must for the true Chinese art lover. ✉ *94 Bonham Rd., Pokfulam, Western* ☎ *2241–5500* ⊕ *www.hku.hk/hkumag* ✉ *Free* ☽ *Mon.–Sat. 9:30–6, Sun. 1–6* Ⓜ *Sheung Wan.*

### WORTH NOTING

**Western Market.** The Sheung Wan district's iconic market, a hulking brown-and-white colonial structure, is a good place to get your bearings. Built in 1906, it functioned as a produce market for 83 years. Today it's a shopping center selling trinkets and fabrics—the architecture is what's worth the visit. Nearby are the Chinese herbal medicine on Ko Shing Street and Queen's Road West; dried seafood on Wing Lok Street and Des Voeux Road West; and ginseng and bird's nest on Bonham Strand West. ✉ *323 Des Voeux Rd. Central, Sheung Wan, Western* ☽ *Daily 10 am–midnight* Ⓜ *Sheung Wan, Exit B or C.*

## CENTRAL

Shopping, eating, drinking—Central lives up to its name when it comes to all of these. But it's also Hong Kong's historical heart, packed with architectural reminders of the early colonial days. They're in stark contrast to the soaring masterpieces of modern architecture that the city is famous for. Somehow the mishmash works. With the harbor on one side and Victoria Peak on the other, Central's views—once you get high enough to see them—are unrivaled. It's a hot spot for both locals and expatriates, packed with people, sights, and life.

The streets between Queen's Road Central and the harbor are laid out more or less geometrically. On the south side of Queen's Road, however, is a confusion of steep lanes. Overhead walkways connect Central's major buildings, an all-weather alternative to the chaotic streets below.

### GETTING HERE AND AROUND

Central MTR station is a mammoth underground warren with a host of far-flung exits. A series of travelators join it with Hong Kong Station, under the IFC Mall, where Tung Chung Line and Airport Express trains

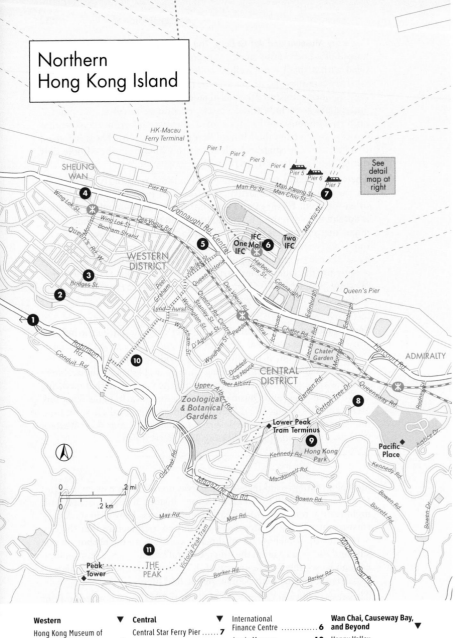

# Northern Hong Kong Island

**Western** ▼

Hong Kong Museum of Medical Sciences ........... 2

Man Mo Temple ............. 3

University Museum and Art Gallery, The University of Hong Kong .................. 1

Western Market ............. 4

**Central** ▼

Central Star Ferry Pier ...... 7

Flagstaff House Museum of Tea Ware ....... 8

Hong Kong Park ............ 9

International Finance Centre ............. 6

Jamia Mosque ............ 10

Mid-Levels Escalator ....... 5

Victoria Peak ............. 11

**Wan Chai, Causeway Bay, and Beyond** ▼

Happy Valley Racecourse ............... 13

Hong Kong Convention and Exhibition Centre ......... 12

Law Uk Folk Museum ..... 14

KOWLOON

Watertours Pier

Tsim Sha Tsui Public Pier

HK-Macau Ferry Terminal

SHEUNG WAN

Pier 1 Pier 2 Pier 3 Pier 4 Pier 5 Pier 6 Pier 7

**4** Wing Lok St. Bonham Strand West

Pier Rd.

Connaught Rd. Central

Man Po St. Man Kwong St. Man Chiu St.

**7** Star Ferry Pier

Morrison

Wing Lok St. Bonham Strand

Des Voeux Rd. Central

WESTERN DISTRICT

One-IFC **6** IFC Mall Two IFC

Queen's Rd. W. Cleverly Hillier

Upper Lascar Row Queen Victoria

Harbour View St.

Tai Ping Shan **3** Upper Hollywood Rd.

Gough Jubilee St. Queen's Rd. Central

Connaught Pl.

**2** Caine Rd. Ladder Bridges St.

Aberdeen Peel Graham St. Gage St. Cochrane Stanley St. Pottinger St. Li Yuen St. W. Li Yuen St. E.

Queen's Pier

Queen's Pl.

Edinburgh

Seymour Rd. Staunton Lyndhurst Wellington St. Wyndham St.

Causeway Bay

Victoria Park

**12** Wan Chai Ferry Pier

Hung Hing Rd. Hung Hing Rd. Marsh Rd. Causeway Bay Rd. Gloucester Rd.

Victoria Park Rd. Food Patterson St.

Seafront Rd. Wan Chai Sports Ground

CAUSEWAY BAY

Fenwick Pier St. Harbour Rd. Harbour Dr. Gloucester Rd.

Jaffe Rd. Lockhart Rd. Lee Wo

WAN CHAI Gloucester Rd.

Hennessy Rd. Percival St. Lee Garden Rd. Yun Ping Rd. Jardine's Cr.

■ Market

Arsenal St. Fenwick Rd. O'Brien Jaffe Rd. Lockhart Rd. Stewart Rd. Tonnochy Rd. Heard Rd. Bowrington Rd. Canal Rd. West

Tanlung St. Russell St. Hysan Ave.

**14**

Hennessy Rd. Johnston Rd. Luard Rd. Thomson Rd. Johnston Rd. Wanchai Rd. ◆ Times Square Mall

Queensway Rd. East Ship St. Swatow Amoy Cross St. Wanchai St. Tai Yuen St. Yat Sin St. Qi Kwen Rd. Leighton Rd.

Wong Nai Chung Rd. Lmk Rd.

Kennedy Rd. Morrison Hill Swimming Pool

Queensway Rd. East

Bowen Rd. HAPPY VALLEY

Kennedy Rd. **13** Stubbs Rd.

Wan Chai Gap Rd. Wong Nai Chung Rd.

| KEY | |
|---|---|
| ✳ | MTR (Metro) |
| ⋯⋯⋯ | Escalator |
| ⋯⋯⋯ | Tramway |
| ⛴ | Ferry |

arrive and depart. Rattling old trams along Des Voeux Road have you at Sheung Wan, Admiralty, and Wan Chai in minutes.

### TOP ATTRACTIONS

**Central Star Ferry Pier.** Take in the view of the Kowloon skyline from this pier, from which sturdy green-and-white Star Ferries cross the harbor. Naturally, the views are even better from the open water. ✉ *Man Kwong St. between Rumsey and Man Yiu Sts., Central* ☎ *2367–7065 for ferries, 2118–6201 for tours* ⊕ *www.starferry.com.hk* Ⓜ *Hong Kong Station, Exit A2.*

Fodor'sChoice ★ **Flagstaff House Museum of Tea Ware.** All that's good about British colonial architecture is exemplified in the simple white facade, wooden monsoon shutters, and colonnaded verandas. More than 600 pieces of delicate antique teaware from the Tang (618–907) through the Qing (1644–1911) dynasties fill rooms that once housed the commander of the British forces. ■TIP➡ **Skip the lengthy, confusing tea-ceremony descriptions; concentrate on the porcelain itself.** Look out for the unadorned brownish-purple clay of the Yixing pots: unglazed, their beauty hinges on perfect form. There's a playroom on the ground floor with interactive computer stations on the history of tea. ✉ *Hong Kong Park, 10 Cotton Tree Dr., Central* ☎ *2869–0690* ⊕ *www.lcsd.gov.hk/ce/Museum/Arts/en/tea/tea01.html* 🎫 *Free* ☉ *Wed.–Mon. 10–6* Ⓜ *Admiralty, Exit C1.*

FAMILY Fodor'sChoice ★ **Hong Kong Park.** A welcome respite from the Central skyscrapers occupies the site of Victoria Barracks, a garrison; the buildings from 1842 and 1910 still stand. The park is home to the Flagstaff House Museum of Tea Ware and the Edward Youde Aviary. ✉ *19 Cotton Tree Dr., Central* ☎ *2521–5041* 🎫 *Free* ☉ *Daily 6 am–11 pm* Ⓜ *Admiralty, Exit C1.*

**Mid-Levels Escalators.** The unimaginatively named Mid-Levels district is midway up the hill between Victoria Peak and the Western and Central districts. Running through it is the escalator, which connects the now-defunct Central Market (at the border of Central and Western) with several main residential roads. Free of charge and protected from the elements, this series of moving walkways makes the uphill journey a cinch. Before 10 am they move only downward, carrying workers bearing coffee to work. ✉ *Next to 100 Queen's Rd. Central, Central* ☉ *6–midnight* Ⓜ *Central, Exit D1.*

Fodor'sChoice ★ **Victoria Peak and the Victoria Peak Tram.** As you step off the Peak Tram, a sharp intake of breath and bout of sighing over the view will cure the feeling that you left your stomach somewhere down in Central. Whatever the time, whatever the weather, be it your first visit or your 50th, this is Hong Kong's one unmissable sight. Spread below you is a glittering forest of skyscrapers; beyond them the harbor and—on a clear day—Kowloon's eight mountains. At the top you enter the Peak Tower, a mall full of restaurants and shops; there's a viewing platform on the roof. Outside the Tower, another mall faces you. Well-signed nature walks around the Peak are wonderful respites from the commercialism. On a rainy day wisps of cloud catch on the buildings' pointy tops; at night both sides of the harbor burst into color. Consider having dinner at one of the restaurants near the Upper Terminus.

A clear day on the Victoria's Peak.

**TIP→** Bypass the overpriced tourist traps inside Sky Terrace and Gallery and head straight up the escalators to the rooftop, which looks down over the Pok Fu Lam country park and reservoir, and, on a clear day, Aberdeen.

Soaring 550 meters (1,805 feet) above sea level, the peak looks over Central and beyond. The steep funicular tracks up to the peak start at the **Peak Tram Terminus,** near St. John's Cathedral on Garden Road. Hong Kong is proud that its funicular railway is the world's steepest. Before it opened in 1888, the only way to get up to Victoria Peak was to walk or take a bumpy ride in a sedan chair on steep steps. At the Lower Terminus, the Peak Tram Historical Gallery displays a replica of the first-generation Peak Tram carriage. On the way up, grab a seat on the right-hand side for the best views of the harbor and mountains. The trams, which look like old-fashioned trolley cars, are hauled the whole way in seven minutes by cables attached to electric motors. En route to the Upper Terminus, 396 meters (1,300 feet) above sea level, the cars pass four intermediate stations, with track gradients varying from 4 to 27 degrees.

Before buying a return ticket down on the tram, consider taking one of the beautiful low-impact trails back to Central. Buses also go down. You'll be treated to spectacular views in all directions on the **Hong Kong Trail,** an easygoing 40- to 60-minute paved path that begins and ends at the Peak Tram Upper Terminus. Start by heading north along fern-encroached Lugard Road. There's another stunning view of Central from the lookout, 20 minutes along, after which the road snakes west to an intersection with Hatton and Harlech roads. From here Lantau,

Lamma, and—on incredibly clear days—Macau come into view. The longer option from here is to wind your way down Hatton to the University of Hong Kong campus in Western District.

Bus 15C, usually, but not always, a red double-decker with an open top, shuttles you between the Peak Tram Lower Terminal and Central Bus Terminal near the Star Ferry Pier, every 15 to 20 minutes, for HK$4.20. ⊠ *Tram between Garden Rd. and Cotton Tree Dr., Central* ☎ *2522– 0922* ⊕ *www.thepeak.com.hk* ☑ *HK$28 one-way, HK$40 round-trip* ⊙ *tram daily every 10–15 mins, 7 am–midnight.*

### WORTH NOTING

**International Finance Centre.** One building towers above the rest of Central's skyline: Two IFC, or the second tower of the International Finance Centre. The tall, tapering structure has been compared to at least one— unprintable—thing and is topped with a clawlike structure straight out of Thundercats. Designed by Argentine architect Cesar Pelli (of London's Canary Wharf fame), its 88 floors top a whopping 1,362 feet. Opposite stands its dinky little brother, the 38-floor One IFC. The massive IFC Mall stretches between the two, and Hong Kong Station is underneath. If you wish to see the breathtaking views from Two IFC, you can visit the Hong Kong Monetary Authority (⊠ *55/F, Two IFC* ☎ *2878–1111* ⊕ *www.info.gov.hk/hkma*). While there, take a quick look at exhibits tracing the history of banking in Hong Kong. Upon arrival, you may need to register your passport with the concierge. ⊠ *8 Finance St., Central* ⊕ *www.ifc.com.hk* ☑ *Free* ⊙ *Hong Kong Monetary Authority weekdays 10–6, Sat. 10–1* Ⓜ *Hong Kong Station, Exit A2.*

**Jamia Mosque.** The Mid-Levels Escalator goes right by the religious institution on Shelley Street. The original 1840s structure was rebuilt in 1915 and shows its Indian heritage in the perforated arches and decorative facade work. The mosque isn't open to non-Muslims, but it occupies a small verdant enclosure that's a welcome retreat. ⊠ *30 Shelley St., above Caine Rd. next to escalator, Central* Ⓜ *Central, Exit D1.*

## WAN CHAI, CAUSEWAY BAY, AND BEYOND

The Happy Valley horse races are a vital part of Hong Kong life, so it's only fitting that they're in one of the city's most vital areas. A few blocks back from Wan Chai's new office blocks are crowded alleys where you might stumble across a wet market, a tiny furniture-maker's shop, or an age-old temple. Farther east, Causeway Bay pulses with Hong Kong's best shopping streets and hundreds of restaurants. At night the whole area comes alive with bars, restaurants, and discos, as well as establishments offering some of Wan Chai's more traditional services (think red lights and photos of seminaked women outside).

### GETTING HERE AND AROUND

Both Wan Chai and Causeway Bay have their own MTR stops, but a pleasant way to arrive from Central is on the tram along Hennessy Road. All the lines go through Wan Chai, but check the sign at the front if you're going beyond. Some continue to North Point and Shau Kei Wan, via Causeway Bay, while others go south to Happy Valley.

## TOP ATTRACTIONS

Fodor's Choice
★
**Happy Valley Racecourse.** The biggest attraction east of Causeway Bay for locals and visitors alike is this local legend, where millions of Hong Kong dollars make their way each year. The exhilarating blur of galloping hooves under jockeys dressed in bright silk jerseys is a must-see. The races make great Wednesday nights out on the town. Aside from the excitement of the races, there are restaurants, bars, and even a racing museum to keep you amused. The public entrance to the track is a 20-minute walk from Causeway Bay MTR Exit A (Times Square), or simply hop on the Happy Valley tram, which terminates right in front. ⊠ *Sports Rd. at Wong Nai Chung Rd., Happy Valley, Causeway Bay* ☎ *HK$10* ⊙ *Wed. 5:15 or 5:30 during racing season* Ⓜ *Causeway Bay, Exit A.*

## WORTH NOTING

**Hong Kong Convention and Exhibition Centre.** Land is so scarce in Hong Kong that developers usually only build skyward, but the HKCEC is an exception, sitting on a spit of reclaimed land jutting into the harbor. Curved-glass walls and a swooping roof make it look like a tortoise lumbering into the sea or a gull taking flight, depending on whom you ask. Of all the international trade fairs, regional conferences, and other events held here, by far the most famous was the 1997 Handover ceremony. An obelisk commemorates it on the waterfront promenade, which also affords great views of Kowloon.

Outside the center stands the *Golden Bauhinia*. This gleaming sculpture of the Bauhinia flower, Hong Kong's symbol, was a gift from China celebrating the establishment of the Hong Kong SAR in 1997. The police hoist the SAR flag daily at 7:50 am; on the first of every month there is an enhanced flag rasing ceremony at 7:45 am. ⊠ *1 Expo Dr., Wan Chai* ☎ *2582–8888* ⊕ *www.hkcec.com.hk* Ⓜ *Wan Chai, Exit A.*

**Law Uk Folk Museum.** This restored Hakka house was once the home of the Law family, who arrived here from Guangdong in the mid-18th century. It's the perfect example of a triple-*jian*, double-*lang* residence. Jian are enclosed rooms—here, the bedroom, living room, and workroom at the back. The front storeroom and kitchen are the *lang*, where the walls don't reach up to the roof, and thus allow air in. Although the museum is small, informative texts outside and displays of rural furniture and farm implements inside give a powerful idea of what rural Hong Kong was like. It's definitely worth a trip to bustling industrial Chai Wan, at the eastern end of the MTR, to see it. Photos show what the area looked like in the 1930s—these days a leafy square is the only reminder of the woodlands and fields that once surrounded this buttermilk-color dwelling. ⊠ *14 Kut Shing St., Chai Wan, Eastern* ☎ *2896–7006* ⊕ *www.lcsd. gov.hk/CE/Museum/History/en/luf.php* ☎ *Free* ⊙ *Mon.–Wed., Fri.–Sat. 10–6, Sun. 1–6* Ⓜ *Chai Wan, Exit B.*

6

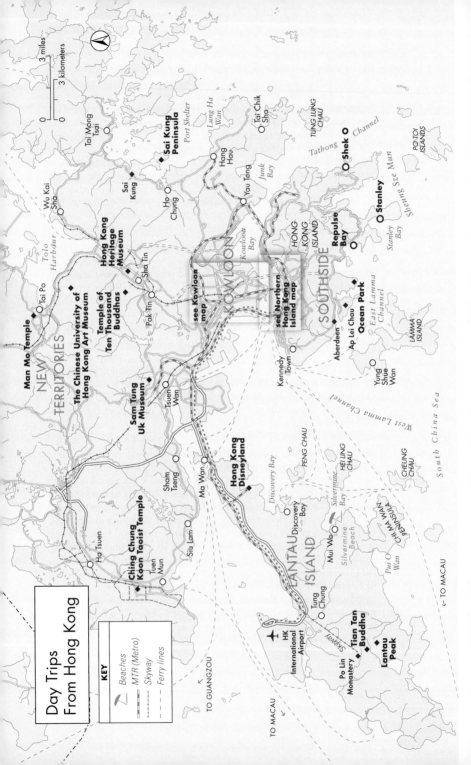

Day Trips From Hong Kong

KEY
Beaches
MTR (Metro)
Skyway
Ferry lines

# KOWLOON

There's much more to the Kowloon than rock-bottom prices and goods of dubious provenance. Just across the harbor from Central, this piece of Chinese mainland takes its name from the string of mountains that bound it in the north: *gau lung,* "nine dragons" (there are actually eight mountains, the ninth represented the emperor who named them). Although less sophisticated and wilder than its island-side counterpart, Kowloon's dense, gritty urban fabric is the backdrop for Hong Kong's best museums and most interesting spiritual sights. And there's street upon street of hard-core consumerism in every imaginable guise.

Kowloon's southernmost district is Tsim Sha Tsui (TST), home to the Star Ferry Pier. The waterfront extends a few miles to TST East. Shops and hotels line Nathan Road, which runs north from the waterfront through the market districts of Jordan, Yau Ma Tei, and Mong Kok.

New Kowloon is the unofficial name for the sprawl beyond Boundary Street. The district just north is Kowloon Tong. Two spiritual sights—Wong Tai Sin and Lok Fu—are a little farther east. The tongue sticking out into the sea to the south was the runway of the old Kai Tak Airport. Kowloon City is a stone's throw west.

### GETTING HERE AND AROUND

The most romantic way from Hong Kong Island to southern Tsim Sha Tsui (TST) is by Star Ferry. There are crossings from Central every 6–12 minutes and a little less often from Wan Chai.

TST is also accessible by MTR. Underground walkways connect the station with the Tsim Sha Tsui East station on the East Rail Line, where trains depart every 10–15 minutes for the eastern New Territories.

## TSIM SHA TSUI

You'll probably come to this district hugging the waterfront at the southern tip of Kowloon (in Chinese the name means "pointed sandy mouth") to see one or more of Hong Kong's top museums. These collections are within easy reach of one another amid high-rises, hotels, shops, and Kowloon Park, a coveted parcel of green space.

### TOP ATTRACTIONS

**Duk Ling.** The *Duk Ling* is a fully restored authentic fishing junk, originally built in Macau in the 1950s, whose large red sails are a sight to behold. The Hong Kong Tourist Board offers visitors aged 3 to 75 one-hour sails from Kowloon Pier (Thursday at 2 pm and 4 pm, Saturday at 10 am and noon) and from Central's Pier 9 (Thursday at 3 pm and 5 pm, Saturday at 11 am and 1 pm). Register first at the HKTB Visitor Centre in Tsim Sha Tsui, and bring your passport to prove you're from out of town. ⊠ *Tsim Sha Tsui* ☎ *2573–5282* ⊕ *www.dukling.com.hk or www.discoverhongkong.com.*

Fodor's Choice ★ **Hong Kong Museum of Art.** An extensive collection of Chinese art is packed inside this boxy tiled building on the Tsim Sha Tsui waterfront in Kowloon. The collections contain a heady mix of Qing ceramics, 2,000-year-old calligraphic scrolls, and contemporary canvases. It's all well organized into thematic galleries with clear, if uninspired, explanations. Hong Kong's biggest visiting exhibitions are usually held here too. The museum is a few minutes' walk from the Star Ferry and Tsim Sha Tsui MTR stop.

### Highlights

**The Chinese Antiquities Gallery** is the place to head if ceramics are your thing. A series of low-lit rooms on the third floor houses ceramics from Neolithic times through the Qing dynasty. Unusually, they're displayed by motif rather than by period: dragons, phoenixes, lotus flowers, and bats are some of the auspicious designs. Bronzes, jade, lacquerware, textiles, enamel, and glassware complete this collection of decorative art.

In the **Chinese Fine Art Gallery** you get a great introduction to Chinese brush painting, often difficult for the Western eye to appreciate. Landscape paintings from the 20th-century Guangdong and Lingnan schools form the bulk of the collection, and modern calligraphy also gets a nod.

The **Contemporary Hong Kong Art Gallery** showcases a mix of traditional Chinese and western techniques. Paintings account for most of the pieces from the first half of the 20th century, when local artists used the traditional mediums of brush and ink in innovative ways. Western techniques dominate later work, the result of Hong Kong artists' having spent more time abroad.

### Tips

Traditional Chinese landscape paintings are visual records of real or imagined journeys—a kind of travelogue. Pick a starting point and try to travel through the picture, imagining the journey the artist is trying to convey.

There is a collection search system on the first floor, as well as a research center.

Guided tours can help you understand art forms with which you're not familiar (in English Tuesday through Sunday at 11 am). Check the website for the schedule of more detailed visits to specific galleries—they change every month. If you prefer to tour alone, consider an English-language audio guide: it's informative, if a little dry, and it costs only HK$10. ⊠ *10 Salisbury Rd., Tsim Sha Tsui* 🖀 *2721–0116* ⊕ *hk.art. museum* 🖭 *HK$10* ⊙ *Fri. and Mon.–Wed. 10–6, Sat. and Sun 10–7* Ⓜ *Tsim Sha Tsui MTR, Exit F.*

**Hong Kong Museum of History.** The permanent Hong Kong Story features spectacular life-size dioramas that include village houses and a Central shopping street in colonial times, while the ground-floor Folk Culture section is a Technicolor introduction to the history and customs of Hong Kong's main ethnic groups. Upstairs, gracious stone-walled galleries whirl you through the Opium Wars and the beginnings of colonial Hong Kong. ■TIP➡ Unless you're with kids who dig models of cavemen and bears, skip the prehistory and dynastic galleries. Reserve energy for the last two galleries: a chilling account of life under Japanese occupation and a colorful look at Hong Kong life in the '60s.

Budget at least two hours to stroll through—more if you linger in each and every gallery. Pick your way through the gift shop's clutter to find

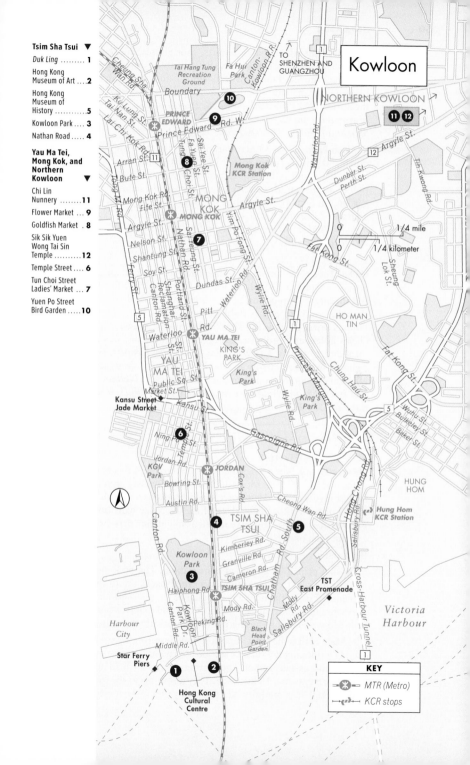

# Kowloon

**Tsim Sha Tsui** ▼

Duk Ling ......... 1

Hong Kong Museum of Art ....2

Hong Kong Museum of History ...........5

Kowloon Park .... 3

Nathan Road ..... 4

**Yau Ma Tei, Mong Kok, and Northern Kowloon** ▼

Chi Lin Nunnery ........11

Flower Market ... 9

Goldfish Market . 8

Sik Sik Yuen Wong Tai Sin Temple ..........12

Temple Street .... 6

Tun Choi Street Ladies' Market ... 7

Yuen Po Street Bird Garden .....10

NORTHERN KOWLOON

TO SHENZHEN AND GUANGZHOU

KEY

MTR (Metro)

KCR stops

Victoria Harbour

local designer Alan Chan's T-shirts, shot glasses, and notebooks. His retro-kitsch aesthetic is based on 1940s cigarette-girl images. To get here from the Tsim Sha Tsui MTR walk along Cameron Road, then left for a block along Chatham Road South. A signposted overpass takes you to the museum. ⊠ *100 Chatham Rd. S, Tsim Sha Tsui* ☎ *2724–9042* ⊕ *hk. history.museum* ⊠ *HK\$10; free Wed.* ☉ *Mon. and Wed.–Sat. 10–6, Sun. and holidays 10–7* Ⓜ *Tsim Sha Tsui, Exit B2.*

FAMILY **Kowloon Park.** These 33 acres are just behind Nathan Road, at TST's north end. They're crisscrossed by paths and meticulously landscaped but this is a still refreshing retreat after a bout of shopping. In addition to a fitness trail, soccer pitch, playgrounds, an aviary, and a maze garden, on Sundays and public holidays there are stalls with arts and crafts. ⊠ *22 Austin Rd., Tsim Sha Tsui* ☎ *2724–3344* ⊕ *www.lcsd.gov. hk/parks/kp/en* ⊠ *Free* ☉ *5 am–midnight* Ⓜ *Tsim Sha Tsui MTR, Exit A1, Jordan, Exit C1.*

### WORTH NOTING

**Nathan Road.** The famous Kowloon road runs several miles north from Salisbury Road in TST, all the way to Mong Kok. It's filled with hotels, restaurants, shopping malls, and boutiques—retail space is so costly that the southern end is dubbed the Golden Mile. The mile's most famous tower block is ramshackle Chungking Mansions, packed with cheap hotels and Indian restaurants. The building was a setting for local director Wong Kar-Wai's film *Chungking Express.* To the left and right are mazes of narrow streets with even more shops selling jewelry, electronics, clothes, souvenirs, and cosmetics. ⊠ *Nathan Rd. between Salisbury Rd. and Boundary St., Tsim Sha Tsui* Ⓜ *Tsim Sha Tsui, Jordan, Yau Ma Tei, Mong Kok, Prince Edward.*

## YAU MA TEI, MONG KOK, AND NORTHERN KOWLOON

### TOP ATTRACTIONS

Fodor'sChoice **Chi Lin Nunnery.** Not a single nail was used to build this nunnery, which
★ dates from 1934. Instead, traditional Tang Dynasty architectural techniques involving wooden dowels and bracket work hold its 228,000 pieces of timber together. Most of the 15 cedar halls house altars to *bodhisattvas* (those who have reached enlightenment)—bronze plaques explain each one.

**Highlights**

**Feng shui principles governed construction.** The buildings face south toward the sea, to bring abundance; their backs are to the mountain, provider of strength and good energy. The temple's clean lines are a vast departure from most of Hong Kong's colorful religious buildings—here polished wood and gleaming Buddha statues are the only adornments.

The **Main Hall** is the most imposing—and inspiring—part of the monastery. Overlooking the smaller second courtyard, it honors the first Buddha, known as Sakyamuni. The soaring ceilings are held up by 28 cedar columns, measuring 18 feet each. They also support the roof—no mean feat, given that its traditionally made clay tiles make it weigh 176 tons.

**Courtyards and gardens,** where frangipani flowers scent the air, run beside the nunnery. The gardens are filled with bonsai trees and artful rockeries. Nature is also present inside: the various halls and galleries all look onto two courtyards filled with geometric lotus ponds and manicured bushes.

**Tips**

Left of the Main Hall is a don't-miss hall dedicated to Avalokitesvra, better known in Hong Kong as Kwun Yum, goddess of mercy and child-bearing, among other things. She's one of the few exceptions to the rule that bodhisattvas are represented as asexual beings.

Be sure to keep looking up—the latticework ceilings and complicated beam systems are among the most beautiful parts of the building. Combine Chi Lin Nunnery with a visit to Sik Sik Yuen Wong Tai Sin Temple, only one MTR stop or a short taxi ride away. ⊠ *5 Chi Lin Dr., Diamond Hill, Northern Kowloon* ☎ *2354–1888* 🖾 *Free* ☉ *Nunnery daily 9–4:30, lotus-pond garden daily 7–7* Ⓜ *Diamond Hill, Exit C2.*

Fodor's Choice ★ **Sik Sik Yuen Wong Tai Sin Temple.** There's a practical approach to prayer at one of Hong Kong's most exuberant places of worship. Here the territory's three major religions—Taoism, Confucianism, and Buddhism—are all celebrated under the same roof. You'd think that ornamental religious buildings would look strange with highly visible vending machines and LCD displays in front of them, but Wong Tai Sin pulls it off in cacophonous style. The temple was established in the early 20th century, on a different site, when two Taoist masters arrived from Guangzhou with the portrait of Wong Tai Sin—a famous monk who was born around AD 328—that still graces the main altar. In the '30s the temple was moved here; continuous renovations make it impossible to distinguish old from new.

Start at the incense-wreathed main courtyard, where the noise of many people shaking out *chim* (sticks with fortunes written on them) forms a constant rhythmic background. After wandering the halls, take time out in the Good Wish Garden—a peaceful riot of rockery—at the back of the complex. At the base of the complex is a small arcade where soothsayers and palm readers are happy to interpret Wong Tai Sin's predictions for a small fee. At the base of the ramp to the Confucian Hall, look up behind the temple for a view of Lion Rock, a mountain in the shape of a sleeping lion. ■TIP➜ **If you feel like acquiring a household altar of your own, head for Shanghai Street in Yau Ma Tei, the Kowloon district north of Tsim Sha Tsui, where religious shops abound.** ⊠ *Wong Tai Sin Rd., Wong Tai Sin, Northern Kowloon* ☎ *2327–8141* 🖾 *Donations expected. Good Wish Garden HK$2* ☉ *Daily 7–5:30* Ⓜ *Wong Tai Sin, Exit B2 or B3.*

**Temple Street.** Temple Street, in the heart of Yau Ma Tei, is home to Hong Kong's biggest night market. Stalls selling kitsch of all kinds set up in the late afternoon in the blocks north of Public Square Street. Fortune-tellers, prostitutes, and street doctors also offer their services here. ⊠ *Temple St. between Jordan Rd. and Kansu St., Yau Ma Tei* Ⓜ *Yau Ma Tei, Exit C; Jordan, Exit A.*

6

**WORTH NOTING**

**Flower Market.** Stalls containing local and imported fresh flowers, potted plants, and even artificial blossoms cover Flower Market Road, as well as parts of Yuen Po Street, Yuen Ngai Street, Prince Edward Road West, and Playing Field Road. ⊠ *Flower Market Rd. between Yuen Ngai St. and Yuen Po St., Mong Kok* ▨ *Free* ☉ *Daily 7–7* Ⓜ *Mong Kok East, Exit C; Prince Edward, Exit B1.*

FAMILY **Goldfish Market.** A few dozen shops on Tung Choi Street and Nullah Road sell the ubiquitous fish, which locals believe to be lucky. In addition to feed and aquariums, the market is home to other varieties of animals. ⊠ *Tung Choi St. and Nullah Rd., Mong Kok* ▨ *Free* ☉ *10:30–10* Ⓜ *Mong Kok East, Exit C; Prince Edward, Exit B2.*

**Tung Choi Street Ladies' Market.** Despite the name, stalls are filled with no-brand clothes and accessories for both sexes. The shopping is best between Dundas and Argyle. ⊠ *Tung Choi St. between Dundas St. and Argyle St., Mong Kok* ▨ *Free* Ⓜ *Mong Kok.*

FAMILY **Yuen Po Street Bird Garden.** Next to the Flower Market, more than 70 stalls sell different types of twittering, fluttering birds of numerous colors, shapes, and sizes. Birdcages and food, from seeds to live grasshoppers, are also for sale. ⊠ *Yuen Po St. between Boundary St. and Prince Edward Rd. West, Mong Kok* ☉ *Daily 7 am–8 pm* Ⓜ *Mong Kok East, Exit C; Prince Edward, Exit B1.*

# DAY TRIPS FROM HONG KONG

## SOUTHSIDE

For all the unrelenting urbanity of Hong Kong Island's north coast, its south side consists largely of green hills and a few residential areas around picturesque bays. With beautiful sea views, real estate is at a premium; some of Hong Kong's wealthiest residents live in beautiful houses and luxurious apartments here. Southside is a breath of fresh air—literally and figuratively. The people are more relaxed, the pace is slower, and there are lots of sea breezes.

### GETTING HERE AND AROUND

You can get here by bus from the center of the city, and the trip will take anywhere from 20 to 50 minutes. Note that express buses skip Aberdeen and Deep Water Bay, heading directly to Repulse Bay and Stanley. Buses run less frequently in the evening, so it's more convenient to grab a taxi (they're everywhere).

### TOP ATTRACTIONS

FAMILY **Ocean Park.** Most Hong Kongers have fond childhood memories of this aquatic theme park. It was built by the omnipresent Hong Kong Jockey Club on 170 hilly acres overlooking the sea just east of Aberdeen. Highlights include the four resident giant pandas; Marine World's enormous aquarium; Ocean Theatre, where dolphins and seals perform; and such thrill rides as the gravity-defying Abyss Turbo. The park is accessible by a number of buses including the 72, 72A, 260, and 629; get off at the stop after the Aberdeen tunnel. ■TIP➔ If you have kids, plan to spend the whole day here. ⊠ *Ocean Park Rd., Aberdeen, Southside*

☎ 3923–2323 ⊕ www.oceanpark.com.hk ✉ HK$280 adults; HK$140 kids ⊙ Daily 10–7.

**Stanley.** This peninsula town lies south of Deep Water and Repulse bays. There's great shopping in the renowned Stanley Market, whether you want casual clothes, sneakers, cheap souvenirs, cheerful bric-a-brac— even snow gear. Stanley's popular beach is the site of the Dragon Boat Races every June. To get here from Exchange Square Bus Terminus in Central, take Bus 6, 6A, 6X, 66, 64, or 260. ✉ Southside.

### WORTH NOTING

**Repulse Bay.** The tranquil area is home to a landmark apartment building with a hole in it. Following the principles of feng shui, the opening was incorporated into the design so the dragon that lives in the mountains behind can readily drink from the bay. The popular restaurant The Verandah (⇨ Quick Bites) is a great place for a meal with majestic bay views. The beach is large and wide, but be warned: it's the first stop for most Southside visitors. Huge statues of Tin Hau—Goddess of the Sea and Goddess of Mercy—at the east end of the beach border on gaudy. In the 1970s, when worshippers were planning to erect just one statue, they worried she'd be lonely, so an additional statue was created to keep her company. To get here, take Bus 6, 6A, 6X, 66, 64, or 260 from Exchange Square Bus Terminus in Central. ✉ Beach Rd. at Seaview Promenade, Repulse Bay, Southside ☎ 2812–2483.

**Shek O.** The seaside locale is Southside's easternmost village. Weekend beachgoers and hikers crowd the Thai restaurant on the left as you enter town. Every shop here sells the same inflatable beach toys—the bigger the better, it seems. Cut through town to a windy road that takes you to the "island" of Tai Tau Chau, really a large rock with a lookout over the South China Sea. Just over a century ago, this open water was ruled by pirates. You can hike through nearby Shek O Country Park, where the bird-watching is great, in less than two hours. To get here from Central, take the MTR to Shau Kei Wan, then take Bus 9 to the last stop (about 30 min). ✉ Southside.

## LANTAU ISLAND

A decade of manic development has seen Lantau become more than just "the place where the Buddha is." There's a mini-theme park at Ngong Ping to keep the Buddha company. Not to be outdone, Disney has opened a park and resort on the northeast coast. And, of course, there's the airport, built on a massive north coast reclamation. At 55 square mi, Lantau is almost twice the size of Hong Kong Island, so there's room for all this development and the laid-back attractions—beaches, fishing villages, and hiking trails—that make the island a great getaway.

### GETTING HERE AND AROUND

The speediest way to Lantau from Central is the MTR's Tung Chung line (HK$18), which takes about half an hour. A trip by ferry is a 35-minute crossing from Central with great views.

**DID YOU KNOW?**

Lantau is the largest island in Hong Kong. In spite of all the recent development, it's often referred to as the lungs of Hong Kong, thanks to lush forests and dearth of high-rise housing developments. Strap on your hiking boots and take a day to explore the island.

## TOP ATTRACTIONS

FAMILY **Hong Kong Disneyland.** Though Hong Kong's home to Mickey Mouse is tame compared with other Magic Kingdoms, it's fast bringing Mai Kei Lo Su—as the world's most famous mouse is known locally—to a mainland audience. Younger kids will find plenty of amusement, but their older siblings and parents will have to settle for just one thrill ride, Space Mountain. If you need to visit a theme park in Hong Kong, Ocean Park in Aberdeen (⇨ *Southside, above) is a better bet.* ⊠ *Fantasy Rd., Lantau Island* ⊕ *park.hongkongdisneyland.com* ☎ *HK$399 adults, HK$285 kids* ⊙ *Daily 10–8 or 9* Ⓜ *Disneyland Resort.*

Fodor'sChoice **Tian Tan Buddha.** Hong Kongers love superlatives, even if making them ★ true requires strings of qualifiers. So the Tian Tan Buddha is the world's largest Buddha—that's seated, located outdoors, and made of bronze. Just know the vast silhouette is impressive. Steep stairs lead to the lower podium, essentially forcing you to stare up at all 202 tons of Buddha as you ascend. At the top, cool breezes and fantastic views over Lantau Island await.

### Highlights

**Po Lin Monastery.** It's hard to believe today, but from its foundation in 1927 through the early '90s, this monastery was virtually inaccessible by road. These days, it's at the heart of Lantau's biggest attraction. The monastery proper has a gaudy, commercial, orange temple complex. Still, it's the Buddha people come for.

**Wisdom Path.** This peaceful path runs beside 38 halved tree trunks arranged in an infinity shape on a hillside. Each is carved with Chinese characters that make up the Heart Sutra, a 5th-century Buddhist prayer that expresses the doctrine of emptiness. The idea is to walk around the path—which takes five minutes—and reflect. Follow the signposted trail to the left of the Buddha.

**Ngong Ping Village.** People were fussing about this attraction before its first stone was laid. Ngong Ping Village is a moneymaking add-on to the Tian Tan Buddha. Walking With Buddha is intended to be an educational stroll through the life of Siddhartha Gautama, the first Buddha, but it's more of a multimedia extravaganza that shuns good taste with such kitsch as a self-illuminating Bodhi tree and piped-in incense. No cost has been spared in the dioramas that fill the seven galleries—ironic, given that each represents a stage of the Buddha's path to enlightenment and the eschewing of material wealth.

### Tips

You can get here on the Ngong Ping 360 sky rail from a terminal adjacent to the MTR station in Tung Chung or via Buses 2 and 23 from Mui Wo and Tung Chung, respectively.

The only way to the upper level, right under the Buddha, is through an underwhelming museum inside the podium. You only get a couple of feet higher up.

The booth at the base of the stairs is only for tickets for lunch—wandering around the Buddha is free.

6

The monastery's vegetarian restaurant is a clattering canteen with uninspiring fare. Pick up sandwiches at the Citygate Mall, Tung Chung, or eat at a restaurant in Ngong Ping Village. ⊠ *Ngong Ping, Lantau Island* ☎ *2109–9898 Ngong Ping hotline* ⊕ *www.plm.org.hk/eng/home.php* 🖅 *Monastery and path free. Walking with Buddha: HK$35* ⊙ *Buddha daily 10–5:30, monastery and path daily 8–6* Ⓜ *Tung Chung.*

### WORTH NOTING

**Lantau Peak.** The most glorious views of Lantau—and beyond—are from atop Fung Wong Shan, or Lantau Peak, but at 3,064 feet, the mountaintop experience is not for the faint-hearted. The ascent requires a strenuous 7½-mi hike west from Mui Wo, or you can begin at the Po Lin Monastery—still a demanding two hours. You can also take a bus to a trail that is closer to the summit, and climb from stage three of the Lantau Trail. ⊠ *Lantau Island.*

# THE NEW TERRITORIES

Rustic villages, incense-filled temples, green hiking trails, pristine beaches—the New Territories have a lot to offer. Until a generation ago the region was mostly farmland with the occasional walled village. Today, thanks to a government housing program that created "new towns" like Sha Tin and Tuen Mun with up to 500,000 residents, parts of the region are more like the rest of Hong Kong. Within its expansive 518 square km (200 square miles), however, you'll still feel far removed from urban congestion. Here you can visit the area's lushest parks and glimpse traditional rural life in the restored walled villages and ancestral clan halls.

### GETTING HERE AND AROUND

Between the bus and MTR, you can get close to many sights. Set off on the MTR from Central to Tsuen Wan; from there, taxis, buses, and minibuses will take you to places such as the Yuen Yuen Institute and Tai Mo Shan. For Sha Tin and other spots in the east, take the MTR to Kowloon Tong; transfer to the East Rail line to Sha Tin station. To reach the Sai Kung Peninsula, take the MTR from Central to Choi Hung, then the green Minibus 1A to Sai Kung Town.

### TOP ATTRACTIONS

Fodor's Choice ★ **Hong Kong Heritage Museum.** This fabulous museum is Hong Kong's largest, yet it still seems a well-kept secret: chances are you'll have most of its 10 massive galleries to yourself. They ring an inner courtyard, which pours light into the lofty entrance hall.

#### Highlights

The **New Territories Heritage Hall** is packed with local history—6,000 years of it. See life as it was in beautiful dioramas of traditional villages—one on land, the other on water (with houses on stilts). The last gallery documents the rise of massive urban New Towns. There's even a computer game that lets you design your own.

In the **T.T. Tsui Gallery of Chinese Art,** exquisite antique Chinese glass, ceramics, and bronzes fill nine hushed second-floor rooms. The curators have gone for quality over quantity. Look for the 4-foot-tall terra-cotta

**DID YOU KNOW?**

The Tian Tan Buddha is surrounded by six smaller bronze statues known as "The Offering of the Six Devas." These offerings of flowers, incense, lamp, ointment, fruit, and music symbolize charity, morality, patience, zeal, meditation, and wisdom—all necessary traits if one wishes to reach Nirvana.

*Horse and Rider*, a beautiful example of the figures enclosed in tombs in the Han Dynasty (206 BC–AD 220). The Tibetan religious statues and *thankga* paintings are unique in Hong Kong.

The **Cantonese Opera Heritage Hall** is all singing, all dancing, and utterly hands-on. The symbolic costumes, tradition-bound stories, and stylized acting of Cantonese opera can be impenetrable: the museum provides simple explanations and stacks of artifacts, including century-old sequined costumes that put Vegas to shame. Don't miss the virtual makeup display, where you get your on-screen face painted like an opera character's.

Kids love the **Children's Discovery Gallery,** where hands-on activities for 4- to 10-year-olds include putting a broken "archaeological find" together. The Hong Kong Toy Story charts more than a century of local toys.

**Tips**

Look for the audio tours in English, which are available for special exhibitions.

There's lots of ground to cover: Prioritize the New Territories Heritage, the T.T. Tsui Gallery, and the Cantonese Opera Halls, all permanent displays, and do the temporary history and art exhibitions if energy levels permit.

The museum is a five-minute signposted walk from Che Kung Temple station. If the weather's good, walk back along the leafy riverside path that links the museum with Sha Tin station, in New Town Plaza mall, 15 minutes away. ⊠ *1 Man Lam Rd., Sha Tin, New Territories* ☎ *2180–8188* ⊕ *hk.heritage.museum* ✉ *HK\$10; free on Wed.* ☉ *Mon. and Wed.–Sat. 10–6, Sun. and holidays 10–7* Ⓜ *Che Kung or Sha Tin.*

**Temple of Ten Thousand Buddhas.** You climb some 400 steps to reach this temple: but look on the bright side, for each step you get about 32 Buddhas. The uphill path through dense vegetation is lined with life-size golden Buddhas in all kinds of positions. If you're dragging bored kids along, get them to play "Spot the Celebrity Lookalike" on the way. ■TIP➔ **In summer bring water and insect repellent.** Prepare to be dazzled inside the main temple, where walls are stacked with gilded ceramic statuettes. There are actually nearly 13,000 Buddhas here, made by Shanghai craftsmen and donated by worshippers over the decades. Kwun Yum, goddess of mercy, is one of several deities honored in the crimson-walled courtyard.

Look southwest on a clear day and you can see nearby **Amah Rock,** which resembles a woman with a child on her back. Legend has it that this formation was once a faithful fisherman's wife who climbed the mountain every day to wait for her husband's return, not knowing he'd been drowned. Tin Hau, goddess of the sea, took pity on her and turned her to stone.

The temple is in the foothills of Sha Tin, in the central New Territories. Take Exit B out of Sha Tin station, walk down the pedestrian ramp, and take the first left onto Pai Tau Street. Keep to the right-hand side of the road and follow it around to the gate where the signposted path starts. ■TIP→ Don't be confused by the big white buildings on the left of Pai Tau Road. They are ancestral halls, not the temple. ⊠ *Off Pai Tau St., Sha Tin, New Territories* ☒ *Free* ☼ *Daily 9–5:30* Ⓜ *Sha Tin, Exit B.*

### WORTH NOTING

**The Chinese University of Hong Kong Art Museum.** Located in the Institute of Chinese Studies building, the museum has paintings and calligraphy from the Qing period to modern times. There are also collections of bronze seals, carved jade flowers, and ceramics from South China. Take the East Rail line to University station, then a campus bus or taxi. ⊠ *Tai Po Rd., Sha Tin, New Territories* ☎ *3943–7416* ⊕ *www.cuhk.edu.hk/ics/amm* ☒ *Free* ☼ *Daily 10–5* Ⓜ *University.*

**Ching Chung Koon Taoist Temple.** Adjacent to the Ching Chung LRT station near the town of Tuen Mun, this temple has room after room of altars filled with the heady scent of incense. On one side of the main entrance is a cast-iron bell with a circumference of about 5 feet—all large monasteries in ancient China rang such bells at daybreak to wake the monks and nuns for a day of work in the rice fields. On the other side of the entrance is a huge drum that was used to call the workers back in the evening. Inside, some rooms are papered with small pictures; people pay the temple to have these photos displayed so they can see their dearly departed as they pray. Colorful plants and flowers, hundreds of dwarf shrubs, ornamental fishponds, and pagodas bedeck the grounds. The temple's entrance isn't obvious, so ask for directions. ⊠ *Tuen Mun, New Territories* ☎ *2462–1507* ⊕ *www.discoverhongkong.com/eng/attractions/nt-chingchungkoon.html* Ⓜ *Siu Hong, Exit B.*

**Man Mo Temple.** Adjacent to the Tai Po Market is the 100-year-old temple that was built to commemorate the establishment of the town of Tai Po. As you draw near, you'll smell the incense offered by worshippers. ⊠ *Fu Shin St., Tai Po, New Territories* ⊕ *www.lcsd.gov.hk/ce/Museum/Monument/en/monuments_23.php* ☒ *Free* ☼ *Daily 9–6* Ⓜ *Tai Wo.*

**Sai Kung Peninsula.** To the east of Sha Tin, this landmass has a few small towns and Hong Kong's most beloved nature preserve. The hikes through the hills surrounding High Island Reservoir are spectacular, and Sai Kung Country Park has several hiking trails that wind through majestic hills overlooking the water. Seafood restaurants dot the waterfront at Sai Kung Town as well as the tiny fishing village of Po Toi O in Clear Water Bay. At Sai Kung Town you can rent a sampan that will take you to one of the many islands in the area for a day at the beach. Take the MTR to Choi Hung and then Bus 92 or 96R, or Minibus 1A or 1S to Sai Kung Town. Instead of taking the bus, you can also catch a taxi along Clearwater Bay Road, which will take you into forested areas and land that's only partially developed with Spanish-style villas overlooking the sea. This excursion will take a full day, and you should only go if it's sunny. ⊠ *Sai Kung Peninsula, Kowloon.*

**Sam Tung Uk Museum.** A walled Hakka village from 1786 was saved from demolition to create this museum. It's in the middle of industrial Tsuen Wan, in the western New Territories, so its quiet whitewashed courtyards and small interlocking chambers contrast greatly with the nearby residential towers. Hakka villages were built with security in mind, and this one looks more like a single large house than a village. Indeed, most Hakka village names end in *uk,* which literally means "house"—Sam Tung Uk translates as "Three Beam House." Rigid symmetry dictated the village's construction: the ancestral hall and two common chambers form the central axis, which is flanked by the more private areas. The front door is angled to face west–southwest, in keeping with feng shui principles of alignment between mountain and water. Traditional furniture and farm tools are displayed in each room. ▬TIP➔ **Head through the courtyards and start your visit in the exhibition hall at the back, where a display gives helpful background on Hakka culture and pre-industrial Tsuen Wan—explanations are sparse elsewhere. You can also try on a Hakka hat.** ✉ *2 Kwu Uk Lane, Tsuen Wan, New Territories* ☎ *2411–2001* ⊕ *www.heritagemuseum.gov.hk/eng/museums/ samtunguk.aspx* ▦ *Free* ⊙ *Wed.–Mon. 10–6* Ⓜ *Tsuen Wan, Exit B3.*

# WHERE TO EAT

No other city in the world boasts quite as eclectic a dining scene as the one in Hong Kong. Luxurious fine-dining restaurants opened by celebrity chefs, such as Gray Kunz and Joël Robuchon, are just a stone's throw away from humble local eateries doling out thin noodles served with some of the best wonton shrimp dumplings, or delicious slices of tender barbecued meat piled atop bowls of fragrant jasmine rice.

Never judge a book by its cover—the most unassuming eateries are often the ones that provide the most memorable meals. At noodle-centric restaurants, fishball soup with ramen noodles is an excellent choice, and the goose, suckling pig, honeyed pork, and soy-sauce chicken are good bets at the roast-meat shops. A combination plate, with a sampling of meats and some greens on a bed of white rice, is a foolproof way to go. Street foods are another must-try; for just a couple of bucks, sample curry fishballs, skewered meats, stinky tofu, and all sorts of other delicious tidbits. If you have the chance, visit a *dai pai dong* (outdoor food stall) and try the local specialties.

For fine dining with a unique Hong Kong twist, you can always hit up places like the exclusive and extravagant Krug Room or try Alvin Leung's one-of-a-kind "X-treme Chinese" fare at Bo Innovation.

Finally, remember that Hong Kong is the world's epicenter of dim sum. While you're here you must have at least one dim sum breakfast or lunch in a teahouse. Those steaming bamboo baskets you see conceal delicious dumplings, buns, and pastries—all as comforting and delicious as they are exotic.

## MEAL TIMES

Locals eat lunch between noon and 1:30 pm; dinner is around 8. Dim sum begins as early as 10 am. Reservations aren't usually necessary except during Chinese holidays or at of-the-moment or high-end hotel restaurants like Alain Ducasse's SPOON or the Caprice. There are certain classic Hong Kong preparations (e.g., beggar's chicken, whose preparation in a clay pot takes hours) that require reserving not just a table, but the dish itself. Do so at least 24 hours ahead.

You'll also need reservations for a meal at one of the so-called private kitchens—unlicensed culinary speakeasies, which are often the city's hottest tickets. Book several days ahead, and if possible, join forces with other people. Some private kitchens only take reservations for parties of four, six, or eight.

> **WORD OF MOUTH**
>
> "Lunch at Amber in the Landmark Hotel is a set tasting menu with wine matched. What a great restaurant; service was the best from all the staff. The food was amazing. It really was the best meal!"
> —aussiedreamer

### PRICES

*Prices in the reviews are the average cost of a main course at dinner or, if dinner is not served, at lunch.* That said, the custom of sharing dishes affects the ultimate cost of your dinner. Further, we exclude outrageously expensive dishes—abalone, bird's-nest soup, shark's-fin soup.

Don't be shocked that you've been charged for everything, including tea, rice, and those side dishes placed automatically on your table. At upmarket and Western-style restaurants, tips are appreciated (10% is generous); the service charge on your bill doesn't go to the waitstaff.

## HONG KONG ISLAND

*Reviews listed alphabetically within neighborhoods. Use the coordinate (✛ B2) at the end of each listing to locate a site on the Where to Eat and Stay in Hong Kong map.*

### WESTERN

$$$
CANTONESE
Fodor's Choice
★

✕ **Tim's Kitchen.** Some of the homespun dishes at this restaurant require at least a day's advanced ordering but the extra fuss is worth it. One signature dish pairs a meaty crab claw with winter melon—a clean and simple combo that allows the freshness of the ingredients to shine. The fist-size "glassy" king prawn looks unassuming, paired with nothing but a slice of Yunnan ham on a plain, ungarnished plate. Take a bite though, and you'll be amazed at how succulent and delectably creamy it is. Word of warning—some of the more intricate dishes can get pretty pricy. But simpler (and cheaper) options are also available, such as pomelo skin sprinkled with shrimp roe, and stir-fried flat rice noodles with beef. $ *Average main: HK$300* ⊠ *84–90 Bonham Strand E, Sheung Wan, Western* ☎ *2543–5919* ⊕ *www.timskitchen.com.hk* ☙ *Reservations essential* ⊘ *Closed Sun.* Ⓜ *Sheung Wan* ✛ *A3.*

$$
JAPANESE
Fodor's Choice
★

✕ **Yardbird.** This bustling bi-level eatery is one of the hottest places to eat. Chef-owner Matt Abergel plates perfectly cooked *yakitori* (Japanese-style grilled chicken) as well as a repertoire of salads and small plates designed for sharing. Definitely try the Korean fried cauliflower (KFC) and the liver mousse served with milk bread and crispy shallots. Drinking is another important part of the experience so try the house brand junmai sake or choose from the well-selected Japanese beer and whiskey list. The only downside here is that the restaurant doesn't take reservations so arrive early or risk waiting for a table. $ *Average main: HK$130* ⊠ *33–35 Bridges St., Sheung Wan, Western* ☎ *2547–9273*

🌐 *www.yardbirdrestaurant.com* ✍ *Reservations not accepted* ⏲ *No lunch. Closed Sun.* ✣ *A2*

## CENTRAL

$$$$ ITALIAN Fodor's Choice ★ 🍴 **8½ Otto e Mezzo.** Spearheaded by chef Umberto Bombana (the ex-Ritz Carlton chef, often lauded as "the best Italian chef in Asia"), this glitzy space delivers everything it promises. The service is hotel grade, the wine list is extensive, and the interior is nothing less than glamorous. Most importantly, the authentic Italian food here is magnificent. Chef Bombana's famed handmade pastas live up to the hype; the burrata cheese ravioli in black-olive and eggplant sauce being particularly stellar. Mains are solid—the beef tongue and beef cheek is excellently executed, but seafood options are even better. If you can't make up your mind, the degustation menu offers a neat sampling of Bombana's best. [$] *Average main: HK$340* ✉ *Shop 202, 2nd fl., Alexandra House, 18 Chater Rd., Central* ☎ *2537–8859* 🌐 *www.ottoemezzobombana.com* ✍ *Reservations essential* ⏲ *Closed Sun.* [M] *Central* ✣ *B3.*

$$$$ FRENCH 🍴 **Amber.** When the Landmark Mandarin Oriental hotel opened in 2005, its aim was to be seen as the preeminent hotel on Hong Kong Island. So it made sense that it would house an award-winning flagship restaurant with a similar level of impeccable, modern style. The restaurant and the concept are no longer new, but Chef Richard Ekkebus's menu of creative European dishes still doesn't fail to impress, and guests can look forward to signature creations such as foie gras lollipops, line-caught *amadai* (tilefish) with orange and fennel confit and *bottarga* grated potatoes bouillabaisse, as well as sea urchin set in lobster gelatin with cauliflower, caviar, and seaweed waffle. [$] *Average main: HK$460* ✉ *Landmark Mandarin Oriental Hotel, 15 Queen's Rd., Central* ☎ *2132–0066* 🌐 *www.amberhongkong.com* [M] *Central* ✣ *B3.*

$$$ ITALIAN 🍴 **Ammo.** Few places in Hong Kong have the kind of stunning garden views that you'll find at Ammo. In a former ammunition compound (hence the name) that was converted into the Asia Society museum, Ammo's interiors and menus blend the old with the new and East with West, resulting in an impressive and dynamic dining experience. Dishes tout Italian roots, but you'll find plenty of Asian flourishes, as in the slow-cooked egg with toro, sea urchin, and roman zucchini sauce; and burrata cheese ravioli doused in Peking duck ragout. Save room for dessert because the panfried brioche is insanely satisfying. [$] *Average main: HK$200* ✉ *9 Justice Drive, Admiralty, Central* ☎ *2537–9888* 🌐 *www.ammo.com.hk* ✍ *Reservations essential* ✣ *C5.*

$$ ECLECTIC FAMILY 🍴 **Café Deco Bar & Grill.** As is often the case where there's a captive audience, dining up at the Peak Galleria mall can be unpredictable—and this huge eatery is no exception. You'll come mostly for the views, though the menu is eclectic enough to keep everyone happy. Menu options traverse five or six continents and there is also a dessert station. Oysters are good, and the pizzas and pastas are okay, but you should avoid the insipid Southeast Asian fare and overpriced steaks. When you book (and you must), be sure to request a table with a view, as many tables in the place have none, which defeats the purpose of coming here. [$] *Average main: HK$190* ✉ *1st fl., Peak Galleria, 118*

*Peak Rd., The Peak, Central* ☎ *2849–5111* 🌐 *www.cafedecogroup.com* ✍ *Reservations essential* ✣ *A6.*

$$ PERUVIAN 🍴 **Chicha.** Expect complex, chili-fueled flavors from Hong Kong's first Peruvian restaurant. The menu has multicultural influences, from Chinese-style *lomo saltado* (a beef, scallion, and rice stir-fry) to the Spanish paella-like *marisco jugoso* flavored with an umami sea urchin and citrus reduction. Be sure to order a platter of *anticuchos* (grilled skewers) to share; the cod with ponzu miso and chili aioli is close to addictive. If you want to cap your meal off in true Peruvian fashion, finish with a pisco brandy cocktail at the bar. [$] *Average main: HK$198* ✉ *26 Peel St., Central* ☎ *2561–3336* 🌐 *www.conceptcreations.hk* ✍ *Reservations essential* ⏲ *No lunch Sat. Closed Sun.* ✣ *A4.*

$$$ SHANGHAINESE Fodor's Choice ★ 🍴 **Fa Zu Jie.** This place is good, really, *really* good. Tucked away in a nondescript building in a hidden alley off Lan Kwai Fong, this reservations-only private kitchen plates up inventive French-inspired Shanghainese dishes that are prepped in a polished open kitchen. The prix-fixe menu is tweaked on a regular basis but you'll probably be treated to trademark items such as drunken quail (cooked in Chinese Hua Diao wine) served with al dente Sanuki udon, and plump scallops slicked in shrimp roe oil. The dining room has only a handful of tables so try to book a few weeks in advance if you can. [$] *Average main: HK$538* ✉ *1st fl., 20A D'Aguilar St., Central* ☎ *3487–1715* ✍ *Reservations essential* 💳 *No credit cards* ⏲ *No lunch. Closed Sun.* ✣ *A5.*

$$$$ FRENCH Fodor's Choice ★ 🍴 **L'Atelier de Joël Robuchon.** Joël Robuchon, one of the most iconic chefs in the world, claims that his atelier (or "artist's workshop") is for contemporary casual dining. Diners sit on barstools around a counter designed like a modern Japanese sushi bar so that everyone can watch the chefs preparing the food in the open kitchen. Though entrées are available, diners typically order small plates for sharing. Everything from the freshly baked bread to desserts is immaculately presented. The quail with foie gras, served with the deservedly famous mashed potatoes; and the sea urchin in a lobster jelly, topped with cauliflower cream, are all standouts. Those who don't want to splurge on a full meal should try the superb croissants and cakes at the salon one floor down from the restaurant. [$] *Average main: HK$500* ✉ *Shop 315 (salon) and 401 (restaurant), The Landmark Mandarin Oriental Hotel, 15 Queen's Rd., Central* ☎ *2166–9000* 🌐 *www.robuchon.hk* [M] *Central* ✣ *B3.*

$$$ CHINESE 🍴 **Lung King Heen.** Lung King Heen has made a serious case for being the best Cantonese restaurant in Hong Kong, especially after winning three Michelin stars for three consecutive years. Where other contenders tend to get too caught up in prestige dishes and name-brand chefs, Lung King Heen focuses completely on taste. When you try a steamed lobster-and-scallop dumpling, or a dish of house-made XO sauce that is this divine, you'll be forced to reevaluate your entire notion of Chinese cuisine. [$] *Average main: HK$250* ✉ *4th fl., Four Seasons Hotel, 8 Finance St., Central* ☎ *3196–8880* 🌐 *www.fourseasons.com* ✍ *Reservations essential* [M] *Central* ✣ *B2.*

$ CHINESE 🍴 **Mak's Noodles Limited.** Mak's may look like any other Hong Kong noodle shop, but this tiny store is one of the best known in town, with a reputation that belies its humble decor. The staff is attentive, and the menu includes a wide range of delicious dishes, such as various sauce-tossed noodles with pork. The real test of a good Cantonese noodle shop, however, is its wontons, and here they're fresh, delicate, and filled with whole shrimp. And don't miss the *sui kau*—a slightly larger and heavier dumpling that has diced mushrooms mixed in to the shrimp filling. $ *Average main: HK$40* ⊠ *77 Wellington St., Central* ☎ *2854–3810* 🖿 *No credit cards* Ⓜ *Central* ✛ *A3.*

$$$$
FRENCH
✕ **Restaurant Petrus.** Commanding breathtaking views atop the Island Shangri-La, Restaurant Petrus scales the upper Hong Kong heights of prestige, formality, and price. This is one of the city's few flagship hotel restaurants that have not attempted to reinvent themselves as fusion; sometimes traditional French haute cuisine is the way to go. Likewise, the design of the place is in the old-school restaurant-as-ballroom mode. The kitchen has a particularly good way with foie gras, and the wine list is memorable, listing more than 1,500 celebrated labels. The dress here is business casual—no jeans or sneakers. $ *Average main: HK$500* ⊠ *56th fl., Island Shangri-La, Pacific Place, Supreme Court Rd., Admiralty, Central* ☎ *2820–8590* ⊕ *www.shangri-la.com* Ⓜ *Admiralty* ✛ *C4.*

$$
CHINESE
✕ **Yung Kee.** Close to Hong Kong's famous nightlife and dining district of Lan Kwai Fong, Yung Kee has become a local institution since it first opened shop as a street-food stall in 1942. The food is authentic Cantonese, served amid riotous decor and writhing gold dragons. Locals come here for roast goose with beautifully crisp skin and tender meat, as well as dim sum. Other excellent dishes include the "cloudy tea" smoked pork, which needs to be reserved a day in advance, and deep-fried prawns with mini crab roe. More adventurous palates may wish to check out the thousand-year-old preserved eggs. $ *Average main: HK$200* ⊠ *32–40 Wellington St, Central* ☎ *2522–1624* ⊕ *www.yungkee.com.hk* Ⓜ *Central* ✛ *A3.*

## WAN CHAI, CAUSEWAY BAY, AND BEYOND

### WAN CHAI

$$$$
CHINESE
Fodor'sChoice
★
✕ **Bo Innovation.** The mastermind behind this renowned, Michelin-approved restaurant is Alvin Leung, who dubbed himself the "demon chef" and had the moniker tattooed on his arm. Bo Innovation serves what he calls "X-treme Chinese" cuisine, applying molecular gastronomy, French, and Japanese cooking techniques to traditional Cantonese dishes. The Australian Wagyu strip loin with black-truffle *cheung fun*, or rice roll, is a winner, as is the signature molecular *xiao long bao* (soup dumpling). At dinner you must choose between the eight-course tasting menu or the 12-course chef's menu; à la carte dining is not available. Tables are often full on Friday and Saturday, so book in advance. $ *Average main: HK$680* ⊠ *Shop 13, 2nd fl., J Residence, 60 Johnston Rd., Wan Chai* ☎ *2850–8371* ⊕ *www.boinnovation.com* ⚁ *Reservations essential* ⊗ *No lunch Sat. Closed Sun.* Ⓜ *Wan Chai* ✛ *A4.*

$$
CHINESE
✕ **Liu Yuan Pavilion.** Often regarded as one of the best Shanghainese restaurants in town, Liu Yuan's cooking style stays loyal to tradition with a no-fuss mentality that has worked in their favor for years. Easy favorites include sweet strips of crunchy eel, panfried meat buns, and steamed *xiao long bao* dumplings plumped up with minced pork and broth. Diners also wax lyrical about the house special crispy rice soup and

rice crackers smothered in salted egg yolk. Come hungry, since you'll need plenty of room to stomach all of these deliciously carby dishes. $ *Average main: HK$120* ✉ *3rd fl., The Broadway, 54–62 Lockhart Rd., Wan Chai* ☎ *2804–2000* ✛ *E4.*

### CAUSEWAY BAY

$$
INTERNATIONAL
✕ **Goldfinch Restaurant.** Travel back to the romantic 1960s as you dine at this retro restaurant. Film buffs might recognize this spot as the backdrop to renowned director Wong Kar-wai's most famous films (*In the Mood for Love, 2046*). Like the decor, the food here has remained largely unchanged since the restaurant's heyday, and you'll find local interpretations of Western dishes such as borscht or cream of mushroom soup and gravy-covered steaks served on sizzling iron plates. Don't come here if you're looking for an authentic steakhouse experience, though: this place is strictly for those who want to relive the nostalgic charm of Hong Kong's swinging era. $ *Average main: HK$120* ✉ *13–15 Lan Fong Rd., Causeway Bay* ☎ *2577–7981* ✛ *H4.*

$
CHINESE
Fodor'sChoice
★
✕ **Man Sing.** Hong Kong's top foodies swear by the steamed meat cake from this cheap and cheerful roadside eatery—the trademark dish consists of a towering mound of minced fatty pork that's been drizzled in soy sauce and topped with a golden orb of salted egg yolk. But the meat cake is not the only thing that makes this place a worthwhile visit; also try the spicy "saliva" chicken (a classic Sichuan poultry dish named after its complex, mouthwatering flavors), spice-tossed lamb rack, and silken steamed egg with fresh crab. Come early though because it gets extremely packed at peak mealtimes. $ *Average main: HK$60* ✉ *16 Wun Sha St., Tai Hang, Causeway Bay* ☎ *2576–7272* ▭ *No credit cards* ✆ *No lunch.* Ⓜ *Tin Hau* ✛ *H5.*

### EASTERN

$
CHINESE
Fodor'sChoice
★
✕ **Tung Po.** Arguably Hong Kong's most famous—if not most perpetually packed—indoor *dai pai dong*, Tung Po has communal tables large enough to fit 18 guests and the restaurant's walls are scribbled with their ever-growing list of specials. The food is Hong Kong cuisine with fusion innovations. Try the spaghetti with cuttlefish, which is flavored with aromatic jet-black fresh squid ink. The seafood dishes and stir-fries are all satisfying, but it's really the atmosphere that makes Tung Po a must-visit. Owner Robby Cheung is one of the most delightful characters in the Hong Kong dining biz. Later in the evening, he'll blast the latest pop songs from the sound system. And if you're lucky, you might just catch him in one of his moonwalking moods. $ *Average main: HK$70* ✉ *2nd fl., Java Road Cooked Food Centre, 99 Java Rd., North Point, Eastern* ☎ *2880–9399* ▭ *No credit cards* ✆ *No lunch.* Ⓜ *North Point* ✛ *H5.*

## SOUTHSIDE

$$$
SEAFOOD
✕ **Aberdeen Fish Market Canteen.** If you have a Cantonese-speaking friend, your lunch here will be easier to navigate, but trust us, it's worth the effort. First off, the canteen is housed within the Aberdeen Fish Market, which is a bit of a trek if you're not familiar with the area. Secondly, there's no set menu; you'll have to set a budget with the boss and he'll design your multicourse lunch based on the day's freshest catch. Expect anything from blanched shrimp served with soy sauce to abalone with chili and salt. It's a bit of a hassle and it's not exactly cheap for lunch

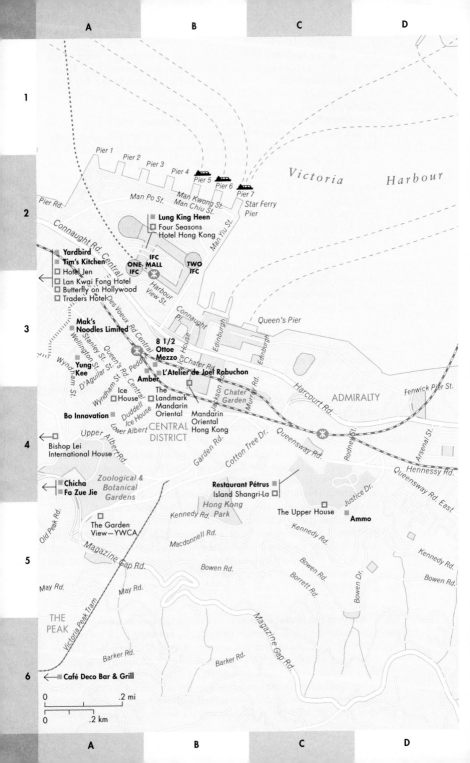

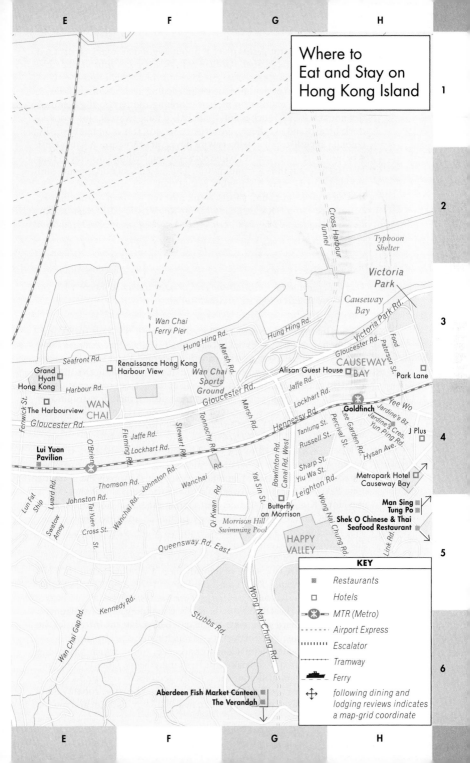

## Where to Eat and Stay on Hong Kong Island

**KEY**

- ■ Restaurants
- □ Hotels
- ⊗ MTR (Metro)
- - - - Airport Express
- ''''''' Escalator
- ++++++ Tramway
- 🚢 Ferry
- ✥ following dining and lodging reviews indicates a map-grid coordinate

but if you like seafood, this place is about as good as it gets. $ *Average main: HK$300* ⊠ *102 Shek Pai Wan Rd., Aberdeen, Southside* ☎ *2552–7555* ⌲ *Reservations essential* ▭ *No credit cards* ◷ *No dinner* ✛ *G6.*

**$$$$**
EUROPEAN

✕ **The Verandah.** You will not forget an evening at the Verandah. From the well-spaced, candlelit tables overlooking the bay to the menu of delicious classics (French onion soup, baked milk-fed veal, slow-cooked duck breast) and excellent, unobtrusive service, this is an unabashedly colonial experience that delivers with finesse at every turn. A live pianist sets the scene for romance, while slow-moving ceiling fans add to that hazy feeling that time is standing still. The food doesn't disappoint, and the wine list is more reasonably priced than you might expect. Note that sleeveless shirts and shorts aren't allowed for men during dinner. $ *Average main: HK$330* ⊠ *1st fl., The Repulse Bay, 109 Repulse Bay Rd., Southside* ☎ *2292–2822* ⊕ *www.therepulsebay.com* ◷ *Closed Mon and Tue.* ✛ *G6.*

## KOWLOON PENINSULA

*Use the coordinate (✛ B2) at the end of each listing to locate a site on the Where to Eat and Stay in Kowloon map.*

### TSIM SHA TSUI

**$$$**
CHINESE
Fodor'sChoice
★

✕ **Dong Lai Shun.** This Northern Chinese restaurant is known for its mutton hot pot, but it's the oxtail in black vinegar sauce that will really win you over. The generous pot arrives with tender meat and bits of cartilage immersed in a sweet and tangy sauce that's close to addictive. Be sure to finish the carrots and potatoes sitting at the bottom of the pot. Dong Lai Shun also offers a host of other great dishes, including traditional Peking duck and tea-leaf-smoked eggs boasting creamy, yolky centers. $ *Average main: HK$200* ⊠ *2nd fl., The Royal Garden, 69 Mody Rd., Tsim Sha Tsui* ☎ *2733–2020* ⊕ *www.rghk.com.hk* ✛ *B5.*

**$$$**
CHINESE

✕ **Hutong.** It's not hard to see why Hutong is one of the hottest tables in Hong Kong: it has some of the most imaginative food in town, yet it's completely Chinese. Meanwhile, its spot at the top of the dramatic One Peking Road Tower overlooks the entire festival of lights that is the Hong Kong island skyline. Best among the sensational selection of northern Chinese creations are crispy, deboned lamb ribs, whose crackling skin conceals a deep, tender gaminess. More subtle dishes include the abalone carpaccio in spring onion oil, and delicate scallops with fresh pomelo. Hutong is a good choice for a memorable meal in Hong Kong. Make sure to reserve well in advance. $ *Average main: HK$354* ⊠ *28th fl., 1 Peking Rd., Tsim Sha Tsui* ☎ *3428–8342* ⊕ *www.aqua.com.hk* ⌲ *Reservations essential* Ⓜ *Tsim Sha Tsui* ✛ *C2.*

**$$$$**
JAPANESE

✕ **Inakaya.** On the 101st floor of the ICC building, Inakaya flaunts a jaw-dropping, bird's-eye view of the city below, but the interior of the restaurant is equally extravagant—the highlight is the specialized *robatayaki* (the Japanese equivalent to barbecue) room, which has a long counter decorated with baskets of fresh ingredients. Choose your prey and the chefs will grill your meat/fish/vegetables to order and serve it the traditional way, on long wooden paddles. Because robatayaki is served in bite-sized morsels, prices can add up but it's a fun and unique

Street food in Hong Kong is cheap and delicious.

experience. If you don't want to splurge on grilled goods, Inakaya also offers other *washoku* (Japanese cuisines) such as sushi and traditional, multicourse *kaiseki* meals. [$] *Average main: HK$500* ✉ *Shop A, 101st fl., ICC, 1 Austin Rd West, Tsim Sha Tsui* ☎ *2972–2666* ⏲ *No lunch Fri and Sat.* ✥ *B1.*

$$ CHINESE 🍴 **Spring Deer.** The pastel blue and green interior and the waiters in bland uniforms make this Peking duck specialist look like something from 1950s Beijing. The crowd, too, is hilariously old-school, which only adds to the experience. You'll see locals with noodle dishes, stir-fried wok meat dishes, and so forth, but the Peking duck is the show-stopper—it might be the best in town. Even the peanuts for snacking, which are boiled to a delectable softness, go above and beyond the call of duty. This place is extremely popular, so it's best to book your table at least a week in advance. [$] *Average main: HK$160* ✉ *1st fl., 42 Mody Rd., Tsim Sha Tsui* ☎ *2366–4012, 2366–5839* ✍ *Reservations essential* [M] *Tsim Sha Tsui* ✥ *C4.*

## YAU MA TEI, MONG KOK, AND NORTHERN KOWLOON

$ CHINESE 🍴 **Islam Food.** This halal restaurant may not be the prettiest restaurant you've ever seen, and you should expect to wait a while for a table (lines get extremely crazy during peak meal hours), but we promise that the pan-fried beef patties (translated as "veal goulash" on the menu) here are well worth the pilgrimage. The browned pastry packets arrive at the table piping hot and bursting with tender, minced beef. Good luck trying to stop at just one, but other excellent dishes include the delicious lamb brisket curry, the pan-fried mutton dumplings, and the hot and sour soup. [$] *Average main: HK$35* ✉ *1 Lung Kong Rd., Kowloon City*

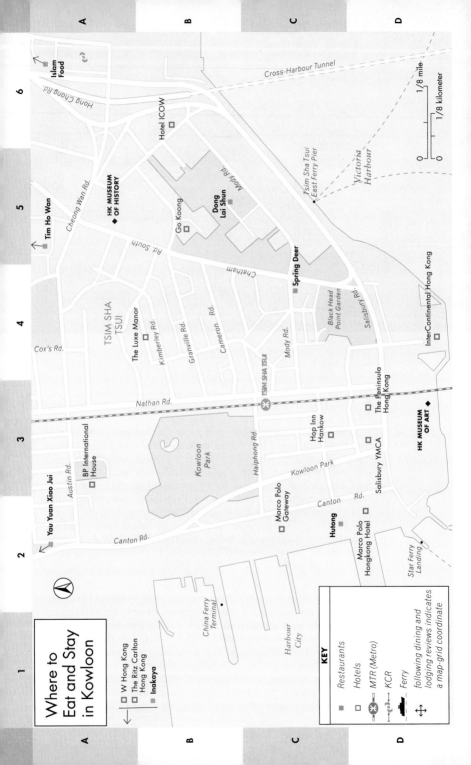

Where to Eat and Stay in Kowloon

W Hong Kong
The Ritz Carlton Hong Kong
Inakaya

Yau Yuan Xiao Jui

Islam Food

Tim Ho Wan

Hotel ICOW

HK MUSEUM OF HISTORY

Cheong Wan Rd.

Hong Chong Rd.

Cross-Harbour Tunnel

Go Koong

Dong Lai Shun

Mody Rd.

Rd. South

Chatham

Spring Deer

Tsim Sha Tsui East Ferry Pier

Victoria Harbour

Cox's Rd.

TSIM SHA TSUI

The Luxe Manor

Kimberley Rd.

Granville Rd.

Cameron Rd.

Mody Rd.

Black Head Point Garden

Salisbury Rd.

InterContinental Hong Kong

Austin Rd.

BP International House

Nathan Rd.

TSIM SHA TSUI

Kowloon Park

Haiphong Rd.

Hop Inn Hankow

The Peninsula Hong Kong

Kowloon Park

Salisbury YMCA

HK MUSEUM OF ART

Canton Rd.

Marco Polo Gateway

Canton Rd.

Hutong

Marco Polo Hongkong Hotel

Star Ferry Landing

China Ferry Terminal

Harbour City

1/8 mile

1/8 kilometer

KEY

Restaurants
Hotels
MTR (Metro)
KCR
Ferry

following dining and lodging reviews indicates a map-grid coordinate

☎ *2382–2822, 2382–8928* ▭ *No credit cards* ✉ *33–35 Tak Ku Ling Rd., Kowloon City* ☎ *2382–1882* 🌐 *www.islamfood.com.hk* ✥ *A6.*

$ CHINESE Fodor's Choice ★ 🍴 **Tim Ho Wan.** Don't let the undiscerning storefront fool you—Tim Ho Wan is an award-winning eatery that serves some of the city's best dim sum. Opened by a former Four Seasons Hotel chef, this humble Mong Kok eatery makes all of its shrimp dumplings, rice rolls, baked cha siu buns, and such, fresh to order. It's top-quality food at dirt-cheap prices. But be warned—the shop is small, and its popularity is immense, so go at off hours between 2:30 pm and 5 pm, or you might find yourself waiting up to half an hour for a seat. There are Tim Ho Wan branches in Sham Shui Po, North Point, and Central, but this Mong Kok flagship remains the most popular. [$] *Average main: HK$15* ✉ *2–8 Kwong Wah St., Mong Kok* ☎ *2332–2896* ▭ *No credit cards* [M] *Mong Kok* ✥ *A5.*

$ CHINESE Fodor's Choice ★ 🍴 **Yau Yuan Xiao Jui.** This tiny storefront may look like any other noodle joint, but its humble appearance belies its culinary prowess. The restaurant plates up authentic Shaanxi snacks, which can be best described as some of the heartiest and delicious chow that China has to offer. The handmade dumplings are amazing, especially if they're fattened up with lamb and umami scallion oil. Then there's the signature *biang biang mien*, which translate into (extremely) long and wide al dente noodle sheets designed to be anointed with chili oil, scallions, and marinated spare ribs. Definitely check this place out. [$] *Average main: HK$28* ✉ *Shop 3, ground fl., Keybond Commercial Building, 38 Ferry St., Jordan, Yau Ma Tei* ☎ *5300–2682* ▭ *No credit cards* ⏲ *Closed Tue.* ✥ *A2.*

6

## WHERE TO STAY

Whether you're a business traveler or a casual tourist, you'll inevitably be caught up with the manic pace of life in Hong Kong. Luckily, hotels are constantly increasing their efforts to provide their guests with a restful haven, often bundling spectacular views of the famous skyline and harbor with chic luxury, snazzy amenities, and soothing ambience.

From budget guesthouses to gleaming towers, you're sure to find a style and site to fit your needs. Prices tend to reflect quality of service and amenities as well as location, so it's worth the effort to examine neighborhoods closely when making your choice—you may end up paying the same to stay exactly where you want to be as you would to be off the beaten path.

The rock stars of Hong Kong's hotel industry are perfectly situated around Victoria Harbour, offering unobstructed harbor views, sumptuous spas, and reputable service to compete for the patronage of business-suited jet-setters, status-sensitive mainland tourists, and any visitor willing to splurge for uncompromised luxury. Farther up the hills on both Kowloon and Hong Kong Island, cozy hotels have blossomed over the past five years and seduce travelers who simply want a safe and practical place to crash in a trendy locale.

Travelers familiar with European cities might be surprised by the lack of provenance among Hong Kong hotels—the 80-plus-year-old Peninsula passes as the venerable old timer in this brashly new city where most hotels are perched in modern towers. And the scene keeps changing: Hong Kong's continued growth as a top tourist destination and business capital means that when it comes to choice of lodging, the next big thing is always around the corner. The Ritz-Carlton, Hong Kong, recently hit the heights when it began hosting guests on the 102nd through 118th floors of the ICC tower in Kowloon, suggesting that on the Hong Kong hotel scene the sky really is the limit.

> **WORD OF MOUTH**
>
> "Tim Ho Wan is awesome! We went there a few months ago and the wait is super long (get there early in the morning to get your number if you hope to wait less than two hours) but it's very delicious. Pork buns are their specialty." —katrinab

### RESERVATIONS AND RATES

Most hotels have reliable online booking systems but phone reservations are also accepted, and receptionists speak English.

Specify arrival and departure dates, number of guests, room type (standard, deluxe, suite), and any specific preferences. Make sure to find out what is, and what is not, included in the room rate, such as breakfast, in-room Wi-Fi, and local calls. A credit-card deposit is generally required to secure reservations.

*Prices in the reviews are the lowest cost of a standard double room in high season.*

Flights from the United States often arrive in the evening, so it's a good idea to inform the hotel when you plan to arrive. Some hotels will not otherwise hold a booking after 6 pm.

## HONG KONG ISLAND

*Reviews listed alphabetically within neighborhood. Use the coordinate (✛ B2) at the end of each listing to locate a site on the Where to Eat and Stay in Hong Kong map.*

### WESTERN

$ **Butterfly on Hollywood.** A charming location alone is reason enough
HOTEL to stay in one of these snug but stylishly contemporary rooms in a cozy neighborhood full of antique shops, galleries, cafés, and up-and-coming restaurants. **Pros:** excellent location for wandering; a 10-minute walk from the hub of Hong Kong nightlife; free Wi-Fi throughout. **Cons:** cramped lobby and few hotel facilities; no views. $ *Rooms from: HK$1040* ✉ *263 Hollywood Rd., Sheung Wan, Western* ☎ *2850–8899* ⊕ *www.butterflyhk.com* ✄ *142 rooms* ❍ *No meals* Ⓜ *Sheung Wan* ✛ *A3.*

$$ **Traders Hotel.** Most guest quarters, soothingly decorated in simple
HOTEL shades of beige and white, come with cushioned seats set into bay windows that are perfect for reading while taking in the city and harbor views—which you may have plenty of time to do, since the surrounding area is quiet at night. **Pros:** rooftop pool and a gym with a view; free shuttle bus to locations around Hong Kong; short walk to the galleries and antique shops around Hollywood Road. **Cons:** a long walk to the

## WHERE SHOULD I STAY?

| | NEIGHBORHOOD VIBE | PROS | CONS |
|---|---|---|---|
| Western | A sprawling neighborhood with hidden alleyways, antique shops, Chinese medicine markets and temples. | Western is akin to the residential extension of Central, with less traffic and similarly spectacular views. Most accessible on foot, and a leisurely tram ride during off-peak hours. | May require steep footwork if your destination is not near the main road, where the trams and MTR run. Even taxis have difficulty navigating many narrow, one-way streets. |
| Central | A dense international finance center full of banks, shopping malls, and footbridges above traffic. High up the escalators, Midlevels is an exclusive residential getaway. | Home to major luxury brands' flagship stores, as well as grand hotels, fine restaurants, and famous nightlife area Lan Kwai Fong. Midlevels offers quiet views from above the fray. | Congested streets by day, crowded bars by night. Midlevels escalators only run uphill after morning rush hour. |
| Wan Chai, Causeway Bay, and Beyond | Wan Chai hosts a strip of street-level bars in addition to the designer Star Street area. Causeway Bay is the haven of hip young locals who come to eat, shop, and hang out in upstairs cafes. | Wan Chai has stylish restaurants, the convention center, and some performing-arts venues. Causeway Bay, home to Victoria Park, is conveniently situated with hotels in all price ranges. | The Wan Chai bar strip can get seedy, while Causeway Bay is extremely crowded on weekends. Eastern is mostly for business or residents. |
| Southside | Lower building density means more space and fewer people, with a fishing-village atmosphere around Aberdeen. | Proximity to great beaches right on Hong Kong Island, as well as to Stanley Market and Cyberport. | Be prepared for a lot of car and bus rides along winding roads, often in slow traffic. |
| Lantau Island | Hong Kong's largest island hosts disparate attractions: an international airport, an outlet shopping mall, natural scenery, Hong Kong Disneyland, and AsiaWorld-Expo. | MTR end-of-the-line town Tung Chung is the point of access to the Ngong Ping scenic cable-car ride and Citygate outlet shopping. Some may prefer a more resortlike setting inside Disneyland. | Inconvenient for exploring the rest of Hong Kong, as even Tung Chung is a half-hour MTR ride out from Central. |
| Kowloon | The "wild" side of Hong Kong, culminating in the commercial centers of Mong Kok and Tsim Sha Tsui—if not the air-conditioned mall in West Kowloon. | Shopping paradise indeed, for both malls and markets. The TST promenade, including the touristy Avenue of Stars, offers postcard views of the Hong Kong skyline. | Kowloon is not everyone's idea of a holiday—outside residential areas the streets (even pedestrian) are generally noisy, crowded and congested. |

6

nearest subway station. $ *Rooms from: HK$1900 ✉ 508 Queen's Road W., Western ☎ 2974–1234 🌐 www.shangri-la.com/hongkong/traders ⇨ 283 rooms 🍴 No meals Ⓜ Western ✥ A3.*

## CENTRAL

$ HOTEL Fodor's Choice ★ **Bishop Lei International House.** If you've ever dreamed of living a life of privilege in the Mid-Levels without having to pay through the nose for it, this is your chance—all the better if you go for a slightly pricier harbor-view room. **Pros:** unique perch near escalators, saving you countless steps up and down to SoHo and Central; good value. **Cons:** escalator runs only upward after 10 am so lots of steps down in the morning. $ *Rooms from: HK$1400 ✉ 4 Robinson Rd., Mid-levels ☎ 852/2868–0828 🌐 www.bishopleihtl.com.hk ⇨ 227 rooms Ⓜ Central ✥ A4.*

$$$$ HOTEL Fodor's Choice ★ **Four Seasons Hotel Hong Kong.** Few comforts are neglected, with amenities ranging from sumptuous Chinese-accented furnishings to all sorts of high-tech gadgetry, but the main features are the knockout views of the harbor and Victoria Peak through walls of glass. **Pros:** elite service and attention to detail; outstanding 24-hour business center. **Cons:** breakfast not included in high rates; some views are better than others. $ *Rooms from: HK$4500 ✉ International Finance Centre, 8 Finance St., Central ☎ 3196–8888 🌐 www.fourseasons.com/hongkong ⇨ 399 rooms 🍴 No meals Ⓜ Central ✥ B2.*

$$ HOTEL **The Garden View – YWCA.** Rooms in this attractive, cylindrical, high-rise guesthouse overlook the peaceful Hong Kong Zoological and Botanical Gardens and are clean, well designed, and affordable. **Pros:** nice park views; value for money; kitchenettes in some suites; walking distance to Central. **Cons:** traffic can get bad during rush hours; limited amenities. $ *Rooms from: HK$1950 ✉ 1 MacDonnell Rd., Mid-levels ☎ 2877–3737 🌐 hotel.ywca.org.hk ⇨ 141 rooms 🍴 No meals Ⓜ Central ✥ A5.*

$$$$ HOTEL **Island Shangri-La.** A city icon towering above Pacific Place drips with old-world charm and offers spacious and luxurious accommodations with an Asian twist, along with fine dining and impeccable service. **Pros:** grand lobby; beautiful pool deck with a great close-up view of the skyline; elevator access to Pacific Place Mall. **Cons:** no real spa. $ *Rooms from: HK$4500 ✉ Pacific Place, Supreme Court Rd., Admiralty, Central ☎ 2877–3838 🌐 www.shangri-la.com/island ⇨ 565 rooms 🍴 No meals Ⓜ Admiralty ✥ C4.*

$$ HOTEL **Lan Kwai Fong Hotel.** The scent of lemongrass and cozy feel of an old Hong Kong apartment building extend to the small but beautiful rooms enlarged by bay windows and plunging views of the surrounding cityscape. **Pros:** hotel and neighborhood have lots of character. **Cons:** narrow roads surrounding the hotel are often congested. $ *Rooms from: HK$2200 ✉ 3 Kau U Fong, SoHo, Central ☎ 3650–0000 🌐 www.lankwaifonghotel.com.hk ⇨ 162 rooms 🍴 No meals Ⓜ Sheung Wan ✥ A3.*

$$$$ HOTEL Fodor's Choice ★ **The Landmark Mandarin Oriental.** Some of the city's most beautifully designed and spacious rooms are equipped with massive, circular spa-style bathtubs, the centerpieces of huge, view-filled bathrooms. **Pros:** you can't get more central in Central; beautiful rooms. **Cons:** relatively small lobby; no harbor views. $ *Rooms from: HK$4500 ✉ 15 Queen's*

*Rd., Central* ☎ *2132–0188* ⊕ *www.mandarinoriental.com/landmark* ➪ *113 rooms* ⊘ *No meals* Ⓜ *Central* ✛ *B4.*

**$$$$**
HOTEL
Fodor's Choice
★
☷ **Mandarin Oriental Hong Kong.** Hong Kong's most famous hotel has lost none of its opulence, colonial charm, and shine over the past 50 years and is still known for spacious and luxurious accommodation and impeccable service. **Pros:** spacious, open, and beautifully designed rooms; old-world ambience at its finest; exquisite spa. **Cons:** in-room Wi-Fi isn't free. Ⓢ *Rooms from: HK$4500* ⊠ *5 Connaught Rd., Central* ☎ *2522–0111* ⊕ *www.mandarinoriental.com/hongkong* ➪ *501 rooms* ⊘ *No meals* Ⓜ *Central* ✛ *B3.*

**$$$$**
HOTEL
Fodor's Choice
★
☷ **The Upper House.** Even standard rooms in this haven of stylish luxury are suites—tranquil havens of design and indulgence that feature huge windowside bathtubs, walk-in rain showers, personal iPod touch with everything on it, free mini-bars, and high-end wine fridges. **Pros:** high design and filled with work of contemporary Asian artists; feels worlds away from Central below; incredible personalized service. **Cons:** no spa or pool; can be difficult to get a taxi. Ⓢ *Rooms from: HK$4600* ⊠ *Pacific Place, 88 Queensway, Admiralty, Central* ☎ *2918–1838* ⊕ *www.upperhouse.com* ➪ *117 rooms* ⊘ *No meals* Ⓜ *Admiralty* ✛ *C5.*

## WAN CHAI, CAUSEWAY BAY, AND BEYOND

### WAN CHAI

**$$$$**
FAMILY
☷ **Grand Hyatt Hong Kong.** A direct connection to the Hong Kong Convention and Exhibition Centre makes this a business-first hotel, but leisure travelers also enjoy the elegant rooms, with sweeping harbor views and accented by curving wooden desks and black marble. **Pros:** excellent service; extensive sports facilities; Plateau spa is a beautiful sanctuary. **Cons:** quiet outside the hotel at night but complimentary taxi service available. Ⓢ *Rooms from: HK$5200* ⊠ *1 Harbour Rd., Wan Chai* ☎ *2588–1234* ⊕ *www.hongkong.grand.hyatt.com* ➪ *549 rooms* ⊘ *Breakfast* Ⓜ *Wan Chai* ✛ *E3.*

**$$$**
HOTEL
FAMILY
☷ **Renaissance Hong Kong Harbour View Hotel.** These modest guest rooms in the Hong Kong Convention and Exhibition Centre complex are simply outfitted with attractive modern decor, and many have harbor views. **Pros:** harborside recreational garden. **Cons:** a little walk away from the subway but near the Star Ferry. Ⓢ *Rooms from: HK$2800* ⊠ *1 Harbour Rd., Wan Chai* ☎ *2802–8888* ⊕ *www.renaissancehotels.com/hkghv* ➪ *857 rooms* ⊘ *No meals* Ⓜ *Wan Chai* ✛ *E3.*

### CAUSEWAY BAY

**$**
B&B/INN
Fodor's Choice
★
☷ **Alisan Guest House.** Some of these no-frills rooms nestled into an old apartment building in Causeway Bay have nice views of the yachts just across Gloucester Road, and all offer cleanliness, safety, and friendly hospitality at a budget price. **Pros:** friendly, English-speaking staff; pride in cleanliness; good location; free Wi-Fi. **Cons:** small rooms and windows; surcharge to pay with credit card (pay with cash or via PayPal instead). Ⓢ *Rooms from: HK$380* ⊠ *Flat A, 5/F, Hoi To Court, 275 Gloucester Rd., Causeway Bay* ☎ *2838–0762* ⊕ *www.alisanguesthouse.com* ➪ *30 rooms* ⊘ *No meals* Ⓜ *Causeway Bay* ✛ *H3.*

**$**
HOTEL
☷ **Butterfly on Morrison.** Standard rooms are small and housed on lower floors with no views, so consider upgrading to a larger room on the upper floors where the surrounding skyline and even Happy Valley

Racecourse form a dramatic backdrop. **Pros:** chic contemporary-style rooms with decent neighborhood views from some. **Cons:** few in-hotel facilities. $ *Rooms from: HK$1200* ✉ *39 Morrison Hill Rd., Causeway Bay* ☎ *3962–8333* ⊕ *www.butterflyhk.com* ⇆ *93 rooms* ⍥ *No meals* Ⓜ *Causeway Bay* ✛ *G5.*

**$$**
**HOTEL**
**Fodor's Choice**
**★**

🏨 **J Plus.** Designer Philippe Starck's incredible ability to blend seemingly unblendable themes makes every corner an exercise in eye candy, but it isn't all style over substance: each white-swathed room is like a mini suite, full of cozy corners that combine old Hong Kong, Alice in Wonderland, and everyday practicalities. **Pros:** great value for money; a design geek's dream; complimentary breakfast; kitchenettes; laundry facilities. **Cons:** no views. $ *Rooms from: HK$1700* ✉ *1–5 Irving St., Causeway Bay* ☎ *3196–9000* ⊕ *www.jplushongkong.com* ⇆ *56 rooms* ⍥ *Breakfast* Ⓜ *Causeway Bay* ✛ *H4.*

**$**
**HOTEL**

🏨 **Metropark Hotel Causeway Bay.** The views of the skyline and adjacent Victoria Park are beautiful, whether enjoyed from the simple but effectively designed modern rooms with all the basics or the pleasant rooftop pool. **Pros:** spectacular views for less; across from Victoria Park. **Cons:** limited hotel facilities; small lobby; few in-room amenities. $ *Rooms from: HK$1200* ✉ *148 Tung Lo Wan Rd., Causeway Bay* ☎ *2600–1000* ⊕ *www.metroparkhotel.com* ⇆ *266 rooms* ⍥ *No meals* Ⓜ *Tin Hau* ✛ *H4.*

**$$**
**HOTEL**

🏨 **Park Lane.** Guest rooms are as airy as the views at this elegant landmark overlooking Victoria Park, with glass-topped furnishings and glass walls that accent the open outlooks over greenery, the harbor, and the skyline. **Pros:** sprawling views; close to Causeway Bay shopping. **Cons:** often crowded; no pool; showing its age in places. $ *Rooms from: HK$1700* ✉ *310 Gloucester Rd., Causeway Bay* ☎ *2293–8888* ⊕ *www.parklane.com.hk* ⇆ *809 rooms* ⍥ *No meals* Ⓜ *Causeway Bay* ✛ *H3.*

## KOWLOON

### TSIM SHA TSUI

**$**
**HOTEL**

🏨 **BP International House.** These small and no-frills rooms in a modern tower on the north side of Kowloon Park come with a bonus: views over an extensive swath of greenery or the harbor; quarters vary in size considerably, so be sure to ask for a spacious room. **Pros:** coffee shop, restaurant, and lounge on premises; self-service coin laundry. **Cons:** can get crowded with business and tour groups; modest with few amenities. $ *Rooms from: HK$1200* ✉ *8 Austin Rd., Tsim Sha Tsui* ☎ *2376–1111* ⊕ *www.bpih.com.hk* ⇆ *529 rooms* ⍥ *No meals* Ⓜ *Tsim Sha Tsui* ✛ *A3.*

**$**
**HOTEL**

🏨 **Hop Inn Hankow.** Much like the affiliated Hop Inn Carnarvon, this appealing guest house is a budget traveler's dream, with loads of personality in the guest rooms designed by a local artists. **Pros:** friendly service and amazing personality for budget lodgings; private bathrooms. **Cons:** no common hangout areas; comically small elevator. $ *Rooms from: HK$400* ✉ *2/F, Hanyee Building, Flat A, Tsim Sha Tsui* ☎ *2881–7331* ⊕ *www.hopinn.hk* ⇆ *9 rooms* ⍥ *No meals* Ⓜ *Tsim Sha Tsui* ✛ *C3.*

JIA

The Upper House

$$
HOTEL
Fodor's Choice
★

**Hotel ICON.** Here's a stunning design statement, from the vertical garden hanging above the lobby café to the stylish, panoramic lounge on the top floor—in between are gorgeous, view-filled guest rooms outfitted with cozy woods and natural fabrics and all the high-tech amenities. **Pros:** a designer's dream; dedication to guest experience; tranquil feel with no tour groups allowed. **Cons:** surrounding area is thick with crowds at times. $ *Rooms from: HK$2000* ✉ *17 Science Museum Rd., Tsim Sha Tsui* ☎ *3400–1000* ⊕ *www.hotel-icon.com* ➲ *262 rooms* ⊗ *No meals* Ⓜ *Tsim Sha Tsui East* ✛ *B6.*

> ### WORD OF MOUTH
>
> "There are also hotels in Causeway Bay, the far eastern section of Wan Chai. I am not a huge fan of this area for a first-time tourist, as there are no major tourist sights in the area, so you will spend time getting to sights (and then back to your hotel to collect luggage, etc). If you are here *exclusively* for clothes shopping, then Causeway Bay is a good location." —Cicerone

$$$
HOTEL
Fodor's Choice
★

**InterContinental Hong Kong.** A location at the tip of the Kowloon peninsula ensures panoramic, front-row harbor views from most of the contemporary rooms, designed with Asian accents that include deep, sunken tubs in the marbled bathrooms. **Pros:** exceptional views; modern design; extravagant spa. **Cons:** the Avenue of Stars just outside is one of the most crowded tourist scenes in Hong Kong. $ *Rooms from: HK$3000* ✉ *18 Salisbury Rd., Tsim Sha Tsui* ☎ *2721–1211* ⊕ *www.hongkong-ic.intercontinental.com* ➲ *495 rooms* Ⓜ *Tsim Sha Tsui* ✛ *D4.*

$$$
HOTEL

**The Luxe Manor.** In the absence of views, rooms are a show in themselves, with audacious design themes (gold, frilly picture frames around flat-screen TVs) that don't sacrifice comfort and luxury. **Pros:** a trippy experience for the eyes; close proximity to more mellow nightlife and easy shopping. **Cons:** no views; lobby feels deserted at times. $ *Rooms from: HK$2800* ✉ *39 Kimberley Rd., Tsim Sha Tsui* ☎ *3763–8880* ⊕ *www.theluxemanor.com* ➲ *159 rooms* ⊗ *No meals* Ⓜ *Tsim Sha Tsui* ✛ *B4.*

$$$
HOTEL

**Marco Polo Hongkong Hotel.** Spacious rooms with sweeping views of Hong Kong Island are near the shopping hub along Canton Road and linked to Harbour City's immense shopping complex. **Pros:** westward views; convenient to Star Ferry and other transports. **Cons:** full in late March during the Hong Kong Rugby Sevens tournament; boisterous crowds during Oktoberfest. $ *Rooms from: HK$2600* ✉ *Harbour City, Canton Rd., Tsim Sha Tsui* ☎ *2113–0088* ⊕ *www.marcopolohotels.com* ➲ *665 rooms* ⊗ *Some meals* Ⓜ *Tsim Sha Tsui* ✛ *D2.*

$$$$
HOTEL
Fodor's Choice
★

**The Peninsula Hong Kong.** Even in a city with so many world-class hotels, the Peninsula manages to stand above the rest, an oasis of old-world glamour, with high-ceiling apartmentlike suites in the old wing and newer rooms in the upper wing, where Kowloon and harbor views make you feel like you own Hong Kong. **Pros:** state-of-the-art room facilities; impeccable service; tons of character; world-class dining, facilities, and entertainment. **Cons:** price; a bit rarified for some tastes. $ *Rooms from: HK$5600* ✉ *Salisbury Rd, Tsim Sha Tsui* ☎ *2920–*

*2888 🌐 www.peninsula.com 🛏 354 rooms 🍴 Some meals [M] Tsim Sha Tsui ✥ D3.*

$ HOTEL FAMILY 🏨 **Salisbury YMCA.** Little wonder this upscale YMCA is a popular budget choice: it sits next to the mighty Peninsula and across from the city's three biggest museums on Tsim Sha Tsui's harborfront, and most rooms have at least partial harbor views. **Pros:** prime views at modest prices; pool and fitness activities to occupy the whole family. **Cons:** busy lobby. [$] *Rooms from: HK$1100 ✉ 41 Salisbury Rd., Tsim Sha Tsui ☎ 2268–7000 🌐 www.ymcahk.org.hk 🛏 363 rooms 🍴 No meals [M] Tsim Sha Tsui ✥ D3.*

### NORTHERN KOWLOON

$$$$ HOTEL FAMILY Fodor's Choice ★ 🏨 **The Ritz-Carlton, Hong Kong.** From the world's highest hotel, perching on the 102nd through the 118th floors of the ICC skyscraper in West Kowloon, every large and luxurious guest room enjoys a stupendous vantage point. **Pros:** earth-shattering views; top-class service and amenities. **Cons:** extremely pricey; surrounding Kowloon area lacks nightlife. [$] *Rooms from: HK$6800 ✉ International Commerce Center, 1 Austin Rd. W, Northern Kowloon ☎ 2263–2263 🌐 www.ritzcarlton.com/en/Properties/HongKong 🛏 312 rooms 🍴 No meals [M] West Kowloon ✥ A1.*

$$$ HOTEL Fodor's Choice ★ 🏨 **W Hong Kong.** A hip, young vibe prevails, but guest rooms are veritable urban oases—soundproof and spacious, alternately colorful or sleek on even and odd floors, with mood lighting, surround audiovisual systems, big mirrors, and even bigger views of the harbor. **Pros:** friendly service; spacious and colorful rooms; panoramic views; exciting bars and restaurants. **Cons:** noisy atmosphere outside rooms; removed shopping-mall location. [$] *Rooms from: HK$2700 ✉ 1 Austin Rd. W, Kowloon Station, Northern Kowloon ☎ 3717–2222 🌐 www.whotels.com/hongkong 🛏 393 rooms 🍴 No meals [M] West Kowloon ✥ A1.*

6

## NIGHTLIFE

A riot of neon, heralding frenetic after-hours action, announces Hong Kong's nightlife districts. Clubs and bars fill to capacity, evening markets pack in shoppers looking for bargains, restaurants welcome diners, cinemas pop corn as fast as they can, and theaters and concert halls prepare for full houses.

The neighborhoods of Wan Chai, Lan Kwai Fong, and SoHo are packed with bars, pubs, and nightclubs that cater to everyone from the hippest trendsetters to bankers ready to spend their bonuses and more laid-back crowds out for a pint. Partying in Hong Kong is a way of life; it starts at the beginning of the week with a drink or two after work, progressing to serious barhopping and clubbing on the weekends. Wednesday is a big night out here, too. Work hard, play harder is the motto in Hong Kong, and people follow it seriously.

Fodor's Choice ★

Intercontinental

The Peninsula

The Luxe Manor

## HONG KONG ISLAND

### WESTERN

#### BARS

**Club 71.** This bohemian diamond-in-the-rough was named in tribute to July 1, 2003, when half a million Hong Kongers successfully rallied against looming threats to their freedom of speech. Tucked away on a terrace down a market side street, the quirky, unpretentious bar is a mainstay of artists, journalists, and left-wing politicians. The outdoor area closes around midnight. ⊠ *B/F, 67 Hollywood Rd., Sheung Wan, Western* ☎ *2858–7071* ⊘ *Closes 2 am* Ⓜ *Central.*

#### GAY AND LESBIAN SPOTS

**Volume Beat.** A friendly, mixed crowd of gays, lesbians, and their friends enjoys free entry and the club's open-door policy. New Arrivals Wednesdays are a staple of the scene, welcoming tourists and newbies and attracting locals with free vodka between 7 and 9 pm. Weekends are reliably hyper, with dance anthems filling the floor till the wee hours. Regular events include '70s and '80s retro nights and quiz nights. ⊠ *Ground fl., 62 Jervois St., Sheung Wan, Western* ☎ *2857–7683* ⊘ *Closes late* Ⓜ *Sheung Wan.*

### CENTRAL

On weekends the streets of Lan Kwai Fong are liberated from traffic, and the swilling hordes from both sides of the street merge into one heaving organism. Hong Kong is proud of this très chic area, a warren of streets stuffed with commensurately priced restaurants, bars, and late-night boutiques. Midway between Lan Kwai Fong's madness and SoHo's bohemian glamour is Wyndham Street, home to an array of sophisticated bars, nightclubs, and restaurants and strict domain of the over 25s.

#### BARS

**Le Jardin.** For an otherworldly, cosmopolitan vibe, check out this casual bar with a terrace overlooking the gregarious outdoor dining lane known locally as Rat Alley. Walk through the dining area and up a flight of steps. It's a little tricky to find, but the leafy, fairy-lit setting is worth it. ⊠ *1st fl., 10 Wing Wah Lane, Lan Kwai Fong, Central* ☎ *2877–1100* ⊘ *Closes 4 am* Ⓜ *Central.*

**Lux.** This two-story bistro and bar recently enjoyed a face-lift. Decorated in lush red and deep wooden tones, the busy street-level bar is separated from the restaurant by an internal staircase. Upstairs, the cuisine is modern European, with signature dishes including roasted lobster spaghetti, while downstairs the cocktail menu has 20 different kinds of martinis. The daily happy hour is popular with the after-work crowd and runs from 5 to 9 pm. ⊠ *Upper ground fl. and 1st fl., The Plaza, 21 D'Aguilar St., Lan Kwai Fong, Central* ☎ *2868–9538* ⊕ *www. luxhongkong.com* ⊘ *Closes 4 am.*

**MO Bar.** This plush bar in the Landmark Mandarin Oriental is where the banking set goes to relax. You'll pay top dollar for the signature drinks (up to HK$200), but the striking interior makes it worthwhile. A huge, red-light circle dominates an entire wall, the "O" being a

6

Chinese symbol of shared experience. ✉ *The Landmark Mandarin Oriental, 15 Queen's Rd. Central, Central* ☎ *2132–0077* ⊕ *www.mandarinoriental.com* ⊙ *Closes 2 am* Ⓜ *Central.*

**RED Bar.** Although its shopping mall location, outdoor terrace self-service policy, and incongruous affiliation with the next-door gym may not seem appealing, once you arrive, you'll throw all your preconceived notions into the harbor. On the roof of IFC Mall, RED has breathtaking views of the city, making it a great place to grab an early dinner and relax with a cocktail while watching the sunset. ✉ *Level 4, Two IFC, 8 Finance St., Central* ☎ *8129–8882* ⊕ *www.pure-red.com* ⊙ *Closes 2 am* Ⓜ *Hong Kong.*

Fodor's Choice ★ **Solas.** Positioned a floor below super-club dragon-i, this red-lit, always crowded bar is Wyndham Street's party central. Expect a mostly expat crowd of twenty- and thirtysomethings, who come straight from work on weekdays. To avoid the excited crush on Wednesday's ladies night and on weekends, head for the booths along the walls and leave before the DJ starts to spin at around 11 pm. ✉ *60 Wyndham St., SoHo, Central* ☎ *3162–3710* ⊕ *www.solas.com.hk* ⊙ *Closes late* Ⓜ *Central.*

**Staunton's Wine Bar & Cafe.** Adjacent to Hong Kong's famous outdoor escalator is this popular bistro-style café and bar. It's the perfect place to people-watch, whether from the balcony or the steps, where you can hang out on foam picnic mats. You can come for a drink at night or coffee during the day. It's also a Sunday-morning favorite for nursing hangovers over brunch. ✉ *10–12 Staunton St., SoHo, Central* ☎ *2973–6611* ⊕ *www.stauntonsgroup.com* ⊙ *Closes 3 am* Ⓜ *Central.*

### DISCOS AND NIGHTCLUBS

**Azure.** Head skyward to this cosmopolitan, bi-level club at the top of the 30-story Hotel LKF. The downstairs lounge is a sophisticated space with pool tables, couches, and a soundtrack of ambient tunes. Upstairs, take in a 270-degree panorama of the harbor from the smoker's terrace, or dance to funky-house music inside. ✉ *29th fl., Hotel LKF, 33 Wyndham St., Central* ☎ *3518–9330* ⊕ *www.azure.hk* ⊙ *Closes 3 am* Ⓜ *Central.*

Fodor's Choice ★ **dragon-i.** This hotspot has been around for a decade and lost none of its popularity, which is rare for a nightclub in Hong Kong. Have a drink on the deck by the doorway or step inside the rich, red playroom, which doubles as a Chinese restaurant at lunchtime and in the early evening. It's the domain of the city's young, rich, and beautiful (if not necessarily classy) and attracts a busy roster of international acts and DJs. The club's notorious Models' Night takes place on Wednesdays. ✉ *The Centrium, 60 Wyndham St., Central* ☎ *3110–1222* ⊕ *www.dragon-i.com.hk* ⊙ *Closes 3 am* Ⓜ *Central.*

## HONG KONG'S TOP FIVE NIGHTLIFE SPOTS

**dragon-i:** The door's clipboard-wielding glamazons will not make entry easy, but this remains the kingpin of the big Central clubs, and second home to the city's extravagant elite.

**Felix:** Aqua Spirit may be trendier, but Philippe Starck–designed Felix, at the Peninsula, is an institution. The best view of the skyline is marketing currency in Kowloon, and this penthouse bar really matches its claim.

**The Pawn:** Modern panache and history's charm combine to make this one of the most unique establishments in town. Order a bottle of

wine and settle onto one of the vintage couches in the ever-popular "living room."

**Socialito:** A recent addition to the Wyndham Street nexus and right next door to Solas (below), this casual taqueria—slash—hidden nightclub was one of 2012's favorite new openings. Never underestimate a skirt-steak taco as the perfect midnight pick-me-up.

Solas: Stronghold of Wyndham Street's after-dark action, Solas is great if you're looking for somewhere loud and lively to meet new people over well-mixed drinks.

**Drop.** This pint-size gem is where celebrities party—usually until sunrise—when they're in town. Hidden down an alley beside a late-night food stand, Droplet, its location only adds an air of exclusivity to the speakeasy feel. Excellent fresh-fruit martinis are its forte. Drop has two incarnations: after-dinner cocktail lounge before midnight, and impenetrable fortress later on, so arrive early to avoid disappointment. Happy hour is from 6 pm to 10 pm, Tuesday through Friday. ⊠ *Basement, On Lok Mansion, 39–43 Hollywood Rd., entrance off Cochrane St., Central* ☎ *2543–8856* ⏱ *Closes 6 am* Ⓜ *Central.*

**Midnight & Co.** This tiny space is the den of local DJ talent, and one of only a few clubs in Central that play underground electronic tunes. As such, it has garnered a band of fiercely loyal regulars, who have frequented the venue since its early, darker days as Yumla and can make the casual visitor feel out of place. Even with a cover charge of up to HK$200 on weekends, the place can get packed, but if you're there for the music it's worth it. ⊠ *Lower basement, Harilela House, 79 Wyndham St., Central* ☎ *2147–2012* ⊕ *www.midnight.hk* ⏱ *Closed Sun.–Mon.* Ⓜ *Central.*

### GAY AND LESBIAN SPOTS

**Propaganda.** Off a quaint but steep cobblestone street is a popular gay nightclub with an art-deco bar area that hosts quite the flirt-fest, while the sunken dance floor has poles on either side for go-go boys to flaunt their wares. It's pretty empty during the week, and the crowds arrive well after midnight on weekends. The entrance is in an alleyway, Ezra Lane, which runs parallel to Hollywood Road and is best accessed from Pottinger Street. Happy hour is Tuesday to Thursday, 10 pm to 1:30 am. ⊠ *Basement, 1 Hollywood Rd., Central* ☎ *2868–1316* ⏱ *Closes 5 am* Ⓜ *Central.*

Fodor'sChoice **Fringe Club.** The arts-minded mingle in this historic redbrick building
★ that also houses the members-only Foreign Correspondents' Club,
next door. The Fringe is the headquarters for Hong Kong's alternative
arts scene, and stages regular live music events at the recently opened
Cabaret Theater. The outdoor roof bar or Fotogalerie, with its potted
plants and fairy lights, is laid-back and serves reasonably priced drinks.
✉ *2 Lower Albert Rd., Central* ☎ *2521–7251* ⊕ *www.hkfringe.com.hk*
☾ *Closes 2 am.*

## WAN CHAI

Wan Chai is the pungent night flower of the nocturnal scene, where the
way of life served as inspiration for the novel *The World of Suzie Wong*.
It now shares the streets with hip wine bars, salsa nights, old men's
pubs, and after-parties that continue past sunrise. The seedy "hostess
bars" in this neighborhood are easy to spot and avoid, with curtained
entrances guarded by old ladies on stools and suggestive names in neon.
But some things never change: the busiest nights are still when there's
a navy ship in the harbor on an R&R stopover. Wednesday's ladies'
night, with half-price drinks, is also a big draw.

### BARS

**1/5 nuevo.** Popular tapas lounge and cocktail bar 1/5 nuevo occupies a
prime spot in Wan Chai's ever-growing Star Street neighborhood. High-
flyers, financiers, and expats populate this sleek hangout. ✉ *9 Star St.,
Wan Chai* ☎ *2529–2300* ☾ *Closes 2 am* Ⓜ *Wan Chai.*

**Carnegie's.** Named after the Scotsman and steel baron Andrew Carnegie,
whose family sailed to America in the late 1800s, this rock-and-roll bar
lives up to its name. Although Carnegie himself probably didn't imagine
bar-top dancing to classic rock tunes at an establishment bearing his
name, the Scottish owners feel that the spirit of his love of music lives
on regardless. ✉ *53–55 Lockhart Rd., Wan Chai* ☎ *2866–6289* ⊕ *www.
carnegies.net/hongkong* ☾ *Closes 2 am* Ⓜ *Wan Chai.*

**Mes Amis.** In the heart of Wan Chai, on the corner of Lockhart and
Luard roads, Mes Amis is a friendly, high-ceilinged bar that also serves
food. Its corner setting and open bifold doors mean that none of the
action outside is missed, and vice versa: the perpetual crowd inside is
on display to those on the street. Happy hour is all day until 9 pm, until
10 pm on weekends. ✉ *83–85 Lockhart Rd., Wan Chai* ☎ *2527–6680*
⊕ *www.mesamis.com.hk* ☾ *Closes 4 am* Ⓜ *Wan Chai.*

Fodor'sChoice **The Pawn.** In a district plagued by controversial redevelopment, this
★ attractive historic building, a former pawnshop, has been preserved
with minimal fuss. The stylish interior is outfitted with retro furniture,
while carefully selected items from its less salubrious days give the
space a decadent, vintage feel. The long balcony overlooking the iconic
Hong Kong tramway is a great place for spying on bustling everyday
life below. Upstairs is the restaurant, serving quality gastro-pub fare.
✉ *62 Johnston Rd., Wan Chai* ☎ *2866–3444* ⊕ *www.thepawn.com.hk*
☾ *Closes 2 am* Ⓜ *Wan Chai.*

Lan Kwai Fong is Hong Kong's famous bar and dining district.

### DISCOS AND NIGHTCLUBS

**Joe Bananas.** This disco and bar has a reputation for all-night partying and general good times. People dressed too casually are strictly excluded: no shorts, sneakers, or T-shirts (the only exception is the Rugby Sevens weekend, when even Joe can't turn away the thirsty swarm). Arrive before 11 pm to avoid the line. ✉ *23 Luard Rd., Wan Chai* ☎ *2529–1811* ⊕ *www.joebananas.com* ☯ *Closes 4 am* Ⓜ *Wan Chai.*

### KOWLOON

Central and Wan Chai are undoubtedly the king and queen of nightlife in Hong Kong. If you're staying in a hotel, however, or having dinner across the water in Kowloon, Ashley Road and Knutsford Terrace still make for a fun night out.

### BARS

Fodor's Choice ★ **Aqua Spirit.** Inside One Peking, an impressive curvaceous skyscraper, this very cool bar is on the mezzanine level of the top floor. The high ceilings and raking glass walls offer up unrivaled views of Hong Kong Island and the harbor filled with ferries and ships. ✉ *29th fl. and 30th fl., One Peking, 1 Peking Rd., Tsim Sha Tsui* ☎ *3427–2288* ⊕ *www.aqua.com.hk* ☯ *Closes 2 am* Ⓜ *Tsim Sha Tsui.*

**Bahama Mama's.** You'll find tropical rhythms at the Caribbean-inspired bar, where world music plays and the kitsch props include a surfboard over the bar and the silhouette of a curvaceous woman showering behind a screen over the restroom entrance. ✉ *4–5 Knutsford Terr., Tsim Sha Tsui* ☎ *2368–2121* ☯ *Closes 4 am* Ⓜ *Tsim Sha Tsui.*

**Delaney's.** Both branches of Hong Kong's pioneer Irish pub have interiors that were shipped here from the Emerald Isle, and the mood is as authentic as the furnishings. Guinness and Delaney's ale (a specialty microbrew) are on tap, there are corner snugs (small private rooms) and an Irish menu. The crowd includes some genuine Irish regulars; get ready for spontaneous outbursts of fiddling and other Celtic traditions. Happy hour runs from 5 to 9 pm daily in Kowloon, noon to 9 pm in Wanchai. ⊠ *Basement fl., 71–77 Peking Rd., Tsim Sha Tsui* ☎ *2301–3980* ⊕ *www.delaneys.com.hk* Ⓜ *Tsim Sha Tsui* ⊠ *Ground fl. and 1st fl., One Capital Place, 18 Luard Rd., Wan Chai* ☎ *2804–2880* ◯ *Closes 3 am* Ⓜ *Wan Chai.*

**ARTFUL DATES**

**Hong Kong Arts Festival (February and March).** Hong Kong Arts Festival (February and March): Past visitors have included Mikhail Baryshnikov, Pina Bausch, and José Carreras. The focus is on performing arts. ⊕ *www.hk.artsfestival.org.*

**Hong Kong International Film Festival (March and April).** Asian cinema accounts for many of the 280-plus new films shown at this festival, which includes citywide exhibitions and parties. ⊕ *www.hkiff.org.hk.*

Fodor'sChoice ★ **Felix.** High up in the Peninsula Hotel, this bar is immensely popular with visitors; it not only has a brilliant view of the island, but the interior was designed by the visionary Philippe Starck. Don't forget to check out the padded mini-disco room. Another memorable feature, the urinals in the men's restroom are situated right by glass windows overlooking the city. ⊠ *28th fl., Peninsula Hong Kong, Salisbury Rd., Tsim Sha Tsui* ☎ *2920–2888* ⊕ *www.peninsula.com* ◯ *Closes 2 am* Ⓜ *Tsim Sha Tsui.*

# SHOPPING

They say the only way to get to know a place is to do what the locals do. When in Rome, scoot around on a Vespa and drink espresso. When in Hong Kong, shop. For most people in this city, shopping is a leisure activity, whether that means picking out a four-figure party dress, rifling through bins at an outlet, upgrading a cell phone, or choosing the freshest fish for dinner.

Shopping is so sacred that sales periods are calendar events, and most stores close on just three days a year—Christmas Day and the first two days of Chinese New Year. Imagine that: 362 days of unbridled purchasing. Opening hours are equally conducive to whiling your life away browsing the racks: all shops are open until 7 or 8 pm; many don't close their doors until midnight.

It's true that the days when everything in Hong Kong was mindbogglingly cheap are over. It *is* still a tax-free port, so you can get some good deals. But it isn't just about the savings. Sharp contrasts and the sheer variety of experiences available make shopping here very different from back home.

You might find a bargain or two elbowing your way through a chaotic open-air market filled with haggling vendors selling designer knockoffs, the air reeking of the *chou tofu* ("stinky" tofu) bubbling at a nearby food stand. But then you could find a designer number going for half the usual price in a hushed marble-floor mall, the air scented by designer fragrances worn by fellow shoppers. What's more, in Hong Kong the two extremes are often within spitting distance of each other.

**WHY PAY RETAIL?**

As Central becomes Sheung Wan, a little lane called Wing Kut Street (between Queen's Road Central and Des Voeux Road) is home to costume-jewelry showrooms and wholesalers, many of whom accept retail customers and offer bargain-basement prices.

Needless to say, thanks to travelers like you running out of space in their suitcases, Hong Kong does a roaring trade in luggage. No need to feel guilty, though—shopping here is practically cultural research. All you're doing is seeing what local life is really like.

## WESTERN

6

### DEPARTMENT STORES

**Wing On.** Great values on household appliances, kitchenware, and crockery have made Wing On a favorite with locals on a budget since it opened in 1907. It also stocks clothes, cosmetics, and sportswear, but don't expect to find big brands (or even brands you know). Though prices have risen over time, you *can* count on rock-bottom clearance deals and an off-the-tourist-trail experience. ⊠ *211 Des Voeux Rd., Central, Sheung Wan, Western* ☎ *2852–1888* ⊕ *www.wingonet.com* Ⓜ *Sheung Wan* ⊠ *Cityplaza Units 074 and 144, 18 Taikoo Shing Rd., Tai Koo, Eastern* ☎ *2884–1529* ⊕ *www.wingonet.com* Ⓜ *Tai Koo Shing* ⊠ *Wing On Kowloon Centre, 345 Nathan Rd., Jordan, Kowloon* ☎ *2710–6288* ☎ *2374–0476* Ⓜ *Jordan.*

### MARKETS

**Western Market.** This redbrick Edwardian-style building in the Sheung Wan district is a declared monument and the oldest existing market building in Hong Kong; when built in 1906 it was used as a produce market. These days, its classical facades are filled with kitschy commerce, with a few unmemorable shops selling crafts, toys, jewelry, and collectibles on the ground floor. Skip these and head up the escalator, where you'll find a remarkable selection of fabric: satins, silks, sequins are all here and worth a look. A more surreal experience is lunch, dinner, or high tea in the Grand Stage Ballroom Restaurant on the top floor. After a great Chinese meal you can while away the afternoon with the old-timers trotting around the room to a live band belting out the cha-cha and tango. The restaurant is also a popular spot for weddings and receptions. Visit in the evening and you're likely to snap up cashmere and chiffon while a violin sings overhead. ⊠ *323 Des Voeux Rd., Central, Sheung Wan, Western* ☎ *6029–2675* ⊕ *www.westernmarket. com.hk* Ⓜ *Sheung Wan.*

### SPECIALTY SHOPS
#### CLOTHING

**15squarestreet.** If you stumble upon an urbane block party while wandering around Sheung Wan's evolving Square Street neighborhood, you're probably outside 15squarestreet. This low-key workshop and boutique features slick Scandinavian watches, shoes, and lots of leather bags from Swedish designers David Ericsson and Alexis Holm. ⊠ *15 Square St., Sheung Wan, Western* ☎ *2362–1086* ⊕ *www.squarestreet. se* Ⓜ *Sheung Wan, Exit A2.*

Fodor's Choice ★ **Moustache.** Brainchild of Alex Daye and Ellis Kreuger, Moustache is perched atop steep Aberdeen Street on the edge of SoHo. Find reasonably priced lightweight men's cotton shirts, Bermuda shorts, and unique finds from the owners' jaunts around Asia. The ready-to-wear garments are housed in a cozy and charismatic shop that's outfitted with an eclectic mix of maritime accents and vintage curiosities from '70s Hong Kong. You can also order locally made tailored suits and bespoke denim, but expect several weeks of production time. ⊠ *31 Aberdeen St., SoHo, Central* ☎ *2541–1955* ⊕ *www.moustachehongkong.com* Ⓜ *Sheung Wan.*

**Select 18 and Mido Eyeglasses.** Across from sprawling Oolaa restaurant are two of Hong Kong's best vintage hangouts in one convenient store. Select 18 has everything from typewriters to 1970s Hermès blouses. If you can tear yourself from the heaps of jewelry and handbags, a treasure trove awaits. Tucked in back, you'll find literally thousands of retro-styled specs from Mido Eyeglasses, priced from a couple of hundred to several thousand Hong Kong dollars. The big question: tortoise-shell cat eyes or classic wayfarers? If you need a second opinion, ask affable owner Thomas Lee to weigh in. ⊠ *18 Bridges St., NoHo, Western* ☎ *9127–3657* ⊕ *www.select-18.com.*

**Sin Sin Atelier.** Sin Sin's conceptual, minimalist clothes, jewelry, and accessories retain a Hong Kong character, while drawing from other influences—especially Indonesian. She also has a fine-art gallery across the street. ⊠ *Ground fl., 52 Sai St., off Hollywood Rd. at Cat St. end, Western* ☎ *2521–0308* ⬥ *Sheung Wan, Exit A2* ⊕ *www.sinsin.com.hk.*

## CENTRAL

### DEPARTMENT STORES

Fodor's Choice ★ **City'super.** Wherever you're from and whatever you're missing, whether it's fresh oysters from France or Japanese cosmetics, this gourmet supermarket and international variety store is the place to begin your search. Locals and tourists looking for gadgets, inexpensive jewelry and accessories, and quirky products like bottled water for pets often find them here, and this store will never bore you. The Times Square location often has international-theme food festivals. Be sure to check out the Japanese imported sweets like Royce Chocolate's unusual chocolate chips. ⊠ *IFC Mall, Shop 1041–1049, 8 Finance St., Central* ☎ *2234–7128* ⊕ *www.citysuper.com.hk* Ⓜ *Hong Kong, Exit A1* ⊠ *Basement One, Times Square, Causeway Bay* ☎ *2506–2888* ⊕ *www.citysuper.com.hk* Ⓜ *Causeway Bay, Exit A* ⊠ *Harbour City, 3rd fl., 3 Canton Rd., Tsim*

*Sha Tsui, Kowloon* ☎ *852–2375* ⊕ *www.citysuper.com.hk* Ⓜ *Tsim Sha Tsui, Exit A1.*

**Sincere.** Hong Kong's most eclectic department store stocks everything from frying pans to jelly beans. Run by the same family for more than a century, Sincere has several local claims to fame: it was the first store in Hong Kong to give paid days off

> ### LAW ON YOUR SIDE
>
> Although mainland law forbids that any item more than 120 years old leave China, the SAR isn't held to this rule. It's perfectly legal to ship your antique treasures home.

to employees, the first to hire women in sales positions—beginning with the founder's wife and sister-in-law—and the first to establish a fixed-price policy backed up by the regionally novel idea of issuing receipts. Although you probably won't have heard of its clothes or cosmetic brands, you might come across a bargain in one of its four locations strewn throughout Hong Kong. ✉ *173 Des Voeux Rd. Central, Central* ☎ *2544–2688, 2830–1016 Customer Service Hotline* ⊕ *www.sincere. com.hk/department/lang_en* Ⓜ *Sheung Wan.*

### MALLS AND CENTERS

Fodor's Choice ★ **IFC Mall.** A quick glance at the directory—Tiffany & Co., Kate Spade, Prada, Gieves & Hawkes—lets you know that the International Finance Centre isn't for the faint of pocket. Designer department store Lane Crawford has its flagship store here, and agnès b.'s whimsical multi-boutique fashion and lifestyle flagship sits under a large skylight styled after the shop owner's summer house in the south of France. Even the mall's cinema multiplex is special: the deluxe theaters have super-comfy seats with extra legroom and blankets for those chilled by the air conditioning. If you finish your spending spree at sunset, go for a cocktail at RED or Isola, two posh rooftop bars with fabulous harbor views. The Hong Kong Airport Express station (with in-town check-in service) is under the mall, and the Four Seasons Hotel connects to it. Avoid the mall between 12:30 and 2, when it's flooded with lunching office workers from the two IFC towers. ✉ *8 Finance St., Central* ☎ *2295–3308* ⊕ *www.ifc.com.hk* Ⓜ *Hong Kong, Exit F.*

### SPECIALTY SHOPS

#### ANTIQUES DEALERS

**Altfield Gallery.** If only your entire home could be outfitted by Altfield. Established in 1980, the elegant gallery carries exquisite antique Chinese furniture, Asia-related maps and topographical prints, Southeast Asian sculpture, and decorative arts from around Asia, including silver and rugs. Altfied Interiors, on nearby Queen's Road, features a selection of larger furniture pieces, framed art, and contemporary décor. ✉ *2nd fl., Prince's Bldg., 10 Chater Rd., Central* ☎ *2537–6370* ⊕ *www.altfield. com.hk* Ⓜ *Central.*

**Chine Gallery.** Dealing in antique furniture and rugs from China, this dark, stylish gallery accommodates international clients by coordinating its major exhibitions with the spring and fall auction schedules of Christie's and Sotheby's. ✉ *42A Hollywood Rd., Central* ☎ *2543–*

It's easy to spend money in Hong Kong.

0023 ✍ info@chinegallery.com ⊕ www.chinegallery.com ⊗ Closed Sun. Ⓜ Central.

**Teresa Coleman Fine Arts Ltd.** Specialist Teresa Coleman sells embroidered costumes from the Imperial Court, antique textiles, painted and carved fans, lacquered boxes, and engravings and prints in her centrally located gallery. She has a streetside shop at the same address for walk-ins, but this space is appointment only. ⊠ 4th fl., 55 Wyndham St., Central ☎ 2526–2450 ✍ tc@teresacoleman.com ⊕ www.teresacoleman.com Ⓜ Central.

**Yue Po Chai Antique Co.** One of Hollywood Road's oldest shops is at the Cat Street end, next to Man Mo Temple. Its vast and varied stock includes porcelain, stone carvings, and ceramics. ⊠ Ground fl., 132–136 Hollywood Rd., Central ☎ 2540–4374 Ⓜ Central.

### ART GALLERIES

**Alisan Fine Arts.** In a relatively quiet corner of Hong Kong Island is this established authority on contemporary Chinese artists. Styles range from traditional to modern abstract, and mediums include oil, acrylic, and Chinese ink. Founded in 1981 by Alice King, this was one of the first galleries in Hong Kong to promote the genre. ⊠ Room 2305, Hing Wai Centre, 7 Tin Wan Praya Rd., Aberdeen, Southside ☎ 2526–1091 ⊕ www.alisan.com.hk ⊗ Closed Sun.–Mon.

**Grotto Fine Art.** Director and chief curator Henry Au-yeung writes about, curates, and gives lectures on 20th-century Chinese art. His tucked-away gallery focuses exclusively on local Chinese artists, with an interest in the newest and most avant-garde works. Look for paintings, sculptures, prints, photography, mixed-media pieces, and conceptual installations. ⊠ *2nd fl., 31C–D Wyndham St., Central* ☎ *2121–2270* ⊕ *www.grottofineart.com* Ⓜ *Central.*

**Hanart TZ Gallery.** This is a rare opportunity to compare and contrast cutting-edge and experimental art from mainland China and Hong Kong selected by one of the field's most respected authorities. Unassuming curatorial director Johnson Chang Tsong-zung also cofounded the Asia Art Archive, and has curated exhibitions at the São Paolo and Venice biennials. ⊠ *4th fl., Pedder Building, 12 Pedder St., Central* ☎ *2526–9019* ⊕ *www.hanart.com* Ⓜ *Central.*

**Schoeni on Old Bailey Street.** Known for vigorously promoting Chinese art on a global scale, this gallery, founded by Manfred Schoeni in 1992, has represented and supported various artists from mainland China with styles ranging from neorealism to conceptualism. Manfred's daughter Nicole now pinpoints exciting new artists for her prominent clientele. You're likely to pass the Hollywood Road branch first, but the Old Baily Street gallery, up the hill, is the bigger and better of the two. ⊠ *21–31 Old Bailey St., Central* ☎ *2869–8802* ⊕ *www.schoeniartgallery.com* ⊙ *Closed Sun.* Ⓜ *Central.*

### BEAUTY

**Sa Sa Cosmetics.** The fuchsia-pink signs that announce Hong Kong's best and largest cosmetic discounter will become familiar sights on any shopping expedition. Look for deals on everything from cheap glittery makeup to sleek designer lines. Fragrances are a particularly good buy; prices are usually even lower than those at airport duty-free shops. ⊠ *Shop G01, Hang Lung Centre, 2–20 Paterson St., Causeway Bay* ☎ *2577–2286, 2505–5023 customer service and branch info* ⊕ *www. sasa.com* Ⓜ *Causeway Bay* ⊠ *1st fl., Chung King Express, 36–44 Nathan Rd., Tsim Sha Tsui, Kowloon* Ⓜ *Tsim Sha Tsui.*

### CLOTHING

**Barney Cheng.** One of Hong Kong's best-known, local designers, Barney Cheng creates haute-couture designs and prêt-à-porter collections with wit and elegance. When the Kennedy Center in Washington, D.C., hosted an exhibition titled "The New China Chic," Cheng was invited to display his works alongside those by the likes of Vera Wang and Anna Sui. His more recent pieces have drifted toward simplicity, with sophisticated cuts and exotic prints, such as alligator jackets and skirts. Cheng has made many a bride's dream gown, and his masterfully tailored suits of award-winning Milano wool cost from HK$100,000 to HK$400,000. Consultations are available on weekdays by appointment, but Cheng will open his doors on weekends for special occasions and VIPs. ⊠ *12th fl., World Wide Commercial Bldg., 34 Wyndham St., Central* ☎ *2530–2829* ⊕ *www.barneycheng.com* ⊙ *Closed weekends* Ⓜ *Central.*

**Lu Lu Cheung.** A fixture on the Hong Kong fashion scene for more than a decade, Lu Lu Cheung creates designs that ooze comfort and warmth. In both daytime and evening wear, natural fabrics and forms are represented in practical yet imaginative ways. ⊠ *Ground fl., 50 Wellington St., Central* ☎ *2537–7515* ⊕ *www.lulucheung.com.hk* Ⓜ *Central.*

**Ranee K.** Designer Ranee Kok Chui-Wah's showrooms feature one-off dresses and eclectic women's wear that bring new meanings to "East meets West." Known for her quirky cheongsams and dresses, she also collaborates with brands such as Furla. Special clients and local celebrities enjoy her custom tailoring, too. ⊠ *Ground fl., 25 Aberdeen St., Central* ☎ *2108–4068* ⊕ *www.raneek.com* Ⓜ *Central.*

Fodor's Choice ★  **Shanghai Tang.** Make your way past the perfumes, scarves, and silk-embroidered Chinese souvenirs to the second floor, where you'll find live Canaries tweeting from golden cages and a rainbow of fabrics at your fingertips. In addition to the brilliantly hued—and expensive—silk and cashmere clothing, you'll find custom-made suits starting at around HK$30,000, including fabric. You can also have a cheongsam (a sexy slit-skirt silk dress with a Mandarin collar) made for around HK$10,000, including fabric. Ready-to-wear Mandarin suits are in the HK$15,000–HK$20,000 range. You can find outlets scattered across Hong Kong, including the airport's Terminal One. ⊠ *1 Duddell St., Central* ☎ *2525–7333* ⊕ *www.shanghaitang.com* Ⓜ *Central.*

### JEWELRY

**Chocolate Rain.** The collections—dreamed up by a Hong Kong fine arts graduate—consist of pieces handcrafted of recycled materials, such as fabrics, bottle lids, paint buckets, and other funky finds. Head here for unique iPhone cases, one-of-a-kind bags, illustrations, and jewelry, as well as an ever-changing array of works by the designer's friends. ⊠ *Ground fl., 67a Peel St., SoHo, Central* ☎ *2975–8318* ⊕ *www. chocolaterain.com* Ⓜ *Central.*

**Edward Chiu.** Everything about Edward Chiu is *fabulous,* from the flamboyant way he dresses to his high-end jade jewelry. The minimalist, geometric pieces use the entire jade spectrum, from deep greens to surprising lavenders. Inspired in part by Art Deco, Chiu is also famous for contrasting black-and-white jade, setting it in precious metals, and adding diamond or pearl touches. ⊠ *Shop 2023, IFC Mall, 8 Finance St., Central* ☎ *2525–2618* ⊕ *www.edwardchiu.com* Ⓜ *Central.*

**Eldorado Watch Co Ltd.** At this deep emporium of watch brands, seek the advice of one of the older staffers who look like they've been there since the British landed. Brands include Rolex, Patek Philippe, Girard-Perregaux, etc. ⊠ *Ground fl., Peter Bldg., 60 Queen's Rd. Central, Central* ☎ *2522–7155* Ⓜ *Central, Exit D2.*

**Qeelin.** With ancient Chinese culture for inspiration and *In the Mood for Love* actress Maggie Cheung as the muse, something extraordinary was bound to come from Qeelin. Its name was cleverly derived from the Chinese characters for male ("qi") and female ("lin"), and symbolizes harmony, balance, and peace. The restrained beauty and meaningful creations of designer Dennis Chan are exemplified in two main collections: Wulu, a minimalist form representing the mythical gourd as well as the lucky number eight; and Tien Di, literally "Heaven and Earth," symbolizing everlasting love. Classic gold, platinum, and diamonds mix with colored jades, black diamonds, and unusual materials for a truly unique effect. A sweeter addendum to the collection was added recently in the form of Bo Bo, the panda bear. ⊠ *IFC Mall, 8 Finance St.,*

*Central* ☎ *2389–8863* ⊕ *hk.qeelin.com* Ⓜ *Central* ✉ *Peninsula Shopping Arcade, Salisbury Rd., Tsim Sha Tsui, Kowloon* Ⓜ *Tsim Sha Tsui.*

**Ronald Abram.** Looking at the rocks in these windows can feel like a visit to a natural history museum. Large white- and rare-color diamonds sourced from all over the world are a specialty here, but the shop also deals in emeralds, sapphires, and rubies. With years of expertise, Abrams dispenses advice on both the aesthetic merits and the investment potential of each stone or piece of jewelry. ✉ *Mezzanine, Mandarin Oriental, 5 Connaught Rd., Central* ☎ *2810–7677* ⊕ *www. ronaldabram.com* Ⓜ *Central.*

**Super Star Jewelry.** Discreetly tucked in a corner of Central, Super Star looks like any other small Hong Kong jewelry shop—with walls lined by display cases filled with the usual classic designs (old-fashioned to some) in predominantly gold and precious stones. What makes them stand out are the good prices and personalized service. The cultured pearls and mixed strands of colored freshwater pearls are not all shown, so ask Lily or one of her colleagues to bring them out. ✉ *The Galleria, 9 Queen's Rd. Central, Central* ☎ *2521–0507* Ⓜ *Central.*

**Tayma Fine Jewellery.** Unusual colored "connoisseur" gemstones are set by hand in custom designs by Hong Kong–based jeweler Tayma Page Allies. The collection is designed to bring out the personality of the individual wearer, and includes oversize cocktail rings, distinctive bracelets, pretty earrings, and more. ✉ *Prince's Bldg., 10 Chater Rd., Central* ☎ *2525–5280* ⊕ *www.taymajewellery.com* Ⓜ *Central.*

### TAILOR-MADE CLOTHING

**Blanc de Chine.** Blanc de Chine has catered to high society and celebrities, such as actor Jackie Chan, for years. That's easy when you're housed in the Prince's Building and you rely on word of mouth. The small, refined tailoring shop neatly displays exquisite fabrics from Switzerland and Italy, lovely ready-made women's wear, menswear, and home accessories. With newer stores in New York and Beijing, it appears the word is getting out. Items here are extravagances, but they're worth every penny. ✉ *Shop 123, Prince's Bldg., 10 Chater Rd., Central* ☎ *2104–7934* ⊕ *www.blancdechine.com* Ⓜ *Central, Exit K.*

**Linva Tailors.** It's one of the best of the old-fashioned cheongsam tailors, in operation since the 1960s. Master tailor Mr. Leung takes clients through the entire process and reveals a surprising number of variations in style. Prices are affordable, but vary according to fabric, which ranges from basics to special brocades and beautifully embroidered silks. ✉ *38 Cochrane St., Central* ☎ *2544–2456* Ⓜ *Central.*

MEN'S TAILORS **A-Man Hing Cheong Co., Ltd.** People often gasp at the very mention of A-Man Hing Cheong, in the Mandarin Oriental Hotel. For some it symbolizes the ultimate in fine tailoring, with a reputation that extends back to its founding in 1898. For others it's the lofty prices that elicit a reaction. Regardless, this is a trustworthy source of European-cut suits, custom shirts, and excellent service. ✉ *Mezzanine, Mandarin Oriental, 5 Connaught Rd., Central* ☎ *2522–3336* Ⓜ *Central.*

**Ascot Chang.** This self-titled "gentleman's shirtmaker" makes it easy to find the perfect shirt, even if you could get a better deal in a less prominent shop. Ascot Chang has upheld exacting Shanghainese tailoring traditions in Hong Kong since 1955, and now has stores in New York, Beverly Hills, Manila, and Shanghai. The focus here is on the fit and details, from 22 stitches per inch to collar linings crafted to maintain their shape. Among the countless fabrics, Swiss 200s two-ply Egyptian cotton by Alumo is one of the most coveted and expensive. Like many shirtmakers, Ascot Chang does pajamas, robes, boxer shorts, and women's blouses, too. It also has developed ready-made lines of shirts, T-shirts, neckties, and other accessories available for online ordering. ✉ *Shop 131, Prince's Bldg., 10 Chater Rd., Central* ☎ *2523–3663* ⊕ *www.ascotchang.com* Ⓜ *Central* ✉ *IFC Mall, 2nd fl., 1 Harbour View St., Central* ☎ *2295–3833* ⊕ *www.ascotchang. com* Ⓜ *Central* ✉ *The Peninsula Hong Kong, Salisbury Rd., Tsim Sha Tsui, Kowloon* ☎ *2366–2398* ⊕ *www.ascotchang.com* Ⓜ *Tsim Sha Tsui* ✉ *Kowloon Station, 2nd fl., 1 Austin Rd. West, Tsim Sha Tsui, Kowloon* ☎ *2196–8438* ⊕ *www.ascotchang.com* Ⓜ *Tsim Sha Tsui.*

**Jantzen Tailor.** Catering to expatriate bankers since 1972, this reputable yet reasonable tailor specializes in classic shirts; it also makes suits and women's garments. The comprehensive website displays its commitment to quality, such as hand-sewn button shanks, customizable interlinings, and Coats brand thread. ✉ *5th fl., 25 Des Voeux Rd., Central* ☎ *2570–5901* ⊕ *www.jantzentailor.com* Ⓜ *Central.*

**Yuen's Tailor.** Need a kilt? This is where the Hong Kong Highlanders Reel Club comes for custom-made kilts. The Yuen repertoire, however, extends to well-made suits and shirts. The tiny shop is on an unimpressive gray walkway and is filled from floor to ceiling with sumptuous European fabrics. It's a good place to have clothes copied; prices are competitive. ✉ *2nd fl., Escalator Link Alley, 80 Des Voeux Rd., Central* ☎ *2815–5388* Ⓜ *Central.*

# ADMIRALTY

## DEPARTMENT STORES

Fodor'sChoice **Chinese Arts & Crafts.** Head to this long-established mainland company ★ to blitz through that tiresome list of presents in one fell swoop. It stocks a huge variety of well-priced brocades, silk clothing, and cheap porcelain. In direct contrast to the thrill of digging through dusty piles at the open-air Jade Market, it provides a clean, air-conditioned environment in which to shop for classic jade jewelry—the prices aren't too outrageous. Incongruously scattered throughout the shops are specialty items like large globes with lapis oceans and landmasses inlaid with semiprecious stones for a mere HK$70,000. Other more accessible—and more packable—gifts include appliqué tablecloths and cushion covers or silk dressing gowns. ✉ *Pacific Place, 88 Queensway, Admiralty, Central* ☎ *2827–6667* ⊕ *www.cacgift.com* Ⓜ *Admiralty, Exit F* ✉ *Ground fl., Hip Shing Hong Centre, 55 Des Voeux Rd. Central, Central* ⊕ *www. cacgift.com* Ⓜ *Central* ✉ *28 Harbour Rd., Wan Chai* ⊕ *www.cacgift. com* Ⓜ *Wan Chai, Exit A5* ✉ *Star House, 3 Salisbury Rd., Tsim Sha Tsui, Kowloon* ⊕ *www.cacgift.com* Ⓜ *Tsim Sha Tsui, Exit F.*

**LAB Concept.** Pacific Place may have put Admiralty on the map, but LAB Concept has breathed new life into the otherwise uneventful neighborhood. This 64,000-square-foot "fashion playground"—from the same masterminds behind Joyce and Lane Crawford—comprises a network of shops in the formerly forgettable Queensway Plaza and is fast becoming a major shopping destination. The white, contemporary space introduces some playful touches you won't find elsewhere, such as concierge facial stations and vending machines selling American Apparel tanks. Expect young and edgy brands, including Theory, JBrand, Scotch & Soda, Michael by Michael Kors, and Alexander Wang. Beloved beauty brands populate the FACES department, but the highlight is the mix of must-have boots, heels (even for bigfoot Americans), and accessories at Shoespace. ⊠ *Queensway Plaza, 93 Queensway, Admiralty* ☎ *2118–6008* ⊕ *www.labconcepthk.com* Ⓜ *Admiralty, Exit C2.*

## SPECIALTY SHOPS
### CLOTHING

**Harvey Nichols.** When this legendary British retailer announced its Hong Kong opening, locals were skeptical, saying nothing would ever live up to the original London store. But Harvey Nicks quickly had them eating their (Philip Treacy) hats with the sheer volume of hyper-cool labels the store stocks. The menswear section has been a particularly big hit with local celebs, while local *tai-tais* (ladies who lunch) have declared the fourth-floor restaurant *the* place for mid-shopping-spree coffee breaks. In 2011, the department store opened a second sprawling spot, located in Admiralty's Pacific Place mall. Head to this flagship store for quiet surrounds and 83,000 sq. ft. of top-shelf brands. ⊠ *The Landmark, 15 Queen's Rd., Central* ☎ *3695–3388* ⊕ *www.harveynichols.com* Ⓜ *Central* ⊠ *Pacific Place, 88 Queensway, Admiralty* ☎ *3968–2668.*

**Vivienne Tam.** You know it when you walk into a Vivienne Tam boutique—the strong Chinese-motif prints and modern updates of traditional women's clothing are truly distinct. Don't let the bold, ready-to-wear collections distract you from the very pretty accessories, which include leather bags with Asian embellishments. Tam is one of the best-known Hong Kong designers and, even though she's now based outside the SAR, the city still claims her as its own. ⊠ *Pacific Place, 88 Queensway, Admiralty, Central* ☎ *2918–0238* ⊕ *www.viviennetam. com* Ⓜ *Admiralty* ⊠ *Ocean Centre, Harbour City, 2–27 Canton Rd., Tsim Sha Tsui, Kowloon* Ⓜ *Tsim Sha Tsui* ⊠ *Festival Walk, 80 Tat Chee Ave., Kowloon Tong, Kowloon* Ⓜ *Kowloon Tong.*

## WAN CHAI, CAUSEWAY BAY, AND BEYOND

### SPECIALTY SHOPS
### CLOTHING

**45R.** Around since 1978, Japanese brand 45R has garnered a reputation for ultracomfortable, exquisitely crafted jeans. Following the successes of outposts in Paris and New York, a flagship store opened on Star Street in 2009. Amid the minimalist surrounds, find heaps of its famous hand-dyed denim as well as breezy button-downs, wooly sweaters, and understated frocks. ⊠ *7 Star St., Wan Chai* ☎ *2861–1145* ⊕ *www.45rpm.jp* Ⓜ *Wan Chai, Exit B2.*

**Giordano.** Hong Kong's version of the Gap is the most established and ubiquitous local source of basic T-shirts, jeans, and casual wear. Like its U.S. counterpart, the brand now has a bit more fashion sense and slick ad campaigns, but still offers reasonable prices. A few of its hundreds of stores are listed here, but you'll have no problem finding one on almost every major street. A new line, **Giordano Concepts,** offers more stylish (and pricier) urban wear in neutral colors like black, gray, and white. Customer service is generally good, even if the young, energetic staff screeches "hello" then "bye-bye" at every customer in a particularly jarring way. ⊠ *Ground fl., Island Beverly, 1 Great George St., Causeway Bay* ☎ *2923–7445* ⊕ *www.giordano.com.hk* Ⓜ *Causeway Bay* ⊠ *Ground fl., Manson House, 74–78 Nathan Rd., Tsim Sha Tsui, Kowloon* ☎ *2926–1028* ⊕ *www.giordano.com.hk* Ⓜ *Tsim Sha Tsui.*

**Giordano Ladies.** If Giordano is the Gap, Giordano Ladies is the Banana Republic, albeit with a more Zen approach. Find clean-line modern classics in neutral black, gray, white, and beige; each collection is brightened by a single highlight color, red one season, blue the next, and so on. Everything is elegant enough for the office and comfortable enough for the plane. ⊠ *Shop 32A, JP Plaza, 22 and 32 Paterson St., Causeway Bay* ☎ *2922–1018* ⊕ *www.giordanoladies.com* Ⓜ *Causeway Bay* ⊠ *1st fl., Manson House, 74–78 Nathan Rd., Tsim Sha Tsui, Kowloon* ☎ *2926–1331* ⊕ *www.giordano.com.hk* Ⓜ *Tsim Sha Tsui.*

**Kapok.** Hip messenger bags, soft fabrics, funky watches, comfy kicks, music, stationery—Kapok has it all. This bright local favorite is a one-stop shop for classic cotton and knits. Meanwhile, its café and gallery space on Sun Street serves up steamy French coffee, chocolate croissants, and freshly baked cupcakes. ⊠ *5 St. Francis Yard, Wan Chai* ☎ *2549–9254* ⊕ *www.ka-pok.com* Ⓜ *Wan Chai, Exit B2.*

**Olivia Couture.** The surroundings are functional, but the gowns, wedding dresses, and *cheongsams* by local designer Olivia Yip are lavish. With a growing clientele, including socialites looking to stand out, Yip is quietly making a name for herself and her Parisian-influenced pieces. ⊠ *Ground fl., Bartlock Centre, 3 Yiu Wah St., Causeway Bay* ☎ *2838–6636* ⊕ *www.oliviacouture.com* Ⓜ *Causeway Bay.*

**Russell Street.** Gatekeeper of the up-and-coming, Russell Street aims to introduce fresh labels to Hong Kong's style savants. Taking cues from New York and London's top fashion students, as well as established international labels—think Victoria Beckham and House of Holland—the boutique showcases eclectic designs ranging from fancy furs to colorful graphic-print dresses. Among the mix of envy-inducing pieces, look for Sophie Hulme's gorgeous leather bags and lively animal print cardigans from Sibling and Sister. ⊠ *6 St. Francis Yard, Wan Chai* ☎ *2886–0800* ⊕ *www.russell-street.com* Ⓜ *Wan Chai, Exit B2.*

**Spy Henry Lau.** Local bad boy Henry Lau brings an edgy attitude to his fashion for men and women. Bold and often dark, with a touch of bling, his clothing and accessories lines are not for the fainthearted. ⊠ *1st* *fl., Cleveland Mansion, 5 Cleveland St., Causeway Bay* ☎ *2317–6928* ⊕ *www.spyhenrylau.com* Ⓜ *Causeway Bay, Exit E.*

**Vie.** Modern and minimalist, Vie's decor is in perfect harmony with its Nordic apparel. The combination boutique and gallery on St. Francis Yard is a spinoff of Vein, and offers up a mix of Scandinavian luxury labels and home accessories. The lineup changes every four to six weeks, but you can usually find at least a dozen stalwart, simple-yet-elegant brands, including Filippa K, Aarikka, and Won Hundred. Expect straight lines, a gray-scale palette, and unexpected pops of color. ✉ *Shop 2, St. Francis Yard, Wan Chai* ☎ *2804–1038* ⊕ *www.bvein.com* Ⓜ *Wan Chai, Exit B2.*

### GIZMOS, GADGETS, AND ACCESSORIES

**Broadway.** Like its more famous competitor, Fortress, Broadway is a large electronic-goods chain. It caters primarily to the local market, so some staff members speak better English than others. Look for familiar name-brand cameras, computers, sound systems, home appliances, and mobile phones. Just a few of the many shops are listed here. ✉ *7th fl., Times Square, 1 Matheson St., Causeway Bay* ☎ *2506–0228* ⊕ *www. ibroadway.com.hk* Ⓜ *Causeway Bay, Exit A* ✉ *3rd fl., Ocean Centre, Harbour City, Canton Rd., Tsim Sha Tsui, Kowloon* ☎ *2736–7733* ⊕ *www.broadway.com.hk* Ⓜ *Tsim Sha Tsui* ✉ *Ground fl., 78 Sai Yeung Choi St. S, Mong Kok, Kowloon* ☎ *2381–6760* ⊕ *www.broadway.com. hk* Ⓜ *Mong Kok.*

Fodor's Choice ★ **Fortress.** Part of billionaire Li Ka-shing's empire, this extensive chain of shops sells electronics with warranties—a safety precaution that draws the crowds. It also has good deals on printers and accessories, although selection varies by shop. You can spot a Fortress by looking for the big orange sign. For the full list of shops, visit the website. ✉ *Times Square, 7th and 8th fl., 1 Matheson St., Causeway Bay* ☎ *2506–0031* ⊕ *www. fortress.com.hk* Ⓜ *Causeway Bay* ✉ *3rd fl., Ocean Centre, Harbour City, 5 Canton Rd., Tsim Sha Tsui, Kowloon* ☎ *3101–1413* Ⓜ *Tsim Sha Tsui* ✉ *Chung Kiu Commercial Bldg., 47–51 Shan Tung St., Mong Kok, Kowloon* ☎ *2781–1730* Ⓜ *Mong Kok* ✉ *Lower ground fl., Melbourne Plaza, 33 Queen's Rd., Central* ☎ *2121–1077* Ⓜ *Central.*

**DG Lifestyle Store.** An appointed Apple Center, DG carries Mac and iPod products. High-design gadgets, accessories, and software by other brands are add-ons that meld with the sleek Apple design philosophy. ✉ *9th fl., Times Square, 1 Matheson St., Causeway Bay* ☎ *2506–1338* ⊕ *www.dg-lifestyle.com* Ⓜ *Causeway Bay* ✉ *Shop 120, Pacific Place, Admiralty, Central* ☎ *2918–4811* ⊕ *www.dg-lifestyle.com* Ⓜ *Admiralty* ✉ *Ground fl., Mikiki Mall, 638 Prince Edward Rd. East, San Po Kong, Kowloon* ☎ *2331–8628* ⊕ *www.dg-lifestyle.com* Ⓜ *Kowloon Bay.*

**Monocle.** A London-based media brand that does it all: magazine publishing, online news, radio, CDs, cafés, plus retail outlets in Tokyo, Toronto, and New York. Hong Kong devotees rejoiced when the brand opened a retail-cum-office on Star Street's St. Francis Yard in 2010. This contemporary spot offers up stylish accessories like beloved linen-bound notebooks, greeting cards, embossed card cases, and walnut-trimmed heritage radios. Whether shopping for trendy tote bags or excellent

Shopping for bargains at Stanley Village Market.

reading material, you'll be in good company. ⊠ *Shop 1, Bo Fung Mansion, 1–4 St. Francis Yard, Wan Chai* ☏ *2804-2323* ⊕ *www.monocle. com* Ⓜ *Wan Chai.*

Fodor'sChoice ★ **Wanchai Computer Centre.** You'll find honest-to-goodness bargains on computer goods and accessories in the labyrinth of shops spanning several floors. And you can negotiate prices. Your computer can be put together by a computer technician in less than a day if you're rushed; otherwise, two days is normal. The starting price is HK$3,000 depending on the hardware, processor, and peripherals you choose. This is a great resource, whether you're a techno-buff who's interested in assembling your own computer (a popular pastime with locals), or a technophobe looking for discounted earphones. ⊠ *130 Hennessy Rd., Wan Chai* Ⓜ *Wan Chai, Exit A5.*

## SOUTHSIDE

### MARKETS

Fodor'sChoice ★ **Stanley Market.** This was once Hong Kong's most famed bargain trove for visitors, but its ever-growing popularity means that Stanley Village Market no longer has the best prices around. Still, you can pick up some good buys in sportswear, casual clothing, textiles, and paintings if you comb through the stalls. Good-value linens—especially appliqué tablecloths—also abound. Dozens and dozens of shops line a main street so narrow that awnings from each side meet in the middle, and on busy days your elbows will come in handy. Weekdays are a little more relaxed. One of the best things about Stanley Market is getting here: the winding bus ride from Central (routes 6, 6X, 6A, or 260) or

Tsim Sha Tsui (route 973) takes you over the top of Hong Kong Island, with fabulous views on the way. ⊠ *Stanley Market, Southside* ⊕ *www. hk-stanley-market.com.*

## KOWLOON PENINSULA

### DEPARTMENT STORES

Fodor's Choice ★ **Yue Hwa Chinese Products Emporium.** Five floors contain Chinese goods, ranging from clothing and housewares through tea and traditional medicine. The logic behind the store's layout is hard to fathom, so go with time to rifle around. As well as the predictable tablecloths, silk pajamas, and chopstick sets, there are cheap and colorful porcelain sets and offbeat local favorites like mini-massage chairs. The top floor is entirely given over to tea— you can pick up a HK$50 packet of leaves or an antique Yixing teapot stretching into the thousands. ⊠ *301–309 Nathan Rd., Jordan, Yau Ma Tei* ☎ *3511–2222* ⊕ *www.yuehwa.com* Ⓜ *Jordan.*

> **CATWALK HONG KONG**
>
> Local and regional talent is showcased at Hong Kong Fashion Week, held at the Hong Kong Convention & Exhibition Centre every January and July. For more information on fashion week or featured designers such as Guo Pei, Dorian Ho, and Frankie Xie, visit ⊕ *www.hkfashionweekfw. com.* To read profiles of Hong Kong designers, visit ⊕ *www. hkfda.org,* the website of the Hong Kong Fashion Designers Association.

### MALLS AND CENTERS

Fodor's Choice ★ **Festival Walk.** Don't be put off by Festival Walk's location in residential Kowloon Tong—it's 20 minutes from Central on the MTR. Make the effort to get here: Festival Walk has everything from Giordano (Hong Kong's answer to the Gap) to Vivienne Tam. By day the six floors sparkle with sunlight, which filters through the glass roof. Marks & Spencer and DKNY serve as anchors; Armani Exchange and ck Calvin Klein draw the elite crowds; while Camper and agnès b. keep the trend spotters happy. Hong Kong's best bookstore, Page One, has a big branch downstairs. The mall also has one of the city's largest ice rinks, as well as a multiplex cinema, perfect if you're shopping with kids who want a respite from the sometimes scorching-hot weather. ⊠ *80 Tat Chee Ave., Kowloon Tong, Northern Kowloon* ☎ *2844–2200* ⊕ *www.festivalwalk. com.hk* Ⓜ *Kowloon Tong.*

Fodor's Choice ★ **Harbour City.** The four interconnected complexes that make up Harbour City contain almost 500 shops between them—if you can't find it here, it probably doesn't exist. Pick up a map on your way in, as it's easy to get lost. **Ocean Terminal,** the largest section, runs along the harbor and is divided thematically, with kids' wear and toys on the ground floor, and sports and cosmetics on the first. The top floor is home to white-hot street-wear store LCX *(⇨ above).* Near the Star Ferry pier, the **Marco Polo Hong Kong Hotel Arcade** has branches of the department store Lane Crawford. Louis Vuitton, Prada, and Burberry are some of the posher boutiques that fill the **Ocean Centre** and **Gateway Arcade,** parallel to Canton Road. Most of the complex's restaurants are here, too. A cinema and three hotels round up Harbour City's offerings. Free Wi-Fi is available. ⊠ *3–27 Canton Rd., Tsim Sha Tsui* ⊕ *www.harbourcity.com.hk* Ⓜ *Tsim Sha Tsui.*

> **IT'S GOOD TO BE JADED**
>
> The Chinese believe that jade brings luck, and it's still worn as a charm in amulets or bracelets. A jade bangle is often presented to newborns, and homes are often adorned with jade statues or other carved decorative items.

**Rise Commercial Building.** Many a quirky Hong Kong street-wear trend is born in this fabulous micromall. Don't let its grubby exterior put you off: this arcade is a haven of Asian cool. Japanese designers are particularly well represented—look out for überhip brand A Bathing Ape, which does some of the funkiest T-shirts around. Handmade shoes and oversized retro jewelry are other fixtures—and all at bargain prices. ⊠ *5–11 Granville Circuit, off Granville Rd., Tsim Sha Tsui* Ⓜ *Tsim Sha Tsui.*

**MARKETS**

**Flower Market.** Huge bucketfuls of roses and gerbera spill out onto the sidewalk along Flower Market Road, a collection of street stalls selling cut flowers and potted plants. Delicate orchids and vivid birds of paradise are some of the more exotic blooms. During Chinese New Year there's a roaring trade in narcissi, poinsettias, and bright yellow chrysanthemums, all auspicious flowers. ⊠ *Flower Market Rd., off Prince Edward Rd. W, Mong Kok* Ⓜ *Prince Edward.*

FAMILY **Goldfish Market.** Goldfish are considered auspicious in Hong Kong (though aquariums have to be positioned in the right place to bring good luck to the family), and this small collection of shops is a favorite local source. Shop fronts are decorated with bag upon bag of glistening, pop-eyed creatures, waiting for someone to take them home. Some of the fishes inside shops are serious rarities and fetch unbelievable prices. ⊠ *Tung Choi St., Mong Kok* Ⓜ *Mong Kok.*

**Kansu Street Jade Market.** From priceless ornaments to fake pendants, if it's green and shiny, it's here. Quality and prices at the stalls vary hugely, so if you're not with a jade connoisseur, stick with the cheap and cheerful. ⊠ *Kansu St. between Battery St. and Reclamation St., Yau Ma Tei* 🖃 *Free* ⊙ *Daily 10–5* Ⓜ *Yau Ma Tei, Exit C.*

**Ladies' Market.** Block upon block of tightly packed stalls overflow with clothes, bags, and knickknacks along Tung Choi Street in Mong Kok. Despite the name, there are clothes for women, men, and children here. Most offerings are imitations or no-name brands; rifle around enough and you can often pick up some cheap and cheerful basics. Haggling is the rule here: a poker face and a little insistence can get you dramatic discounts. At the corner of each block and behind the market are stands and shops selling the street snacks Hong Kongers can't live without. Pick a place where locals are munching and point at whatever takes your fancy. Parallel **Fa Yuen Street** is Mong Kok's unofficial sportswear market. ⊠ *Tung Choi St., Mong Kok* Ⓜ *Mong Kok.*

Fodor's Choice ★ **Temple Street Night Market.** Each night, as it gets dark, the lamps strung between the stalls of this Yau Ma Tei street market slowly light up, and the air fills with the smells wafting from myriad food carts. Hawkers try to catch your eye by flinging clothes up from their stalls. Cantonese opera competes with pop music, and vendors' cries and shoppers' haggling fills the air. Adding to the color here are the fortune-tellers and the odd magician or acrobat who has set up shop in the street. Granted, neither the clothes nor cheap gadgets on sale here are much to get excited about, but it's the atmosphere people come for—any purchases are a bonus. The market stretches for almost a mile and is one of Hong Kong's liveliest nighttime shopping experiences. ⊠ *Temple St., Mong Kok* Ⓜ *Jordan.*

## SPECIALTY SHOPS

### CLOTHING

Fodor'sChoice
★

**Pearls & Cashmere.** Warehouse prices in chic shopping arcades? It's true. This old Hong Kong favorite is elegantly housed in hotels on both sides of the harbor. In addition to quality men's and women's cashmere sweaters in classic designs and in every color under the sun, they also sell reasonably priced pashminas, gloves, and socks, which make great gifts for men and women. In recent years the brand has developed the more fashion-focused line, BYPAC. ⊠ *Mezzanine, Peninsula Hotel Shopping Arcade, Salisbury Rd., Tsim Sha Tsui* ☎ *2723–8698* Ⓜ *Tsim Sha Tsui* ⊠ *Mezzanine, Mandarin Oriental, 5 Connaught Rd., Central* ☎ *2525–6771* Ⓜ *Central.*

### JEWELRY

**Artland Watch Co Ltd.** Elegant but uncomplicated, the interior of this established watch retailer is like its service. The informed staff will guide you through the countless luxury brands on show and in the catalogs from which you can also order. Prices here aren't the best in Hong Kong, but they're still lower than at home. ⊠ *Ground fl., Mirador Mansion, 54-64B Nathan Rd., Tsim Sha Tsui* ☎ *2366–1074* Ⓜ *Tsim Sha Tsui.*

**Sandra Pearls.** You might be wary of the lustrous pearls hanging at this little Jade Market stall. The charming owner, Sandra, does, in fact, sell genuine and reasonably priced cultured and freshwater pearl necklaces and earrings. Some pieces are made from shell, which Sandra is always quick to point out, and could pass muster among the snobbiest collectors. ⊠ *Stall 437 and 447, Jade Market, Kansu St., Yau Ma Tei* ☎ *9485–2895* Ⓜ *Yau Ma Tei.*

**TSL Jewellery.** One of the big Hong Kong chains, TSL (Tse Sui Luen) specializes in diamond jewelry, and manufactures, retails, and exports its designs. Its range of 100-facet stones includes the Estrella cut, which reflects nine symmetrical hearts and comes with international certification. Although its contemporary designs use platinum settings, TSL also sells pure, bright, yellow-gold items targeted at Chinese customers. ⊠ *G5–G7, Park Lane Blvd., Nathan Rd., Tsim Sha Tsui* ☎ *2332–4618* ⊕ *www.tsljewellery.com* Ⓜ *Tsim Sha Tsui* ⊠ *Ground fl., 1 Yee Woo St., Causeway Bay* Ⓜ *Causeway Bay.*

## TAILOR-MADE CLOTHING

MEN'S TAILORS **David's Shirts Ltd.** Customers have been enjoying the personalized service of David Chu since 1961. All the work is done in-house by Shanghainese tailors with at least 20 years' experience each. There are more than 6,000 imported European fabrics to choose from, each pre-washed. Examples of shirts, suits, and accessories—including 30 collar styles, 12 cuff styles, and 10 pocket styles—help you choose. Single-needle tailoring; French seams; 22 stitches per inch; hand-picked, double-stitched shell buttons; German interlining—it's all here. Your details, down to on

> **WORD OF MOUTH**
>
> "Go to the bird market and flower market early in the morning, with a stop at the Jade Market and then a visit to the Wong Tai Sin temple to get your fortune told, and that is a morning in Kowloon."
> —Cicerone

which side you wear your wristwatch, are kept on file should you wish to use its mail-order service in the future. ⊠ *Ground fl., Wing Lee Bldg., 33 Kimberley Rd., Tsim Sha Tsui* ☎ *2367–9556* ⊕ *www.davidsshirts. com* Ⓜ *Tsim Sha Tsui* ⊠ *Mezzanine, Mandarin Oriental, 5 Connaught Rd., Central* ☎ *2524–2979* Ⓜ *Central.*

**Maxwell's Clothiers Ltd.** After you've found a handful of reputable, high-quality tailors, one way to choose between them is price. Maxwell's is known for its competitive rates. It's also a wonderful place to have favorite shirts and suits copied and for straightforward, structured women's shirts and suits. It was founded by third-generation tailor Ken Maxwell in 1961 and follows Shanghai tailoring traditions, while also providing the fabled 24-hour suit upon request. The showroom and workshop are in Kowloon, but son Andy and his team take appointments in the United States, Canada, Australia, and Europe twice annually. The motto of this family business is, "Simply let the garment do the talking." ⊠ *7th fl., Han Hing Mansion, 38–40 Hankow Rd., Tsim Sha Tsui* ☎ *2366–6705* ⊕ *www.maxwellsclothiers.com* Ⓜ *Tsim Sha Tsui.*

Fodor's Choice ★ **Sam's Tailor.** Unlike many famous Hong Kong tailors, you won't find the legendary Sam's in a chic hotel or sleek mall. But don't be fooled. These digs in humble Burlington House, a tailoring hub, have hosted everyone from U.S. presidents (back as far as Richard Nixon) to performers such as the Black Eyed Peas, Kylie Minogue, and Blondie. This former uniform tailor to the British troops once even made a suit for Prince Charles in a record hour and 52 minutes. The men's and women's tailor does accept 24-hour suit or shirt orders, but will take about two days if you're not in a hurry. Founded by Naraindas Melwani in 1957, "Sam" is now his son, Manu Melwani, who runs the show with the help of his own son, Roshan, and about 57 tailors behind the scenes. In 2004 Sam's introduced a computerized bodysuit that takes measurements without a tape measure. (It uses both methods, however.) These tailors also make biannual trips to Europe and North America. (Schedule updates are listed on the website.) ⊠ *Burlington House, 94 Nathan Rd., Tsim Sha Tsui* ☎ *2367–9423* ⊕ *www.samstailor.com* Ⓜ *Tsim Sha Tsui.*

**W. W. Chan & Sons Tailors Ltd.** Chan is known for excellent-quality suits and shirts and classic cuts and has an array of fine European fabrics. It's comforting to know that you'll be measured and fitted by the same master tailor from start to finish. The Kowloon headquarters features a mirrored, hexagonal changing room so you can check every angle. Tailors from here travel to the United States several times a year to fill orders for their customers; if you have a suit made here and leave your address, they'll let you know when they plan to visit. ✉ *2nd fl., Burlington House, 92–94 Nathan Rd., Tsim Sha Tsui* ☎ *2366–9738, 2366–2634* ⊕ *www.wwchan.com* Ⓜ *Tsim Sha Tsui.*

WOMEN'S **Mode Elegante.** Don't be deterred by the somewhat dated mannequins in
TAILORS the windows. Mode Elegante is a favorite source for custom-made suits among women and men in the know. Tailors here specialize in European cuts. You'll have your choice of fabrics from the United Kingdom, Italy, and elsewhere. Your records are put on file so you can place orders from abroad. It'll even ship the completed garment to you almost anywhere on the planet. Alternatively, you can make an appointment with director Gary Zee, one of Hong Kong's traveling tailors, who make regular visits to North America, Europe, and Japan. ✉ *11th fl., Star House, 3 Salisbury Rd., Tsim Sha Tsui* ☎ *2366–8153* ⊕ *www.modeelegante.com* Ⓜ *Tsim Sha Tsui.*

# SIDE TRIP TO MACAU

Enter the desperate, smoky atmosphere of a Chinese casino, where frumpy players bet an average of five times more than the typical Vegas gambler. Sit down next to grandmothers who smoke like chimneys while playing baccarat—the local game of choice—with visiting high rollers. Then step out of the climate-controlled chill and into tropical air that embraces you like a warm, balmy hug. Welcome to Macau.

The many contrasts in this tiny enclave of 555,000 people serve as reminders of how different cultures have embraced one another's traditions for hundreds of years. Though Macau's population is 95% ethnic Chinese, there are still vibrant pockets of Portuguese and Filipino expats. And some of the thousands of Eurasians—who consider themselves neither Portuguese nor Chinese, but something in between—can trace the intermarriage of their ancestors back a century or two.

Macau's old town, while dominated by the buildings, squares, and cobblestone alleyways of colonial Portugal, is tinged with eastern influences as well. In Macau you can spend an afternoon exploring Buddhist temples before feasting on a dinner of *bacalhau com natas* (dried codfish with a cream sauce), grilled African chicken (spicy chicken in a coconut-peanut broth—a classic Macanese dish), Chinese lobster with scallions, or fiery prawns infused with Indian and Malaysian flavors. Wash everything down with *vinho verde,* the crisp young wine from northern Portugal, and top it all off with a traditional Portuguese *pastel de nata* (egg-custard tart) and dark, thick espresso.

## GETTING TO MACAU

### AIR TRAVEL

International flights (from Asia) come into Macau, but there are no planes from Hong Kong. Fifteen-minute helicopter flights fly between Hong Kong's Shun Tak Centre and the Macau Ferry Terminal on Sky Shuttle; they leave every 30 minutes from 9 am to 11 pm daily. Prices are HK$3,700 Monday to Thursday with an HK$200 surcharge on Friday, Saturday, Sunday, and holidays. Reservations are essential.

Contacts **Sky Shuttle** ☎ *853/2872–7288 Macau Terminal, 2108–9898 Shun Tak Centre* ⊕ *www.skyshuttlehk.com.* **Macau International Airport** ☎ *853/2886–1111* ⊕ *www.macau-airport.com/en.*

### FERRY TRAVEL

Ferries run between Hong Kong and Macau every 15 minutes with a reduced schedule from midnight to 7 am. Prices for economy/ordinary and super/deluxe run HK\$151–HK\$291. VIP cabins begin at HK\$1,164 (four seats) to HK\$1,746 (six seats). Weekday traffic is usually light, so you can buy tickets right before departure. Weekend tickets often sell out, so make reservations.

Most ferries leave from Hong Kong's Shun Tak Centre Sheung Wan MTR station in Central, though limited service is available from First Ferry at Kowloon's Tsim Sha Tsui terminal. In Macau most ferries disembark from the main Macau Ferry Terminal, but CotaiJet services the terminal on Taipa Island. The trip takes one hour each way. Buses, taxis, and free shuttles to most casinos and hotels await on the Macau side.

Contacts **CotaiJet** ☎ *853/2885–0595 in Macau, 2359–9990 in Hong Kong* ⊕ *cotaijet.com.mo.* **First Ferry** ☎ *2131–8181* ⊕ *www.nwff.com.hk.* **TurboJET** ☎ *2859–3333 information* ⊕ *www.turbojet.com.hk/en.*

## GETTING AROUND MACAU

### BUS TRAVEL

Public buses are clean and affordable; trips to anywhere in the Macau Peninsula cost MOP\$3.20. Service to Taipa Island is MOP\$4.20, service to Coloane is MOP\$5, and the trip to Hác Sá is MOP\$6.40. Buses run 6:30 am–midnight and require exact change upon boarding. But you can get downtown for free, via casino shuttles, from the official Border Gate crossing just outside mainland China, from the airport, and from the Macau Ferry Terminal.

### TAXI TRAVEL

Taxis are inexpensive but not plentiful in Macau. The best places to catch a cab are the major casinos—the Wynn, Lisboas, Sands, and Venetian. Carry a bilingual map or ask the concierge at your hotel to write the name of your destination in Chinese. All taxis are metered, air-conditioned, and reasonably comfortable. The base charge is MOP\$15 for the first 1.6 km (1 mile) and MOP\$1.50 per additional 230 meters. Trips between Coloane and either the Macau Peninsula or Taipa incur respective surcharges of MOP\$5 and MOP\$2. Drivers don't expect a tip.

## RESTAURANTS

Macau's medley of Portuguese and Cantonese cuisine—spicy and creamy Macanese interpretations of traditional Cantonese dishes such as baked prawns, braised abalone, and seafood stews—has made the peninsula one of Asia's top fine-dining destinations for decades.

Now, thanks to the spate of new casino-hotels, Macau has also become an exciting world-class culinary frontier. But Macau dining isn't all highbrow. Near the Largo do Senado, in the villages of Taipa or Coloane, wander the back alleys for *zhu-bao-bao,* a slab of fried pork

Pedestrian-only Largo do Senado preserves the Portuguese influence that shaped Macau for centuries.

on a toasted bun served with milk tea, or the signature *pasteis de nata* (custard tart): simple and delicious, and classic Macau.

### HOTELS

An influx of luxury hotels has transformed Macau into a posh place to stay. The musty three-stars are still out there, but the five-stars are generally worth the splurge. For a true Macau experience, try staying in *pousadas,* restored historic buildings that have been converted into intimate hotels with limited facilities but lots of character.

### VISITOR INFORMATION

To enter Macau, Americans, Canadians, and EU citizens need only a valid passport for stays of up to 90 days. The Macau Government Tourist Office (MGTO) is well managed.

**Contacts Macau Government Tourist Office** (*MGTO*). ✉ *335–341, Alameda Dr. Carlos d'Assumpção* ☎ *853/2833-3000 in Macau, 8238-8680 in Hong Kong* ⊕ *www.macautourism.gov.mo.*

## EXPLORING MACAU

Macau is a small place, where on a good day you could drive from one end to the other in 30 minutes. This makes walking and bicycling ideal ways to explore winding city streets, nature trails, and long stretches of beach. Most of Macau's population lives on the peninsula attached to mainland China. The region's most famous sights are here—Senado Square, the Ruins of St. Paul's, A-Ma Temple—as are most of the luxury hotels and casinos. As in the older sections of Hong Kong, cramped older buildings stand comfortably next to gleaming new structures.

### DOWNTOWN MACAU

Chances are you'll arrive at the Macau Ferry Terminal after sailing from Hong Kong. There's not much to see around the terminal itself, so hop into one of the many waiting casino or hotel shuttles and head straight downtown, less than 10 minutes away. From there it's a short walk to the city's historic center, along the short stretch of road named Avenida Almeida Ribeiro, more commonly known as San Ma Lo, which is Macau's commercial and cultural heart.

### TOP ATTRACTIONS

Fodor's Choice **Fortaleza da Guia.** This fort built between 1622 and 1638 on Macau's
★ highest hill was key to protecting the Portuguese from invaders. You can walk the steep, winding road up to the fortress or take a five-minute cable-car ride from the entrance of Flora Garden on Avenida Sidónio Pais. Once inside, notice the gleaming white Guia Lighthouse (you can't go up, but you can get a good look at the exterior) that's lit every night. Next to it is the Guia Chapel, built by Clarist nuns to provide soldiers with religious services. Restoration work in 1998 uncovered elaborate frescoes mixing western and Chinese themes. They're best seen when the morning or afternoon sun floods the chapel, which is no longer used for services. ⊠ *Guia Hill, Downtown* ☎ *853/8399–6699* ⊡ *Free* ⊙ *Daily 9–5:30.*

**Igreja de São Domingos** (*St. Dominic's Church*). The cream-and-white interior of one of Macau's most beautiful churches takes on a heavenly golden glow when illuminated for services. St. Dominic's was originally a convent founded by Spanish Dominican friars in 1587. In 1822 China's first Portuguese newspaper, *The China Bee,* was published here, and the church became a repository for sacred art in 1834 when convents were banned in Portugal. ■TIP→ **Admission to all churches and temples is free, though donations are suggested.** ⊠ *Largo de São Domingos, Downtown* ⊙ *Daily 8–6.*

Fodor's Choice **Largo do Senado.** The charming hub of Macau for centuries, open only
★ to pedestrians and paved in shiny black-and-white tiles, is lined with neoclassical-style colonial buildings painted in bright pastels. The **Edifício do Leal Senado** (Senate Building) that gives the square its name was built in 1784 as a municipal chamber and continues to be used by the government today. An elegant meeting room on the first floor opens onto a magnificent library based on one in the Mafra Convent in Portugal, with books neatly stacked on two levels of shelves reaching to the ceiling, and art and historical exhibitions are frequently hosted in the beautiful foyer and garden. Alleys adjacent to the square are packed with restaurants and shops. ■TIP→ **Visit on a weekday to avoid the crowds, and try to come back at night, when locals of all ages gather to chat and the square is beautifully lit.** ⊠ *Downtown.*

**NEED A BREAK?**

**Margaret's Café e Nata.** Not far off the main drag but somewhat hidden down an alleyway, Margaret's Café e Nata offers a cool—albeit increasingly crowded—place to sit, outside under fans and awnings, with some of the best custard tarts in town, plus fresh juices, sandwiches, homemade tea blends, and pizza slices. ⊠ *Rua Comandante Mata e Oliveira, Downtown* ☎ *853/2871–0032.*

**Leitaria i Son.** Look for the small cow sign marking the out-of-the-ordinary Leitaria i Son milk bar. The decor is cafeteria-style and Spartan, but the bar whips up frothy glasses of fresh milk from its dairy and blends them with all manner of juices: papaya, coconut, apricot, and more. ⊠ *Largo do Senado 7, Downtown* ☎ *853/2857–3638.*

**Macau Canidrome.** The greyhound track looks rundown and quaint compared to the bigger Jockey Club and glitzy casinos, but it offers a true taste of Macau in a popular neighborhood near the China border crossing. The Canidrome opened in 1932; it tends to attract a steady crowd of older gamblers several times a week for the slower-pace, lower-stakes gambling rush of betting on fast dogs chasing an electronic rabbit. Check out the parade of race dogs before each race. You can sit on benches in the open-air stadium, at tables in the air-conditioned restaurant, or in an upstairs box seat. ⊠ *Av. do Artur Tamagnini Barbosa at Av. General Castelo Branco, Downtown* ☎ *853/2833–3399, 853/2826–1188 to place bets* ⊕ *www.macauyydog.com* ⌦ *Public stands MOP$10, private box seats MOP$120* ☉ *Mon., Tues., Thurs., and weekends 6 pm–11:45 pm; first race at 7:30.*

Fodor'sChoice
★ **Macau Tower Convention & Entertainment Centre.** Rising above peaceful San Van Lake, the 335-meter (1,100-foot) freestanding tower recalls Sky Tower, a similar structure in New Zealand—and it should, as both were designed by New Zealand architect Gordon Moller. The Macau Tower offers a variety of thrills, including the Mast Climb, which challenges the daring and strong of heart and body with a two-hour climb on steel rungs 105 meters (344 feet) up the tower's mast for incomparable views of Macau and China. Other thrills include the Skywalk X, an open-air stroll around the tower's exterior—without handrails; the SkyJump, an assisted, decelerated 233-meter (765-foot) descent; and the world's highest bungee jump. More subdued attractions inside the tower are a mainstream movie theater and a revolving lunch, high tea, and dinner buffet at the 360-degree Café. ⊠ *Largo da Torre de Macau, Downtown* ☎ *853/2893–3339* ⊕ *www.macautower.com.mo* ⌦ *MOP$688 for Skywalk X to MOP$2,488 for the Mast Climb; photos extra.* ☉ *Observation deck, weekdays 10–9, weekends and holidays 9–9.*

Fodor'sChoice
★ **Ruínas de São Paulo** (*Ruins of St. Paul's Church*). Only the magnificent, towering facade, with its intricate carvings and bronze statues, remains from the original Church of Mater Dei, built between 1602 and 1640 and destroyed by fire in 1835. The church, an adjacent college, and Mount Fortress, all Jesuit constructions, once formed East Asia's first western-style university. The ruins are now the widely adopted symbol

6

of Macau, a tourist attraction with snack bars and antiques and other shops at the foot of the site. The small **Museum of Sacred Art and Crypt** tucked behind the facade of São Paulo holds statues, crucifixes, and the bones of Japanese and Vietnamese martyrs. There are also some intriguing Asian interpretations of Christian images, including samurai angels and a Chinese Virgin and Child. ⊠ *Top end of Rua de São Paulo, Downtown* ☏ *853/8399–6699* 🖅 *Free* ☉ *Ruins, daily 8–5; museum, daily 9–6.*

**Santa Casa da Misericordia.** Founded in 1569 by Dom Belchior Carneiro, Macau's first bishop, the Holy House of Mercy is the China coast's oldest Christian charity, and it continues to take care of the poor with soup kitchens and health clinics, as well as providing housing for the elderly. The exterior, with its imposing white facade, is neoclassical, but the interior is done in a contrasting opulent, modern style. A reception room on the second floor contains paintings of benefactress Marta Merop. ⊠ *2 Travessa da Misericordia, Downtown* ☏ *853/2857–3938* 🖅 *MOP$5* ☉ *Mon.–Sat. 10–1 and 2:30–5:30.*

Fodor's Choice ★ **Templo de A-Ma.** One of Macau's most picturesque temples is thought to be Macau's oldest building. Properly Ma Kok Temple but known to locals as simply A-Ma, the structure originated during the Ming Dynasty (1368–1644) and was influenced by Confucianism, Taoism, and Buddhism, as well as local religions. Vivid red calligraphy on large boulders tells the story of the goddess A-Ma (also known as Tin Hau), the patron of fishermen. A small gate opens onto prayer halls, pavilions, and caves carved directly into the hillside. ⊠ *Rua de São Tiago da Barra, Largo da Barra, Downtown* ☉ *Daily 7–6.*

**WORTH NOTING**

**Fortaleza do Monte** (*Mount Fortress*). On the hill overlooking the ruins of São Paulo and affording great peninsular views, this renovated fort was built by the Jesuits in the early 17th century. In 1622 it was the site of Macau's most legendary battle, when a priest's lucky cannon shot hit an invading Dutch ship's powder supply, saving the day. The interior buildings were destroyed by fire in 1835, but the outer walls remain, along with several large cannons and artillery pieces. Exhibits at the adjoining **Macau Museum** (daily 10–6, MOP$15) take you through the territory's history, from its origins to modern development. ⊠ *Monte Hill, Downtown* ☏ *853/2835–7911* ⊕ *www.macaumuseum. gov.mo* 🖅 *Free* ☉ *Daily 6 am–7 pm.*

**Igreja de São Lourenço** (*Church of St. Lawrence*). One of Macau's three oldest churches, the Church of St. Lawrence was founded by Jesuits in 1560 and has been lovingly rebuilt several times. Its present appearance dates to 1846. It overlooks the South China Sea amid pleasant, palm-shaded gardens. Families of Portuguese sailors used to gather on the front steps to pray for the sailors' safe return; hence its Chinese name, Feng Shun Tang (Hall of the Soothing Winds). Focal points of its breathtaking interior are the elegant wood carvings, a baroque altar, and crystal chandeliers. ⊠ *Rua de São Lourenço, Downtown* ☏ *8399– 6699* ☉ *Mon.–Fri. 10–4, Sat. 10–1.*

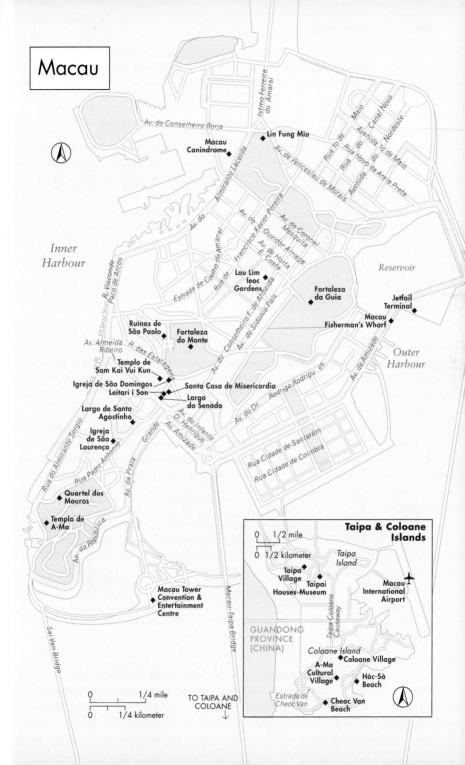

# Macau

Inner Harbour

Av. do Conselheiro Borja

Macau Canindrome

Lin Fung Miu

Av. de Venceslau de Morais

Rua To de Maio

Canal Novo

Avenida To de Maio

do Nordeste

Rua Novo do Areia Preta

Avenida

Almirante Lacerda

Av. do

Av. do Coronel Mesquita

Av. do Francisco Xavier Pereira

Av. do Ouvidor Arriaga

Av. de Horta E. Costa

Estrada de Coelho do Amaral

Rua de

Lou Lim leoc Gardens

Fortaleza da Guia

Reservoir

Jetfoil Terminal

R. Visconde Paço de Arcos

Av. do Conselheira F. de Almeida

Av. de Sidónio Pais

Macau Fisherman's Wharf

Ruínas de São Paolo

Fortaleza do Monte

Av. Almeida Ribeiro

R. das Estalagens

Outer Harbour

Av. da Amizade

Templo de Sam Kai Vui Kun

Igreja de São Domingos

Santa Casa de Misericordia

Leitari i Son

Largo do Senado

Av. do Dr. Rodrigo Rodrigu es

Largo de Santo Agostinho

Av. do Infante D. Henrique

Av. da Amizade

Igreja de São Lourenço

Rua do Almirante Sergio

Rua Padre Antonio

Rua da Prata

Grande

Rua Cidade de Santarém

Rua Cidade de Coimbra

Quartel dos Mouros

Templo de A-Ma

Av. da Republica

Sai Van Bridge

Macau Tower Convention & Entertainment Centre

Macau Taipa Bridge

0       1/4 mile

0       1/4 kilometer

TO TAIPA AND COLOANE ↓

## Taipa & Coloane Islands

0       1/2 mile

0       1/2 kilometer

Taipa Island

Taipa Village

Taipai Houses-Museum

Macau International Airport

Taipa-Coloane Causeway

GUANDONG PROVINCE (CHINA)

Coloane Island

A-Ma Cultural Village

Coloane Village

Hàc-Sà Beach

Estrada de Cheoc Van

Cheoc Van Beach

**Largo de Santo Agostinho.** Built in the pattern of traditional Portuguese squares, St. Augustine Square is paved with black-and-white tiles laid out in mosaic wave patterns and lined with leafy overhanging trees and lots of wooden benches. It's easy to feel as if you're in a European village, far from South China. One of the square's main structures is the **Teatro Dom Pedro V,** a European-style hall with an inviting green-and-white facade built in 1859. It's an important cultural landmark for Macanese and was regularly used until World War II, when it fell into disrepair. The 300-seat venue once again hosts concerts and recitals—especially during the annual Macau International Music Festival—as well as important public events, the only times you can go inside. It does, however, have a garden that's open daily, and admission is free. **Igreja de Santo Agostinho (Church of St. Augustine),** to one side of the square, dates from 1591, and has a grand, weathered exterior and a drafty interior with a high wood-beam ceiling (open daily 10–6). There's a magnificent stone altar with a statue of Christ on his knees, bearing the cross, with small crucifixes in silhouette on the hill behind him. The statue, called Our Lord of Passos, is carried in a procession through the streets of downtown on the first day of Lent. ⊠ *Off R. Central, Downtown.*

**Lin Fung Miu.** Built in 1592, the Temple of the Lotus honors several Buddhist and Taoist deities, including Tin Hau (goddess of the sea), Kun Iam (goddess of mercy), and Kwan Tai (god of war and wealth). The front of the temple is embellished with magnificent clay bas-reliefs of renowned figures from Chinese history and mythology. Inside are several halls, shrines, and courtyards. The temple is best known as a lodging place for Mandarins traveling from Guangzhou. Its most famous guest was Commissioner Lin Zexu, whose confiscation and destruction of British opium in 1839 was largely responsible for the First Opium War. ⊠ *Av. do Almirante Lacerda, Downtown* ☽ *Daily dawn–dusk.*

**Lou Lim Ieoc Gardens.** These beautiful gardens were built in the 19th century by a Chinese merchant named Lou Kau. Rock formations, water, vegetation, pavilions, and sunlight were all carefully considered, and the balanced landscapes are the hallmark of Suzhou garden style. The government took possession and restored the grounds in the mid 1970s, so that today you can enjoy tranquil walks among delicate flowering bushes framed with bamboo groves and artificial hills. A large auditorium frequently hosts concerts and other events, most notably recitals during the annual Macau International Music Festival. Adjacent to the gardens, a European-style edifice contains the **Macau Tea Culture House,** a small museum with exhibits on the tea culture of Macau and China (Tues.–Sun. 9–7, free). ⊠ *Estrada de Adolfo Loureiro, at Av. do Conselheiro Ferreira de Almeida, Downtown* ☎ *853/2835–6622* ▱ *Free* ☽ *Daily 6 am–9 pm.*

FAMILY **Macau Fisherman's Wharf.** This sprawling complex of rides, games, and other minor attractions has an appealing Old World aura. The centerpiece is the Roman Amphitheatre, which hosts outdoor performances, but the main draws are the lively themed restaurants on the west side, such as AfriKana, serving up Macau's best African brews and barbecues. Come for the food, and stay after dark, as Fisherman's Wharf is most active at night. ✉ *Av. da Amizade, at Av. Dr. Sun Yat-Sen, Downtown* ☎ *853/8299–3300* ⊕ *www.fishermanswharf.com.mo* 🖅 *Admission free, games MOP$1–MOP$32* ⊙ *Open 24 hours.*

**Templo de Sam Kai Vui Kun.** Built in 1750, this temple is dedicated to Kuan Tai, the bearded, fierce-looking god of war and wealth in Chinese mythology. Statues of him and his two sons sit on an altar. A steady stream of people comes to pray and ask for support before they go wage battle in the casinos. May and June see festivals honoring Kuan Tai throughout Macau. ✉ *Rua Sui do Mercado de São Domingos, Downtown* ⊙ *Daily 8–6.*

### TAIPA ISLAND

The island directly south of peninsular Macau was once two small islands that were, over time, joined by deposits from the Pearl River Delta. It's connected to peninsular Macau by three long bridges. The region's two universities, horse-racing track, scenic hiking trails, and its international airport are all here.

Like downtown Macau, Taipa has been greatly developed in the past few years, yet it retains a visual balance between old Macau charm and modern sleekness. Try to visit on a weekend, so you can shop for clothing and crafts in the traditional flea market that's held every Sunday from morning to evening in Taipa Village.

**Taipai Houses-Museum.** These five sea-green houses are interesting examples of Porto-Chinese architecture and were originally residences of wealthy local merchants. They now house changing art exhibitions. Paths lead into the beautiful adjoining **Carmel Garden,** where palm trees provide welcome shade. Within the garden stands the brilliant white-and-yellow **Nossa Senhora do Carmo** (Church of Our Lady of Carmel), built in 1885 and featuring a handsome single-belfry tower. ✉ *Av. da Praia, Carmo Zone, Taipa* ☎ *853/2882–7103* 🖅 *Museum MOP$5, free Sun.; garden free* ⊙ *Museum Tues.–Sun. 10–6; garden daily, 24 hours.*

Fodor's Choice ★ **Taipa Village.** The narrow, winding streets are packed with restaurants, bakeries, shops, temples, and other buildings with traditional South Chinese and Portuguese design elements. The aptly named Rua do Cunha (Food Street) has many great Chinese, Macanese, Portuguese, and Thai restaurants. Several shops sell homemade Macanese snacks, including steamed milk pudding, almond cakes, beef jerky, and coconut candy.

### COLOANE ISLAND

Centuries ago, Coloane was a wild place, where pirates hid in rocky caves and coves, awaiting their chance to strike at cargo ships on the Pearl River. Early in the 20th century the local government sponsored a huge planting program to transform Coloane from a barren place to a green one. The results were spectacular—and enduring. Today this island is idyllic, with green hills and clean sandy beaches.

Once connected to Taipa Island by a thin isthmus, Coloane is now almost completely fused with Taipa via the huge Cotai reclaimed land project, where the "Strip" was completed in 2010. Regardless of the recent development boom, Coloane remains the destination of choice

**DID YOU KNOW?**

When the Portuguese landed on Macau, just outside the Templo de A-Ma, they asked the natives the name of the place. They told them the temple name, *Mā Gé Miào,* which sounds suspiciously like *Macau.*

for anyone seeking natural beauty and tranquility.

FAMILY
Fodor's Choice
★
**A-Ma Cultural Village.** A huge complex built in a traditional Qing Dynasty style pays homage to Macau's namesake, the goddess of the sea. The vibrancy and color of the details in the bell and drum towers, the tiled roofs, and the carved marble altars are truly awe-inspiring. It's as if you've been transported back to the height of the Qing Empire and can now see temples in their true state of greatness. Other remarkable details include the striking rows of stairs leading to Tian Hou Palace at the entrance. Each row features painstakingly detailed marble and stone carvings of auspicious Chinese symbols: a roaring tiger, double lions, five cranes, the double phoenix, and a splendid imperial dragon.

> ### WORD OF MOUTH
>
> "I do enjoy the old town parts of Macau city, and also find that Taipa and Coloane (especially Coloane), have much less of a city feel, offer some nice beaches and parks, and are mostly devoid of the hordes of tourists you can find in the old town in Macau. The little town near Hác Sá is cute and the village of Coloane itself has a Tin Hau temple and the famous and very good egg tarts at the Lord Stow Bakery. In Macau city itself, once you get out of the main historic core around the cathedral and the steps of St Paul's, it can be very quiet indeed and much less crowded."
> —Cicerone

The grounds here also have a recreational fishing zone and an arboretum with more than 100 species of local and exotic flora.

Behind A-Ma Cultural Village is the 560-foot-tall **Coloane Hill,** crowned by a gleaming white-marble statue of A-Ma (commemorating the year of Macau's handover), soaring 65 feet and visible from miles away. You can make the short hike up to the top or take one of the shuttle buses that leave from the foot of the hill every 30 minutes. ⊠ *Off Estrada de Seac Pai Van, Coloane Island South* ☉ *Daily 8–6.*

Fodor's Choice
★
**Coloane Village.** Quiet, relaxed Coloane Village is home to traditional Mediterranean-style houses painted in pastels, as well as the baroque-style Chapel of St. Francis Xavier and the Taoist Tam Kung Temple. The narrow alleys reveal surprises at every turn; you may well encounter fishermen repairing their junks or a baptism at the chapel. At the village's heart is a small square adorned with a fountain with a bronze Cupid. The surrounding Macanese and Chinese open-air restaurants are among the region's best; some are the unheralded favorites of chefs visiting from Hong Kong and elsewhere in Asia.

## WHERE TO EAT

### DOWNTOWN MACAU

$$
PORTUGUESE
✕ **Afonso III.** After four years at the Hyatt Regency, Chef Afonso Carrao Pereira decided to open his own place and cook the way his grandmother did. The result is his modest café in the heart of downtown near Senado Square, with an intimate space downstairs of dark wood and stucco, and a more expansive upstairs. The food consists of simple, hearty, traditional dishes served in huge portions, mostly to Portuguese

expatriates and Macanese locals. Your best bets are the daily specials, which invariably include *bacalhau* (Portuguese salted codfish), braised pork, or beef stew probably better than any other you'll taste in Macau. The wine list is extensive, and comes in generous goblets or by the bottle. $ *Average main: MOP$150* ⊠ *11A Rua Central, Downtown* ☎ *853/2858–6272* ▬ *No credit cards* ⊘ *Closed Sun.*

$$$
FRENCH

✕ **Aux Beaux Arts.** A 1930s-style Parisian brasserie in the MGM Grand is one of the trendiest restaurants in Macau. Chinese diners are particularly fond of its fresh, catch-of-the-day seafood—the lobster is especially choice. So, too, are the French mains, such as beef tartare with french fries. Oysters and caviar are also exclusive, at prices reaching MOP$2,950 for 50 grams. In-house sommeliers are at hand to pair the latest wines with dishes. With tan wood, private booths, and a terrace, the decor is as much old French Concession Shanghai as it is old Paris. Either way, the place has raised the bar for Macau's restaurant scene. $ *Average main: MOP$300* ⊠ *MGM Grand, Av. Dr. Sun Yat Sen, Downtown* ☎ *853/8802–3888* ⊕ *www.mgmmacau. com* ⊘ *Closed Mon.*

$$
PORTUGUESE

✕ **Clube Militar de Macau (The Macau Military Club).** Founded in 1870 as a private military club, the stately pink-and-white structure was restored in 1995 and reopened as a restaurant. The languid Old World atmosphere perfectly complements the extensive list of traditional Portuguese dishes, such as *bacalhau dourado* ("golden cod," a specialty of fried cod and potatoes), African chicken, and *arroz de marisco* (flavored rice and seafood). Leave room for dessert—the options include Portuguese sweet rice pudding with mango, warm chestnut tart, and coconut ice cream with caramelized pineapple. $ *Average main: MOP$150* ⊠ *975 Av. da Praia Grande, Downtown* ☎ *853/2871–4000* ⊕ *www. clubemilitardemacau.net.*

$
PORTUGUESE
Fodor's Choice
★

✕ **Dom Galo.** "Quirky" springs to mind when describing the colorful decor, with plastic monkey puppets and funky chicken toys hanging from the ceilings. A wide clientele includes graphic designers, gambling-compliance lawyers, and 10-year-old Cantonese kids celebrating birthdays. The owner is Portuguese and the food is usually spot-on, with *insalada de polvo* (octopus salad), king prawns, and steak fries served with a tangy mushroom sauce among the stand-outs. Pitchers of sangria are essential with any meal here. So, too, are reservations, as this place is increasingly popular with tourists. $ *Average main: MOP$100* ⊠ *Av. Sir Andars Ljung Stedt, Downtown* ☎ *853/2875–1383* ⊜ *Reservations essential.*

$$
CANTONESE
Fodor's Choice
★

✕ **Fat Siu Lau.** Well known to both locals and visitors from Hong Kong, Fat Siu Lau has kept its customers coming back since 1903 with delicious Macanese favorites and modern creations. Try ordering whatever you see the chatty Cantonese stuffing themselves with at the surrounding tables, and you won't be disappointed. Your meal might well consist of whole curry crab, grilled prawns in a butter garlic sauce, and the famous roasted pigeon dressed in a secret marinade. Fat Siu Lau 2 is on Macau Lan Kwai Fong Street, and the newer Fat Siu Lau 3 is near the Venetian—both offer the same great food. $ *Average main:*

*MOP$125* ✉ *64 Rua da Felicidade, Downtown* ☎ *853/2857–3580* 🌐 *www.fatsiulau.com.mo* ✍ *Reservations essential.*

$ MACANESE 🍴 **Pastelaria Koi Kei.** Walking toward the Ruins of St. Paul's, you will likely be accosted by salespeople forcing Macanese snacks into your hands, and enticed to step into one of the street's *pastelarias* (pastry shops), serving traditional almond cakes, ginger candy, beef jerky, and egg rolls,. Have a taste or two—competition is fierce, and one of the oldest and best is Pastelaria Koi Kei. Hong Kong residents regularly haul the distinctive tan bags, heavy with snacks—and in particular, the Portuguese custards—back home for friends and relatives. Other branches are on nearby Rua de São Paulo and on Rua do Cunha in Taipa. Cash is preferred. [$] *Average main: MOP$35* ✉ *70–72 Rua Felicidade, Downtown* ☎ *853/2893–8102* 🌐 *www.koikei.com.*

## MACAU OUTER HARBOUR

$ AFRICAN 🍴 **AfriKana Bar.** Macau's historical contacts with Africa, especially Angola and Mozambique, come into sharp focus in one of the few places on the peninsula where you can eat roasted coconut chicken under a thatched roof. Scores of Portuguese-speaking residents who were born in Portugal's African colonies come here for parties or cultural events. The eight thatched pavilions feature resilient colors, from dark blues to mustard yellows to sandy reds. [$] *Average main: MOP$75* ✉ *Fisherman's Wharf, Outer Harbour* ☎ *853/8299–3678* ⏲ *No lunch.*

6

## MACAU INNER HARBOUR

$$ PORTUGUESE Fodor's Choice ★ 🍴 **A Lorcha.** Vastly popular A Lorcha (the name means "wooden ship") celebrates the heritage of Macau as an important port with a maritime theme for the menu. Don't miss the signature dish, Clams Lorcha Style, with tomato, beer, and garlic. Other classics include *feijoada* (Brazilian pork-and-bean stew), steamed crab, and perfectly smoky and juicy fire-roasted chicken. Save room for *serradura* (aka Macau sawdust pudding, made from biscuits and vanilla whipped cream). Watch for racers during the Grand Prix, as the Macanese owner Adriano is a fervent Formula fan. [$] *Average main: MOP$140* ✉ *289 Rua do Almirante Sérgio, Inner Harbour* ☎ *853/2831–3193* ✍ *Reservations essential* ⏲ *Closed Tues.*

$$ MACANESE 🍴 **Litoral.** In tastefully decorated environs with whitewashed walls and dark-wood beams, one of the most popular local restaurants serves authentic Macanese dishes that are simple, straightforward, and deliciously satisfying. Must-try dishes include the tamarind pork with shrimp paste, as well as codfish baked with potato and garlic, and a Portuguese vegetable cream soup. For dessert, try the *bebinca de leite,* a coconut-milk custard, or the traditional egg pudding, *pudim abade de priscos.* Variously priced set menus are also available, and reservations are recommended on weekends. [$] *Average main: MOP$180* ✉ *261 Rua do Almirante Sergio, Inner Harbour* ☎ *853/2896–7878* 🌐 *www.restaurante-litoral.com.*

## COLOANE

$$ PORTUGUESE 🍴 **Restaurante Espaço Lisboa.** Portuguese-owned and with a Portuguese chef, this is a favorite among local Portuguese, occupying a converted two-story house with a small but pleasant outdoor balcony overlooking

Coloane Village. Menu highlights include codfish cakes, savory duck rice, monkfish rice, boiled bacalhau with cabbage, sausage flambé, steak topped with ham and fried egg, and smoked ham imported from Portugal. Take your pick from an extensive list of hearty Portuguese wines, and finish the meal with homemade mango ice cream with a cherry flambé. [$] *Average main: MOP$200* ✉ *8 Rua das Gaivotas, Coloane Island West* ☎ *853/2888–2226* ⊙ *No lunch.*

$$ PORTUGUESE Fodor's Choice ★ 🍴 **Restaurante Fernando.** Everyone in Hong Kong and Macau knows about Fernando's, but the vine-covered entrance close to Hác-Sá Beach is difficult to spot. The open-air dining pavilion and bar have attracted beachgoers for years now, and the enterprising Fernando has built a legendary reputation for his Portuguese fare. The menu focuses on seafood paired with homegrown vegetables, and diners choose from among the bottles of Portuguese reds on display rather than from a wine list or opt for the beloved sangria. The informal nature of the restaurant fits in with the satisfying, home-style food such as grilled fish, baked chicken, and huge bowlfuls of spicy clams, all eaten with your fingers and washed down with crisp vinho verde. [$] *Average main: MOP$150* ✉ *Hác-Sá Beach 9, Coloane Island South* ☎ *853/2888–2531* 🌐 *www.fernando-restaurant.com* ✍ *Reservations not accepted* 💳 *No credit cards.*

## WHERE TO STAY

### DOWNTOWN MACAU

$$ HOTEL 🏨 **Hotel Lisboa.** In Macau's infamous landmark, redolent with history and intrigue, labyrinthine hallways and salons display jade and artworks, and an ostentatiously gilded staircase leads to luxurious guestrooms with hardwood floors and Jacuzzi baths. [$] *Rooms from: MOP$1850* ✉ *2–4 Av. de Lisboa, Downtown* ☎ *853/2888–3888* 🌐 *www.hotelisboa.com* 🛏 *950 rooms, 50 suites.*

$$ HOTEL Fodor's Choice ★ 🏨 **MGM Macau.** Rooms are everything you'd expect in the way of comfort and elegance from a luxury accommodation, with decor adhering to a muted cream, brown, and beige color palette, but it's the classy world around them that distinguishes this hotel from the rest. **Pros:** tasteful architecture; fine artwork; refined dining and lounge options. **Cons:** inseparable from the casino, which can get smoky and loud; high-traffic location. [$] *Rooms from: MOP$1788* ✉ *Av. Dr. Sun Yat Sen, Downtown* ☎ *853/8802–8888* 🌐 *mgmmacau.com* 🛏 *468 rooms, 99 suites, 15 villas.*

### MACAU OUTER HARBOUR

$$ HOTEL 🏨 **Sands Macao.** The Sands is nothing if not luxurious, with spacious rooms that have deep, soft carpets, large beds, and huge marble bathrooms with Jacuzzis. **Pros:** heated outdoor pool; across the street from Fisherman's Wharf. **Cons:** not as new as the Venetian; near lots of vehicle traffic. [$] *Rooms from: MOP$1698* ✉ *203 Largo de Monte Carlo, Outer Harbour* ☎ *853/2888–3388* 🌐 *www.sands.com.mo* 🛏 *238 suites, 51 VIP suites.*

### MACAU INNER HARBOUR

$$$$

B&B/INN

Fodor'sChoice

★

⌂ **Pousada de São Tiago.** This romantic lodging's origins as a 17th-century fortress permeate every corner, from the tunnel-like entrance to 12 modern luxury suites, each with Jacuzzi bathrooms and large balconies for room-service breakfast. **Pros:** all the modern comfort of a luxury hotel; complimentary minibar and WiFi; intimate, sunset views of the Inner Harbour. **Cons:** small pool; limited facilities; you'll need to call a taxi to go out and, even then, it's hit or miss. $ *Rooms from: MOP$3000* ⊠ *Fortaleza de São Tiago da Barra, Av. da República, Inner Harbour* ☎ *853/2837–8111* ⊕ *www.saotiago.com.mo* ⇨ *12 suites.*

### TAIPA

$$$

HOTEL

Fodor'sChoice

★

⌂ **Altira.** Towering over northern Taipa, the Altira offers stunning sea views of the Macau Peninsula from each and every room, each one like a suite, with a dedicated lounge, walk-in wardrobe, and circular stone bath. **Pros:** panoramic-view pool; open-air rooftop bar. **Cons:** may sometimes be noisy from nearby construction; still a taxi (or shuttle) ride from the peninsula. $ *Rooms from: MOP$1888* ⊠ *Av. de Kwong Tung, Taipa* ☎ *853/2886–8888* ⊕ *www.altiramacau.com* ⇨ *284 rooms, 24 suites, 8 villas.*

### COLOANE

$$

RESORT

FAMILY

Fodor'sChoice

★

⌂ **Westin Resort.** This is where you truly get away from it all: built into the side of a cliff, every room faces the ocean, and the vast private terraces are ideal for alfresco dining and afternoon naps. **Pros:** green surroundings on Hác-Sá Beach; golf-club access; fun for kids. **Cons:** isolated location; limited access. $ *Rooms from: MOP$1150* ⊠ *1918 Estrada de Hác Sá, Coloane Island South* ☎ *853/2887–1111, 800/228–3000 in Hong Kong* ⊕ *www.starwoodhotels.com/westin* ⇨ *200 rooms, 8 suites.*

## NIGHTLIFE

Old movies, countless novels, and gossip through the years have portrayed Macau's nightlife as a combustible mix of drugs, wild gambling, violent crime, and ladies of the night. Up until the 1999 handover back to mainland China, this image of Macau was mostly accurate, and worked to drive away tourists.

Outside of the casinos and a few restaurants, today's Macau shuts down after 11 pm. You can slip into any dark, elegant lounge bar inside the larger hotels and enjoy live music and expensive cocktails, but don't expect much energy or big crowds. And most late-night saunas are glorified brothels, with "workers" from China, Vietnam, Thailand, and Russia. Because casino-hotel lounges often double as coffee shops in the morning or around midday, some "nightlife" hot spots may open as early as 7 am.

### CASINOS

Gambling is lightly regulated, so there are only a few things to remember. No one under age 18 is allowed into casinos. Most casinos use Hong Kong dollars in their gaming and not Macau patacas, but you can easily exchange currencies at cashiers. High- and no-limit VIP rooms are

Rickshaws await the gamblers leaving the Casino Lisboa, the gambling den that started it all.

available on request, where minimum bets range from HK$50,000 to HK$100,000 per hand. You can get cash from credit cards and ATMs 24 hours a day, and every casino has a program to extend additional credit to frequent visitors. Most casinos don't have strict dress codes outside of their VIP rooms, but men are better off not wearing shorts or sleeveless shirts. Minimum bets for most tables are higher than those in Las Vegas, but there are lower limits for slots and video gambling.

The players here may not look sophisticated, but don't be fooled. Many of Macau's gamblers are truly hard-core. Average bets are in the hundreds per hand, and many people gamble until they're completely exhausted or completely broke, usually the latter.

**DOWNTOWN**

**Casino Lisboa.** Welcome to the casino that started it all. Opened in 1965 by Dr. Stanley Ho, this iconic Macau gaming den is replete with ancient jade ships in the halls, gilded staircases, and more baccarat tables than you can shake a craps stick at. It's great for a few rounds of dai-siu—dice bets over cups of iced green tea. Most of the gamblers are from neighboring Guangdong province, and Cantonese is the lingua franca. Other popular pastimes at this storied casino revolve around international fine-dining venues and colorful coffee shops, if you care to wander around a maze of marbled floors and low ceilings. ⊠ *Av. de Lisboa, Downtown* ☎ *853/2888–3888* ⊕ *www.hotelisboa.com.*

**Galaxy StarWorld.** As you enter the StarWorld empire you're greeted by tall girls in high heels, while a mariachi band serenades you from across the lobby. The gaming floors are small and have a couple of Chinese-style diners if you get peckish, but the cool Whisky Bar (⇨ *After*

*Dark)* on the 16th floor of the adjacent hotel is an atmospheric place to either begin or wind down your evening. The neon-blue building is just across from the Wynn and down the block from the MGM Grand. Live lobby entertainment and local holiday attractions add a kitschy, friendly feel. ⊠ *Av. da Amizade, Downtown* ☎ *853/2838–3838* ⊕ *www.starworldmacau.com.*

**Grand Lisboa.** With more than 300 tables and about 750 slot machines, the main gaming floor is anchored with a glowing egg statue and a leggy Paris cabaret show every 15 minutes. The second floor features craps and sports betting, and has a great bar. The Grand also has a variety of dining choices, from the baroque Don Alfonso 1890 to the Round-the-Clock Coffee Shop between the first and second gaming floors. If the slots have been kind, head up to the Grand Lisboa's crown jewel — the three-Michelin-starred Robuchon au Dôme on the 43rd floor. ⊠ *2–4 Av. de Lisboa, Downtown* ☎ *853/2838–2828* ⊕ *www.grandlisboa.com.*

**MGM Macau.** A stylish part of Macau's gambling scene offers lavish lounges, Dale Chihuly glass sculptures, Portuguese-inspired architecture, and fine dining. The gambling floor itself is popular with high rollers from Hong Kong, including business tycoons who are just in for a few days, and one of the owners, Pansy Ho (like her brother Lawrence Ho), is the daughter of Macau's "gambling godfather," Dr. Stanley Ho. She is a high-octane business professional in her own right and a woman's classy touch shows up in this place's glitz-and-glam energy and high-society appeal. ⊠ *Av. Dr. Sun Yat Sen, Downtown* ☎ *853/8802–8888* ⊕ *www.mgmmacau.com.*

Fodor's Choice ★ **Sands Macao.** The Sands Macao was the largest casino on earth until its sibling, the Venetian, stole the spotlight. It's the first casino you'll see on the peninsula even before debarking from the ferry. Past the sparkling 50-ton chandelier over the entrance, the grand gaming floor is anchored with a live cabaret stage above an open bar and under a giant screen. Several tiers are tastefully linked with escalators leading to the high-stakes tables upstairs. The friendly atmosphere and handy location, just across from Fisherman's Wharf and near the bar street in NAPE, makes this place a good choice for a warm-up to your night out. ⊠ *203 Largo de Monte Carlo, Downtown* ☎ *853/2888–3333* ⊕ *www.sands.com.mo.*

Fodor's Choice ★ **Wynn Macau.** Listen for theme songs such as "Diamonds are Forever," "Luck Be a Lady," or "Money, Money" as Wynn's outdoor Performance Lake dazzles you with flames and fountain jets of whipping water every 15 minutes from 11 am to midnight. Inside the "open hand" structure of Steve Wynn's Macau resort, the indoor Rotunda Tree of Prosperity also wows guests with feng shui glitz. Wynn's expansive, brightly lit gaming floor, fine dining, buffet meals, luxury shops, deluxe spa, and trendy suites make this one of the more swish resorts in Macau. ⊠ *Rua Cidade de Sintra, Downtown* ☎ *853/2888–9966* ⊕ *www.wynnmacau.com.*

**TAIPA**

Fodor's Choice ★ **Altira Macau.** Touting itself as Macau's first "six-star" integrated resort, the Altira is indeed stellar. The only classy casino on the island of Taipa faces the glow of casinos to the north on the peninsula and offers swank, '70s-style gaming floors decked out in browns and taupes with mod-style chandeliers. The selection of game play is abundant, from baccarat to straight-up slots to posh VIP gaming rooms. The VIP resort suites, fine-dining, and elegantly discreet 38 Lounge on the roof add to the overall ambience. ⊠ *Av. de Kwong Tung, Taipa* ☎ *853/2886–8888* ⊕ *www.altiramacau.com.*

Fodor'sChoice ★ **Venetian Macao-Resort-Hotel.** The Macau Venetian is twice the size of its namesake in Las Vegas, offering gambling, shopping, eating, and sleeping, along with faux-Renaissance decoration, built-in canals plied by crooning gondoliers, live carnival acts, plenty of sheer spectacle, and more than a touch of pretension. The 534,000-square-foot gaming floor has some 2,000 slot machines and more than 550 tables of casino favorites. The sprawling property also includes nearly 3,000 suites, a 15,000-seat arena, and the multi-purpose Venetian Theater. It's no wonder the Venetian is the must-see megacomplex that everyone's talking about. ⊠ *Estrada da Baía de N. Senhora da Esperança, Cotai* ☎ *853/2882–8888* ⊕ *www.venetianmacao.com.*

## SHOPPING

Macau, like Hong Kong, is a free port for most items, which leads to lower prices for electronics, jewelry, and clothing than other international cities. But the experience is completely different, with a low-key atmosphere, small crowds, and compact areas. It is a hub for traditional Chinese arts, crafts, and even some antiques (but be aware that there are many high-quality reproductions in the mix, too). Macau's major shopping district is along its main street in the downtown area, Avenida Almeida Ribeiro, more commonly known by its Chinese name, **San Ma Lo**; there are also shops downtown on **Rua Dos Mercadores** and its side streets; in **Cinco de Outubro**; and on the **Rua do Campo.**

Most of Macau's shops operate year-round with a short break in late January for Chinese New Year and are open from 10 am to 8 pm and later on weekends. While most shops accept all major credit cards, specialty discount shops usually ask for cash, and street vendors accept only cash. For most street vendors and some smaller stores, some friendly bargaining is expected; ask for the "best price," which ideally produces instant discounts of 10%–20%. The shopping mantra here is "bargain hard, bargain often."

# PEARL RIVER DELTA

# WELCOME TO PEARL RIVER DELTA

## TOP REASONS TO GO

★ **Feel the buzz:** This region is the engine driving China's economic boom, and whether you're in older Guangzhou or the "instant city" of neon-lit Shenzhen you're sure to feel the buzz of a communist nation on a capitalist joyride.

★ **Explore the ancient:** Though thoroughly modern, the Pearl River Delta has not lost touch with its ancient roots. From the temples of Guangzhou to the Ming Dynasty walled city of Dapeng in Shenzhen, this is a journey through the centuries.

★ **Soak up some colonial splendor:** Guangzhou's architecture dates back to the 19th century, when European merchants amassed fortunes in the opium trade, and the buildings from which they once plied their trade still stand on Shamian Island.

★ **Culinary treats:** You can sample a rich variety of foods in the Pearl River Delta from classic Cantonese fare such as dim sum and wonton noodles to seafood fresh from the neighboring South China Sea.

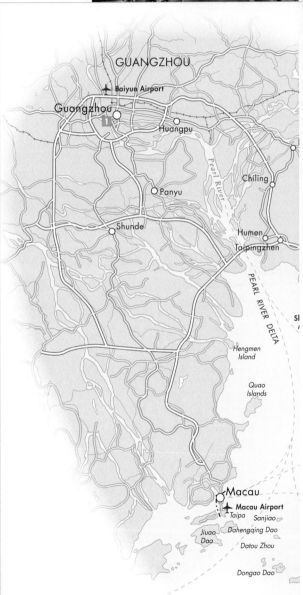

**1** Guangzhou. After you've adjusted to the crowds, traffic, and pollution, turn to the city's unique cuisine, sights, culture, and history, such as Colonial Shamian and the nearby Baiyun Mountain, where there's a panoramic view of the city from the cable car.

**2** Shenzhen. Come to Shenzhen for excellent local shopping and dining at affordable prices. Or head to Overseas Chinese Town to take in some art and culture. The city, directly over the border from Hong Kong, offers a variety of top-notch golf courses. The city's Mission Hills Golf Club promises to blow your mind.

## GETTING ORIENTED

The Pearl River Delta is a massive triangle. Guangzhou is at the top and Shenzhen on the east corner. The area as a whole is just a bit too spread out for any one corner to make a good base of operations from which to explore the others. We recommend beginning at one corner and making your way around. Guangzhou is fairly dense, so leave yourself at least three days in which to soak it all in before heading down to Shenzhen, where you should spend a day and night shopping, eating, and enjoying the spa before heading to Hong Kong.

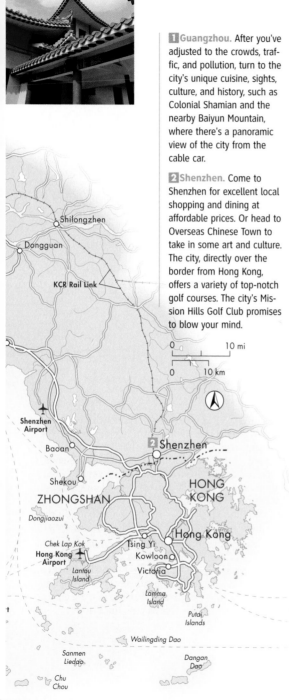

Updated by
Amy Wu

Why visit the Pearl River Delta? History enthusiasts head to Guangzhou, Guangdong Province's ancient capital and the historic center of Cantonese culture. Gourmands flock to both Guangzhou and Shenzhen to indulge in some of the best examples of contemporary Chinese cuisine. Culture vultures take in the many temples, shrines, and museums scattered throughout the region. A visit to the Pearl River Delta will quickly dismiss any lingering notions that China is still a nation bound by the tenets of Marx and Mao.

The hard-working Pearl River Delta is one of China's fastest-growing and most affluent regions. With a GDP that outranks that of Saudi Arabia, Guangdong Province has been the industrial engine powering China's meteoric economic rise. It's also among China's most polluted regions, and that's saying a lot. From the southern suburbs of Guangzhou city to the northern edge of Shenzhen, industry stretches in all directions. Tens of thousands of factories churn out the lion's share of the world's consumer products. This hyper-industry has polluted the entire area's soil, water, and air so badly that in Hong Kong (on the region's southern tip) pollution is an overriding public concern.

But much has changed in recent years as municipal governments struggle to upgrade the quality of life for residents and visitors. Pollution levels are slowly improving as some factories are being shuttered or moved inland. Guangzhou's clean and efficient subway system has been expanded. In Shenzhen the subway system doubled in size at the end of 2011, and several new lines were under construction in 2013.

## PLANNING

### WHEN TO GO

The best time to go is spring and autumn, when temperatures and humidity are much lower than in the summer, but this is complicated by a few factors. Unless you have friends in the hotel industry, don't even think about visiting Guangzhou during the annual China Import and Export Fair typically held in April and May, when hotel prices double or triple. Don't travel anywhere in China during the Golden Week holiday, which takes place annually from October 1 through 7. And avoid China during Lunar New Year, generally in February, as the trains and buses and packed with workers headed home for the holidays. In addition, many businesses are closed. So what do we recommend? September, October (excluding Golden Week), and early to mid-November.

### GETTING HERE AND AROUND

The best way to get around the Pearl River Delta is by train and bus. With a little assistance from your hotel, you should be just fine.

#### AIR TRAVEL

With Hong Kong, Macau, and Shenzhen all in such close proximity, the Pearl River Delta airspace is one of the most heavily trafficked in the world. This will give you plenty of options, depending on where you are flying in from and where you want to go. Flying from another mainland city to Shenzhen or Zhuhai is usually cheaper than flying to Hong Kong or Macau. Cathay Pacific out of Hong Kong is one of the best airlines going, and can get you around the Southeast Asia region or further abroad, while Shenzhen Air and China Southern are quality mainland airlines linking Shenzhen and Zhuhai with many other cities throughout China. The major airports are the Baiyun International Airport north of Guangzhou, and Bao'an Shenzhen International Airport northwest of Shenzhen.

#### BUS TRAVEL

Bus travel through the area can often be the best way to go, although it can be complicated for the uninitiated. At the Guangzhou main railway station, where metro Lines 2 and 5 cross, you can go to the Guangdong Automobile Long Distance Bus Station and catch buses to most other cities in the Pearl River Delta. There is an English-speaking ticket window for foreigners, and all the waiting areas have the names of the destinations in pinyin. Your hotel might be able to help you by writing a detailed note about where you want to go.

#### CAR TRAVEL

You can't legally drive yourself in China, but you could hire a driver for around Y500–Y600 per day and up, depending on whether the driver speaks English and what kind of car you want.

#### TRAIN TRAVEL

It is quick and easy to get from Guangzhou to Shenzhen or Hong Kong by train. Rail service has come a long way, and the Guangzhou-Kowloon Express Train lives up to its name. The train features comfortable seats with ample leg space. Tickets can be purchased at travel agencies such as China Travel Service or at the station. By around 2015 there will be a high-speed rail train that burrows under Hong Kong's Kowloon district, cuts through Shenzhen, and terminates in Guangzhou that should cut travel times between the two major hubs considerably.

## HEALTH AND SAFETY

Take the usual precautions against appearing conspicuously wealthy, and carry with you only the amount of cash you need. Crowded places, such as bus and train stations, often harbor pickpockets, so keep your eyes on your bags and your wallet in your front pocket. If you see a local wearing a backpack on the front of his or her body, it's probably a good idea to do the same.

## MONEY MATTERS

ATMs abound in the more developed areas of Guangzhou and Shenzhen, and most take foreign cards, so getting cash is relatively simple. A wide range of hotels and stores now accept credit cards.

## RESTAURANTS

Most Cantonese dishes are stir-fried or steamed, although roasted meats such as barbecued chicken and pork are also popular. A Cantonese mid-morning favorite is dim sum, consisting of bite-sized dishes like dumplings, steamed buns, and pastries. Filled with meat and vegetables, they are a perfect way to start the day, and many traditional dim sum places stop serving by mid-afternoon. In Cantonese culture, dim sum on weekends is a family affair.

While Guangzhou is more of a Cantonese-food capital, you can find many other types of food in Shenzhen. Since the city is growing so quickly, most residents are from elsewhere in China, and Hunan, Sichuan, Jiangsu and Fujian-style dishes can be found easily. Also, more specific styles of food such as Chiu Chow, with its seafood porridges and fish-ball soups, and Hakka, with its more home-style soups and excellent tofu dishes, are plentiful.

*Prices in the reviews are the average cost of a main course at dinner or, if dinner is not served, at lunch.*

## HOTELS

Over the past few years, the hotel scene in Guangzhou and Shenzhen has grown rapidly, with local hotels providing reasonably priced lodgings and international chains dominating the high end of the market. English is now spoken at many mid-priced hotels, and at luxury hotels the staff often speak excellent English.

*Prices in the reviews are the lowest cost of a standard double room in high season.*

## VISITOR INFORMATION

While China is a large tourist destination, visitor information facilities are not widely available. The best place to check for information is online at China-specific travel websites or on places like the Fodors. com forum for the latest information.

## TOURS

**Splendid Tours** (缤纷旅游 *Bīnfēn xíng*). Hong Kong–based Splendid Tours runs good Shenzhen and Guangzhou tours. The company can also arrange same-day service for single-entry or multiple-entry visas into China. ✉ *Sheraton Hong Kong Hotel & Towers, 20 Nathan Rd., 2nd fl., Kowloon, Hong Kong* ☎ *852/2316–2151* ⊕ *www.splendid.hk.*

**China Travel Service Limited** (香港中国旅行社*Xiānggǎng Zhōngguó lǚxíngshè*). CTS can arrange just about any type of travel in the Pearl River Delta. With more than 40 locations in and around Hong Kong, CTS has an efficient staff that can assist with everything from securing visas to booking hotel rooms. ☎ *852/2853–3533, 852/2522–0450* ⊕ *www.ctshk.com* ⊗ *Weekdays 9–7; Sat. 9–5; Sun. 9:30–12:30 and 2–5.*

# GUANGZHOU

*120 km (74½ miles; 1½ hrs) north of Hong Kong.*

Guangzhou (also known as Canton), the capital of Guangdong Province, is both a modern boomtown and an ancient port city. This metropolis of more than 13 million people has all the expected accoutrements of a competitive, modern Chinese city: skyscrapers, heavy traffic, efficient metro, and serious crowds. Guangzhou is an old city with a long history. Exploring its riverfront, parks, temples, and markets, one is constantly reminded of the impact its irrepressible culture, language, and cuisine has made on the world.

In the early 20th century Guangzhou was a hotbed of revolutionary zeal, first as the birthplace of the movement to overthrow the last dynasty (culminating in the 1911 Revolution), and then as a battleground between Nationalists and Communists in the years leading to the 1949 Communist Revolution. Following the open-door policy of Deng Xiaoping in 1979, the port city was able to resume its role as a commercial gateway to China.

The Asian Games in 2010 spurred the city to extend the subway system, clean up ramshackle neighborhoods, and institute air-pollution controls. Guangzhou's parks, temples, winding old-quarter backstreets, and river islets are pleasant places to explore.

## GETTING HERE AND AROUND

Most travelers enter Guangzhou either by train or plane. Long-distance trains pull in at two railway stations, the Guangzhou Railway Station and the Guangzhou East Station. The East Station has a handy connection to the city's subway system. One-way tickets to or from Hong Kong cost in the ballpark of Y190.

Guangzhou is connected to Shenzhen, approximately 100 km (62 miles) to the south, by the aptly named Guangzhou–Shenzhen Express Train. Tickets cost Y75 to Y100, depending on the class of service.

AIR TRAVEL Guangzhou's Baiyun International Airport currently offers at least five flights per day to Hong Kong and around 10 to Beijing. The airport has direct flights to Paris, London, Moscow, Singapore, Bangkok, Sydney, Jakarta, and Phnom Penh, and a number of cities in North America including Los Angeles.

BOAT TRAVEL One of the best ways to see Guangzhou is to take a nighttime Pearl River Delta Cruise offered by the Zhujiang Yeyou Company. The two-hour

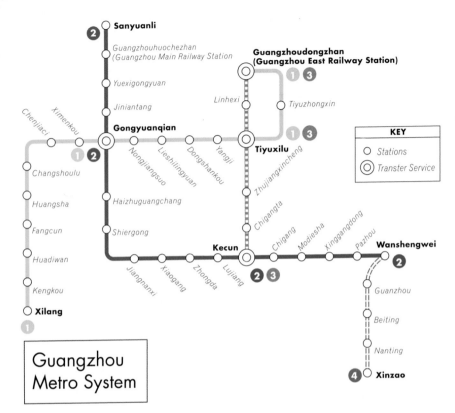

Guangzhou
Metro System

ride passes all of the city's major sites, including Shamian Island, Ersha Island, and the Canton Tower. Guangzhou's ever-growing number of bridges is a pretty accompaniment to an already colorful skyline. Ticket price includes reserved seating and tea.

BUS TRAVEL Guangzhou Provincial Passenger Bus Station is the largest bus station in Guangdong Province. Buses depart from here daily to the neighboring Guangxi, Hunan, Fujian, and Jiangxi provinces. There are also deluxe buses to Shenzhen, Hong Kong, and Macau. The easiest way from Guangzhou to Hong Kong is by the deluxe bus. Buses also depart from the Guangzhou Main Train Station for many areas throughout Guangdong and elsewhere in China.

SUBWAY TRAVEL The metro system is the fastest, cheapest, and most efficient way to travel around Guangzhou. The underground network currently has six lines connecting more than 98 stations. Tickets range from Y2 for short trips to Y14 for the longest leg.

TAXI TRAVEL Although taxis in Guangzhou are cheap and plentiful, traffic can sometimes be a nightmare, as it is in most major Chinese cities. Make sure you have the name of the destination written in Chinese.

TRAIN TRAVEL About a dozen express trains (Y234 first class, Y190 second class) depart daily for Guangzhou East Railway Station from Hong Kong's Kowloon Station. The trip takes about 1¾ hours. The last train back

CLOSE UP

## Guangzhou by Underground

Guangzhou's ever expanding subway system is cheap, clean, and (unlike Beijing's) reasonably efficient. It's divided into six lines that span both sides of the Pearl River, but most casual visitors will spend most of their time on Lines 1 and 2 (the red and yellow lines on the maps). The most interesting temples and shrines are within walking distance of stations along Line 1, with signs in English pointing the way.

The terminus of Line 1 is Gongyuanqian Station, where you'll find the

Guangzhou East Train Station. This area is also the heart of the Tianhe, Guangzhou's financial and business district and is close to Beijing Pedestrian Road, the hip, trendy shopping district. Gongyuanqian Station is also the transfer point for Lines 1 and 2.

English-language subway maps are available. Make sure to ask at your hotel. Consider buying the Transportation Smart Card, which costs Y10 and allows you to add money as you need it.

to Hong Kong leaves at 9:32 pm. Trains between Shenzhen's Luohu Railway Station and Guangzhou East Railway Station run every hour and cost between Y80 and Y100.

### SAFETY AND PRECAUTIONS
Foreigners who over-imbibe at clubs and bars can be the target of opportunists trying to separate you from your wallet, so watch how much you drink or stay with the group.

### TIMING
Two or three days in Guangzhou and two days in Shenzhen are probably enough to get a good taste of each city.

### REGIONAL TOURS
**GZL International Travel Service** (广之旅国际旅行社股份有限公司 *Guǎngzhīlǚ guójì lǚxíngshè gǔfèn yǒuxiàn gōngsī*). Guangzhou-based GZL International Travel Service has tours focusing on everything from nightlife to traditional medicine. ✉ *1 Lejia Rd., Jichang Rd. W* ☎ *020/8633–8680, 020/8634-6903* ⊕ *www.myorientours.com.*

### ESSENTIALS
**Air Contacts China Southern Airlines** (中国南方航空 *Zhōngguó nánfāng hángkōng*). ✉ *181 Huanshi Lu, near Guangzhou Railway Station* ☎ *020/40066–95539 24-hr hotline* ⊕ *www.csair.com.* **Guangzhou Baiyun International Airport** (ôôBái yúnguó jì jī cháng). ☎ *020/3606–6999, 020/8613-7273* ⊕ *www.baiyunairport.com.* **Zhuhai International Airport** (珠海国际机场 *Zhūhǎi guójì jīcháng*). ☎ *0756/777–1111* ⊕ *www.zhairport.com.*

**Banks HSBC** (汇丰银行 *Huìfēng yínháng*). ✉ *Garden Hotel, No. 368 Huan Shi Dong Lu* ☎ *020/8391–8133 outside China, 800/830–2880 from within China* ⊕ *www.hsbc.com.cn.* **Bank of China** (中国银行 *Zhōngguó yínháng*). ✉ *197 Dongfeng Xilu* ☎ *020/8333–8080* ⊕ *www.boc.cn.*

**Boat Contacts Bus Contacts Citybus** (城巴 *Chéng bā*). ☎ *0852/2873-0818* ⊕ *www.nwstbus.com.hk.* **Guangdong Long-Distance Provincial Bus Station**

(广东省汽车客运站 *Guǎngdōng shěng qìchē kèyùnzhàn*). The largest bus station in the Guangdong Province. ⊠ *145-149 West Huanshi Xi Lu* ☏ *020/8666-1297*. **Guangzhou Bus Station** (广州公车站 *Guǎngzhōu gōngchēzhàn*). ⊠ *158 Huanshi Xi Lu* ☏ *020/8668-4259*. **Tianhe Interstate Bus Terminal** (天河客运站 *Tiānhé kèyùnzhàn*). ⊠ *633 Yanling Lu, Tianhe District* ☏ *020/3708-5070* ⊕ *www. tianhebus.com*.

**Medical Assistance Shenzhen People's Hospital** ⊠ *1017 Dongmen Bei Lu N, Shenzhen* ☏ *0755/2553-3018, 1387 [Outpatient Dept.]*.

**Subway Contact Guangzhou Metro** (广州地铁 *Guǎngzhōu dìtiě*). ☏ *020/8328-9999* ⊕ *www.gzmtr.com*.

**Train Contacts Guangzhou East Railway Station** (广州东站 *Guǎngzhōu dōngzhàn*). ⊠ *Linhe Zhong Lu, Tianhe District* ☏ *020/6134-6222*. **Guangzhou Railway Station** (广州火车站 *Guǎngzhōu huǒchēzhàn*). ⊠ *159 Huanshixi Lu* ☏ *020/6135-7222*.

## EXPLORING

Guangzhou is a massive, sprawling metropolis divided into several districts and many more neighborhoods. Roughly speaking, the city is divided in half by the Pearl River, which runs from east to west and separates the Haizhu District (a large island) from the districts in the north. Most tourist destinations are north of the Pearl River.

### TOP ATTRACTIONS

**Bright Filial Piety Temple** (光孝寺 *Guāngxiào Sì*). Better known to locals as the Guangxiao Temple, this is the oldest and most charming Buddhist temple in Guangzhou. The gilded wooden laughing Buddha at the entrance heralds the temple's welcoming atmosphere. A huge bronze incense burner stands in the main courtyard. Beyond the main hall, noted for its ceiling of red-lacquer timbers, is another courtyard with several treasures, among them a small brick pagoda said to contain the tonsure hair of Hui-neng (the sixth patriarch of Chan Buddhism), and a couple of iron pagodas that are the oldest of their kind in China. Above them spread the leafy branches of a myrobalan plum tree and a banyan, called Buddha's Tree because it is said Hui-neng became enlightened in its shade. ⊠ *109 Guangxiao Lu, 2 blocks north of Ximenkou subway station, Liwan* 🚊 *Y10* ⊙ *Daily 6–5:30* Ⓜ *Ximenkou*.

**Canton Tower** (广州塔 *Guǎngzhōu tǎ*). Guangzhou's skyline wouldn't be as colorful without the Canton Tower, one of the world's tallest TV towers. The 108-story building—also known as the Guangzhou Ta—outstretches even Toronto's CN Tower. Resembling a thin champagne bottle, the building turns into a kaleidoscope of color at night. There are excellent photo opportunities on the observation decks and

A nighttime Zhujiang River cruise

a section of transparent floors where you can get an eagle's view of the cityscape. The tower features the world's tallest Ferris wheel, which has 16 transparent passenger cars. One revolution takes 30 minutes. There are also two revolving restaurants and a coffee shop. ✉ *222 Yuejiang West Lu, Haizhu District* ☎ *020/8933–8222* ⊕ *gztvtower.info* ✉ *Y50–Y150* ⊗ *Daily 9 am–10 pm.*

**Guangdong Museum of Art** (广东美术馆 *Guǎngdōng měishùguǎn*). This gallery regularly hosts the works of painters, sculptors, and other artists from around China and the world. With a dozen exhibition halls and a sculpture garden, the museum is located on Er Sha Island, which is also home to the Xinghai Concert Hall. One excellent way to enjoy the amazing architecture is by boat cruise. ✉ *38 Yanyu Lu, Er Sha Island* ☎ *020/8735–1468* ⊕ *www.gdmoa.org* ✉ *Free* ⊗ *Tues.–Sun. 9–5.*

**Museum of the Tomb of the Nan Yue King** (西汉南越王博物馆 *Xīhàn nányuèwáng bówùguǎn*). In 1983 bulldozers clearing ground for the China Hotel uncovered the intact tomb of Emperor Wen Di, who ruled Nan Yue (southern China) from 137 to 122 BC. The tomb was restored and its treasures placed in the adjoining Nan Yue Museum. The tomb contained the skeletons of the king and 15 courtiers—guards, cooks, concubines, and a musician—who were buried alive to attend him in death. Also buried were several thousand funerary objects, clearly designed to show off the accomplishments of the southern empire. The tomb—built of stone slabs—is behind the museum and is remarkably compact. ✉ *867 Jiefang Bei Lu, around the corner from the China Hotel, Liwan* ☎ *020/3618–2920* ⊕ *www.gznywmuseum.org* ✉ *Y12* ⊗ *Daily 9–5:30; last admission 4:45.*

Zhenhai Tower, in Yuexiu Park, was built 1380 and later incorporated into the city wall.

**Shamian Island** (沙面岛 *Shāmiàn dǎo*). More than a century ago the Mandarins of Guangzhou designated a 44-acre sandbank outside the city walls in the Pearl River as an enclave for foreign merchants. The foreigners had previously lived and done business in a row of houses known as the Thirteen Factories, near the present Shamian, but local resentment after the Opium Wars—sometimes leading to murderous attacks—made it prudent to confine them to a protected area, which was linked to the city by two bridges that were closed at 10 every night.

The island soon became a bustling township, as trading companies from Britain, the United States, France, Holland, Italy, Germany, Portugal, and Japan built stone mansions along the waterfront. With spacious gardens and private wharves, these served as homes, offices, and warehouses. There were churches for Catholics and Protestants, banks, a yacht club, football grounds, a cricket field, and the Victory hotel.

Shamian was attacked in the 1920s but survived until the 1949 Revolution, when its mansions became government offices or apartment houses and the churches were turned into factories. In recent years, however, the island has resumed much of its old character. Many colonial buildings have been restored, and churches like Our Lady of Lourdes Catholic Church have been beautifully renovated and reopened to worshippers.

Shamian is now a particularly popular place for expatriates to reside, as it has a relaxing atmosphere. Especially worth visiting is a park with shady walks and benches has been created in the center of the island, where local residents come to chat with friends, walk around with their caged birds, or practice tai chi .

**Sacred Heart Cathedral** (石室耶稣圣心主教坐堂 *Shíshì yēsū shèngxīntáng*). In the heart of the old city, this Catholic church is the seat of the archbishop of the Archdiocese of Guangzhou. The church is known to the locals as ShiShi, which translates as "Stone House." The Gothic-style cathedral was opened in 1863, and is one of the largest in Southeast Asia. Masses are popular with the city's expatriate community. ⊠ *56 Yide Lu, Yuexiu District* ☎ *020/8333–6761* Ⓜ *Haizhu Square.*

**NEED A BREAK?**

**Shamian Island Blenz Coffee.** Enjoy an espresso or latte in Chinese colonial splendor at this coffee house in a building dating back to the late Qing Dynasty. Comfy couches, strong coffee, and free Internet access are available in this café inside an old building that housed Guangzhou's U.S. Bank in the pre-revolutionary days. ⊠ *46 Shamian Ave.* ☎ *020/8121–5052.*

**Sun Yat-sen Memorial Hall** (孙中山纪念堂 *Sūn Zhōngshān jìniàn tàng*). This handsome pavilion stands in a garden behind a bronze statue of the leader. Built in 1929–31 with funds mostly from overseas Chinese, the building is a classic octagon, with sweeping roofs of blue tiles over carved wooden eaves and verandas of red-lacquer columns. The Memorial Hall is split into four grand buildings, and includes an auditorium with seating for 5,000. Worth noting are the golden characters reading *Tian Xia Wei Gong* ("Peace and Harmony Universally") on the front door. ⊠ *Jiefang Lu, Yuexiu District* 🚇 *Y5–10* ☉ *Daily 8–6* Ⓜ *Sun Yat-Sen Memorial Hall.*

**7**

**Temple of the Six Banyan Trees** (六榕寺 *Lùróng sì*). Look at any ancient scroll painting or lithograph by early Western travelers, and you'll see two landmarks rising above old Guangzhou. One is the minaret of the mosque; the other is the 56-meter (184-foot) pagoda of the Six Banyan Temple. Still providing an excellent lookout, the pagoda appears to have nine stories, each with doorways and encircling balconies. Inside, however, there are 17 levels. Thanks to its arrangement of colored, carved roofs, it is popularly known as the Flowery Pagoda. The temple was founded in the 5th century, but because of a series of fires, most of the existing buildings date from the 11th century. It was built by the Zen master Tanyu, and is still a very active place of worship, with a community of monks and regular attendance by Zen Buddhists. It was originally called Purificatory Wisdom Temple, but changed its name after a visit by the Song Dynasty poet Su Dongpo, who was so delighted by six banyan trees growing in the courtyard that he left an inscription with the characters for six banyans. ⊠ *87 Liurong Lu, south of Yuexiu Park, Liwan* ☎ *020/8339–2843* 🚇 *Y5–10* ☉ *Daily 8:30–5.*

**WORTH NOTING**

**Chen Clan Academy** (陈家祠 *Chénjiā cí*). The Chen family is one of the Pearl River Delta's oldest clans. In the late 19th century local members, who had become rich merchants, decided to build a memorial temple. They invited contributions from the Chens—and kindred Chans—who had emigrated overseas. Money flowed in from 72 countries, and no expense was spared. One of the temple's highlights is a huge ridgepole frieze. It stretches 90 feet along the main roof and depicts scenes from

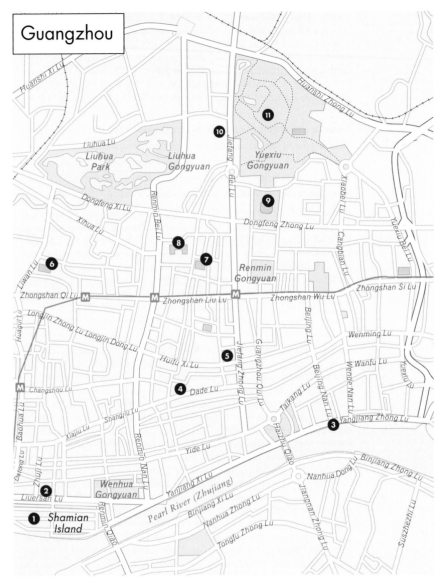

Guangzhou

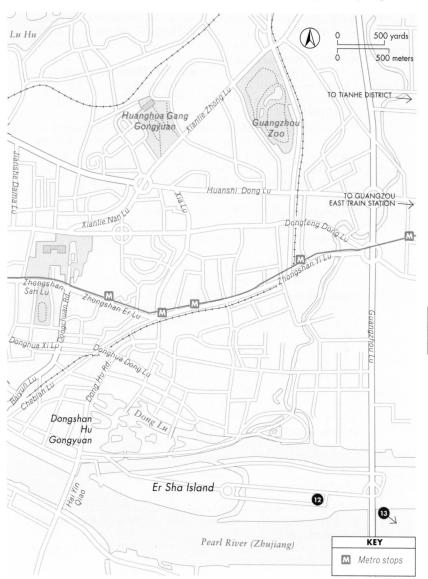

KEY

Ⓜ Metro stops

the epic *Romance of Three Kingdoms,* with thousands of figures against a backdrop of ornate houses, monumental gates, and lush scenery. Elsewhere in the huge compound of pavilions and courtyards are friezes of delicately carved stone and wood, ceramic sculptures, fine iron castings, and a dazzling altar covered with gold leaf. The temple also houses a folk-arts museum and shop that sells handicrafts of the local province. ☒ *7 Zhongshan Qi Lu, Liwan* 🕿 *Y15* ⊗ *Daily 8:30–5:20* Ⓜ *Chen Clan Academy Station.*

Fodor's Choice ★ **Five Celestials Shrine (五仙观** *Wŭxīan guàn).* According to local legend, a quintet of gods in the form of goats blessed the city with rice and bountiful harvest. This temple was built to celebrate the origin of Guangzhou's name, which means "City of Goats." Bring your passport to gain admission. ☒ *Huifu West Lu, Yuexiu District* 🕿 *020/8332–3508* 🕿 *Free* ⊗ *Tues.–Fri. 9–5; weekends 8:30–5:30* Ⓜ *Gongyuanqian.*

**Qingping Market (清平市场** *Qīngpíng shìchǎng).* This market has always had a good selection of knickknacks, as well as a large section of medicinal goods (ginseng, fungi, and the like). The older outdoor section of the market still exists, but a large section of the old market has been cleared away to make room for a mall dedicated to traditional medicines. ☒ *Qingping Lu and Tiyun Lu* ⊕ *Huangsha.*

FAMILY **Yuexiu Park (越秀公园** *Yuèxiù gōngyuán).* Guangzhou's largest park covers 247 rolling acres and includes landscaped gardens, artificial lakes, an Olympic-sized swimming pool, an amusement park, and playgrounds. The famous Sculpture of Five Rams (五羊塑像*Wŭyáng sùxiang)* celebrates the legend of the five celestials who appeared riding on goats to bring grain to the people. Another must-see is the Zhenhai Tower, now converted into a museum featuring archaeological findings in Guangzhou. ☒ *Jiefang Bei Lu, across from China Hotel, Liwan* 🕿 *020/8666–1950* ⊕ *www.yuexiupark-gz.com* 🕿 *Free* ⊗ *Daily 6 am–11 pm* Ⓜ *Yuexiu Park.*

**Zhujiang Yeyou Company (珠江夜游** *Zhūjiāng yèyóu)* ☒ *Tianzhi Wharf, Central Riverside Rd., northern bank of the Pearl River, Yuexiu District* 🕿 *020/8366–1476* ⊕ *www.zhujiangyeyou.com.cn* 🕿 *Y80–Y150.*

## WHERE TO EAT

The city is famous both in and outside of China for its fresh and diverse selection of seafood, due to its close proximity to the South China Sea. Amazing braised and barbecued meats are available in delicious variety, and succulent dim sum still rules the roost as the city's hometown favorite.

Guangzhou has numerous Indian, Italian, Thai, and Vietnamese restaurants, and owing to the recent influx of Middle Eastern traders, in some parts of town it's easier to find a falafel than a shrimp dumpling.

*Use the coordinate (⊕ B2) at the end of each listing to locate a site on the Where to Eat and Stay in Guangzhou map.*

$$$ CANTONESE ✕ **Bei Yuan Cuisine (北园酒家** *Běiyuán jiŭjiā).* Worth a visit for the decor alone, Bei Yuan is a throwback to 1928, the year the restaurant opened. The two-story dining room wraps around a traditional Chinese

courtyard and includes a well-manicured garden and a pond with gold-fish. The restaurant's interior is jazzed up with Chinese screens, lanterns and chandeliers. The menu—specializing in Cantonese cuisine and dim sum—is on the pricier side (Y31 for a bowl of wonton noodles) but it's well worth the experience and photo-taking opportunities. $ *Average main: Y100* ⊠ *202 Xiaobei Lu, Yuexiu District* ☎ *020/8356–3365* ⌕ *Reservations essential* ⊘ *Closed Sun.* ✛ *D2.*

**$$$$**
**EUROPEAN**
✕ **The Connoisseur** (名仕阁 *Míngshì gé*). With its arched columns, gilded capitals, gold-framed mirrors, lustrous drapes, and immaculate table settings, this top-notch restaurant feels like Regency-era France. The menu has become decidedly more European as of late, with non-French items such as Irish stew now included. The menu changes every six months or so. $ *Average main: Y300* ⊠ *Garden Hotel, 368 Huanshi Dong Lu, 3rd fl.* ☎ *020/8333–8989* ⊕ *www2.thegardenhotel.com.cn* ⌕ *Reservations essential* ⌂ *Jacket and tie* ⊘ *No lunch* ✛ *F2.*

**$**
**CANTONESE**
✕ **Datong Restaurant** (大同酒店 *Dàtóng jiǔdiàn*). Occupying all eight stories of an old riverfront building with an open terrace on the top floor, this restaurant is popular with locals all hours of the day, so arrive early to be guaranteed a seat. The atmosphere is chaotic and noisy, but the morning and afternoon dim sum is well worth it, especially for the low prices. Famous dishes include stewed chicken feet (delicious, we'll have you know), crispy-skin chicken, and roasted duck. $ *Average main: Y40* ⊠ *Nanfang Dasha, 63 Yanjiang Xi Lu, Colonial Canton* ☎ *020/8188–8447* ✛ *C5.*

**$$$$**
**INTERNATIONAL**
**FAMILY**
✕ **Four Seas International House** (四海一家 *Sìhǎi yījiā*). Famous for its massive buffet, this colorful place offers a memorable culinary and cultural experience. It can be easy to get lost among the hundreds of food stations, which have themes that match the cuisines—such as a sushi station shaped like a treasure ship. There's no need to reserve ahead, as seating is in more than 1,000 booths. $ *Average main: Y168* ⊠ *Yingbin Lu with intersection at 296 Provincial Lu, Panyu District* ☎ *020/3482–2266* ⌕ *Reservations essential* Ⓜ *Hanxi Changlong* ✛ *G6.*

**$$**
**CANTONESE**
✕ **Guangzhou Restaurant** (广州酒家 *Guǎngzhōu jiǔjiā*). Earning a string of culinary awards since it opened in 1936, this legendary place is one of the best-known restaurants in town. The setting is classic Canton, with flower-filled courtyards surrounded by dining rooms of various sizes. The food is some of the finest in the city, with house specialties like "Eight Treasures," a mix of poultry, pork, and mushrooms served in a bowl made of melon. Other Cantonese dishes include duck feet stuffed with shrimp, roasted goose, and of course, dim sum. Meals can be cheap or very expensive, depending on how exotic your tastes are. $ *Average main: Y150* ⊠ *2 Wenchang Nan Lu, Ancestral Guangzhou* ☎ *020/8138–0388* ✛ *B4.*

**$$$**
**ITALIAN**
✕ **The Italian Restaurant** (小街风情 *Xiǎojiē fēngqìng*). This aptly named eatery has a cheerful home-away-from-home feel, complete with flags from various countries hanging from the ceiling and beers from around the world. The food is inexpensive and good, with pizzas, pastas, and excellent brochette prepared by an Italian chef. Food from the menu is much better than the buffet, which is Y138 per person. $ *Average main:*

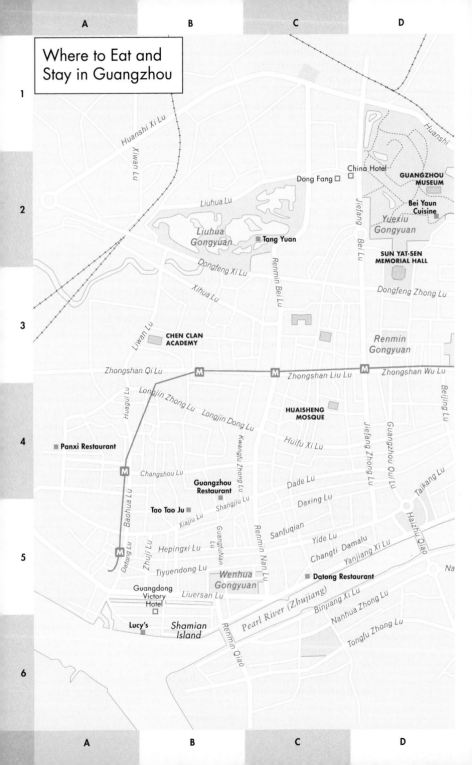

Where to Eat and Stay in Guangzhou

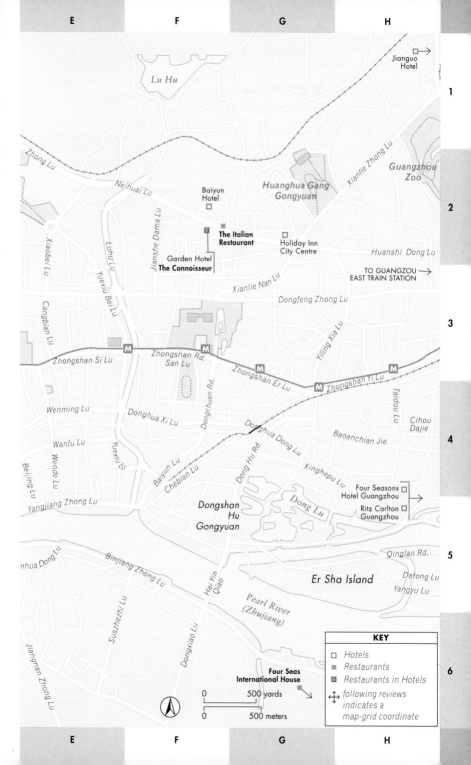

E F G H

1
2
3
4
5
6

Lu Hu

Jianguo Hotel

Zhong Lu

Neihuai Lu

Baiyun Hotel

Huanghua Gang Gongyuan

Xianlie Zhong Lu

Guangzhou Zoo

The Italian Restaurant

Holiday Inn City Centre

Huanshi Dong Lu

Garden Hotel
**The Connoisseur**

Jianshe Dama Lu

Luhu Lu

Yuexiu Bei Lu

Xiaobei Lu

Xianlie Nan Lu

TO GUANGZOU →
EAST TRAIN STATION

Dongfeng Zhong Lu

Cangbian Lu

Yiling Xia Lu

M

Zhongshan Si Lu

Zhongshan Rd.
San Lu

M

Zhongshan Er Lu

M

M

Zhongshan Yi Lu

M

Taidou Lu

Wenming Lu

Donghua Xi Lu

Dongchuan Rd.

Donghua Dong Lu

Baoanchian Jie

Cihou Dajie

Wanfu Lu

Yuexiu Lu

Baiyun Lu

Chebian Lu

Dong Hu Rd.

Xinghepu Lu

Four Seasons
Hotel Guangzhou →

Beiling Lu

Wende Lu

Dongshan
Hu
Gongyuan

Dong Lu

Ritz Carlton
Guangzhou

Yangjiang Zhong Lu

Qinglan Rd.

nhua Dong Lu

Binjiang Zhong Lu

Hai Yin Qiao

Er Sha Island

Datong Lu

Yangyu Lu

Suszhezhi Lu

Dongxiao Lu

Pearl River
(Zhujiang)

Jiangnan Zhong Lu

Four Seas
International House

0       500 yards

0       500 meters

**KEY**

☐ Hotels
■ Restaurants
■ Restaurants in Hotels
↔ following reviews
indicates a
map-grid coordinate

E F G H

*Y130* ✉ *Pearl Building, East Tower, 360 Huanshi Zhong Lu., 3rd Fl.* ☎ *020/8386–3840* ✣ *F2.*

$$$ ECLECTIC ✕ **Lucy's** (露丝酒吧 *Lùsī jiǔbā*). With so many cuisines represented on its menu (Asian curries, Tex-Mex favorites, British fish-and-chips, and much more), a UN think tank could happily share a table here. Steak is one of Lucy's signature dishes. A favorite among foreigners, this eatery in the old Shamian District has a lovely outdoor dining area; even the dining room has a few trees growing through the roof. A friendly and helpful staff is at your service. [$] *Average main: Y100* ✉ *3 Shamian Nan Jie, 1 block from White Swan Hotel* ☎ *020/8136–6203* ▭ *No credit cards* ✣ *B6.*

## TO YOUR HEALTH!

Good-bye Starbucks, hello Wong Chun Loong! For decades the Loong beverage franchise has dominated the Guangzhou scene, and for good reason. They serve drinks that are thirst-quenching, healthy, and taste good (sometimes). The most popular drinks are *huomaren,* a beverage made from crushed hemp seeds (it's the brown beverage displayed on the counter) and *yezi,* or coconut milk. A cup of either costs only Y5.

$$$ CANTONESE ✕ **Panxi Restaurant** (泮溪酒家 *Bànxī jiǔjiā*). On the edge of Liwan Lake, this famous restaurant has a series of teahouse rooms and landscaped gardens interconnected by paths and bridges that have the feel of a Taoist temple. One room is built on a floating houseboat. Signature dishes include scallop and crab soup, and quail eggs cooked with shrimp roe on a bed of green vegetables. The dim sum, especially popular with Southern Chinese, is highly recommended, as the restaurant is known for its beautiful presentation along with its fresh flavors. Make reservations or expect long lines. [$] *Average main: Y150* ✉ *151 Longjin Xi Lu, Liwan Park* ☎ *020/8181–5955* ✍ *Reservations essential* ✣ *A4.*

$$$$ CANTONESE ✕ **Tang Yuan** (唐苑 *Táng yuàn*). The location alone beats out most other restaurants in Guangzhou. It is in a faux colonial-style mansion on an island in Liuhuahu Park. The cuisine is pure old-school Cantonese, with expensive dishes like abalone and shark's fin soup served alongside more rational staples like crispy fried pigeon, roasted mackerel, and stuffed garlic prawns. Naturally, there's plenty of dim sum, and the "Cantonese combo plate" features a variety of roasted meats. Although the food at Tang Yuan is excellent, most people come here for the opulent dining room. A golf cart waits at the park's entrance on Liuhua Road to whisk diners to the restaurant's palatial front door. [$] *Average main: Y200* ✉ *Lihuahu Park, Dongfeng Xi Lu and Renmin Bei Lu, 2 blocks west of Yuexiu Gongyuan metro station, Yuexiu District* ☎ *020/3623–6993* ✣ *C2.*

$$ CANTONESE ✕ **Tao Tao Ju** (陶陶居 *Táotáo Jū*). With a name that means "House of Happiness," this is one of the city's most revered traditional Cantonese restaurants. Opening its door more than a century ago, Tao Tao Ju is famous for its dim sum, especially *the nai huang bao* (buns made with milk and egg yolks). Tao Tao Ju's cakes are filled with 20 different ingredients, including ham, roast duck, shrimp, peanuts, mushrooms and lotus seeds. The menu, available in English, has many items that you're unlikely to find elsewhere, including tasty kudzu and snakehead

soup. $ *Average main: Y50* ✉ *20 Dishifu Lu, Shangxiajiu* ☎ *020/8139–6111* ✛ *B5.*

## WHERE TO STAY

*Use the coordinate (✛ B2) at the end of each listing to locate a site on the Where to Eat and Stay in Guangzhou map.*

**$$$**
**HOTEL**
**Baiyuan Hotel** (广州白云宾馆 *Guǎngzhōu báiyún bīnguǎn*). Located in Guangzhou's Central Business District, this luxurious lodging is ideal for both business and leisure travelers. **Pros:** easy access to premium shopping spots; close to public transportation. **Cons:** A little pricey. $ *Rooms from: Y1690* ✉ *367 Huanshi Dong Lu, Yuexiu District* ☎ *020/8333–3998* ⊕ *www.baiyun-hotel.com* ↘ *590 rooms, 30 suites* ▐◯▌ *Breakfast* Ⓜ *Taojin* ✛ *F2.*

**$**
**HOTEL**
**China Hotel** (中国大酒店 *Zhōngguó dàjiǔdiàn*). Part of a shopping mall big enough to get lost in, the China Hotel gives you easy access to a range of restaurants that will satisfy any appetite. **Pros:** close to subway; handy location; nicely renovated rooms. **Cons:** appeals to business travelers. $ *Rooms from: Y900* ✉ *Liuhua Lu, Liwan* ☎ *020/8666–6888* ⊕ *www.marriott.com* ↘ *736 rooms, 114 suites* ▐◯▌ *No meals* Ⓜ *Yuexu Gongyuan* ✛ *D2.*

**$$**
**HOTEL**
**Dong Fang** (东方宾馆 *Dōngfāng bīnguǎn*). Across from Liuhua Park, this conveniently located hotel features a subtropical 22-acre garden with pavilions, carp-filled pools, and rock gardens. **Pros:** spacious gardens; choice of restaurants; lovely setting. **Cons:** impersonal feel. $ *Rooms from: Y538* ✉ *120 Liuhua Lu* ☎ *020/8666–9900* ↘ *699 rooms, 101 suites* ▐◯▌ *No meals* ✛ *C2.*

**$$$$**
**HOTEL**
**Four Seasons Hotel Guangzhou** (广州四季酒店 *Guǎngzhōu sìjì fàndiàn*). You can't beat the views at the Four Seasons Hotel Guangzhou, ensconced in the 100-story Guangzhou International Finance Center. **Pros:** chic and innovative business lounge; spacious rooms with magnificent views; top-notch restaurants. **Cons:** pricey rates; outside of the central business district. $ *Rooms from: Y2000* ✉ *5 Zhujiang West Rd., Tianhe District* ☎ *020/8883–3888* ⊕ *www.fourseasons.com/guangzhou* ↘ *344 rooms; 42 suites* ▐◯▌ *No meals* ✛ *H4.*

**$**
**HOTEL**
**Fodor's Choice**
★
**Guangdong Victory Hotel** (广东胜利宾馆 *Guǎngdōng shènglì bīnguǎn*). This lodging on Shamian Island hotel is continually making improvements, and it shows. **Pros:** historic building; peaceful area; great view of the city from the rooftop pool. **Cons:** shabby fitness center. $ *Rooms from: Y600* ✉ *53 Shamian Bei Lu, Shamian Island* ☎ *020/8121–6688* ⊕ *www.vhotel.com* ↘ *300 rooms, 28 suites* ▐◯▌ *Breakfast* ✛ *B5.*

**$**
**HOTEL**
**Holiday Inn City Centre** (文化假日酒店 *Wénhuà jiàrì jiǔdiàn*). With large, tastefully decorated rooms arranged according to Chinese feng shui principles, this hotel has flat-screen TVs and wireless Internet access. **Pros:** a solid practical hotel especially for business folks; spacious rooms; friendly staff; central location; short walk to the subway. **Cons:** not what you'd call quaint; business center and sauna could use an upgrade. $ *Rooms from: Y500* ✉ *28 Guangming Rd., Huanshi Dong* ☎ *020/6128–6868* ⊕ *www.guangzhou.holiday-inn.com* ↘ *430 rooms, 38 suites* ▐◯▌ *No meals* ✛ *G2.*

7

Qingping Market is not for the squeamish.

$ HOTEL Fodor's Choice ★ 🏨 **Jianguo Hotel** (天伦万怡酒店 *Guǎngzhōu jiàn guó fàn diàn*). Next to the Guangzhou East Railway Station, this upscale boutique hotel in the Tianhe District offers large luxurious rooms with a cutting-edge design. **Pros:** near subway and train stations; centrally located; clean and comfortable rooms; includes breakfast. **Cons:** lack of English TV channels. [$] *Rooms from: Y800* ✉ *172 Linhe Lu Central, next to Guangzhou East Railway Station, Tianhe District* ☎ *020/8393–6388* 🌐 *www.jianguohotelgz.com* 🛏 *403 rooms, 20 suites* 🍴 *Breakfast* ⊕ *H1.*

$$$$ HOTEL 🏨 **Ritz-Carlton Guangzhou** (广州富力丽思卡尔顿酒店 *Guǎngzhōu fùlì lìsī kǎ'ěrdùn jiǔdiàn*). Bringing five-star luxury to Guangzhou's Pearl River New City, the Ritz-Carlton Guangzhou features posh rooms with marble baths, six international restaurants and bars, and a swank spa. **Pros:** unique cuisine; bar with fine cognacs and cigars. **Cons:** books up fast during conferences. [$] *Rooms from: Y1980* ✉ *3 Xing An Lu, Pearl River New City* ☎ *20/3813–6688* 🌐 *www.ritzcarlton.com* 🛏 *351 rooms, 35 suites* 🍴 *Breakfast* ⊕ *H5.*

## NIGHTLIFE AND THE ARTS

Bingjiang Xilu is the street for barhopping. Very popular with a younger crowd, it has great views, and if you get bored with looking north across the river you can always cross the bridge to Yanjiang Xilu and drink at some of the bars on that side.

## NIGHTLIFE
### PUBS AND BARS

**1920 Restaurant and Bar** (1920 餐厅 *1920 Cāntīng*). This Bavarian-themed bar is known for its vast selection of imported wheat beers, ale (the menu includes a dozen or more), and beverages like champagne, wine, and cocktails that are

> **IN THE NEWS**
>
> Some good publications to check out for regularly updated info on ongoing cultural happenings are *Paper, In the Red, and That's PRD.*

best enjoyed on the lovely spacious outdoor patio. The atmosphere inside is chic yet cozy, with a long bar and warm lighting. ✉ *Haizhu Sq., 183 Yanjiang Zhong Lu* ☎ *020/8333–6156* ⊕ *www.1920cn.com.*

**Café Lounge.** The Café Lounge has a mellow vibe, big comfortable bar stools, quiet tables for two, live music on weekends, and a fine selection of cigars. ✉ *China Hotel, lobby* ☎ *020/8666–6888.*

**Hare and Moon.** The big attraction of the Hare and Moon—the lobby bar of the historic White Swan Hotel—is the panorama of the Pearl River as it flows past the picture windows. ✉ *White Swan Hotel, Yi Shamian Lu, Shamian Island* ☎ *020/8188–6968* ⊕ *www.whiteswanhotel.com.*

**The Paddy Field** (爱尔兰餐吧 *Àiěrlàn cānbā*). The games of darts, pints of Guinness and Kilkenny, and football matches on a massive screen make you long for Ireland. It's a popular gathering spot for Guangzhou's expat community. ✉ *38 Huale Lu, 2nd fl.* ☎ *020/8398–6181* ⊕ *www.thepaddyfield.com.*

### DANCE CLUBS

**Deep Anger Music Power House** (咆哮 *Páoxiào*). This cool dance club is located in a building that was a theater back in the days of Sun Yat-sen. Lounge lizards and history buffs will enjoy sipping a beer here. ✉ *183 Yanjiang Lu* ☎ *020/8317–7158.*

**Soho Bar** (苏荷酒吧 *Sūhé jiǔbā*). The biggest and hippest dance club in Guangzhou, Soho bar lets you get your jive on to house and electronica inside or chill out on the terrace. Admission is Y50 to Y100, depending on the night. ✉ *87 Changdi Dama Lu, Yuexiu District* ☎ *020/8319–5095, 020/8336–6611* ⊕ *www.sohobar.com.cn.*

## THE ARTS

**Friendship Theater** (友谊剧院 *Yǒuyì jùyuàn*). Operating since 1965, the Friendship Theater has hosted many art organizations from nearly 100 countries. The performance fare includes drama, theater, opera, symphony, and concerts. Almost all of the performances are in Chinese. ✉ *696 Renmin Bei Lu, Haizhu District* ☎ *020/8666–8991* ⊕ *www.gzyyjy.com.cn.*

**Guangdong Modern Dance Company** (广东现代舞团 *Guǎngdōng Xiàndàiwǔ Tuán*). Mainland China's first professional modern-dance company, Guangdong Modern Dance Company is regularly praised for its cutting-edge style. ✉ *13 Shuiyinhenglu, Shaheding* ☎ *020/8704–7117* ⊕ *www.gdmdc.com.*

FAMILY **Guangzhou Puppet Art Center** (广东木偶艺术中心 *Guǎngdōng mùǒu yìshù zhōngxīn*). Live puppet shows are presented every Saturday and

Beijing Lu is one of Guangzhou's busiest shopping districts.

Sunday at 10:30 am and 3 pm inside Guangzhou Puppet Art Center's two theaters. ⊠ *43 Hongde Lu, Haizhu District* ☎ *020/8431–0235.*

### GALLERIES AND PERFORMANCE SPACES

**Vitamin Creative Space** (维他命艺术空间 *Wéitāmìng yìshù kōngjiān*). If eclectic art is your thing, then Vitamin Creative Space might be worth the trip. But be warned: it's located in the back of a semi-enclosed vegetable market and not easy to find even if you speak Chinese. Call ahead for directions or have someone to lead you to the door. ⊠ *Xinggang Cheng, 29 Hengyi Jie, Room 301, Haizhu District* ☎ *020/8429–6760* ⊕ *www.vitamincreativespace.com.*

**Xinghai Concert Hall** (星海音乐厅 *Xīnghǎi yīnyuètīng*). Home of the Guangzhou Symphony Orchestra, Xinghai Concert Hall puts on an amazing array of concerts featuring national and international performers. Next to the Guangzhou Museum of Art, the concert hall is surrounded by a fantastic sculpture garden. ⊠ *33 Qingbo Lu, Er Sha Island* ☎ *020/8735–2222* ⊕ *www.concerthall.com.cn.*

## SHOPPING

Shangxiajiu Pedestrian Road is a massive warren of old shops in the heart of Old Guangzhou. There's a wide variety of street stalls selling a large selection of delicious edibles. Beijing Pedestrian Road makes no pretense at being anything other than a neon-draped pedestrian mall, similar to Beijing's Wangfujing Street or Shanghai's Nanjing Street. Noisy and fun, the street is lined with cheap food stalls, cozy cafés, and fast-food chains.

### MALLS AND MARKETS

FAMILY **Grandview Mall** (正佳广场 *Zhèngjiā guǎngchǎng*). This mega mall (one of the largest in Guangzhou) is worth a visit if you want to get a sense of Guangzhou's rapidly growing middle class. There are more than 500 stores, many of them well-known international chains including the three-story Nike anchor store. ⊠ *228 Tianhe Rd.* ☎ *020/3833-0812* ⊕ *www.zhengjia.com.cn* Ⓜ *Tianhe Sports Center.*

**La Perle** (丽柏广场 *Lìbǎi Guǎngchǎng*). This upscale shopping mall sits in the city's central business district. Luxury brands include Versace, Louis Vuitton, Polo, Burberry, Fendi, Armani, and Prada. ⊠ *367 Huanshi Dong Lu, across from the Garden Hotel* ☎ *020/8336-0222* ⊕ *www.laperle-global.com.*

**Zhanxi Clothing Wholesale Market** (站西市场 *Zhànxī shìchǎng*). At this wholesale and retail market you can get bargains on jeans and many other kinds of casual clothing. Be prepared to bargain, though sellers are not as aggressive as in Beijing. ⊠ *Zhan Xi Rd., near Guangzhou Railway Station.*

## SIDE TRIP TO BAIYUN MOUNTAIN

*17 km (10½ miles) north of central Guangzhou.*

**Baiyun Mountain** (白云山 *Báiyúnshān*). Also known as White Cloud Mountain, Baiyun Mountain gets its name from the halo of clouds that, in the days before heavy pollution, appeared around the peak following a rainstorm. The mountain is part of a 28-square-km (17-square-mile) resort area, and consists of six parks, 30 peaks, and myriad gullies. **Santailing Park** is home to the enormous Yuntai Garden, of interest to anybody with a thing for botany. **Fei'eling Park** has a nice sculpture garden, and **Luhu Park** is home to Jinye Pond, as pure and azure a body of water as you're likely to find within 100 miles. All in all, a trip to Baiyun Mountain is a good way to get out of the city center—maybe for a day of hiking—without traveling too far. The cable car is an excellent way to get an expansive view of the cityscape and take photos with the backdrop of Guangzhou's skyline. The outdoor restaurant is a good place for simple dishes such as fried rice, noodles, and tea and conversation on a sunny day. ⊕ *www.baiyunshan.com.cn* 🎫 *Y5* ⊘ *Daily 9–5.*

# SHENZHEN

*112 km (70 miles; 1 hr by express train, 2½ hrs by express bus) from Guangzhou.*

Shenzhen may be China's youngest city, but this is one metropolis that's definitely come of age. A small farming town until 1980, Shenzhen was chosen by Deng Xiaoping as an incubator in which the seeds of China's economic reform were to be nurtured. The results are the stuff of legend; a quarter century later Shenzhen is now China's richest, and, according to some, its most vibrant city.

Until recently, most visitors thought of China's youngest city as a place to pass through on the way from Hong Kong to Guangzhou. But over

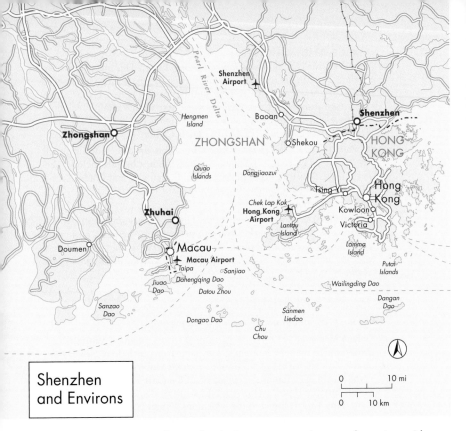

## Shenzhen and Environs

0       10 mi

0       10 km

the last several years the city has seen a complete transformation, with zippy subways, beaming modern shopping malls, and an uptick in top-notch restaurants.

**GETTING HERE AND AROUND**

Tens of thousands of people cross from Hong Kong into Shenzhen (and back) daily, usually over the Luohu border crossing. Over the weekends, numbers can triple. Most visitors take the metro from Kowloon to the crossing and walk into Shenzhen.

A more expensive—but infinitely more pleasant—way is to take the ferry from Hong Kong's Central ferry pier to Shekou Harbor. Here immigration lines are a fraction of what they can be in Luohu. Another way to beat the border crowds is to cross at the Lok Ma Chau Station, which channels you straight into Shenzhen's Futian District.

AIR TRAVEL    Shenzhen's Bao'an International Airport is very busy, with flights to more than 50 cities. There is bus service between the airport and Hong Kong, as well as a ferry link between the Shenzhen and Hong Kong airports. Bus service links the Shenzhen Railway Station, via Huaren Dasha, direct to Shenzhen Airport for Y25 each way.

BOAT AND    The Turbojet Company runs regular ferries connecting Hong Kong, FERRY TRAVEL    Shenzhen, Macau, and Zhuhai. One-way trips from Hong Kong to Shenzhen are around Y70.

## AVOID THE BORDER-CROSSING CRUSH

At Luohu (the main border crossing between Hong Kong and mainland China) the masses are funneled through a three-story building. From the outside this building looks huge, but from the inside—especially when you're surrounded by a quarter of a million people waiting to be processed—the crossing is reminiscent of a scene from *Soylent Green*.

If you're going through Shenzhen on your way to Guangzhou, take the through train from Kowloon to Guangzhou. The immigration line at the Guangzhou East Station is a comparative piece of cake, even on the worst days. It's possible to buy tickets on the fly on this commuter

train, but we advise booking anywhere from a few hours to a day or two in advance.

If you're heading into Shenzhen, why not trade the mad crush of Luohu for an hour-long ferry ride followed by a quick trip through the much less popular border crossing at Shekou Harbor? Ferries are usually not more than half full.

Another way to get to Shenzhen is to take the East Rail Line to the Lok Ma Chau station, built by Hong Kong's MTR to make crossing the border easier for travelers. The station is expansive and efficient, and the crowds are considerably smaller.

BUS TRAVEL Air-conditioned express buses crisscross most of the Pearl River Delta region several times a day. Buses for Shenzhen leave from a number of locations, including the China Travel Service branches in Central and Wan Chai.

SUBWAY TRAVEL Shenzhen's metro has five lines, and tickets range between Y2 and Y8. The most up-to-date information can be found at the Shenzhen Metro's website at ⊕ *www.szmc.net.*

TRAIN TRAVEL Shenzhen can easily be reached from Hong Kong by taking the metro to Luohu Railway Station and then crossing over to Shenzhen on foot. Trains between Guangzhou East Railway Station and Shenzhen's Luohu Railway Station depart every hour and cost between Y80 and Y100.

### SAFETY AND PRECAUTIONS
Shenzhen is safe for the most part, but keep an eye on your bags, especially in crowded spots like Luohu Station. Take care around the expat bar areas; pickpockets have been known to prey on drunken foreigners.

### TIMING
Shenzhen is an excellent place for a one- or two-night stay if you are looking for good food, international shopping, or an expert massage. The spas remain less expensive than those in Hong Kong.

### ESSENTIALS
**Air Contacts Civil Aviation Administration of China** ⊠ *181 Huanshi Lu, on left as you exit Guangzhou railway station [Guangzhou main station metro]* ☎ *020/8668–2000, 24-hr hotline.* **Shenzhen Airport (深圳机场** *Shēnzhèn jīchǎng).* ☎ *0755/2777–7821, 0755/2345–6789* ⊕ *eng.szairport.com.*

**Banks HSBC** ⊠ *Shangri-la Hotel, 1002 Jianshe Rd., Shop No. 9* ☎ *755/8266–3228* ⊕ *www.hsbc.com.cn.* **Bank of China** ⊠ *International Finance*

*Building, 2022 Jianshe Lu, Luohu District* ☎ *755/2233–8888* ⊕ *www.boc.cn.*

**Boat and Ferry Contacts Hong Kong-Macau Ferry Terminal** (港澳码头 *Gǎng'ào mǎtóu*). ⊠ *Shun Tak Centre, Connaught Rd., Sheung Wan, Hong Kong* ☎ *852/2546–3528* ⊕ *www.gov.hk/en/residents/transport/crossboundary/ferryservices.* **Shenzhen Party** ⊕ *www.shenzhenparty.com/travel.* **Turbojet Company** (喷射飞航 *Pēnshè fēiháng*). ⊠ *83 Hing Wah St. W, Lai Chi Kok, Hong Kong, Hong Kong–China* ☎ *852/2859–3333* ⊕ *www.turbojet.com.hk.*

**Bus Contact Shenzhen Luohu Bus Station** (深圳罗湖汽车站 *Shēnzhèn luóhú qìchēzhàn*). ⊠ *East Plaza, 1st–2nd fls., Luohu District* ☎ *755/8232–1670.*

**Medical Assistance Shenzhen People's Hospital** (深圳人民医院 *Shēnzhèn rénmín yīyuàn*). ⊠ *Dongmen Bei Lu N* ☎ *0755/2553–3018* ⊕ *www.szhospital.com.*

**Subway Contact Shenzhen Metro** (深圳地铁 *Shēnzhèn dìtiě*). ☎ *0755/8896–0600.*

**Train Contacts Mass Transit Rail** (港铁 *Xiānggǎng Gǎngtiě*). ☎ *852/2881–8888* ⊕ *www.mtr.com.hk.* **Shenzhen Railway Station** (深圳火车站 *Shēn zhèn huǒ chē zhàn*). ⊠ *Luohu District* ☎ *0755/8232–6560* ⊕ *www.szstation.net.*

**PLAY TIME**

The themed exhibitions in OCT Park, an urban expanse of greenery and sculptures, could all be visited in a single day, but for the sake of sanity, we recommend visiting only two for the day. They are connected by an elevated monorail that costs Y20.

## EXPLORING SHENZHEN

Sprawling Shenzhen is composed of numerous districts. Luohu and Futian are the "downtown" districts, with most of the major shopping areas and hundreds of hotels. A foray outside the sprawl of Shenzhen proper is worth the trip if you have the time; Yantian and Longgang are great destinations for beaches and atmospheric historical buildings.

Futian, Shenzhen's commerical hub, is where Shenzhen's gourmands go for a night of gastronomic pleasure. The Zhenhua Road area has scores of excellent restaurants competing for the patronage of Shenzhen's very discriminating diners. The Shekou neighborhood in the Nanshan district is known for its many bars and restaurants. It's famous for Sea World Plaza, a pedestrian mall featuring restaurants, bars, and a completely landlocked oceangoing vessel (now transformed into a bar, hotel, and nightclub complex).

### TOP ATTRACTIONS

FAMILY **Window of the World** (世界之窗 *Shìjiè zhīchuāng*). With miniature versions of more than 130 of the world's most famous landmarks, Window of the World is China's biggest and busiest homegrown theme park. Divided into eight geographical areas connected by winding paths and a monorail, it includes—randomly scaled—the Taj Mahal, Mount Rushmore, the Sydney Harbor Opera House, and a 100-meter-high (328-foot-high) Eiffel Tower that can be seen from miles away. There is also a fireworks show at 9 pm on weekends and holidays. ⊠ *9037*

Don't miss the floor show at Minsk World.

*Shennan Dadao, Nanshan District* ☎ *0755/2660–8000* ⊕ *www.szwwco. com* ✉ *Y160* ☺ *Daily 9–10:30* Ⓜ *Window of the World Station.*

**WORTH NOTING**

**Hexiangning Art Museum** (何香凝美术馆 *Héxiāngníng měishùguǎn*). This museum features contemporary and classical art from all over China. ✉ *Shenzhen shi Huaqiaocheng, 9013 Shennan Dadao, Nanshan District* ☎ *0755/2660–4540* ⊕ *www.hxnart.com* ✉ *Free* ☺ *Tues.–Sun. 10–5* Ⓜ *Huaqiaocheng.*

**OCT Contemporary Art Terminal** (OCT当代艺术中心 *OCT dāngdài yìshù zhōngxīn*). This is where you'll find works from the hippest artists from Beijing and beyond. ✉ *Enping Rd., Nanshan District* ☎ *0755/2691– 6199* ✉ *Free* ☺ *Tues.–Sun. 10–5:30* Ⓜ *Huaqiaocheng.*

**OUTER SHENZHEN**

Just east of Luohu, Yantian is Shenzhen's beach district. **Dameisha** and **Xiaomeisha** are two beaches adjacent to one another, which offer sun, surf, and strange statues of colorful winged men doing what appears to be beachfront taiji. Dameisha is a public beach, whereas Xiaomeisha has a Y20 admission price. Both are about 40 minutes from Luohu by taxi. **Xichong Beach**, another 30 minutes by taxi to the east, is larger and much more secluded than its neighbors close to town.

Dapeng Fortress and the Hakka Folk Customs Museum and Enclosures are slices of ancient China; they are about an hour by taxi from the modern heart of Luohu.

**TOP ATTRACTIONS**

**Dapeng Fortress** (大鹏古城 *Dàpéng gǔchéng*). Like the rapidly disappearing hutong neighborhoods of Beijing, Dapeng Fortress in the Longgang district is a living museum. The Old Town contains homes, temples, shops, and courtyards that look pretty much the way they did when they were built over the course of the Ming (1368–1644) and Qing (1644–1911) dynasties. For the most part, the residences are occupied, the shops are doing business, and the temples are active houses of worship. Dapeng's ancient city is surrounded by an old stone wall, and entered through a series of gates. ✉ *Pengcheng Village, Dapeng Town, Longgang District* ☎ *0755/8431–9269* ⊕ *www.szdpsc.com* 🎫 *Y20* ⊙ *Daily 9:30–5:30.*

> **ADVENTUROUS EATING**
>
> The Futian District's Zhenhua Road, just two blocks north of the Hua Qiang metro station, is one of the few food streets that has not succumbed to the franchise blight of McDonald's and KFC. There are very few English menus and even less Western food, so be prepared to be adventurous. Two good choices are the North Sea Fishing Village Restaurant, whose staff speaks a bit of English, and has live seafood in tanks out front allowing diners to point and choose, and Lao Yuan Zi, a restaurant with a definite *Crouching Tiger, Hidden Dragon* vibe.

**Hakka Folk Customs Museum and Enclosures** (客家民俗博物馆和围屋 *Kèjiā mínsú bówùguǎn hé wéiwū*). Hakka Folk Customs Museum and Enclosures is a large series of concentric circular homes built inside an exterior wall that basically turns the whole place into a large fort. Inside the enclosure are a large number of old Hakka residences, some of which are still filled with tools and furniture left over from the Qing Dynasty. While some restoration projects elsewhere might pretty things up to the point of making the site look unreal, the opposite is true here. ✉ *Luoruihe Village, Longgang Township, 1 Luoruihe Beijie, Longgang District* ☎ *0755/8429–6258* 🎫 *Y10* ⊙ *Daily 9–5.*

**WORTH NOTING**

**Dafen Oil Painting Village** (大芬油画世界 *Dàfēn yóuhuà shìjiè*). If you're interested in watching art in the making, spend an afternoon at the Dafen Oil Painting Village, a small town 20 minutes by taxi from Luohu, which employs thousands of artists painting everything from originals to copies of classics. Where do all those oil paintings you find in motels come from? Visit Dafen and you'll know. Be aware that opening hours are sporadic. ✉ *Shen Hui Rd., Bu Ji St., Longgang District* ☎ *0755/8473–2633* ⊕ *www.cndafen.com* ⊙ *Daily 9:30–9.*

**Minsk World** (明思克航母世界 *Míngsîkè hàngmǔ shìjiè*). This is Shenzhen's most popular—and perhaps strangest—tourist attraction. It's pretty cheesy but young kids might get a kick out of it. Essentially, it's a decommissioned Soviet-era aircraft carrier that a group of business executives bought in the late 1990s. Parked in perpetuity on the top deck of the ship (which is as long as three football fields placed end to end, and gets wickedly hot in the summer) are several Soviet fighter planes and helicopters. Every hour on the hour comely young ladies in military costumes perform a dance routine combining sensuality with martial flair and twirling rifles. ⊠ *Shatoujiao, Dapeng Bay, Yantian District* ☎ *0755/2535–5333* ⊕ *www.szminsk.com* 🎫 *Y130* ⊙ *Daily 9:30–7:30.*

## WHERE TO EAT

From the heavy mutton stews of Xinjiang to the succulent seafood dishes of Fujian, Shenzhen is home to thousands of restaurants existing not to please the fickle palates of visitors but to alleviate the homesickness of people pining for native provinces left behind.

$   ✗ **1881** (*Yī bābā yī*). The classy
NORTHERN   decor, cozy atmosphere, and warm
CHINESE   ambience are good reasons to dine at 1881. Located inside the Grand Hyatt Shenzhen, 1881 specializes in classic Northern Chinese and Sichuan cuisine, and features a vast choice of Chinese wine. $ *Average main: Y200* ⊠ *Grand Hyatt Shenzhen, 1881 Baoan Nan Lu, Luohu* ☎ *0755/2218–7338* ⊕ *www.shenzhen.grand.hyatt.com.*

$$$   ✗ **360** (360度酒吧 *Sānliùlíng dù jiǔbā*). One of the brighter stars on the
ECLECTIC   Shenzhen haute-cuisine scene, 360 takes up the top two floors of the
**Fodor's**Choice   Shangri-la Hotel and offers sumptuous western dishes like homemade
★   pasta with eggplant, zucchini, and pesto, and ginger-crusted-salmon fillet with couscous and lemon-celery sauce. The steak stands out on the menu. The ambience is chic, and the view from any table in the house is breathtaking. For food, decor, and view we can't recommend this place highly enough. $ *Average main: Y300* ⊠ *Shangri-la Hotel, 1002 Jianshe Rd., 31st fl., Luohu* ☎ *0755/8396–1380* ⊕ *www.shangri-la.com* Ⓜ *Luohu.*

$$$   ✗ **Blue** (意大利餐厅 *Yìdàlì cāntīng*). As the name suggests, the decor
ITALIAN   here in various shades of blue—walls, ceilings, and even the mellow lighting. One of the finest Italian restaurants in China, it's especially well known for its expertly prepared fish dishes. The food is expensive, but worth every penny. If you're really in the mood for decadence, try the dessert tray: chocolates, pastries, and eight different types of mousse surround a caramelized sugar statue of David. $ *Average main: Y300* ⊠ *Crowne Plaza Hotel, 9026 Shen Nan Rd., 3rd fl., Nanshan District* ☎ *0755/2693–6888* ⊕ *www.crowneplaza.com* 🍽 *Reservations essential* ⊙ *No lunch* Ⓜ *Window of the World.*

$   ✗ **Fangdu Restaurant** (芳都酒楼 *Fāngdu jiǔlóu*). This Cantonese-styled
CANTONESE   restaurant is one of the few in Shenzhen that offers the feel of a grand ballroom. In Shenzhen's fast-changing restaraunt scene, such old-style *jiu lou* eateries are becoming quite rare. Fangdu's two floors are decorated

7

with chandeliers and opulent car-pets. This is a good place to fill your stomach with decent dim sum, especially if you are traveling to or from the nearby Lok Ma Chau Sta-tion. Other dishes tend to be a bit heavy on the sauce. The service is speedy. Open for dinner. $ *Average main: Y60* ✉ *Luo Fang Lu, Luohu* ☎ *0755/2224–3777* Ⓜ *Xinxiu.*

**OUT IN SHENZHEN**

One of the byproducts of China's rapid modernization has been the shedding of old taboos. Although it's an overstatement to say that being gay is no longer taboo, it is safe to say that the closet door has been opened in a big way. And nowhere is this truer than in Shenzhen, which has always prided itself on being ahead of the curve.

$$$
CONTEMPORARY

✕ **Greenland Lounge** (绿涧廊大堂吧 *Lǜjiànlàng dàtángbā*). This favorite is known for its international-style buffet and truly unique selection of Chinese teas. The glass-domed roof and smart-casual ambience make it a popular spot for Shenzhen's movers and shakers. Afternoon tea is highly recommended. $ *Average main: Y100* ✉ *Pavilion Hotel, 4014 Huaqiang Rd. N, Futian District* ☎ *0755/8207–8888* ⊕ *www.pavilionhotel.com.*

$$
INDIAN

✕ **Little India** (小印度餐厅 *Xiǎo Yìndù*). This is definitely not your aver-age curry house. The Nepalese chef offers cuisine from both Northern India and Nepal. The restaurant is especially known for its tandoori dishes and for its selection of baked naan breads. Little India is also the only restaurant in the Sea World Plaza that offers hookahs, though the staff will gently ask you to smoke on the outdoor pavilion during peak hours. $ *Average main: Y80* ✉ *138 Mingtian Rd., Futian District* ☎ *0755/8317–4827* ⊕ *www.shenzhenindianrestaurant.com* Ⓜ *Guo Wu Gong Yuan.*

$$$
NORTHERN
CHINESE

✕ **Shui Zu Yi Xiang** (水煮鱼乡 *Shuǐ zhǔ yú xiāng*). This is a hidden treasure amid Shenzhen's vast number of restaurants. It's famous for its Peking duck, said to be just as good as that in Beijing, and for its fish soups, served in hubcap sized bowls. The catfish and pickled veg-etable soup is velvety and the fish melts in your mouth. The smaller side dishes, mostly vegetables, offset the heavier fare. The waiting area in the front has birds in cages, and you're offered tea and pumpkin seeds while you wait. $ *Average main: Y120* ✉ *Xinghua Seaside Garden, Hoi Fai House, Nanshan District* ☎ *0755/8230–3704, 0755/8230–3695* ⊕ *www.szyx1982.com* Ⓜ *Huangbeiling.*

$$
BAKERY

✕ **Sugar Box** (糖立方 *Tánglì fāng*). This patisserie is a great place to take a break while shopping at the nearby malls. Sugar Box offers a wide variety of cakes, breads, coffees, and teas. The relaxing atmosphere makes it great for people-watching. Lunch might include two mini sand-wiches and tea. $ *Average main: Y60* ✉ *Grand Hyatt Shenzhen, 1881 Baoan Nan Lu, 1st fl., Luohu* ☎ *0755/2218–7212, 0755/2218–7338* ▭ *No credit cards* Ⓜ *Daju Yuan.*

$$
JAPANESE

✕ **Yokohama** (横滨日本料理 *Héngbīn Rìběn liàolǐ*). Amazing views of the fishing boats and ferries of Shekou Harbor to the east and Nanshan Mountain to the north are yours at Yokohama. This is a good place to rest before taking the ferry to Hong Kong or Macau. The sashimi is the freshest around, and the other dishes are the real deal. The clientele is

A pedestrian walkway in the center of Shenzhen City

mostly Japanese, which is always a good sign. Try a side dish of *oshinko* (traditional Japanese pickles)—unlike many lesser Japanese restaurants in China, Yokohama takes no shortcuts with its oshinko, and offers eight different types. $ *Average main: Y70* ⊠ *Nanhai Hotel, 1 Gongye Yilu, 10th fl., Shekou District* ☎ *0755/2669–5557* Ⓜ *Shekou Gang.*

## WHERE TO STAY

$$
HOTEL
Fodor's Choice
★

🍽 **Crowne Plaza** (威尼斯皇冠假日酒店 *Wēinísî huàngguān jiàrì jiǔdiàn*). This hotel holds its own among the best hotels in Asia. **Pros:** near metro; stylish decor; good restaurants. **Cons:** you may not have been thinking Italy when you came to China. $ *Rooms from: Y1118* ⊠ *3018 Nanhu Lu, across from Windows of the World metro station, Nanshan District* ☎ *0755/2693–6888* ⊕ *www.crowneplaza.com* 🛏 *368 rooms, 47 suites* ⊙ *No meals* Ⓜ *Windows of the World.*

$$$$
HOTEL
Fodor's Choice
★

🍽 **InterContinental Shenzhen** (深圳华侨城洲际大酒店 *Shēnzhèn huáqiáochéng zhōujì dàiǔdiàn*). An intoxicating blend of fun, flair, and sophistication, the Spanish-themed InterContinental Shenzhen has everything from bellmen dressed in toreador costumes to a massive Pirates of the Caribbean–style ship serving as a bar and restaurant. **Pros:** eye-catching design; playful atmosphere; ship-shaped bar is a memorable sight. **Cons:** staff can be inattentive. $ *Rooms from: Y1858* ⊠ *9009 Shennan Rd., Nanshan District* ☎ *0755/3399–3388* ⊕ *www.intercontinental.com* 🛏 *540 rooms, 61 suites* ⊙ *No meals* Ⓜ *Huaqiao Cheng.*

$
HOTEL

🍽 **Nan Hai** (深圳南海酒店 *Shēnzhèn nánhǎi jiǔdiàn*). This hotel's retro space-age exterior, featuring rounded balconies that look as if they might detach from the mother ship at any moment, greets visitors

Wu Xiangbin, the head of Mission Hills Golf Academy, gives a student some pointers.

arriving on the ferry from Hong Kong. **Pros:** near the Hong Kong Island ferry terminal. **Cons:** dated decor. $ *Rooms from: Y759* ⊠ *1 Gongye Yilu, Shekou/Nanshan District* ☏ *0755/2669–2888* ⊕ *www.nanhai-hotel.com* ⤴ *369 rooms* ❐ *No meals* Ⓜ *She Kou Gang.*

$
HOTEL
Ⓣ **The Pavilion** (圣廷苑酒店 *Shèngtíngyuàn jiǔdiàn*). With a great location in the heart of the business district and a gorgeous interior (check out the domed-glass roof over the piano bar and teahouse), the Pavilion is one of the top international-class hotels in Shenzhen. **Pros:** good location; doting service; several dining options. **Cons:** rooms don't have much character. $ *Rooms from: Y899* ⊠ *4002 Huaqiang Bei Lu, Futian District* ☏ *0755/8207–8888* ⊕ *www.pavilionhotel.com* ⤴ *297 rooms and suites* ❐ *No meals* Ⓜ *Huaxin.*

$$
HOTEL
Ⓣ **Shangri-La Shenzhen** (深圳香格里拉酒店 *Shēnzhèn xiānggélǐlā jiǔdiàn*). The unbeatable location—practically straddling the border with Hong Kong—has made the Shangri-La a popular meeting place and a longtime landmark. **Pros:** near shopping malls; luxurious rooms. **Cons:** noisy and crowded neighborhood. $ *Rooms from: Y1188* ⊠ *1002 Jianshe Lu, Luohu, east side of train station, Luohu District* ☏ *0755/8233–0888* ⊕ *www.shangri-la.com* ⤴ *552 rooms, 30 suites* Ⓜ *Luohu.*

$
HOTEL
Ⓣ **Shenzhen Wuzhou Guest House** (五洲宾馆 *Wǔzhōu bīnguǎn*). The word "grand" defines every aspect of the Shenzhen Wuzhou Guest House, built by the municipal government to house dignitaries and now open to the public. **Pros:** a unique experience; prime location; beautifully manicured garden. **Cons:** expensive rates. $ *Rooms from: Y988* ⊠ *6001 Shennan Lu, Futian District* ☏ *0755/8293–8000* ⊕ *www.wuzhouguesthouse.com* ⤴ *334 rooms; 11 suites* ❐ *No meals.*

## NIGHTLIFE AND THE ARTS

Shenzhen's nightlife is so happening that it's not unusual to run into people—expats and Chinese—who have come in from Hong Kong and Guangzhou just to party. The two major nightlife centers are Coco Park in the Futian District (a flashy crowd) and Shekou in the Nanshan District (a bit more laid-back), but a couple of cool spots are in the OCT District as well.

> **FORE!**
>
> Although manufacturing is undoubtedly the Pearl River Delta's raison d'être, golfing may well come in as a close second with more than 30 courses.

**Club Viva!** (喂哇俱乐部 *Viva* 酒吧Viva jùlèbù).From salsa to hip-hop, you can dance the night away inside this hot spot or enjoy a drink on the outdoor patio while you mingle with Shenzhen's young professional crowd. Tell your taxi driver "Guowugongyuan," which translates to Coco Park Shopping Park. ⊠ *Coco Park Shopping Park, No. 140 Futian Road, Futian District* ☏ *186/2531–3763.*

**Terrace** (露台 *Lù tái*). The Filipino house band rocks the joint almost every night at the Terrace, but you can also find blues, reggae, and other music here all week. If you need a rest from dancing, slip out to the outdoor balcony for a cocktail and a view over the Shekou area. ⊠ *Sea World Square, Tai Zi Lu, Shekou District* ☏ *0755/2682–9105* ⊕ *www.theterrace.com.cn.*

**True Color** (本色音乐 *Běnsè yīnyuè*). One of the coolest party scenes in Shenzhen, True Color attracts top-name international DJs. Music ranges from trance to house, and the party usually doesn't break up until dawn. ⊠ *3/4 F Dongyuan Mansion, 1 Dongyuan Lu, Luohu District* ☏ *0755/8227–4834.*

**V-Bar** (V 吧 *V-bā*). Without a doubt the hottest nightspot in the OCT, V-Bar boasts a holographic globe hovering over a circular bar. It's the only bar in town with an attached swimming pool. ⊠ *Crowne Plaza, 3018 Nanhu Lu, Nanshan District* ☏ *0755/2693–6888* ☾ *8 pm–2 am.*

## SHOPPING

**CITIC City Plaza** (深圳中信大厦 *Shēnzhèn zhōngxìn dàshà*). This upscale shopping has more than 100 stores, include Japanese department stores Seibu and Jusco. There's also a food court on the lower level that's not a bad place to take a break over some coffee or a bowl of noodle soup. ⊠ *1093 Shennan Rd.* ☏ *0755/2594–1502* ⊕ *www.zxcityplaza.com* Ⓜ *Kexueguan.*

**The Mixc** (华润中心 *Huárùn zhōngxīn*). This high-end shopping mall includes many luxury brands, including Cartier, Prada, and Miu Miu. ⊠ *500 Shennan East Lu, Luohu District* ☏ *0755/8266–8266* ⊕ *www.themixc.com* Ⓜ *Da Ja Yuan.*

## GOLF

**Lakewood Golf Club** (珠海翠湖高尔夫球会 *Zhūhǎi cuìhú gāoěrfū qiúhuì*). The Lakewood Golf Club is about 20-30 minutes from the Zhuhai Ferry Terminal, and is the most popular of the city's five golf clubs. Both its Mountain Course and its Lake Course are 18 holes or 36 holes, and are said to be challenging. Visitor packages, including greens fees and a caddy, are Y1,080 weekdays and Y1,780 weekends. ⊠ *Da'nan Mountain, Jinding District* ☎ *0756/338–3666* ⊕ *www.lakewoodclub.com.cn.*

**Mission Hills Golf Club** (*Guānlàn Gāoěrfū*). Widely considered by golfers as one of the top golf courses and clubs in Southern China, Mission Hills Golf Club has 12 18-hole courses (two of which offer nighttime playing), as well as a spectacular clubhouse, a tennis court, two restaurants, and an outdoor pool. ⊠ *Nan Shan, Da Wei, Sha He, Bao'an District* ☎ *0755/2690–9999, 852/2826–0238 in Hong Kong* ⊕ *www.missionhillschina.com* ⊙ *6 am–dark.*

**Sand River Golf Club** (沙河高尔夫球会 *Shāhé gāoěrfū qiúhuì*). The Sand River Golf Club offers two courses, one of which was designed by Gary Player and is floodlighted for night playing. Other facilities include a large driving range and various resort amenities. ⊠ *1 Shahe Donglu, Nanshan District* ☎ *0755/2690–0111* ⊕ *www.sandrivergolfclub.com* ⊙ *Daily 6–8:30.*

## SIDE TRIPS TO ZHONGSHAN AND ZHUHAI

Two other cities worth visiting in the Pearl River Delta are Zhongshan and Zhuhai. Though some casual visitors might chose to spend more than one day in this region, both are small enough to be seen in an afternoon.

### ESSENTIALS

**Bus Contacts Zhongshan Bus Station** ⊠ *Fuhua Rd., Shiqiben West District* ☎ *760/863–3825.* **Zhuhai Gongbei Bus Station** ⊠ *No. 1 Lianhua Rd., Gongbei District* ☎ *756/888–8554.*

# THE SOUTHWEST

Guangxi, Guizhou, and Yunnan

# WELCOME TO THE SOUTHWEST

## TOP REASONS TO GO

★ **Lose yourself in Lijiang:** Treasured by the Chinese and home to a UNESCO World Heritage Site, the winding cobblestone lanes of Lijiang beckon to all.

★ **Lush Xishuangbanna rain forests:** Hugging the borders of Laos and Myanmar, this small city in Yunnan is home to the legendary Dai minority people, who make you feel far from the rest of China.

★ **Trek Tiger Leaping Gorge:** Explore the deepest gorge in the world, and one of the most scenic spots in all of Yunnan, and possibly China.

★ **Guizhou's eye-popping Huangguoshu Falls:** Travel to the Baishui River in Guizhou, where the largest waterfall in China plummets 230 feet.

★ **Cycling around Yangshuo:** Snake your way through this strange lunar landscape of limestone karsts.

**1** Guangxi. Having inspired countless paintings and poems in the past, the spectacular karst scenery of Guilin and Yangshuo today inspires travelers who are in search of an unforgettable Chinese experience. Capital city Nanning is being groomed as China's gateway to Vietnam. Guangxi is officially Guangxi Zhuang Minority Autonomous Region, not a province.

**2** Guizhou. Off the beaten path, this fascinating province is known for its undulating mountains, terraced fields, traditional villages, frequent festivals, and China's largest waterfall, Huangguoshu. More than a third of the population is made up of Dong, Hui, Yao, Zhuang, and Miao (known in the West as the Hmong) peoples.

CHONGQING
Chongqing

Zunyi
GUIZHOU
2

HUNAN

Huangguoshu Falls
Guiyang  Kaili
Anshun  Duyun

Longsheng

Xingyi

Guilin

Yishan  Yangshuo

Liuzhou

Bose

GUANGXI
1  Hechi

Yulin

Nanning

GUANGDONG

Fangcheng  Qinzhou

Beihai
*Gulf of
Tonkin*

## GETTING ORIENTED

Southwest China can be summed up in one word: diversity. The regions of Guangxi, Guizhou, and Yunnan offer some of China's most singular travel experiences. Guilin and Yangshuo in Guangxi are surrounded by other-worldly karst mountains and idyllic rivers. Qianling Park in Guizhou's capital, Guiyang, has a beautiful Buddhist temple, hundreds of monkeys, and amazing city views. Stretching between Tibet and Vietnam, Yunnan Province's geographic, biological, and ethnic diversity is unparalleled anywhere else in China. This part of the world must be seen to be believed.

8

**3** Yunnan. The ancient towns of Lijiang and Dali offer glimpses into the centuries-old traditions of the Naxi and Bai ethnic groups. For a more rugged experience, hike through the breathtaking Tiger Leaping Gorge. If a slow boat on the Mekong appeals, head south to Jinghong and chill out in the tropics.

Updated by Sander Van de Moortel

The southwestern provinces are among the most alluring destinations in the country. This region lays claim to some of the most breathtaking scenery in all of China—from the moonscape limestone karsts and river scenery of Yangshuo, to China's mightiest waterfall in Guizhou, to Yunnan's tropical rain forests and spectacular Tiger Leaping Gorge.

Rich in ethnic diversity and culture, Yunnan is home to almost a third of China's ethnic minorities. In 1958 Guangxi became an autonomous region in an attempt to quell the friction between the Zhuang minority and the ethnic Han majority. Yunnan, Guangxi, and Guizhou represent the complex tapestry of China's ethnic diversity.

In Kunming, Dali, and villages around Yunnan, the Yi and Bai peoples hold their Torch Festivals on the 24th day of the sixth lunar month. They throw handfuls of pine resin into bonfires, lighting the night sky with clouds of sparks. The Dai Water Splashing Festival in the rain forests of Xishuangbanna on the 22nd day of the third lunar month is liquid pandemonium. Its purpose is to wash away the sorrow of the old year and refresh you for the new.

Dali has two festivals of note: the Third Moon Fair (middle of third lunar month) during which people from all around Yunnan come to Dali to sell their wares; and the Three Temples Festival (usually May). The Sister's Meal Festival, celebrated in the middle of the third lunar month by Miao people throughout Guizhou, is dedicated to unmarried women. During the great rice harvest, special brightly colored dishes are made, and at nightfall there's much ado about courtship, dancing, and old-fashioned flirting. The Zhuang Singing Festival turns Guangxi's countryside into an ocean of song. On the third day of the third lunar month, the Zhuang gather and sing to honor Liu Sanjie ("Third Sister Liu"), the goddess of song. Singing "battles" ensue between groups who sing—often improvising—at each other until one group concedes.

## PLANNING

### WHEN TO GO

When you are packing for travel in Southwest China, think of the region as three distinct zones separated by altitude. Steamy tropical lowlands spread across the southern halves of Yunnan and Guangxi. The mountainous highlands of central and northwest Yunnan are characterized by intense sun, long rainy seasons, and cold winters. Somewhere in between are the cloudy mountain scenes found throughout Guizhou and northern Guangxi. Each zone requires a different packing strategy.

In summer the monsoon rains can be heavy, so keep abreast of weather reports as you travel. Temperatures don't get as hot as the tropics or as cold as the highlands, but summers can be quite hot in Guilin and Yangshuo, and winters in Guiyang can be cold enough for snow. The best time of year is spring, in April or early May. Winter months can be surprisingly cold (except in southern Guangxi and Yunnan), and the summertime heat is stifling. Mid-September can also be a comfortable time to travel. The falls at Huangguoshu are at their best in the rainy season from May through October.

### GETTING HERE AND AROUND

With new roads, faster trains, and more airports every year, traveling around Southwest China is becoming increasingly convenient. If you're short on time, flying within the region is the best option, with most flights taking an hour or less. If you're not in a hurry, trains and buses are a cheap and scenic option.

### AIR TRAVEL

Southwest China's air network is constantly expanding, with most popular travel destinations served by their own airports. China Eastern Airlines is the dominant carrier in the region. Kunming, Guilin, Nanning, Jinghong, and Guiyang all have international airports, and cities such as Lijiang and Dali are reachable by air.

### BUS TRAVEL

Traveling around Southwest China by bus is a good way to cover the shorter distances in your travels. The regional bus network is efficient and is primarily served by luxury coaches. Keep in mind that in general there is no English spoken on buses here.

### CAR TRAVEL

There are no legal car-and-driver services, only buses and taxis.

### HEALTH AND SAFETY

Gastrointestinal problems are the main health concern in this part of the country—make sure that your food is cooked thoroughly in a hygienic environment. A new rating system, giving restaurants grades from A to C, will help you find the better places. Altitude sickness can be a problem if you're flying into northwest Yunnan; make sure to take it easy for the first day or two after arriving.

8

### MONEY MATTERS

Money can be changed in the major hotels or at the Bank of China. The Guilin and Nanning airports have branches with ATMs that accept foreign cards. The Kunming airport has a foreign exchange counter just outside the international arrivals gate.

Bank cards on the Cirrus or Plus systems can be used at ATMs displaying their respective logos. Bank of China and ICBC are your best bets. When traveling to remote parts of the region, have cash on hand, as ATMs accepting foreign cards are rare.

### RESTAURANTS

In addition to great Chinese food, usually on the spicier side, Southwest China is home to a rainbow of ethnic cuisines, with Dai, Bai, and Tibetan being some of the most notable. Yunnan has the most diverse culinary offerings, which even include some breads and cheeses. Wild mushrooms are available every May through September.

### HOTELS

Locally run hotels in Southwest China's larger cities offer adequate service and amenities for a reasonable price, but don't expect an English-speaking staff. There is a growing number of international luxury hotels in Kunming, Guiyang, and Nanning that offer personal service and well-regarded restaurants. Cities like Dali, Lijiang, and Yangshuo have plenty of comfortable and cheap small hotels and guesthouses where you can get home-cooked local meals.

### VISITOR INFORMATION

This part of China has virtually nothing in the way of useful English-language tourist information. Cafés and guesthouses are usually good places to ask about travel in the region.

### TOURS

Although they can be cheaper, Chinese package tours tend to be noisy, crowded, and aimed at getting you to buy junk. In Southwest China's larger cities, hotels are the most convenient places to make transportation arrangements. In travel hot spots such as Yangshuo, Lijiang, and Dali there are plenty of English-speaking travel agents.

**China Minority Travel.** One of the oldest travel agencies in Southwest China, China Minority Travel offers tours exploring virtually every corner of Southwest China. ⌂ *63 Bo'ai Lu, Dali* ☎ *0872/267–7824* ⊕ *www.china-travel.nl.*

**Wild China.** This company specializes in unique itineraries in Yunnan, Guizhou, and Guangxi, and can create journeys tailored to specific interests. ⌂ *Oriental Place, 9 Dongfang Dong Lu, Room 801, Chaoyang, Beijing* ☎ *010/6465–6602* ⊕ *www.wildchina.com.*

# GUANGXI

Known throughout China for its fairy-tale scenery, Guangxi's rivers, valleys, and stone peaks have inspired painters and poets for centuries. From the distinctive terraced rice fields of Longsheng, which resemble a dragon's spine, to the karst rock formations that surround Guilin and

Watching a Dragon Boat race at the Water Splashing Festival in Xishuangbanna

Yangshuo and rise from the coastal plain in the south, Guangxi is quite possibly the most picturesque of China's regions.

A significant portion of Guangxi's population consists of ethnic minorities: the Dong, Gelao, Hui, Jing, Miao, Shui, Yao, Yi, and, in particular, the Zhuang people, who constitute about a third of the province's population. Guangxi has often seen conflict between these indigenous peoples and the Han, who established their rule only in the 19th century. Today it is one of five autonomous regions, which, in theory, have an element of self-government.

The climate is subtropical and affected by seasonal monsoons, with long, hot, humid, and frequently wet summers and mild winters. Guangxi is one of the most popular travel destinations in China.

## GUILIN

*500 km (310 miles; 13 hrs by train) northwest of Hong Kong; 1,675 km (1,039 miles; 22 hrs by train) southwest of Beijing.*

Guilin has the good fortune of being situated in the middle of some of the world's most beautiful landscapes. This region of limestone karst hills and mountains, rising almost vertically from the earth, has a dreamy, hypnotic quality. They were formed 200 million years ago, when the area was under the sea. As the land beneath began to push upward, the sea receded, and the effects of the ensuing erosion over thousands of years produced this sublime scenery.

Architecturally, the city lacks charm, having been heavily bombed during the Sino-Japanese War and rebuilt in the utilitarian style popular in

Guangxi

the 1950s. Still, the river city is replete with beautiful parks and bridges, and has a number of historic sites that make it worthy of exploration. It's also a good base from which to explore northern Guangxi.

### GETTING HERE AND AROUND

AIR TRAVEL About 28 km (17 miles) southwest of the city center, Guilin Liangjiang International Airport has flights to cities throughout China as well as throughout Asia. An airport shuttle bus, which operates daily from 6:30 am to 8 pm, runs between the airport and the Aviation Building at 18 Shanghai Lu, across from the main bus station. The cost is Y20 per person.

BUS TRAVEL The main bus station in Guilin is just north of the train station on Zhongshan Nan Lu. Short- and long-distance buses connect Guilin to nearby cities, including Yangshuo, Liuzhou, and Nanning. For Longsheng, you need the Qingtan Bus Station. Long-distance sleeper coaches travel to cities throughout the Pearl River Delta.

TRAIN TRAVEL Guilin is linked by daily rail service with most major cities in China. Most long-distance trains arrive at Guilin's South Railway Station.

### SAFETY AND PRECAUTIONS

Like most cities in Southwest China, Guilin is generally safe, but one should be careful when crossing the street, as pedestrians don't get much respect from drivers.

**TIMING**

Although it is increasingly overshadowed by nearby Yangshuo, Guilin is a pleasant city that's well worth a stop. Most of the sights can be taken in within a couple of days.

**ESSENTIALS**

**Air Contact Guilin Liangjiang International Airport** ☎ *0773/284–5359.*

**Banks Bank of China** ✉ *5 Shanhu Bei Lu* ☎ *0773/280–2867.*

**Bus Contact Guilin Bus Station** ✉ *Off Zhongshan Nan Lu* ☎ *0773/382–2153.*

**Medical Assistance Guilin People's Hospital** ✉ *12 Wenming Lu* ☎ *0773/282–8712.*

**Public Security Bureau PSB Guilin** ✉ *16 Shi Jia Yuan Rd.* ☎ *0773/282–3334.*

**Train Contact Guilin Railway Station** ✉ *Off Zhongshan Nan Lu* ☎ *0773/216–4842.*

**Visitor and Tour Info China International Travel Service** ✉ *11 Binjiang Lu* ☎ *0773/288–0319.* **China Travel Service** ✉ *11 Binjiang Lu* ☎ *0773/283–3986* ⊕ *en.guilincits.com.*

**EXPLORING**

**TOP ATTRACTIONS**

**Elephant Trunk Hill** (象鼻山 *Xiàngbí shān*). On the banks of the river in the southern part of the city, Elephant Trunk Hill takes its name from a rock formation arching into the water like the trunk of an elephant. Nearby is a grotto covered in poetic inscriptions inspired by the beauty of the place, some by the greatest poets of the Song Dynasty. ✉ *Binjiang Lu, across from Golden Elephant Hotel* ☎ *0773/258–6602* 🎫 *Y75* ⏰ *Daily 7 am–9:30 pm.*

**Peak of Solitary Beauty** (独秀峰 *Dúxiù fēng*). The 492-foot Peak of Solitary Beauty, with carved stone stairs leading to the top, offers an unparalleled view of Guilin—and a short but intense workout for your legs. It's one of the attractions of the **Prince City Solitary Beauty Park** *(Wáng chéng)*. Surrounded by an ancient wall, outside of which vendors hawk their wares, sits the heart of Old Guilin. Inside are the decaying remains of an ancient Ming Dynasty palace built in 1393 and Guilin's Confucius temple. Sun Yat-sen lived here for a few months in the winter of 1921 (a fact duly noted on the wall by the outside gate). Cixi, the former empress dowager of China, inscribed the character for "longevity" on a rock within these walls. ✉ *2 blocks north of Zhengyang Lu Pedestrian Mall* 🎫 *Y70* ⏰ *Daily 7:30–6:30.*

**Seven Star Park** (七星公园 *Qīxīng gōngyuán*). This park gets its name from the arrangement of its hills, said to resemble the Big Dipper. At the center of this huge park is **Putuo Mountain** (Pǔtuóshān), atop which sits a lovely pavilion housing a number of famous examples of Tang calligraphy. Indeed, calligraphy abounds on the side of this hill, mostly the work of Ming Dynasty Taoist philosopher Pan Changjing. Nearby is **Seven Star Cave** (Qīxīng yán), with several large caves open for exploration. The largest contains rock formations that are thought to resemble a lion with a ball, an elephant, and other figures. An inscription in the

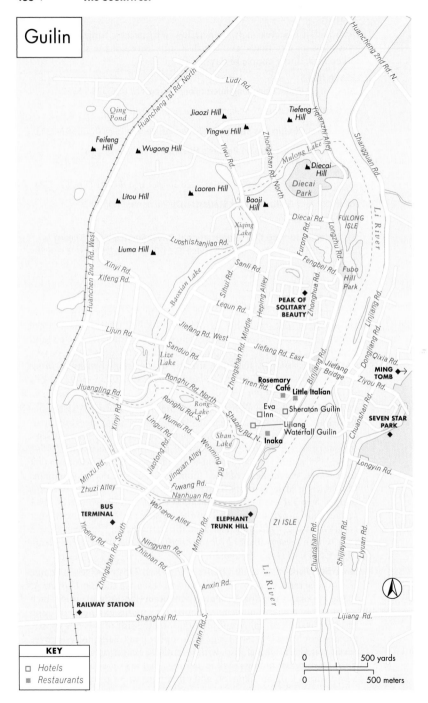

# Guilin

**KEY**
- □ Hotels
- ■ Restaurants

0 — 500 yards
0 — 500 meters

cave dates from AD 590. Seven Star Park also contains the Guilin City Zoo, only worth a stop if you have kids in tow. It costs an additional Y30. ✉ *East side of the Li River, 1 km (½ mile) east of downtown Guilin* 🎫 *Y75* 🕒 *Daily 6–9:30.*

**WORTH NOTING**

**Ming Tomb** (靖江王陵 *Jìngjiāngwáng líng*). East of downtown is the tomb of Zhu Shouqian, the nephew of the first Ming emperor, who founded a principality here. It makes a pleasant excursion by bicycle and its gates combine with the surrounding hills for good photo opportunities. To get here, take Jiefang Dong Lu east about 9 km (5 miles). ✉ *Jiefang Dong Lu* ☎ *0773/589–7276* 🎫 *Y20* 🕒 *Daily 8:30–4:30.*

## WHERE TO EAT

Guilin's notable local dishes are limited to horse meat and rice noodles. Freshwater fish is popular with locals, but eat it only if you dare. The Zhengyang Lu pedestrian street has the best variety of dining spots.

$$ JAPANESE 🍴 **Inaka** (田舍日本料理 *Tiánshè rìběn liàol*). Resembling a Japanese home, this excellent restaurant sits at the southern end of the Zhengyang Lu Pedestrian Mall. The interior, which recalls that of a temple, has a low-key vibe. The sashimi and sushi—not easy to find in cities away from the coast—are fresh and excellent. The best deals are the four-course lunch specials, which begin with miso soup and end with a dessert made from sweetened bean curd. [$] *Average main: Y50* ✉ *1 Zhengyang Lu* ☎ *0773/280–2888.*

$ ITALIAN 🍴 **Little Italian** (唐纳德 *Tángnàdé*). This little restaurant may have the best Western food in Guilin. The menu is straightforward: pizza, pasta, and sandwiches made fresh when you order. The cozy urban decor creates an ideal environment for reading a book, checking your email, or planning the next step in your trip. Most of the young, friendly staff speaks English. [$] *Average main: Y45* ✉ *1–4, 18 Binjiang Lu* ☎ *0773/311–1068.*

$ INTERNATIONAL 🍴 **Rosemary Café.** Just a hop, skip, and a jump away from the Sheraton Hotel, the Rosemary Cafe has outside seating in the middle of a calm pedestrian street, making it a nice place to while away an evening. It may not have the most inspired decor, but don't let that deceive you: the Western menu includes delicious burritos and salads which you can wash down with a glass of freshly pressed pineapple juice. [$] *Average main: Y45* ✉ *1–3 Yiren Lu* ☎ *0773/281–0063.*

## WHERE TO STAY

$ HOTEL Fodor's Choice ★ 🏨 **Eva Inn** (四季春天酒店 *Sìjì chūntiān jiǔdiàn*). The best budget lodging in Guilin, the Eva Inn offers clean, modern rooms at very reasonable rates. **Pros:** great location; good value; pleasant views. **Cons:** rooms could be a bit bigger. [$] *Rooms from: Y300* ✉ *66 Binjiang Lu, on west bank of Li River* ☎ *0773/283–0666* 🛏 *113 rooms* 🍽 *No meals.*

$ HOTEL 🏨 **Lijiang Waterfall Guilin** (漓江大瀑布酒店 *Líjiāng dàpùbù jiǔdiàn*). With a privileged perch overlooking the river, this luxury hotel has breathtaking views of Elephant Trunk Hill and Seven Star Park. **Pros:** reasonable rooms for reasonable rates. **Cons:** occasionally chaotic due to conferences. [$] *Rooms from: Y680* ✉ *1 Shanhu Bei Lu, southern*

**CLOSE UP**

# The Zhuang and the Miao

The famous Miao hair pieces.

The Zhuang are China's largest minority population, totaling more than 16 million. Most Zhuang are in Guangxi Zhuang Autonomous Region (where they constitute more than 85% of the population), Guizhou, Yunnan, and Guangdong provinces. The Zhuang language is part of the Tai-Kadai family, related to Thai and fellow Chinese minority the Dai. Historically, the Zhuang have had almost constant friction with China's Han majority, but that's improved since the Guangxi Zhuang Autonomous region was established in 1958. In many ways the Zhuang are becoming assimilated into the dominant Han Chinese culture, but they have still preserved their strong culture and its music and dance traditions. Clothing varies from region to region, but mostly consists of collarless embroidered jackets buttoned to the left, loose wide trousers or pleated skirts, embroidered belts, and black square headbands.

The Miao are also a large minority group spread across much of southern China. Throughout their history, the Miao have had to deal with Han China's southward expansion, which drove them into marginal, chiefly mountainous areas in southern China and northern areas of Myanmar, Thailand, Laos, and Vietnam (where they are known as the Hmong). Living in such isolated regions, the Miao group developed into several subsets, including Black, Red, Green, and Big Flowery Miao. Most of China's nearly 10 million Miao are in Guizhou Province, where local markets feature their intricate and expert craftsmanship, especially jewelry, embroidery, and batik. The Miao are also renowned for their festivals, particularly the Lusheng festival, which occurs from the 11th to the 18th of the first lunar month. Named after a Miao reed instrument, Lusheng is a week of lively music, dancing, horse races, and bullfights. The Guizhou city of Kaili is the center of Miao festivals, hosting more than 120 each year.

*end of Zhengyang Lu Pedestrian Street* ☎ *0773/282–2891* 🌐 *www.waterfallguilin.info/en/index.html* 🛏 *651 rooms, 23 suites* 🍴 *No meals.*

$$ HOTEL 🏨 **Sheraton Guilin** (贵阳喜来登饭店 *Guìlín xǐláidēng fàndiàn*). Easily the most elegant hotel in town, the Sheraton Guilin welcomes you with a chic lobby with a sunny atrium and glass elevators that whisk you upstairs. **Pros:** plenty of creature comforts; good restaurants; English-speaking staff. **Cons:** slightly overpriced. [$] *Rooms from: Y1320* ✉ *15 Binjiang Lu, on west bank of Li River* ☎ *0773/282–5588* 🌐 *www.sheraton.com/guilin* 🛏 *389 rooms, 19 suites* 🍴 *No meals.*

### NIGHTLIFE AND THE ARTS

**Back Garden Irish Pub** (后园爱尔兰酒吧 *Hòuyuán Àiěrlán jiǔbā*). This place offers occasional live music, a well-stocked bar, and a friendly owner. Guinness is available only in bottles, there's none on tap—yet. ✉ *Mingcheng Hotel, Zhengyang Lu* ☎ *773/280–3869.*

## LONGSHENG LONGJI RICE TERRACES

*120 km (74 miles; 3 hrs by bus) northwest of Guilin.*

**Longsheng Longji Rice Terraces** (龙胜龙脊梯田 *Lóngshèng lóngjí tītián*). A mesmerizing pattern of undulating fields has been cut into the hills at the Longsheng Longji Rice Terraces. These terraces, known as the "Dragon's Backbone," are amazing in both their scale and their beauty. They are worked, and have been for generations, by rice farmers from the local Yao, Dong, Zhuang, and Miao communities, who build their houses in villages on the terraced hills. 🎫 *Y80.*

### GETTING HERE AND AROUND

Buses are the best way to get to Heping, gateway to the Longsheng scenic area. The only alternative to a bus is to pay a premium to retain a taxi's services for the day, which will set you back at least Y500.

Buses heading to Heping from Guilin's Qintan Bus Station leave every 15 minutes and take about 2 hours (Y20). The express bus back to Guilin departs from Longsheng every two hours.

### SAFETY AND PRECAUTIONS

If you're hiring a cab to take you to Heping, avoid making the trip at night, as the road is full of sharp corners and is not well lit. Make sure your shoes have plenty of ankle support if you plan on hiking in the rice terraces; you'll avoid a twist or sprain.

### TIMING

The Longji Rice Terraces make for a fulfilling day trip from Guilin, but shutterbugs may want to catch the terraces at sunrise and sunset over the course of two or three days to maximize the chance of getting that perfect shot.

### TOURS

Longsheng is not home to any local tour companies. Travel plans in Longsheng are best arranged in Guilin. The stretch of Binjiang Lu south of the Sheraton has several English-speaking travel agencies.

**DID YOU KNOW?**

Most of the magnificent Longji terraced fields were built about 500 years ago, during the Ming Dynasty. They're called Dragon's Backbone because the peaks of the mountain range resemble the backbone of the dragon, and the water-filled terraces shimmer like a dragon's scales. If you stand at the summit, you can see the dragon's backbone curving off to the horizon.

CLOSE UP

## Guangxi's Silver-Toothed Touts

Aggressive touts are a fact of life for Western travelers in hyper-capitalist China. Guangxi Province is known for the tenacity of its touts—mostly older tribal women with silver teeth (as is the local custom). To these wandering merchants a Western traveler is a coin purse with legs.

It's not uncommon for half a dozen of these women to surround you at any given site, shouting "water" and "postcard." They'll follow you around until you buy something from each of them.

It's hard for travelers to maintain equilibrium when confronted with a gaggle of old women who seem doggedly intent on turning a hiking trip around, say, the Longsheng Rice Terraces into a no-win trinket-buying binge. Polite

"no, thank you's" can soon escalate into expletive-laden tirades, inevitably leading to remorse for cursing a poverty-stricken old woman.

What's worse, it accomplishes nothing. No sooner will the last bitter word leave your lips than someone will thrust a pack of commemorative postcards at you and shout "10 yuan!"

Consider the purchasing of minor souvenirs or unwanted sodas as part of the experience; keep a few yuan handy for just that, and deal with it smilingly. Failing that, you can always run. But remember, these old women know all the shortcuts, and you'll tire out and need to buy a beverage anyway. And maybe some postcards as well.

### WHERE TO EAT AND STAY

$
CHINESE
✕ **Li Qing Restaurant** (丽晴饭店 *Lìqíng fàndiàn*). In addition to well-known Chinese dishes, this extremely popular restaurant serves a number of less-common dishes like bamboo stuffed with sticky rice, or stir-fried mountain vegetables. $ *Average main: Y25* ✉ *Ji Lu, Ping'an* ☎ *0773/758–3048* 🚫 *No credit cards.*

$
B&B/INN
🛏 **Li Qing Guesthouse** (丽晴客站 *Lìqíng kèzhàn*). In the village of Ping'an, the Li Qing Guesthouse is run by sisters Liao Yan Li and Liao Yan Qing. **Pros:** friendly staff; reasonable rates; popular restaurant. **Cons:** can be noisy on weekends. $ *Rooms from: Y180* ✉ *Ji Lu, Ping'an* ☎ *0773/758–3048* 🛏 *30 rooms* 🍴 *No meals.*

## YANGSHUO

*70 km (43 miles; 90 min by bus) south of Guilin.*

Yangshuo has taken center stage as Guangxi's top tourist destination. At the heart of the city is West Street, a pedestrian mall extending to the Li River. Many visitors are content to spend a few days eating, drinking, and gazing over the low-slung traditional structures facing toward the fang-shaped peaks that surround the town. Yangshuo is fast becoming a destination for adventure travel, and the countryside is filled with opportunities for biking, hiking, rock climbing, and caving.

Keep in mind that Yangshuo isn't off the beaten path. It's part and parcel of the Southeast Asia backpacker circuit that was forged in the 1970s, and remains well-trodden to this day. The main drag throbs with the cacophony of Hong Kong canto-pop, reggae, hip-hop, and classic rock. In restaurants competing for the tourist trade you can order everything from lasagna to enchiladas to pad thai noodles.

### GETTING HERE AND AROUND

Arriving via train or airplane means traveling via Guilin. You can also get from Guilin to Yangshuo by bus or minibus, or via a costly but pleasant boat trip.

AIR TRAVEL Guilin Liangjiang International Airport is the gateway to Yangshuo. Taxis from Guilin Airport to Yangshuo cost around Y250.

BOAT TRAVEL The boat from Guilin takes approximately four hours. At Y380 for a round-trip ticket, it's costlier than other modes of travel, but the trip is pleasant and scenic. Tickets are available from any of the countless travel agents in Guilin.

BUS TRAVEL Departing from the Guilin Train Station, express luxury buses travel between Guilin and Yangshuo every half hour between 7 am and 8 pm. The trip in air-conditioned and smoke-free buses takes just under two hours and cost Y18.

### SAFETY AND PRECAUTIONS

Yangshuo is quite safe, but it is worth being extra careful if cycling outside of town, where cars tend to be faster and not always willing to yield much road space.

### TIMING

Two or three days is enough time to take in Yangshuo's town and surrounding areas.

### TOURS

If getting wet and muddy underground is your idea of a good time, look no farther than Water Cave, the deepest and largest underground grotto in the area. Accessible only by flat-bottom boat, it includes a mud bath and a number of crystal clear pools perfect for washing off. Tours can be arranged through any of the travel agencies in the Xi Jie area, including Charm Yangshuo Tour.

### ESSENTIALS

**Bank Bank of China** ✉ *93 Pantao Lu* ☎ *0773/882–0260.*

**Bus Contact Yangshuo Bus Station** ✉ *Pantao Lu, across from Yangshuo Park* ☎ *0773/882–2188.*

**Public Security Bureau PSB Yangshuo** ✉ *Pan Tao Lu* ☎ *0773/882–2178.*

**Visitor and Tour Info China International Travel Service** ✉ *Xi Jie, near Pantao Lu* ☎ *0773/882–7102.* **Charm Yangshuo Tour** ✉ *Pantao Lu* ☎ *0773/881–4355.*

### EXPLORING

**Moon Hill** (月亮山 *Yuèliàng shān*). Probably the most popular destination in Yangshuo, Moon Hill is named after the large hole through the center of this karst peak. Amazing vistas await at the top of the several trails that snake up the hill's side. ✉ *Yangshuo–Gaotian Lu* 🎟 *Y15* ⊙ *Daily 6 am–7:30 pm.*

8

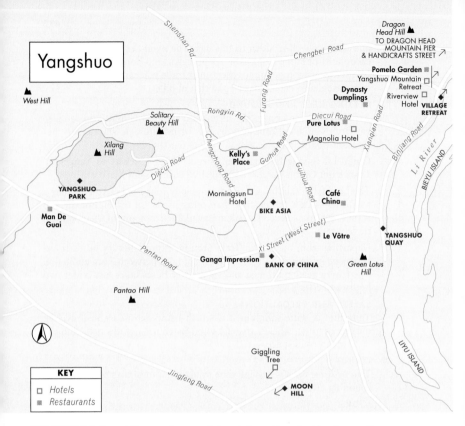

Yangshuo

West Hill

Solitary Beauty Hill

Xilang Hill

YANGSHUO PARK

Man De Guai

Pantao Hill

Shenshan Rd.

Chengbei Road

Dragon Head Hill
TO DRAGON HEAD MOUNTAIN PIER & HANDICRAFTS STREET

Pomelo Garden
Yangshuo Mountain Retreat
Riverview Hotel

Dynasty Dumplings

Furong Road

Rongyin Rd.

Diecui Road
Pure Lotus

Magnolia Hotel

VILLAGE RETREAT

Xianqian Road

Li River

BIEYU ISLAND

Binjiang Road

Kelly's Place

Chengzhong Road

Diecui Road

Guihua Road

Morningsun Hotel

Café China

BIKE ASIA

Xi Street (West Street)

Le Vôtre

YANGSHUO QUAY

Pantao Road

Ganga Impression

BANK OF CHINA

Green Lotus Hill

LIYU ISLAND

Giggling Tree

KEY
□ Hotels
■ Restaurants

Jingfeng Road

MOON HILL

---

**NEED A BREAK?**

**Sweet Heaven.** Lovers of chocolate and beer looking for an afternoon break should stop by Sweet Heaven. Belgian transplant to China Kathy will keep your palate entertained with imported Belgian pralines and beer as well as ice cream, milk shakes and coffee. Upstairs and rooftop seating means that these treats come served with pretty Li river views. ⊠ *12 Binjiang Lu* ☎ *0136/778–62400.*

**Yangshuo Park** (阳朔公园 *Yángshuò gōngyuán*). In the center of town, Yangshuo Park is where older people come to play chess while children scamper about in small playgrounds. The park has a number of statues and ponds worth seeing, and Yangshuo Park Peak has a small pagoda offering excellent views of the surrounding town. For a more intense climb with even better views, ascend the television tower across the street from the park's entrance. ⊠ *Diecui Lu, at Pantao Lu* 🖾 *Free* ☉ *Daily.*

### WHERE TO EAT

$

ECLECTIC

✕ **Café China** (原始人咖啡厅 *Yuánshǐrén kāfēitīng*). Located on a cozy corner on bustling West Street, Café China serves an addictive rotisserie chicken that is made from a highly guarded local recipe. The kitchen roasts between 12 and 18 chickens each night, so in-the-know diners call at least an hour in advance. One whole chicken will set you back

Y50. In addition, the kitchen also turns out shepherd's pie and sandwiches on baguettes. $ *Average main: Y35* ⊠ *34 Xi Jie* ☏ *138/0783–0498* ▭ *No credit cards.*

$

NORTHERN CHINESE

✕ **Dynasty Dumplings** (一品饺子 *Yīpǐn jiǎozi*). This local favorite serves some of the area's best northern-style dumplings. Don't leave town without trying them, either steamed or fried. You'll also find excellent local specialties like *pijiu yu* (beer fish) and *tian luo niang* (stuffed river snails). English menus are available, and the Beijing couple who own this place is very friendly. $ *Average main: Y15* ⊠ *21 Xianqian Jie, across from Magnolia Hotel* ▭ *No credit cards.*

$

MODERN INDIAN

✕ **Ganga Impression** (恒河印象 *Hénghé yìnxiàng*). A relative newcomer in town, Ganga Impression offers Indian classics of excellent quality and in large portions. Its rice, spices, and chefs come directly from India. The restaurant opens as early as 7 am, making this one of the few places to try an authentic Indian breakfast. ■TIP→ **If asked whether you want your food spicy, just say no. The food here could bring you to tears.** $ *Average main: Y45* ⊠ *Sunshine 100, Guihua Lu* ☏ *0773/881–1456.*

$

ECLECTIC

✕ **Kelly's Place** (灯笼风味馆 *Dēnglóng fēngwèiguǎn*). Beloved by expats, this closet-size café is an escape from the hustle and bustle of West Street. On any given night, English teachers can be found sampling tasty Chinese-style dumpling soups and drinking beer in the cobblestone pavilion. $ *Average main: Y30* ⊠ *43 Guihua Lu, 1 block north of Xi Jie* ☏ *0773/881–3233* ▭ *No credit cards.*

$

FRENCH

✕ **Le Vôtre** (乐德法式餐厅 *Lèdé fǎshì cāntīng*). A restored building dating from the Qing Dynasty is the setting for this French restaurant. With its slender wooden columns, the dining room subtly blends East and West. French specialties like grilled lamb chops and duck breast are nicely prepared, as are the pastas and pizzas. $ *Average main: Y40* ⊠ *79 Xi Jie* ☏ *0773/882–8040* ▭ *No credit cards.*

$

CHINESE

✕ **Man De Guai** (满得拐 *Mǎnde guǎi*). Popular with locals but almost unknown to travelers, this family-owned restaurant serves an amazing array of local dishes. There are no English menus, but the owners will bring you into the kitchen and let you pick out what you want. This place is hard to find: look for it on the small street two blocks north of the bus station, next to the large statue of Guanyin, the Buddha of Compassion. They also have a second restaurant on Jingfeng Lu. $ *Average main: Y25* ⊠ *41 Yangshuo Xie Bilian Dong* ☏ *0773/691–0959* ▭ *No credit cards.*

$

✕ **Pomelo Garden** (罗马假日山庄 *Luómǎ jiàrì yòuzi shānzhuāng*). A 20-minute walk from Yangshuo's center, the Village Retreat is an excellent place to enjoy a healthy breakfast, filling lunch, or a romantic dinner with views of the surrounding scenery. Trained by European masters, the chef clearly understands how Western food ought to taste—without neglecting the Chinese menu. Find yourself astonished by signature dishes such as sirloin steak served with Belgian-style fries. Finish your meal with coffee or a milk shake and a piece of their magnificent chocolate cake. $ *Average main: Y45* ⊠ *Village Retreat, Shi Ban Qiao Village* ☏ *073/888–8766* ⊕ *www.yangshuo-village-retreat.com.*

$

CHINESE

✕ **Pure Lotus** (暗香疏影素菜馆 *Ànxiāng shūyǐng sùcàiguǎn*). Yangshuo's only vegetarian restaurant serves a variety of mouthwatering creations,

8

Li river and the limestone karsts of Yangshuo

including almond rolls, crispy tofu skin in a spicy sauce, and a vegetarian version of the famous Shanghainese *shizi tou* (meatballs). The zen-like interior adds to the calm atmosphere which makes diners forget about the hubbub outside. The staff is helpful, there's an English menu, and the prices are very affordable. [$] *Average main: Y35* ✉ *Magnolia Hotel, 7 Die Cui Lu* ☎ *0773/881–8995* 🌐 *www.yangshuomagnolia.com/purelotus.htm* 💳 *No credit cards.*

## WHERE TO STAY

$ B&B/INN FAMILY Fodor's Choice ★ 🏨 **The Giggling Tree.** Nestled among the karst mountains outside of Yangshuo, the Giggling Tree is one of China's coolest guesthouses. **Pros:** beautiful views; quiet countryside; good food. **Cons:** a bit remote; taxis are sometimes hard to come by. [$] *Rooms from: Y250* ✉ *Aishanmen Village* ☎ *136/6786–6154* 🌐 *www.gigglingtree.com* 🛏 *22 rooms* 💳 *No credit cards* 🍴 *Breakfast.*

$ HOTEL 🏨 **Magnolia Hotel** (白玉兰酒店 *Báiyùlán jiǔdiàn*). Built around a traditional courtyard, the Magnolia welcomes you with a glass-roofed lobby overlooking a lovely carp pond. **Pros:** comfortable rooms; lovely views; good value. **Cons:** uninspiring decor; noisy area of town. [$] *Rooms from: Y300* ✉ *7 Diecui Lu* ☎ *0773/881–9288* 🌐 *www.yangshuomagnolia.com* 🛏 *29 rooms, 1 suite* 🍴 *No meals.*

$ HOTEL 🏨 **Riverview Hotel** (望江楼客站 *Wàngjiānglóu kèzhàn*). With its curvaceous tile roof and balconies with stunning views of the Li River, this is one of the town's nicest budget hotels. **Pros:** comfortable rooms; tasty restaurant; river views. **Cons:** slightly isolated from the rest of town. [$] *Rooms from: Y300* ✉ *15 Binjiang Lu* ☎ *0773/882–2688* 🌐 *www.riverview.com.cn* 🛏 *52 rooms* 🍴 *Breakfast.*

$

B&B/INN

FAMILY

Fodor's Choice

★

**⚐ Village Retreat** (罗马假日山庄 *Luómǎjiàrì yòuzi shānzhuāng*). In Shi Ban Qiao, a village around 20 minutes walking from Yangshuo's center, sits one of the town's more eccentric hotels. **Pros:** great views; excellent restaurant; superb value. **Cons:** eclectic decor may not appeal to all. $ *Rooms from: Y278* ⊠ *Shi Ban Qiao Village* ☎ *0773/888–8766* ⊕ *www.yangshuo-village-retreat.com* ⮡ *13 rooms, 2 suites, 1 penthouse* ⦿| *No meals.*

$

RESORT

FAMILY

**⚐ Yangshuo Mountain Retreat** (阳朔胜地渡假山庄 *Yángshuò shèngdì dùjiǎ shānzhuāng*). Far away from the hubbub of Yangshuo, the Yangshuo Mountain Retreat is one of the area's most relaxing lodgings. **Pros:** quiet atmosphere; some of the best views around. **Cons:** too remote for some. $ *Rooms from: Y350* ⊠ *Gaotian Town* ☎ *773/877–7091* ⊕ *www. yangshuomountainretreat.com* ⮡ *29 rooms* ⦿| *No meals.*

## NIGHTLIFE

**The Alley** (阿里酒吧 *Ālǐ jiǔbā*). With its impressive selection of beers and spirits, the Alley also happens to serve excellent pub grub like burgers and pizza. Open until late at night, it's an excellent alternative for those seeking a quieter hangout. ⊠ *Guihua Lu* ☎ *0136/678–66922* ⊕ *www. yangshuo-beer-bar.com.*

## SPORTS AND THE OUTDOORS

### BIKING

**Bike Asia.** Cheaply made mountain bikes are available all over Yangshuo for about Y10 per day. For a better-quality ride, Bike Asia rents all sizes for Y70 per day. The company also leads short trips to the villages along the Li River that start at Y150. In the evening, the shop is transformed into a bar popular with expats called the Rusty Bolt. ⊠ *22 Guihua Lu* ☎ *0773/882–6521* ⊕ *www.bikeasia.com.*

### BOATING

Starting as a humble spring at the top of Mao'er Mountain, the majestic Li River snakes through Guangxi, connecting Yangshuo to many other towns along the way. One of the country's most scenic—and less polluted—rivers, its banks are lined with stone embankments where people practice tai chi. Several local companies offer rides on bamboo rafts along the river. You can bargain with them at the stone quay at the end of West Street.

### ROCK CLIMBING

**Black Rock Climbing.** Yangshuo is the undisputed rock-climbing capital of China. Run by an American-Chinese couple, Blackrock is the go-to place for guided climbs suited for all skill levels. The experienced crew takes care of all necessary equipment and transportation. Half-day climbs are Y220 per person; a full day will set you back Y450. ⊠ *19 Guihua Lu* ☎ *773/881–9656* ⊕ *www. blackrockclimbing.net.*

8

### SHOPPING

West Street is filled with shops selling everything from tourist junk to high-quality handicrafts. Also explore Dragon Head Mountain Pier Handicrafts Street, a cobblestone street running along the river. You can bargain merchants down to half the original asking price or even less.

### SIDE TRIPS FROM YANGSHUO

Yangshuo is an exceptional base from which to explore the villages along the Li River, many of which date back hundreds of years.

> **WORD OF MOUTH**
>
> "I went on a small boat down the Li River, which was beautiful. I enjoyed the small boat because you could get outside of it and sit on the top of it rather than the large tourist boats. There's plenty of outdoor activities in Yangshuo and it's not a big city like Guilin."
> —aquawink

## NANNING

*350 km (217 miles; 5 hrs by train) southwest of Guilin; 440 km (273 miles; 24 hrs by train) southeast of Guiyang; 600 km (372 miles; 16 hrs by train) west of Hong Kong.*

Built along the banks of the Yong River, Nanning is the capital of Guangxi Zhuang Autonomous Region. The city isn't a major tourist draw, but it is a pleasant place to stop for a day or two. Many travelers come here for a visa before continuing into Vietnam.

### GETTING HERE AND AROUND

Nanning is most accessible by bus from elsewhere in Guangxi. For anything beyond, it's a flight or an overnight train.

AIR TRAVEL  Nanning Wuxu International Airport is 31 km (19 miles) southwest of the city and has flights throughout China, including to Guilin.

BUS TRAVEL  There are frequent buses between Nanning and Guilin, taking at least four hours. There is no direct service from Yangshuo.

TRAIN TRAVEL  Nanning's train station is at the northwestern edge of town, and offers frequent service to Guilin. The fastest of these takes five hours.

### SAFETY AND PRECAUTIONS

Nanning is a quiet and safe city, but some areas can be poorly lit at night—make sure you watch where you're going after sundown.

### TIMING

Nanning doesn't have much going on tourism-wise, but is an otherwise pleasant city with nice parks.

### ESSENTIALS

**Air Contact Nanning Wuxu International Airport** ☎ *0771/209–5160.*

**Banks Bank of China** ✉ *39 Gu Cheng Lu* ☎ *0771/281–1267.*

**Bus Contact Nanning Bus Station** ✉ *65 Huadong Lu* ☎ *0771/242–4529.*

**Medical Assistance Nanning First Municipal People's Hospital** ✉ *89 Qixing Lu* ☎ *0771/267–7885.*

**Public Security Bureau PSB Nanning** ✉ *5 Ke Yuan East Rd., Xi Xiang Tang* ☎ *110, 0771/289–1302.*

**Train Contact Nanning Railway Station** ✉ *North end of Chaoyang Lu* ☎ *0771/243–2468.*

**Visitor and Tour Info China International Travel Service** ✉ *40 Xinmin Lu* ☎ *0771/532–0165.*

## EXPLORING

**Guangxi Zhuang Autonomous Region Museum** (广西自治区博物馆 *Guǎngxi zhuàng zìzhìqū bówùguǎn*). This museum focuses on Guangxi's numerous ethnic minorities. In the back are magnificent full-size reconstructions of houses, pagodas, and drum towers set among attractive pools and bridges. A collection of more than 300 bronze drums made by local people is also on display. ✉ *34 Minzu Dadao* ☎ *0771/281–0907* 🌐 *www.gxmuseum.com* 🎫 *Free* 🕒 *Tues.–Sun. 9–5.*

**People's Park** (人民 *Rénmín gōngyuán*). Surrounding White Dragon Lake, People's Park has some 200 species of rare trees and flowers. Here you'll find the remains of fortifications built by a warlord in the early part of the 20th century. ✉ *1 Renmin Dong Lu* 🎫 *Free* 🕒 *Daily 8:30–6.*

**South Lake** (南湖 *Nánhú*). In the southeastern part of the city, South Lake covers more than 200 acres. A bonsai exhibit and an orchid garden are in the surrounding park. The park is encircled by a wide path that's ideal for strolling or jogging. ✉ *Gucheng Lu* 🎫 *Free* 🕒 *Daily.*

## WHERE TO EAT

$ CHINESE 🍴 **Beifang Renjia** (北方人家 *Běifāng rénjiā*). Tired of the local rice noodles? This is where many transplants from northeastern China come to dine on traditional *dongbei cai*. A large dumpling menu is complemented by a full range of northeastern favorites such as moo shu pork and *disanxian* (eggplant, potatoes, and green peppers in a brown sauce). Wash it all down with a cold Harbin beer. The staff is friendly, and the menu has photos and descriptions in English. [$] *Average main: Y25* ✉ *Hong Men Hotel, 6 Huichun Lu, 3rd fl.* ☎ *0771/530–4263* 💳 *No credit cards.*

$$ ITALIAN FAMILY Fodor's Choice ★ 🍴 **The Here** (*Zhèlǐ*). Homemade pastas and pizzas, delicious salads and sandwiches, a great beer selection, and the best coffee in Guangxi—The Here serves the finest Western food you'll find for hundreds of miles in any direction. In addition to the amazing food and drinks, the staffers are friendly and seem to genuinely enjoy themselves. The decor is plush and comfortable, and the music is chilled out. [$] *Average main: Y55* ✉ *131 Minzu Dadao, behind the Admiral City Mall* ☎ *0771/588–7183* 💳 *No credit cards.*

$ CHINESE 🍴 **Xuyuan** (*Xùyuán*). Inside what was once the residence of General Huang Xuchu, this much acclaimed restaurant serves excellent versions of classic dishes, such as cold beef slices drenched in lemon juice, pork rolls, and roast duck. The menu includes plenty of pictures for easy ordering. The restaurant accommodates guests in private dining rooms, so noise levels are kept relatively low. [$] *Average main: Y30* ✉ *53 Mingde Jie, next to the Yongjiang Hotel* ☎ *0771/280–8228.*

8

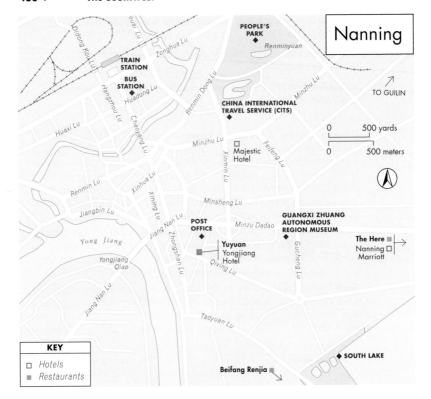

### WHERE TO STAY

**$**
**HOTEL**
**Fodor's Choice**
★

🛏 **Majestic Hotel** (明园新都大酒店 *Míngyuán xīndū dàjiǔdiàn*). Close to the main square, this luxury hotel has been refurbished reasonably well and is efficiently run. **Pros:** professional staff; well-outfitted gym; pleasant pool. **Cons:** in a tough place to catch a cab; not much of interest in the immediate vicinity. $ *Rooms from: Y280* ✉ *38 Xinmin Lu* ☎ *0771/283–0808* 🛏 *290 rooms* 🍽 *Breakfast.*

**$$**
**HOTEL**

🛏 **Nanning Marriott** (南宁金伟万豪酒店 *Nánníng jīnwěiwànháo jiǔdiàn*). In an eye-catching cylindrical tower, the Marriott is located in the city's northeastern reaches. **Pros:** good service; high-tech touches; good for business travelers. **Cons:** far from the city center. $ *Rooms from: Y1050* ✉ *131 Minzu Dadao* ☎ *771/536–6688* 🌐 *www. nanningmarriott.com* 🛏 *328 rooms* 🍽 *No meals.*

**$**
**HOTEL**

🛏 **Yongjiang Hotel** (邕江宾馆 *Yōngjiāng bīnguǎn*). With nice views of the bridge crossing the Yongjiang River, this is one of Nanning's most venerable luxury hotels. **Pros:** central location; reasonable rates; excellent service. **Cons:** pool not open all year; little personal touch. $ *Rooms from: Y385* ✉ *1 Linjiang Lu* ☎ *0771/282–9585* 🌐 *www.yongjianghotel. com* 🛏 *130 rooms* 🍽 *No meals.*

# GUIZHOU

With its undulating mountains, terraced fields, and traditional villages, Guizhou is among China's most interesting provinces. It has less tourism infrastructure than neighboring Guangxi or Yunnan, so Guizhou attracts visitors intent on heading off the beaten path.

More than a third of Guizhou's population belongs to one of a dozen ethnic minorities, including the Dong, Hui, Yao, Zhuang, and Miao (known in the west as the Hmong) peoples. The countryside is sprinkled with villages dominated by impressive towers—most notably those of the Dong. The province is known for its festivals, and it's hard to travel through Guizhou without running into at least one celebration.

**REGIONAL TOURS**

**Dylan Gu.** Fluent in English, Mandarin, Miao, and Dong, this tour guide knows Guizhou like the back of his hand. He is happy to custom tailor an excursion to meet your needs. Guided trips start at Y400 a day. ⊠ *Kaili* ☎ *0137/655–505–010.*

**WildChina Travel.** Founded by a native of neighboring Yunnan Province, WildChina Travel runs several high-end tours that either pass through Guizhou or are entirely dedicated to the province. Most focus on the province's incredible minority cultures and include village homestays. A one-week tour of Guizhou is $1,760, including food and lodging. ☎ *0106/465–6602* ⊕ *www.wildchina.com.*

## GUIYANG

*350 km (217 miles; 12 hrs by fastest train) northwest of Guilin; 425 km (264 miles; 12 hrs by train) northwest of Nanning; 850 km (527 miles; 20½ hrs by train) northwest of Hong Kong; 1,650 km (1,023 miles; 21 hrs by train) southwest of Beijing.*

The capital Guiyang is a pleasant place to begin an exploration of the province. Like most cities in China, it is fast losing its older buildings, but even in the heart of downtown enough remain to make a short stay here worthwhile. The main streets of the sprawling city are Zunyi Lu, Ruijin Lu, Zhonghua Lu, and Yan'an Lu.

**GETTING HERE AND AROUND**

AIR TRAVEL  Guiyang Airport lies 15 km (9 miles) to the southeast of the city. There are direct flights between Guiyang and most of China's main cities.

BUS TRAVEL  Guiyang East Passenger Terminal, the city's main long-distance bus station, has been relocated to the remote airport district southeast of the city. Luckily, the smaller bus station on Jiefang Lu just north of Guiyang's train station still has regular bus service to Anshun (2 hrs), Kaili (2 hrs), and other destinations around Guizhou and the rest of China.

TRAIN TRAVEL  Direct trains link Guiyang with Chongqing (9 hrs), Guilin (12 hrs), Kunming (10 hrs), Liuzhou (8 hrs), Nanning (12 hrs), and Shanghai (26 hrs). The train station is at the southwest edge of the city at the southern end of Zunyi Lu.

### SAFETY AND PRECAUTIONS

The biggest threat to personal safety in Guiyang is the frenetic traffic. Use the city's numerous pedestrian tunnels whenever possible, and never expect drivers to follow traffic rules or exercise sound judgment. Be careful with your valuables and stay vigilant for pickpockets and bag snatchers.

### TIMING

A day or two is enough time to visit most of the sights and sample some local delicacies.

### ESSENTIALS

**Air Contact Guiyang Airport** ☎ *0851/549–8908.*

**Bank Bank of China** ✉ *347 Ruijin Nan Lu* ☎ *0851/581–3954.*

**Bus Contact Guizhou Stadium Bus Station** ✉ *Jiefang Lu, 1 block north of the train station* ☎ *0851/579–3381.*

**Public Security Bureau PSB Guiyang** ☎ *0851/798–7284.*

**Train Contact Guiyang Railway Station** ✉ *Zunyi Lu* ☎ *0851/818–1222.*

**Visitor and Tour Info China International Travel Service** ✉ *1 Hequn Lu* ☎ *0851/690–1506.*

### EXPLORING

### TOP ATTRACTIONS

FAMILY **Qianling Park** (黔灵公园 *Qíanlíng gōngyuán*). Dominating this 740-acre park is a 4,265-foot-high mountain that has fine views of the town from its western peak. The park itself has a bit of everything, including thousands of plants and a collection of birds and monkeys (many of which roam freely through the park). ✉ *187 Zaoshan Lu, 2½ km (1 mile) northwest of city* 🚗 *Y5* ⏲ *Daily 6:30 am–10 pm.*

　**Unicorn Cave** (麒麟洞 *Qílín dòng*). Discovered in 1531, Unicorn Cave was used as a prison for the two Nationalist generals, Yang Hucheng and Chang Xueliang, who were accused of collaborating with the Communists when Chiang Kai-shek was captured at Xi'an in 1937.

**Underground Gardens** (地下公园 *Dìxià gōngyuán*). In this poetically named cave, 1,925 feet below the ground, a path weaves its way past the various rock formations, which are illuminated to emphasize their similarity with animals, fruits, and other living things. ✉ *25 km (15 miles) south of Guiyang* ☎ *0851/511–4014* 🚗 *Free* ⏲ *Daily 9–5.*

### WORTH NOTING

FAMILY **Hebin Park** (河滨公园 *Hébīn gōngyuán*). Filled with bamboo groves, Hebin Park sits on the banks of the Nanming River. In many ways it's the architypical Chinese park, with senior citizens practicing tai chi in the pavilions, young couples strolling hand in hand, and the omnipresent sound of music and public announcements playing from loudspeakers. For children, there's a Ferris wheel and other rides. ✉ *Ruijin Nan Lu* 🚗 *Free* ⏲ *Daily 5 am–midnight.*

*Continued on page 490*

# FOR ALL THE TEA IN CHINA

Legend has it that the first cup dates from 2737 BC, when Camellia sinensis leaves fell into water being boiled for Emperor Shenong. He loved the result, tea was born, and so were many traditions.

Historically, when a girl accepted a marriage proposal she drank tea, a gesture symbolizing fidelity. Betrothal gifts were known as "tea gifts," engagements as "accepting tea," and marriages as "eating tea." Today the bride and groom kneel before their parents, offering cups of tea in thanks.

Serving tea is a sign of respect. Young people proffer it to their parents or grandparents; subordinates do the same for their bosses. Pouring tea also signifies submission, so it's a way to say you're sorry. When you're served tea, show your thanks by tapping the table with your index and middle fingers.

And forget about adding milk or sugar. Not only is most Chinese tea best without it, but why dilute and sweeten a beverage long known by herbalists to be good for you? Even modern medicine acknowledges that tea's powerful antioxidants reduce the risk of cancer and heart disease. It's also thought to be such a good source of fluoride that Mao Zedong eschewed toothpaste for a green-tea rinse. Smiles, everyone.

In China, tea was first discovered by the Emperor Shennong.

## HISTORICAL BREW

Tea preparation is a careful affair.

### THE RISE AND FALL OF EMPIRES

Tea has a long and tumultuous history, making and breaking empires in both the East and the West. Bricks of tea were used as currency, and Chinese statesmen kept rebellious northern nomads in check by refusing to sell it to them.

Rumor has it that tea caused the downfall of the Song Empire. Apparently, tea-whisking was Emperor Huizong's favorite pastime: he was so obsessed with court tea culture that he forgot all about trivial little matters like defense. The country became vulnerable to invasion and fell to the Mongols in 1279.

Genghis preferred airag (fermented mare's milk), but after the Mongol's defeat, the drink of kings returned with a vengeance to the court of the Ming Dynasty (1368–1644). Tea as we know it today dates to this period: the first Ming emperor, Hongwu, set the trend of using loose-leaf tea by refusing to accept tea tribute gifts in any other form.

### TEA GOES INTERNATIONAL

The first Europeans to encounter the beverage were navigators and missionaries who visited China in the mid-16th century. In 1610, Dutch traders began importing tea from China into Europe, with the Portuguese hot on their heels. It was initially marketed as a health drink and took a while to catch on. By the 1640s, tea had become popular among both the Dutch and Portuguese aristocracy, initially the only ones who could afford it.

Although we think of tea as a quintessentially British drink, it actually arrived in America two years before it appeared in Britain. When the British acquired New Amsterdam (later New York) in 1664, the colony consumed more tea than all the British isles put together.

Tea was available in Britain from about 1554 onward, but Brits were wary of the stuff at first. What tipped the scales in tea's favor was nothing less than celebrity product endorsement. King

All types of tea come from one plant.

Charles II married the Portuguese princess Catherine of Braganza in 1662. She arrived in England with tea and fine porcelain tea ware in her dowry and a healthy addiction to the stuff. Members of the royalty were the 16th century's trendsetters: tea became the thing to drink at court; pretty soon the general public was hooked, too.

## STORMS IN A TEACUP

Tea quickly became a very important—and troublemaking—commodity. Religious leaders thought the drink sinful and doctors declared it a health risk. In Britain, ale-brewers were losing profits and pressure groups successfully persuaded the government to tax tea at 119%. On top of all this, the immensely powerful British East India Company held the monopoly on tea importation.

Tea's value skyrocketed: by 1706, the retail price of green tea in London was equivalent to $300 for 100 g (3.5 oz), far beyond the reach of normal people. Tea smuggling quickly became a massive—and often cut-throat—business. To make sought-after tea supplies stretch even further, they were routinely mixed with twigs, leaves, animal dung, and even poisonous chemicals.

Back in the New World, Americans were fed up with paying taxes that went straight back to Britain. Things came to a head when a group of patriots dressed as Native Americans peacefully boarded British ships in Boston harbor and emptied 342 chests of tea into the water. The act came to be known as the Boston Tea Party and was a vital catalyst in starting the American Revolution.

The War of Independence wasn't the only war sparked by tea. In Britain, taxes were axed and, as tea was suddenly affordable for everyone, demand grew exponentially. But China remained the world's only supplier, so that by the mid-19th century, tea was causing a massive trade deficit. The British started exporting opium into China in exchange for tea, provoking two Opium Wars. In the 1880s, attempts to grow tea in India were finally successful and Indian tea began to overtake Chinese tea on the market.

These days, over 3.2 million metric tons of tea are produced annually worldwide. After water, tea is the world's favorite drink. Though Britain and Ireland now consume far more tea per capita than China, tea is still a regular presence at the Chinese table and is inextricably bound to Chinese culture.

## ANCIENT TRADE ROUTES

The Ancient Tea and Horse Caravan Road, also known as the Southern Silk Road, is a trade corridor dating back to the Tang Dynasty (618–907). The 4,000-km route emerged more than 1,200 years ago and was actually still in use until recently.

Back in the heyday of the Caravan Road, Xishuangbanna, Dali, Lijiang, and many other parts of Yunnan were important outposts on the route. Tea, horses, salt, medicinal herbs, and Indian spices all featured prominently in this massive network.

During World War II, the route was used to smuggle supplies from India into the interior of Japanese-occupied China.

## DRINKING IN THE CULTURE

The way tea was prepared historically bears little resemblance to the steep-a-teabag method many westerners employ today. Tea originally came in bricks of compressed leaves bound with sheep's blood or manure. Chunks were broken, ground into a powder, and whisked into hot water. In the first tea manual, *Cha Jing (The Way of Tea)*, Tang-dynasty writer Lu Yu describes preparing powdered tea using 28 pieces of teaware, including big brewing pans and shallow drinking bowls.

The potters of Yixing (near Shanghai) gradually transformed wine vessels into small pots for steeping tea. Yixing pottery is ideal for brewing: its fine unglazed clay is highly porous, and if you always use the same kind of tea, the pot will take on its flavor.

Today the most elaborate Chinese tea service—which requires only two pots and enough cups for all involved—is called *gong fu cha* (skilled tea method). Although you can experience it at many teahouses, most people consider it too involved for every day. They simply brew their leaf tea in three-piece lidded cups, called *gaiwan*, tilting the lid as they drink so that it acts as a strainer.

### THE CEREMONY

1 Rinse teapot with hot water.

2 Fill with black or oolong to one third of its height.

3 Half-fill teapot with hot water and empty immediately to rinse leaves.

4 Fill pot with hot water, let leaves steep for a minute; no bubbles should form.

5 Pour tea into small cups, moving the spout continuously over each, so all have the same strength of tea.

6 Pour the excess into a second teapot.

7 Using the same leaves, repeat the process up to five times, extending the steeping time slightly.

Green Tea leaves in a Chinese gaiwan

## TEA TIMELINE

Japanese tea ceremony

| | |
|---|---|
| 350 AD | "Tea" appears in Chinese dictionary. |
| 618–1644 | Tea falls into and out of favor at Chinese court. |
| 7th c. | Tea introduced to Japan. |
| 1610–1650 | Dutch and Portuguese traders bring tea to Europe. |
| 1662 | British King Charles II marries Portugal's Catherine of Braganza, a tea addict. Tea craze sweeps the court. |
| 1689 | Tea taxation starts in Britain; peaks at 119%. |

## HOW TEA IS MADE

Chinese tea is grown on large plantations and nearly always picked by hand. Pluckers remove only the top two leaves. A skilled plucker can collect up to 35 kg (77 lbs) of leaves in a day; that's 9 kg (almost 20 lbs) of tea, or 3,500 cups. After a week, new top leaves will have grown, and bushes can be plucked again. Climate and soil play an important role on a tea plantation, much as they do in a vineyard. But what really differentiates black, green, and oolong teas is the way leaves are processed.

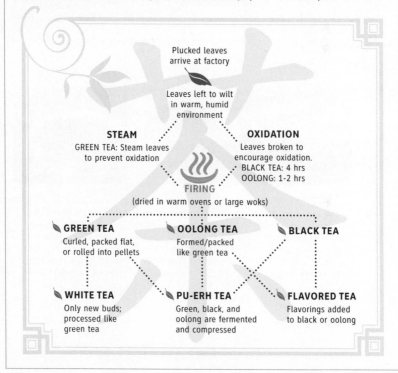

Plucked leaves arrive at factory

Leaves left to wilt in warm, humid environment

**STEAM**
GREEN TEA: Steam leaves to prevent oxidation

**OXIDATION**
Leaves broken to encourage oxidation.
BLACK TEA: 4 hrs
OOLONG: 1-2 hrs

**FIRING**
(dried in warm ovens or large woks)

**GREEN TEA**
Curled, packed flat, or rolled into pellets

**OOLONG TEA**
Formed/packed like green tea

**BLACK TEA**

**WHITE TEA**
Only new buds; processed like green tea

**PU-ERH TEA**
Green, black, and oolong are fermented and compressed

**FLAVORED TEA**
Flavorings added to black or oolong

Boston Tea Party

| 1773 | Boston Tea Party: Americans dump 342 chests of tea into Boston Harbor, protesting British taxes. |
| 1784 | British tea taxes slashed; consumption soars. |
| 1835 | Tea cultivation starts in Assam, India. |
| 1880s | India and Ceylon produce more tea than China. |
| 1904 | Englishman Richard Blechynden creates iced tea at St. Louis World's Fair. |
| 1908 | New York importer Thomas Sullivan sends clients samples in silk bags—the first tea bags. |
| 2004 | Chinese tea exports overtake India's for the first time since the 1880s. |

## TYPES OF TEA

Some teas are simply named for the region that produces them (Yunnan or Assam); others are evocatively named to reflect a particular blend. Some are transliterated (like Keemun); others translated (Iron Goddess of Mercy). Confused? Keep two things in mind. First, the universal word for tea comes from one Chinese character—pronounced either "te" (Xiamen dialect) or "cha" (Cantonese and Mandarin).

| | BLACK | PU-ERH | GREEN |
|---|---|---|---|
| Overview | It's popular in the West so it makes up the bulk of China's tea exports. It has a stronger flavor than green tea, though this varies according to type. | Pu-erh tea is green, black, or oolong fermented from a few months to 50 years and formed into balls. Pu-erh is popular in Hong Kong, where it's called Bo Le. | Most tea grown and consumed in China is green. It's delicate, so allow the boiling water to cool for a minute before brewing to prevent "cooking" the tea. |
| Flavor | From light and fresh to rich and chocolatey | Rich, earthy | Light, aromatic |
| Color | Golden dark brown | Reddish brown | Light straw-yellow to bright green |
| Caffeine per Serving | 40 mg | 20–40 mg | 20 mg |
| Ideal Water Temperature | 203°F | 203°F | 160°F |
| Steeping Time | 3–5 mins. | 3–5 mins. | 1–2 mins. |
| Examples | Dian Hong (chocolatey aftertaste; unlike other Chinese teas, can take milk). Keemun (Qi Men; mild, smoky; once used in English breakfast blends). Lapsang Souchong (dried over smoking pine; strong flavor). Yunnan Golden (full bodied, malty). | Buying Pu-erh is like buying wine: there are different producers and different vintages, and prices vary greatly. | Bi Luo Chun (Green Snail Spring; rich, fragrant). Chun Mee (Eyebrow; pale yellow; floral). Hou Kui (Monkey Tea; nutty, sweet; floral aftertaste). Long Ding (Dragon Mountain; sweet, minty). Long Jing (Dragon's Well; bright green; nutty). |

Black
Pu-erh
Green
White
Oolong
Flavored

| | WHITE | OOLONG | FLAVORED |
|---|---|---|---|
| Overview | The rare white tea is made from the newest buds, picked unopened at daybreak and processed like green tea. Small batches mean high prices. It's a tea for refined palates. | Halfway between green and black tea, this tea is more popular in China than elsewhere. The gong fu cha ceremony best reveals its complexities. | Petals, bark, and other natural ingredients are added to black or green tea to create these brews. Earl Grey is black tea scented with bergamot (a recipe supposedly given to the tea's 18th-century namesake by a Mandarin). Jasmine tea is green tea dried with jasmine petals. Others include lychee congou and rose congou: black tea dried with lychee juice or rose petals. Flavor, color, caffeine content, and ideal preparation depend on the tea component of the blend. Don't confuse flavored teas with the caffeine-free herbal teas made from herbs, roots, and blossoms (e.g., chamomile, peppermint, rosehips, licorice, ginger). |
| Flavor | Very subtle | Aromatic, lighter than black tea | |
| Color | Very pale yellow | Pale green to pale brown | |
| Caffeine per Serving | 15 mg | 30 mg | |
| Ideal Water Temperature | 185°F | 203°F | |
| Steeping Time | 4–15 mins | 1–9 mins. | |
| Examples | Bai Hao Yin Zhen (Silver Needle; finest white tea; sweet and very delicate, anti-toxin qualities). Bai Mu Dan (White Peony; smooth and refreshing). | Da Hong Pao (Scarlet Robe; comes from only 4 bushes; full bodied, floral). Tie Guan Yin (Iron Goddess of Mercy; legend has it a farmer repaired statue of the goddess, who rewarded him with the tea bush shoot; golden yellow; floral). | |

8

IN FOCUS FOR ALL THE TEA IN CHINA

## WHERE TO EAT

Every province has a number of dishes that locals point to with pride. In Guizhou this is unquestionably *suan tang yu,* or fish in a sour soup. It combines a mouth-numbing number of herbs, spices, and local vegetables to make a dish that is at once spicy and savory. Another wonderfully named dish is *lian ai doufu guo,* or "the bean curd in love." It's a strip of vegetable- or meat-stuffed tofu toasted to a golden brown and sprinkled with sesame oil. It's a popular dish with couples.

$ INTERNATIONAL 🍴 **Highlands Coffee** (高原咖啡 *Gāoyuán kāfēi*). Understated decor, comfy seating, and high-quality imported coffee turned into tasty beverages by skilled baristas are the highlights here. There are also savory paninis on homemade bread, as well as a wide selection of teas, smoothies, and desserts. The affable American owner is often present, and always tries to make visitors feel at home. The smoking area is separated from the rest of the dining area. [$] *Average main: Y30* ✉ *1 Liudong Jie, Bo'ai Lu* ☎ *0851/582–6222* 🌐 *www.highlands-coffee.com.*

$$$ SEAFOOD Fodor's Choice ★ 🍴 **Old Kaili Sour Fish Restaurant** (老凯里酸汤鱼 *Lǎo kǎil suāntāngyú*). Sour fish soup, Guiyang's signature dish, is the specialty at this venerated local joint. Choose a fish from the tanks, select your other ingredients, and mix your own sauce. The soup—an import from the city of Kaili—and the fish will then be cooked at your table. Should yours

be too spicy, remember that a bit of white rice—*not* water—is the best method for dousing culinary flames. There are no reservations, so expect to queue a bit on weekends or holidays. Because of increasing popularity, the restaurant has recently added branch on nearby Shengfu Bei Jie. $ *Average main: Y150* ✉ *55 Shengfu Lu* ☎ *0851/584–3665* ⚏ *Reservations not accepted* ▭ *No credit cards* ⊘ *No lunch.*

## WHERE TO STAY

$ ▦ **Amber Hotel** (时光驿 *Shíguāng yì*). A 10-minute walk from the city
B&B/INN center, this tasteful boutique hotel has unique and spacious rooms fur-
Fodor'sChoice nished with dark wood and natural stone. **Pros:** exceptional value; very
★ comfortable rooms. **Cons:** slightly outside the center. $ *Rooms from: Y400* ✉ *47 Dongshan Lu* ☎ *0851/688–0777* ⤳ *25 rooms* ▭ *No credit cards* ⦿ *No meals.*

$ ▦ **Nenghui Jiudian** (能辉酒店 *Nénghuī jiǔdiàn*). With a central location,
HOTEL cozy accommodations, and reasonable prices, this handsome, mod-
ern hotel offers a lot of bang for the yuan. **Pros:** close to the sights; nice rooms; bargain rates. **Cons:** noisy part of town. $ *Rooms from: Y450* ✉ *38 Ruijin Nan Lu* ☎ *0851/589–8888* ⊕ *www.nenghuihotel. com* ⤳ *125 rooms* ⦿ *Breakfast.*

$$ ▦ **Sheraton Guiyang Hotel** (喜来登贵酒店 *Xǐláidēng guìháng jiǔdiàn*).
HOTEL Among the city's best lodgings, this chain hotel has everything a high-end traveler needs, and more: a full-service spa, a bar with amazing city views, great international dining, and an attentive staff. **Pros:** excellent city views; near a pretty park; soothing spa. **Cons:** a bit impersonal. $ *Rooms from: Y1100* ✉ *49 Zhonghua Nan Lu* ☎ *0851/588–8888* ⊕ *www.sheraton.com/guiyang* ⤳ *335 rooms, 41 suites* ⦿ *Breakfast.*

## SIDE TRIP TO HUANGGUOSHU FALLS

Fodor'sChoice **Huangguoshu Falls** (黄果树瀑布 *Huángguǒshù pùbù*). The Baishui River
★ tumbles over nine sets of rocks, creating nine waterfalls over a course of 2 km (1 mile). At the highest point, Huangguoshu Falls drops an eye-popping 230 feet. The largest in China, these falls are set in lush countryside where you'll find numerous villages. You can enjoy them from afar or by wading across the Rhinoceros Pool *(Xiniu Jian)* to the Water Curtain Cave *(Shuilian Dong)* hidden behind the main falls. Seven km (4½ miles) downstream is the **Star Bridge Falls** *(Xingqiao Pu)*. The falls are at their best from May through October. To avoid switching buses en route at the city of Anshu, book a tour with a local agency or at your hotel. ✉ *160 km (99 miles) southwest of Guiyang* ☎ *400/683–3333* ◪ *Y180* ⊘ *Daily dawn–dusk.*

# KAILI

*200 km (124 miles; 3 hrs by train) east of Guiyang.*

Capital of the Qian Dongnan Miao and Dong Autonomous Region, Kaili serves as the starting point for a journey to the Miao and Dong villages that dominate eastern Guizhou. More than two-thirds of the population is Miao, and their villages are along the eastern and north-eastern outskirts of Kaili. The Dong communities are to the southeast.

Outside town the local villages are of great interest. To the north is the Wuyang River, which passes by many mountains, caves, and Miao

Huangguoshu Falls, the largest of a series of nine waterfalls

villages. At **Shibing** you can take boat rides through spectacular limestone gorges and arrange stops at these towns. South of Kaili are the Dong villages of **Leishan, Rongjiang,** and **Zhaoxing.** The latter village, set in a beautiful landscape, is known for its five drum towers.

### GETTING HERE AND AROUND
The fastest way to get from Guiyang to Kaili is often by bus, which can take as little as two hours. The train takes about three hours.

BUS TRAVEL From the long-distance bus station just north of the Guiyang Train Station, Kaili-bound buses depart every 20 minutes or so. Buses usually don't leave until they're full. Tickets are about Y60.

TRAIN TRAVEL Kaili's small train station is three hours from Guiyang. Trains passing through Kaili connect to Guilin, Kunming, Beijing, Shanghai, and much of the rest of China.

### SAFETY AND PRECAUTIONS
Kaili remains relatively poor and off the beaten path: take special care, especially if out alone at night. Also keep an eye on the city's taxi drivers, who frequently refuse to start their meters and try to charge highly inflated rates for short rides.

### TIMING
Though the sites in Kaili could conceivably occupy a day's time, the city is better viewed as a stepping-off point for multiday tours of the surrounding countryside and its scenic ethnic villages.

CLOSE UP

# Festivals of Guizhou

Since the province is comprised of various ethnic groups—including the Dong, Hui, Yao, Zhuang, and Miao peoples—Guizhou is a gallery of traditional customs. Festivals are held throughout the year in Guiyang and elsewhere in the province. Many of these festivals are named after the dates on which they're held. These dates are according to a lunar calendar, so the festival called Eighth Day of the Fourth Month is not on April 8, but on the eighth day of the fourth lunar month (usually sometime in May).

**Siyueba,** which translates as Eighth Day of the Fourth Month, is when the Miao, Buyi, Dong, Yao, Zhuang, Yi, and other peoples of the province celebrate spring. Similar to Mardi Gras (but without the drinking or bawdy behavior), the festival is a major holiday in the region. Guiyang is a great place to check out the festival. The area around the fountain in the city center erupts with music, dancing, and general merrymaking.

An important traditional festival of Guiyang's Buyi population is **Liuyueliu,** or Sixth Day of the Sixth Month. Held in midsummer, as the name implies, this festival sees thousands of Buyi people from the region gathering on the banks of the Huaxi River. As the story goes, a beautiful Buyi maiden embroidered an image of mountains and rivers of immense beauty. It was so inspiring that a miscreant plotted to steal it, and on the sixth day of the sixth lunar month he sent his minions to take it by force. The maiden cast her embroidery into the air, where it was transformed into the beautiful mountains and rivers seen here today.

Among the Miao people who live in and around Kaili a bullfight is a contest between the bulls themselves. The **Miao Bullfight Festival** traditionally takes place between the planting of rice seedlings and their harvest a few months later, usually between the sixth and eighth lunar months. Owners of bulls meet beforehand to size up the competition prior to agreeing to the fight. The atmosphere on fight day is lively, with drinking, music, and exchanging of gifts. Fireworks entice the bulls into combat until one falls down or runs away.

An important fertility festival among the Miao people is the **Sister's Meal Festival,** when unmarried women harvest rice from the terraced fields and prepare a special dish of sticky rice colored blue, pink, and yellow. Men arrive to serenade the women, and the women offer gifts of rice wine and small packets of rice wrapped in cloth. In the evening, women dress up for a night of dancing.

8

## TOURS
Tour operator WildChina offers trips that take travelers from Guiyang to Kaili via several minority villages. Guizhou can sometimes be difficult for tourists to navigate, particularly for non-Chinese speakers: this tour offers a hassle-free and off-the-beaten-path look at Guizhou minority culture with English-speaking guides.

## ESSENTIALS
**Bank Bank of China** ✉ *Beijing Dong Lu.*

**Bus Contact Kaili Bus Station** ✉ *Wenhua Bei Lu.*

**Train Contact Kaili Train Station** ✉ *Qingjiang Lu.*

### EXPLORING

**Drum Tower** (鼓樓 *Gǔ lóu*). In Jinquanhu Park, the Drum Tower is the Dong people's gathering place for celebrations.

**Minorities Museum** (州民族 *Zhōu mínzú bówùguǎn*). This museum displays arts, crafts, and relics of the local indigenous peoples. ✉ *5 Guangchang Lu* 🎟 *Free* 🕒 *Mon.–Sat. 9–5.*

### WHERE TO STAY

**$** 🍴 **Guotai Dajiudian** (国泰大酒店 *Guótài dàjiǔdiàn*). With a downtown
**HOTEL** location and comfortable guest rooms, the Guotai Dajiudian compares favorably with flashier options that have appeared on the outskirts of town. **Pros:** ideal location; reasonable rates; cozy rooms. **Cons:** restaurant service can be slow. 💲 *Rooms from: Y250* ✉ *6 Beijing Dong Lu* ☎ *0855/826–988* ⤷ *73 rooms* ▭ *No credit cards* 🍴 *No meals.*

# YUNNAN

Hidden deep in southwestern China, Yunnan is one of the country's most fascinating provinces. Its rugged and varied terrain contains some of China's most beautiful natural scenery, as well as the headwaters of three of Asia's most important rivers: the Yangtze, Mekong, and Salween. Stunning mountains, picturesque highland meadows, and steamy tropical jungles are inhabited by Bai, Dai, Naxi, Hani, and dozens of other ethnic groups, many of which can only be found in Yunnan.

Yunnan sits atop the Yunnan-Guizhou Plateau, with the Himalayas to the northwest and Myanmar, Laos, and Vietnam to the south. Yunnan was central to the Ancient Tea and Horse Caravan Route, an important trade route that connected China with the rest of Southeast Asia for thousands of years. Today Yunnan is one of the top travel destinations in China, with Lijiang, Dali, and Jinghong getting most of the attention. Countless lesser-known but equally amazing places are scattered throughout the province.

Roughly the size of California, Yunnan is becoming increasingly accessible to the outside world. More convenient air travel makes it possible to have breakfast by the Mekong in Jinghong and dinner overlooking the old mountain town of Lijiang the same day. Yunnan still has plenty of places that are off the beaten path.

### REGIONAL TOURS

**China Minority Travel.** This company offers tours of Yunnan that include the province's lesser-known gems, including Yuanyang, Lugu Lake, and Zhongdian. The agency, based in Dali, has been organizing Yunnan tours for more than a decade. Multiple-day treks, family-oriented tours, and custom itineraries are all available. ✉ *63 Bo'ai Lu, Dali* ☎ *0872/267–9549* ⊕ *www.china-travel.nl.*

**Zouba Tours.** If you're longing to venture off the beaten track in Yunnan, consult with Frank Hitman at Zouba Tours. Having lived in

**DID YOU KNOW?**

During the Sisters' Meal festival, Miao women express interest (or rejection) by giving parcels of brightly colored sticky rice labeled with one of three images, each with a meaning. A pair of chopsticks says "let's get married now!" A single chopstick means "maybe." And an image of a chili means "get lost."

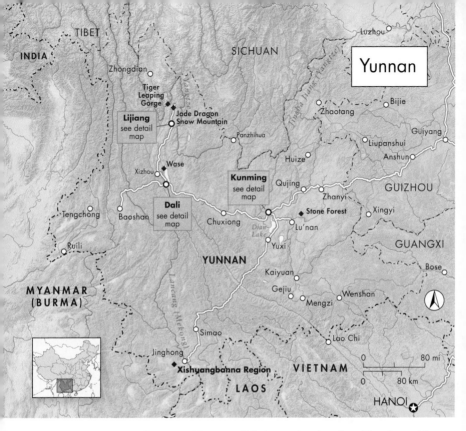

Yunnan for years, Hitman will help you break cultural barriers with local minority cultures. The company offers tailored trips focusing on cultural and culinary experiences. ✉ *Dali* ☎ *0152/8814–5939* ⊕ *www.zoubatours.com.*

## KUNMING

*400 km (248 miles; 10½ hrs by train) southwest of Guiyang; 650 km (403 miles; 18½ hrs by train) southwest of Chengdu; 1,200 km (744 miles; 28 hrs by train) west of Hong Kong.*

With its cool mountain air and laid-back locals, Kunming is one of China's most comfortable big cities, and is an ideal base for Yunnan travels. It's one of the few cities in the country that regularly has blue skies, and is nicknamed the "Spring City." Despite this moniker, weather can be gray and soggy during the summer monsoon season and cold in January and February.

Kunming is changing rapidly as the city is transforming into China's gateway to Southeast Asia. But despite the disappearance of the Old City and increasingly congested traffic, Kunming retains its unique character as a relaxed and somewhat idiosyncratic metropolis.

### GETTING HERE AND AROUND

AIR TRAVEL  An architectural highlight of the city, the new international airport is about 30 km (19 miles) east of the city center. Taxis take 30 to 40 minutes and cost Y80 to Y120, depending on traffic. Kunming is a busy air hub, with flight links all over China, as well as direct routes to Southeast Asia, Nepal, India, and the United Arab Emirates, among others.

BUS TRAVEL  Kunming has five long-distance bus stations: the north, east, south, west and northwest stations. All buses bound for Dali, Lijiang and Shangri-la depart from the west station; buses to Laos depart from the south station; and buses to Guangxi Province and the Yunnan-Vietnam border crossing at Hekou depart from the east station.

CAR TRAVEL  If you need a car and driver while you're in Kunming, make arrangements through your hotel. Expect to pay at least Y500 for a car to the Stone Forest.

TRAIN TRAVEL  The main station is at the southern end of Beijing Lu. There are day and overnight trains to both Dali (6 to 8 hours) and Lijiang (9 hours), as well as other Southwest China destinations.

### SAFETY AND PRECAUTIONS

Watch out for pickpockets, especially on crowded city buses. When riding overnight on long-distance buses be careful with your valuables, as thieves sometimes steal money and electronics from sleeping passengers.

Negotiate Kunming's frenetic traffic carefully, and watch out for noiseless electric scooters, which, not unlike other vehicles, often illegally travel in the wrong direction. Kunming drivers frequently ignore pedestrian right-of-way laws.

### TIMING

A day or two in Kunming should suffice for most travelers.

### TOURS

No group tours of Kunming are recommended, as most spend more time in shops than at attractions.

### ESSENTIALS

**Air Contact Kunming Airport** ⊠ *Changshui* ☎ *0871/6735–8125* ⊕ *www. newkma.com.*

**Bank Bank of China** ⊠ *515 Beijing Lu* ☎ *0871/6319–2910.*

**Bus Contact West Bus Transit Station** ⊠ *Chunyu Lu, at Yining Lu* ☎ *0871/6532–7326.*

**Medical Assistance Kunming First People's Hospital** ⊠ *504 Qingnian Lu* ☎ *0871/6318–8200.*

**Public Security Bureau PSB Kunming** ⊠ *411 Beijing Lu* ☎ *110.*

**Train Contact Kunming Train Station** ⊠ *Beijing Lu* ☎ *0871/6534–9414, 0871/6351–1534.*

**Visitor and Tour Info Kunming Tourism Authority** ⊠ *17 Dongfeng Dong Lu, 8th fl.* ☎ *0871/6314–9748* ⊕ *www.kmta.gov.cn.* **GoKunming** ⊕ *www.gokunming. com.*

8

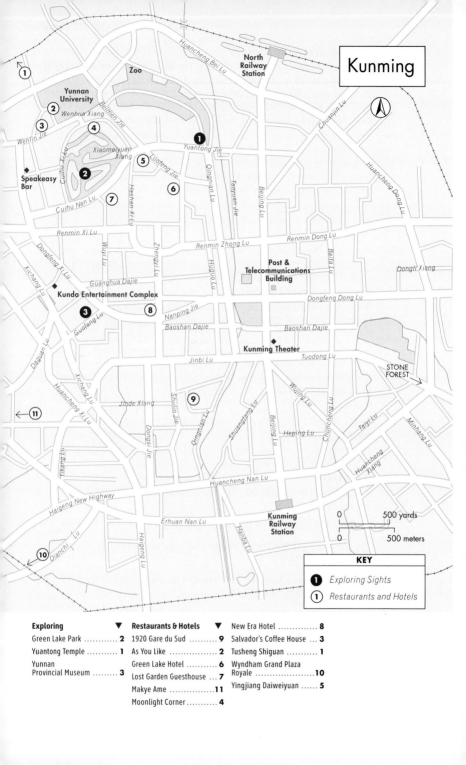

# Kunming

Zoo

North Railway Station

Yunnan University

Speakeasy Bar

Kunda Entertainment Complex

Post & Telecommunications Building

Kunming Theater

STONE FOREST

Kunming Railway Station

0     500 yards
0     500 meters

**KEY**

1 Exploring Sights
(1) Restaurants and Hotels

| Exploring ▼ | Restaurants & Hotels ▼ | |
|---|---|---|
| Green Lake Park ........... 2 | 1920 Gare du Sud ......... 9 | New Era Hotel .............. 8 |
| Yuantong Temple ........... 1 | As You Like ................. 2 | Salvador's Coffee House ... 3 |
| Yunnan Provincial Museum ... 3 | Green Lake Hotel .......... 6 | Tusheng Shiguan ........... 1 |
| | Lost Garden Guesthouse ... 7 | Wyndham Grand Plaza Royale .....................10 |
| | Makye Ame .................11 | Yingjiang Daiweiyuan ...... 5 |
| | Moonlight Corner........... 4 | |

**EXPLORING**

Fodor's Choice ★ **Green Lake Park** (翠湖公园 *Cuìhú gōngyuán*). Filled with willow- and bamboo-covered islands connected by stone bridges, Green Lake was once part of Dianchi Lake, but it was severed from that larger body of water in the 1970s. The park is a favorite gathering place for Kunming's older residents, who begin to congregate in the park for singing and dancing in the late morning and stay until the gates close at 11 pm. In summer the lake is filled with pink and white lotus blossoms. In winter the park fills with migrating seagulls from Siberia. ⊠ *Cuihu Nan Lu* 🎫 *Free* ⊙ *Daily 7–11.*

**Yuantong Temple** (圆通寺 *Yuántōng sì*). The largest temple in the city, Yuantong Temple dates back some 1,200 years to the Tang Dynasty. The compound consists of a series of gates leading to the inner temple, which is surrounded by a pond brimming with fish and turtles. The chanting of worshippers in the serene environment makes it hard to believe you're in the middle of a big city. In the back of the compound a temple houses a statue of Sakyamuni, a gift from the king of Thailand. ⊠ *30 Yuantong Jie* 🎫 *Y6* ⊙ *Daily 8–5.*

**Yunnan Provincial Museum** (云南省博物馆 *Yúnnánshěng bówùguǎn*). The museum focuses primarily on the Dian Kingdom, which ruled much of Yunnan from 1000 BC to 1 BC. Most of what you'll see here is more than 2,000 years old. Exhibits have good English captions. ⊠ *118 Wuyi Lu* 🕿 *0871/6617–9656* ⊕ *www.ynbwg.cn* 🎫 *Free* ⊙ *Daily 9:30–4:30.*

**WHERE TO EAT**

$$
YUNNAN
Fodor's Choice
★
✕ **1910 La Gare du Sud** (火车南站 *Huǒchēnánzhàn*). Located in a renovated railroad station, this restaurant's historic ambience and ample outdoor seating are just as appealing as the menu full of tasty Yunnan dishes. The structure was built in the early 20th century by French colonists, and was once the terminus of the 535-mile railroad linking Hanoi to Kunming. Try a spicy salad of chrysanthemum greens, fried rubing cheese, or grilled tilapia. Don't pass up anything made with Yunnan's prized cured ham. The menu is in English, with photos of most of the options. $ *Average main: Y50* ⊠ *8 Houxin Jie* 🕿 *0871/6316–9486* ▭ *No credit cards.*

$$
VEGETARIAN
✕ **As You Like** (有佳面包店 *Yǒujiā miànbāo diàn*). Tucked away in an alley off bustling Wenlin Jie, As You Like is a quaint vegetarian restaurant and deli. Freshly baked bread, healthy salads and all kinds of pastries will make your mouth water, and the pizzas are some of the best around. It's in an old house, so tall people will have to mind their heads, but the food more than makes up for it. $ *Average main: Y45* ⊠ *5 Tianjundian Xiang, up the alley next to Dune Cafe* 🕿 *0871/6541–1715.*

$$
TIBETAN
✕ **Makye Ame** (马吉 *Mǎjí āmǐ*). As much a cultural experience as a gastronomical adventure, Makye Ame is known for its Tibetan and Indian song-and-dance performances. The shows are enjoyable, but hard on the eardrums. For a quieter meal, ask for one of the rooms in the back or in the cozy teahouse upstairs. Food-wise, Makye Ame serves a large variety of Tibetan dishes, including stone-cooked yak, *malai kafta* (large potato and cashew balls in a curried yogurt sauce), and an incomparable platter of *xianggu* (shiitake mushrooms). A cold Lhasa beer or some homemade yogurt wine rounds out one of the city's more memorable

8

The Yuantong Temple is the largest temple in Kunming.

meals. $ *Average main: Y60* ✉ *Jinhuapu Lu, 2nd fl.* ☎ *0871/6833–6300* ⊕ *www.makyeame.cn* ▭ *No credit cards* ☾ *No lunch.*

**$$$** ✕ **Moonlight Corner** (月亮弯 *Yuèliàng wān*). With Thai owners, Thai
THAI  chefs, and imported Thai ingredients, Moonlight Corner is arguably
the best Thai restaurant in China. This spot on the north side of Green
Lake Park has been booming with locals and foreigners since it opened.
Try favorites such as Thai barbecued chicken, pineapple fried rice, green
papaya salad, or grilled fish, or go for lesser-known gems such as lemon-
grass salad. Wash it all down with Thai-style iced tea. If the sun is out,
sit out front and enjoy one of the neighborhood's best park views. $ *Av-
erage main: Y160* ✉ *16 Cuihu Dong Lu* ☎ *0871/6513–8088* ⊕ *www.
moonlightcorner.com* ▭ *No credit cards.*

**$** ✕ **Salvador's Coffee House** (萨尔瓦多咖啡馆 *Sà'ěrwǎduō kāfēiguǎn*).
CAFÉ  Regularly packed to capacity and brewing some of Kunming's best
FAMILY  coffee out of a custom blend of Yunnan beans, Salvador's also has an
Fodor's Choice  extensive food menu and is in the vanguard of China's burgeoning
★  organic food movement. About half of its ingredients are organic, and
more are being added regularly, with the goal of becoming one of the
few entirely organic eateries in China. Popular main dishes include
burritos, quesadillas, and falafel. The place has comfy sofas for loung-
ing and outdoor seating ideal for people-watching on bustling Wenhua
Xiang. $ *Average main: Y40* ✉ *76 Wenhua Xiang* ☎ *0871/6536–3525*
⊕ *www.salvadors.cn* ▭ *No credit cards.*

**$** ✕ **Tusheng Shiguan** (土生使馆 *Tǔshēng shíguǎn*). Without a doubt the
YUNNAN  best organic Chinese restaurant in town, Tusheng Shiguan is a must
Fodor's Choice  for anyone who wants to try the finest Yunnan cuisine. Don't miss the
★  *erkuai* (rice pancakes) or the *fuzhu* (a tofu skin dish whose misleading

name translates to "rotten bamboo"), and ask which vegetables are in season. The inside and outside seating is comfortable, and the service is most hospitable. Make sure to order rice if you're having spicy dishes, and try a small jug of their home-brewed corn liquor. $ *Average main: Y30* ⊠ *Loft Jinding 1919 Complex, 15 Jindingshan Lu* ☎ *0871/6542–0010* ▭ *No credit cards.*

$
YUNNAN
Fodor's Choice
★

✕ **Yingjiang Daiweiyuan** (盈江傣味园 *Yíngjiāng dǎiwèiyuán*). This sometimes hectic eatery may be the best place in Kunming to enjoy Dai cuisine, which is known for its liberal use of chili peppers. If you want to go straight for the heat, try the *gui ji* or "ghost chicken," a cold salad that is slightly sour and extremely spicy. Tamer options include pineapple rice, fennel omelets, dried beef, wild mushrooms, fried fish, and tapioca with cookies in coconut milk. Dai cuisine features many dishes and ingredients that are foreign even to coastal Chinese residents. It has another branch on Cuihu Bei Lu. $ *Average main: Y25* ⊠ *6 Luofeng Jie* ☎ *0871/512–2251* ▭ *No credit cards.*

### BIKING KUNMING

Although traffic may seem a bit daunting at first, Kunming is one of the best cities in China for biking. Small brown signs point to historical and cultural sights. The signs are in Chinese, but just follow the arrows. Explore the winding lanes at Green Lake Park; heading south, you'll find pockets of Old Kunming, including parks, temples, and pagodas.

**Xiong Brothers Bike Shop.** Decent rental bikes are available here for about Y40 per day. Group tours leave Saturday morning at 9. ⊠ *51 Beimen Jie* ☎ *0871/6519–1520.*

## WHERE TO STAY

$$$$
HOTEL

🏨 **Green Lake Hotel** (翠湖宾馆 *Cuìhú bīnguǎn*). Adjacent to Green Lake Park, this is one of Kunming's most elegant lodgings. **Pros:** great location; good service; comfortable rooms. **Cons:** many staff members speak little or no English. $ *Rooms from: Y2277* ⊠ *6 Cuihu Nan Lu* ☎ *0871/6515–8888* ⊕ *www.greenlakehotel.cn* ⤳ *301 rooms, 6 suites* ❡ *Breakfast.*

$
B&B/INN

🏨 **Lost Garden Guesthouse** (一丘田七号客栈 *Yīqiūtián qīhào kèzhàn*). If you manage to book a room in this always-packed guesthouse, you'll find yourself a stone's throw from Green Lake. **Pros:** close to Green Lake; personal service; surprising amenities in the rooms. **Cons:** basic furnishings; common areas shared with diners from outside. $ *Rooms from: Y160* ⊠ *7 Yi Qiu Tian* ☎ *0871/6511–1127* ⊕ *www. lostgardenguesthouse.com* ✉ *Yīqiūtián qī hào kèzhàn* ⤳ *24 rooms* ❡ *No meals.*

$
HOTEL

🏨 **New Era Hotel** (新纪元大酒店 *Xīnjìyuán dàjiǔdiàn*). Conveniently located on Kunming's main pedestrian streets, the New Era Hotel has well-furnished rooms with views of the west mountains and the crawling crowd below. **Pros:** excellent value; sensational breakfast. **Cons:** views disturbed by construction. $ *Rooms from: Y520* ⊠ *1 Dongfeng Xi Lu, on Nanping square* ☎ *0871/6363–6556* ⊕ *www.erahotel.com* ⤳ *315 rooms* ❡ *Breakfast.*

8

CLOSE UP

# Yunnan Cuisine

Dian cuisine is the term for Han Chinese cuisine found in Yunnan, especially around Kunming. Dian-style dishes are similar to Sichuan dishes and tend to favor spicy and sour flavors. Rice is a staple here, as is a type of rice noodle called *mixian*. A favorite dish is *guoqiao mixian*, a boiling broth served with raw pork and vegetables that you cook yourself. *Qiguo ji* (steampot chicken), another trademark Dian-style dish, uses a special earthenware pot to steam chicken and vegetables into a savory soup.

One thing that sets Dian cuisine apart from that of the rest of China is the dairy products. *Rubing* is made from goat's milk, and is typically fried

and served with dried chili peppers or sugar. It is a little drier and less pungent than regular goat cheese. *Rushan*, or "milk fan," is a long strip of a cheese that is spread with a salty or sweet sauce. Wrapped around a chopstick, it makes a handy snack.

Street barbecue is a major part of the Yunnan culinary experience. Every kind of meat and vegetable is on offer, as well as quail eggs, *chou doufu* (stinky tofu), and *erkuai* (rice pancakes with sweet or savory fillings). Most restaurants in Yunnan close early, but barbecue stands stay open until the wee hours, making them a good place for a late-night snack.

**$$$**
HOTEL
Fodor's Choice
★

Wyndham Grand Plaza Royale (昆明七彩云南温德姆至尊豪廷 *Kūnmíng qīcǎi Yúnnán wēndémǔzhìzūn háotíng dàjiǔdiàn*). Without a doubt the city's most luxurious hotel, the Wyndham Grand Plaza Royale brings taste and style to everything from the grand lobby to the soothing spa to the selection of six globe-trotting restaurants. **Pros:** attentive staff; excellent restaurants; tasteful touch to everything. **Cons:** far from the city center; views disturbed by construction. $ *Rooms from: Y1600* ⊠ *569 Dianchi Lu* ☎ *0871/6817–7777* ⊕ *www.wyndham. com* ⊃ *374 rooms* ⊠ *Breakfast.*

## NIGHTLIFE AND THE ARTS

### ARTS

**Dynamic Yunnan** (云南映象 *Yúnnán yìngxiàng*). Chinese dance legend Yang Liping may have retired, but the Yunnan native's award-winning dance and musical production Dynamic Yunnan still plays to full-capacity crowds. It's an impressive fusion of the storytelling, songs, and dances of indigenous groups. ⊠ *Kunming Arts Theatre, 132 Dongfeng Xi Lu, near Xiao Xi Men* ☎ *087/6313–0033* ⊕ *www.dynamicyunnan.com.*

**Livstone House** (石榴 *Shíliú*). Founded by Yunnanese prodigy Liu Lifen, Livstone house is often buzzing with activity, offering everything from art exhibits to theater productions. ⊠ *Loft Jinding 1919 Complex, 15 Jindingshan Bei Lu* ☎ *0871/6538–5159.*

**Mu Yu Studio** (木鱼摄影棚 *Mùyú shèyǐngpéng*). A small art studio and bar hidden off Wenlin Jie, Mu Yu Studio is where Kunming's creative crowd gathers to exhibit an eclectic collection of art. ⊠ *202 Wenlin Jie, enter through the gate* ☎ *0135/7705–6433.*

The Stone Forest in Yunnan is a UNESCO World Heritage Site.

### NIGHTLIFE

When evening falls, Kunming's growing expat population tends to congregate at the bars, cafés, and restaurants of Wenlin Jie and Wenhua Xiang. After midnight, the clubs and bars around the Kundu Night Market attract the crowds.

**Alei Lounge Club & Tapas Bar** (ALEI酒廊精致小点 *ALEI jiǔláng jīngzhì xiǎodiǎn*). A posh yet unpretentious lounge, Alei is the best place to enjoy mix drinks and tapas. ✉ *3 A1 Building, Zheng Yi Fang* ☎ *0871/6836–9099.*

**Chapter One.** This Western-style bar attracts a largely Chinese clientele and offers a decent selection of drinks and snacks. English-spoken trivia night happens every other Thursday. ✉ *146 Wenlin Jie* ☎ *0871/6536–5635.*

**Dune Café** (沙丘咖啡馆 *Shāqiū kāfēiguǎn*). This expat boasts an impressive selection of Belgian ales, chilled to exactly the right temperature. ✉ *138 Wenlin Jie* ☎ *0871/6534–7236.*

**Moondog** (月亮狗 *Yuèliàng gǒu*). Open until the wee hours, this bar on a pleasant side street has Kunming's widest selection of whiskeys. It's a favorite with expats for darts, cards, and other games. ✉ *138-5 Wacang Nan Lu* ☎ *0158/8714–6080.*

**O'Reilly's Irish Pub** (O'Reilly's爱尔兰酒吧 *O'Reilly's ài'ěrlán jiǔbā*). Run by a trio who claims never to have set foot on Irish soil, O'Reilly's Irish Pub serves cold Guinness and Kilkenny on tap, as well as a remarkable selection of Belgian ales. The obligatory pub grub is of the highest quality. ✉ *13 Beichen Pedestrian Street* ☎ *0871/6561–5661* ⊕ *www. oreillys.cn.com.*

8

CLOSE UP

## Kunming's Flying Tigers

Despite being in the hinterland of Southwest China, Kunming played a crucial role in World War II by preventing Japanese forces from taking control of all of China. At the center of this role was the American Volunteer Group, best known by its local nickname *feihu*, or the Flying Tigers, because of the shark faces painted on their fuselages.

The group of around 300 American servicemen was led by the mysterious Claire L. Chennault. A retired captain in the U.S. Air Force, Chennault first came to Kunming in 1938, when Madame Chiang Kai-shek, wife of the country's leader, asked him to organize a Chinese air force to counter the relentless attacks from the Japanese, who were busily bombing much of China with little opposition.

Supply routes to China's capital were being taken out one after another, leaving just one road. Chennault argued that a group of American pilots could defend this crucial supply artery, as well as push the Japanese out of the region.

The Flying Tigers were tenacious fighters. They swept through much of China to combat the constant bombing by Japanese forces. Their record was second to none in World War II. They had more than 50 enemy encounters and were never defeated.

### SHOPPING

If you're looking for a good deal on tea, look no farther than the wholesale tea market at the southeast corner of Beijing Lu and Wujing Lu. Within the market you'll find an amazing variety of green teas, black teas, flower teas, and herbal teas. It's a wholesale market, but vendors will sell you small quantities.

Qianju Jie, near the intersection of Wenlin Jie and Wenhua Xiang, is one of the more popular shopping streets in the city.

**Bird and Flower Market** (花鸟市场 *Huāniǎo shìchǎng*). For all kinds of trinkets and oddities, head to the Bird and Flower Market. Consisting of a bunch of street stalls along Jingxing Jie, this market is the ultimate place to sharpen your haggling skills—and perhaps find that one special gift for the folks back home. ⊠ *Jingxing Jie, off Zhengyi Lu, nearby Nanping square.*

**Mandarin Books** (漫林书苑 *Mànlín shūyuàn*). On Wenhua Xiang is Mandarin Books, one of the best foreign-language bookstores in all of Yunnan. ⊠ *52 Wenhua Xiang 9–10* ☎ *0871/6551–6579* ⊕ *www.mandarinbooks.cn.*

### SIDE TRIP TO THE STONE FOREST

Fodor's Choice ★ **Stone Forest** (石林 *Shílín*). One of the most interesting sites near Kunming is a geological phenomenon known as the Stone Forest. This cluster of dark gray-limestone karst formations has been twisted into unusual shapes since being formed beneath the sea 270 million years ago. Many have been given names to describe their resemblance to creatures real (turtles) or mythological (phoenixes).

Walking through the park you'll find plenty of Sani women eager to act as guides and sell you their handicrafts. The main trail has become rather commercialized, but there are plenty of similar formations in other parts of the park. Stone Forest-bound Buses depart every 15 to 30 minutes from Kunming's East Bus Station, although

> **WORD OF MOUTH**
>
> "In Dali you'll see many minorities dressed in their own dress and many natural areas of great beauty. The people appear to be much more Tibetan than Chinese."
> —merckxxx

hiring a car and driver is more convenient. ⊠ *Lu'nan* 🚌 *Y175* ⊘ *24 hrs.*

**GETTING HERE AND AROUND**

The Stone Forest is 125 km (78 miles) southeast of Kunming. There are several ways to get here, the best being a car and driver. One can be arranged through your hotel and should cost between Y500 and Y600. Bus tours (Y20 round-trip) leave each morning from near the train station. This trip takes at least four hours, as the driver makes numerous stops at souvenir stands and junk stores along the way.

## DALI

*250 km (155 miles; 5 hrs by bus) northwest of Kunming; 140 km (87 miles; 3 hrs by bus) south of Lijiang.*

Dali is one of those rare places that feel completely cut off from the rest of the world yet has high-speed Internet access. The rustic town is perched at the foot of the towering Cangshan Mountains and overlooks lovely Erhai Lake. Its typically sunny weather, sleepy artistic atmosphere, and gorgeous sunsets have made it one of Yunnan's most popular destinations

Home to the Bai people, Dali has been inhabited for more than 4,000 years, serving as a major rice-production base for the region. Today tourism is rejuvenating the town. The upside of this building boom is a greater variety of restaurants and hotels; the downside is that the Old Town is constantly being demolished and reconstructed. A planned high-speed rail link with Kunming means now is the time to see Dali before it changes even more.

**GETTING HERE AND AROUND**

AIR TRAVEL There are multiple daily flights from Kunming to Dali. Dali's airport is at the southern tip of Erhai Lake. Taxis between the airport and the Old Town cost Y90 and take just under an hour.

BUS TRAVEL Buses from Kunming to Dali take five hours and cost Y110. Most drop you off in "New Dali," the nondescript city of Xiaguan. From there, a 25-minute cab ride gets you to the Old Town. It should cost Y40 to Y6, depending on the time of day and your haggling skills.

TRAIN TRAVEL Trains between Kunming and Dali cost around Y100, but the trip takes seven hours, about two hours longer than taking a bus.

**SAFETY AND PRECAUTIONS**

Several solo hikers have died in the mountains above Dali in recent years. If you do any hiking—other than the paved tourist paths—do so with at least one other person.

**TIMING**

Most of the major sites in and around Dali can be enjoyed within two or three days. Many travelers find themselves arriving in Dali with ambitious itineraries, but end up staying to enjoy the town's lazy vibe.

**TOURS**

China Minority Travel lets you explore the villages surrounding Erhai Lake. The trip is Y2,000 for up to four people, including a guide, transportation, and lunch.

**THE TORCH FESTIVAL**

One of the more exciting festivals in Southwest China is the Torch Festival, celebrated by both the Yi and Bai minorities on the 24th day of the sixth lunar month (in June or July). Dali's Old Town is one of the best (and worst) places to catch the festival. Many local children like to frighten travelers with the flames, especially on Foreigner Street. Anyone who wants to see the festival without worrying about getting singed by pyromaniac children might want to go to Xizhou—the first town north of Dali.

**ESSENTIALS**

**Air Contact Dali Airport** ☎ *0872/242–8909.*

**Medical Assistance Dali First Municipal People's Hospital** ✉ *217 Tai'an Lu* ☎ *0872/212–4462.*

**Banks Bank of China** ✉ *Fuxing Lu.* **ICBC** ✉ *Huguo Lu.*

**Public Security Bureau PSB Dali** ✉ *Huguo Lu* ☎ *110.*

**Train Contact Xiaguan Train Station** ✉ *Dianyuan Lu, Xiaguan.*

Visitor and Tour Info

**EXPLORING**

Dali's Old Town, called Dali Gucheng, is surrounded by attractive reconstructions of the old city wall and gates. Go to the wall's southwest corner and take the stairs to the top for a great view of the city and the surrounding mountains. Outside the bustling center of the Old Town are countless little alleys lined with old Bai-style homes.

Dali has two popular pedestrian streets, Huguo Lu and Renmin Lu, both of which run east–west, or uphill–downhill. Huguo Lu, better known as Foreigner Street, is lined with the cafés that made Dali famous in the 1990s, but the street has begun to lose its luster. High rents and cutthroat competition have taken a toll on quality and service. Nightlife is concentrated on Renmin Lu.

**Three Pagodas** (三塔寺 *Sāntǎ sì*). The most famous landmark in Dali, the Three Pagodas appear on just about every calendar of Chinese scenery. The largest, 215 feet high, dates from AD 836 and is decorated on each of its 16 stories with Buddhas carved from local marble. The other two pagodas, also richly decorated, are more elegant in style. When the water is still, you can ponder their reflection in a nearby pool. A massive

**CLOSE UP**

# Dali and the Nanzhao Kingdom

The idyllic scenery belies Dali's importance as the center of power for the Nanzhao Kingdom. The easily defensible area around Erhai Lake was the kingdom's birthplace, which began as the Bai- and Yi-dominated Damengguo in 649. Almost a century later, Damengguo was expanded to include the six surrounding kingdoms ruled by powerful Bai families. This expansion was supported by the ruling Chinese Tang Dynasty, and the kingdom was renamed Nanzhao.

The primarily Buddhist Nanzhao Kingdom was essentially a vassal state of the Tang Dynasty until AD 750, when it rebelled. Tang armies were sent in 751 and 754 to suppress the insurgents, but they suffered humiliating defeats. Emboldened by their victories, Nanzhao troops helped the kingdom acquire a significant amount of territory. Before reaching its high point with the capture of Chengdu and Sichuan in 829, the Nanzhao Kingdom had expanded to include all of present-day Yunnan, as well as parts of present-day Burma, Laos, and Thailand.

Although the capture of Chengdu was a major victory for Nanzhao, it appears to have led directly to its decline. The Tang Dynasty couldn't stand for such an incursion and sent large numbers of troops to the area. They eventually evicted Nanzhao forces from Sichuan by 873. About 30 years later the Nanzhao leaders were finally overthrown, ending the story of their meteoric rise and fall.

Chan Buddhist Temple has been built behind the pagodas. The pagodas are a 20-minute walk from the Old Town. ⊠ *1 km (½ mile) north of Dali Gucheng* ☎ *Y128* ☉ *Daily 7 am–8 pm.*

**8**

### WHERE TO EAT

For a taste of authentic local Bai dishes like *paojiao zhurou* (pork with pickled peppers) or *chao rubing* (fried goat cheese), try any of the local restaurants on Renmin Lu just east of Fuxing Lu. Most of these restaurants lack English menus, but they generally have their ingredients on display.

$
CAFÉ ✕ **The Bakery No. 88** (八八号西点店 *Bābā hàoxī diǎndiàn*). The dessert counter here boasts some of Dali's best cakes, which can be enjoyed with a coffee and a book on the second floor if you desire a quiet environment. It's one of the best places in town for good Western food and take-away stuffed baguettes. $ *Average main: Y30* ⊠ *52 Bo'ai Lu* ☎ *0872/267–9129.*

$
ECLECTIC ✕ **Bill's Place** (*Huǒchái rén*). From the rooftop, you are treated to some of the most splendid views of the Old Town. The main dining area, accessible from the street through a small door and a flight of stairs, features a little balcony with tables for two, perfect for a romantic tête-à-tête. The focus of the kitchen is on Italian and Mexican cuisine, proof being some very tasty fajitas and burritos. $ *Average main: Y35* ⊠ *105 Bo'ai Lu, corner of Renmin Lu* ☎ *00872/251–8323.*

$
ECLECTIC ✕ **Café de Jack** (樱花园西餐厅 *Yīnghuā yuánxī cāntīng*). A longtime favorite specializing in Western and Chinese classics as well as some

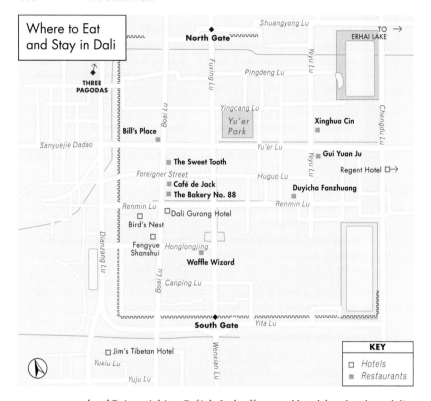

Where to Eat and Stay in Dali

**KEY**

□ *Hotels*
■ *Restaurants*

local Bai specialties, Café de Jack offers good breakfast, lunch, and dinner and the strongest cup of coffee in Yunnan. All three floors are a bit different: the first floor feels like a bar, the second floor is more like a restaurant, and the rooftop is a perfect place to kick back with a beer. Catch up with the rest of the world via computer terminals or Wi-Fi. $ *Average main: Y30* ⊠ *82 Bo'ai Lu* ☎ *0872/267–1572.*

$ ✕**Duyichu Fanzhuang** (独一处饭庄 *Dúyīchù fànzhuāng*). Hidden inside
NORTHERN a leaning shack, this little dumpling palace is not your typical fine-
CHINESE dining restaurant. The owners, both from China's freezing northeastern reaches, wrap the best *jaozi* in Dali and the surrounding region. Other dishes are on offer, depending on what's available in the local markets. The menus have been kindly translated into English by expat regulars, but they don't mention the selection of splendid house-made liquor. $ *Average main: Y15* ⊠ *Renmin Lu, across from Mayana Restaurant* ▭ *No credit cards.*

$ ✕**Gui Yuan Ju** (桂苑居 *Guì yuàn jū*). A bit removed from the crowds
KOREAN is the city's best bet for Korean food. Dishes include Korean hotpot, barbecued meats, and almost all other Korean specialties, to be enjoyed from a relaxing albeit somewhat dull dining area. $ *Average main: Y35* ⊠ *189 Yeyu Lu* ☎ *0872/267–1889.*

$ ✕**The Sweet Tooth** (甜点屋 *Tiāndiǎnwū*). Dali's expat community
MEXICAN indulges its love of pastries at this low-profile little eatery. Surprisingly

enough, it also cooks up some of the best Mexican food in town. The prices are more than reasonable, but the seating is limited. [$] *Average main: Y25* ✉ *52 Bo'ai Lu* ☎ *0872/266–3830* 🌐 *Tiándiǎn wū.*

$ CAFÉ 🍴 **Waffle Wizard** (比利时挖福饼 *Bǐlìshí wāfúbǐng*). Here you'll find authentic Belgian waffles topped with whipped cream, ice cream, or just a dusting of powdered sugar. If you don't have a sweet tooth, sip a cold Belgian ale while you watch the people stroll past. It's easy to miss, as this place is no more than a cutaway in the street with some chairs out front. The Wi-Fi connection is a plus. [$] *Average main: Y20* ✉ *Corner of Honglongjing Lu and Fuxing Lu* ☎ *137/0060–6575* 🌐 *www.wafflewizard.com.*

$ YUNNAN 🍴 **Xinghua Cun** (目录村 *Xìnghuā cūn*). In business for decades, Xinghua Cun is a no-nonsense Chinese restaurant with the usual revolving-top tables and a counter filled with all kinds of homemade liquor. If can look past the Spartan decor, you'll notice what this place does best: tasty Yunnanese and local Bai dishes, all served with a smile. The menus are in Chinglish, but ordering is easily done by pointing at pictures. [$] *Average main: Y35* ✉ *Yeyu Lu* ☎ *0872/267–0082.*

## WHERE TO STAY

$ HOTEL 🏨 **Bird's Nest** (鸟窝 *Niǎo wō*). Owned by a couple of young artists from northern China, the Bird's Nest is centered around a tranquil courtyard on the westernmost part of Renmin Lu. **Pros:** dynamic staff; comfortable rooms; chilled-out courtyard. **Cons:** tall people need to mind their heads. [$] *Rooms from: Y180* ✉ *22 Renmin Lu* ☎ *0872/266–1843* 🌐 *www.birdbardali.com* 🛏 *9 rooms, 2 suites* 🍽 *No meals.*

$ HOTEL Fodor's Choice ★ 🏨 **Dali Gurong Hotel** (大理古榕会馆 *Dàlǐ gǔróng huìguǎn*). One of the most pleasant hotels in Dali's Old Town, the upscale Dali Gurong offers spacious and well-furnished rooms in a cluster of villas in a parklike setting. **Pros:** luxurious feel; helpful staff; central location. **Cons:** somewhat expensive for the area. [$] *Rooms from: Y880* ✉ *59 Bo'ai Lu* ☎ *0872/268–5999* 🌐 *www.dlgrhotel.com* 🛏 *61 rooms* 🍽 *Breakfast.*

$ HOTEL 🏨 **Fengyue Shanshui** (风月山水客栈 *Fēngyuè shānshuǐ kèzhàn*). Owned by acclaimed Chinese artist Fang Lijun, this guesthouse is in a class by itself. **Pros:** unique style; great views; quiet at night. **Cons:** rooms may feel a little empty; often booked solid; staff does not speak English. [$] *Rooms from: Y200* ✉ *3 Honglongjing* ☎ *0872/266–3741* 🛏 *17 rooms, 1 suite* 💳 *No credit cards* 🍽 *No meals.*

$ B&B/INN FAMILY 🏨 **Jim's Tibetan Hotel** (吉姆藏式酒店 *Jímǔzàngshì jiǔdiàn*). Outside the south gate, this quiet lodging is ideal if you want to avoid the hubbub of Dali's Old Town. **Pros:** kid-friendly vibe; unique interior. **Cons:** a bit dusty; a little far from the sights. [$] *Rooms from: Y220* ✉ *13 Yuxiu Lu* ☎ *0872/267–7824* 🌐 *www.china-travel.nl* 🛏 *15 rooms* 🍽 *Breakfast.*

## NIGHTLIFE

**Bad Monkey** (坏猴子 *Huàihóuzi*). One of the town's oldest establishments, this is Dali's most popular watering hole. In addition to an extensive bar, Bad Monkey brews its own beer, with every batch selling out quickly. Drinks aside, the kitchen stays open until early morning and cooks up decent fish-and-chips and pizzas. There's live music almost every night. ✉ *74–76 Renmin Lu* 🌐 *www.badmonkeybar.com.*

8

Bai fishermen on Erhai Lake.

**Kaki Cofe** (柿子树咖啡馆 *Shìzǐshù kāfēiguǎn*). Tucked away in an alley off busy Renmin Lu, this daytime café gets a bit more lively when the bottles come out at night. There's a standard selection of drinks, completed with the obligatory Belgian ales. This is an excellent place to find a quiet spot. ⊠ *164 Huguo Lu, off Renmin Lu* ☎ *0872/536–5688.*

**September Bar** (九月 *Jiǔyuè*). With its jazzy atmosphere, loungy decor, and wall of wine bottles behind the bar, September Bar is a nice alternative if you're seeking a more intimate environment. There's regular live music and a selection of Belgian and German beers. ⊠ *225 Renmin Lu* ☎ *0136/8878–3009.*

**Sun Island** (太阳岛 *Tàiyáng dǎo*). One of Old Town's most pleasant bars, the civilized Sun Island draws a crowd that's young, alternative, and mostly Chinese. Grab a seat at the wooden bar and strike up a conversation with the friendly staffers. ■TIP→ **For a local specialty, ask for the plum wine—it's actually plum liquor—on the rocks.** ⊠ *324 Renmin Lu.*

## SHOPPING

Foreigner Street is lined with Bai women who have been selling the same jewelry, fabrics, and Communist kitsch for nearly two decades. Don't be afraid to walk away when bargaining; vendors will often drop their prices at the last minute.

Bo'ai Lu and Renmin Lu are peppered with a variety of shops featuring outdoor clothing and equipment; handicrafts from India, Nepal, and Southeast Asia; as well as Chinese antiques. Fuxing Lu, aimed primarily at Chinese tourists, is where you'll find local teas, specialty foods, and, most prominently, jade. Much of it is of low quality, so buy only if you know something about jade.

## CAFÉ SOCIETY

Dali has some of the best coffee shops in China, particularly on Renmin Lu.

**Bird Bar** (鸟吧 *Niǎo bā*). For a taste of Yunnan's cash crop, head to the Bird Bar. The place grows, roasts and grinds its own coffee beans. The owner's love for antique buildings clearly shines through in the bar's cozy, old-fashioned interior.

✉ *22 Renmin Lu* ☏ *0872/266–1843* ⊕ *www.birdbardali.com.*

**Guiqu Laixi** (归去来兮 *Guīqù láixī*). The owner of Guiqu Laixi collects Chinese antiques. This place serves Dali's best coffee and tea. ✉ *258 Renmin Lu* ☏ *0872/267–6737.*

### SIDE TRIPS FROM DALI

Fodor's Choice ★ **Cangshan** (苍山 *Cāngshān*). With a peak that rises to more than 4,500 meters (14,765 feet), "Green Mountain" can be seen from just about anywhere in Dali. A 16-km (10-mile) path carved into the side of the mountain offers spectacular views of Dali and the surrounding villages. There are also several temples, grottoes, and waterfalls just off the main trail. To get to the footpath, follow Yu'er Lu to the foot of the mountain. If you don't want to climb, there are two cable cars to take you up the mountain.

**Erhai Lake** (洱海 *Ěrhǎi hú*). Almost any street off Fuxing Lu will bring you to the shore of Erhai Lake. You may catch a glimpse of fishermen with teams of cormorants tied to their boats. In good weather, ferries are a wonderful way to see the lake and the surrounding mountains. The ferries cost between Y30 and Y70 (depending on your ability to bargain). More interesting—and cheaper—is hiring fishermen to paddle you wherever you want to go. Boats depart from the village of Zhoucheng.

On the shores of the lake, the village of Shaping has a popular market every Monday morning. Wase is the place to go for Bai clothing.

DID YOU KNOW?

**The cormorants used by fishermen on Erhai Lake have a collar around their necks that prevents them from swallowing the fish they have caught.**

**Xizhou.** Among the prettiest towns in the area is Xizhou, about 20 km (12 miles) north of Dali. It has managed to preserve a fair amount of its Bai architecture. The daily morning market and occasional festivals of traditional music attract a fair number of tourists from neighboring Dali. Minibuses leave from Dali's west gate and cost Y7.

8

# LIJIANG

*150 km (93 miles; 3 hrs by bus) north of Dali; 320 km (198 miles; 7 hrs by bus) northwest of Kunming; 550 km (341 miles; 20 hrs by bus) southwest of Chengdu.*

Lijiang is probably the most famous travel destination in Yunnan, as its Old Town was named a UNESCO World Heritage Site. At the base of majestic Jade Dragon Snow Mountain, Lijiang is home to the Naxi people, who are related to Tibetans but have their own language and culture.

Lijiang's Old Town is a labyrinth of winding alleys, fish-filled streams, and old Naxi houses with tile rooftops. Traditional Naxi singing and dancing are on display nightly at Sifang Jie, the square in Old Town's center.

## GETTING HERE AND AROUND

AIR TRAVEL There are multiple daily flights from Kunming. The airport is 48 km (30 miles) south of Lijiang. A Y20 bus from the airport takes you to the edge of the Old Town. A taxi to the Old Town will run you Y80.

BUS TRAVEL Lijiang's main bus stations are on Xin Dajie and on Xiangelila Dadao. Trips from Kunming take just over eight hours.

TRAIN TRAVEL There are day and night trains from Kunming. The ride takes nine hours and costs about Y150. A train from Dali takes 2 hours and costs Y29. Don't expect much in the way of views, as much of the route goes through tunnels.

## SAFETY AND PRECAUTIONS

Lijiang gets a lot of foot traffic, which has made the cobbled paths in the Old Town quite slippery. Also, if taking a taxi, make sure they use the meter, as some drivers may try to pull a fast one.

Visiting Tiger Leaping Gorge during rainy weather is not advised, as large rocks regularly come crashing down.

## TIMING

Lijiang is good for two or three days of taking in the Old Town and surrounding areas. If you're feeling active, head to Tiger Leaping Gorge for a day or two.

## TOURS

Lijiang has plenty of English-language signs in the Old Town, and tour guides aren't needed on Jade Dragon Snow Mountain or in Tiger Leaping Gorge. If you want to hike the surrounding mountains, however, a guide is strongly recommended.

## ESSENTIALS

**Air Contact Lijiang Airport** ☎ *0888/517–3088.*

**Bank Bank of China** ✉ *Dong Dajie.*

**Bus Contact Xianggelila Bus Station** ✉ *Xiangelila Dadao.*

**Medical Assistance Lijiang People's Hospital** ✉ *Fuhui Lu* ☎ *0888/512-2393.*

**Public Security Bureau PSB Lijiang** ✉ *Fuhui Lu* ☎ *110.*

The old town in Lijiang at dusk

**Visitor and Tour Info China International Travel Service** ✉ *Xin Dajie* ☎ *0888/512-3508.*

### EXPLORING

With so many shops and markets selling the same things, much of Lijiang's Old Town feels more like a Special Economic Zone than a UNESCO-protected site. However, it's still possible to get away for an interesting stroll. Helpful English maps available around town help you navigate the maze. ■TIP➜ **Most sites in and around Lijiang are free for holders of a "maintenance ticket," available for Y80 from most hotels and attractions.**

**Black Dragon Pool Park** (黑龙潭 *Hēilóngtán gōngyuán*). Outside the Old Town, Black Dragon Pool Park has a tranquil pavilion where locals come to play cards and drink tea. Sadly, recent droughts mean that the pool is almost entirely devoid of water during the dry winter season. The rest of the year, the park is one of the most popular places to photograph nearby Jade Dragon Snow Mountain. The park is home to the Dongba Research Institute Museum *(Dōngba wénhuà bówùguǎn)*, devoted to Naxi Dongba culture. ✉ *Xinde Lu* 🎫 *Y80* 🕑 *Daily 6:30 am–8 pm.*

**Pujian Temple** (普贤寺 *Pǔxián sì*). If you can find it, the Pujian Temple is a tranquil place to get away from the crowds. At the temple's vegetarian restaurant, try the *jidoufen*, a bean concoction that can be eaten hot as a porridge or cold and cut up like noodles. The ubiquitous *baba* bread is also quite good. Wash it all down with a pot of Tibetan yak butter tea. ✉ *Qi Yi Jie* 🎫 *Free* 🕑 *Daily 8–6.*

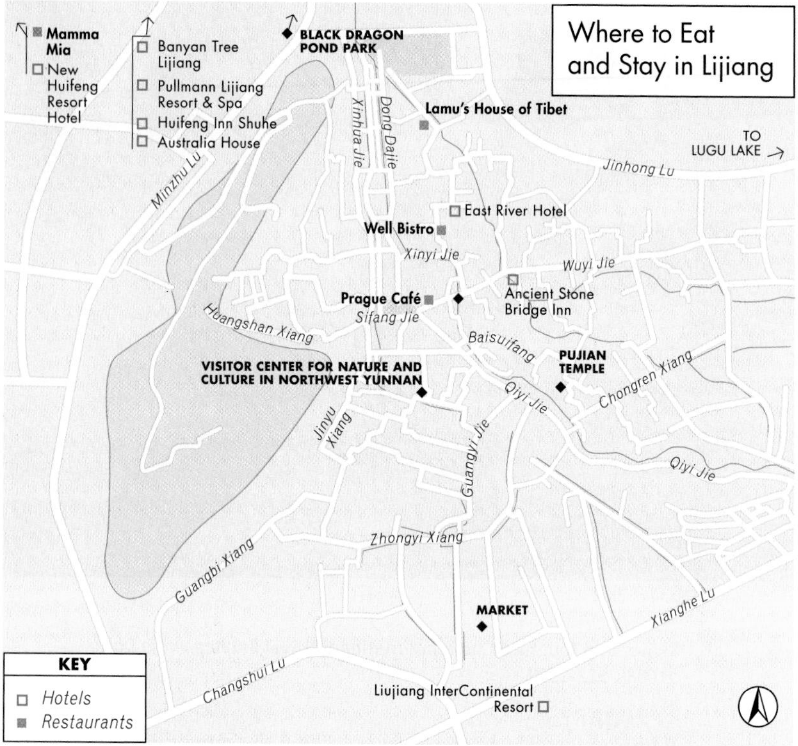

Where to Eat and Stay in Lijiang
Mamma Mia
New Huifeng Resort Hotel
Banyan Tree Lijiang
Pullmann Lijiang Resort & Spa
Huifeng Inn Shuhe
Australia House
BLACK DRAGON POND PARK
Lamu's House of Tibet
TO LUGU LAKE
Jinhong Lu
Minzhu Lu
Xinhua Jie
Dong Dajie
East River Hotel
Well Bistro
Xinyi Jie
Wuyi Jie
Prague Café
Sifang Jie
Ancient Stone Bridge Inn
Huangshan Xiang
Baisuifang
PUJIAN TEMPLE
Chongren Xiang
VISITOR CENTER FOR NATURE AND CULTURE IN NORTHWEST YUNNAN
Qiyi Jie
Jinyu Xiang
Guangyi Jie
Qiyi Jie
Zhongyi Xiang
Guangbi Xiang
MARKET
Xianghe Lu
Changshui Lu
Liujiang InterContinental Resort
KEY
Hotels
Restaurants


**Visitor Center for Nature and Culture in Northwest Yunnan** (滇西北自然与文化之窗暨绿色旅游推广中心 *Diān xīběi zìrányǔwénhuà zhīchuāng jì lǜsè lǚyóutuī guǎng zhōngxīn*). This small but fascinating museum highlights the region's cultural and biological diversity. Exhibits include one in which villagers were given cameras to document their daily lives. Another compares photos taken in the 1920s with those taken more recently. The museum is funded by the Nature Conservancy. ✉ *42 Xianwen Xiang, at Guangyi Jie* ☎ *0888/511–5969* 🎫 *Free* ⏲ *Daily 9–6.*

## WHERE TO EAT

$ CHINESE 🍴 **Lamu's House of Tibet** (西藏屋 *Xīzàngwū xīcānguǎn*). The traditional Tibetan decor, pleasant atmosphere, and helpful staff make this one of Lijiang's better dining options. The kitchen serves Tibetan, Chinese, and Naxi cuisine, as well as familiar dishes like lasagna and french fries. [$] *Average main: Y35* ✉ *56 Jishan Xiang, Xinyi Jie* ☎ *0888/511–5776* 💳 *No credit cards.*

$$ ITALIAN Fodor's Choice ★ 🍴 **Mamma Mia** (妈妈咪呀餐吧 *Māmāmīya cānbā*). This is the place to go for excellent Italian cuisine, complete with an impressive selection of fine wines. The Italian chef and owner runs an import business aimed at distributing Italian specialities in southwest China, which means you're getting the real deal here. ■ **TIP→ Try the tiramisu, which is made**

CLOSE UP

# Naxi Music of Lijiang

The Naxi culture is rich in artistic elements—the Naxi pictographs, architecture, Dongba shamans, and, not least of all, the music. It is a complex and intricate musical blending of Han and Naxi musical traditions that has commonly served as entertainment, as well as a measuring stick for Confucian social relationships. Naxi musicians and members of social clubs related to the music were considered to be of a higher status than the average Naxi villager.

Today Naxi music, with its 500 years of history, is a sonic time capsule, giving us the opportunity to hear songs dating as far back as the Tang, Song, and Yuan Dynasties. Most of the Naxi-inhabited counties around Lijiang feature their own orchestras specializing in the two extant versions of Naxi music: Baisha fine music and Dongjing music. A third type, Huangjing music, fell out of practice over the centuries and has since been lost.

### THE ROOTS OF RHYTHM

Legend has it that Baisha fine music developed as a result of Kublai Khan's gratitude for Naxi assistance during his conquest of Yunnan during the Yuan Dynasty. The Khan is believed to have left a group of his best musicians and their musical canon with the Naxi in Lijiang. Baisha fine music is one of the grander Chinese musical styles, with large orchestras including the Chinese flute, the lute, and the zither.

Dongjing music came to this region from central China during the Ming and Qing dynasties, and is based on Taoist classics. It is the better preserved of the two musical styles, most likely because the Naxi incorporated more of their indigenous music into it.

### BEAUTY IS IN THE EAR OF THE BEHOLDER

Naxi orchestras have their own standards for what makes for a quality Naxi musical experience, the key factor being age. In the eyes of the Naxi, the older the musicians, the better. Perhaps this is because fewer and fewer are learning the traditional styles. The musicians' instruments are also old, often much older than the septuagenarians playing the music—the craftsmanship 100 years ago was better than today. Naxi orchestras refuse to play any modern music. They only jam to centuries-old tunes.

For many travelers, Naxi music is an aural step back in time. Others find it screechy and grating. You can catch a show at a number of venues in Lijiang's Old Town and the new city. The most famous groups are the Baihua and Dayan orchestras. Tickets can typically be purchased starting at Y100 at most hotels and guesthouses.

8

with real mascarpone from Italy. $ *Average main: Y60* ⊠ *Feihachushui* ☎ *0888/544-5777* ⊕ *www.mammamiabar.com.*

$$ ✕ **Prague Café** (布拉格咖啡馆 *Bùlāgé kāfēiguǎn*). A favorite with
CAFÉ expats, this bright, sunny eatery serves international favorites like Japanese-style *katsudon* (pork cutlets in a savory sauce). This is also the town's top choice for fresh bread, good coffee, and especially American-style breakfasts. It's a nice place to hang out with a cup of tea or a beer at night. There's a good book collection and free Internet access.

$ *Average main: Y60* ⊠ *80 Mishi Xiang, at Xinyi Jie* ☎ *0888/512–3757* 🖃 *No credit cards.*

$ ✕ **Well Bistro** (井卓餐馆 *Jǐngzuó*
CAFÉ *cānguǎn*). This second-story eatery serves a nice variety of international food at reasonable prices. It's in a pretty setting, away from the hustle and bustle of the town square. The coffee is very good, and it's a top choice for breakfast. This is one of the best places in town to hunker down with a hot drink and a good book on a cold or rainy day. $ *Average main: Y35* ⊠ *32 Mishi Xiang, at Xinyi Jie* ☎ *0888/518–6431* 🖃 *No credit cards.*

> **WORD OF MOUTH**
>
> "We made the decision to tour Yunnan over the Yangtze cruise and I now feel that we definitely made the right choice. The Naxi and Tibetan people are warm and inviting. They are proud of their heritage." —Syl

### WHERE TO STAY

$ 🏠 **Ancient Stone Bridge Inn** (大石桥 *Dàshíqiáo kèzhàn*). Two of the
HOTEL rooms in this guesthouse look directly out over a brook crossed by a pair of bridges. **Pros:** good location; inexpensive rates. **Cons:** in slight need of a renovation. $ *Rooms from: Y580* ⊠ *71 Wuyi Jie Xingrenxia* ☎ *0888/518–4001, 0135/7839–4460* 🛏 *10 rooms* 🖃 *No credit cards* ❤️*No meals.*

$ 🏠 **Australia House** (澳洲部落精品客站 *Àozhōu bùluò jīngpǐn kèzhàn*).
B&B/INN Run by a warm Greek-Australian owner and his Chinese family, this boutique hotel on a quiet side street in Shuhe offers nice rooms similar to the ones found elsewhere in the area, each with their own unique touch. **Pros:** warm owners; peaceful location. **Cons:** a bit remote; certain guest areas a bit claustrophobic. $ *Rooms from: Y580* ⊠ *52/7 Dongkang Jie, Shuhe* ☎ *0888/518–8671* ⊕ *www.aussietribe.com* 🛏 *20 rooms* ❤️*Breakfast.*

$$$$ 🏠 **Banyan Tree Lijiang** (丽江悦榕庄 *Lìjiāng Yuèróng zhuāng*). The area's
RESORT only luxury resort, the Banyan Tree is made up of villas designed to resemble traditional courtyard houses. **Pros:** nearly perfect service; upscale accommodations; breathtaking scenery. **Cons:** very expensive. $ *Rooms from: Y1500* ⊠ *Yuerong Lu, Shuhe* ☎ *0888/533–1111* ⊕ *www.banyantree.com* 🛏 *55 villas* ❤️*No meals.*

$ 🏠 **East River Hotel** (东河 *Dōng hé kèzhàn*). Well hidden in the maze
HOTEL of streets in Old Town, the East River Hotel offers some of the area's most comfortable rooms. **Pros:** quiet atmosphere; idyllic courtyard. **Cons:** hard to find. $ *Rooms from: Y380* ⊠ *44 Mishi Xiang, off Xinyi Jie* ☎ *0888/515–1668* ⊕ *www.ljdhkz.com* 🛏 *40 rooms* 🖃 *No credit cards* ❤️*No meals.*

$ 🏠 **Huifeng Inn Shuhe** (回峰 *Huífēng kèzhàn*). With each room uniquely
B&B/INN decorated to represent one of Yunnan's many different ethnic minorities, the Huifeng Inn is one of the most remarkable hotels in Lijiang. **Pros:** splendid interior design; nice swimming pool. **Cons:** low ceilings. $ *Rooms from: Y380* ⊠ *56 Jiewei Alley, near to Old Sifang Square, Shuhe* ☎ *0888/511–7879* ⊕ *lijianghuifeng.taobao.com* 🛏 *16 rooms* ❤️*No meals.*

$ 🏠 **New Huifeng Resort Hotel** (新回峰 *Xīn huífēng dùjià jiǔdiàn*). Although
HOTEL the term "resort" may be a bit misleading, the New Huifeng offers

plenty of peace and quiet. The soothing smell of polished wood is the first thing to greet you when entering the spacious and comfortable rooms, all of which are individually decorated. The snowcapped Jade Dragon Snow Mountain is visible from most rooms and from the rooftop terrace. **Pros:** great views; swimming pool; unique architecture. **Cons:** some low ceilings, so mind your head. $ *Rooms from: Y380* ✉ *30 Zhonghe Cun, Shuhe* ☎ *1588/756–9046* 🛏 *34 rooms* ⦿ *Breakfast*

$$ 🏨 **Lijiang Intercontinental Resort** (*Lìjiāng zhōujì dùjià jiǔdiàn*). Filling the gap between the small hotels and guesthouses in the Old Town and the ultraluxurious Banyan Tree, the Lijiang Intercontinental was the beginning of a wave of international five-stars moving into Lijiang. **Pros:** comfortable; high level of service. **Cons:** a bit removed from the Old Town; reception understaffed. $ *Rooms from: Y1280* ✉ *276 Xianghe Lu* ☎ *888/558–8888* ⦿ *www.ichotelsgroup.com* 🛏 *270 rooms* ⦿ *Breakfast.*

RESORT

FAMILY

$$$$ 🏨 **Pullman Lijiang Resort & Spa** (丽江珀尔曼度假酒店 *Lìjiāng bórěmàn dùjià jiǔdiàn*). With a hard-to-beat location, the Pullman Lijiang Resort offers views of the Jade Dragon Snow Mountain so beautiful that it has a dedicated viewing area. **Pros:** stupefying views; ultimate comfort; efficent service. **Cons:** expensive rates; almost clinically perfect. $ *Rooms from: Y3000* ✉ *Entrance to Shuhe Old Town* ☎ *0888/530– 0111* ⦿ *www.pullmanhotels.com/7231* 🛏 *130 villas* ⦿ *Breakfast.*

RESORT

Fodor's Choice

★

### NIGHTLIFE AND THE ARTS

Traditional Naxi music and dancing can be found in the town square at Sifang Jie beginning in the afternoon and lasting into the evening.

**Lijiang Impression** (丽江印象 *Lìjiāng yìnxiàng*). The city's most impressive cultural event is Lijiang Impression, a music and dance performance that makes full use of the spectacular location. There are four performances a day, and admission is Y190 to Y260, depending on how close you want to be to the front. ✉ *Ganhai Scenic District* ☎ *0888/888–8888.*

**Mountain Spirit Show** (丽水金沙 *Lìshuǐjīnshā*). At the Meeting Hall of Lijiang, the Mountain Spirit Show offers fire eating and other extraordinary feats. The 8 pm performances cost Y120. ✉ *Minzu Lu.*

**Stone The Crows** (乌鸦飞了酒吧 *Wūyāfēile jiǔbā*). Run by an eccentric Irishman, Stone The Crows offers some interesting cocktails and a selection of imported beer. Pub grub is also available, if the staff is in the mood. ✉ *134-2 Wenzhi Alley, Yangshuo* ☎ *0131/5066–2289.*

### SIDE TRIPS FROM LIJIANG

**Jade Dragon Snow Mountain** (玉龙雪山 *Yùlóng xuěshān*). Towering majestically over Lijiang, the 18,360-foot Jade Dragon Snow Mountain is one of China's most spectacular peaks. The mountain's jagged, snow-covered face is one of the defining sights of a trip to Lijiang. The well-maintained road to the scenic area passes numerous villages and offering fine views of the valley. The park entrance is about a 30-minute drive from Old Town. Taxis should cost around Y40 one way, or Y100 or more if you want the driver to wait for you. 🎫 *Y105* ⊙ *Daily 7–5.*

Fodor's Choice **Tiger Leaping Gorge** (虎跳峡 *Hǔtiàoxiá*). A 2½-hour drive from Lijiang, ★ Tiger Leaping Gorge is home to some of China's most breathtaking

8

Black Dragon Pool Park with Jade Dragon Snow Mountain in the distance

mountain scenery. By water, the gorge winds about 16 km (10 miles); if you're hiking along the upper trail, the 40-km (25-mile) route can be finished in a day or two. The upper trail connects the towns of Qiaotou in the west and Daju in the east, and there is a ferry across the river near Daju. The easiest way to tackle the walk from Lijiang is to take the 8:30 am or 9 am bus on Xin Dajie to Qiaotou and hike toward Daju.

There are several guesthouses in the gorge, scattered at distances to accommodate hikers at any stage of their trek. All offer food, hot showers, and beds for Y20 to Y40. Many of the guesthouses have expanded and upgraded accommodations in the past couple of years, so there is more selection and even some higher-end rooms for Y150. The guesthouses have put up signs and arrows to let hikers know how much farther until the next lodging. If you don't mind not hiking the whole gorge, stop in Walnut Garden, where you can take one of the regular buses back to Lijiang. If you continue to Daju, there are only two buses a day to Lijiang, at 8:30 am and 1 pm.

For those only interested in seeing the point where the tiger is supposed to have leapt, there are two options: the prettier one is on the Lijiang side of the gorge, includes a nice 4-km (3-mile) walk along a path cut out of the cliffside and costs Y50 to enter; the Shangri-La side can be reached directly by minivan but will include a few hundred steps down to where the water rages most fiercely. The entrance fee costs Y65, which also includes the rest of the gorge. Most hotels will also gladly arrange tours in minivans—expect to pay more than Y140 per person each way. ▣ Y65.

**Lugu Lake** (泸沽湖 *Lúgū hú*). If you have a few days to spare, Lugu Lake is a great getaway from Lijiang. The lake straddles the border of Sichuan and Yunnan provinces and is dotted with dreamy little towns belonging mostly to the Mosuo, a subgroup of the ubiquitous Naxi. Exploring the Lake's 80 km (50 miles) of stunning lake and mountain scenery is possible by bus, but biking and hiking provide better views.

Buses taking about five hours depart each morning from Lijiang. Depending on your destination on the lake, tickets cost Y74 to Y97. An airport, slated to open by 2014, will likely turn this into a major tourist hot spot. ✉ *Lugu Lake.*

### WHERE TO STAY

$ B&B/INN 🏨 **Wenhai Ecolodge** (文海生态旅馆 *Wénhǎishēngtài lǚguǎn*). One of the country's first "green" resorts, Wenhai Ecolodge is located in the mountain valley that is home to Lake Wenhai, a seasonal lake that appears between July and March. **Pros:** fascinating for nature lovers; gorgeous setting. **Cons:** remote location; rougher than some travelers can handle; no private bathrooms. [$] *Rooms from: Y120* ✉ *Lake Wenhai* ☎ *139/888–26672* 🌐 *www.northwestyunnan.com/wenhai_ecolodge.htm* 🛏 *12 rooms* 💳 *No credit cards* 🍴 *All meals.*

## XISHUANGBANNA REGION

*380 km (238 miles; 8 hrs or 10 at night by bus) southwest of Kunming; 400 km (250 miles; 12 hrs by bus) south of Dali.*

Jinghong is the capital of southern Yunnan's Xishuangbanna Dai Autonomous Region, which borders Laos and Myanmar. Xishuangbanna is home to the Dai, a people related to Thais and Laotians, who, like their cousins to the south, love very spicy food.

The city sits on the banks of the muddy Mekong, although this stretch of the legendary river is known locally as the Lancang. This is where China meets Southeast Asia; it looks and feels more and more like Laos or Thailand the farther you travel from Jinghong. Even inside the city the architecture, the clothing, and even the barbecue seem much more like what you'd find in Vientiane or Chiang Mai.

Jinghong has experienced a tourism explosion, with the city completely filling up with visitors from all over China and hotel prices skyrocketing during the holidays. It has its own international airport, connecting it to Kunming and other major cities. But despite the increase in economic activity, the pace of life in Jinghong still moves at about the same speed as the Mekong.

### GETTING HERE AND AROUND

AIR TRAVEL Jinghong's international airport has service to and from Kunming, Chengdu, Beijing, Shanghai as well as destinations in Thailand. The international terminal is about 15 minutes west of the city center. From the airport, take the Number 1 bus into town for Y2, or opt for a taxi for Y30.

BUS TRAVEL Jinghong's three main bus stations are Jinghong Bus Station, north of Zhuanghong Lu on Mengle Avenue, Banna Bus Station, just north of the intersection of Mengle Avenue and Xuanwei Avenue, and the South Bus

Station at the intersection of Mengle Avenue and Menghai Road. The former two both have services to Kunming and Dali. For shorter routes, head to Banna Bus Station. The South Station has connections to Laos.

### SAFETY AND PRECAUTIONS

Be sure to drink plenty of water—Jinghong gets hot, and dehydration is a risk as you explore town.

### TIMING

Spend a day exploring downtown Jinghong, and add an extra day or two if you plan to tour out to the surrounding countryside.

### TOURS

Tours organized by Sara Lai and Stone Chen from Forest Café are your best bet for a tailored English-language tour of Xishuangbanna.

### THE WATER SPLASHING FESTIVAL

The Dai Water Splashing Festival is held in Dai-inhabited areas of southern Yunnan, including the cities of Jinghong and Ruili.

Originally, water was poured gently upon the backs of family members to wash away the sins of the past year and provide blessings for the coming year. Today it has become a water war, replete with squirt guns, buckets of ice water, and other weapons. It is quite a bit of fun, and a great way to cool off. Just remember to leave any cameras, watches, and cell phones back in your room, as foreigners are a beloved target.

### ESSENTIALS

**Air Contact Jinghong Airport** ☎ *0691/212–3003.*

**Bus Contacts Jinghong Bus Station.** Jinghong Bus Station ✉ *Mengle Dadao* ☎ *0691/212–2487.* **Banna Bus Station** ✉ *Minhang Lu* ☎ *0691/212–4427.*

**Medical Assistance Xishuangbanna People's Hospital** ✉ *4 Galan Zhong Lu* ☎ *0691/212–3221.*

**Bank Bank of China** ✉ *96 Galan Zhong Lu.*

**Public Security Bureau PSB Jinghong** ✉ *Xuanwei Dadao* ☎ *110.*

**Visitor and Tour Info China International Travel Service** ✉ *Galan Zhong Lu* ☎ *0691/213–1165.* **Forest Cafe** (森林咖啡屋 *Sēnlín kāfēi*). ✉ *23 Mengla Lu* ☎ *0691/898–5122* ⊕ *www.forest-cafe.org.*

### EXPLORING

Even a short walk around Jinghong reveals its colorful mix of Dai, Chinese, Thai, and Burmese influences. It's small enough that you can cover most of it on foot in a day. Bordered by the Lancang River to the east, the city quickly begins to thin out as you head west. Once you're in the new city area, marked with dozens of high-rises, it's about time to turn back.

**Lancang River** (澜沧江 *Láncāngjiāng*). The Lancang River is the name of the Mekong River in China, where it originates before flowing through Southeast Asia. It is easiest to access the river from Jinghong at the Xishuangbanna Bridge. The southern bank is lined with bars and really livens up at night.

**Manting Park** (曼听公园 *Màntīng gōngyuán*). On the southeastern edge of Jinghong is Manting Park, where you can have a closer look at some of the area's indigenous plants. Also worth exploring is the large peacock aviary. The park is especially lively around mid-April, when people gather to celebrate the Water Splashing Festival. ✉ *35 Manting Lu* ☎ *0691/216–1061* 🎫 *Y40* 🕒 *Daily 7:30 am–7:30 pm.*

**Xishuangbanna Tropical Flower and Plant Garden** (西双版纳热带卉园 *Xīshuāngbǎnnà rèdài huā huìyuán*). This is an interesting place to spend several hours walking among fragrant frangipani, massive lily pads, drooping jackfruit, and thousands of other colorful and peculiar plants. This is one of China's finest gardens, featuring a well-designed layout. Don't walk through too fast, or you'll miss out on some of the more unique plants such as *tiaowu cao,* or "dancing grass," which actually stands up if you sing at it. Each plant's placard features English and Latin names. ✉ *99 Xuanwei Dadao* 🎫 *Y40* 🕒 *Daily 7:30–6.*

## WHERE TO EAT

$$ YUNNAN 🍴 **Foguang Yuan** (佛光园 *Fóguāng yuán*). Tucked away behind a school and a police station, Foguang Yuan is a true oasis of peace and quiet. The restaurant is actually several dining areas built around a patch of jungle. The traditional architecture and tropical setting merit a visit, but the restaurant also serves an excellent array of Dai and Chinese classics. English menus are available, but not necessarily up to date. If in doubt, you can always venture into the kitchen and point to what looks good. [$] *Average main: Y50* ✉ *2 Jiaotong Xiang, near Yiwu Lu* ☎ *0691/213–8608* 💳 *No credit cards.*

$ INTERNATIONAL 🍴 **Meimei Café** (美美咖啡厅 *Měiměi kāfēitīng*). This is a good place to compare notes with other travelers, as many people come here to buy tickets, book tours, or get travel information. One of the few places in Jinghong with an English-speaking staff, Meimei Café serves Western and Chinese favorites, as well as great coffee and juices. Open from early morning to late at night, the terrace is a splendid place to enjoy the sunrise. [$] *Average main: Y45* ✉ *2 Menglong Lu* ☎ *0691/216–1221* 💳 *No credit cards.*

## WHERE TO STAY

$$$$ RESORT FAMILY 🏨 **Anantara Xishuangbanna Resort & Spa** (西双版纳安纳塔拉度假酒店 *Xīshuāngbǎnnà ānnàtǎlādùjìa jiǔdiàn*). On the banks of the Luosuo River, this luxury resort is in Menglun, about 60 km (37 miles) from Jinghong. **Pros:** perfect service; great views; sparkling pool. **Cons:** expensive rates. [$] *Rooms from: Y2000* ✉ *Country Road 009, Menglun* ☎ *691/893–6666* 🌐 *xishuangbanna.anantara.com* 🛏 *80 rooms, 23 villas* 🍽 *Breakfast.*

$ HOTEL 🏨 **Crown Hotel** (皇冠大酒店 *Huángguàn dàjiǔdiàn*). In the heart of Jinghong, the Crown Hotel has several low-slung buildings in a parklike setting with a lily-leaf shaped swimming pool. **Pros:** central location; night market nearby; good value. **Cons:** wired Internet only. [$] *Rooms*

CLOSE UP

# Ethnic Minorities of the Southwest

With 26 of the country's 56 ethnic minorities living within its borders, Yunnan is like no other place in China. Many of the groups in this region have long resisted Han influence.

## NAXI

Living primarily in the area around Lijiang and neighboring Sichuan, the Naxi culture is unique, even when compared with other minority groups in China. The society is traditionally matriarchal, with women dominating relationships, keeping custody of children, and essentially running the show. Some Naxis practice Buddhism or Taoism, but it is the shamanistic culture of the Dongba and Samba that set their spiritualism apart from other groups. The Dongba (male shamans) and Samba (female shamans) serve their communities as mediators, entering trancelike states and communicating with the spirit world in order to solve problems on earth. Naxi script, like Chinese script, is made up of ideograms. These pictographs are vivid representations of body parts, animals, and geography used to express concrete and abstract concepts. Despite numbering fewer than 300,000, the

Naxi are one of the better-known ethnic groups in China.

## BAI

The Bai, also known as the Minjia, are one of the more prominent minorities in Yunnan, although they are also found in Guizhou and Hunan provinces. Primarily centered around Dali prefecture, the Bai are known for their agricultural skills and unique architecture style. The Bai also have some of the most colorful costumes, particularly the rainbow-colored hats worn by women. The Bai, along with the Yi people, were part of the Nanzhao Kingdom, which briefly rose to regional dominance in Southwest China and Southeast Asia during the Tang Dynasty, before giving way to the Kingdom of Dali. The Dali region and the Bai have essentially been a part of the Chinese sphere of influence since the Yuan Dynasty, during which the Yuan's Mongolian armies conquered the area in the 13th century. The Bais' highly productive rice paddies were seen as an asset by the Yuan, who let them operate under relative autonomy. Today the Bai and their festivals, including the Third Moon Festival and Torch Festival, are major attractions for domestic and international tourists.

### DAI

Related to Thais and speakers of languages belonging to the Tai-Kadai family, the Dai seem much more Southeast Asian than Chinese. In China they are primarily located in the Xishuangbanna, Dehong, and Jingpo regions of southern Yunnan, but can also be found in Myanmar, Laos, and Thailand. They practice Theravada Buddhism, the dominant form of Buddhism in Southeast Asia. The linguistic, cultural, and religious connections with Southeast Asia give Dai-inhabited regions a decidedly un-Chinese feel. Within China, they are most famous for their spicy and flavorful food and their Water Splashing Festival (water is used to wash away demons and sins of the past and bless the future). Many grow rice and produce such crops as pineapples, so villages are concentrated near the Mekong (Lancang) and Red (Honghe) rivers. The Dai population here has ebbed and flowed with China's political tide, and many are now returning after the turmoil of the 1960s and '70s.

### YI

Descendants of the Qiang people of northwestern China, the Yi (aka Sani) are scattered across southwestern China in Yunnan, Sichuan, and Guizhou provinces as well as Guangxi Zhuang Autonomous Region. The largest concentration of the more than 6.5 million Qiang descendants are in Sichuan's Liangshan region. They live in isolated, mountainous regions and are known for being fierce warriors. Notable traits include their syllabic writing system, ancient literature, and traditional medicine—all of which are still being used today. The Yi also sport extravagant costumes that vary according to geographical region. Massive black mortarboard-style hats, blue turbans, ornate red headdresses, and other headwear complement brilliantly colored vests and pants. Their language is part of the Tibeto-Burman language family and similar to Burmese. Some Yi also live in Vietnam, where they are called the Lolo.

*from: Y350 ✉ 70 Mengle Dadao ☎ 0691/219–9888 🌐 www.newtgh.com 🛏 121 rooms 🍴 No meals.*

$$ RESORT Fodor's Choice ★ 🏨 **Yourantai** (悠然台 *Yōurán tái*). The "Terrace of Serenity" more than lives up to its name. **Pros:** excellent atmosphere; gorgeous setting; amazing mattresses. **Cons:** minimum stay required; steps to climb. [$] *Rooms from: Y1280 ✉ 2 Galan North Rd. ☎ 138/8793–4096 🌐 www.yourantai.com 🛏 6 rooms 💳 No credit cards 🍴 Breakfast.*

## SHOPPING

On Zhuanghong Lu in the northern part of town, there's a handicrafts market filled with Burmese jade jewelry and goods from Vietnam and Thailand. There is a small but vibrant night market on Mengla Lu outside the Crown Hotel. Genuine Pu'er tea can be safely bought from the tea shop in the Golden Zone hotel.

## SIDE TRIPS FROM JINGHONG

**Ganlan Basin** (橄榄坝 *Ganlanba*). One of the more scenic areas of Xishuangbanna is Ganlan Basin, 37 km (23 miles) from Jinghong. Locals still live in bamboo huts in the beautiful rain forest. The area is famous in Yunnan for its tropical flowers and the millions of butterflies that inhabit this valley.

**Sanchahe Nature Reserve.** One of China's first serious attempts at ecotourism, the 900-acre Sanchahe Nature Reserve is home to wild elephants. Two hours north of Jinghong, the park also features a butterfly farm and a cable car that offers breathtaking views. Lodging is in "tree houses" about 25 feet above ground—a unique place to spend a night.

**Xishuangbanna Tropical Botanical Garden** (西双版纳热带植物园 *Xishuāngbǎnnà rèdài zhíwùyuán*). China's largest botanical garden has a gorgeous setting on a peninsula in the Luosuo River. It's home to more than 13,000 tropical and subtropical plant species and a section of dense, unspoiled tropical rain forest. A museum tells about the local flora and fauna, as well as the humans that have inhabited the region. Families enjoy the humid and fragrant air of the tropics, picknicking in pavilions, and observing rare plants and animals. Visits can take anywhere from a few hours to an entire day, so there are also dining and lodging options here. Electric buses help you explore, and hop-on, hop-off tickets are available for Y100. ■ **TIP→ Buses only run until 6 pm, so start at the eastern park and make your way back toward the entrance.** ✉ *Menglun* 🎫 *Y80.*

# SICHUAN AND CHONGQING

Visit Fodors.com for advice, updates, and bookings

# WELCOME TO
# SICHUAN AND CHONGQING

## TOP REASONS TO GO

★ **Emeishan:** Hike 10,000 feet to the top of one of China's holy mountains and a UNESCO World Heritage Site.

★ **Giant Panda Breeding Research Base:** Stroll through the bamboo groves, bone up on the latest in genetic biology and ecological preservation, and check out cute baby pandas.

★ **Horseback riding in Songpan:** Marvel at the raw beauty of northern Sichuan's pristine mountain forests and emerald-green lakes from the backs of these gentle beasts.

★ **Liquid fire:** Savor some of the spiciest food on the planet in Chongqing's many hotpot restaurants.

★ **An engineering miracle or madness:** Enjoy a lazy riverboat ride through the surreal Three Gorges, and stand in awe of one of China's latest engineering feats, the mighty Three Gorges Dam.

**1 Chengdu.** Sichuan's capital and culinary hub is also one of the last bastions of the art of tea drinking. While bent on modernizing, the capital city still retains its laid-back character. Kick back and enjoy!

**2 Emeishan.** One of China's holy mountains, it has almost 50 km (31 miles) of paths leading to the summit. Take time out to enjoy the lush mountains around Emeishan, which also produce some of the world's best tea.

GANSU
SHAANXI

Three Gorges
Reservoir
Wanzhou
THREE GORGES
HUBEI

Jinyun
Mountian
CHONGQING
Neijiang
Fengdu
4 Chongqing
Dazu
HUNAN
Luzhou
Yibin
GUIZHOU

0 ———— 50 mi
0 ———— 50 km

## GETTING ORIENTED

If you're after a China experience where the cuisine is fiery and pandas can be found in the forests gnawing on bamboo, Sichuan Province in southwestern China is a good bet. Smack-dab in the middle of Sichuan, the capital city of Chengdu is easy to navigate, thanks to its subway system and plentiful taxis. It's also acclaimed for its many outdoor gear shops that can equip one for any of Sichuan's local and neighboring natural wonders. For those interested in witnessing the mighty Three Gorges Dam, the city of Chongqing, 240 km (150 miles) southeast of Chengdu, is where the best Yangtze tour boats begin their journey downriver.

9

3 **Juizhaigou Natural Preserve.** Nestled between the snowcapped peaks of the Aba Autonomous Prefecture in northern Sichuan lies the Jiuzhaigou Reserve, a wonderland of turquoise.

4 **Chongqing.** Formerly part of Sichuan proper, Chongqing is its own exploding municipality with more than 15 million residents. Chongqing's meandering alleys will appeal to those who love getting lost in Venice-like twisting streets. This is also the jumping-off point for the Three Gorges river ride.

Updated by Daniel Garber and Dana Kaufman

Renowned for spicy cuisine, giant pandas, and fiery tempers, Sichuan is one of China's most interesting and influential provinces. Chongqing is known as China's "mountain city." Vast and modern, while still retaining many of its old buildings—for now—Chongqing features a fascinating balance of modern Chinese dynamism and Sichuan spice.

With a population of more than 100 million, Sichuan is known for its people's proud, independent spirits. One of the most famous Sichuanese ever, former paramount leader of China Deng Xiaoping, was purged from the Communist Party twice before taking control and launching the reforms that have converted the country from economic pariah to the second-largest economy in the world.

Often referred to as Szechuan cooking in the West, Sichuan's cuisine is famous in China for its liberal use of the chili pepper as well as the curious, numbing flavor of the *huajiao*, also known as the Sichuan pepper. Such popular dishes such as eggplant in fish sauce, kung pao chicken, and the ubiquitous hotpot originated in this part of the country.

The variety of ingredients found in Sichuan cooking are a reflection of the province's diverse topography. The eastern half of Sichuan is dominated by the Sichuan Basin, an area of high agricultural output that in dynastic times was fought over by rival kingdoms. Heading westward, the basin gives way to mountains that become increasingly awe-inspiring as Han Sichuan yields to the province's Tibetan regions.

Sichuan's capital of Chengdu is currently one of the country's most happening cities. During the day, leisure-loving residents sip on tea while chatting or playing mah-jongg. When the sun goes down, there is plenty of amazing food to sample from around China and the world, with one of China's best live music scenes waiting afterward.

Once the capital of Sichuan—and China—the megacity of Chongqing sits to the east of the province and now answers directly to Beijing. With the completion of the Three Gorges Dam, which allows seagoing barges to make it all the way to Chongqing, the city is now changing faster than ever in its new role as Western China's seaport.

## PLANNING

### WHEN TO GO

Chengdu and eastern Sichuan are hot and humid, with temperatures of 35° to 50°F in winter and 75° to 85°F in summer. Chongqing is known for its broiling summer temperatures—sometimes over 100°F. The western plateau is cold but intensely sunny (bring sunscreen and sunglasses). In winter temperatures drop to -15°F. Summers are around 65°F.

### GETTING HERE AND AROUND

Traveling in and out of Sichuan and Chongqing has never been more convenient. The rapid modernization of the two cities and their surrounding rural areas has changed what was once a difficult area for traveling into a corridor of connectivity within and without the region.

#### AIR TRAVEL

Chengdu and Chongqing are both modern cities with international airports serving regional, national, and international destinations. Since the launch of a high-speed rail link, the two cities are no longer connected by flights. Sichuan Airlines is the largest local airline and serves smaller destinations throughout the province, including Jiuzhaigou. A brand-new domestic passenger terminal in Chengdu was just completed to handle the increasing passenger volume. New international routes are constantly being added to Chengdu including direct flights to Bangkok (Thai Airlines), Amsterdam (KLM) and Abu Dhabi (Etihad).

#### BUS TRAVEL

Taking buses around Sichuan is a convenient and economical option for short-distance travel. It is worth keeping abreast of the weather situation in western Sichuan, as heavy rains in the area can cause large—occasionally fatal—landslides that can close roads for days.

#### TRAIN TRAVEL

Chengdu and Chongqing are both major hubs in China's national rail network. The two cities are connected by a bullet train that takes about two hours. It's usually possible to buy tickets at the station on the day you want to travel if you don't mind a bit of pushing and long lines. Reserve at least two weeks in advance if you plan to travel during major Chinese holidays.

### MONEY MATTERS

Banks and ATMs are plentiful in cities and tourist destinations throughout this region. It is advisable to secure sufficient cash before going into remote areas, just in case.

### RESTAURANTS

Eating out in Sichuan and Chongqing can be a boisterous affair, with the tables surrounding you filled with loud, animated diners. Almost anything in these parts comes with some serious spice, so if you can't take the heat it's worthwhile to learn the phrase *bu lade* (boo-lah-duh, meaning "not spicy"). In addition to great Sichuan cuisine, Chengdu and Chongqing also have a growing number of international restaurants.

*Prices in the reviews are the average cost of a main course at dinner or, if dinner is not served, at lunch.*

### HOTELS

Chinese-run hotels in Sichuan and Chongqing offer adequate accommodations at a reasonable price, but the staff usually won't speak English. There are more and more international five-star hotels in Chengdu and Chongqing. In destinations such as Jiuzhaigou and Ciqikou, guesthouses are also an option.

*Prices in the reviews are the lowest cost of a standard double room in high season.*

### VISITOR INFORMATION

Chengdu and Chongqing don't offer much useful English-language visitor information, but hotels, cafés, and guesthouses are good places to ask around.

# SICHUAN

Throughout history, Sichuan has been known as the "Storehouse of Heaven," due not only to its abundance of flora and fauna, but also to its varied cuisine, culture, and customs.

Geographically, it's dominated by the Sichuan Basin, which covers much of the eastern part of the province. The Sichuan Basin—also known as the Red Basin because of the reddish sandstone that predominates in the region—accounts for almost half its area. On all sides the province is surrounded by mountains: the Dabashan in the northeast, the Wushan in the east, the Qinghai Massif in the west, and the Yunnan and Guizhou plateaus in the south.

Sichuan's relative isolation made communication with the outside world difficult and fostered the development of valley, plains, and mountain cultures with distinct characteristics. The Tibetans living deep in the foothills of the Himalayas share space with Qiang, Hui, and Han settlers. In the mountains to the south toward Yunnan, there are dozens of peoples living side by side, such as the Yi, Naxi, Mosu, Miao, and Bai. These cultures all have their own religions and philosophies, with Buddhism and Taoism the dominant religions in the area.

The mountain of Emeishan is a pilgrimage site for millions of Buddhists, as is the Great Buddha in nearby Leshan. Its distance from the epicenter spared the area from any major quake damage. In Songpan, north of the capital city of Chengdu, Muslims, Buddhists, Christians, and Taoists live alongside each other in harmony. One of China's most famous national parks is in Jiuzhaigou, far to the north in Aba Prefecture. The natural springs, dense forests, dramatic cliffs, and sprawling waterfalls make Jiuzhaigou Nature Reserve one of the country's most popular tourist destinations. And if you need more urban comforts, Chengdu is an increasingly international city with food from all over the world, top-notch hotels, dizzying nightlife, and what must be more teahouses per square inch than any other city in the world.

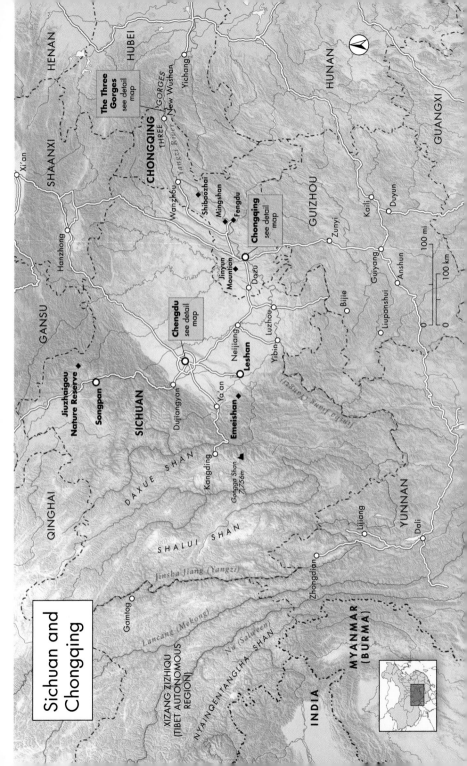

Sichuan and Chongqing

## CLOSE UP · Plight of the Panda

Mysterious, endangered, and cuddly are a few of the monikers typically associated with China's best-known symbol. Dwindling in population would be another. Given China's recent economic reforms, pandas face a mixed future. On the one hand, economic growth and overpopulation are increasingly affecting their habitat. On the other hand, more state and international resources are pouring into special research institutes like Sichuan's Panda Breeding Research

Base. What will be the ultimate fate of these stoic creatures? It's hard to say. One thing is certain though: those who visit ecological panda preserves are part of the solution.

## CHENGDU

*240 km (149 miles; 2 hrs by train) northwest of Chongqing; 1,450 km (900 miles; 25 hrs by train) southwest of Beijing; 1,300 km (806 miles; 27 hrs by train) northwest of Hong Kong.*

Home to more than 14 million people, Chengdu is what you want it to be: while some visitors seek out the pulsating nightlife, others are happy to while away the days strolling through the city's many parks or sipping tea and cracking sunflower seeds in one of its multitude of tea gardens.

Upon arrival, you may be a bit disappointed. Much of the traditional architecture of the charming Old Town has been razed to make room for modern high-rises. The city has been torn in half, literally, for the last several years as new expressways, a modern airport, and gleaming office towers push locals' tolerance and pollution levels sky-high.

Despite the rush to modernize, there is still much to see in terms of history and culture. Temples and memorials demonstrate Chengdu's position as the cosmopolitan capital of Western China. The city is also a great center for Sichuan cooking, famous for its spicy peppers, which many believe is the best in China. Chengdu has too many good restaurants to list, and the hole-in-the-wall around the corner may serve the tastiest Sichuan dishes you'll eat.

All roads into Southwest China lead through Chengdu. As the gateway to Tibet, this city is the place to secure the permits and supplies needed for your trip there. Journeys south to Yunnan or north to Xi'an pass through here as well. Lying in the middle of Sichuan Province, Chengdu is also a good base for excursions to the scenic spots dotting Sichuan. ■ TIP→ **Like many big cities in China, Chengdu suffers from pollution. Bring eye drops, anti-bacterial wipes, and possibly even a face mask.**

**GETTING HERE AND AROUND**

Chengdu is the transportation hub of Western China. Bus, train, and plane connections are as convenient as they get in China. The Chengdu Tourism Bureau has a shuttle bus between the city's three major sights: Du Fu's Cottage, the Memorial of the Marquis of Wu, and the Tomb of Emperor Wang Jian. With your ticket stub, you can hop aboard the bus free of charge. The bus leaves every 20 minutes.

Chengdu is built along a main north–south artery and surrounded by three ring roads. Cheap taxis and the subway system are the best ways to get around. If you are on foot, many of the city's sights are within walking distance of Tian Fu Plaza.

AIR TRAVEL Chengdu Shuangliu International Airport is about 16 km (10 miles) southwest of the city. From here you can fly to Beijing (2½ hours), Guangzhou (2 hours), Kunming (1 hour), Shanghai (2½ hours), or many other domestic destinations. There are a few international connections, but these may be canceled without notice.

Bus service links the airport terminal and downtown Chengdu, with Bus 303 traveling to the center of town. Taxis should cost about Y55.

BUS TRAVEL There are three main bus stations in Chengdu. The Xinnanmen Bus Station, in the city center, has buses to almost every town in Sichuan. The Wuguiqiao Bus Station, east of the city, is used mainly for travelers to Chongqing or Yibin. The Chadianzi Bus Station, in the northwestern part of the city, has buses to destinations in the mountains to the north and west (including Jiuzhaigou and Songpan).

TRAIN TRAVEL Chengdu sits on the Kunming–Beijing railway line, and connections are reliable. The Chengdu Railway Station is in the northern part of the city. The Chengdu East Railway Station, now accessible by subway line 2, is where all the bullet trains arrive and depart. It's a Y20 cab ride from Tianfu Plaza.

**SAFETY AND PRECAUTIONS**

Stay alert for vehicles on both streets and sidewalks, and do not assume that drivers will follow traffic laws. Pickpockets, bag-snatchers, and other thieves can also be a problem. Stay alert on the street and while riding trains and buses, and don't leave valuables unsecured in hotel rooms.

**TIMING**

Chengdu deserves at least a few days, but travelers coming from remote areas of China may wish to stay longer to take a break in the city's increasingly cosmopolitan atmosphere.

**TOURS**

A good resource for package and individual tours in Chengdu and throughout Sichuan is the tour agency Intowestchina.

**ESSENTIALS**

**Air Contact Chengdu Shuangliu International Airport** ☎ *028/8520–5555* ⊕ *www.cdairport.com.*

**Bank Bank of China** ✉ *Renmin Nan Lu.*

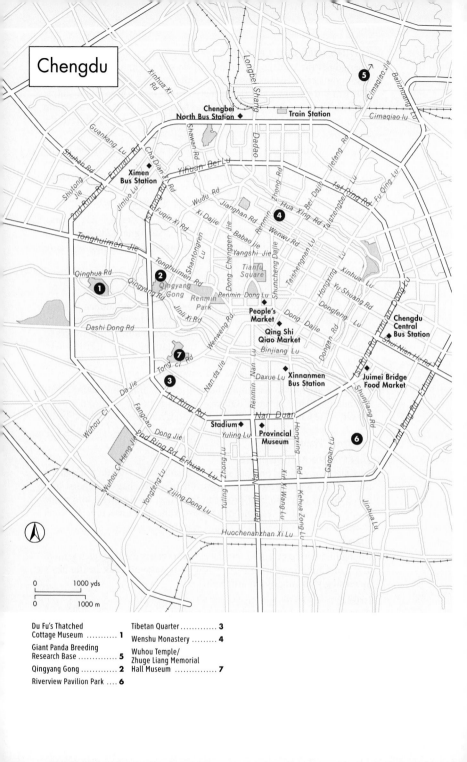

# Chengdu

Du Fu's Thatched
Cottage Museum ........... 1

Giant Panda Breeding
Research Base .............. 5

Qingyang Gong ............. 2

Riverview Pavilion Park .... 6

Tibetan Quarter ............. 3

Wenshu Monastery ......... 4

Wuhou Temple/
Zhuge Liang Memorial
Hall Museum ............... 7

**Bus Contacts Chadianzi Bus Station** ✉ *Sanhuan Lu* ☎ *028/870–6610.*
**Wuguiqiao Bus Station** ✉ *Dongguicun Sanzhu* ☎ *028/8471–1692.* **Xinanmen Bus Station** ✉ *57 Linjiang Lu.*

**Consulate U.S. Consulate** ✉ *4 Lingshiguan Lu* ☎ *028/8558–3992* ⊕ *chengdu. usembassy-china.org.cn.*

**Medical Assistance Chengdu Medical Center.** This modern clinic is staffed with English-speaking doctors. Most international insurance is accepted. ✉ *Chengdu No. I Peoples Hospital, 18 Wanxiang Bei Lu* ☎ *028/8331–7899* ⊕ *www.parkwayhealth.cn.* **For emergency medical assistance.** For emergency medical assistance anywhere in China, dial 120; for all other emergencies call 110. ✉ *PSB; Foreigner's Police, Wenwu Lu, part of Xinhua Dong Lu;, 40 Wenmiaohou Jie* ☎ *110, 028/8674–4683.*

**Train Contact Chengdu Railway Station** ✉ *Second Ring Rd., Third North Section* ☎ *028/8337–2608.* **Chengdu East Railway Station** ✉ *Chengdu, Jinjiang District* ☎ *028/8513–6245.*

**Visitor and Tour Info Intowestchina** ✉ *71 Qinglong Jie* ☎ *028/8558–2963* ⊕ *www.intowestchina.com.*

## EXPLORING CHENGDU

### TOP ATTRACTIONS

**Du Fu's Thatched Cottage Museum** (杜甫草堂 *Dùfǔ cǎotáng*). This museum is named for the famous poet Du Fu (712–770) of the Tang Dynasty, whose poetry continues to be read today. A Manchurian, he came to Chengdu from Xi'an and built a small hut overlooking the bamboo and plum tree–lined Huanhua River. During the four years he spent here he wrote more than 240 poems. After his death the area became a garden; a temple was then added during the Northern Song Dynasty (960–1126). A replica of his cottage now stands among several other structures, all built during the Qing Dynasty. Some of Du Fu's calligraphy and poems are on display here. ✉ *37 Qinghua Lu* ☎ *028/8731–9258* ⊕ *www. dfmuseum.org.cn* 🎫 *Y60* 🕐 *Daily 8–6.*

FAMILY **Giant Panda Breeding Research Base** (大熊猫博物馆 *Dàxióngmāo bówùguǎn*). The Giant Panda Breeding Research Base is worth the 45-minute drive to walk the peaceful bamboo groves, snap pictures of the lolling pandas, and catch a glimpse of the tiny baby pandas that are born with startling regularity. Crews of scientists help pandas breed and care for the young in a safe, controlled environment. Guests can also briefly hold a baby or juvenile giant panda for a donation to the center of Y2,000. ■TIP→ **Visit early in the morning, when the pandas are most active.** To get here, book a driver through your hotel for Y300 to Y400 round-trip. A taxi will cost about Y80 each way. ✉ *26 Jiefang Lu* ☎ *028/8351–0033* ⊕ *www.panda.org.cn/english* 🎫 *Y58* 🕐 *Daily 8–5.*

**Qingyang Gong** (青羊宫 *Qīngyáng gōng*). Built during the Tang Dynasty, Qingyang Gong is the oldest Taoist temple in the city, and one of the most famous in China. Six courtyards open out onto each other before arriving at the sculptures of two goats, which represent one of the earthly incarnations of Lao Tzu (the legendary founder of Taoism). If you arrive mid-morning, you can watch the day's first worshippers

The Wenshu Monastery in Chengdu

before the stampede of afternoon pilgrims. The temple grounds are filled with nuns and monks training at the Two Immortals Monastery, the only such facility in Southwest China. A small teahouse is on the premises. ⊠ *9 Yihuan Lu, at Xi Erduan* ☎ *028/8776–6584* ⊕ *www.qingyanggong.org* ⊠ *Y5* ⊙ *Mar.–Sept., daily 8–6; Oct.–Feb., daily 8–5.*

**Wenshu Monastery** (文殊院 *Wénshūyuàn*). Named after Manjusri, the bodhisattva of transcendent wisdom, Wenshu Monastery is one of the most important Zen Buddhist monasteries in China, and has been around almost as long as the religion itself. It was originally constructed during the Sui Dynasty, around the same time of Zen Buddhism's emergence in China. The monastery and accompanying temples have since been destroyed several times, most notably during the Ming Dynasty, after which the monks are said to have continued sitting among the ruins chanting sutras. It is notable for hundreds of antique statues crafted from a variety of materials that have survived upheavals of times past better than the actual buildings. The attractive 11-tiered Thousand Buddha Peace Pagoda is actually a rather late addition—it was built in 1988 based off an original Sui Dynasty pagoda. The on-site tea garden is a great place to relax in the afternoon. ⊠ *15 Wenshu Yuan Jie, off Renmin Zhong Lu* ⊠ *Free* ⊙ *Daily 8:30–6.*

**Wuhou Temple** (武侯祠 *Wǔhòu sì*). The Wuhou Temple complex houses the **Zhuge Liang Memorial Hall Museum**, a shrine to the heroes that made the Shu Kingdom legendary during the Three Kingdoms Period. The temple here was constructed in 221 to entomb the earthly remains of Shu Emperor Liu Bei. During the Ming Dynasty, Liu Bei's subjects were also housed here, most notably Zhuge Liang. Liu Bei's most trusted adviser during the Three Kingdoms Period, Zhuge Liang is a legendary figure in Sichuan, and in some respects more honored than his master. The temple burned during the wars that toppled the Ming Dynasty and was rebuilt in 1671–72 during the Qing Dynasty. The main shrine, Zhaolie Temple, is dedicated to Liu Bei; the rear shrine, Wu Hou Temple, to Zhuge Liang. There is also the Sworn Brotherhood Shrine, which commemorates Liu Bei, Zhang Fei, and Guan Yu's "Oath in the Peach Garden." The Sichuan Opera performs here nightly from 7:30 to 10. The Y180 ticket is expensive, but the face-changing, fire-breathing, lyre-playing ensemble may help justify the price tag. ⊠ *231 Wuhou Ci Da Jie* ☏ *028/8555–2397* ⊕ *www.wuhouci.net.cn* ⊠ *Y60* ⊙ *Daily 8–9.*

> **WORD OF MOUTH**
>
> "Lots to see inside Chengdu with significant historical importance. Plus the pandas. All easy to get to by cheap taxis." —rkkwan

**WORTH NOTING**

Fodor's Choice ★ **Riverview Pavilion Park** (望江楼公园 *Wàngjiānglóu gōngyuán*). The four-story wooden pavilion in Riverview Pavilion Park, dating from the Qing Dynasty, offers splendid views of the Fu River. The poet Xue Tao, who lived in Chengdu during the Tang Dynasty, was said to have spent time near the river, from which she apparently drew water to make paper for her poems. The pavilion stands amid more than 150 species of bamboo, a plant revered by the poet. ⊠ *30 Wangjiang Lu* ☏ *028/8522–3389* ⊕ *www.wangjianglou.com* ⊠ *Y20* ⊙ *Daily 6:30–8:30.*

Fodor's Choice ★ **Tibetan Quarter** (小拉萨 *Xiǎolásà*). Chengdu's tiny Tibetan Quarter is a fascinating place to explore. Shop for colorful Tibetan clothing and art, including religious objects such wooden beads, Buddhist prayer flags, and Tibetan scrolls. Make sure to bargain hard. If you can't make it to Tibet, stop for a cup of salty yak milk tea at one of the many restaurants lining the main drag. ⊠ *Wuhuoci Heng Jie, Wu Hou Ci.*

**■ NEED A BREAK?**

**Big Foot** (大脚板 *Dàjiǎobǎn*). After a long day exploring Chengdu's many parks, temples, and markets, head over to Big Foot for an invigorating break. You'll be taken to a cozy room with huge reclining chairs and offered a fruit platter and your choice of green or flower tea. Your feet are submerged in a bamboo bucket of steaming water, then are carefully kneaded, stretched, and worked with hot rocks. If the pressure is a bit too strong, say *qing yi dian*; if it's strong enough say *zhong yi dian*. The cost is Y98 for 100 minutes. ⊠ *2 Tong Zi Lin Nan Lu* ☏ *028/8517–0383.*

**WHERE TO EAT**

In Chengdu, hotpot is easy to find. A walk down just about any street will turn up at least one restaurant serving this local specialty: a boiling vat of chili oil, red peppers, and mouth-numbing spices into which you dip duck intestines, beef tripe, chicken livers, or (for the less adventurous) bamboo shoots and mushrooms. Hotpot restaurants tend to be open-air affairs, often spilling out onto the sidewalk.

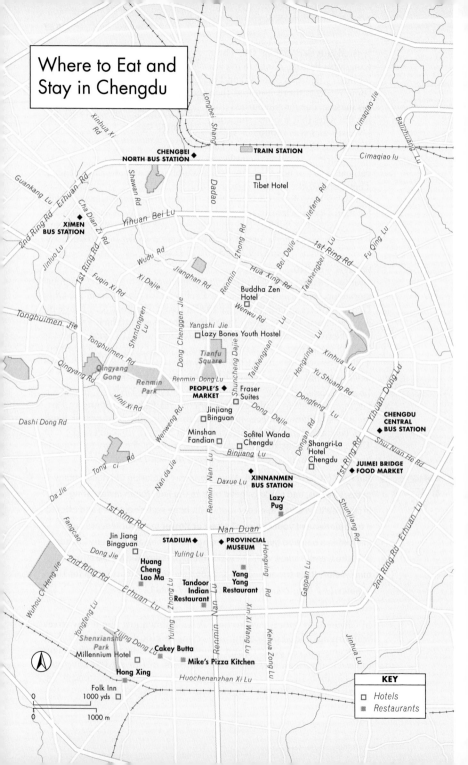

# Where to Eat and Stay in Chengdu

KEY

☐ Hotels

■ Restaurants

$ BAKERY 🍴 **Cakey Butta** (卡卡吡哒 *Kǎ kǎ bì dā*). Run by two Texas natives, this tiny café serves great sandwiches, salads, and mouthwatering desserts that are hard to find elsewhere in the city. Both local and expats rave about the ever-expanding selection of homemade cheesecakes, with pumpkin and caramel-apple highly recommended. [$] *Average main: Y40* ✉ *29 Zijing Dong Lu, Wu Hou Ci* 💳 *No credit cards* 🕒 *Closed Sun.*

$$ SICHUAN 🍴 **Hong Xing** (红杏酒家 *Hǒngxìng jiǔjiā*). Eat like a local at Hong Xing, where Sichuan cuisine is done consistently well. The useful picture menu has amusing English translations and makes ordering a pointing game. With a dining room that resembles an enormous ballroom, you'll feel like you're crashing a wedding reception. Favorites on offer include eggplant with garlic and ginger, pork with peanuts and peppers, or the house signature dish called Hong Xing Ji, which is tender bits of chicken floating in a sea of sesame oil topped with peanuts and mouth-numbing pebbles of Sichuan peppercorns. There are lots of unique vegetarian options, including shredded white bamboo. [$] *Average main: Y80* ✉ *137 Ziwei Dong Lu* ☎ *028/8517–5388* 💳 *No credit cards.*

$$$ SICHUAN 🍴 **Huang Cheng Lao Ma** (皇城老妈 *Huàngchéng lǎomǎ*). Run by artists, this amazing restaurant occupies a massive brick-and-stone building with sculpted pillars flanking either side and a facade depicting scenes from old Chengdu. The hotpot comes in the traditional spicy varieties, as well as a *qing tang*, or "soft soup," style without the spices. You can also opt for those prepared with wild mushrooms or seafood. There are often photo exhibitions from local artists. The top floor is a high-end teahouse and a performance space. [$] *Average main: Y100* ✉ *20 Erhuan Lu Nan* ☎ *028/8513–9999* 🌐 *www.hclm.net* 💳 *No credit cards.*

$$ ECLECTIC 🍴 **Lazy Pug** (懒巴哥西餐厅 *Lǎnbāgè xīcāntīng*). Chengdu's only American-owned restaurant and bar, Lazy Pug serves globe-trotting fare ranging from hummus and pita bread to chicken or steak fajitas. Great blues music and the owner's travel photos decorating the brick walls will make you feel like you've momentarily stepped out of China. There's a long list cocktails, beer, and wine hard to find elsewhere. Sunday brunch is a hit with the city's large expat communtiy. [$] *Average main: Y60* ✉ *Master Building, 48 Ren Min Nan Lu* ☎ *028/13881782604* 🌐 *www.thelazypug.com* 💳 *No credit cards* 🕒 *Closed Mon.*

$$ PIZZA 🍴 **Mike's Pizza Kitchen** (麦克比萨厨房 *Màikè bǐsà chúfáng*). A truly incredible find in Southwestern China, this tiny pizza kitchen is owned by an animated Canadian chef (whose dough-tossing delights guests) and his friendly and charming Chinese wife. The creative menu includes pizza-shaped cookie desserts. Delivery is available within a small range of the city. [$] *Average main: Y65* ✉ *9 Tongzilin Nan Lu* ☎ *028/8522–6453* 🌐 *www.mikespizzakitchen.com* 💳 *No credit cards* 🕒 *Closed Sun.*

DID YOU KNOW?

**Not many people know that some of the best green tea comes from the mountains of western Sichuan. In Chengdu, *hua cha* (flower tea) is the most popular. Hua cha has such a potent aroma because it has been doctored up with jasmine or chrysanthemum.**

**Chengdu's most celebrated green tea, grown row upon row on Sichuan's Emei Mountain, is called Zhu Ye Qing (Bamboo Leaf Green). Slightly bitter,**

9

**crisp and earthy in flavor, Zhu Ye Qing is also the name of a ritzy tea franchise with several outlets in Chengdu and generous sample tastings.**

**If you want to sample some good tea, head to People's Park, Wenshu Temple, or the recently redeveloped *kuan xiangzi* and *zhai xiangzi* (wide and narrow alley) area.**

$$$ INDIAN 🍴 **Tandoor Indian Restaurant** (天都里印度餐厅 *Tiāndùlǐ Yìndù cāntīng*). Just a couple of blocks southwest from the American Consulate, this northern Indian restaurant serves Chengdu's best Indian fare. The decor, a sophisticated combination of wood and mirrors, makes a meal here seem like a special occasion. Tandoor is named after the traditional clay oven used in India, so it's no surprise the grilled meats and chicken are consistently tender and delicious. [$] *Average main: Y100* ✉ *34 Renmin Nan Lu Si Duan, behind the Sunjoy Inn* ☎ *028/8555–1958* 🌐 *www.tandoorchina.cn.*

$$ SICHUAN 🍴 **Yang Yang Restaurant** (杨杨餐馆 *Yángyáng cānguǎn*). This New York Times–raved about restaurant offers what is considered Sichuan 'soul food.' Mouth-watering dishes are created from simple ingredients such as eggplant and potatoes. Yang Yang is a perfect place to sample many dishes in a lively, authentically Sichuanese environment. From the sweet and sour pork to thinly sliced beef soaked in chili oil the menu is tourist friendly complete with pictures. [$] *Average main: Y100* ✉ *32 Jin Yuan Xiang, Wu Hou Ci* ☎ *028/8523-1394.*

## WHERE TO STAY

$ HOTEL 🏨 **Buddha Zen Hotel** (成都圆和圆佛禅文化酒店 *Fóshēn wénhuà jiǔdiàn*). Drawing inspiration from the nearby Wenshu Zen Buddhist monastery, this boutique hotel has carefully designed antique wooden decorations, a peaceful courtyard, wonderful staff, and good food. **Pros:** good location; crisp service; reasonable prices. **Cons:** street can be noisy. [$] *Rooms from: Y700* ✉ *B6-6 Wenshu Fang, near Wenshu Temple* ☎ *028/8692–9898* 🌐 *www.buddhazenhotel.com* 🛏 *35 rooms* 🍽 *No meals.*

$ HOTEL 🏨 **Folk Inn** (附近饭店 *Fǔjīn fàndiàn*). In the southern part of Chengdu near leafy Shen Xian Shu Park, this boutique hotel has temple-style architecture and antique wooden furniture that give it plenty of character. **Pros:** plenty of charm; reasonable rates; near a pretty park. **Cons:** staff doesn't speak English; hard beds. [$] *Rooms from: Y500* ✉ *63 Shenxianshu Nan Lu* ☎ *028/8123–8888* 🛏 *98 rooms, 12 suites* 🍽 *No meals.*

$$$ HOTEL 🏨 **Fraser Suites** (成都仁恒辉盛阁国际公寓 *Rènhéng huīshènggé guójì góngyǔ*). This Singaporean-managed skyscraper in the heart of downtown puts you within walking distance of Tian Fu Square; it's also a two-minute walk to the nearest subway station, so getting around the city is a breeze. **Pros:** great location; luxe rooms; English-speaking staff. **Cons:** expensive rates; lack of dining options. [$] *Rooms from: Y1500* ✉ *111 Zhihui Lu* ☎ *028/8516–6999* 🌐 *chengdu.frasershospitality.com* 🛏 *360 residences* 🍽 *Breakfast.*

$ HOTEL 🏨 **Jinjiang Binguan** (锦江宾馆 *Jǐnjiāng bīngguǎn*). For years this was the city's best hotel—foreign dignitaries and bigwigs from Beijing could always be found milling around the lobby. **Pros:** great riverside location; large rooms, next to subway. **Cons:** no longer the best in town. [$] *Rooms from: Y900* ✉ *80 Renmin Nan Lu, 2nd section* ☎ *028/8550–6666* 🌐 *www.jjhotel.com* 🛏 *456 rooms* 🍴 *No meals.*

$ 🏨 **Lazy Bones Hostel.** The exceedingly helpful staff members here speak better English than those at most of Chengdu's five-star hotels, which might make the basic private rooms and occasionally frat house–like atmosphere a passable choice for Western travelers. **Pros:** good value; helpful English-speaking staff. **Cons:** small rooms; lacks many amenities. [$] *Rooms from: Y1500* ✉ *16 Yangshi Jie, Renmin Zhong Lu* ☎ *028/6537–7889* 🌐 *www.chengduhostel.com* 🛏 *20 private rooms* 💳 *No credit cards.*

$$ HOTEL 🏨 **Millennium Hotel** (新东万千喜大酒店 *Xín dǒng wānqián huàn dǎjiǔdiàn*). Located south of the city center in the Tongzilin residential district, this hotel faces a slender park that's a great place to watch elderly couples practice tai chi while their grandchildren fly homemade kites. **Pros:** great amenties; pretty pool; peaceful location. **Cons:** disappointing breakfast buffet. [$] *Rooms from: Y1100* ✉ *41 Shenxianshu Lu* ☎ *028/8512–7777* 🌐 *www.millenniumhotels.com.cn* 🛏 *359 rooms* 🍴 *Multiple meal plans.*

$ HOTEL 🏨 **Minshan Fandian** (岷山饭店 *Mǐnshān fàndiàn*). This elegant hotel seems out to prove a point: a locally owned lodging can match and even outdo the international chains. **Pros:** great value; excellent service; feels like you're pampering yourself. **Cons:** noisy streets outside. [$] *Rooms from: Y800* ✉ *55 Renmin Nan Lu, 2nd section* ☎ *028/8558–3333* 🌐 *www.minshan.com.cn* 🛏 *370 rooms, 13 suites* 🍴 *No meals.*

$$$ HOTEL Fodor's Choice ★ 🏨 **Shangri-La Hotel Chengdu** (香格里拉大酒店 *Xiǎnggēlílà dàjiǔdiàn*). Opulent style and exceptional service are hallmarks of the Singapore-based Shangri-La chain, and the Chengdu property delivers both. **Pros:** great service; good restaurants; soothing spa. **Cons:** slightly inconvenient location; expensive rates. [$] *Rooms from: Y1400* ✉ *9 Binjiang Dong Lu* ☎ *028/8888–9999* 🌐 *www.shangri-la.com* 🛏 *593 rooms* 🍴 *No meals.*

$$ HOTEL 🏨 **Sofitel Wanda Chengdu** (索菲特万达大饭店 *Shàfěisí wǎndá dàfǎndiàn*). A modern glass tower situated in the city center, the Sofitel Wanda seems to thrive on the consistency of a major international brand. **Pros:** modern vibe; good location. **Cons:** subpar food; noise from street. [$] *Rooms from: Y1100* ✉ *15 Binjiang Zhong Lu* ☎ *028/6666–9999, 800/830–2688 toll free in U.S.* 🌐 *www.sofitel.com* 🛏 *262 rooms, 100 suites* 🍴 *No meals.*

$ HOTEL 🏨 **Tibet Hotel** (西藏饭店 *Xīzàng fàndiàn*). Located near the train station, this inexpensive hotel is a good option for those planning trips to Tibet. **Pros:** good value; handy travel office. **Cons:** far from many dining and nightlife areas. [$] *Rooms from: Y380* ✉ *10 Renmin Bei Lu* ☎ *028/8318–3388, 800/886–5333* 🌐 *www.tibet-hotel.com* 🛏 *238 rooms, 22 suites* 🍴 *No meals.*

### NIGHTLIFE AND THE ARTS

Chengdu has an increasingly chic and sophisticated bar scene, with more Western-style establishments serving imported beer, wine, and mixed drinks.

Zhai Xiangzi, or Narrow Alley, is a pedestrian street packed with restaurants, bars, and shops, all built in a traditional Chinese style. Flanked by the parallel Kuan Xiangzi and Jing Ziangzi (Wide Alley and Well Alley), it is popular among tourists and locals alike.

For a more local experience, visit the cluster of bars running along the river on Wangjiang Lu. Beers are purchased warm and mixed with ice cubes. Young business executives wheel and deal and occasionally slip into karaoke joints for some tipsy crooning.

**Bookworm Cafe** (老书虫咖啡 *Lǎoshùchóng*). South of the U.S. Consulate you'll find the Bookworm, a relaxed haven for thousands of the city's expats to drink, eat, and browse through over 1,000 books. It's the only place in the city to buy English language books, travel guides, and magazines. An annual literary festival (usually held in March) draws famous authors like humorist David Sedaris. The Worm is also a great place to enjoy a pint of Guinness or decent imported wine. ✉ *Yujie Dong Jie 2–7, off Renmin Nan Lu* ☎ *028/8552–0117* ⊕ *www. chengdubookworm.com.*

**Jellyfish Bar** (水母酒吧 *Shuǐmǔ jiǔbā*). A staple of the Chengdu nightlife scene, this lively club draws both expats and young locals. The adjoining burger joint, the Spot, is open around the clock on weekends and makes excellent burgers on homemade buns. ✉ *Blue Carribean Shopping Complex, 143 Kehua Bei Lu* ☎ *028/8525–1789.*

**Underground Bar** (随到酒吧 *Suì dǎo jiǔbā*). Tucked away in Jiu Yan Qiao, one of the city's biggest areas for nightclubs, this small and smoky British-owned bar draws in a good mix of young locals and expats. The beer list is constantly expanding, and offers Chengdu's largest selection of Belgian beers. The place is also gay friendly. ✉ *Tai Ping Nan Xin Jie, Jiu Yan Qiao* ☎ *135/4022–1774* ⊕ *www.undergroundchengdu.com.*

**Zhai Xiangzi.** The redeveloped old Zhai Xiangzi, or Narrow Alley, is a walking street packed with restaurants, bars, shops, and one of the city's many Starbucks outlets—all built in a traditional Chinese style. Flanked by the parallel Kuan Xiangzi and Jing Ziangzi (Wide Alley and Well Alley), it is popular among tourists and locals alike. Chengdu has an increasingly chic and sophisticated bar scene, with more Western-style establishments serving high-quality beer, wine, and mixed drinks.

### SHOPPING

The main shopping street is Chunxi Lu, east of Tianfu Square. Near Wenshu Monastery, Wenshu Fang is another of the city's pedestrian streets lined with traditional-style architecture. Many shops selling flavorful tea and local handicrafts can be found here.

**Song Xian Qiao Antique City** (送仙桥 *Sóngxiānqiáo*). A good place to shop for souvenirs is Song Xian Qiao Antique City, the country's second-largest antiques market, with more than 500 separate stalls selling everything from Mao-era currency to fake Buddha statues to wonderful watercolor paintings. It's near Du Fu's Cottage and Wu Hou Temple. Always counter with less than half the asking price and proceed from there. ✉ *416 Qingyang Shangjie.*

The Wannian monastery at Emeishan

**Wenshu Fang.** Wenshu Fang near Wenshu Monastery is another of the city's redeveloped pedestrian areas built with traditional architecture. It has a lot of shops for buying souvenirs like tea and local handicrafts, as well as restaurants and hotels.

## EMEISHAN

*100 km (62 miles) southwest of Chengdu.*

**Emeishan** (峨眉山 *Éméishān*). The 10,000-foot-high Emeishan (literally translated as Lofty Eyebrow Mountain) in southern Sichuan is one of China's holiest Buddhist pilgrimage sites. The temples here survived the Cultural Revolution better than most others in China, due in part to courageous monks. Still, of the hundreds of temples that once were found here, only 20 remain. Today it is one of the better-known tourist attractions in the country. ■TIP→ **A bamboo walking stick is very useful when ascending the mountain. It's also a good way to scare off the fearless gangs of Tibetan macaques that inhabit the area.**

### GETTING HERE AND AROUND

Most people get to Emeishan Town via a shuttle bus from Chengdu or Leshan, but you can also take the train. The trip from Chengdu takes about two to three hours by bus or three hours by train. Inexpensive public buses travel between destinations, but schedules vary and stops are often unmarked.

BUS TRAVEL    There are departures from Chengdu's Xinnanmen station every half hour and from Leshan every hour on the hour between 7 am and 6 pm. One-way tickets cost between Y35 and Y45, and the trip takes two hours. Also departing from Leshan are buses that travel directly to Emeishan's Baoguo Si. They depart every half hour between 9 and 5 for about Y10.

Most buses coming from Chengdu and Leshan bypass Emei altogether and head directly for the base of the mountain.

TRAIN TRAVEL A Kunming-bound train from the Chengdu North Railway Station passes through Emeishan Town; it takes two to three hours and costs about Y40.

> **MONKEY BUSINESS**
>
> The mountain is known for its wily golden monkeys, who have been known to steal items (such as cameras) and hang them in trees. They will try to surround you, screaming, pointing, and jumping in an intimidating manner. A sound strategy is to walk quickly through the band before they can increase in number.

**SAFETY AND PRECAUTIONS**

The biggest threat here is the unpredictable weather on top of the mountain, so bring warm clothes and dress in layers. Also, be careful of falls or twisted ankles on the slippery stone staircases that run up the mountain.

**TIMING**

Climbing the mountain from base to peak and back again can take anywhere from three to six days, depending on your fitness level. A day of relaxation and recovery for tender joints and muscles will likely be in order afterward. Taking a shuttle bus most of the way and then transferring to a chairlift requires as little as a day.

**TOURS**

Relatively clear English signage makes organized tours of Emeishan unnecessary, but guides can be booked through hotels in Emeishan Town, the cluster of hotels and restaurants at the base of the mountain.

**ESSENTIALS**

**Bank Agricultural Bank of China** ⊠ *Near Baoguo Monastery, Emeishan* ☏ *083/3559–3397.*

**Medical Assistance Emeishan Renmin Hospital** ⊠ *94 Santaishan Jie, Emeishan* ☏ *083/3553–4524, 083/3552–2725.*

**Train Contact Emeishan Railway Station** ⊠ *Emeishan* ☏ *083/3516–8609.*

**Visitor and Tour Info Emeishan Travel Agency** ⊠ *94 Ningshan Lu, Emeishan* ☏ *083/3552–4244.*

**EXPLORING EMEISHAN**

You can hike the 25 miles of stone staircase to the Golden Summit of Emeishan in two to three days. It's a difficult climb—the stairs up the mountain somehow make it seem more arduous. On the first day, hike until a bit before nightfall and walk into one of the temples along the way to sleep for Y20 to Y40 per person. Most hikers can reach the summit by nightfall of the second day or sometime on the third day. Stay a night near the top of the mountain and rise early: the clouds that often obscure views during the day are bathed in a breathtaking amber color at sunrise.

The most common route to the top is past Long Life Monastery. This route takes you past the Elephant Bathing Pool, once used by Bodhisattva Puxian to wash the grime off his white elephant. Once you ascend from here you will be mostly free of the madding crowd. A recommended route down is the long shoulder of the mountain past Magic Peak Monastery, where the scenery is beyond compare. Sharing a simple meal with monks in the courtyard and then staying the night in the monastery is magical.

DID YOU KNOW?

**The mountain is part of a range that stretches from Ya'an in the north to Xichang in the south. These mountains produce some of the world's best green tea. Emei's local tea is called Zhu Ye Qing (Jade Bamboo Leaf), and there are several types and grades. It's possible to buy organic Zhu Ye Qing around the mountain and in more than a dozen ultra-sleek shops in Chengdu.**

For an easier pilgrimage, take advantage of the Y40 minibus service from the Mount Emeishan Tourist Transportation Center below Declare Nation Temple up to the Leidong Terraces, from where your climb will take about two hours. To avoid climbing altogether, ride the cable car (Y70 round-trip) to the summit from Jieyin Dian.

Regardless how you ascend, the best times to climb are in the spring or fall. Bring a change of clothes for the sweaty part of the journey and a warm jacket for the summit. Water and food are available on the mountain, carried by pipe-puffing porters to the stalls along the way.

### WHERE TO EAT AND STAY

$ SICHUAN 🍴 **Emei Kaoyu** (峨眉烤鱼 *Éméi kǎoyú*). Set among several other decent restaurants on "Good Eats Street," Emei Kaoyu lays out a variety of fresh vegetables every day. After you've selected your favorites, the cooks turn them into delicious stir-fries. Try fiddlehead ferns fried with local bacon. The street is just up the hill from the bus station at the base of the mountain. [$] *Average main: Y35* ✉ *Haochi Jie, Emeishan* ☎ *138/0813–5338* 💳 *No credit cards.*

$ HOTEL 🏨 **Baoguo Monastery** (报国寺 *Bàoguó sì*). This monastery at the foot of the mountain is one of the many accommodations available to those journeying to the Golden Summit. **Pros:** monastic experience; handy location; reasonable rates. **Cons:** pretty basic. [$] *Rooms from: Y75* ✉ *Baoguo Si, Emeishan* 🛏 *30 rooms* 💳 *No credit cards* 🍽 *No meals.*

$ HOTEL Fodor's Choice ★ 🏨 **Teddy Bear Hotel** (小熊咖啡 *Xiǎoxióng kāfēi*). Arriving at the Emei Bus Station, you will likely be approached by tours offering to take you to the Teddy Bear Café. **Pros:** free maps and information; congenial owners; Wi-Fi connections. **Cons:** hard beds. [$] *Rooms from: Y250* ✉ *43 Baoguosi Lu, Emeishan* ☎ *0833/559–0135* 🌐 *www.teddybear.com.cn* 🛏 *40 rooms* 💳 *No credit cards* 🍽 *No meals.*

## LESHAN

*165 km (102 miles; 3 hrs by bus) south of Chengdu.*

Leshan is famous for the Great Buddha, carved into the mountainside at the confluence of the Dadu, Qingyi, and Min rivers. The Great

**DID YOU KNOW?**

The Giant Buddha of Leshan has a sophisticated, built-in drainage system of hidden gutters and channels embedded on the head, arms, behind the ears, and in the clothes. This helps displace rainwater and cut back on erosion.

Buddha—a UNESCO World Heritage Site—was initiated by the monk Haitong in 713, but he didn't live to see its completion in 803. The statue, blissfully reclining, has overlooked the swirling, choppy waters for 1,200 years. The city's museum, up the Dadu River from the Great Buddha, is worth a stop.

Although the Great Buddha is the city's main attraction, it's worth spending some time exploring the area. Xiao Gong Zui is an atmospheric stretch of the waterfront lined with local restaurants and teahouses with stunning views of the Great Buddha. Rub elbows with locals cracking sunflower seeds and playing mah-jongg.

#### GETTING HERE AND AROUND

BUS TRAVEL  Leshan-bound buses leave from Chengdu's Xinnanmen station every 30 minutes between 7:30 and 7:30. Buses from Chongqing leave every hour from 6:30 to 6:30. From Leshan's Xiao Ba Bus Station, take public bus Line 13 directly to the Great Buddha's main gate.

TRAIN TRAVEL  The train trip between Chengdu and Leshan takes between 1½ and 2½ hours and costs Y8 to Y109.

#### SAFETY AND PRECAUTIONS

Watch out for slippery paths, and make sure you're well hydrated for long walks in the steamy forested park that surrounds the Great Buddha.

#### TIMING

One day is sufficient to see the Buddha and the surrounding park and pavilions.

#### TOURS

Boats at a dock about 1,500 feet up the river from the main gate will take you for a bumpy ride to within camera distance of the Giant Buddha. The 40-minute trip is Y40 per person. From the boat you will be able to see two heavily eroded guardians that flank the main statue.

#### ESSENTIALS

**Bank Bank of China** ✉ *35 Huangjiashan* ☎ *0833/212–5246.*

**Medical Assistance Leshan Renmin Hospital** ✉ *76 Baita Jie* ☎ *0833/211–9310.*

### EXPLORING LESHAN

**Giant Buddha** (乐山大佛极 *Lèshān dàfó*). Rising 233 feet, this is the tallest stone Buddha and among the tallest sculptures in the world. The big toes are each 28 feet long. A monk who wished to placate the rivers that habitually took local fishermen's lives started the construction of the Giant Buddha in 713. The project took more than 90 years to complete, and it had no noticeable effect on the waters. It's possible to clamber down, via a stairway hewn out of rock, down to the platform where the feet rest. ☎ *0833/230–2121* ⊕ *whc.unesco.org* ✍ *Y95 (includes Wu You Temple)* ☉ *Daily 8–5:30.*

**Wu You Temple** (乌尤寺 *Wūyóu sì*). There are several temples and pagodas in the park that houses the Giant Budda, including this Ming Dynasty structure with a commanding view of the city. You might find yourself staring at the lifelike figures and wonder about the people who served as the models. ⓢ *Y95 (includes Giant Budhda)* ⊙ *Daily 8–5:30.*

### WHERE TO EAT AND STAY

$$ ╳**Deng Qiang** (邓强饭店 *Dèngqiǎng fàndiàn*). This always-packed
SICHUAN FAMILY
family-run restaurant near the river is only a five-minute walk from the Giant Buddha. Local Sichuan dishes, including Leshan's famous cold chicken in a spicy sauce, can be sampled here. Consistently delicious food, a friendly staff, and a laid-back atmosphere make Deng Qiang by far the best choice in the town. ⓢ *Average main: Y50* ⊠ *158 Binjiang Lu Xia Duan* ☎ *0833/212–5110* ▭ *No credit cards.*

$ ⌂**Jinrui Hotel** (乐山金瑞酒店 *Lèshān jīnruí jiǔdiàn*). Set back from the main road, this newly renovated hotel is as good as it gets in Leshan! ⓢ *Rooms from: Y250* ⊠ *342 Baiyang Dong Lu* ☎ *0833-242-2222* ⇱ *34 rooms* ▭ *No credit cards* ⍩*No meals.*

## JIUZHAIGOU NATURE PRESERVE

*350 km (217 miles; 8–10 hrs by bus) north of Leshan; 225 km (140 miles; 4–6 hrs by bus) northwest of Chengdu.*

Fodor's Choice **Jiuzhaigou Nature Reserve** (九寨沟自然保护区 *Jiǔzhàigōu zìrán bǎohùqū*). High among the snowcapped peaks of the Aba Autonomous Prefecture of northern Sichuan lies the Jiuzhaigou Nature Reserve, a spectacular national park filled with lush valleys, jagged peaks, a dozen large waterfalls, and most famously, a collection of iridescent lakes and pools. Jiuzhaigou has become one of the country's most popular tourist destinations, with more than 1.5 million people visiting every year.

This UNESCO World Heritage site preserve's cerulean and aqua pools are among the most beautiful in the world, and the park's raw natural beauty has been compared to Yellowstone National Park. Also similar to Yellowstone are the crowds—throngs of Chinese tourists descend daily on this 800-km (497-mile) stretch of lush forests, piercing peaks, languid lakes, and clear pools.

Jiuzhaigou is a natural reserve and a collection of villages, mostly of Tibetan and Qinang origin. (The name Jiuzhaigou means Nine Villages.) The park shelters 76 mammal species, including pandas, black bears, and deer. The climate is wet in the spring and fall, very snowy and cold in the winter, and bright and warm in the summer. ☎ *0837/773–9753* ⊕ *www.jiuzhai.com* ⊠ *Apr.–mid-Nov. Y220; mid-Nov.–Mar., Y80* ⊙ *Apr.–mid-Nov., daily 7–6; mid-Nov.–Mar., daily 8–5.*

### GETTING HERE AND AROUND

AIR TRAVEL You can fly to Jiuhuang Huanglong Airport, one hour south of Jiuzhaigou in Huanglong. Your hotel should arrange a transfer; otherwise a shuttle bus will cost Y45.

BUS TRAVEL Several buses a day shuttle passengers from Chengdu's Xinnanmen Bus Station or Chadianzi Bus Station.

### TIMING

The park can be seen in one day, although it is a hectic day. If you want to go camping and explore sites outside the national park, three days should suffice.

**TOURS**

If you want to experience Jiuzhaigou as the Chinese do, sign up with any of the numerous package tours in Chengdu and Chongqing. A word to the wise: be prepared to be herded along by a guide armed with a flag and a bullhorn. General information on tours from Chengdu and Chongqing is available from China Travel Service.

**WORD OF MOUTH**

"Jiuzhaigou was really something else—there really aren't words to describe this place. It's superb scenery, absolutely gorgeous. What makes it even better is there are several beautiful Tibetan villages and temples in the valley where Tibetans go about their everyday lives." —Neil_Oz

**ESSENTIALS**

**Air Contact Jiuzhaigou Huanglong Airport** ☎ *0837/724–3700* 🌐 *www.jzairport.com.*

**Bank Contacts Agricultural Bank of China** ☎ *0837/773–9717.*

**Visitor and Tour Info China Travel Service** ☎ *028/6866–3866, 028/6866–3138* 🌐 *www.chinatravelservice.com.* **Jiuzhaiguo Park Office** ☎ *0837/773–9753* 🌐 *www.jiuzhai.com.*

## EXPLORING JIUZHAIGOU

Exploring the park is made easier by frequent ranger stations and signs in English. As you explore the Y-shaped Jiuzhaigou Nature Reserve, your first stop will undoubtedly be the Zaru Valley, on your left. Deeper in the valley you'll pass the stunning Shunzheng Terrace Waterfall before you reach Mirror Lake and Nuorilang Falls. On the right side of this path you'll find the fabled Nine Villages, where it is possible to have a meal with the locals.

From Mirror Lake, veer left to the Zechawa Village, an impossibly beautiful small Tibetan community. From the village, the path travels through a temperate rain forest interspersed with dozens of turquoise-colored pools. At the far end of the left branch of the Y is Long Lake, a beautiful and peaceful place. Down the right branch of the Y is a series of amazing small lakes, including Five Flower Lake and Arrow Bamboo Lake, crisscrossed by wooden walkways.

9

## WHERE TO EAT AND STAY

Did someone say yak? Near the main gate of Jiuzhaigou Reserve you'll find restaurants selling dried yak, cured yak, pickled yak, smoked yak, fried yak, and—well, you get the point. Sample the *sampas* (barley-and-yak-butter tea cakes).

$$$ HOTEL **Intercontinental Resort Jiuzhai Paradise** (九寨沟天堂洲国际大酒店 *Jiŭzhàigōu tiăntàngzhōu guóji dàjiŭdiàn*). The region's most luxurious lodging, the Intercontinental Resort Jiuzhai Paradise is tucked away in a valley 20 km (12 miles) from the Jiuzhaigou Nature Reserve. **Pros:** stunning location; amazing architecture; plush rooms. **Cons:** less-than-stellar food and service. [$] *Rooms from: Y1500* ✉ *Near Jiuzhaigou Nature Preserve* ☎ *0837/778–9999* 🌐 *www.intercontinental.com* 🛏 *1,020 rooms, 131 suites* 🍴 *No meals.*

$$$ RESORT **Sheraton Jiuzhaigou Resort** (九寨沟喜来登国际大酒店 *Jiŭzhàigōu xĭláidēng guóji dàjiŭdiàn*). The region's first luxury hotel, the Sheraton

Jiuzhaigou Resort sits about 1,000 feet from the mouth of the Jiuzhai Valley. **Pros:** top-notch service; hard-to-beat location; plush rooms. **Cons:** some dated decor. $ *Rooms from: Y1500* ⊠ *Jiuzhaigou Scenic Spot* ☎ *800/810–3088* ⊕ *www.sheraton.com/jiuzhaigou* ⇦ *482 rooms, 20 suites* ❘◎❘ *No meals.*

$ 🏠 **YouU Hostel** (悠游度假连锁酒店 *Yōuyóu dùjià liánsuǒ jiǔdiàn*). All things considered, this may be the best value in the area. **Pros:** helpful staff. **Cons:** sporadic hot water. $ *Rooms from: Y300* ⊠ *Building 4, Khampa Lingka Plaza* ☎ *0837/776–3111* 🖨 *0837/776–3966* ⇦ *60 rooms, 6 suites* ⊟ *No credit cards.*

## SONGPAN

*350 km (217 miles; 8–10 hrs by bus) northwest of Chengdu.*

Songpan has experienced quite a construction boom over the past five years. The village with a couple of dirt roads and no accommodations has become a small, ever-growing town with several hotels and even Western-style restaurants. The locals have spruced up the streets and built nice new wooden signs, often with English translations. The old town is not that old any longer, but the mosque by the river is a beautiful sight in the morning when the sunlight reflects off of the minaret.

Most people visit Songpan for the horses, and they do not leave disappointed. These horseback-riding treks through the surrounding countryside go on and on, the longest being 10 days.

### GETTING HERE AND AROUND

AIR TRAVEL     Don't be fooled by the name of Songpan's Jiuzhaigou Huanglong Airport—it's about 88 km (55 mi) from Jiuzhaigou. Aggressive cabbies compete to take you on the 60-minute trip to Songpan (Y100).

BUS TRAVEL     Buses from Chengdu's Xinnanmen and Chadianzi bus stations shuttle passengers daily, with several buses departing between 6:30 am and 9:30 am. Tickets cost Y123.

### SAFETY AND PRECAUTIONS

When hiring a car to go between Songpan and Jiuzhaigou, do not switch cars midway through the journey, as both drivers will try to claim your agreed-upon fare.

### WHERE TO EAT AND STAY

$ ✕ **Emma's Kitchen.** On the main drag not far from the bus station,
CONTEMPORARY     Emma's Kitchen serves both Western and Chinese fare. The prices are reasonable, and the very friendly staff speaks English. The proprietor is a great source of information about the area. With no actual address simply go about 30 meters from the bus station, then turn left onto the main road. $ *Average main: Y40* ⊠ *Main road, near the bus station* ☎ *0837/723–1088* ⊟ *No credit cards.*

$ 🏠 **Old House Hotel** (老房子 *Lǎofángzi*). Also known as the Guyun Inn,
B&B/INN     this guesthouse has a café with good coffee and online access. **Pros:** convenient location; helpful staff. **Cons:** small rooms. $ *Rooms from: Y200* ⊠ *Shunjiang Lu, near the bus station* ☎ *0837/723–1368* ⇦ *15 rooms* ⊟ *No credit cards* ❘◎❘ *No meals.*

A bridge in Songpan

# CHONGQING AND THE YANGTZE RIVER

Called the Mountain City (also the name of the local beer), Chongqing is the major jumping-off point for the Three Gorges cruise down the Yangtze River. The classic novel *The Three Kingdoms* takes place along this stretch of the river, and the cliffs are lined with caves and tombs dating back to the Yellow Emperor. The controversial Three Gorges Dam is now complete, and the water level is steadily rising—millions of people have been displaced, entire villages swamped, and countless historical artifacts lost forever—but China needs energy, and the western regions need a reliable inland port, therefore the dam stays.

**DID YOU KNOW?** Chongqing is the heart of the Ba Yu Culture—vibrant, colorful, and proud—with its own version of Sichuan Opera, its own cuisine, and a history of rebelliousness. The Chongqingese are known for their directness and fiery tempers.

## CHONGQING

*240 km (149 miles; 4 hrs by bus) southeast of Chengdu; 1,800 km (1,116 miles; 3 hrs by plane) southwest of Beijing; 1,025 km (636 miles; 34 hrs by train) northwest of Hong Kong.*

With a layout reminiscent of Hong Kong and a distinct Sichuanese vibe, Chongqing is one of the most interesting and dynamic cities in Western China. The "Mountain City," as it is known, is much more three-dimensional than your average Chinese metropolis, so prepare for plenty of hills and stairs. It is also one of China's hottest cities in the summer,

9

but the plentiful trees and growing numbers of skyscrapers offer plenty of shade in the afternoon.

The central peninsula area of Yuzhong district, between the Jialing River to the north and the Yangtze River to the south, is the most interesting and dynamic area of Chongqing. Within Yuzhong, most of the action is centered around the

Jiefang Bei (Liberation Monument) area, where you will find the bulk of Chongqing's top hotels, restaurants, bars, and clubs.

There's plenty to do outside of the city center, however, with scenic mountains in the south, the old Ming town of Ciqikou to the northwest, and the fantastic Buddhist caves at Dazu, farther afield.

**GETTING HERE AND AROUND**

Chongqing is smack-dab in the middle of China, connected by rail, bus, and plane to every major city in the country. Chongqing's Jiangbei International Airport is among the busiest in the region, with daily flights to all major cities in China. For trips to Chengdu, the high-speed rail link is the best bet.

Chongqing's light-rail line from the city center to the zoo in the south is worth the Y10 round-trip ticket price. The two stations in the city center (Jiao Chang Kou and Lin Jiang Men) are easily accessible from Jiefang Bei. The line curves north to the Jialing River—above ground—and goes through six riverside stations before it heads south to the terminal station at the zoo.

AIR TRAVEL Traffic permitting, Chongqing's Jiangbei International Airport is a 40-minute drive north by taxi from the city center. The airport has flights to every major domestic, and some international hubs, mostly within Asia.

BOAT AND FERRY TRAVEL Boats go on the Yangtze from Chongqing all the way to Shanghai (seven days), but the most popular route is the cruise downstream from Chongqing to Yichang or Wuhan (three to four days) or upstream from Wuhan to Chongqing. Most major sights, including the Three Gorges and Three Little Gorges, lie between Chongqing and Yichang. Tourist boats offer air-conditioned cabins with a television and private bath.

BUS TRAVEL The shared train and bus station may be the most inconvenient, crowded, and annoying station in the world. Once your taxi has maneuvered through the corrugated tin walls and piles of baggage, finding your bus or train is not hard, however.

Chongqing to Chengdu is a well-trodden path. The bus departs every hour, takes five to six hours, and costs Y120. Buses are viable options as far as Yibin, but trains are recommended for all other destinations.

CAR TRAVEL A taxi is often the most convenient way to navigate the winding roads and long distances. Meters start at Y5, and even long cab rides tend to be much cheaper than they would be elsewhere in China. There is a Y3 fuel surcharge added to every fare.

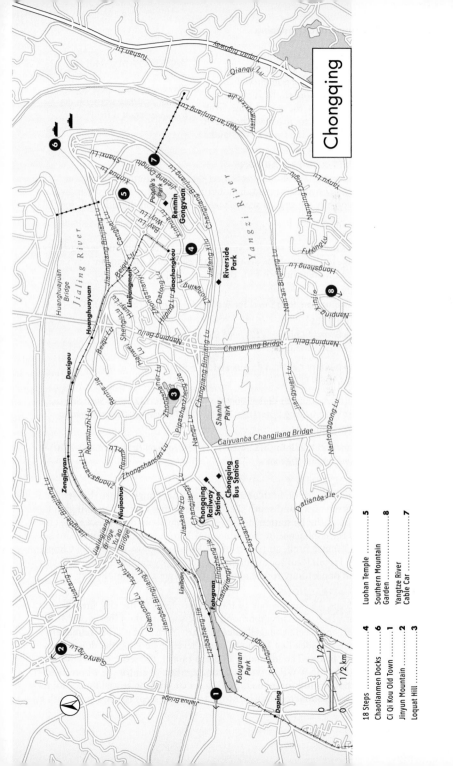

Chongqing

18 Steps ............... **4**
Chaotianmen Docks ...... **6**
Ci Qi Kou Old Town ........ **1**
Jinyun Mountain .......... **2**
Loquat Hill .............. **3**

Luohan Temple ......... **5**
Southern Mountain
Garden .............. **8**
Yangtze River
Cable Car ............ **7**

TRAIN TRAVEL Trains leave Chongqing every minute for every conceivable city in China. If you're going to Chengdu, the ultra-modern high-speed rail link has cut the travel time from four hours to just two hours. A hard seat on the train is Y98 and a soft seat is Y117.

> **WORD OF MOUTH**
>
> "Beware of the hotpots in Chongqing—they teach you the true meaning of H O T !"
> —Marija

**SAFETY AND PRECAUTIONS**
Despite its size, Chongqing is a very safe city in terms of crime. But with all the construction and demolition taking place above street level, it is worth being careful where you walk when on the sidewalk for falling debris.

**TIMING**
You could easily stay in Chongqing for a week without seeing everything, but most of the sights of interest in and around the city can be visited within three or four days.

**TOURS**
**Chongqing Dongfang Travel Service** ⊠ *5 Chaoqiang Lu* ☎ *0236/371–0326.*

**ESSENTIALS**
**Bank Bank of China** ⊠ *218 Zhong Shan Yi Lu, YuZhong District* ☎ *023/6388–9453.*

**Train Contact Cai Yuan Ba Bus and Train Station** ⊠ *Off of Nan Qu Lu* ☎ *023/6168–1114.*

**Medical Assistance Global Doctor** ⊠ *Hilton Hotel, 139 Zhong Shan San Lu, Room 701, YuZhong District* ☎ *023/8903–8837* ⊕ *www.globaldoctor.com.au* ⊙ *Weekdays 9–6.*

**Visitor and Tour Info CITS** ⊠ *151 Jiefangbei Zourong Lu* ☎ *023/6372–7120* ⊕ *www.hikeyangtze.com.*

## EXPLORING CHONGQING

Be sure to ride on both of the cable cars that dangle above the city. One links the north and south shores of the Jialing River, from Cangbai Lu to the Jinsha Jie station, and gives excellent views of the docks, the city, and the confluence of the Jialing and Yangtze rivers. The other crosses the Yangtze itself, and starts off of Xinhua Lu, just west of the Chongqing Hotel. Ideal for taking photos of the city and the two rivers, it's a good opportunity to rise above it all and get a grip on the city.

**TOP ATTRACTIONS**
**18 Steps.** 18 Steps is one of the coolest places in the city, literally and figuratively. The neighborhood is just south of the Liberation Monument, and hasn't changed since the early 20th century. The name refers to the steps leading from the upper level of Jie Fang Bei down to the slums below. The infamous 18 Steps tunnel, the scene of horrible carnage during WWII, serves as a congregation point for the whole neighborhood. Find the tunnel, pull up a mat, and sip tea while the locals stare at you incredulously. At the top of the steps is a teahouse with a

*Continued on page 561*

# A CULINARY TOUR OF CHINA

For centuries the collective culinary fragrances of China have drifted far beyond its borders and tantalized the entire world. Now with China's arms open to the world, a vast variety of Chinese flavors—from the North, South, East, and West—are more accessible than ever.

In dynasties gone by, a visitor to China might have to undertake a journey of a thousand li just to feel the burn of an authentic Sichuanese hotpot, and another to savor the crispy skin and juicy flesh of a genuine Beijing roast duck. Luckily for us, the vast majority of regional Chinese cuisines have made successful internal migrations. As a result, Sichuanese cuisine can be found in Guangzhou, Cantonese dim sum in Urumuqi, and the cumin-spiced lamb-on-a-stick, for which the Uigher people of Xinjiang are famous, is now grilled all over China.

**Four corners of the Middle Kingdom**

Before you begin your journey, remember, a true scholar of Middle Kingdom cuisine should first eliminate the very term "Chinese food" from their vocabulary. It hardly encompasses the variety of provincial cuisines and regional dishes that China has to offer, from succulent Shanghainese dumplings to fiery Sichuanese hotpots.

To guide you on your gastronomic journey, we've divided the country's gourmet map along the points of the compass—North, South, East, and West. Bon voyage and bon appétit!

Following the revolution, it was hard to find authentic Chinese cuisine.

# NORTH

## THE BASICS
Cuisine from China's Northeast is called dongbei cai, and it's more wheat than rice based. Vegetables like kale, cabbage, and potatoes are combined with robust, thick soy sauces, garlic (often raw), and scallions.

Even though many Han Chinese from southern climates find mutton too gamey, up north it's a regular staple. In many northern cities, you can't walk more than a block without coming across a small sidewalk grill with yang rou chua'r, or lamb-on-a-stick.

Peking duck sliced table-side.

## NOT TO BE MISSED
The most famous of all the northern dishes is Peking duck, and if you've ever had it well prepared, you'll know why Beijingers are proud of the dish named for their city.

The fowl is cleaned, stuffed with burning millet stalks and other aromatic combustibles, and then slow-cooked in an oven heated by a fire made of fragrant wood. Properly cooked, Peking duck should have crispy skin, juicy meat, and none of the grease. Peking duck is served with pancakes, scallions,

and a delicious soy-based sauce with just a hint of sweetness.

## LEGEND HAS IT
Looking for the best roast duck in Beijing? You won't find it in a luxury hotel. But if you happen to find yourself wandering through the Qianmendong hutong just south of Tiananmen Square, you may stumble upon a little courtyard home with a sign in English reading Lɪ QUN ROAST DUCK. This small and unassuming restaurant is widely considered as having the best Peking roast duck in the capital. Rumor has it that the late leader Deng Xiaoping used to send his driver out to bring him back Li Qun's amazing ducks.

## THE CAPITAL CITY'S NAMESAKE DISH

A perfectly prepared duck

Scallions

Soy based hoisin sauce

Pancakes

# SOUTH

(left) Preparing for the feast. (top right) Dim sum as art. (bottom right) Place your order.

## THE BASICS

The dish most associated with Southern Chinese cuisine is dim sum, which is found in great variety and abundance in Guangdong province, as well as Hong Kong and Macau. Bite-size dim sum is usually eaten early in the day. Any good dim sum place should have dozens of varieties. Some of the most popular dishes are *har gao*, a shrimp dumpling with a rice-flour skin, *siu maai*, a pork dumpling with a wrapping made of wheat flour, and *chaa-habao*, a steamed or baked bun filled with sweetened pork and onions. Adventurous eaters should order the chicken claws. Trust us, they taste better than they look.

The Cantonese saying *"fei qin zou shou"* roughly translates to "if it flies, swims or runs, it's food."

For our money, the best southern food comes from Chaozhou (Chiuchow), a coastal city only a few hours' drive north of its larger neighbors. Unlike dim sum, Chaozuo cuisine is extremely light and understated. Deep-fried bean curd is also a remarkably fresh Chaozuo dish.

## NOT TO BE MISSED

One Chaozuo dish that appeals equally to the eye and the palate is the plain-sounding mashed vegetable with minced chicken soup. The dish is served in a large bowl, and resembles a green-and-white yin-yang. As befitting a dish resembling a Buddhist symbol, a vegetarian version substituting rice gruel for chicken broth is usually offered.

## SOUTHWEST AND FAR WEST

### Southwest

**THE BASICS**

When a person from the Southwest asks you if you like spicy food, consider your answer well. Natives of Sichuan and Hunan take the use of chilies, wild pepper, and garlic to blistering new heights. These two areas have been competing for the "spiciest province in China" title for centuries. The penchant for fiery food is likely due to the weather—hot and humid in the summer and harshly cold in the winter. But no matter what the temperature, if you're eating Sichuan or Hunan dishes, be prepared to sweat.

Southwest China shares some culinary traits with both Southeast Asia and India. This is likely due to the influences of travelers from both regions in centuries past. Traditional Chinese medicine also makes itself felt in the regional cuisine. Theory has it that sweating expels toxins and equalizes body temperature.

As Chairman Mao's province, Hunan has a number of dishes with revolutionary names. The most popular are red-cooked Hunan fish *(hongshao wuchangyu)* and red-cooked pork *(hongshao rou)*, which was said to have been a personal favorite of the Great Helmsman.

Sichuan pepper creates a tingly numbness.

**NOT TO BE MISSED**

One dish you won't want to miss out on in Sichuan is *mala zigi*, or "peppery and hot chicken." It's one part chicken meat and three parts fried chilies and a Sichuanese wild pepper called *huajiao* that's so spicy it effectively numbs the tongue. At first it feels like eating Tiger Balm, but the hot-cool-numb sensation produced by crunching on the pepper is oddly addictive.

### KUNG PAO CHICKEN

One of the most famous Chinese dishes, Kung Pao chicken (or gongbao jiding), enjoys a legend of its own.

Though shrouded in myth, its origin exemplifies the improvisational skills found in any good Chinese chef. The story of Kung Pao chicken has to do with a certain Qing Dynasty era (1644–1911) provincial governor named Ding Baozhen, who arrived home unexpectedly one day with a group of friends in tow. His cook, caught in between

shopping trips, had only the chicken breast and a few vegetables he was planning to cook for his own dinner. The crafty chef diced the chicken into tiny bits and fried it up with everything he could find in the cupboard—some peanuts, sugar, onion, garlic, bits of ginger, and a few handfuls of dried red peppers—and hoped for the best.

(top left) Tibetan dumplings. (center left) Uyghur-style pilaf. (bottom left) Monk stirring tsampa barley. (right) Juggling hot noodles in the Xinjiang province.

## Far West

### THE BASICS

Religion is the primary shaper of culinary tradition in China's Far West. Being a primarily Muslim province, chefs in Xinjiang don't use pork products of any kind. Instead, meals are likely to be heavy on spiced lamb. Baked flat breads coated in sesame seeds are a specialty. Whole lamb roasted on a spit, fine spicy tomato salads, and lightly spiced mutton and vegetable soups are also favorites.

### NOT TO BE MISSED

In Tibet, climate is the major factor dictating cuisine. High and dry, the Tibetan plateau is hardly suited for rice cultivation. Whereas a Han meal might include rice, Tibetan cuisine tends to include tsampa, a ground barley usually cooked into a porridge. Another staple that's definitely an acquired taste is yak butter tea. Dumplings, known as *momo,* are wholesome and filling. Of course, if you want to go all out, order the yak penis with caterpillar fungus.

## EAST

(top left) Cold tofu with pork and thousand-year-old eggs. (top right) Meaty dumplings. (bottom right) Letting off the steam of Shanghai: soup dumplings. (bottom left) Steamed Shanghai hairy crabs.

### THE BASICS

The rice, seafood, and fresh vegetable-based cooking of the southern coastal provinces of Zhejiang and Jiangsu are known collectively as huiyang cai. As the area's biggest city, Shanghai has become a major center of the culinary arts. Some popular dishes in Shanghai are stir-fried freshwater eels and finely ground white pepper, and red-stewed fish—a boiled carp in sweet and sour sauce. Another Shanghai favorite are xiaolong bao, or little steamer dumplings. Similar to Cantonese dim sum, xiaolong bao tend to be more moist. The perfect steamed dumpling is meant to explode in your mouth in a juicy burst of meat.

### NOT TO BE MISSED

Drunken anything! Shanghai chefs are known for their love of cooking with wine. Dishes like drunken chicken, drunken pigeon, and drunken crab are all delectable meals cooked with prodigious amounts of Shaoxing wine. People with an aversion to alcohol should definitely avoid these. Another meal not to be missed is hairy freshwater crabs, which only come into season in October. One enthusiast of the dish was 15th-century poet and essayist Li Yu, who wrote of the dish in near-erotic terms. "Meat as white as jade, golden roe . . . to use seasoning to improve its taste is like holding up a torch to brighten the sunshine."

treasure trove of WWII memorabilia. ✉ *Jie Fang Bei District, south of the Liberation Monument.*

**Ciqikou Old Town** (磁器口古镇 *Cíqìkǒu gǔzhèn*)Perched in the western area of the city overlooking the Jialing River, this district dates back to the late Ming Dynasty. There is a main drag with dozens of souvenir and snack shops, including the peaceful Baolun Temple, which dates back 1,500 years. If you do stay until late into the evening, head down the alleys off the main drag and have a bowl of "night owl noodles." They're spicy, meaty, and filling. The taxi ride from downtown takes approximately 30 minutes and costs around Y30.

**18 STEPS**

Chongqing has the dubious distinction of being the most-bombarded city ever. During WWII people would hide in the tunnels throughout the city to escape devastation. One of these tunnels is in the district known as 18 Steps, in present-day Jiefang Bei District. The tunnel still exists, but serves a very different purpose. It emits a constant flow of cool air, and area residents gather here to cool themselves on sweltering summer days.

**Jinyun Mountain** (缙云山 *Jìnyún shān*). Just north of the city, Jinyun Mountain has some pretty views and a smattering of pavilions from the Ming and Qing dynasties. Three contain imposing statues: the Giant Buddha, the Amitabha Buddha, and the famous general of the Three Kingdoms period, Guan Yu. The park also has a set of **hot springs,** where you can swim in a pool or soak in the private cubicles. ✉ *50 km (30 miles) by bus north of the city, Beibie* 🎫 *Y15* ☉ *Daily 8:30–6.*

**Luohan Temple** (罗汉寺 *Luóhàn sì*). Originally built about 1,000 years ago, then rebuilt in 1752 and again in 1945, the Luohan Temple is a popular place of worship, and a small community of monks is still active here. One of the main attractions is the 500 lifelike painted clay arhats—Buddhist disciples who have succeeded in freeing themselves from the earthly chains of delusion and material greed. At the back of the temple you can order tea, get a massage, and enjoy a vegetarian lunch. ✉ *7 Luohan Si, across from Carrefour* 🎫 *Y10* ☉ *Daily 8 am–5 pm.*

**Southern Mountain Garden** (重庆南山公园 *Chóngqìng nánshān gōngyuán*). Southern Mountain is the highest point in the city, and at 935 feet it's the most popular place from which to view Chongqing. For a thousand years Nan Shan has been the route over which travelers and traders of medicine, tea, spices, and silk entered the city and headed on to Sichuan. The best place to enjoy the views and the feel of the mountain is in this very traditional Chinese garden with oddly shaped rocks and bonsai trees. ✉ *101 Nan Shan Gong Yuan Lu* 🎫 *Y30* ☉ *Daily 8–5.*

Fodor's Choice ★ **Yangtze River Cable Car** (电缆车 *Diànlǎnchē*). The Yangtze River Cable Car is a great way to experience the enormous scale of the city, sky, and mountains and a bird's eye-view of Chongqing, one of the world's biggest cities. Ideal for taking photos of the city and the two rivers, it's a good opportunity to rise above it all and get a grip on the massive scale of the metropolis. ✉ *Jiefang Dong Lu, west of the Chongqing Hotel* 🎫 *Y2* ☉ *Daily 7 am–10 pm.*

9

DID YOU KNOW?

**There are dozens of hole-in-the-wall restaurants all along the stone steps that serve the cheapest, tastiest food in town.**

### CHONGQING NOODLES

Southern China was not always known for its noodles, as such fare was traditionally the domain of northerners. But during the mass migrations south and west over the past century, noodle culture has been introduced to the Mountain City. Now Chongqing has some of the tastiest bowls anywhere in the nation. Chongqing noodles come in all varieties, and there are too many noodle stands to count.

### WORTH NOTING

**Chaotianmen Docks** (朝天门码头 *Cháotiānmén mǎtóu*). Not as busy and bustling as once upon a time, Chaotianmen Docks lets you get a glimpse of China at work. Here you can witness the merging of the muddy-brown Yangtze River and the blue-green Jialing River. Chaotianmen Square has great skyline views. ✉ *Shaanxi Lu.*

**Loquat Hill** (枇杷山 *Pípá shān*). The 804-foot Loquat Hill has great views of the river below. At night, enjoy the city lights. There's also a small park with no entrance fee. ✉ *Zhongshan Er Lu* 🎟 *Free* 🕒 *Daily 8–7.*

### WHERE TO EAT

$$ MEXICAN
🍴 **Cactus Tex-Mex** (仙人墨西哥餐厅 *Xiānrén mòxīgē cāntīng*). Anyone craving something other than mouth-numbing local dishes will be thrilled to find this American-owned Tex-Mex restaurant. Sip from your favorite of the premium tequilas and watch locals mingle with expats or take in views of the Yangtze River. Decked out with a large wooden bar, the atmosphere makes the food almost beside the point. [$] *Average main: Y80* ✉ *9F Hong Ya Dong, YuZhong District* ☎ *03/6382–8187* 🌐 *www.cactustexmex.com* 💳 *No credit cards.*

$ CAFÉ
🍴 **Nenlu Tea** (嫩绿茶 *Nēnlǜ chá*). Slick, comfortable, and modern, this teahouse is the city's answer to Starbucks. With several locations around the city (with the Jiabin Lu branch boasting awesome river views), Nenlu is the perfect place to escape the heat, crowds, and general pandemonium of navigating the hilly streets. Loose leaf teas from around the world and creative drink options make this place worth the visit. Snacks are also available, but the tea is the highlight. [$] *Average main: Y30* ✉ *88 Jiabin Lu, Hong Ya Cave* ☎ *023/6373–4860* 🌐 *www.nenlu.com.*

$$ SICHUAN
🍴 **Qiqi Shanyu Hot Pot** (琪琪上虞火锅 *Qíqí shàngyú huǒguò*). If you ask a local about classic Chongqing-style hotpot, you might be steered to this restaurant. Sure enough, it serves up a highly authentic version of the city's signature dish. The big pot of broth is served hot, and soon comes to a boil over a burner in the center of your table. Choose from tofu, vegetables, or raw shaved beef and mutton and cook them by placing them in the broth. Qiqi Shanyu has all the classic ingredients, but also has a few tricks up its sleeve, such as compartmentalized pots for cooking different ingredients with different cooking times. Unusual but highly recommended ingredients include duck and eel. [$] *Average main: Y85* ✉ *Zourong Plaza, 69 Linjiang Lu, 2nd fl.* ☎ *023/6379–9369* 💳 *No credit cards.*

$$$ SICHUAN 🍴 **Xiaotian'e Sichuan Restaurant** (重庆小天鹅 *Chóngqìng xiǎotiān'é*). Some of Chongqing's most authentic Sichuanese dishes are served in this restaurant on the bank of the Yangtze. An after-dinner stroll along the banks of the river is a great cap to the meal. A house specialty is water-boiled fish slices: the "water" actually has liberal amounts of oil, dried chilies, whole Sichuan peppercorns, and other spices that create an explosion of flavor. Other good choices are cold rice noodles, tofu-stuffed dumplings, and spicy fried chicken. If you want a seat overlooking the river, try to beat the dinner rush and arrive by 6 pm. [$] *Average main: Y100* ✉ *88 Jiabin Lu, 11th Fl.* ☎ *023/6303–9958* 💳 *No credit cards.*

## WHERE TO STAY

$$ HOTEL 🏨 **Hilton Chongqing** (重庆希尔顿酒店 *Chóngqìng shà'érdùn jiǔdiàn*). In a leafy, quiet neighborhood near Lianglukou Stadium, the Hilton Chongqing has plush rooms with the firmest beds in town and fabulous bathrooms. **Pros:** modern design; nice views; helpful staff. **Cons:** not very close to shopping. [$] *Rooms from: Y1100* ✉ *139 Zhongshan San Lu* ☎ *023/8903–9999* 🌐 *www.hilton.com.cn* 🛏 *400 rooms, 35 suites* 🍽 *No meals.*

$$ HOTEL 🏨 **InterContinental Chongqing** (]重庆洲际大酒店 *Chóngqìng zhōují dàjiǔdiàn*). With one of the city's top breakfast buffets and a trio of top-notch restaurants, the InterContinental is a favorite with locals and visitors. **Pros:** convenient downtown location; lots of amenities; plush rooms. **Cons:** upper-level views tend to be obscured. [$] *Rooms from: Y1200* ✉ *101 Minzu Lu* ☎ *023/8906–6888* 🌐 *www.intercontinental.com* 🛏 *308 rooms, 30 suites* 🍽 *No meals.*

$$ HOTEL 🏨 **JW Marriott** (重庆JW万豪酒店 *JWwǎnhào jiǔdiàn*). Just off the city's main drag, this gleaming glass tower puts you within walking distance of virtually anywhere near Liberation Monument. **Pros:** great location; elegant rooms; good pool. **Cons:** poor breakfast buffet; some air-conditioning problems. [$] *Rooms from: Y1200* ✉ *77 Qing Nian Lu, YuZhong District* ☎ *023/6388–8888* 🌐 *www.marriotthotels.com* 🛏 *428 rooms, 32 suites* 🍽 *No meals.*

9

$$ HOTEL Fodor's Choice ★ 🏨 **Le Méridien Chongqing** (艾美大酒店 *Àiméi dàjiǔdiàn*). Successfully blending French hospitality and Chinese architectural flourishes, the upscale Le Méridien Chongqing is truly a gem. **Pros:** spacious rooms; great design; stellar service. **Cons:** not in the center of town. [$] *Rooms from: Y1000* ✉ *10 Jiang Nan Ave., Nan An District* ☎ *023/8638–8888* 🌐 *www.lemeridien.com/chongqingnanan* 🛏 *288 rooms, 31 suites* 🍽 *No meals.*

$ HOTEL 🏨 **Radisson Blu** (雷迪森酒店 *Ruīdìsà jiǔdiàn*). For the price, this is an excellent option in downtown Chongqing. **Pros:** comfortable rooms; great location. **Cons:** predictable design. [$] *Rooms from: Y500* ✉ *22 Nan Bin Lu, Nan An District* ☎ *023/8866–8888* 🌐 *www.radissonblu.com* 🛏 *280 rooms, 28 suites* 🍽 *No meals.*

$ HOTEL 🏨 **Somerset Jiefangbei Chongqing** (重庆盛捷解放碑服务公寓 *Shèngjiějiéfàngbēi*). This sleek hotel's

**WORD OF MOUTH**

"One of the highlights was going to Luohan Temple. . . . It was amazing. Inside there are over 500 various Buddhas, all life-size and of every description." —NeoPatrick

prime location makes it easy to see the best of the city. **Pros:** great location; modern feel; memorable river views. **Cons:** often fully booked. $ *Rooms from: Y700* ⊠ *108 Minzu Lu, YuZhong District* ☎ *023/8677-6888* ⊕ *www.somerset.com* ⇥ *157 Rooms* ⑪ *No meals.*

> **BEFORE YOU GO**
>
> The Three Gorges area is steeped in legends and history. To best appreciate the trip, read the classic book *The Three Kingdoms.*

### NIGHTLIFE AND THE ARTS

Fodor's Choice ★

**Hong Ya Cave** (洪崖洞 *Hóngyá dòng*). This complex overlooks the Jialing River and has a brightly lit waterfall and paved streets built right into the mountainside. The main attraction is the Ba Yu Theater, a rather cheesy performance of Chongqing customs and folklore. The historical aspects of Bayu culture have been dumbed down, but the costumes, choreography, and the bit on the Devil Town of Fengdu make it an evening well spent. ⊠ *56 Cangbai Lu, south bank of the Jialing River* ☎ *023/6303-9968.*

### SHOPPING

**Carrefour** (家乐福超市 *Jiālèfú chāoshì*). Near Chaotianmen Port, Carrefour is the largest foreign-owned department store chain in China. The France-based giant sells everything from congee to caviar, plus there's a decent import section with all the goodies from back home. Carrefour is the best place in Chongqing to stock up on Western food and drink before a Yangtze cruise. ⊠ *Cangbai Lu* ☎ *023/6378-8852.*

### SIDE TRIP TO DAZU

Fodor's Choice ★

**Baoding Shan** (保定山 *Bǎodìng shān*). A UNESCO World Heritage site, these Buddhist caves rival those at Datong, Dunhuang, and Luoyang. The sculptures, ranging from teeny-tiny to gigantic, contain unusual domestic details, as well as purely religious works. There are two major sites at Dazu—Bei Shan and Baoding Shan. Work at the caves began in the 9th century during the Song and Tang Dynasties, and continued for more than 250 years.

Baoding Shan is the more impressive of the two sites, where the carvings were completed according to a plan. Here you will find visions of hell reminiscent of similar scenes from medieval Europe; the Wheel of Life; a magnificent 100-foot reclining Buddha; and a gold statue of the 1,000-armed goddess of mercy.

The best way to reach Dazu is to book a tour from Chongqing. Every agency offers the Dazu tour for between Y220 and Y250, which includes transportation, lunch, and admission. You could also go on your own, but you won't save much. Minibuses departing from Chongqing's Liberation Monument cost Y180 to Y230 round-trip. ✉ *Mar.–Dec., Y180; Jan. and Feb., Y130* ☉ *Daily 8–6.*

#### WHERE TO STAY

$ HOTEL

**Dazu Binguan** (大足宾馆 *Dàzú bīngguǎn*). If you find yourself staying overnight in Dazu, your best bet is this serviceable but unimaginative hotel. **Pros:** prime location. **Cons:** uncomfortable beds. $ *Rooms from: Y250* ⊠ *350 Longgang Zhonglu* ☎ *023/4372–1888* 🖷 *023/4372–2907* ⇥ *132 rooms* ⑪ *No meals.*

## THE THREE GORGES

The third-longest river in the world after the Amazon and the Nile, the Yangtze cuts across 6,380 km (3,956 miles) and seven provinces before flowing out into the East China Sea. After descending from the mountain ranges of Qinghai and Tibet, the Yangtze crosses through Yunnan to Sichuan, winding its way through the lush countryside between Sichuan and Hubei before flowing northward toward Anhui and Jiangsu. Before the 20th century, many lost their lives trying to pass through the fearsome stretch of water running through what is known as the Three Gorges—the complicated system of narrow cliffs between Fengjie, in Sichuan, and Yichang, in Hubei.

> **WORD OF MOUTH**
>
> "Meals on the Victoria Queen are eaten at assigned tables. Breakfast and lunch are buffets. Dinner is served family-style at the tables. We were very pleasantly surprised by the quality of the food. There was good variety, both Chinese and European, and the food was well prepared." –Marija

The spectacular scenery of the Three Gorges—Qutang, Wu, and Xiling—has survived the rising waters of the newly dammed Yangtze River. A trip through the Three Gorges offers a glimpse of the new China moving full steam ahead. Almost all of the cities and towns in the area are in the middle of a construction and tourism boom. The Yangtze itself has endless streams of passenger and cargo boats moving up and downstream.

While there is no doubt that much of the charm has been diminished by the flooding of the area, what's done is done, and the Gorges are still scenic and fascinating. Sitting on deck and taking in the moon and stars on a clear night while heading downstream is a great way to escape the hustle and bustle of Chinese cities.

### BOAT TOURS

Riverboat rides essentially come in two forms: luxury and domestic. Domestic cruises are much cheaper and have few amenities. No matter which option you choose, book ahead, as berths are limited.

#### LUXURY CRUISE BOATS

The foreign-owned ships, such as the Victoria Series boats, are big, quadruple-decker liners and by far the most comfortable option. In addition to spacious decks from which to soak up the breathtaking views, many boats are equipped with a gym, a ballroom, a business center with Internet connection, and bars and restaurants. There are also a few shops in case you run out of film or other necessities.

The ticket price includes the admission cost for most of the sites along the way, except the Little Three Gorges. A one-way package tour ranges from Y3,793 to Y4,583, and the boats themselves are divided into three-, four-, and five-star service.

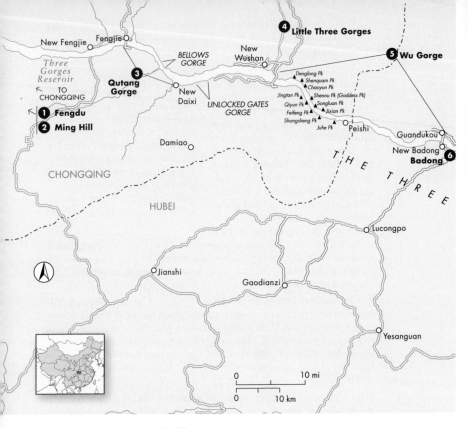

## DOMESTIC BOATS

These less expensive, less luxurious boats are divided into four classes. Suites offer almost all of the amenities of Luxury Cruise Boats and are available for Y2,084 each way. First class sleeps two people and costs Y1,042 each way. Spartan rooms come with two beds, a private bathroom, TV, and air-conditioning. Second and third classes, costing Y503 and Y347 each way, have bunk beds, shared bathrooms that aren't always kept clean, and limited views. The domestic boats usually serve good Chinese food, depending on the class you choose.

The tour operators have been consolidated into one company called Chongqing Port International Travel Service, and most tours get booked through them. Offices can be found throughout the Chaotianmen District. Prices range from Y476 for the least expensive tour to Y4,600 for the costliest.

**Contact Chongqing Port International Travel Service** ✉ *18 Xinyi St., Chaotianmen, Yu Zhong District, Chongqing* ☎ *023/6310-0595* ⊕ *www.cqpits.com.*

## HYDROFOIL

This option is used by those returning from Yichang to Chongqing, who don't want to do the whole trip over again in reverse. Prices vary, but currently it is Y280 from Yichang to Chongqing and takes about six hours. You have to get off at Wanxian and take a bus back into

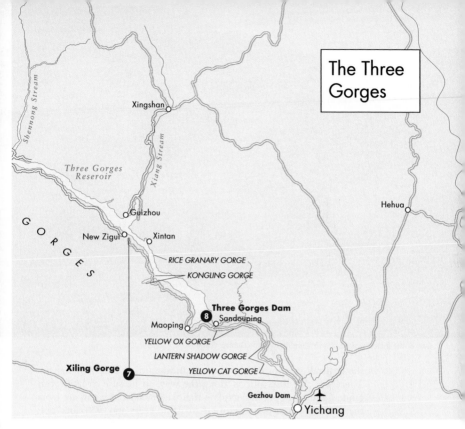

The Three Gorges

Chongqing. This costs Y120 and takes another 3½ hours. If you're pressed for time, an airport in Yichang has daily flights to Chongqing.

## SIGHTS EN ROUTE

Fodor's Choice ★ **Fengdu** (丰都 *Fēngdū*). Also known as Guicheng or the "city of devils," this city on the banks of the Yangtze is filled with temples, buildings, and statues depicting demons and devils. During the Tang Dynasty, the names of two local princely families, Yin (meaning "hell") and Wang (meaning "king"), were linked through marriage, making them known as Yinwang, or the "king of hell." Part of the old city has been submerged in the Three Gorges Dam project. You can take a series of staircases or a cable car to the top of the mountain. ✈ *Y80* ⊙ *Daily 6–6.*

**Ming Hill** (名山 *Míngshān*). The bamboo-covered Ming Hill is home to a Buddhist temple, a pavilion, and pagodas with brightly painted dragons and swans emanating from the eaves. The hill has a nice view of the Yangtze River.

**Three Gorges** (三峡 *Sānxiá*). The Three Gorges lie along the fault lines of what once were flourishing kingdoms. Those great kingdoms vanished into history and became, collectively, China.

**Qutang Gorge** (瞿塘峡 *Qūtángxiá*). The westernmost gorge, Qutang Gorge is also the shortest. The currents here are quite strong due to

One of the Victoria cruise ships sailing through the Qutang Gorge

the natural gate formed by the two mountains, Chijia and Baiyan. There are cliff inscriptions along the way, so be sure to have your guide point them out and explain their significance. Several are from the Warring States period more than 1,000 years ago. Warriors' coffins from that period were discovered in the caves on these mountains, and some still remain.

**Fodor's Choice** ★ **Little Three Gorges** (小三峡 *Xiǎo sānxiá*). At the entrance to Wu Gorge, you can take a smaller boat navigated by local boatmen to the Little Three Gorges. These three gorges—Dragon Gate Gorge, Misty Gorge, and Emerald Gorge—are spectacular and not to be missed. They are striking and silent, rising dramatically out of the river. If you have time, take a trip to the old town of Dachang. ✉ *Y240*.

**Wu Gorge** (巫峡 *Wūxiá*). The impressive Wu Gorge is 33 km (20 miles) long. Its cliffs are so sheer and narrow that they seem to be closing in on you as you approach in the boat. Some of the cliff formations are noted for their resemblances to people and animals. Most notable is the Goddess Peak, a beautiful pillar of white stone.

**Badong** (巴东 *Bādōng*). At the city of Badong, just outside the eastern end of Wu Gorge, boats leave for Shennongjia on the Shennong River, where you can take in the costumes and traditions of Tujia and Miao ethnic minorities.

**Xiling Gorge** (西岭峡 *Xīlíngxiá*). About 66 km (41 miles) long, Xiling Gorge is the longest and deepest of all the gorges, with cliffs that rise up to 4,000 feet. It is undoubtedly the most peaceful and contemplative leg of the journey.

CLOSE UP

# Dam the Yangtze

Nearly a century ago, Chinese leader Sun Yat-sen first proposed damming the Three Gorges area of the Yangtze River, a project that subsequently appealed to Chiang Kai-shek and even the invading Japanese, both of whom prepared plans for the project.

It wasn't until the 1990s under the Communist government that China began building the world's largest power generator, the Three Gorges Dam. In addition to power generation, the dam's locks are big enough to handle containerized sea barges, allowing Chongqing to be the world's farthest inland seaport.

Construction of the main body of the Three Gorges Dam was finished in 2006, and the 26th generator was installed in late 2008. Eight additional generators bring total power generation capacity to an unmatched 22.5 gigawatts.

Even in China, the sheer scale of this project is staggering. The $26 billion dam is more than 600 feet high and a mile wide. By 2010 it had an installed capacity of 18.2 gigawatts and was able to generate 80,000 gigawatt-hours of power annually.

As with any infrastructure project of its scope, the dam has been controversial from the beginning, with critics focusing on its massive social, cultural, and environmental costs.

The reservoir created by the flooding of the Three Gorges area was preceded by the forced relocation of more than 1.2 million people. Many of these people are now migrant workers in nearby cities.

The rising river levels also resulted in the submerging of many significant and valuable relics and buildings

dating back to the beginning of Chinese civilization. Although some artifacts and buildings were moved uphill, it is widely acknowledged that the flooding of the gorges incurred major cultural losses.

It is the environmental impact of the dam project that has attracted the most negative publicity, with serious potential ramifications both upstream and downstream from the dam.

Behind the dam, millions of acres of forest were drowned, and landslides have become a bigger problem than before. The reduced ability of the Yangtze to flush itself clean of wastewater and other pollution has led to the reservoir's containing higher levels of pollution than the river did before damming.

Downstream, it is the lack of sediment that threatens riverbanks, which could become more prone to flooding. The economic dynamo of Shanghai, which is built on the river's floodplain, could also become more vulnerable to inundation after being deprived of normal silt deposits.

While disaster has been averted so far, heavy rains have provided a jittery first major test for the dam, which almost filled to capacity. There are also concerns about cracks already appearing in the dam and its seismological impact.

9

**Three Gorges Dam** (长江三峡大坝 Chángjiāng *sānxià dǎbá*). Xiling Gorge ends at the Three Gorges Dam. Nothing that you've seen or read about this project can possibly prepare you for its massive scale. Sit back in awe as the boat approaches this great dam and then slowly slips down the locks into the lower reaches of the river. ✈ *Y180.*

# THE SILK ROAD

10

Shaanxi, Gansu, Quinghai, and Xinjiang

# WELCOME TO THE SILK ROAD

## TOP REASONS TO GO

★ **Terracotta warriors:** Take in one of the nation's most haunting and memorable sites—the vast life-size army of soldiers, built to outlast death.

★ **Discover Dunhuang:** Satisfy your inner archaeologist at the magnificent Mogao caves and scale the shifting slopes of Singing Sand Mountain.

★ **Seek Solace at Kumbum Monastery:** Visit one of the six great monasteries of the Tibetan Buddhist sect known as Yellow Hat, reputedly the birthplace of the sect's founder, Tsong Khapa.

★ **Tour Turpan:** Discover the ruins of the ancient city-states Jiaohe and Gaochang, destroyed by Genghis Khan and his unstoppable Mongol hordes.

★ **Kashgar and the Karakorum Highway:** Explore Central Asia's largest and liveliest bazaar before heading south to the snowcapped Pamir Mountains and crystal clear Karakul Lake.

**1 Shaanxi.** Visit the tomb of China's first emperor and its army of thousands of terra-cotta warriors in Xian. Shaanxi is the starting point of the fabled Silk Road that brought silks and spices from China to Rome more than two millennia ago.

**2 Gansu.** Arid and mountainous, Gansu has served as a corridor to the West for thousands of years. Heralded sites include the Mogao Grottoes, Singing Sand Mountain, and the remote Labrang Monastery.

## GETTING ORIENTED

There was no single "Silk Road," but scores of trading posts that formed an overland trade network that linked China, Central Asia, and Europe. The current "Silk Road" received its moniker from German scholar Baron Ferdinand von Richtofen in the mid-19th century, when the Chinese section of the route stretched to Xian in Shaanxi Province. After passing through the famed Jade Gate, which divided China from the outside world, it webbed out in three directions to several key cities in Xinjiang: Ürümqi in the north, Korla in the center, Hotan in the south, and Kashgar in the west.

10

**3 Qinghai.** Away from the industrialized cities, on the vast open plains, seminomadic herders clad in brown robes slashed with fluorescent pink sashes still roam the grasslands.

**4 Xinjiang.** Chinese in name only, Xinjiang is a land of vast deserts and ancient Silk Road settlements, including legendary Kashgar. The region is populated by Uyghurs, China's largest minority group.

# SHAANXI

Updated by
Kit Gillet

Shaanxi has more often than not been the axis around which the Chinese universe revolved. It was here more than 6,000 years ago that Neolithic tribes established the earliest permanent settlements in China. In 221 BC the territories of the Middle Kingdom were unified here under the Qin Dynasty (from which the name "China" is derived). Propitiously located at the eastern terminus of the famed Silk Road, Shaanxi later gave birth to one of the ancient world's greatest capitals, Chang'an, a city enriched financially and culturally by the influence of foreign trade.

But nothing lasts forever: as the Silk Road fell into disuse and China isolated itself from the outside world, Shaanxi's fortunes declined. Flood, drought, and political unrest among the province's large Muslim population made Shaanxi a very difficult place to live for most of the past 1,000 years. It's only since the founding of the People's Republic in 1949 that the area has regained some of its former prominence, both as a center of industry and as a famed travel destination.

## PLANNING

### WHEN TO GO

The best time to visit is from early May to late October, when it's warm and the land is in bloom with grasses and flowers. It's also high tourist season, when many festivals take place.

In spring, wildflowers make a colorful, riotous appearance on the mountain meadows, rolling grasslands, and lush valleys.

Dry, sunny summers provide blue skies and long days, optimal for exploring and photographing the region. Afternoons, however, can be insufferably hot, and most tourists follow the locals' lead in taking a midday siesta. Clear skies last usually through October, while winter brings subfreezing temperatures and a dearth of travelers. Although solitude may have its charms, a few sights close for the off-season.

### GETTING HERE AND AROUND

Xian, the capital of Shaanxi province, is also its main travel hub, where you can board trains and buses to most corners of the region

### WOMEN'S WEAR

Many places along the Silk Road have large Muslim communities, and it's courteous to dress appropriately when there. Women will feel less conspicuous in Xinjiang if they dress as most locals do and wear long trousers and cover their shoulders. Scarves aren't necessary, but they can be good protection against dust.

and planes to just about anywhere in the country. To avoid long and back-breaking journeys by bus, it's worth flying at least occasionally, and with tickets often heavily discounted there's not always a huge price difference. The train is also more comfortable than buses and extremely efficient—and with the great scenery, time passes quickly.

### AIR TRAVEL

Air China, China Southern, and Hainan Airlines are the main airlines that fly to Xian and Lanzhou from major cities in China. From Ürümqi there are daily flights from Kashgar, Hami, Korla, and Hotan. Tickets are easy to come by, frequently at discounted rates.

### BUS TRAVEL

Spectacular scenery and time for contemplation are the rewards for taking bus journeys. The negatives include long journeys, regular breakdowns, and, often, smoking on board. In Xinjiang, long-distance bus routes crisscross the province, and from Ürümqi there are sleeper buses for the 24-hour journey to Kashgar (flying is often a similar price). In addition, there are handy tourist buses from Ürümqi to Heavenly Lake and from Xian to the Terracotta Warriors.

### CAR TRAVEL

It's simple to hire a car and driver in major tourist destinations such as Xian, Ürümqi, Kashgar, and Turpan; ask your hotel or contact a local travel agency. It's unlikely that your driver will speak English, so agree on your destination beforehand and whether tolls and other sundry costs are included in the price. Expect to pay around Y800 a day for a modern, comfortable car.

### TRAIN TRAVEL

Shaanxi and Gansu provinces are well connected to major cities in the rest of China, with direct trains from Beijing and Shanghai to Xian, Lanzhou, and Dunhuang. Xinjiang and Qinghai are more isolated, though there are trains from all the above cities to Xining and Ürümqi. From Xining and Lanzhou, there's daily service to Lhasa in Tibet. The trip takes around 24 hours, and you must book in advance and secure a Tibet Travel Permit. From Ürümqi there is regular service to Kashgar, Korla, Hotan, Turpan, and Hami, as well as Almaty in Kazakstan.

10

■TIP→ For all train travel, save yourself the hassle and ask your hotel or travel agency to book your ticket.

### HEALTH AND SAFETY

In an emergency, your first stop should be a good hotel. Even if you are not a guest, or if you don't speak Chinese or have a Chinese friend to call on, get a hotel involved to arrange treatment and provide translation. If you call them directly, you will find that the emergency services do not speak any English.

### TRAVELING IN THE DESERT

Things change quickly from uncomfortable to dangerous in the intense heat of northwest China's expansive deserts. Temperatures in the summer reach 100°F (40°C), with some areas—the depression around Turpan in particular—soaring to 120°F (50°C). Many of the sites you'll be visiting are remote and lack even the most basic facilities.

In conditions like these, it's unwise to travel without abundant water, as well as strong sunscreen, sunglasses, hand sanitizer, a good hat, toilet paper, and some heat-resistant snacks (dried fruit and nuts). If you're a fan of cold water, buy frozen plastic bottles in the morning and they'll stay cool until lunchtime.

### MONEY MATTERS

You can use foreign bank cards in all major cities in the region, including Xian, Ürümqi, and Lanzhou. But the farther away you get from metropolitan areas, the less likely it is that your card will work in a local ATM. Have a supply of cash to avoid getting stranded. Traveler's checks can be cashed and foreign currency converted at Bank of China branches and major hotels. Tipping is unnecessary in restaurants and hotels: some more expensive hotels will add a service charge, but there is no need to add anything extra.

### RESTAURANTS

Restaurants vary from street-side stalls to modern restaurants with air-conditioning and English menus, though don't expect cutting-edge style and ambience in any of the eateries in this part of the country.

The cuisine in Shaanxi revolves around noodles and *jiaozi* (dumplings) rather than rice, and lamb is the meat of choice. A Xian Muslim specialty is *yangrou paomo,* a spicy lamb soup poured over broken pieces of flat bread. Other popular Muslim street foods are *heletiao* (buckwheat noodles marinated in soy sauce and garlic) and *roujiamo* (pita bread filled with beef or pork and topped with cumin and green peppers).

Gansu and Qinghai don't offer many culinary surprises, but in Xinjiang, where temperatures can reach scorching levels, you'll find a variety of local ices, ice cream, and *durap* (a refreshing mix of yogurt, honey, and crushed ice). ⚠ While delicious, ices might not be as pure or hygienic as you'd like. Traditional Uyghur dishes like *bamian* (lamb and vegetables served over noodles) and *kevap* (spicy lamb kebabs) are ubiquitous, and often washed down with fresh pomegranate juice. Grapes from Turpan and melons from the oasis town of Hami are famous throughout China.

*Prices in the reviews are the average cost of a main course at dinner or, if dinner is not served, at lunch.*

## HOTELS

Cities that see a regular influx of tourists, such as Xian and Ürümqi, offer the full spectrum of lodging options. The more remote the area, the fewer the choices, and standards are lower than you might be used to; also, don't expect your credit cards to be accepted. There are almost no boutique options in the region, though in Kashgar there are some dusty hotels that have historic interest, remnants from when the city was a center for trade between the east and west.

*Prices in the reviews are the lowest cost of a standard double room in high season.*

## VISITOR INFORMATION

Travelers should use guidebooks, travel agencies, and online forums like Fodors.com for information. As in the rest of China, official tourist information is hard to come by.

## TOURS

**Sino NZ Tourism Group.** Run out of Xian Apartment Guesthouse, this well-managed tour agency offers highly recommended walking tours of Xian City. Prices depend on the size of your group, but expect to pay upwards of Y300 per person, which includes an English-speaking guide, transportation, and lunch. The company also offers tours to the Terracotta Warriors. ⊠ *Hong Cheng Guoji Gong Yu Building A, Xi Hua Men, Xian* ☎ *0131/4925–0037* ⊕ *www.xianapartmentshq.com.*

**CITS.** The Xian branch of the state-run travel service gets good reviews, thanks to the friendliness of its young, well-trained staff. Its tours might be more expensive, but they include nicer cars and smaller groups. Tours head to key Silk Road destinations. ⊠ *48 Changan Bei Lu, Xian* ☎ *029/8669–2055* ⊕ *www.chinabravo.com.*

# XIAN

*2 hrs by plane or 6 hrs by high-speed train southwest of Beijing; 11 hrs by fast train west of Shanghai.*

Many first-time visitors to Xian are seeking the massive terra-cotta army standing guard over the tomb of China's first emperor. Xian was known in ancient times as Chang'an (meaning Long Peace), and was one of the largest and most cultured cities in the world. During the Tang Dynasty—considered by many Chinese to be the nation's cultural pinnacle—the city became an important center for the arts. Not surprisingly, this creative explosion coincided with the height of trade on the Silk Road, bringing Turkish fashions to court and foreigners from as far away as Persia and Rome. Although the caravan drivers of yesteryear have long since turned to dust, their memory lives on in the variety of faces seen in Xian.

## GETTING HERE AND AROUND

AIR TRAVEL Although Xian's Xianyang Airport is an inconvenient 47 km (29 miles) northwest of the city center in neighboring Xianyang, it has daily flights to and from Beijing, Shanghai, Hong Kong, Guangzhou, Chengdu,

Shaanxi

Kunming, Dunhuang, and Ürümqi. International destinations include Japan, South Korea, Singapore, and Thailand. The airport has recently expanded, with a third terminal opening in 2012. If your hotel doesn't arrange transportation, taxis will try to squeeze every last yuan out of your wallet; head to the official taxi rank and know that a decent price is around Y130. Buses are a far more economical option, costing Y26 and running every 20 minutes. There are six routes to choose from, with Route 1 to the Bell Tower and 2 to the train station the most useful—make sure you have the name in Chinese.

BUS TRAVEL  Just about every bus in Xian passes through the traffic circle around the Bell Tower. If your Chinese is shaky, it's best to stick to taxis.

The long-distance bus station on Jiefang Lu, across the street and just west of the train station, has buses to Lanzhou, Xining, and other destinations throughout Shaanxi and Henan. Tourist destinations like the Terracotta Warriors Museum are served from the parking lot between the train station and the Jiefang Hotel.

CAR TRAVEL  Because so many of the sights lie outside the city proper, hiring a taxi or a car and driver gives you the freedom to depart when you like instead of waiting for the rest of the tour. Prices start at about Y800 per day, but vary widely based on the type of vehicle and whether you need an English-speaking guide. Every major hotel can arrange car services.

TRAIN TRAVEL The train station lies on the same rail line as Lanzhou. Those arriving in Xian by train disembark north of the old city walls. The train station is close to most hotels; a taxi should cost less than Y10. The foreigners' ticket window, on the second floor above the main ticket office, is open daily 8:30 to 11:30 and 2:30 to 5:30. It sometimes closes without explanation. For a small booking fee, hotels and travel agencies can get tickets.

**SAFETY AND PRECAUTIONS**
All normal precautions here apply, especially when it comes to pickpocket prevention at tourist destinations.

**TIMING**
If you're in a rush, you can see the main city sights plus a day trip to the Warriors in two days; however, Xian is one of China's more appealing cities, and is a rewarding place to stay for longer periods of time. Stay a few days longer, and enjoy the unique ambience of the city's Muslim quarter and great food.

> **TREASURES OF SHAANXI**
>
> Shaanxi gave birth to 13 major Chinese dynasties, including the Zhou, Qin, Han, and Tang states. The Tang is considered China's Golden Age. Consider first hitting the Shaanxi History Museum. Once you've steeped yourself in its chronology, local "must-see" destinations like Xian's Drum Towers, Muslim Quarter, and Great Goose Pagodas will make much more sense. So, too, will the awe-inspiring army of terracotta warriors at the tomb of China's first emperor. True fans of history can even make the trip to China's own "Valley of the Kings" near Xianyang.

**TOURS**
Most hotels offer their own guided tours of the area, usually dividing them into eastern area, western area, and city tours. Most tour operators have special English-language tour guides.

Bargaining may get you a much better deal. And check more than one company to make sure you are being charged the going rate. One of the best places to comparison shop is on the second floor of the Bell Tower Hotel, where several tour companies vie for your business. Try Golden Bridge first, but there are other good options.

EASTERN TOUR By far the most popular option from Xian, tours that head east of the city usually visit the Tomb of the First Qin Emperor, the Terracotta Warriors Museum, and the Huaqing Hot Springs, all in the town of Lintong. Many tours also stop at the Banpo Matriarchal Clan Village in eastern Xian. The China International Travel Service (CITS) offers this tour for Y500, which includes all admission tickets and an English-speaking guide. The journey takes most of the day; plan on leaving after breakfast and returning in time for dinner.

If you don't want a guide, you're better off taking Bus 306 (travel bus no. 5), which leaves constantly from the parking lot between the Xian train station and the Jiefang Hotel. The 60-minute journey costs Y7; you can buy tickets on the bus. The Terracotta Warriors are the last stop. To travel between any of the sites in Lintong, a taxi should cost between Y5 and Y10 (although drivers ask foreigners for Y15). To get back to Xian, simply wait along the road for a bus headed to the city.

10

The Bell Tower in Xian

WESTERN TOUR Less popular than the eastern tour, this excursion varies wildly from operator to operator. Find out what you're getting for the money. Amateur archaeologists and would-be tomb raiders will hardly be able to tear themselves away from the sites in what's been called China's own Valley of the Kings; others will appreciate some of the relics, but may tire of what appear to be mounds of dirt or holes in the ground. Know there is no English-language signage.

Of the 18 imperial tombs on the plains west of Xian, a list of the best should include the Qian Tomb, resting place of Tang Dynasty Empress Wu Zetian, China's only female sovereign. A number of her relatives—many sentenced to death by her own decree—are entombed in the surrounding area. The tomb of Prince Yi De contains some beautifully restored frescoes. Other stops on the western tour might include the Xianyang City Museum in Xianyang and the Famen Temple in Famen. Sino NZ Tourism Group offers a customizable western tour for between Y400 and Y800, depending on the number of people. Plan on spending the whole day visiting these sites.

**ESSENTIALS**

**Air Contact Xian Xianyang Airport** ☎ 029/8879–8450.

**Bank Bank of China.** Bank of China ⊠ 396 Dong Da Jie ☎ 029/8741–5624 ⊠ 157 Jiefang Lu ☎ 029/8742–5916 ⊠ 21 Xianning Xi Lu ☎ 029/8249–2382.

**Bus Contact Xian Bus Station** (西安汽车站 Xīān qìchēzhàn). ⊠ 354 Jiefang Lu ☎ 029/8742–7420.

**Internet Hai An Xian Internet Bar** (海岸西安网吧 Hǎi'àn Xīān wǎngbā). ⊠ 232 Jiefang Lu ☎ 029/8741–0555 💷 Y4 per hour ⊗ 8 am–midnight.

**Medical Assistance Ambulance** ☒ *Xian* ☎ *120.* **Police** ☎ *110.* **People's Hospital** (西安人民医院 *Xī'ān rénmín yīyuàn*). ☒ *214 Youyi Xi Lu* ☎ *029/8525–1331.*

**Train Contacts Xian Railway Station** (西安火车站 *Xī'ān huǒchēzhàn*). ☒ *Huancheng Bei Lu 15* ☎ *029/8213–1300.*

**Visitor and Tour Info Golden Bridge Travel** ☒ *Xi Da Jie An Ding Plaza, Building 3, Room 503* ☎ *029/8763–9810* ⊕ *www.trip51168.com.*

## EXPLORING

### TOP ATTRACTIONS

**Bell Tower** (钟楼 *Zhōng lóu*). Xian's most recognizable structure, the Bell Tower was built in the late 14th century in what was then the center of the city. It's still good a reference point—the tower marks the point where Xi Da Jie (West Main Street) becomes Dong Da Jie (East Main Street) and Bei Da Jie (North Main Street) becomes Nan Da Jie (South Main Street). To reach the tower, which stands isolated in the middle of a traffic circle, use any of eight entrances to the underground passageway. Once inside the building, you'll see Ming Dynasty bells on display. Concerts are given six times daily (9:10, 10:30, 11:30, 2:30, 3:30, and 4:30). For Y5 you can make your own music by ringing a copy of the large iron bell that gives the tower its name. Don't miss the panoramic views of the city from the third-floor balcony. ☒ *Junction of Dong Da Jie, Xi Da Jie, Bei Da Jie, and Nan Da Jie* ⊕ *www.xazgl.com/ewzjj.asp* ☜ *Y 35; Y50 includes admission to Drum Tower* ☼ *Apr.–Oct., daily 8:30 am–9:30 pm; Nov.–Mar., daily 8:30–6.*

**Big Wild Goose Pagoda** (大雁塔 *Dàyàn tǎ*). This impressively tall pagoda lies 4 km (2½ miles) southeast of South Gate, on the grounds of the still-active Temple of Thanksgiving (Da Ci'en Si). The pagoda was constructed adjacent to the Tang palace in the 7th century to house scriptures brought back from India by monk Xuan Zang. It's been rebuilt numerous times since then, most recently during the Qing Dynasty, in Ming style. A park and huge plaza surround the temple, and locals gather here after work to fly kites, stroll hand in hand, and practice calligraphy. There is a popular water-fountain show synchronized to music at noon and 9 pm. The main entrance gate to the temple is on the plaza's southern edge. ☒ *Yanta Lu* ☎ *029/8552–7958* ☜ *Y50; additional Y30 to climb the pagoda* ☼ *Daily 9–5.*

**Drum Tower** (鼓楼 *Gǔlóu*). Originally built in 1380, this 111-foot-high Ming Dynasty building—which used to hold the alarm drums for the imperial city—marks the southern end of Xian's Muslim Quarter. Various ancient drums are on display inside the building, and concerts are given daily at 9:10, 10:30, 11:30, 2:30, 3:30, and 4:30. After passing through the tower's massive base, turn left down a small side street called Hua Jue Xiang to find everything from shadow puppets to Mao memorabilia—truly a souvenir heaven. After clearing that gauntlet, you'll find yourself deep inside the Muslim Quarter at the entrance to the Great Mosque. ☒ *Bei Yuan Men, 1 block west of the Bell Tower* ⊕ *www.xazgl.com/ewzjj.asp* ☜ *Y 35; Y50 includes admission to Bell Tower* ☼ *Apr.–Oct., daily 8:30 am–9:30 pm; Nov.–Mar., daily 8:30–6.*

10

Fodor's Choice ★ **Forest of Stone Tablets Museum** (碑林博物馆 *Bēilín bówùguǎn*). As the name suggests, there is no shortage here of historical stone tablets engraved with content ranging from descriptions of administrative projects to artistic renditions of landscape, portraiture, and calligraphy. One of the world's first dictionaries and a number of Tang Dynasty classics are housed here. One tablet, known as the Popular Nestorian Stela, dates from 781, and records the interaction between the emperor and a traveling Nestorian priest. After presenting the empire with translated Nestorian Christian texts, the priest was allowed to open a church in Xian. While non-Chinese speakers may feel frustrated that they can't read the tablets, there are some with English translations. ⊠ *15 Sanxue Jie, end of Culture St.* ☎ *029/8721–0764* ⊕ *www.beilin-museum.com* ☞ *Mar.–Nov.,Y75; Dec.–Feb.,Y50* ☉ *Mar.–Nov., daily 8:15–6:45; Dec.–Feb., daily 8:15–5:15.*

**Great Mosque** (西安大清真寺 *Xī'ān dà qīngzhēn sì*). This lushly landscaped mosque with four graceful courtyards may have been established as early as AD 742, during the Tang Dynasty, but the remaining buildings date mostly from the 18th century. Amazingly, it was left standing during the Cultural Revolution. Stone tablets mark the various pavilions, often bearing inscriptions in both Chinese and Arabic. Look above the doors and gates: there are some remarkable designs, including three-dimensional Arabic script that makes the stone look as malleable as cake frosting. Non-Muslims are not allowed in the prayer hall, as the mosque is still an active place of worship. The place is a bit hard to find. After passing through the Drum Tower, follow a small curving market street called Hua Jue Xiang on the left. (You'll see an English sign posted on a brick wall next to the street's entrance reading "Great Mosque.") When you reach a small intersection, the mosque's entrance is on the left. The bustling **Muslim Quarter** surrounding the mosque is the center of the city's Hui (Chinese Muslim) community. It's a great place to wander, and you'll find endless food stalls offering everything from cold sesame noodles to pan-fried dumplings to spicy mutton kebabs. ⊠ *30 Hua Jue Xiang* ☞ *Y25* ☉ *May–Sept., daily 8–7; Oct.–Apr., daily 8–5.*

Fodor's Choice ★ **Shaanxi History Museum** (陕西历史博物馆 *Shǎnxī lìshǐ bówùguǎn*). Although museums in China are often underwhelming, this is a notable exception. The works in this imposing two-story structure, built in 1991, range from crude Paleolithic stone tools to gorgeously sculpted ceramics from the Tang Dynasty. Several terracotta warriors taken from the tombs outside town are on display. The exhibits, which have English descriptions, leave no doubt that China has long been the world's most advanced culture. The museum is free; a limited number of tickets are handed out in the morning and the afternoon. Arrive early, and bring your ID. ⊠ *91 Xiaozhai Dong Lu* ☎ *029/8525–4727* ⊕ *www.sxhm.com* ☞ *Free* ☉ *Tues.–Sun. 8:30–6.*

**South Gate** (南门永宁门 *Nán mén/yǒngníng mén*). Also known as Yong Ning Gate, this is the most impressive of the 13 gates leading through Xian's 39-foot-high city walls. This was the original site of Tang Dynasty fortifications; the walls you see today were built at the beginning of the Ming Dynasty, and they include the country's only remaining example of a complete wall dating to this dynasty. Biking the entire 13.7-km (8.5-mile) route atop the walls takes about 90 minutes. Rental bikes are Y40 for 100 minutes, and you must put down a Y200 deposit. Open-air electric cars cost Y80. ⊠ *Nan Da Jie* ☎ *029/8727–1696* ☜ *Y40* ⊙ *Apr.–Oct: 8 am–10 pm; Nov.–Mar., daily 8–8.*

**WORTH NOTING**

**Banpo Matriarchal Clan Village** (半坡博物馆 *Bànpō bówùguǎn*). About 5 km (3 miles) east of the city are the remains of a 6,000-year-old Yangshao village, including living quarters, a pottery-making center, and a graveyard. The residents of this matriarchal community of 200 to 300 people survived mainly by fishing, hunting, and gathering, although there is ample evidence of attempts at animal domestication and organized agriculture. The small museum contains stone farming and hunting implements, domestic objects, and pottery inscribed with ancient Chinese characters. The archaeological site has captions in English. Unless you're interested in documenting one of China's great tourist oddities, avoid the awful model village that sits in a state of semi-disrepair toward the rear of the property. ⊠ *155 Banpo Lu, off Changdong Lu* ☎ *029/8351–2807* ⊕ *www.bpmuseum.com* ☜ *Y45* ⊙ *Daily 8–5:30.*

**Culture Street** (文化街 *Wénhuà jiē*). Just inside the city wall, this lively but very touristy pedestrian street is lined with houses that have been rebuilt in traditional Ming style. Shops sell a wide variety of wares, including charming calligraphy and watercolors. If you're coming from South Gate, halfway down the first block you'll find Guanzhong Academy, built in 1609. Take a peek through the gates, as entrance is forbidden. Continue east along the city wall to reach the Forest of Stone Tablets. ⊠ *1 block north of South Gate.*

Fodor's Choice
★

**Small Goose Pagoda** (小雁塔 *Xiǎoyàn tǎ*). Once part of the 7th-century Jianfu Temple, this 13-tier pagoda was built by Empress Wu Zetian in 707 to honor her predecessor, Emperor Gao Zong. Much less imposing than the Big Goose Pagoda, the smaller pagoda housed Buddhist texts brought back from India by the pilgrim Yiqing in the 8th century. A tremendous earthquake in 1555 lopped off the top two stories of what was originally a 15-story structure; climbing to the top lets you examine the damage. The Xian Museum (entrance Y10) is part of the same complex, and shows how the ancient capital changed over the centuries. The whole park offers good people-watching opportunities, and is very peaceful compared to other Xian attractions. ⊠ *72 Youyi Xi Lu, west of Nanguan Zhengjie* ☎ *029/8781–1081* ☜ *Y50* ⊙ *Daily 9–5.*

10

**AROUND XIAN**

**Famen Temple** (法门寺 *Fǎmén sì*). Originally built in the 3rd century AD, the temple was the site of an amazing find during renovations in 1981. A sacred crypt housing four of Sakyamani Buddha's finger bones was discovered to hold more than 25,000 coins and 1,000 sacrificial objects of jade, gold, and silver. Many of these objects are now on display in the on-site museum. The temple is in Famen, 125 km (80 miles) west of Xian. ⊠ *Famen* ☎ *0917/525–4002* ⊕ *www.famensi.com* ☜ *Y120* ⊙ *Mar.–Oct., 8–5,30; Nov.–Feb., 8:30–5.*

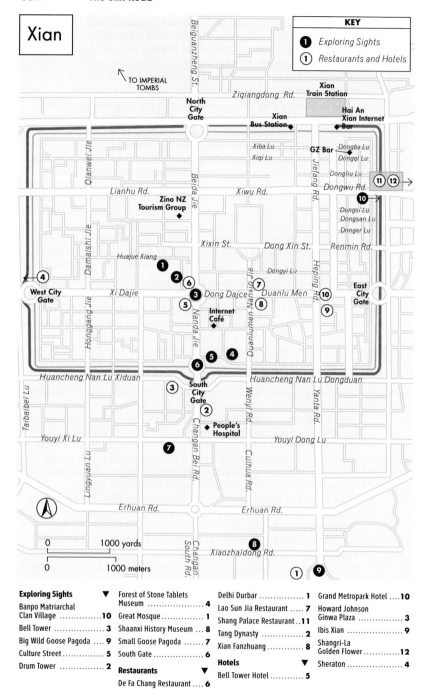

Xian

KEY
- **1** Exploring Sights
- (1) Restaurants and Hotels

**Exploring Sights** ▼

Banpo Matriarchal
Clan Village ............... **10**

Bell Tower ................. **3**

Big Wild Goose Pagoda .... **9**

Culture Street ............. **5**

Drum Tower ............... **2**

Forest of Stone Tablets
Museum .................... **4**

Great Mosque ............... **1**

Shaanxi History Museum .. **8**

Small Goose Pagoda ...... **7**

South Gate ................ **6**

**Restaurants** ▼

De Fa Chang Restaurant .... **6**

Delhi Durbar ............... **1**

Lao Sun Jia Restaurant ..... **7**

Shang Palace Restaurant .. **11**

Tang Dynasty ............... **2**

Xian Fanzhuang ............ **8**

**Hotels** ▼

Bell Tower Hotel ............ **5**

Grand Metropark Hotel ....**10**

Howard Johnson
Ginwa Plaza ................ **3**

Ibis Xian .................... **9**

Shangri-La
Golden Flower .............**12**

Sheraton ................... **4**

**Hua Shan** (华山 *Huáshān*). A few hours east of Xian lies one of China's five sacred mountains, a traditional watercolor come to life. The 7,218-foot mountain has lovely scenery, including pines reminiscent of a Dr. Seuss creation and sheer granite walls that rise shockingly out of the surrounding plains. The five peaks of Huashan reminded ancient visitors of flower petals, hence the name; translated it means

"Flower Mountain." Climbing the mountain is not a trip for the fainthearted: unless you're an Olympic athlete, hiking the main trail to the top will take a good seven to nine hours, some of it along narrow passes on sheer cliffs. Thankfully, there's a cable-car ride to North Peak that brings you most of the way up the trail. Don't worry about looking like a wimp; there's plenty of climbing left to do from the cable-car terminal.

From Xian you can take a D train (Y35) or G train (Y59) to Huashan North Station, situated 5 km (3 miles) from the park entrance; frequent minibuses (Y10) link the two. A better choice might be one of the tour buses that leave hourly every morning from the parking lot in front of the Jiefang Hotel, across from the train station. Provide your passport information when you buy a ticket. ✉ *Mar.–Nov., Y180; Dec.–Feb., Y100* ⊙ *Mar.–Nov., 7–7; Dec.–Feb., 9–5.*

**Huaqing Hot Springs** (华清池 *Huáqīng chí*). A pleasure palace during the Tang Dynasty and later, the living quarters of General Chiang Kai-shek during the Chinese Civil War, the destination gets mixed reviews from visitors. Despite the name, the hot springs are often out of action, leaving visitors to wander around the garden. You'll probably be happier spending your time on **Lishan,** the small mountain directly behind Huaqing Hot Springs. It was on these slopes that Chiang was captured, and it has China's first beacon tower and a number of small temples. If you are here in the evening (8:30 pm), catch the light and sound show that uses the mountain as a backdrop. The attraction is 30 km (19 miles) east of Xian. ✉ *38 Huaqing Chi Rd., Lintong* ☎ *029/8381–2003* ⊕ *www.hqc.cn* ✉ *Dec.–Feb., Y80; Mar.–Nov., Y110* ⊙ *Dec.–Feb., daily 7:30–6:30; Mar.–Nov., daily 7–6.*

Fodor'sChoice **Terracotta Warriors Museum** (兵马俑博物馆 *Bīngmǎyǒng bówùguǎn*). ★ Discovered in 1974 by farmers digging a well, this UNESCO World Heritage site includes more than 7,000 terracotta soldiers standing guard over the tomb of Qin Shihuang, the first emperor of a unified China. The warriors, 1,000 of which have been painstakingly pieced together, come in various forms: archers, infantry, charioteers, and cavalry. Relics are still being found. In 2010, 114 extra warriors were discovered in Pit One. Incredibly, each of the life-size statues is unique, including different mustaches, beards, and hairstyles. An exhibition hall displays artifacts unearthed from distant sections of the tomb, including two magnificently crafted miniature bronze chariots. Allow yourself at

**10**

*Continued on page 594*

# THE TERRACOTTA SOLDIERS

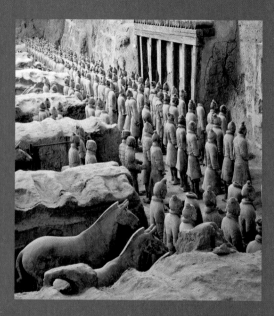

In 1974, Shaanxi farmers digging a well accidentally unearthed one of the greatest archaeological finds of the 20th century—the Terracotta Soldiers of Qin Shihuang. Armed with real weapons and accompanied by horses and chariots, the more than 8,000 soldiers buried in Qin's tomb were to be his garrison in the afterlife.

(top) Statues depict different military units. (right) Note how the faces differ. Each one is sculpted to be unique.

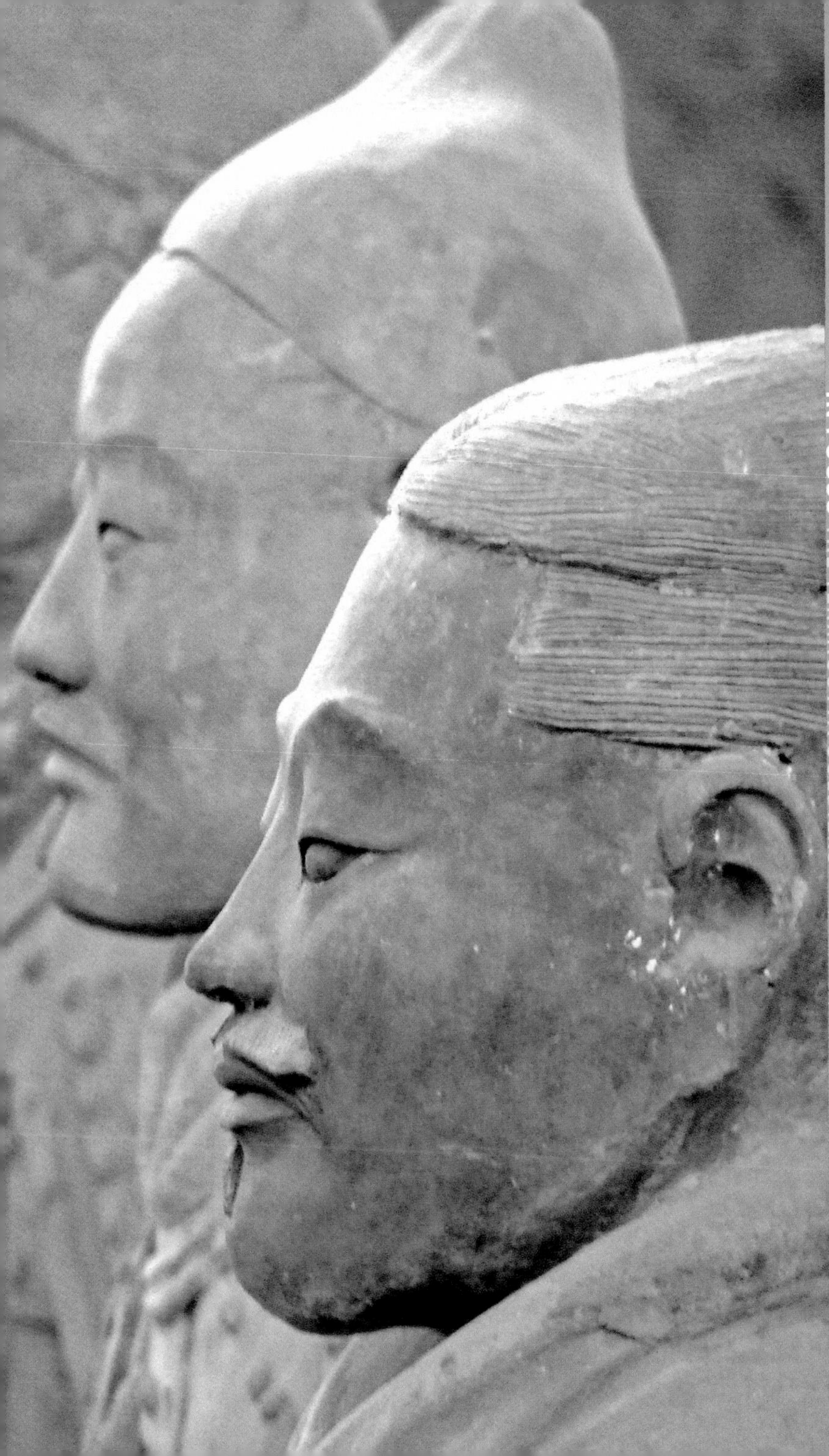

**DID YOU KNOW?**

The thousands of life-size soldiers include charioteers, cavalrymen, archers, and infantrymen. They're all arranged according to rank and duty—exactly as they would have been for a real-life battle. Each one has individual facial features, including different mustaches, beards, and hairstyles.

# UNCOVERING AN ARMY

## WHO WAS QIN SHIHUANG?

After destroying the last of his rivals in 221 BC, Qin Shihuang became the first emperor to rule over a unified China. He established a centralized government headquartered near modern day Xianyang in Shaanxi Province. Unlike the feudal governments of the past under which regional officials developed local bases of power, the new centralized government concentrated all power in the hands of a godlike emperor.

Unfortunately for Qin Shihuang's potential heirs, the emperor's inexhaustible hunger for huge engineering projects created high levels of public unrest. These projects, including a precursor to the Great Wall, his own massive tomb, and numerous roads and canals, required the forced labor of millions of Chinese citizens. In 210 BC, Qin died from mercury poisoning during a failed attempt at making himself immortal. Only four years later, his son was overthrown and killed, bringing an ignominious end to China's first dynasty.

## A THANKLESS JOB

The construction of Qin Shihuang's gargantuan tomb complex—which includes the Terracotta Soldiers—was completed by more than 700,000 workers over a period of nearly 40 years. The warriors themselves are believed to have been created in an assembly line process in which sets of legs and torsos were fired separately and later combined with individually sculpted heads. Most workers were unskilled laborers; skilled craftsmen completed more delicate work such as the decoration of the tomb and the molding of heads. The soldiers were then painted with colored lacquer to make them both more

durable and realistic. It's believed that all of the workers were buried alive inside the tomb (which hasn't yet been excavated) to keep its location and treasures a secret and protect it from grave robbers.

## DISCOVERING THE SOLDIERS

Only five years after the death of Qin Shihuang, looting soldiers set fire to the thick wooden beams supporting the vaults. As wood burned and the structure became unsound, beams and earthen walls came crashing down onto the statues, crushing many soldiers and burying all. In many ways, though, the damage to the vaults was a blessing in disguise. The buried Terracotta Soldiers were forgotten to history, but the lack of oxygen and sunlight preserved the figures for centuries.

Since its rediscovery, only a part of the massive complex has been excavated, and the process of unearthing more warriors and relics continues. No one is sure just how many warriors there are or how far the figures extend beyond the already excavated 700-foot-by-200-foot section. For the time being, most excavation work has stopped while scientists attempt to develop a method of preserving the figures' colored lacquer, which quickly deteriorates when exposed to oxygen.

(top) Warriors were once painted in bright colors.

IN FOCUS THE TERRACOTTA SOLDIERS

10

## VISITING THE SOLDIERS

Be sure to walk around to the rear of Vault 1, which contains most of the figures that have already been unearthed. There you can see archaeologists reassembling the smashed soldiers. Vaults 2 and 3 contain unreconstructed warriors and their weapons and give you an idea of how much work went into presenting Vault 1 as we see it today.

### CIRCLE VISION THEATER

Before heading to the vaults, stop by this 360-degree movie theater and learn how the army was constructed, destroyed, forgotten, and then rediscovered. Although the film is cheesy, it's nonetheless entertaining and informative. It gives a sense of what the area may have been like 2,200 years ago.

### VAULT 1

Here you'll find about 6,000 warriors, although only 1,000 have been painstakingly pieced together by archaeologists. The warriors stand in their original pits and can only be seen from the walkways erected around the digs. Those in the front ranks are well shaped and fully outfitted except for their weapons, whose wooden handles have decayed over the centuries (the chrome-plated bronze blades were still sharp upon excavation). Walk around to the rear of the vault where you can see terracotta soldiers in various states of reconstruction.

Archaeologists have puzzled together almost 1,000 statues, including warriors, chariots, horses, officials, acrobats, strongmen and musicians. The tallest statues are also the highest in rank; they are the generals.

## COLORATION

The colored lacquers that were used not only gave the terracotta soldiers a realistic appearance, but also sealed and protected the clay. Unfortunately, upon exposure to oxygen, these thin layers of color become extremely brittle and flake off or crumble to dust. Chinese scientists are devising excavation methods that will preserve the coloration of warriors unearthed in the future.

Ready on one knee with bow in hand, these archers are poised to rise and fire a deadly salvo at a moment's notice.

Every cavalry rider is accompanied by a life-size terracotta horse.

## VISITING THE SOLDIERS

(top) Statues were made in pieces and then assembled. (right) The statue of an officer. (opposite page) The cavalry horses.

### VAULT 2

This vault offers a glimpse of unreconstructed figures as they emerge from the ground. It has remained mostly undisturbed since 1999 when archaeologists found the first tricolor figures—look closely and you can still see pink on the soldiers' faces and patches of dark red on their armor. As with ancient Greek sculptures, the warriors were originally painted in lifelike colors and with red armor. Around the sides of the vault, you can take a close-up look at excellent examples of soldiers and their weaponry in glass cases.

### VAULT 3

Sixty-eight soldiers and officers in various states of reconstruction stand in what appears to be a military headquarters. Although the condition of the warriors are similar to those in Vault 2, there is one unique figure: a charioteer standing at the ready, though his wooden chariot has been lost to time.

### QINYONG MUSEUM

Near Vault 3, an imposing sand-colored pavilion houses two miniature bronze chariots unearthed in the western section of Qin Shihuang's tomb. Found in 1980, these chariots are intricately detailed with ornate gold and silver ornamentation. In the atrium leading to the bronze chariots, look for a massive bronze urn—it's one of the treasures unearthed by archaeologists in their 1999 excavation of an accessory pit near the still-sealed mausoleum. Other artifacts on display including Qin Dynasty tricolor pottery and Qin jade carvings.

## GETTING THERE

Practically every hotel and tour company in Xian arranges bus trips to the Terracotta Soldiers as part of an Eastern Tour package. If you aren't interested in having an English-speaking guide for the day, you can save a lot of money by taking one of the cheap buses (Y10 one-way) that leave for the town of Lintong from the parking lot between Xian's train station and the Jiefang Hotel. The ride to the Terracotta Warriors Museum should take between 90 and 120 minutes.

**Opening Hours:** Mar.–Nov., daily 8:30–5:30; Dec.–Feb., daily 8:30–5.

**Admission:** Mar.–Nov., Y150 ; Dec.–Feb., Y120. Price includes movie, access to three vaults, and entrance to the Qinyong Museum.

**Phone:** 029/8139–9001 (main office); 029/8139–9126 and 029/8139–9170 (ticket office).

## VISITING TIPS

**Cameras:** You can shoot photographs and videos inside the vaults, a change from previous years when guards brusquely confiscated film upon seeing your camera. You still can't use a flash or tripod, however.

**Souvenirs:** You can buy postcards and other souvenirs in the shops outside the vaults and the Circle Vision Theater. Alternatively, you can face the fearsome gauntlet of souvenir hawkers outside the main gates; miniature replica terracotta soldiers can be found here for as little as Y1 each. If you're intimidated by the aggressive touts, however, there's nothing available here that you can't get back in Xian. So be strong, don't look them in the eyes, and most important, never stop walking.

**Time:** You'll likely end up spending two to three hours touring the vaults and exhibits at the Terracotta Warriors Museum. The time spent here will probably be part of a long day-tour visiting a number of sites—the Hauqing Hot Springs and possibly the Banpo Matriachal Clan Village—clustered around the small city of Lintong, east of Xian.

## RAIDERS OF THE LOST TOMB

Qin started construction on his enormous, richly endowed tomb, said to be boobytrapped with automatic crossbows, almost as soon as he took the throne. According to ancient records, this underground palace contained 100 rivers of flowing mercury as well as ceilings inlaid with precious stones and pearls representing the stars and planets. Interestingly enough, mercury levels in the area's soil are much higher than

normal, indicating that there may be truth to those records. Though the site of the tomb was rediscovered to the east of Xian in 1974 (soon after the Terracotta Soldiers were unearthed), the government didn't touch it because it lacked the sophisticated machinery needed to excavate safely. Authorities also executed any locals foolish enough to attempt a treasure-seeking foray. In 1999, archaeologists finally began excavations

of the area around the tomb and unearthed some fabulous treasures. They've only scratched the surface, however. Most of the tomb still lies buried. In fact, no one is even certain where its main entrance—reportedly sealed with molten copper—is located. Authorities have delayed further excavations until the tomb can be properly preserved rather than risk damaging what may be China's greatest archaeological site.

least three hours if you want to study the warriors in detail. The site is 30 km (19 miles) east of Xian in the town of Lintong. ✉ *Lintong* ☎ *029/8139–9170* 🌐 *bj.bmy.com.cn* 🎫 *Mar.–Nov., Y150; Dec.–Feb., Y120* 🕒 *Mar.–Nov., daily 8:30–5:30; Dec.–Feb., daily 8:30–5.*

**Tomb of the First Qin Emperor** (秦始皇陵 *Qínshǐhuánglíng*). The tomb—consisting mainly of a large burial mound—may pale compared to the Terracotta Warriors Museum, but history buffs will enjoy it. According to ancient records, the underground palace took more than 40 years to build, and many historians believe the tomb contains a wealth of priceless treasures, though perhaps we will never know for sure. You can climb to the top of the burial mound for a view of the surrounding countryside, although most visitors hurry off to see the Terracotta Warriors Museum after watching a mildly amusing ceremony honoring the emperor who united China. The tomb is in Lintong, 30 km (19 miles) east of Xian. ✉ *Lintong* 🎫 *Y40* 🕒 *Apr.–Oct., daily 7–7; Nov.–Mar., daily 8–6.*

## WHERE TO EAT

$$ CHINESE

🍴 **De Fa Chang Restaurant** (德发长饺子馆 *Dé fā chǎng jiǎozi guǎn*). If you think dumplings are just occasional snack food, think again. De Fa Chang, one of Xian's most famous restaurants, is known for its dumpling banquet. Do try the pan-fried *guotie*, stuffed with pork and chives. For the dumpling banquet, head upstairs and choose between the preset menus. Considerably cheaper à la carte dishes can be found downstairs; just grab a plate as a cart passes by your table and be ready to pay on the spot. [$] *Average main: Y60* ✉ *Xi Da Jie, north side of Bell Tower Sq.* ☎ *029/8721–4065* 💳 *No credit cards.*

$$ INDIAN

🍴 **Delhi Darbar** (新德里餐厅 *Xīndélǐ cāntīng*). When you need a change from Chinese food, try this place run by Indian expats for spicy flavors and friendly service. Try the Palak Green Peas Masala with fluffy naan bread. Vegetarians will feel right at home—for once you can rely on waitresses to tell you if there is meat in a dish! [$] *Average main: Y80* ✉ *3 Huan Ta Xi Lu, near Big Wild Goose Pagoda* ☎ *029/8525–5157* 💳 *No credit cards.*

$ NORTHERN CHINESE

🍴 **Lao Sun Jia Restaurant** (孙老家饭庄 *Lǎo sūn jiā fànzhuāng*). This traditional, family-run affair has been serving some of the best local Islamic lamb and beef specialties since 1898; it's become so popular that it's grown into a small Xian chain. The decor isn't special, but the food is popular with Xian's large Muslim community. A few famous offerings, such as the roasted leg of lamb or the spicy mutton spareribs, are pricey, but most dishes are inexpensive. Try *pao mo*, the mutton and bread soup. Ask for an English menu. [$] *Average main: Y30* ✉ *364 Dong Da Jie, near the corner of Duanlu Men* ☎ *029/8742-1858* 💳 *No credit cards.*

$$$$ CANTONESE

🍴 **Shang Palace Restaurant** (香宫 *Xiāng gōng*). All of Xian's top hotels have elegant eateries, but Shang Palace deserves special mention for its Cantonese and Sichuan dishes, which are authentic and approachable. On the menu, classics like honey-barbecued pork and stir-fried chicken with chili sit alongside less familiar dishes; note that drinks are pricey. As you dine, musicians pluck away in traditional costumes. Most of the staff speaks some English. $ *Average main: Y150* ✉ *Shangri-La Golden Flower Hotel, 8 Changle Xi Lu* ☎ *029/8323–2981.*

**$$$$**
CHINESE
Fodor's Choice
★
✕ **Tang Dynasty** (西安唐乐宫 *Xī'ān táng lè gōng*). Don't confuse the cuisine served in the Tang Dynasty's popular dinner theater with the specialties available at the separate restaurant. While the former serves mediocre fare, the latter specializes in Tang Dynasty–imperial cuisine— a taste you're not likely to find back home at your local Chinese restaurant. Locals praise the abalone and other fresh fish dishes as the finest in Xian. You can reserve either for dinner and the show (Y500) or just the show (Y220), which starts every night at 8:30 pm. $ *Average main: Y180* ✉ *75 Changan Bei Lu* ☎ *029/8782–2222* ⊕ *www. xiantangdynasty.com.*

**$$**
CHINESE
✕ **Xian Fanzhuang** (西安饭庄 *Xī'ān fànzhuāng*). This restaurant specializes in Shaanxi snacks with a Muslim flavor, as well as "small eats"—street food spruced up for the visitor. Business executives and T-shirt-clad college students alike head to the bustling first-floor dining room for the all-you-can-eat buffet, a bargain at Y25. An adjacent entrance leads to a second-floor restaurant, where more exotic and expensive dishes—algae flavored with orchid, for example—are prepared. An English menu is available. $ *Average main: Y60* ✉ *Xian Hotel, 298 Dong Da Jie* ☎ *029/8727–3185* ▭ *No credit cards.*

### WHERE TO STAY

**$**
HOTEL
Fodor's Choice
★
🏨 **Bell Tower Hotel** (钟楼饭店 *Zhōnglóu fàndiàn*). Relatively inexpensive compared to other hotels in its class, the very popular Bell Tower has spacious, airy rooms with views overlooking downtown Xian. **Pros:** excellent location. **Cons:** absence of character; hotel restaurants are mediocre. $ *Rooms from: Y520* ✉ *110 Nan Da Jie* ☎ *029/8760–0000* ⊕ *www.belltowerhotelxian.cn* ⤳ *300 rooms, 11 suites* ⫼ *Breakfast.*

**$**
HOTEL
🏨 **Grand Metropark Hotel Xian** (阿房宫维景国际大酒店 *Āfáng gōng wéi jǐng guójì dà jiǔdiàn*). Although there are newer luxury properties, people return to the Grand Metropark because of its friendly staff and central location. **Pros:** walking distance to the city's sights; fun bar, which is an expat hangout; cheerful staff. **Cons:** overpriced breakfast; chirping birds in the atrium lobby can be annoying when you're trying to fall asleep. $ *Rooms from: Y550* ✉ *158 Dong Da Jie* ☎ *029/8723– 1234* ⊕ *www.hyatt.com* ⤳ *315 rooms, 22 suites* ⫼ *No meals.*

**$**
HOTEL
🏨 **Howard Johnson Ginwa Plaza** (金花豪生国际大酒店 *Jīnhuā háoshēng guójì dàjiǔdiàn*). Don't look for the familiar orange roof here. **Pros:** attractive lobby; superb variety at mealtimes. **Cons:** nothing individual about this place; language barriers with staff; no Wi-Fi in rooms. $ *Rooms from: Y600* ✉ *18 Huancheng Nan Lu* ☎ *029/8818–1111* ⊕ *www.ginwaplaza.com* ⤳ *324 rooms, 30 apartments* ⫼ *No meals.*

**$**
HOTEL
🏨 **Ibis Xian** (西安宜必思酒店 *Xī'ān íbìsī jiǔdiàn*). The best bargain in Xian's Old City is part of the French budget hotel chain. **Pros:** great location; friendly service. **Cons:** unappealing breakfast. $ *Rooms from: Y220* ✉ *59 Heping Lu* ☎ *029/8727–5555* ⊕ *www.accorhotels.com* ⤳ *220 rooms* ⫼ *No meals.*

**$**
HOTEL
🏨 **Shangri-La Golden Flower** (西安金花大酒店 *Xī'ān jīnhuā dàjiǔdiàn*). The older of the two Shangri-La's in Xian, this remains one of the city's most luxurious hotels. **Pros:** spacious rooms; excellent room

10

service. **Cons:** layout is confusing; rooms are beginning to show their age. $Rooms from: Y560 ⊠ 8 Changle Xi Lu ☎ 029/8323–2981, 800/8942–5050 in the U.S. ⊕ www.shangri-la.com ⤳ 416 rooms, 16 suites ⦿ No meals.

**$$**
**HOTEL**
⊡ **Sheraton** (喜来登大酒店 Xǐláidēng dàjiǔdiàn). This is a joint venture with high-quality standards and colorfully decorated rooms. **Pros:** glitzy and well-fitted bathrooms; excellent buffet breakfast. **Cons:** located in an uninteresting commercial part of town; difficult to get taxis from hotel. $Rooms from: Y900 ⊠ 262 Fenghao Dong Lu ☎ 029/8426–1888 ⊕ www.starwoodhotels.com ⤳ 365 rooms, 17 suites ⦿ No meals.

### NIGHTLIFE AND THE ARTS

One of the busiest parts of town in the evening, the Muslim Quarter is where crowds converge to shop, stroll, and eat virtually every night of the week. Street-side chefs fire up the stoves and whip up tasty dishes, vendors ply the crowded lanes peddling their wares, and locals and tourists alike jostle in the frenetic pace.

**GZ Groovz Jazz Club** (GZ爵士酒吧 GZ juéshì jiǔbā). The only jazz bar in Xian, GZ Groovz is worth seeking out for its nightly live music and cheap beers. ⊠ Dong Qi Dao Xiang, near He Ping Gate ☎ 133/5920–7823.

**Tang Dynasty** (唐代 Táng dài). The impressive song and dance performance at Tang Dynasty is the city's most popular evening of entertainment for foreign visitors. Shows begin at 8:30. ⊠ 75 Changan Bei Lu ☎ 029/8782–2222 ⊕ www.xiantangdynasty.com.

### SHOPPING

Predictably, Xian is overloaded with terracotta souvenirs. There is more to buy than terracotta souvenirs, however. The shops are filled with carved jade, calligraphy, and Shaanxi folk paintings. Even if you don't buy anything, it's a nice place for a stroll.

**Hua Jue Xiang Market** (化觉巷 Huā juéxiàng). In the alley leading to the Great Mosque, the Hua Jue Xiang Market is one of the best places to find interesting souvenirs. Expect the antique you're eyeing to be fake, no matter how vehemently the vendor insists that your find is "genuine Ming Dynasty." ⊠ Hua Jue Xiang, Lian Hu district.

# GANSU

Gansu is the long, narrow province linking central China with the desert regions of the northwest. For centuries, as goods were transported through the region, Gansu acted as a conduit between China and the Western world. As merchants made their fortunes from silk and other luxuries, the oasis towns strung along the Silk Road became important trade outposts of the Middle Kingdom. But beyond the massive fortress at Jiayuguan lay the end of the Great Wall, the oasis of Dunhuang, and then perdition. Gansu was the edge of China.

What has long been the poorest province in China is essentially dry, rugged, and barren. The decline of the Silk Road brought terrible

suffering and poverty, from which the area has only very recently begun to recover as tourism boosts the local economy. Over the last few years, protests at Labrang Monastery have led to travel restrictions. The area around Xiahe was closed off to foreign tourists in late 2012, but at the time of writing it was open again to foreigners. Check with your travel agent for up-to-date information.

**REGIONAL TOURS**

**John's Information Cafè.** There aren't a lot of choices when it comes to tours in Gansu, but this café owned by the affable John Hu offers tours to Dunhuang and the Mogao Caves led by English-speaking guides. Prices depend on the number of people traveling, but expect to pay about Y200 per person, excluding admission costs. The company can also arrange tours of Lanzhou. ⊠ *21 Mingshan Lu, north of the Feitian Hotel, Dunhuang* ☏ *1399/373–3106* ⊕ *www.johncafe.net.*

## LANZHOU

*8 hrs by train northwest of Xian; 21 hrs by train southeast of Ürümqi; 2½ hrs by train east of Xining, 18 hours by train from Beijing.*

Built on the banks of the Yellow River, the capital of Gansu extends along the base of a narrow gorge whose walls rise to 5,000 feet. A city with a long history, Lanzhou has been nearly ruined by rampant industrialization, and is now one of the world's most polluted urban areas. Though air quality is getting better, in winter the city can be filled with smog.

The ethnic mix of the city's population makes the place interesting for a few hours, but plan to stay here only as long as it takes to arrange transportation to somewhere more pleasant, like Xiahe or Dunhuang.

### GETTING HERE AND AROUND

AIR TRAVEL The city's Zhongchuan Airport is 67 km (42 miles) north of town. From Lanzhou there are daily flights to Dunhuang, Beijing, Guangzhou, Shanghai, Chengdu, Ürümqi, and Xian. A public bus costing Y30 per person takes over an hour to reach the airport from the China Northwest Airlines office at 512 Donggang Xi Lu.

BUS TRAVEL Long-distance buses arrive at the East Station (*qìchēdōngzhàn*) on Pingliang Lu, north of the train station. Leaving the city can be a bit more complicated. Buses to major destinations like Xian, Xining, Jiayuguan, and Dunhuang usually leave from the East Station, while smaller destinations are served by the West Station (*qìchēxīzhàn*). Buses to Xiahe depart from the South Station (*qìchēnánzhàn*).

Buses originating in Lanzhou often require foreigners to show proof of travel insurance bought from the Chinese company PICC (The People's Insurance Company of China—a monstrously large insurance company) before purchasing tickets. It's unclear why this regulation exists, or why there's usually at least one daily bus to each destination that doesn't require the paperwork. You should be able to purchase insurance with your bus ticket, but this is often not the case. For peace of mind, head straight to the main PICC office on the north side of Qingyang Lu, just east of Jingning Lu. They'll know why you're there. A two-week policy costs Y40. At this writing, you were required to show two photocopies of your visa and passport details.

TRAIN TRAVEL The train station (Lanzhou huǒchēzhàn) is at the southern end of Tianshui Lu, 1 km (½ mile) south of the city's main hotels. With few trains originating here, buying sleeper tickets in Lanzhou can be difficult; your best bet is to buy tickets early, or hope for an upgrade once onboard.

### SAFETY AND PRECAUTIONS

Heavy rains in the past few years have led to mudslides that caused 1,500 deaths. It pays to check with a tour company before venturing out to isolated locations or in adverse weather regions. There can also be friction between ethnic Tibetans and Han Chinese in some areas.

### TIMING

Lanzhou's appeal is limited; stay only as long as you need to arrange transportation to the province's other worthier attractions.

### TOURS

Gansu Western Travel Service offers a day trip to Thousand Buddha Temple and Grottoes that includes all transportation and insurance for around Y400 per person. The company also has tours to Xiahe, including a five-day trip that visits the spectacularly beautiful Tibetan temples at Langmusi on the border with Sichuan. A basic two-day tour from Lanzhou costs between Y600 and Y850 per person, including hotel.

**ESSENTIALS**

**Air Contacts Lanzhou Zhongchuan Airport** (兰州中川机场 *Lánzhōu zhōngchuān jīchǎng*). ✉ *Zhongchuan* ☎ *0931/896–8160.*

**Bank Bank of China** (中国银行 *Zhōngguó yínháng*). ✉ *525 Tianshui Lu* ☎ *0931/841–0884.*

**Bus Contacts Lanzhou East Bus Station** (兰州汽车东站 *Lánzhōu qìchēdōngzhàn*). ✉ *12 Pingliang Lu* ☎ *0931/266–3285.* **Lanzhou West Bus Station** (兰州汽车西站 *Lánzhōu qìchēxīzhàn*). ✉ *458 Xijin Dong Lu* ☎ *0931/233–3285.* **Lanzhou South Bus Station** (兰州汽车南站 *Lánzhōu qìchēnánzhàn*). ✉ *Langong Ping, Qi Li He* ☎ *0931/291–4066.*

**Train Contact Lanzhou Train Station** (兰州火车站 *Lánzhōu huǒchēzhàn*). ✉ *Huoche Zhan Dong Jian, at the southern end of Pingliang Lu and Tianshui Lu* ☎ *0931/492–2222.*

**Visitor and Tour Info Gansu Western Travel Service** ✉ *Lanzhou Hotel, 486 Donggang Xi Lu* ☎ *0931/841–6321, 138/9331–8956.*

**EXPLORING**

**Five Springs Mountain Park** (五泉山公园 *Wǔquánshān gōngyuán*). Sip tea among ancient temples and take in impressive views of the city from this pretty park. The five springs that gave the place its name, unfortunately, have dwindled to a trickle. ✉ *10 Wu Quan Nan Lu* ☎ *093/824324* 🏷 *Y6* ⊘ *Daily 6–7.*

Fodor's Choice ★ **Gansu Provincial Museum** (甘肃省博物馆 *Gānsù shěng bówùguǎn*). The most famous item in this excellent museum's collection is the elegant bronze "Flying Horse," considered a masterpiece of ancient Chinese art. Other notable objects include a silver plate documenting contact between China and Rome more than 2,200 years ago, and wooden tablets used to send messages along the Silk Road. Exhibits are subtitled in English. Make sure to bring your passport. ✉ *3 Xijin Xi Lu, across from the Friendship Hotel* ☎ *0931/233–9133* 🏷 *Free* ⊘ *Tues.–Sun. 9–5.*

**Mountain of the White Pagoda Park** (白塔山公园 *Báitǎshān gōngyuán*). Laid out in 1958, the park covers the slopes on the Yellow River's north bank. It's more of a carnival than a place to relax, but it's a great place for people-watching. ✉ *Bei Bin He Zhong Lu, entrance at Zhongshan Qiao, the bridge extending over the Yellow River* ☎ *931/837–1462* 🏷 *Y8* ⊘ *Daily 6–7:30.*

**WHERE TO EAT**

Many of the best restaurants in Lanzhou are found in its upscale hotels; one to try is Zhong Hua Yuan in the Lanzhou Hotel, where an English menu is available. Another place to find a good meal is along Nongmin Xiang Lu, a street that runs behind the Lanzhou Hotel. This is a great place to try *roujiamo,* a small sandwich filled with onion, chili, and flash-fried lamb or beef.

$ ✕ **Chuanwei Wang** (川味王 *Chuānwèi wáng*). You can often tell a good
SICHUAN restaurant by the lack of empty tables; at mealtimes, this Sichuanese

10

eatery is always packed. There's no English menu, but pictures of almost every dish make ordering simple. If you're stuck, order *gongbao jiding,* a slightly spicy dish of chicken stir-fried with peanuts. [$] *Average main: Y40* ✉ *26 Nongmin Xiang Lu, north of Tianshui Lu* ☎ *0931/887–9879* 💳 *No credit cards.*

$$ CHINESE 🍴 **Xinhai Restaurant** (**鑫海大酒店** *Xīnhǎi dàjiǔdiàn*). One of Lanzhou's finest eateries, Xinhai is surprisingly affordable. Lanzhou specialties such as braised beef and hand-pulled noodles, as well as Cantonese and Sichuanese dishes, are pictured on the menu; you can also order from the text-only English menu. [$] *Average main: Y80* ✉ *499 Donggang Xi Lu, next to Legend Hotel* ☎ *0931/886–6078* 💳 *No credit cards.*

## WHERE TO STAY

$ HOTEL 🏨 **Jin Jiang Sun Hotel** (**锦江阳光酒店** *Jǐnjiāng yángguāng jiǔdiàn*). From the marble floors in the lobby to the plush furnishings, this 25-story tower is Lanzhou's top luxury hotel. **Pros:** excellent value; reception staff speak English. **Cons:** expensive Internet and business-center facilities are sparse; in a commercial part of town. [$] *Rooms from: Y450* ✉ *481 Donggang Xi Lu* ☎ *0931/880–5511* 🌐 *www.jinjianghotels.com* 🛏 *236 rooms* 🍽 *No meals.*

$ HOTEL 🏨 **Lanzhou Hotel** (**兰州饭店** *Lánzhōu fàndiàn*). Built in 1956, this concrete behemoth's Sino-Stalinist exterior hides a modern if drab interior. **Pros:** a local landmark that's easy to find. **Cons:** even the no-smoking rooms can be smoky. [$] *Rooms from: Y460* ✉ *486 Donggang Xi Lu, corner of Tianshui Lu* ☎ *0931/841–6321* 🌐 *www.lanzhouhotel.com* 🛏 *41 rooms, 61 suites* 🍽 *No meals.*

## SIDE TRIPS FROM LANZHOU

Fodor's Choice ★ **Labrang Monastery** (**拉卜楞寺** *Lābǔléng sì*). In the remote town of Xiahe, the monastery is a little piece of Tibet along the Gansu-Qinghai border. A world away from Lanzhou, Xiahe has experienced a dizzying rise in the number of travelers over the past decade. Even Tibetan monks clad in traditional fuchsia robes now surf the Internet, play basketball, and listen to pop music. Despite the encroaching modernity, Xiahe is still a wonderful place, attracting large numbers of pilgrims who come to study and to spin the 1,147 prayer wheels of the monastery daily, swathed in their distinctive costume of heavy woolen robes tied with brightly colored sashes. ■ TIP→ **Because of political protests, Labrang Monastery was closed to tourists in October and November of 2012, but the area is open once again. Check with your travel agent for up-to-date information.**

The Labrang Monastery is the largest Tibetan lamasery outside Tibet. Founded in 1710, it once had as many as 4,000 monks, a number much depleted due in large part to the Cultural Revolution, when monks were forced to return home and temples were destroyed. Though the monastery reopened in 1980, the government's continued policy of restricted enrollment has kept the number of monks down to about 1,500. There are guided tours daily at 10:15 am and 3:15 pm.

There are two ways to reach Xiahe: by public bus or by private tour. Buses for Xiahe leave from Lanzhou's South Station (qìchē nánzhàn) in the morning (6:30 and 7:30) and afternoon (2 and 3) and take about

The Great Prayer Festival at the Labrang Monastery

four hours. Make sure to purchase tickets in advance, as some departures require travel insurance (*baoxian*). Also, have two photocopies of your visa and passport information on hand in case they are required. ⊠ *2 km (1 mile) west of long-distance bus station, Xiahe* 🚍 *Y40* ⊙ *Daily sunrise–sunset.*

Fodor's Choice ★ **Thousand Buddha Temple and Grottoes** (炳灵寺 *Bǐnglíng sì*). One of the best day trips is the Thousand Buddha Temple and Grottoes, about 80 km (50 miles) from Lanzhou. More commonly known by its Chinese name Bingling si, it's filled with Buddhist paintings and statuary, including an impressive 89-foot-tall Buddha carved into a cliff face.

The canyon that holds the Thousand Buddha Temple runs along one side of the Yellow River. The journey through a gorge lined by water-sculpted rocks is spectacular. When the canyon is dry you can travel 2½ km (1½ miles) on foot or by four-wheel-drive vehicle to see the small community of Tibetan lamas at the Upper Temple of Bingling. However, it's much easier to book a tour. Gansu Western Travel Service offers a popular day trip that includes all transportation and insurance for about Y400 per person. 🚍 *Y50* ⊙ *July–Nov., daily 8–5.*

## DUNHUANG

*17 hrs by bus or 14 hrs by train northwest of Lanzhou; 6 hrs by bus west of Jiayuguan.*

A small oasis town, Dunhuang was for many centuries the most important Buddhist destination on the Silk Road. Just outside of town, beyond the towering dunes of Singing Sand Mountain, you can see the

10

extraordinary caves of the Mogao Grottoes, considered the richest repository of Buddhist art in the world.

Buddhism entered China via the Silk Road, and as Dunhuang was the point of entry to the Chinese world, it was not long before a temple was established here. By 366, the first caves were being carved and painted at the Mogao oasis. Work continued until the 10th century, after which they were left undisturbed for nearly 1,000 years.

Adventurers from Europe, North America, and other parts of Asia began plundering the caves at the end of the 19th century, yet most of the statuary and paintings remain.

**DON'T MISS**

A highlight of a visit to the Labrang Monastery is the daily gathering of monks for religious debate in the liveliest fashion. The monks charge at each other in groups, hissing good-naturedly, as older monks supervise with a benevolent air. The debate takes place on a lawn in the afternoon; ask at the ticket office for times. Another interesting daily event is the gathering of hundreds of chanting monks on the steps of the main prayer hall, beginning at 11 am.

By far the most astounding find was a "library cave" filled with more than 45,000 forgotten sutras and official documents. The contents were mostly sold to Sir Aurel Stein in 1907, and when translated they revealed the extent to which Dunhuang was an ancient melting pot of cultures and religions.

Today you'll find a rapidly developing small city that is still, in some ways, a melting pot; tourists from every continent converge upon Dunhuang daily to visit one of the most impressive sites in all of China.

**GETTING HERE AND AROUND**

The best way to get around Dunhuang is by bicycle, and you can easily hire one from rental places around town.

AIR TRAVEL   The easiest way to reach Dunhuang is by air, with regular flights from Beijing, Xian, Lanzhou, and Ürümqi. Dunhuang's airport is 13 km (8 miles) east of town, on the road to the Mogao Grottoes. A taxi ride from the airport costs Y20 to Y30.

BUS TRAVEL   Buses from Lanzhou, Turpan, and Jiayuguan depart frequently for Dunhuang, dropping you off at the bus station in the center of town.

TRAIN TRAVEL   Dunhuang's train station is 13 km (8 miles) northeast of the town and serves Lanzhou, Xian, and Jiayuguan. A better-connected station, with services to Beijing and Shanghai, is in the small town of Liuyuan, 120 km (74 miles) away. Taxis from Liuyuan to Dunhuang cost Y120, or you can hop aboard one of the buses that leave hourly for Y15.

**SAFETY AND PRECAUTIONS**

Dunhuang is an expensive place to visit, as admission costs quickly add up. Taxi drivers often charge extortionate prices to take you out into the desert; never take their opening offer!

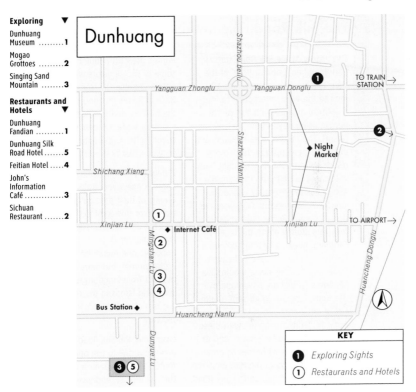

**Exploring** ▼
Dunhuang Museum .........**1**
Mogao Grottoes .........**2**
Singing Sand Mountain ........**3**

**Restaurants and Hotels** ▼
Dunhuang Fandian ..........**1**
Dunhuang Silk Road Hotel .......**5**
Feitian Hotel .....**4**
John's Information Café ..............**3**
Sichuan Restaurant .......**2**

**KEY**
❶ Exploring Sights
① Restaurants and Hotels

**TIMING**

Aim to spend at least two days in Dunhuang: one day to see the Mogao Caves and Singing Sand Mountain, and the other to spend time in the town itself.

**TOURS**

If you only have time for one trip out of town, head to the Mogao Grottoes (Y20 for the round-trip bus fare). Don't bother with a tour to Singing Sand Mountain, as it's easy enough to reach on your own by taxi. If you're able to spend an extra day in town, take a tour of sites relating to ancient Dunhuang (Y130).

**ESSENTIALS**

**Air Contact Dunhuang Airport** (敦煌机场 Dūnhuáng jīchǎng). ✉ 13 km (8 mi) east of Dunhuang, near the Mogao Grottoes ☎ 0937/882–5292.

**Bank Bank of China** (中国银行 Zhōngguó yínháng). ✉ Yangguan Zhonglu ☎ 0937/263–0510.

**Bus Contact Dunhuang Bus Station** (敦煌汽车站 Dūnhuáng qìchēzhàn). ✉ Mingshan Lu 25 ☎ 0937/882–2174.

**Train Contacts Liuyuan Train Station** (柳园火车站 Liǔyuán huǒchēzhàn). ✉ Liuyuan Huoche Zhan ☎ 0937/557–2995. **Dunhuang Train Sta-**

CLOSE UP

# The Silk Road: Then and Now

The history of the Silk Road starts in 138 BC, when Emperor Wudi of the Han Dynasty sent a caravan of 100 men to the west, attempting to forge a political alliance with the Yuezhi people living beyond the Taklamakan Desert. The mission was a failure, and only two men survived the 13-year return journey, but they brought back with them to Chang'an (present-day Xian) tales of previously unknown kingdoms: Samarkand, Ferghana, Parthia, and even Rome. More important, they told stories about the legendary Ferghana horse, a fast and powerful creature said to be bred in heaven. Believing that this horse would give his armies a military advantage over the Huns, Emperor Wudi sent a number of large convoys to Central Asia in order to establish contact with these newly discovered kingdoms—and to bring back as many horses as possible. These envoys of the Han emperor were the first traders on the Silk Road.

The extension of the Silk Road beyond Central Asia to the Middle East and Europe was due to another ill-advised foreign excursion, this time on the part of the Roman Empire. In 55 BC Marcus Licinius Crassus led an army to the east against Parthia, in present-day Syria. The battle was one of

Rome's greatest military defeats, but some of the survivors were able to obtain Chinese silk from the Parthians. Back in Rome, wearing silk became the fashion, and for the first time in history a trade route was established covering the 5,000-mile journey between East and West.

It might seem odd today, but the two empires knew very little about the origins of their precious cargo. The reason for this common ignorance was the complicated supply chain that transported goods over the Silk Road. No one merchant made the entire journey, but wares were instead brought from kingdom to kingdom, switching hands in the teeming bazaars of wealthy oasis cities along the way.

Over time, the Silk Road became less important due to the opening of sea routes, and was dealt a deathblow by the isolationist tendencies of the Chinese Ming Dynasty in the 14th century. Yet today the Silk Road is being resurrected to transport the modern world's most precious commodity: oil. China's rapid development has created an almost insatiable appetite for energy resources. In the last few years pipelines have been completed from Kazakhstan and Xinjiang to Shanghai.

tion (敦煌火车站 *Dūnhuáng huǒchē zhàn*). ⊠ *Dunhuang Huoche Zhan* ☎ *0937/882–2598.*

**Visitor and Tour Info CITS** ⊠ *Feitian Hotel, 22 Mingshan Lu* ☎ *0937/882–2474* ⊕ *www.cits.net.*

## EXPLORING

**Dunhuang Museum** (敦煌博物馆 *Dūnhuáng bówùguǎn*). The small museum displays objects recovered from nearby Silk Road fortifications such as reclining Buddhas, sumptuous wall paintings, and sculptures. If you've visited the Jade Gate or Yangguan Pass, you may enjoy seeing what's been found. ⊠ *8 Yangguan Dong Lu, east of the night market*

☎ *0937/882–2981* ✉ *Free* ⊙ *Daily 8–1 and 2–6.*

Fodor'sChoice ★ **Mogao Grottoes** (莫高窟 *Mógāo kū*). The magnificent Buddhist grottoes lie southeast of Dunhuang. At least 40 of the 700 caves—dating from the Northern Wei in the 4th century AD to the Five Dynasties in the 10th century AD—are open to the public. Which caves are open on a given day depends on the whim of local authorities, but you shouldn't worry too much about missing something. Everything here is stunning. You'll almost certainly visit the giant seated Buddhas in caves 96 and 130, the Tang Dynasty sleeping Buddha in cave 148, and the famous "library" in caves 16 and 17, where 45,000 religious and political documents were uncovered at the turn of the 20th century. A flashlight is a useful item for your visit. Note that photographs are not allowed.

This is one site where you should hire an English-speaking guide. At a cost of Y20, your understanding of the different imagery used in each cave will increase immeasurably. Tours in English take place about three times a day in high season, so you may have to wait to join one. Be sure to verify that the tour is of the same two-hour duration and covers the same number of caves (8–10) as the Chinese tours. After the tour, you'll have time to wander around and revisit any unlocked caves. A fine museum contains reproductions of eight caves not usually visited on the public tour. A smaller museum near the Library Cave details the removal of artifacts by foreign plunderers. If you have a deep interest in the cave art, you may be able to pay Y300 extra to visit other caves that are sealed off to the general public. Ask at the ticket office.

To get here, take a taxi (Y60 to Y80 round-trip) or take the half-hour bus ride that departs from Xinjian Lu, near the corner with Minshan Lu. The bus runs from 8:30 am to 7 pm, and tickets cost Y8 each way. The CITS at the Feitan Hotel offers a daily bus service, leaving Dunhuang at 8 am and returning at noon. A round-trip costs Y20. ✉ *25 km (17 miles) southeast of Dunhuang* ☎ *0937/888-2304* ✉ *Y180 for tour; additional Y20 for English-speaking guide* ⊙ *Daily 8:30–6.*

**Singing Sand Mountain** (鸣沙山 *Míngshāshān*). South of Dunhuang, the oasis gives way to desert. Here you'll find a gorgeous sweep of sand dunes, named for the light rattling sound that the sand makes when wind blows across the surface. At 5,600 feet above sea level, the half-hour climb to the summit is difficult but worth it for the views, particularly at sunset. Nestled in the sand is **Crescent Moon Lake** (月牙泉 *Yuèyáquán*), a lovely pool that by some freak of the prevailing winds never silts up. Camels, sleds, and various flying contraptions are available at steep prices; try your bargaining skills. ✉ *Mingshan*

10

*Lu, 5 km (3 miles) south of town* 🎫 *Y120* 🕒 *8–5.*

> **A TOP ATTRACTION**
>
> China is promoting the Mogao Caves as one of the country's top attractions. The number of visitors jumped from 26,000 in 1979 to 680,000 in 2011. To protect the precious relics, the Dunhuang Academy is building a new state-of-the-art visitor center to enhance understanding of the historic site. The avant-garde building is expected to be finished by 2014.

### WHERE TO EAT

Dunhuang's night market is a 10-minute walk from the most popular hotels. Located between Xinjian Lu and Yangguan Dong Lu, it's worth a visit for cold beer and flavorful lamb kebabs. Small restaurants are clustered together on Mingshan Lu in the center of town.

$$ AMERICAN 🍴 **John's Information Café.** Cool off after a full day of sightseeing on this trellised patio with an ice-cold beer and plate of noodles. Another option is to come early in the day for a Western-style breakfast and a cup of joe. The restaurant can arrange overnight camel rides for Y300–Y500 per person, as well as trips to Yadan National Park and other destinations. [$] *Average main: Y50* ✉ *21 Mingshan Lu, north of the Feitian Hotel* ☎ *1399/373–3106* 🌐 *www.johncafe.net* 💳 *No credit cards.*

$ SICHUAN 🍴 **Sichuan Restaurant** (四川餐厅 *Sìchuān cāntīng*). Delicious Sichuanese classics like chicken with peanuts, sweet-and-sour pork, and spicy fried potato strips are available here at very cheap prices. There's an English menu, but prices are much higher than on the Chinese menu. [$] *Average main: Y20* ✉ *75 Mingshan Lu, next to the Dunhuang Trade Union Hotel* 💳 *No credit cards.*

### WHERE TO STAY

$ HOTEL 🏨 **Dunhuang Fandian** (敦煌饭店 *Dūnhuáng fàndiàn*). If you're looking for something mildly luxurious, this lodging in the center of town will fit the bill. **Pros:** central location; excellent value. **Cons:** some noise from a local nightclub if you're on a low floor; Chinese breakfast options only. [$] *Rooms from: Y190* ✉ *16 Mingshan Lu, corner of Xinjiang Lu* ☎ *0937/885–2999* 🛏 *98 rooms* 🍽 *No meals.*

$$ HOTEL Fodor's Choice ★ 🏨 **Dunhuang Silk Road Hotel** (敦煌山庄 *Dūnhuáng shānzhuāng*). This cross between a Chinese fortress and an alpine lodge is the most interesting place to stay in Dunhuang, and possibly in the whole of the province. **Pros:** rooftop terrace; good hotel food. **Cons:** touts approach guests all the time. [$] *Rooms from: Y700* ✉ *Dun Yue Lu* ☎ *0937/888–2088* 🌐 *www.dunhuangresort.com* 🛏 *292 rooms, 8 suites* 🍽 *Breakfast.*

$ HOTEL 🏨 **Feitian Hotel** (飞天宾馆 *Fēitiān bīnguǎn*). Dunhuang's most popular budget hotel has a variety of clean, comfortable rooms. **Pros:** inexpensive rates. **Cons:** basic rooms; large deposits required upon check-in. [$] *Rooms from: Y168* ✉ *22 Mingshan Lu, ½ block north of the bus station* ☎ *0937/882–2337* 🌐 *www.dunhuangfly.com* 🛏 *90 rooms* 💳 *No credit cards* 🍽 *No meals.*

The dramatic landscape of Qinghai

# QINGHAI

A remote and sparsely populated province on the northeastern border of Tibet, Qinghai's sweeping grasslands locked in by icy mountain ranges are relatively unknown to most Chinese people, who tend to think of the province as their nation's Siberia; a center for prisons and work camps. Yet Qinghai shares much of the majestic scenery of Xinjiang, combined with the rich culture of Tibet.

The opening of the railway linking Tibet with the rest of China led to an influx of travelers to Qinghai, one of the last major stops before the train arrives in Lhasa. Many hoped that tourism would improve Qinghai's struggling economy, but restrictions on travel to Tibet also brought the number of foreigners traveling through this stunning region to a dramatic halt in March 2008. Happily, the region is once again open for independent travel.

Visitors to the region should take in a few of Qinghai's must-see sites. Xining, the compact capital city, has some charming Tibetan flair. On the northwest edge of the city is the famed North Monastery, a solemn Daoist destination. The Kumbum Monastery is a testament to Tibetan tranquillity. For a truly heavenly display, crane your neck skyward at the aptly named Bird Island on Qinghai Lake, several hundred miles to the west of Xining.

10

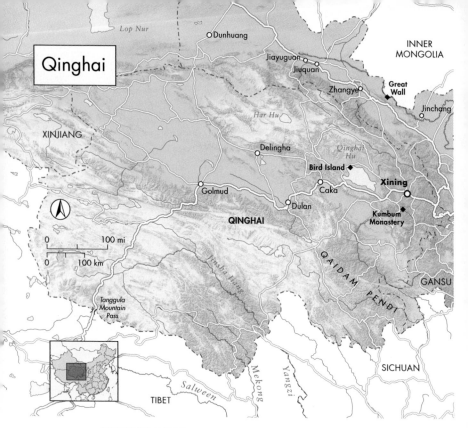

## REGIONAL TOURS

**Tibetan Connections.** This locally owned tour company offers very interesting off-the-beaten-track hikes, camping trips, and tours through one of the region's most fascinating and beautiful areas. ☒ *Lete Youth Hostel, Jiancaixiang, Xining ⊕ www.tibetanconnections.com.*

**CITS.** The local branch of China's state-run travel service offers tours of the city as well as to Bird Island. It's intended for international tourists, but the office has few staffers who speak limited English. ☒ *Xining Guesthouse, 215 Qiyi Lu, Xining ☎ 0971/613–3847 ⊕ www.qhcits.cn.*

## XINING

*3 hrs (225 km [140 miles]) by train or 3 hrs by bus west of Lanzhou; 24 hours (1,900 km [1,200 miles]) by train northeast of Lhasa.*

Its name means "peace in the west," so it's no surprise that Xining started out as a military garrison in the 16th century, guarding the empire's western borders. It was also an important center for trade between China and Tibet. A small city by Chinese standards, with a population slightly more than 2.2 million, Xining is no longer cut off from the rest of China. But the city still feels remote. A far-flung metropolis wedged between dramatic sandstone cliffs, Xining is populated largely by Tibetan and Hui peoples.

For travelers, Xining is a convenient base for visits to the important Kumbum Monastery, which sits just outside the city, and the stunning avian sanctuary of Bird Island, 350 km (217 miles) away on the shores of China's largest saltwater lake. Tibet-bound trains stop in Xining, so this could be a good place to acclimatize to the high altitude.

### GETTING HERE AND AROUND
Xining Caojiabao Airport is 30 km (19 miles) east of the city. Shuttle buses costing Y25 per person can get you to or from the airport in about 40 minutes. If you're traveling with someone else, a taxi (Y80–Y100) is a better option. If you arrive by train or bus, a taxi should be less than Y10.

AIR TRAVEL Daily flights link Xining with Beijing, Shanghai, Chengdu, Guangzhou, Xian, and Shenzhen. There is less frequent service to Lhasa, Ürümqi, Qingdao, and Golmud.

BUS TRAVEL Tickets for the long, bumpy bus ride to Lhasa can be purchased from any travel agent. Tickets for the journey to Lanzhou (3 hours) and Xian (15 hours) are available at the long-distance bus station, a few minutes north of the train station. If your next stop is Dunhuang, but you don't want to backpedal to Lanzhou, take the bus to Jiuquan in Gansu and get a connection farther west; the mountain scenery and small Tibetan villages along the way are spectacular.

TRAIN TRAVEL The train to Lhasa runs every day, but foreign travelers need to arrange permits and book a tour before they can buy train tickets for the 24-hour journey. You can also travel to Beijing, Shanghai, Lanzhou, Guangzhou, and Chengdu by train.

### SAFETY AND PRECAUTIONS
The standard advice for travelers applies here; beware of pickpockets and be on the lookout for taxi drivers with "broken meters."

### TIMING
Xining is not a place to linger, as there are other, more appealing cities in the region. Spending a night here to explore and see the city's sights is enough.

### TOURS
Xining's more upscale hotels have travel offices that can help you arrange expensive private tours with English-speaking guides to Kumbum Monastery or Bird Island. For less expensive tours, contact Tibetan Connections or consider the services of an enterprising individual like Niu Xiaojun, who speaks good English and has been leading foreigners to off-the-beaten-path destinations for years.

### ESSENTIALS
**Air Contact Xining Caojiabao Airport** (曹家堡机场 Cáo jiābǎo jichǎng). ⊠ 30 km (19 miles) east of Xining, Gao Zhai Xiang ☎ 0971/818–8222.

**Bus Contact Xining Main Bus Station** (西宁汽车站 Xíníng qìchēzhàn). ⊠ Jianguo Lu, south of the train station ☎ 0971/719–2222.

10

**Medical Assistance Qinghai People's Hospital** (西宁人民医院 *Xíníng rénmín yīyuàn*). ⊠ *143 Gonghe Lu* ☎ *0971/817–7911.*

**Train Contact Xining Railway Station** (西宁火车站 *Xíníng huǒchēzhàn*). ⊠ *Northern end of Jianguo Lu* ☎ *0971/814–9790* ⊕ *www.xnhcz.com.*

**Visitor and Tour Info Niu Xiaojun** ☎ *1319/579–1105.*

### EXPLORING

Although most travelers don't come to see Xining, there are a few sights in and around the city.

**Dongguan Mosque** (东关清真大寺 *Dōngguān qīngzhēn dàsì*). This is one of the largest mosques in all of China and illustrates the ethnic diversity of Xining. Built in the 14th century, its green and white dome and two tall minarets see some 40,000 to 50,000 people for Friday prayers. ⊠ *Dongguan Jie* 🏷 *Y10* ⏱ *Daily 8–noon and 2–5. Closed to tourists Fri. 10–noon.*

**North Monastery** (北禅寺 *Běi chán sì*). Xining's most important site is the Taoist North Monastery, at the northwest end of town. Construction on this series of mountainside cloisters and pavilions began more than 1,700 years ago during the Northern Wei. Climbing the stairs to the white pagoda at the top gives you a view of the entire city sprawled out beneath you. To get here, take a taxi. ⊠ *North end of Chanjiang Lu* 🏷 *Y10* ⏱ *Daily 8:30–6.*

### AROUND XINING

Fodor'sChoice ★ **Kumbum Monastery** (塔尔寺 *Tǎ'ěr sì*). The magnificent Kumbum Monastery lies 25 km (15 miles) southwest of Xining. One of the six great monasteries of the Tibetan Buddhist sect known as Yellow Hat—and reputedly the birthplace of the sect's founder, Tsong Khapa—construction began in 1560. A great reformer who lived in the early 1400s, Tsong Khapa formulated a new doctrine that stressed a return to monastic discipline, strict celibacy, and moral and philosophical thought over magic and mysticism. Tsong's followers have controlled Tibetan politics since the 17th century. Still a magnet for Tibetan pilgrims and, more recently, waves of tourists, Kumbum boasts a dozen prayer halls, an exhibition hall, and monks' quarters (look out for the yak butter sculptures). No photos are allowed. Public buses (Y6) to Huangzhong depart frequently from Zifang Jie Bus Station. Get off at the last stop and walk 2 km (1 mile) uphill, or take a put-put (Y2) to the monastery's gates. Taxis from Xining are Y30. ⊠ *Huangzhong* ☎ *0971/223–2357* ⊕ *www.kumbum. org* 🏷 *Y80* ⏱ *Daily 8–5.*

### WHERE TO EAT

$ ╳ **Black Tent** (黑帐篷藏吧 *Hēi zhàngpéng cángbā*). This place serves
INTERNATIONAL great Tibetan, Indian, and Nepali food. All of the workers are Tibetans from Amdo and are very friendly. The atmosphere is great. The menu

> **WORD OF MOUTH**
>
> "Luce Boulnois's history of the Silk Road has finally been translated from the French. Susan Whitfield's *Life Along the Silk Road* is a very readable collection of first-person accounts from individuals living at various points on the routes at different periods of its history."
> —PeterN_H

Wenshu Hall in the Kumbum Monastery.

is in Tibetan and English. Don't miss the momo dumplings. $ *Average main: Y40 ⊠ Wenhua Jie ☎ 0971/823–4029 ⊟ No credit cards.*

$$  ✕ **Casa Mia.** If you think it's impossible to get delicious wood-fired piz-
ITALIAN  zas or hearty pastas in Xining, think again. Managed by a local Chi-
nese woman, this eatery is financed by several European expats who
wanted a place to satisfy their cravings for Italian cooking. With free
wireless Internet and real espresso, the place is very popular among
expats. Menus are in English and Chinese, and the staff speak English.
$ *Average main: Y60 ⊠ 10–4 Wu Si Xi Lu ☎ 0971/631–5180 ⊟ No
credit cards.*

$$  ✕ **Jianyin Revolving Restaurant** (建银宾馆旋转餐厅 *Jiànyín bīnguǎn*
ASIAN  *xuánzhuǎn cāntīng*). Perched atop the 28-story Jianyin Hotel, this
slowly revolving restaurant may not serve the finest Asian cuisine, but
the food is really beside the point. People come here for the spectacular
views of the city. There's no minimum, so sipping a cup of tea while
enjoying the scenery or playing cards is perfectly acceptable. $ *Average
main: Y60 ⊠ Jianyin Hotel, 55 Xida Jie, southeast corner of the central
square ☎ 0971/826–1885 ⊟ No credit cards.*

## WHERE TO STAY

$  🏨 **Yinlong Hotel** (银龙酒店 *Yínlóng jiǔdiàn*). This ultramodern hotel is
HOTEL  considered the finest lodging between Xian and Ürümqi, but standards
seem to have fallen recently. **Pros:** central location; good-quality hotel
restaurants; Wi-Fi in rooms. **Cons:** expensive buffet breakfast; small
gym; dearth of English-speakers. $ *Rooms from: Y600 ⊠ 38 Huanghe
Lu, north side of the central square ☎ 0971/616–6666 ⊕ www.ylhotel.
net ⇆ 316 rooms ○ No meals.*

10

**SHOPPING**

Visitors interested in Tibetan handicrafts will want to stroll through Xining's excellent street markets.

**Jianguo Lu Wholesale Market** (建国路小商品批发市场 *Jiànguó lù xiǎo shāngpǐn pīfā shìchǎng*). This market sells everything from traditional Tibetan clothing to favorite local foods. ⊠ *Jianguo Lu, opposite the main bus station.*

**SIDE TRIP FROM XINING**

Fodor's Choice ★    **Bird Island** (鸟岛 *Niǎo dǎo*). Bird Island is the main draw at Qinghai Hu, China's largest inland saltwater lake. The name Bird Island is a misnomer: it was an island until the lake receded, connecting it to the shore. The electric-blue lake is surrounded by rolling hills covered with yellow rapeseed flowers. Tibetan shepherds graze their flocks here as wild yaks roam nearby. Beyond the hills are snowcapped mountains. An estimated 100,000 birds breed at Bird Island, including egrets, speckle-headed geese, and black-neck cranes; sadly, the numbers have been much depleted because of the country's efforts to suppress the spread of avian flu. There are two viewing sites: spend as little time as possible at Egg Island in favor of the much better Common Cormorant Island, where you can see birds flying at eye-level from the top of a cliff. The best months to see birds are May and June.

To get to Bird Island, either contact a tour agency or catch a tourist bus from Xining Railway Station for Y35 each way. If you opt for a tour, make sure that you're not headed to the much closer tourist trap known as Qinghai Hu 151. ⊠ *350 km (215 miles) northwest of Xining* ⊠ *Y115.*

# XINJIANG

The vast Xinjiang Uyghur Autonomous Region, covering more than 1.6 million square km (640,000 square miles), is China's largest province. Even more expansive than Alaska, it borders Mongolia, Russia, Kazakhstan, Kyrgyzstan, Tajikistan, Afghanistan, and Pakistan. Only 41% of Xinjiang's 21.8 million inhabitants are Han Chinese. About 43% are Uyghur (a people of Turkic origin), and the remainder are mostly Kazakhs, Hui, Kyrgyz, Mongols, and Tajiks.

Xinjiang gets very little rainfall except in the northern areas near Russia. It gets very cold in winter and very hot in summer, especially in the Turpan Basin, where temperatures often soar to 120°F. Visitors usually forgive the extreme weather, however, as they're charmed by the locals and awed by the rugged scenery, ranging from the endless sand dunes of the desert to the pastoral grasslands of the north.

Long important as a crossroads for trade with Europe and the Middle East, Xinjiang has nevertheless seldom come completely under Chinese control. For more than 2,000 years the region has been contested and divided by Turkic and Mongol tribes who—after setting up short-lived empires—soon disappeared beneath the shifting sands of time. In the 20th century, Uyghurs continued to resist Chinese rule, seizing power from a warlord governor in 1933 and claiming the land as a separate

republic, which they named East Turkestan. China tightened its grip after the 1949 revolution, however, encouraging Han settlers to emigrate to the province to dilute the Uyghur majority, thus increasing ethnic tensions. In the last few years these tensions have blown up into full-scale social unrest. In 2008 and 2009 Uyghurs took to the streets in Ürümqi, Kashgar, and Hotan, protesting that they were not free to practice their religious beliefs. More than 200 people were killed. Chinese authorities say that the vast majority of the dead were Han Chinese, while Uyghur groups claim that a significant proportion of the dead were demonstrators shot by the police. Tensions boiled over again in 2010, when a Uyghur man detonated explosives in a crowd of police officers, resulting in at least seven casualties.

Renewed unrest in 2012 once again meant tightened security in the area, but no travel restrictions on foreign tourists were imposed.

**DID YOU KNOW?** In the 1980s, archaeologists discovered dozens of tombs in various parts of Xinjiang, with bodies that had been buried for about 3,000 years yet remained remarkably preserved thanks to the arid desert climate. Many of the mummies, believed to be forefathers of the Uyghurs, had northern European features, including fair hair and skin.

The Xinjiang Uyghur Autonomous Region

### REGIONAL TOURS

**Uyghur Tour & Travel Center.** This excellent tour company based in Kashgar organizes tours of the Silk Road, as well as more unusual destinations like traditional Uyghur villages. It can arrange cars to take you along the Karakorum Highway at prices significantly lower than the competition, and goes out of its way to tailor tours to your requirements. ✉ *Qinibagh Hotel, 144 Seman Lu, Kashgar* ☎ *0998/298–1073* ⊕ *www.uighurtour.com.*

**CYTS.** Based in Ürümqi, this English-speaking tour agency offers interesting tailor-made tours to sights across the province, from two-day tours to Heavenly Lake to multistop trips to Turpan and Kashgar. ✉ *Bogda Hotel, 10 Guangming Lu, Ürümqi* ☎ *0991/232–1170.*

## ÜRÜMQI

*35 hrs (3200 km [1988 miles]) by train, 4 hrs by plane northwest of Beijing.*

Xinjiang's capital and largest city, Ürümqi is at the geographic center of Asia, and has the distinction of being the most landlocked city in the world. It's a new city by Chinese standards, little more than barracks for Qing Dynasty troops when it was built in 1763. Once a sleepy trading post, Ürümqi has grown to be a sprawling city, with more than 2.7 million inhabitants. Yet despite this modernization, Ürümqi manages to conjure up the past, especially in the Uyghur-populated area near the International Grand Bazaar.

**GETTING HERE AND AROUND**

AIR TRAVEL Many people fly to Ürümqi from Beijing, Shanghai, Hong Kong, or Xian to begin a journey on the Silk Road. The airport is 20 km (12 miles) north of the downtown area, and can be reached in about 30 minutes by taxi (Y50). Shuttle buses are Y15.

BUS TRAVEL Long-distance buses are often the only way to travel in Xinjiang if you don't want to wait a day or two for the next available train. Every city in the region is served at least daily by buses from Ürümqi. There's even bus service to Almaty, Kazakhstan.

**WHAT TIME IS IT?**

A constant source of confusion for travelers in Xinjiang is figuring out the time. Uyghurs often refer to unofficial Xinjiang time, whereas Han Chinese use standard Beijing time. If in doubt, ask. No matter what time is spoken, you can count on everything in Xinjiang starting two hours later than in Beijing. That is, lunch in Kashgar is usually eaten at 2 pm Beijing time.

It's usually a straightforward affair buying tickets from the only station in town, but Ürümqi is more complicated. Unless you're going to Hotan or Altai—which have their own separate bus stations—your best bet is to first look for tickets at Nianzigou Station. If you don't like what's available there, or if your destination is Kashgar or Turpan, head to the South Station (Nanjiao Qichezhan).

Buses (Y25 each way) leave for Heavenly Lake (Tianchi Hu) at 9 am from the north gate of Renmin Park. They usually leave the lake at 6 pm and arrive back in Ürümqi at 7:30 pm. Be careful to get on a regular bus rather than a tour bus that will take you to minor attractions on the way, limiting your time at the lake.

TRAIN TRAVEL Those arriving by train will find themselves about 2 km (1 mile) southwest of the city center.

**MONEY MATTERS**

In China, there's no place more difficult to run out of money than in off-the-beaten-track Xinjiang. ⚠ There are ATMs in Ürümqi and Kashgar, and all accept international credit cards and debit cards. Most banks will also exchange currency and traveler's checks.

**SAFETY AND PRECAUTIONS**

There remains a heavy police presence after the unrest in 2012. Tourists may be stopped by security personnel, but there are no travel restrictions. And as always, be sure to secure your valuables when in public places.

**TIMING**

While there is plenty to see in Ürümqi, it's fair to say that Xinjiang's best attractions are out of the capital. If the clock is ticking, spend no more than two days enjoying Ürümqi's sights before heading further afield.

**TOURS**

Ürümqi is a popular place to begin a tour of Xinjiang's vast desert expanses. Travel agencies are happy to let you pick and choose from a list of destinations. A four-wheel-drive vehicle will cost around Y1,300 per day.

10

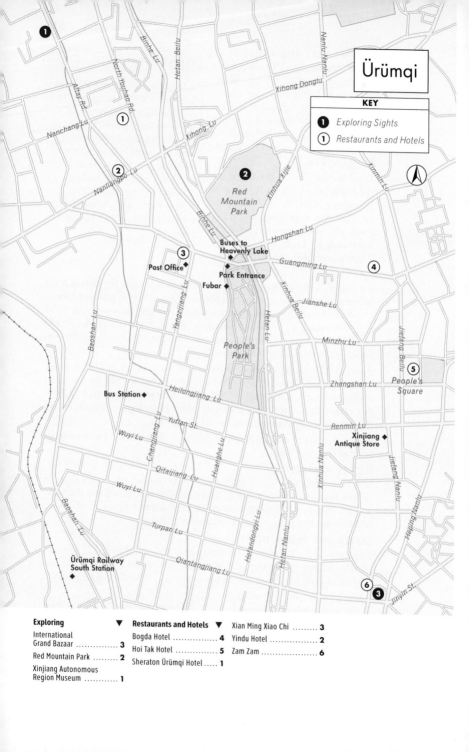

## Ürümqi

**KEY**

- **1** Exploring Sights
- (1) Restaurants and Hotels

Red Mountain Park

Buses to Heavenly Lake

Post Office

Park Entrance

Fubar

People's Park

Bus Station

People's Square

Xinjiang Antique Store

Ürümqi Railway South Station

| Exploring ▼ | Restaurants and Hotels ▼ | Xian Ming Xiao Chi ......... **3** |
|---|---|---|
| International Grand Bazaar ............. **3** | Bogda Hotel ................ **4** | Yindu Hotel ................. **2** |
| Red Mountain Park ........ **2** | Hoi Tak Hotel .............. **5** | Zam Zam ..................... **6** |
| Xinjiang Autonomous Region Museum ............ **1** | Sheraton Ürümqi Hotel ..... **1** | |

**CLOSE UP**

# China's Muslims

**UYGHUR**

The Muslim Turkic people known as Uyghurs (pronounced "WEE-grs") are one of China's largest—and in the eyes of Beijing, most troublesome—minority groups. Uyghurs mostly live in northwest China's Xinjiang, an "autonomous region" that is one of the most tightly controlled parts of the country after Tibet. Uyghurs are descendants of nomadic Turkic Central Asian tribes. Their language, food, music, dance, clothing, and other customs have little or no relation to those found elsewhere in China. Yet despite a population of nearly 10 million people, most foreigners have never heard of them or their troubled independence movement. Protests and occasional violence in the region during the late 1990s brought a severe crackdown from Beijing; limits were placed on religious education and hundreds of suspected Uyghur separatists were executed. The attacks of September 11, 2001, gave the Chinese government further leverage to oppress Uyghurs in the name of fighting terrorism.

**HUI**

Identifiable by their brimless white caps and headscarves, the Hui are descendants of Middle Eastern traders who came to China via the Silk Road, settling down with Chinese wives after their conversion to Islam. Over a thousand years' time, the Middle Eastern influence on the Hui appearance became diluted, but it is still very easy to distinguish between the different facial features of the Hui and Han Chinese. Because of cultural differences associated with their Islamic faith, the Hui tend to associate with others in their largely Muslim neighborhoods. The Hui reject eating several kinds of meat that can be popular with Han Chinese, including pork, horse, dog, and several types of birds. In what could be seen as a form of respect by the business-savvy Han Chinese, the Hui are generally considered to be shrewd businesspeople, perhaps a nod to their being descendants of foreign traders.

10

CLOSE UP

# The Jade Road

The residents of Xinjiang are apt to point out that the Silk Road isn't the first road they knew. That honor goes to the "Jade Road," which was established nearly 7,000 years ago. Running from Hotan into today's Qinghai and Gansu provinces, the Jade Road was the artery for Xinjiang's legendary white jade trade. Primarily mined from the Hotan River, Xinjiang jade comes in a number of hues, although small white stones with a reddish-brown exterior are the most highly valued.

Sensuous and smooth to the touch, this "lamb's fat jade" is cloudy with translucent qualities. Chinese emperors have craved it for centuries. Good places to hunt around for all manner of jade in Ürümqi include the swirling International Grand Bazaar and the Xinjiang Antique Store.

Visitors who wish to know more about this region's heady history of jade, silk, and more should visit the Xinjiang Autonomous Region Museum. Here's a quick tip: buy fast. The availability of quality jade has dropped in recent years, and scientists fear the precious stone is being mined to exhaustion.

## ESSENTIALS

**Air Contacts** Ürümqi Airport (乌鲁木齐地窝堡国际机场 *Wūlūmùqíde wōbǎo guójì jīchǎng*). ⊠ *16 km (10 miles) northwest of Ürümqi, Diwopu* ☎ *0991/380–1949* ⊕ *www.xjairport.com.*

**Bank** Bank of China ⊠ *343 Jiefang Nan Lu, at the corner of Minzhu Lu, behind the Hoi Tak Hotel* ☎ *0991/283–4222.*

**Bus Contacts** Ürümqi Nianzigou Station (乌鲁木齐碾子沟 客运站 *Wūlūmùqí niǎnzigōu kèyùn zhàn*). ⊠ *Western end of Heilongjiang Lu* ☎ *0991/587–8898, 0991/528–2443.* Ürümqi South Station (乌鲁木齐南郊 客运站 *Wūlūmùqí nánjiāo kèyùnzhàn*). ⊠ *Yanerwo Lu* ☎ *0991/286–6635.*

**Internet** Dragon Netbar ⊠ *190 Wuyi Lu.*

**Medical Assistance** Chinese Medicine Hospital of Ürümqi (乌鲁木齐市中 医院 *Wūlūmùqí shìzhōng yīyuàn*). ⊠ *60 Youhao Nan Lu* ☎ *0991/452–0963.*

**Train Contact** Ürümqi Train Station (乌鲁木齐火车站 *Wūlūmùqí huǒchēzhàn*). ⊠ *Qiantangjiang Lu* ☎ *0991/581–4203.*

**Visitor and Tour Info** Grassland Travel Service ⊠ *2 Renmin Gongyuan Bei Jie, southwest of People's Park entrance* ☎ *0991/584–1116.*

## EXPLORING

**International Grand Bazaar** (国际大巴扎 *Guójì dàbāzhā*). The streets around the bazaar were once full of donkey carts and flocks of sheep. Men in embroidered skullcaps and women in heavy brown wool veils remain, and the whole area maintains the bustling atmosphere of a Central Asian street market. You can bargain for Uyghur crafts, such as decorated knives, colorful silks, and carved jade. Small shops are tucked into every nook and cranny. The international bazaar itself has been heavily expanded, and now includes a newly built minaret, which you can climb for Y20. The stalls, while interesting enough, are aimed firmly at tourists; more authentic options are the streets nearby that are filled with traditional ironmongers and Islamic butcher shops. ⊠ *Jiefang Lu, 3 km (2 miles) south of the city center.*

**Red Mountain Park** (红山公园 *Hóngshān gōngyuán*). This park gives you a picture-perfect view of the snowcapped Heavenly Mountains. An array of incongruously grouped objects—including an eight-story pagoda built by the emperor in 1788 to suppress an evil dragon—are reached via a long set of stairs. Arrive in the early evening for the pleasure of seeing the cityscape bathed in the setting sun's golden light. Ignore the cheap carnival rides near the entrance. The park is hard to find, and few tourists venture here, so take a taxi. ⊠ *Off Hongshan Lu* ☎ *991/885–5671* 🎫 *Free* ☾ *Daily 6 am–11 pm.*

Fodor's Choice ★ **Xinjiang Autonomous Region Museum** (新疆自治区博物馆 *Xīnjiāng zìzhìqū bówùguǎn*). Don't miss the perfectly preserved mummies at this superb museum, located 4 km (2½ miles) northwest of the city center. The mummies—including the 4,000-year-old Beauty of Loulan—were excavated from tombs in various parts of Xinjiang. In addition, the museum has a well-executed exhibition on the region's ethnic minorities. If you are lucky, one of the museum's English-speaking guides will accompany you. There's no extra charge, and it's well worth asking. ⊠ *132 Xibei Lu, 1 block west of the Sheraton Hotel* ☎ *0991/453–4453* 🎫 *Free* ☾ *Weekdays 10–6.*

## WHERE TO EAT

Ürümqi is a good place to have your first taste of Uyghur cuisine. For cheap eats and a great scene, the Wuyi night market is best.

$
CHINESE
✗ **Xian Ming Xiao Chi** (西安名小吃 *Xī'ān míng xiǎochī*). If you need a change from Uyghur fare, this cheap and cheerful fast-food joint offers tasty snacks from Xian. Do as the locals do when the temperature rises: try a cooling plateful of cold noodles with cucumber called *liang pi.* Say *bu la* if you don't want your noodles to be spicy. Other specialties include *rou jia mo,* or Chinese-style pork burgers—made from a meat rarely served in this part of the world. Ⓢ *Average main: Y30* ⊠ *33 Yangzi Jiang Lu* ▭ *No credit cards.*

$
NORTHERN
CHINESE
✗ **Zam Zam.** Near the International Bazaar, this smart Uyghur eatery looks as though it should be very pricey. The ornate room is outfitted with carved wood and Arabic-style arches, and the staff is smartly attired. The excellent food is the best bargain in town. Few of the waiters speak Mandarin, let alone English, but there is a picture menu: point to the pilaf or the lamb dumplings. No alcohol is served. Ⓢ *Average main: Y30* ⊠ *423 Heping Nan Lu* ☎ *0991/843–0555* ▭ *No credit cards.*

## WHERE TO STAY

$
HOTEL
🏨 **Bogda Hotel** (博格达宾馆 *Bógédá bīnguǎn*). A good budget option, this hotel has rooms that are cleaner and more comfortable than those offered in similarly priced lodgings. **Pros:** good selection of tours available; convenient to banks and restaurants. **Cons:** noisy lobby; little English spoken. Ⓢ *Rooms from: Y300* ⊠ *10 Guangming Lu* ☎ *0991/886–3910* 🖷 *0991/886–5769* 🛏 *248 rooms* ▭ *No credit cards* ⊠ *Breakfast.*

10

$ HOTEL Fodor's Choice ★ 🏨 **Hoi Tak Hotel** (信达海德酒店 *Xìndá hǎidé jiǔdiàn*). Popular with Chinese tour groups and Hong Kong business travelers, this gleaming white tower offers first-rate views of the snowcapped Tian Shan Mountains. **Pros:** the staff speak English; rooms are good value. **Cons:** not near any attractions or good restaurants. [$] *Rooms from: Y700* ✉ *1 Dongfeng Lu, west side of People's Square* ☎ *0991/232–2828* 🌐 *www.hoitakhotel.com* 🛏 *318 rooms, 38 suites* 🍴 *No meals.*

$$$ HOTEL 🏨 **Sheraton Ürümqi Hotel** (喜来登酒店 *Xǐláidēng jiǔdiàn*). Very popular with both well-heeled business and leisure travelers, this luxury hotel pampers you with an indoor pool illuminated with skylights and a fitness room with the latest generation of equipment. **Pros:** keen staff; rooms have great bathrooms; great gym. **Cons:** inconvenient for Ürümqi's sights. [$] *Rooms from: Y1200* ✉ *669 Youhao Bei Lu* ☎ *0991/699–9999* 🌐 *www.starwoodhotels.com* 🛏 *398 rooms, 22 suites* 🍴 *No meals.*

$$ HOTEL 🏨 **Yindu Hotel** (银都酒店 *Yíndū jiǔdiàn*). Xinjiang's finest hotel, the Yindu is testament to the influx of cash that has transformed Ürümqi over the past decade. **Pros:** comfortable rooms. **Cons:** bad location for exploring the sights. [$] *Rooms from: Y700* ✉ *3179 Xihong Xi Lu* ☎ *0991/453–6688* 🌐 *www.yinduhotel.com* 🛏 *308 rooms* 🍴 *Breakfast.*

## NIGHTLIFE

As with most Chinese cities, every other block in Ürümqi is blighted by high-price karaoke parlors and blaring discos. But there are plenty of quieter places to order a bottle of cold beer, with the best options on Renmin Gongyuan Bei Jie, where there is also a selection of gay bars.

**Fubar** (福吧 *Fú ba*). Fubar is the real thing: a tavern serving imported beer and authentic pub grub. The pizza is especially noteworthy, as are the fish-and-chips. This is the best place in Ürümqi to relax after a day exploring the city. The owners are happy to dispense free travel advice. ✉ *40 Renmin Gongyuan Bei Jie* ☎ *0991/584–4498* 🌐 *www.fubar.com.cn.*

Fodor's Choice ★ **International Grand Bazaar Banquet Performance Theater** (国际大巴扎宴艺大剧院 *Guójì dàbā zhāyànyì dàjùyuàn*). This entertaining song-and-dance performance is preceded by a ho-hum buffet that unsuccessfully tries to capture the delights of Uyghur cuisine. Never mind the food, as this is your best chance to see Uyghur, Uzbek, Kazakh, Tajik, Tartar, and even Irish dancing all in one spectacular evening. Make reservations through your hotel. ✉ *Jiefang Lu, 3 km (2 mi) south of the city center* ☎ *0991/855–6000* 🎫 *Y298.*

## SHOPPING

The International Grand Bazaar is the best place to go for Uyghur items like embroidered skullcaps, brightly colored carpets, and hand-carved knives. If it's inexpensive gifts you're after, you will find them.

**Xinjiang Antique Store** (新疆古玩店 *Xīnjiāng gǔwàndiàn*). This shop has a good selection of genuine antique Chinese bric-a-brac, including jade, jewelry, carpets, and porcelain. As all items come with a state-certified export certificate, you won't have to worry about getting your purchase through customs. There is a smaller branch inside the Xinjiang Autonomous Region Museum. ✉ *325 Jiefang Nan Lu, south of Renmin Lu* ☎ *0991/282–5161.*

### SIDE TRIP FROM ÜRÜMQI

Fodor's Choice ★ **Heavenly Lake** (天池 *Tiānchí*). After a three-hour ride from Ürümqi you'll reach what is quite possibly the prettiest lake in China, surrounded by snow-sprinkled mountains. The water is crystal clear with a sapphire tint. In summer, white flowers dot the hillsides. Unfortunately, tourism is leaving its ugly footprint. The lake's southern shore is crowded with tour groups posing for snapshots with Mount Bogda in the background. To better appreciate the lake's natural beauty, arrive before the hordes, or stay until after the last bus has departed.

Kazakh families still set up traditional felt tents along the shores of Heavenly Lake from early May to late October, bringing their horses, sheep, and cashmere goats. The Kazakh people have a long history as horse breeders and are known to be skilled riders.

From Ürümqi, day-tour buses (Y25 each way after bargaining plus Y100 entrance fee to the lake) to Heavenly Lake leave at 9 am from a small street beside the north gate of People's Park *(Renmin Gongyuan)*. You'll have from about noon to 6 to explore the lake, arriving back in the city at 8 pm. Tickets—usually available up until the bus leaves—can be purchased near the buses. ✉ *Apr.–Oct. Y100; Nov.–Mar. Y40.*

## TURPAN

*2½–3 hrs (184 km [114 miles]) by bus southeast of Ürümqi.*

Turpan, which means "the lowest place" in Uyghur, lies in a desert basin at the southern foot of the Heavenly Mountains. Part of the basin lies 505 feet below sea level, the hottest spot in China and the second-lowest point in the world after the Dead Sea. In summer, temperatures can soar to more than 50°C (120°F), so come prepared with lots of water and sunscreen.

Turpan's claim to fame is its location between the ruins of two spectacular ancient cities, Jiaohe and Gaochang. Most visitors don't linger in Turpan; the best five sites can easily be visited in a single day. But there are other attractions. Surrounded by some of the richest farmland in Xinjiang, Turpan's vineyards are famous for producing several varieties of candy-sweet raisins popular throughout China.

### GETTING HERE AND AROUND

Too close to Ürümqi to have its own airport, Turpan is an inconvenient 60 km (38 miles) south of the nearest train station in Daheyan. A high-speed train link to the town itself is under construction, but no date has been given for its completion. If you arrive by train, head to the city via a taxi (Y40) or public bus (Y7.50). The bus trip from Ürümqi takes 2½ hours. Buses leave every 25 minutes from 7:30 am to 8:30 pm, and cost Y40. The terminal is in the center of town on the north side of Laocheng Lu.

10

Leaving Turpan is more difficult than arriving: one bus daily departs at noon for Kashgar. For any other destination, you'll have to head back to Ürümqi.

**SAFETY AND PRECAUTIONS**

The harsh, dry climate is probably the biggest danger; temperatures here have reached 50°C (122°F) in the height of summer, and have fallen to -28.9°C (-18,4°F) in winter. Drink plenty of water in hot months, slather on that sunscreen, and stay in the shade.

**TIMING**

An overnight stay is enough to see the sights that lie on the outskirts of town.

**TOURS**

You could join an organized group tour around Turpan, but you'll likely spend too much time in annoying tourist traps. With a slightly more expensive taxi tour you can choose your own itinerary and spend hours roaming the ruins of Jiaohe and Gaochang. In the off-season you may be able to secure a taxi for the day for as little as Y150, although prices of Y250 are more common during the summer.

**ESSENTIALS**

**Bus Contact Turpan Bus Station** (吐鲁番汽车站 *Tǔlǔfān qìchēzhàn*). ⊠ *27 Laocheng Lu* ☎ *0995/853–5818.*

**Train Contact Daheyan Train Station** (大河沿火车站 *Dà héyán huǒchē zhàn*). ⊠ *Huoche Zhan Lu, Daheyan* ☎ *0995/864–2233.*

**Visitor and Tour Info CITS** ⊠ *Jiaotong Hotel, 125 Laocheng Lu* ☎ *0995/852–1352* ⊕ *www.xinjiangtour.com.*

**EXPLORING**

**Karez Irrigation System** (坎儿井灌溉系统 *Kǎn'erjǐng guàngài xìtǒng*). The remarkable 2,000-year-old system allowed the desert cities of the Silk Road to flourish despite an unrelentingly arid environment. In the oasis cities of Turpan and Hami, 1,600 km (990 miles) of underground tunnels brought water—moved only by gravity—from melting snow at the base of the Heavenly Mountains. You can view the tunnels at several sites around the city. Most tour guides take visitors to the largely educational Karez Irrigation Museum. Despite being described as the "underground Great Wall," most visitors are completely underwhelmed by what are essentially narrow dirt tunnels. ⊠ *888 Xincheng Lu, on the city's western outskirts* ⊠ *Y40* ☉ *Daily 8–7.*

**Sugong Mosque** (苏公塔 / 额敏塔 *Sūtǎ gōng/Émǐn tǎ*). Sugong Mosque and the adjacent **Emin Tower** form Turpan's most recognizable image, often featured in tourist brochures. Built in 1777, it commemorates a military commander who suppressed a rebellion by a group of aristocrats. The 141-foot conical tower is elegantly spare, with bricks arranged in 15 patterns. The sunbaked roof of the mosque affords a view of the surrounding lush vineyards. You have to pay an extra Y25 if you wish to climb the minaret. This complex lies 4 km (2½ miles) from the city center at the southeast end of town. To get here, head east on Laocheng Lu and turn right on the last paved road before you reach farmland. ⊠ *Off Laocheng Lu* ⊠ *Y50* ☉ *Daily 8–8.*

The Thousand Buddha Caves outside of Turpan

## AROUND TURPAN

Fodor's Choice ★ **Bezeklik Thousand Buddha Caves** (柏孜克里克千佛洞 *Bǎizī kèlǐ kèqiān fúdòng*). In a breathtaking valley inside the Flaming Mountains is this ancient temple complex, built between the 5th and 9th century by slaves whose entire lives went into the construction. Many of the fine examples of Buddhist sculpture and wall frescoes were destroyed after Islam came to the region in the 13th century. Other sculptures and frescoes, including several whole murals of Buddhist monks, were removed by 20th-century archaeologists like German Albert von Le Coq, who shipped his finds back to Berlin. Although they remain a feat of early engineering, the caves are in atrocious condition. Go just to see the site itself and the surrounding valley, which is magnificent. The views of the scorched, lunar landscape leading up to the site, which clings to one flank of a steep, scenic valley, make the trip worth the effort. Avoid the nearby Buddha Cave constructed in 1980 by a local artist; it isn't worth an additional Y20. ⊠ *35 km (22 miles) east of Turpan* ☎ *995/852–3774* ☞ *Y40* ⊘ *Dawn–dusk*.

Fodor's Choice ★ **City of Gaochang** (高昌故城 *Gāochāng gùchéng*). These fascinating city ruins lie in a valley south of the Flaming Mountains. Legend has it that a group of soldiers stopped here in the 1st century BC on their way to Afghanistan, found that water was plentiful, and decided to stay. By the 7th century the city was the capital of the kingdom of Gaochang, which ruled more than 21 other towns, and by the 9th century the Uyghurs had moved into the area from Mongolia, establishing the kingdom of Kharakojam. In the 14th century Mongols destroyed the kingdom, leaving only the ruins seen today. Only the city walls and a

10

partially preserved monastery surrounded by muted, almost unrecognizable crumbling buildings remain, an eerie and haunting excursion into the pages of history. Despite repeated plundering of the site, in the early 1900s German archaeologists were able to unearth manuscripts, statues, and frescoes in superb condition. To make the best of your time here, take a donkey cart (time to use your bargaining skills—Y20 is a fair price) to the monastery in the rear right corner; from there you can walk back toward the entrance through the ruins. It's best to go early, as there is little shade. ⊠ *30 km (19 miles) east of Turpan* ☎ *995/869–3178* 🌐 *Y60* ☾ *Dawn–dusk.*

Fodor'sChoice
★

**City of Jiaohe** (交河故城 *Jiāohé gùchéng*). On an island at the confluence of two rivers, these impressive ruins lie in the Yarnaz Valley west of Turpan. The city, established as a garrison during the Han Dynasty, was built on a high plateau, protected by the natural fortification of cliffs rising 100 feet above the rivers. Jiaohe was governed from the 2nd to the 7th century by the kingdom of Gaochang, and occupied later by Tibetans. Despite destruction in the 14th century by Mongol hordes, large fragments of actual streets and buildings remain, including a Buddhist monastery and Buddhist statues, a row of bleached pagodas, a 29-foot observation tower, and a prison. Guards will make sure you stay on the marked paths. Arrive as early as possible, as there is little shade. ⊠ *8 km (5 miles) west of Turpan* 🌐 *Y40* ☾ *Dawn–dusk.*

### WHERE TO EAT

Most visitors stick to the restaurants in and around the Turpan Hotel on Qingnian Lu, a pleasant side street shaded by grape vines. The bazaar across from the bus station is a good place to grab lunch for around Y10. A lively night market with rows of kebab and spicy hotpot stands is on Gaochang Lu, a 10-minute walk north from the Turpan Hotel, next to the huge public square and near the China Post building.

$$
AMERICAN

✕ **John's Information Café.** Part of a small family-run chain that operates in destinations along the Silk Road, this popular tourist hangout is far from authentic, but people flock here for the familiar Western fare and rock-solid travel advice. The tours are good, but check carefully to see what is included. The place can also rent bikes and wash laundry. Ⓢ *Average main: Y50* ⊠ *Qingnian Lu, rear of the Turpan Hotel* ☎ *0998/258–1186* ⊕ *www.johncafe.net* ▬ *No credit cards.*

$$
NORTHERN
CHINESE

✕ **Muslim Restaurant** (清真餐厅 *Qīngzhēn cāntīng*). Like most hotel restaurants in the region, this one is poorly lighted and lacks ambience, but it does have a hearty variety of standard Uyghur dishes: lamb, noodles, and vegetables. Ⓢ *Average main: Y50* ⊠ *Turpan Hotel, 2 Qingnian Nan Lu* ☎ *099/852–2301* ▬ *No credit cards.*

### WHERE TO STAY

$
HOTEL

🏠 **Jiaotong Hotel** (交通宾馆 *Jiāotōng bīnguǎn*). This budget option isn't a bad place to stay, despite noise from the bus station in the rear and the bazaar across the street. **Pros:** bargain rates; convenient for early buses. **Cons:** bad water pressure; occasional power outages. Ⓢ *Rooms from: Y238* ⊠ *230 Laocheng Xi Lu, next to the bus station* ☎ *0995/625–8008* ⤳ *67 rooms* ▬ *No credit cards* ⦿ *No meals.*

$ HOTEL **Turpan Hotel** (吐鲁番宾馆 *Tŭlŭfān bīnguăn*). This study in basic geometry, covered in white tile, has seen better days, but rooms are relatively clean and large, the restaurant is quite good, and the gift shops are handy. **Pros:** offers good discounts; friendly staff. **Cons:** if you can't get a discount, better values are available elsewhere; Chinese breakfast options only. [$] *Rooms from: Y260* ✉ *2 Qingnian Nan Lu, south of Laocheng Lu* ☎ *0995/852–2301* 🛏 *219 rooms, 5 suites* 🍴 *No meals.*

## KASHGAR

*24 hrs (1,588 km [987 miles]) by train or 1½ hours by plane southwest of Ürümqi.*

Kashgar, the westernmost city in China, is closer to Baghdad than Beijing. More than 3,400 km (2,100 miles) west of the capital, the city has been a center of trade between China and the outside world for at least 2,000 years. Today Kashgar is a hub for merchants coming in over the Khunjerab Pass from Pakistan and the Torugart Pass from Kyrgyzstan. When these two treacherous mountain passes are open from May to October, Kashgar becomes a particularly colorful city, abuzz not only with curious Western tourists but also with visitors from every corner of Central Asia.

Despite an increasing Han presence in central Kashgar (symbolized by one of the largest Mao statues in the country), the city is still overwhelmingly Uyghur. A great deal of modernization has taken place here since the railway from Ürümqi arrived in 1999. Beijing is showering attention and money to boost the local economy and placate Kashgar's Uyghur population. There are still occasional clashes, and in 2008 Uyghurs killed more than a dozen police officers. This led to a heavy security presence that remains today.

Much of the city's Uyghur architecture has been demolished, but there are still some traditional houses with ornately painted balconies, as well as large remaining sections of the Old City. Most visitors come to Kashgar for the amazing Sunday Market, the largest bazaar in Central Asia and one of the best photo-ops in all of China.



### GETTING HERE AND AROUND

Daunted by the long train journey from Ürümqi, many tourists headed for Kashgar travel by air. The airport is 13 km (8 miles) north of the city center; a taxi to your hotel shouldn't cost more than Y30, and shuttle buses are Y15. Trains between Ürümqi and Kashgar (25 or 32 hours) depart three times a day; the slow train is half the price of the fast train, but you'll have to do without air-conditioning. The train station is 10 km (6 miles) east of town, not far from the livestock market. Taxis from here cost about Y15. Kashgar's long-distance bus station is just east of People's Park in the center of town, although many buses arriving in the city will stop somewhere less convenient to drop you off.

### SAFETY AND PRECAUTIONS

Tensions between local Uyghurs and Han Chinese remain, but tourists are not subject to any travel restrictions.

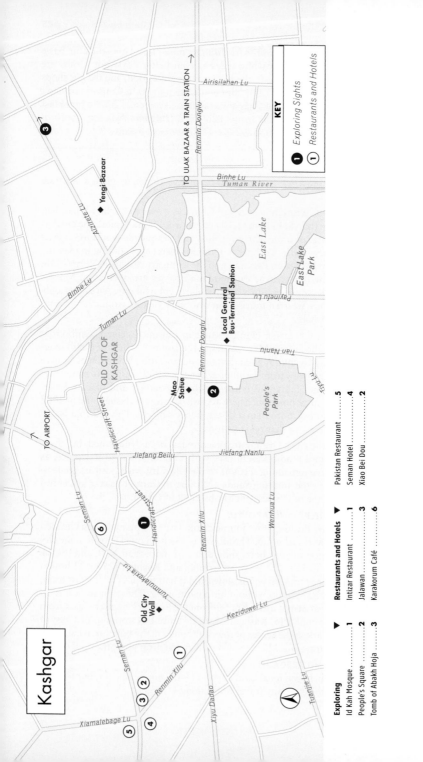

Kashgar

KEY
● Exploring Sights
① Restaurants and Hotels

Exploring ▶
Id Kah Mosque .............. 1
People's Square ............ 2
Tomb of Abakh Hoja ........ 3

Restaurants and Hotels ▶
Intizar Restaurant .......... 1
Jalawan ................... 3
Karakorum Café ............ 6

Pakistan Restaurant ........ 5
Seman Hotel ............... 4
Xiao Bei Dou .............. 2

**TIMING**

Allow two or three days if possible, and try to time your stay to include the famous Sunday market.

**TOURS**

Kashgar is a tourist-friendly city, so you shouldn't have any trouble arranging tours. Uyghur Tour and Travel Center, in the lobby of the Overseas Chinese Hotel, offers a "money-back guarantee." It has received high marks from travelers for years. A day tour of sites within Kashgar will cost about Y400, not including admission tickets. If you're interested in spending a night in the area's only 1,000-star hotel—the Taklamakan Desert—the agency can arrange an all-inclusive overnight camel trek for Y850 per person.

**ESSENTIALS**

**Air Contact Kashgar Airport** (喀什机场 *Kāshí jīchǎng*). ⊠ *13 km (8 miles) north of the city center* ☎ *0998/282–3204.*

**Bus Contact Kashgar Bus Station** (喀什汽车站 *Kāshi qìchēzhàn*). ⊠ *Tiannan Lu, east side of People's Park* ☎ *0998/282–5208.*

**Police Kashgar Police** ⊠ *139 Yumulakexiehai Lu, south of the Qinibagh Hotel* ☎ *0998/282–2028.*

**Medical Assistance No. 1 People's Hospital** (喀什地区第一人民医院 *Kāshi dìqū dì yī rénmín yīyuàn*). ⊠ *Jichang Lu* ☎ *0998/296–2750* ⊕ *www. xjkshospital.com.*

**Train Contact Kashgar Train Station** (喀什火车站 *Kāshi huǒchēzhàn*). ⊠ *Kashi Huoche Zhan* ☎ *0998/256–1298.*

**Visitor and Tour Info CITS** ⊠ *Qinibagh Hotel, 144 Seman Lu* ☎ *0998/298–3156* ⊕ *www.xinjiangtour.com.* **Uyghur Tour and Travel Center** ⊠ *Qinibagh Hotel, 144 Seman Lu, at Renmin Lu* ☎ *0998/298–1073* ⊕ *www.uighurtour.com.*

**EXPLORING**

**Id Kah Mosque** (艾提朵尔清真寺 *Àitíduǒěr qīngzhēn sì*). Start your tour of the city with a visit to the center of Muslim life in Kashgar. One of the largest mosques in China, the ornate structure of yellow bricks is the result of many extensions and renovations to the original mosque, built in 1442 as a prayer hall for the ruler of Kashgar. The main hall has a ceiling with fine wooden carvings and precisely 100 carved wooden columns. When services aren't being held, you are free to wander the quiet shaded grounds and even to enter the prayer hall. As this is an active site of worship, dress modestly. ⊠ *Ai Teaser Guangchang* ☐ *Y20* ⊙ *Dawn–dusk.*

**10**

**People's Square** (人民广场 *Rénmín guǎngchǎng*). If you happen to forget which country Kashgar is in, chances are you aren't standing in this square. A statue of Mao Zedong—one of the largest in China—stands with his right arm raised in perpetual salute. The statue is evidence of an unspoken rule in China that directly relates the size of a Mao tribute to its distance from Beijing; the only Mao statue larger than this one is in Tibet. ⊠ *Renmin Lu, between JieFang Nan Lu and Tian Lu.*

**Tomb of Abakh Hoja** (香妃墓 *Xiāng fēi mù*). About 5 km (3 miles) northeast of the city lies one of the most sacred sites in Xinjiang. The sea-green tiled hall that houses the tomb—actually about two dozen tombs—is part of a massive complex of sacred Islamic structures built around 1640. Uyghurs named the tomb and surrounding complex after Abakh Hoja, an Islamic missionary believed to be a descendant of Mohammed, who ruled Kashgar and outlying regions in the 17th century. Excavations of the glazed-brick tombs indicate that the first occupant was Abakh Hoja's father, who is buried here along with Abakh Hoja and many of their descendants.

The Han, who prefer to emphasize the site's historical connection to their dynastic empire, call it the Tomb of the Fragrant Concubine. When the grandniece of Abakh Hoja was chosen as concubine by the Qing ruler Qianlong in Beijing, Uyghur legend holds that she committed suicide rather than submit to the emperor. In the Han story, she dutifully went to Beijing and spent 30 years in the emperor's palace, then asked to be buried in her homeland. Either way, her alleged tomb was excavated in the 1980s and found to be empty. The tomb is a bit difficult to locate, so take a taxi. ⊠ *Off Aizirete Lu, 2 km (1 mile) east of the Sunday Bazaar* 🎫 *Y30* ⊙ *Daily 8–5.*

## WHERE TO EAT

$ ✕ **Intizar Restaurant** (银提扎尔快餐厅 *Yíntízhā'ěr kuài cāntīng*). Frequented by locals and outfitted with wooden paneling and chandeliers, Intizar is the most formal of Kashgar's Uyghur restaurants. It offers a range of the great cuisine, and the menu is translated into English, including helpful descriptions of each dish. For those tired of typical Uyghur fare, Muslim-friendly stir-fry dishes are also available. Alcohol is not allowed on the premises. Ⓢ *Average main: Y30* ⊠ *33 Renmin Xi Lu, southeast of the Seman Hotel* ☎ *0998/258–5666* ▭ *No credit cards.*

NORTHERN CHINESE

Fodor'sChoice ★

$ ✕ **Jalawan** (吉乌兰美食 *Jíwū án měishí*). It's very easy to join the crowds of locals relaxing at this restaurant, especially underneath the (admittedly) fake trellises of grapes around a fountain. The staff will hand you an English-language menu whose prices are a few yuan higher than on the Chinese-language menu. But when it's all so cheap, you can't complain too much. Try the *lao hu cai*, or tiger salad, an evocatively named dish of cucumber, chilies and tomatoes, or the pilaf with a cooling bowl of yogurt. Ⓢ *Average main: Y30* ⊠ *Seman Lu, on the roundabout opposite the Seman Hotel* ☎ *0998/258–1001* ▭ *No credit cards.*

NORTHERN CHINESE

$$ ✕ **Karakorum Café** (喀拉昆仑咖啡厅 *Kālākūnlún kāfē tīng*). If it's Western food you're craving, head straight to this expat-run café—after weeks of eating noodles, you'll feel it's a veritable breath of fresh air on the Silk Road. The banana smoothies go down well, as does the roast eggplant focaccia. The friendly manager will give you travel advice if asked. Ⓢ *Average main: Y60* ⊠ *87 Seman Lu, opposite the Qinibagh Hotel's entrance gate* ☎ *0998/282-2669* ⊕ *www.crowninntashkorgan. com* ▭ *No credit cards.*

AMERICAN

$ ✕ **Pakistan Restaurant** (巴基斯坦西餐厅 *Bājīsītǎn xī cāntīng*). Foreign restaurants are rare in Kashgar, so this dirt-cheap curry joint is a welcome addition. This is where the city's Pakistani residents while away their evenings playing cards and sipping tea. There's an English menu,

MIDDLE EASTERN

but its function seems to be primarily illustrative—we visited twice and got the wrong dishes both times (in both cases they were delicious). Particularly good were the curries. There are no chopsticks here, as everything is scooped-up using delicious *roti* flat bread. Hot chai tea served with milk is the best way to wash down your meal. This restaurant's sign is covered by a large tree, so look for the tree instead. $ *Average main: Y30* ⊠ *Seman Lu, opposite the Seman Hotel's rear entrance* ⊟ *No credit cards.*

$

SICHUAN

✕ **Xiao Bei Dou** (小北斗 *Xiǎo běidǒu*). When you've grown tired of mutton, head here for the best Sichuan-style dishes in Kashgar. Classic selections like sweet-and-sour pork (*tangcu liji*), chicken with peanuts (*gongbao jiding*), and scallion pancakes (*conghuabing*) are all well prepared. There's plenty of cold beer in the refrigerator, and the second-floor covered terrace is perfect on a warm summer evening. An English menu is available, but the selection is limited. $ *Average main: Y20* ⊠ *285 Seman Lu, east of the Seman Hotel* ⊟ *No credit cards.*

### WHERE TO STAY

$

HOTEL

🏨 **Seman Hotel** (色满宾馆 *Sèmǎn bīnguǎn*). Built in 1890 as the Russian consulate, this edifice served as a center of political intrigue for many years. **Pros:** near some excellent restaurants; competitive prices from the lobby tour agencies. **Cons:** musty bathrooms in the cheaper rooms and dorms. $ *Rooms from: Y180* ⊠ *170 Seman Lu, at Renmin Lu* ☎ *0998/258–2129* 🖨 *0998/258–2150* 🛏 *212 rooms* 🍽 *No meals.*

### SHOPPING

**Handicraft Street** (职人街 *Zhírén jiē*). Running alongside the Id Kah Mosque is a narrow lane known as Handicraft Street. In either direction you'll find merchants selling everything from bright copper kettles to wedding chests to brass sleigh bells.

**Sunday Market** (星期天大巴扎 *Xīngqítiān dàbā zhā*). Kashgar's famous Sunday Market consists of two bazaars with a distance of almost 10 km (6 miles) between them. The **Yengi Bazaar** on Aizilaiti Lu, about 1½ km (1 mile) northeast of the city center, is open every day, but on Sunday the surrounding streets overflow with vendors hawking everything from boiled sheep's heads to trendy sunglasses. In the covered section you can bargain for decorative knives, embroidered fabrics, and all sorts of Uyghur-themed souvenirs. Behind the bazaar, rows of sleepy donkeys nod off in the bright sunlight, their carts lined up neatly beside them. For the best photos, however, you'll need to head over to the **Ulak Bazaar**, a 10-minute taxi ride east. Essentially a livestock market, farmers here tug recalcitrant sheep through the streets, scarf-shrouded women preside over heaps of red eggs, and old Uyghur men squat over baskets of chickens, haggling over the virtues and vices of each hapless hen. In the market for a camel? You can buy one here. On the outskirts of the market you can get an Old World–style straight-razor shave from a Uyghur barber or grab a bowl of *laghman* noodles, knowing that it's flavored with meat that is very, very fresh.

**Uyghur Musical Instruments Workshop** (维吾尔民族乐器制作销售店 *Wéiwú'ěr mínzú yuèqì zhìzuò xiāoshòu diàn*). At this shop you can watch the owner or his apprentice working on Uyghur string instruments—

10

**DID YOU KNOW?**

Karakul Lake is the highest body of water on the Pamir plateau. It is surrounded by snow-covered mountains, with the three highest peaks visible from the lake. Muztagh Ata (shown here) is 24,757 feet (7,546 meters) high.

stretching snakeskin or inlaying tiny bits of shell to make a Uyghur guitar called a *ravap*. ⊠ *272 Kumdarwaza Lu* ☎ *0998/222–8845.*

## SIDE TRIPS FROM KASHGAR

**Karakorum Highway** (喀喇昆仑公路 *Kālǎkūnlún gōnglù*). The Karakorum Highway (KKH), a spectacular road winding across some of the most dramatic and inhospitable terrain on Earth, traces one of the major ancient silk routes, from Kashgar south for 2,100 km (1,300 miles) through three great mountain ranges over the Khunjerab Pass (the highest border crossing in the world) into Pakistan. The journey can be hair-raising in part because of rock- and mudslides and in part because of daredevil driving.

A permit is required for Chinese nationals to travel on KKH, but currently foreigners don't need one. However, bring your passport or you'll be turned back at a border checkpoint in Gezcun or at one of the other checkpoints that have sprung up along the way. Buses headed for Tashkurgan, two hours south of the lake, leave Kashgar's long-distance bus station on Xiyu Dadao every morning at 9:30 Beijing Time (the bus station operates on Xinjiang time, off by two hours). You'll have to pay the full price of Y51 for your ticket even though you're not traveling the full distance. Buses reach the lake in about four hours. To catch the bus back, wait by the side of the highway and flag it down—the bus returning to Kashgar from Tashkurgan passes the lake between 11 am and 1 pm. A seat should only cost Y40, but enterprising drivers may demand Y50. Either way, the bus is much cheaper than private tours, which will set you back about Y600 per day.

**Karakul Lake** (喀拉库勒湖 *Kālā kùlēi hú*). Four hours south of Kashgar, having followed the Gez River valley deep into the heart of the Pamir Mountains, the highway passes alongside this picturesque lake. At an elevation of 3,800 meters (12,500 feet), this crystal-blue jewel is dominated on either side by stunning snowcapped mountains, with the 7,800-meter (25,600-foot) peak of **Muztagata,** the "Father of the Ice Mountains," dominating the landscape. Arriving at the lake, you'll practically be assaulted by would-be hosts on camelback, horseback, and motorcycle. Avoid the expensive yurts near the entrance and head back along the road to the more secluded yurts, where it is possible to stay with a local family for Y50 including simple meals. Standard food will be limited to bread and butter, tea, and fried rice dishes, but there is an expensive Chinese restaurant. Toilet facilities in this area are some of the worst in China, and there are no showers, but the area's beauty makes it worthwhile. Tour the lake via camel, horse, or motorbike, or just walk around, which will take about three hours. Bring warm clothing even in the summer, as it can be downright chilly: during our visit in July, we were applying sunscreen in the morning and battling sleet in the afternoon. ⊠ *Y50.*

# TIBET

The Rooftop of the World

# WELCOME TO TIBET

## TOP REASONS TO GO

★ **Barkhor:** Tibetan Buddhism's holiest pilgrimage circuit, the Barkhor is both the heart of Old Lhasa and one of the liveliest people-watching spots in all of China.

★ **Potala Palace:** Towering over Lhasa, this impressive palace of the Dalai Lamas was once the world's tallest structure, and is still a wonder.

★ **Ganden Monastery:** The most remote of the capital's three great monasteries, Ganden offers stunning views of the Lhasa River Valley and surrounding Tibetan farmland from a height of 14,764 feet.

★ **Gyantse Dzong:** The site of fierce fighting between Tibetan and British troops in 1904, this fortress is one of the few remaining symbols of Tibetan military power.

★ **Everest Base Camp:** Stand in awe beneath the world's tallest mountain.

**1 Lhasa.** Despite the city's rapid modernization, Lhasa is still one of China's must-visit destinations. From the crowded back alleys of the Barkhor to the imposing heights of the Potala Palace, a mix of Westerners, local Tibetans, Nepalese, and Han Chinese give this city an atmosphere unlike any other place in the world.

**2 Gyantse.** Past the sapphire waters of Yamdrok Tso and endless fields of golden highland barley, this small city is the gateway to southern Tibet and the Himalayas. An abandoned fortress high above town is testament to the area's former military importance, while the unique architecture at Pelkor Chode Monastery speaks to the city's history as a melting pot of religious denominations.

11

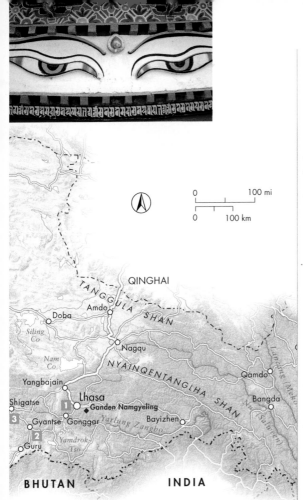

# GETTING ORIENTED

The Tibetan plateau is more than twice the size of France, sandwiched between two Himalayan ridges whose peaks reach an altitude of nearly 9 km (5½ miles). With the opening of the world's highest rail line and significantly improved roads, Tibet is more accessible than ever—once you get the required permits, that is. Lhasa is the best base from which to take day trips to the fertile Kyi-chu Valley or longer jaunts into the southwestern highlands of Tsang to visit Gyantse, Shigatse, and the Everest region. Every hotel and tour operator can arrange four-wheel-drive jeeps with a driver and/or a guide. Tibet is currently undergoing massive infrastructure improvements, and many roads that were once as bumpy as the steep mountain passes have been flattened into perfect stretches of blacktop.

**3** Shigatse. Tibet's second-largest city, Shigatse is the traditional capital of the Tsang region and home to the Panchen Lama's seat of power at Tashilhunpo Monastery. The ruined fortress on a hill above town has been rebuilt based on old photographs, but its concrete construction stands as one of the most glaring symbols of the modern world's encroachment on an ancient and sacred land.

**4** Everest. You may have trouble breathing when you first see the majestic peaks of the Himalayas, and not only because of the high altitude. The roof of the world is a spectacular place, with roaring snowmelt rivers feeding Tibetan farms and fields of wildflowers below.

Updated by Kit Gillet

Tibet is all you've heard and everything you've imagined: a land of intense sunshine and towering snowcapped peaks, where crystal clear rivers and sapphire lakes irrigate terraced fields of golden highland barley. The Tibetan people are extremely religious, viewing their daily toil and the harsh environment surrounding them as challenges along the path to life's single goal, the attainment of spiritual enlightenment. The region's richly decorated monasteries, temples, and palaces—including the Potala Palace—were not constructed by forced labor, but by laborers and artisans who donated their entire lives to the accumulation of good karma.

The death, destruction, and cultural denigration of Tibet that accompanied the Chinese invasion in the early 1950s changed this land forever, as did the Cultural Revolution in the late 1960s. Yet the people remain resilient. Colorfully dressed pilgrims still bring their offerings of yak butter to the temples, and monks work with zeal to repair the damage done to their monasteries. Many young Tibetans, attracted by the wealth and convenience brought by development, have abandoned their ancestors' traditional ways. Coca-Cola, fast food, and pulsing techno music are popular in Lhasa. Yet the changes have not lessened Tibet's allure as a travel destination. Unfortunately, however, tourism has been ever more tightly controlled since violent riots in March 2008, during which protestors railed against the central government's influence over religious practice in the region. Tibetans have also been protesting years of government policies encouraging migration of majority Han Chinese to Tibet, which has stoked ethnic tensions. As the region's infrastructure is built up, Tibet's GDP is growing at 12% every year, and its small towns are quickly turning into cities; people looking for job opportunities naturally gravitate here. With seven packed trains arriving every day in Lhasa, Han Chinese almost certainly outnumber Tibetans in some areas. Still, while the Barkhor in Lhasa and the area around Tashilhunpo Monastery in Shigatse are Tibetan islands in otherwise increasingly Han cities, much of the region remains relatively free of Han Chinese influence.

**11**

---

## PLANNING

### WHEN TO GO

Choosing when to visit Tibet is a matter of balancing your tolerance for extreme weather with your tolerance for tourist hordes, as well as keeping an eye on the current permit situation. The busiest months for tourists are July and August, but pleasant weather is common from May through October. However, bear in mind that Tibet can be abruptly closed to non-Chinese travelers during national holidays, such as the May 1st holiday and the October holiday. If you come at the beginning or end of the high season you'll have plenty of breathing space to take in the golden roofs of Tibet's monasteries and the icy peaks of the Himalayas. You may want to schedule your trip to coincide with one of Tibet's colorful celebrations, including the Birth of Buddha Festival (end of May), the Holy Mountain Festival (end of July), the Yogurt Festival (August), and the Bathing Festival (September). If you travel to Tibet in the off-season, many hotels and restaurants may be closed. Whenever you visit, warm clothing, sunglasses, and sunscreen are essentials for the high-altitude climate.

### GETTING HERE AND AROUND

**Passports and Visas.** A visa valid for the People's Republic of China is required. You will also need a Tibet Tourism Bureau (TTB) travel permit, which is arranged by the travel agent who books your tour or transportation to Lhasa. Travel by train or plane without a permit is next to impossible—on Internet forums you may hear of the odd person who claims to have managed it, but it's more than likely that you will be refused boarding with no refund.

In 2013, the Tibet Tourism Bureau (TTB) relaxed its regulations on travel through the region. It no longer requires that you be a part of a group of five or more, so independent travel is once again possible. It also allows people of different nationalities to travel together. All travel still must be booked through local agencies.

Some regions remain out of reach. The Chamdo region is closed, which makes overland travel from the provinces of Sichuan and Kunming impossible. At this writing the Mt. Everest Base Camp was closed, but contact your travel agent for the latest information regarding access.

The TTB requires that you pay a deposit to your travel agency's account. The amount varies from Y500 to Y1,000, depending on the length of the tour.

### AIR TRAVEL

In line with the government's ambitious infrastructure plans for Tibet, there are now five airports, with another one, Nagqu Dagring, due to open by the end of 2014. When finished, Nagqu Dagring Airport will be the world's highest airport, at an altitude of 4,436 meters (14,500 feet). Currently, 16 domestic airlines fly into Gonggar Airport, about 95 km (59 miles) from Lhasa, connecting Tibet with most major Chinese mainland cities and Hong Kong. The airport is renowned for having terrible facilities and humorless guards, so don't expect much. Tibet also has smaller airports in Chamdo, Shigatse, Nyingchi, and Ngari prefectures. These have frequent flights to Lhasa and less frequent flights to other nearby Chinese cities. Security on flights bound for Lhasa is much tighter than on other internal flights—expect to be thoroughly searched.

### BUS TRAVEL

There are buses in Tibet, of the rickety, bone-shaking sort, but they tend to cater to locals only. Drivers are often very reluctant to pick up foreign travelers. In Lhasa it's easier, but you will be expected to have your tour guide with you. Most visitors hire a land cruiser to get around once outside of Lhasa.

### CAR TRAVEL

A car and driver is usually included in tour packages. Travel costs are high because distances are large and gas is expensive.

### TRAIN TRAVEL

Provided you have a TTB permit, you can travel on the world's highest railway to Tibert. This means that you should book a tour that includes your train trip. Air-conditioned trains, complete with oxygen masks because of the altitude, arrive several times a week from Beijing, Shanghai, Guangzhou, and Xian to Lhasa. Every passenger has to sign a health waiver saying they're fit to travel. The rail link is not without its controversies—some argue that the train encourages Han migration, and that its construction has had a tremendous environmental impact.

### RESTAURANTS

It's fair to say that no one travels to Tibet for its food. Tsampa is Tibet's staple food, which is barley flour mixed with salted butter tea. It's accompanied by an odd servings of meat, vegetables, and dairy products. Lhasa has Tibet's best dining options, so make the most of the competitive market of hybrid restaurants that serve Chinese, Indian, Nepali, Tibetan, and Western fare. Most have sprung up from backpacker haunts serving perennially favorite dishes, from banana pancakes to yak burgers to chicken masala.

Because all your meals are usually included in your tour package, we do not list individual restaurants in this guide.

**11**

### HOTELS

Hotel options in Lhasa have improved significantly in recent times. There are a smattering of boutique hotels and a couple of international-brand properties. Many of the more expensive hotels even equip their rooms with oxygen machines to ease the effects of altitude sickness. Tibetan guesthouses are staffed by locals and are more personable, but some of the shared bathing facilities at the lower-end options can be archaic. Outside of Lhasa, standards are much lower, so be prepared to rough it.

All your accommodations are usually included in your tour package, so we do not list individual lodgings in this guide.

### TOURS

Foreign travelers are required to book a tour when securing a Tibet Travel Bureau permit. Agents should advise you on the latest changes to travel restrictions and permit requirements. Typically, the cost of an organized tour for a week runs $1,000 to $2,000 per person. When booking a tour, be sure to get confirmation in writing, with details about your hotel and meal arrangements.

Popular tours include the two-day trip to Nam Tso Lake (Y1,000–Y1,500), the two-day trip to Samye Monastery (Y800–Y2,500), and the 12-day trip to sacred Mount Kailash (Y7,000–Y14,000).

### VISITOR INFORMATION

Travelers are at the mercy of private travel agents, guidebooks, and online travel forums for the most up-to-date information on Tibet. State-run travel bureaus do exist, but are often downright unhelpful. Such travel agencies as Tibet Travel and Snow Lion Tours are very knowledgeable and offer great service.

# LHASA

*14 hrs by train south of Golmud, 43 hrs by train southwest of Beijing. 2 hrs by plane west of Chengdu, 5 hrs by plane southwest of Beijing.*

The capital of Tibet is a treasure trove of monasteries, palaces, and temples. Geographically, the city is divided into a Chinese Quarter to the west and a Tibetan Quarter to the east. The Chinese neighborhood is where you'll find older hotels and Norbulingka Summer Palace. The more colorful Tibetan Quarter is full of small guesthouses, laid-back restaurants, bustling street markets, and Jokhang Temple. There is also a small Muslim Quarter to the southeast of the Barkhor. The winding lanes in and around the Barkhor are immensely walkable and a great way to rub shoulders with the locals. Don't worry about getting lost: most of the thoroughfares are circular; if you follow the pilgrims, you'll make it back to the circuit.

### GETTING HERE AND AROUND

With the opening of the railway line, travelers can now travel easily and cheaply to Tibet from almost anywhere in China. You'll need a Tibet Travel Bureau permit to purchase a train ticket, and this should be arranged by your tour group. The gleaming Lhasa Train Station is

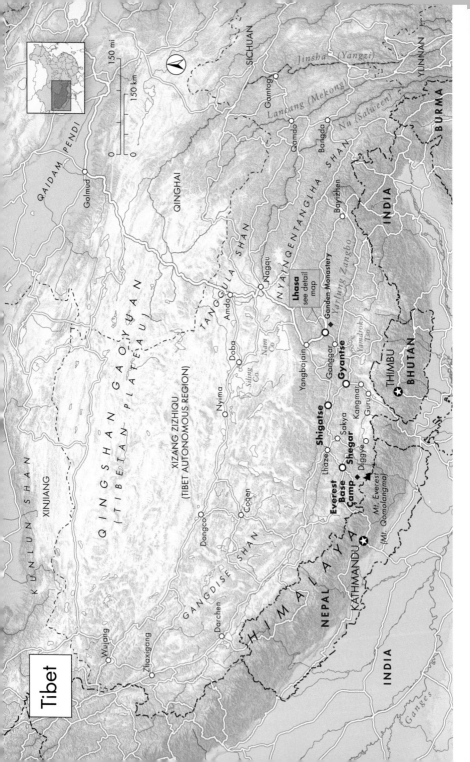

Tibet

15 to 20 minutes southwest of the city center by taxi (Y50).

BY AIR Booking an airline ticket to Lhasa also requires a Tibet Tourism Bureau permit. Even if you can buy a ticket without the permit, it's highly unlikely that you will be allowed to board.

Air China, Sichuan Airlines, China Southern Airlines, and China Eastern Airlines are some of the 16 airlines with frequent service to Lhasa. The easiest direct route is from Chengdu, which has as many as 10 daily flights during the summer months for about Y1,500 each way. Flights to Lhasa depart from Beijing (5 hrs), Guangzhou (5 hrs), Xi'an (3½ hrs), Chongqing (3 hrs), and Chengdu (2 hrs). The airport is 53 km (32 miles) southwest of Lhasa, which takes about 45 minutes by taxi (Y180) or more than an hour by shuttle bus (Y25).

**ABOUT THE WEATHER**

From November to January, temperatures become frightfully cold (–10°F), but the climate is dry and the skies are blue. Many tourist sites in Lhasa shorten their opening hours in winter months. From June to August highs reach 80°F, although it can feel hotter. Summer sees a bit of rain, and occasionally roads will be closed to popular tourist destinations, including the Everest Base Camp. The best touring conditions occur from mid-April through May, as wildflowers bloom and snow begins to melt. September through early November, with its mild weather, is another good option.

If you are coming from Kathmandu, the nonstop flights made four times a week will give you fantastic views of the Himalayas. You must show your permit from the Tibet Tourism Bureau when you check in.

BY BUS Intercity bus travel is not only long and uncomfortable, it's not encouraged for foreigners in almost all of Tibet. You can, however, take the pilgrim buses that leave every day at 6:30 am from Barkhor Square headed to Ganden Monastery. You can also travel to Shigatse from Lhasa Bus station at Jinzhu Lu.

BY CAR When you book a tour, the package will include a car and driver and all the necessary permits. If you're headed to Nepal, make sure you arrange a visa in Lhasa before your departure.

BY TRAIN The train line to Lhasa has rewritten many of the world's records for extreme engineering. It's the world's highest railway, with more than 966 km (600 miles) of track above 13,000 feet, reaching above 16,500 feet in several locations. The line is also home to the world's highest railway station, which at Tangu-la Pass sits at almost 17,000 feet.

The train is comfortable and inexpensive, with free oxygen supplies beneath every seat to combat altitude sickness. Traveling by rail is also the perfect way to see the vast uninhabited expanse of the northern Qinghai-Tibet Plateau, with yaks and antelopes roaming the hills.

**SAFETY AND PRECAUTIONS**
■ **TIP→ Don't talk politics with Tibetans. If they speak out against the government they may be charged with treason and receive a 20-year jail term.** Public Security Bureau personnel are everywhere, sometimes

CLOSE UP

## Lhasa Express

One of history's most audacious engineering projects, the rail line to Lhasa began construction in 2001 after more than 30 years of delays. Chairman Mao first proposed the railroad in the 1960s, along with other infrastructure projects now being realized, like the massive Three Gorges Dam on the Yangtze River. The list of technical challenges confronting the rail line was daunting, as more than 966 km (600 miles) of track needed to be constructed at an altitude of more than 13,000 feet, topping out at Tangula Pass near 17,000 feet. Much of the track rests on semi-frozen and constantly shifting permafrost. The line also crosses through six protected environmental reserves, home to endangered species like the Tibetan antelope and the snow leopard.

Swiss engineers, experts on frozen terrain, said the project was impossible, but the Chinese government was having none of it. The first passenger train, carrying President Hu Jintao and a host of other dignitaries, rolled into Lhasa's shiny new station on July 1, 2006.

The cultural implications of the railroad to ethnic Tibetans—already a minority in their own land—are obvious. The migration of Han Chinese will continue to expand as the traditional Tibetan way of life in many areas rapidly declines in the face of modernization. Politically, the railroad is another firm sign from Beijing that they have no intention of ever letting Tibet break off into a separate political entity; in fact, plans to extend the railway to Tibet's second-largest city, Shigatse, and over the Himalayas to Kathmandu in Nepal are being developed.

However, the railway isn't completely negative for the locals. A large number of Tibetans make their livelihood from tourism, which has increased dramatically since the opening of the line. The relatively cheap, quick, and comfortable ride by train has also made it possible for Tibetans working and studying in faraway parts of China to return home and visit their families during holidays, something that was nearly impossible when the only practical way to reach Lhasa was an expensive flight.

in uniform, sometimes in civilian clothes or even in monks' robes. Beware of the charming Tibetan who may be a secret policeman trying to entrap you into giving him a photograph of the Dalai Lama. You could be detained or even deported. PSB offices are in all towns and many of the smaller townships.

### TIMING

At a minimum, aim to spend four nights in Lhasa: this allows enough time to acclimatize to the altitude as well as see the main attractions such as Jokhang Temple, Potala Palace, and the Sera and Drepung monasteries.

### TOURS

Foreign travelers to Tibet have to purchase tours along with their airline or train tickets, as is required by Chinese law. Once you're here, you may be able to book additional one-day tours through your original travel agent. The city is overflowing with travel agencies, mostly geared toward Chinese tourists. A good local agency is Tibet FIT Travel.

The golden spires of the Jokhang Temple in Lhasa

**ESSENTIALS**

**Air Contact Gongga Airport** (贡嘎机场 *Gòng gā jīchǎng*). ⊠ *Airport Rd., Gongga County* ☎ *0891/624-6114, 0891/624-6009.*

**Bank Bank of China** ⊠ *28 Linkuo Xi Lu* ☎ *0891/682-8547, 0891/683-5311* ⊠ *20 Beijing Dong Lu* ☎ *089/632-6263.*

**Medical Assistance TAR People's Hospital** (拉萨第一人民医院 *Lāsà dì yī rénmín yīyuàn*). ⊠ *18 Linkuo Bei Lu, northeast of Potala Palace* ☎ *0891/632-2200.*

**Train Contact China Tibet Tourism Bureau** (西藏自治区旅游局 *Xīzàng zìzhìqū lǚyóu jú*). ⊠ *3 Luobulingka Lu* ☎ *0891/683-4315* ⊕ *www.xzta.gov.cn/yww* ⊙ *Daily 8:30-6:30.*

**Visitor and Tour Info Access Tibet Tour** ⊠ *Tibet Hotel, Beijing Zhong Lu* ☎ *028/8618-3638* ⊕ *www.accesstibettour.com.* **Tibet FIT Travel** ⊠ *Snowlands Hotel, 4 Zangyiyuan Lu* ☎ *0891/634-9239* ⊕ *www.tibetfit.com.* **Snow Lion Tours** ⊠ *1 Danjielin Lu* ☎ *13439329243* ⊕ *snowliontours.com.* **Tibet Travel** ⊕ *www.tibettravel.info.* **Tibetan Connections** ☎ *18697259259* ⊕ *www.tibetanconnections.com.*

## EXPLORING LHASA

Your main axis of orientation in Lhasa is Beijing Lu, a street that stretches from the Barkhor in the east to as far as Drepung Monastery in the west, passing right in front of the Potala Palace. The easiest way to get from site to site is by taxi, with journeys between most locations in the city costing no more than Y10. Pedicabs are also available, but agreeing on a price before you hop on is essential; most trips should cost about Y10. Many of the most popular attractions are concentrated in and around the Barkhor area, so walking is always an option.

## TOP ATTRACTIONS

**Ani Tsangkung Nunnery** (美洲黑杜鹃女修道院 *Āní cāngkōng nīgū ān*). This small, colorful convent has a livelier atmosphere than what you'll find at Lhasa's monasteries. Beaming nuns encourage you to wander through the courtyards, listen to their chanting, and watch them make ornamental butter flowers. There's a simple outdoor restaurant—popular at lunchtime—where nuns serve up inexpensive bowls of noodles and *momos* (dumplings). The chief pilgrimage site is the meditation hollow where Songtsen Gampo concentrated his spiritual focus on preventing the flood of the Kyi River in the 7th century. You're free to take photos here without charge—an option not available at many monasteries. ⊠ *Waling Lam, southeast of Jokhang Temple* ⚏ *Y30* ⊙ *Daily 8–5.*

**Barkhor** (八廓 *Bākuò*). Circling the walls of the Jokhang Temple, the Barkhor is not only Tibetan Buddhism's holiest pilgrimage circuit but also the best spot in Lhasa for people-watching. Look for monks sitting before their alms bowls while the faithful constantly spin their prayer wheels. Unless you want to shock the devout with your blatant disregard for tradition, flow with the crowd in a clockwise direction. This wide pedestrian street is also souvenir central, crammed with stalls where vendors sell prayer shawls, silver jewelry, wall hangings, and just about anything that screams "I've been to Tibet!" Don't even think about paying what the vendors ask; many of the items can easily be bargained down to less than a quarter of the original price.

Fodor's Choice ★ **Jokhang Temple** (大昭寺 *Dàzhāo sì*). This temple is the most sacred building in Tibet. From the gentle flicker of a butter-lamp light dancing off antique murals, statues, tapestries, and *thangkhas* (scroll paintings) to the air thick with incense and anticipation as thousands of Tibetans pay homage day and night, the temple contains a plethora of sensory delights. Most likely built in 647 during Songtsen Gampo's reign, the Jokhang stands in the heart of the Old Town. The site was selected by Queen Wengcheng, a princess from China who became Songtsen Gampo's second wife. His first wife, Princess Bhrikuti from Nepal, financed the building of Jokhang. In her honor, and in recognition of Tibet's strong reliance on Nepal, the Jokhang's main gate faces west, toward Nepal. Among the bits remaining from the 7th century are the four door frames of the inner temple, dedicated to different deities. ⚠ Remember that photos are not allowed inside the buildings without a Y90 photo permit.

Over the centuries, renovations have enlarged the Jokhang to keep it the premier temple of Tibet. Its status was threatened in the 1950s when the Chinese Army shelled it

> **WORD OF MOUTH**
>
> "For anyone with an interest in Tibet, I highly recommend the documentary *Tibet: Cry of the Snow Lion.* You'll learn what really happened in Tibet when the Chinese invaded and what's happening even now. I didn't see it until after we returned but wish I had seen it before going." —PIPERPAT

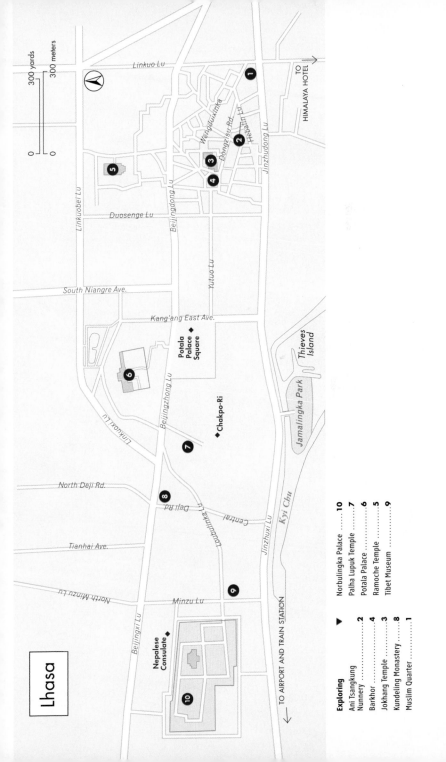

Lhasa

0 — 300 yards
0 — 300 meters

Exploring

Ani Tsangkung
Nunnery .............. 2
Barkhor .............. 4
Jokhang Temple ...... 3
Kundeling Monastery .... 8
Muslim Quarter ........ 1

Norbulingka Palace ...... 10
Palha Lupuk Temple ...... 7
Potala Palace ............ 6
Ramoche Temple ........ 5
Tibet Museum .......... 9

**DID YOU KNOW?**

The tomb of the 13th Dalai Lama can be found west of the Great West Hall in the Potala Palace. Before his death in 1933, he predicted the invasion of Tibet.

and the Red Guards of the Cultural Revolution ransacked it. During this period, the temple was used for various purposes, including as a pigsty. Much of the damage has since been repaired, but a portion of it has been lost forever.

Before entering the Inner Jokhang, you should walk the Nangkhor Inner Circuit in a clockwise direction. It's lined with prayer wheels and murals depicting a series of Buddhist scenes. Continue on to the large Entrance Hall, whose inner chapels have murals depict-

> ### GETTING AROUND
>
> Taxis are plentiful in Lhasa. Y10 will get you almost anywhere within the city limits. Getting to Drepung Monastery will cost about Y40. Minibuses ply a fixed route, with fares of around Y2. Bicycle rickshaws are also available for short trips, and normally cost Y3, although they're famous for trying to charge foreigners higher prices.

ing the wrathful deities responsible for protecting the temple and the city. Straight ahead is the inner sanctum, the three-story **Kyilkhor Thil,** some of whose many columns probably date from the 7th century, particularly those with short bases and round shafts.

The chapels on the ground floor of the Kyilkhor Thil are the most rewarding. The most revered chapel of the inner hall is **Jowo Sakya-muni Lhakhang,** opposite the entrance. Inside rests a bejeweled statue of Jowo Rinpoche—representing the Buddha at age 12—surrounded by adoring disciples. It was brought to Tibet by Queen Wengcheng and somehow has survived, despite a history of being plastered over and buried in sand. On busy days you may wait in line to enter this shrine, but it's worth it. On the second floor there are a number of small chapels, although many are closed to visitors. Before you leave, climb the stairs next to the main entrance up to the Jokhang's ornately decorated golden roof. You'll be rewarded with sweeping views of the Barkhor, the Potala Palace, and the snowcapped mountains beyond Lhasa. ⊠ *Barkhor* ☎ *0891/632–3129* ⊠ *Y85* ⊗ *Daily 7–noon and 3-6:30, but tourists can visit only in the afternoon.*

**Kundeling Monastery** (修道院 *Kūndélín sì*). This monastery is often overlooked by tourists, so it's less crowded than others around Lhasa. If you arrive in the morning, climb to a second-floor chapel to see monks chanting, beating drums, and playing long bronze prayer trumpets. This temple also contains examples of sand painting, in which millions of colorful grains of sand are arranged in a complex pattern over the course of hours or even days. ⊠ *Beijing Zhong Lu and Deji Lu, west of the Potala Palace* ☎ *0891/685–1973* ⊠ *Y10* ⊗ *Daily 9–8.*

**Muslim Quarter** (穆斯林小区 *Mùsīlín xiǎoqū*). In perhaps the most Buddhist of cities, the Muslim Quarter—centered on Lhasa's Great Mosque—is a bit of an anomaly. The district was originally intended for immigrants arriving from Kashmir and Ladakh. The Great Mosque (Dà qīngzhēn sì) with its green minaret was completed in 1716, but very little of the original structure remains. The area is now primarily of interest for its distinct atmosphere, thanks to its Hui Muslim residents

11

and the large concentration of pork-free halal restaurants. ⊠ *Lingkor Nan Lu, west of Lingkor Dong Lu.*

**Palha Lupuk Temple** (石窟寺 *Pàlālǔfǔ shíkǔ sì*). Religious rock paintings dating from as early as the 7th century can be seen at this grotto-style temple. On the third floor you'll find an entrance to a cave with sculptures carved into the granite walls, mostly by Nepalese artists more than a millennium ago. Very few tourists visit, so if you're looking to escape the crowds, head here. ⊠ *On a small street opposite the western end of the Potala Palace, south face of Iron Mountain* 🎫 *Y20* 🕙 *Daily 9–8.*

Fodor's Choice ★

**Potala Palace** (布达拉宫 *Bùdálā gōng*). The awesome sight that is the Potala Palace is quite rightly considered a wonder of the world. However, virtually nothing remains of the original 11-story Potala Palace, built in 637 by Songtsen Gampo. What you see today is a 17th-century replacement. The Fifth Dalai Lama, anxious to reestablish the importance of Lhasa as the Tibetan capital, employed 7,000 workers and 1,500 artisans to resurrect the Potala Palace on the 7th-century foundation. The portion called the White Palace was completed in 1653. The Red Palace was not completed until 1694, 12 years after the Dalai Lama's death (which was kept secret by the regent in order to prevent interruption of the construction). The Potala Palace has been enlarged since then, and has been continually renovated. Once the headquarters of Tibet's theocracy, the vast complex is now a museum and a UNESCO World Heritage site.

The Potala Palace was the world's tallest building before the advent of modern skyscrapers. Towering above the city from the slopes of Mount Marpori, the structure is 384 feet high; its 1,000 rooms house some 200,000 images. The outer section, the White Palace, was the seat of government and the winter residence of the Dalai Lama until 1951. Inside you can pass through the Dalai Lama's spartan quarters. On either side of the palace are the former offices of the government. The Red Palace, looming above the White Palace, is filled with murals that chronicle Buddhist folklore and ancient Tibetan life. Interspersed among the chapels are eight spectacular tombs covered in nearly five tons of gold. These bejeweled rooms contain the remains of the Fifth through 13th Dalai Lamas.

Only 2,300 visitors are allowed in each day. Your ticket allows you up to 90 minutes at the site. To limit the number of visitors, starting in June 2012 the ticket price almost doubled. ⚠ **The legions of Chinese soldiers don't take kindly to being photographed. If they spot you taking pictures in their direction, they're likely to approach and want to see your camera.** ⊠ *Beijing Zhong Lu, Gongtian Xian* ☎ *0891/683–4362* 🎫 *Nov.–Apr., Y200; May–Oct., Y100* 🕙 *Nov.–Apr., daily 9:30–3; May–Oct., daily 9–4.*

DID YOU KNOW?

Underneath the 13-story, 1,000-room fortress of the Potala Palace are the dungeons, inaccessible to tourists. Justice could be harsh—torture and jail time were the punishments for refusing to pay taxes, displaying anger, or insulting a monk. The worst place to be sent was the Cave of Scorpions, where prisoners were the targets of stinging tails.

**WORTH NOTING**

**Norbulingka Palace** (罗布林卡宫 *Luóbùlínkǎ gōng*). The Seventh Dalai Lama (1708–57), a frail man, chose to build a summer palace on this site because of its medicinal spring, and later had his whole government moved here from the Potala Palace. Successive Dalai Lamas expanded the complex, adding additional palaces, a debating courtyard, a pavilion, a library, and a number of landscaped gardens, which are at their best in summer

> **ALTITUDE ALERT**
>
> At 12,000 feet, shortness of breath and mild headaches are common during the first few days in Lhasa. These symptoms can be managed by use of a small oxygen canister, herbal remedies, or an aspirin or two. Drink plenty of water. Severe altitude sickness should immediately be brought to the attention of a physician.

months. The most recent addition, built by the current Dalai Lama between 1954 and 1956, is an ornate two-story building containing his private quarters. It turned out to be the place from which, disguised as a soldier, he fled to India on March 17, 1959, three days before the Chinese massacred thousands of Tibetans and fired artillery shells into every building in the complex. Only after searching through the corpses did they realize that the Dalai Lama had escaped.

The repair work in the aftermath of the March 1959 uprising is not of high caliber, and much of Norbulingka feels run-down. That said, a collection of the Dalai Lama's carriages and automobiles housed in the **Changsam Palace** are worth a look. More fascinating are the personal effects of the current Dalai Lama housed in the **New Summer Palace**, including his radio and phonograph. You can even peek into the Dalai Lama's bathroom. No photos are allowed inside, unfortunately. There is also a small zoo full of pitiable animals, which is worth avoiding. ✉ *Western end of Luobulingka Lu* 🎫 *Y60* ⏲ *Mon.-Sat. 9:30–12:30 and 3:30–6.*

**Ramoche Temple** (小昭寺 *Xiǎo zhāo sì*). This temple was founded by Queen Wengcheng at the same time as the Jokhang Temple. Its three-story structure dates from the 15th century. Despite restorations in the 1980s, it lost much of its former grandeur after the Chinese used it to house the Communist Labor Training Committee during the Cultural Revolution.

The Ramoche Temple was intended to house the most revered statue of Jowo Rinpoche. A threat of a Chinese invasion in the 7th century induced Queen Wengcheng to hide the statue in the Jokhang Temple. Some 50 years later it was rediscovered and placed within the Jokhang Temple's main chapel. As a substitute, Jokhang reciprocated with a Nepalese statue of Jowo Mikyo Dorje—representing Buddha as an eight-year-old—richly layered in gold and precious stones. It was decapitated during the Cultural Revolution and its torso lost in Beijing. Both head and body were found in 1984, put back together again, and placed in a small chapel at the back of the Ramoche Temple's inner sanctum. Be sure to climb to the temple's roof for a spectacular view of the Potala Palace perched high above the rooftops of Lhasa. ✉ *Xiao*

*Zhao Si Lu, off the north side of Beijing Dong Lu* ☎ *0891/633–6163* ✆ *Y25* ⏰ *Daily 8–4:30.*

**Tibet Museum** (西藏博物馆 *Xīzàng bówùguǎn*). For the Chinese interpretation of Tibetan history, politics, and culture, visit this modern museum. The free personal audio guide provides commentary on important pieces from prehistoric times, Chinese dynasties, and traditional Tibetan life. If you are a scholar of history, you may find some of the explanations intriguing. It often hosts temporary Tibetan art exhibitions. ✉ *Corner of Luobulingka Lu and Minzu Nan Lu, across from Norbulingka Palace* ☎ *0891/681–2210* ✆ *Y30* ⏰ *Tue.–Sun. 9–1, 2–6.*

## NIGHTLIFE AND THE ARTS

**Ganglamedo** (冈拉梅朵咖啡吧 *Gānglā méiduǒ kāfēi bā*). If you're looking for a quiet spot near the Barkhor to enjoy a drink or a cup of tea after a long day, try Ganglamedo, across from the Yak Hotel. The bar stocks a wide range of liquors. ✉ *127 Beijing Dong Lu* ☎ *0891/633–3657* ⊕ *www.ganglamedo.com.*

**Tibet Shol Opera Troupe.** Tibetan operas are performed by the Tibet Shol Opera Troupe in a theater at the Himalaya Hotel. Tickets cost Y100, and reservations are required. ✉ *Himalaya Hotel, 6 Lingkor Dong Lu* ☎ *0891/632–1111.*

## SHOPPING

### ARTS AND CRAFTS

For souvenirs varying from prayer flags to jewel-encrusted horse bridles, stop by one of the hundreds of open-air stalls and small shops that line the roads leading to the Jokhang Temple. Bargain in a tough but friendly manner, and the proprietors may throw in extra items for luck. Many of the goods come from around Tibet and Nepal.

**Dropenling.** For quality Tibetan handicrafts, visit Dropenling, down an alley opposite the Muslim Quarter's main mosque. Unlike those at other souvenir shops, all the products here are made by Tibetans, and all profits are returned to the local community. ✉ *11 Chak Tsal Gang Lu* ☎ *0891/636–0558* ⊕ *www.tibetcraft.com.*

**Tanva Carpet Workshop** (毯华手工地毯 *Tǎnhuá shǒugōng dìtǎn*). On the road between Lhasa and Gongga Airport is the Tanva Carpet Workshop. The artisans here use handspun Tibetan highland wool to make both traditional and contemporary carpets using natural dyes. Even if you're not buying, it's interesting to see the whole carpet-making process from start to finish. Tanva makes the carpets that are sold in Torana stores in Beijing and Shanghai. Call ahead to arrange a visit. ☎ *1398/990–8681.*

### OUTDOOR EQUIPMENT

**Third Pole** (第三极 *Dì sān jí*). West of the Potala Palace, the Third Pole can outfit you with everything you'll need to enjoy the great outdoors, from good hiking shoes to walking sticks to sunglasses. ✉ *6 Luobulingka Lu* ☎ *0891/682–0549.*

CLOSE UP

## The Tibetans

Prayer flags are sold in front of the Jokhang, Tibet's holiest temple.

They live primarily on the Tibet-Qinghai Plateau, but they also make their homes in southern Gansu, western and northern Sichuan, and northwestern Yunnan. Their culture is influenced both by Tibet's extreme geography and their unique interpretation of Buddhism, the line between the two often blurred by a "sacred geography," which deifies many of the region's mountains and lakes. Compared with other forms of Buddhism, Tibetan Buddhism (also known as "Lamaism") places far more emphasis on the physical path to enlightenment. This is why the sight of pilgrims prostrating around the base of a sacred mountain or temple for days or weeks on end is a common one in the region.

When Tibet was annexed (or "liberated") by China in 1959, their supreme spiritual leader the Dalai Lama fled in disguise to India, where he set up a Tibetan government-in-exile in Dharamsala, which became known as "little Lhasa." Since then the Dalai Lama has become an international celebrity and has succeeded in making the struggle for Tibetan independence a focus of global attention, drawing strong condemnation—and brutal crackdowns—from Beijing. Few people realize that the Dalai Lama has actually for many years no longer insisted on independence, but a more moderate form of autonomy like that enjoyed by Hong Kong and Macau. Yet despite international pressure—and perhaps even because of the attention—there seems little hope that Tibet's status will change in the near future.

Meanwhile, Tibet continues to modernize at full speed, with seemingly every road between Lhasa and Mount Everest being upgraded simultaneously. The rail link between Beijing and Lhasa completed in 2006 has promoted "Hanification," or a major increase in the Han Chinese population. It's estimated that 60%–70% of the population in Lhasa is Han Chinese. With only 2.5 million Tibetans living in the Tibet Autonomous Region—and 800 million impoverished Han Chinese nationwide looking for a better way of life—it's only a matter of time before ethnic Tibetans become a small minority in their own homeland.

**Toread** (探路者 *Tàn lù zhě*). A Chinese clothing chain, Toread features a wide selection of genuine outdoor equipment, as well as warm clothing if you're planning a trip to the mountains. ⊠ *182 Beijing Zhong Lu* ☎ *0891/682–9365.*

## AROUND LHASA

Many of Lhasa's best sites are clustered around the city center, but three of the most important are more remote. This trio of monasteries are known as the "three pillars of Tibetan Buddhism," having all been founded by religious patriarch Tsongkhapa at the beginning of the 15th century. All three are worth the effort it takes to reach them (especially Ganden Monastery, 90 minutes east of Lhasa) and should be part of any tour of Lhasa.

> **WORD OF MOUTH**
>
> "Remember just about everything you do in Lhasa requires lots of walking and uphill. Potala Palace is incredibly taxing, even if you are in great shape. So too with the other monasteries. We saw lots of people really struggling with breathing. It is very hard work in the high altitude." —Don

**Drepung Monastery** (哲蚌寺 *Zhébàng sì*). The largest of the Gelugpa monasteries was the residence for lesser lamas. Founded in 1416, it was enlarged in the 16th century by the Second Dalai Lama. By the era of the Fifth Dalai Lama it had become the largest monastic institution in the world, with 10,000 residents. During the Cultural Revolution it suffered only minimally, because the Army used the building as its headquarters and therefore didn't ransack it as much as other temples. The monastery was reopened in 1980, although the number of resident monks has been severely depleted.

The monastery's most important building is the Tshomchen, whose vast assembly hall, the **Dukhang**, is noteworthy for its 183 columns, atrium ceiling, and ceremonial banners. Chapels can be found on all three floors, as well as on the roof. In the two-story **Buddhas of Three Ages Chapel** (Düsum Sangye Lhakhang), at the rear of the Dukhang on the ground floor, the Buddhas of past, present, and future are each guarded by two bodhisattvas. ⊠ *Off Beijing Xi Lu, 8 km (5 miles) west of Lhasa* ☎ *0891/686–0011* 🎟 *Y55* ⊙ *Daily 9–1 (afternoon often closed to visitors).*

Fodor's Choice ★ **Ganden Monastery** (甘丹寺 *Gāndān sì*). If you have time for only one side trip from Lhasa, this rambling monastery with ocher-colored walls is your best bet. It was established in 1409 by Tsongkhapa, the founder of the Gelugpa sect, and its abbot is chosen on merit rather than heredity. Of the six great Gelugpa monasteries, Ganden was the most seriously damaged by the Chinese during the Cultural Revolution. Since the early 1980s, Tibetans have put tremendous effort into rebuilding the complex; some 300 monks are now in residence. Pilgrims come daily from Lhasa to pay homage to the sacred sites and religious relics.

The monastery comprises eight major buildings. The most impressive structure is the **Gold Tomb of Tsongkhapa** (Serdhung Lhakhang) in the heart of the complex, easily recognized by the recently built white

CLOSE UP

## Festivals and Celebrations

Try to time your visit with one of the brilliantly colorful traditional Tibetan festivals. Dancing monks whip up a frenzy to dispel the evil spirits of the previous year at the Year End Festival on the 29th day of the 12th lunar month. The first week of the first lunar month includes Losar (New Year Festival), when Lhasa is filled with Tibetan drama performances, incense offerings, and locals promenading in their finest wardrobe. Grand butter lanterns light up the Barkhor circuit during the Lantern Festival on the 15th of the first month. On the seventh day of the fourth month you can join the pilgrims in Lhasa or Ganden to mark the Birth of Sakyamuni (the Buddha), or you may want to wait until the 15th for the celebrations of Saga Dawa (Sakyamuni's enlightenment) and join the pilgrims who climb the Drepung Monastery to burn juniper incense. Picnics at the summer palace of Norbulingka are common during the Worship

of the Buddha in the second week of the fifth month. During Shötun (Yogurt Festival) in the first week of the seventh month, immerse yourself in the operas, masked dances, and picnics from Drepung, about 6½ km (4 miles) out of Lhasa, to Norbulingka. During the festival, giant thangkas of the Buddha are unveiled in Drepung Monastery, and Tibetan opera troupes perform operas at Norbulingka.

The Tibetan calendar is the same as the lunar calendar, so exact dates as they relate to the Western calendar are only published a year in advance. The approximate dates are as follows: Tibetan New Year (February); the Butter Lantern Festival (late February/early March); the Birth of Buddha Festival (late May/early June); the Holy Mountain Festival (late July/early August); the one-week Yogurt Festival (August); and the Bathing Festival (September).

*chorten,* or small shrine, standing before the red building. On the second floor is the chapel of **Yangchen Khang,** with the new golden chorten of Tsongkhapa. The original from 1629, made of silver and later gilded, was the most sacred object in the land. In 1959 the Chinese destroyed it, although brave monks saved some of the holy relics of Tsongkhapa, which are now inside the new gold-covered chorten. Be careful walking around this shrine: the buttery wax on the floor is thick and slippery.

A path that circumambulates the monastery starts from the parking lot. From the path, which leads to the spot where Tsongkhapa was cremated in 1419, you'll be treated to breathtaking views of the Lhasa River Valley. You'll need about an hour to complete the circuit. Photo permits cost Y15-20 extra. ⊠ *Tibet–Sichuan Hwy., 36 km (22 miles) southeast of Lhasa* 🖼 *Y50* ⊙ *Daily 9–4.*

**Nechung Monastery** (乃琼寺 *Nǎiqióng sì*). Many people skip this 12th-century monastery, but that's a big mistake. With a strong focus on beasts, demons, and the afterlife, Nechung is unlike anything else you'll see in Tibet. Murals on the monastery's walls depict everything from humans being dismembered by dogs and vultures to demons wearing long belts of human skulls and engaged in passionate sexual intercourse. Until 1959 this monastery was home to the highly influential Nechung

**DID YOU KNOW?**

The path leading to Choding Khang hermitage is flanked by painted rock carvings of Tsongkhapa (a famous Buddhist teacher), Jamchen (an important disciple), and Dharma Raja (the protector).

Oracle. Every important decision by a Dalai Lama is made after consulting this oracle, which currently resides in Dharamsala as a member of the government-in-exile. The monastery is 1 km (½ mile) southeast of Drepung Monastery. ⊠ *Off Beijing Xi Lu, 8 km (5 miles) west of Lhasa* 🎫 *Y25* ☉ *Daily 9–4.*

**RUSTIC CUISINE**

Outside the capital, the variety of food leaves something to be desired, but in areas commonly visited by tourists you should be able to find a simple meal.

Fodor'sChoice ★ **Sera Monastery** (色拉寺 *Sèlā sì*). This important Gelugpa monastery, founded in 1419, contains numerous temples filled with splendid murals and icons. Originally it was a hermitage for Tsongkhapa and a few of his top students. Within a couple hundred of years it housed more than 5,000 monks.

On the clockwise pilgrimage route, start at the two buildings that will take up most of your visit. **Sera Me Tratsang,** founded in 1419, has a *dukhang* (assembly hall) rebuilt in 1761 with murals depicting Buddha's life. Among the five chapels along the north wall, the one with its exterior adorned with skeletons and skulls is unforgettable. The complex's oldest surviving structure, **Ngagpa Tratsang,** is a three-story college for tantric studies. Here you'll find statues of famous lamas and murals depicting paradise.

Continue to the four-story-high **Sera Je Tratsang,** where Manjashuri, the God of Wisdom, listens to monks engaged in philosophical debate in a courtyard just beyond the temple walls. The extremely animated debates—during which emphatic hand movements signify agreement or disagreement—take place daily starting at 3 am. Whatever your feelings are about the excitement of debates, this is one you don't want to miss. ⊠ *At the base of Mt. Phurbuchok, 5 km (3 miles) north of Lhasa* 🕿 *0891/638–7453* 🎫 *Y55* ☉ *Daily 9–4.*

# TSANG PROVINCE

The Tibetan province of Tsang includes some of the region's most important historic sites outside of Lhasa, but it's also rich in stunning scenery and dotted with small villages and terraced barley fields filled with brightly decorated yaks. This is your chance to get out of the city and experience rural Tibet, where life seems to have changed little over the past 100 years.

**TOURS**

If you're trying to find the majestic valleys and towering peaks that Tibet conjures up in the imagination, a journey through Tsang should be part of your itinerary. Travel agencies offer customized tours typically lasting five to eight days taking you to famous places: the brilliant blue waters of Yamdrok Tso Lake, the Dzong Fortress and Pelkor Chode Monastery in Gyantse, the Tashilhunpo Monastery in Shigatse, and the Base Camp below the world's highest peak at Mount Everest.

Kumbum is one of Tibet's largest stupas.

## GYANTSE

*6 hrs (180 km [110 miles]) by jeep southwest of Lhasa over the Yong-la Pass. 1½ hrs (90 km [55 miles]) southeast of Shigatse.*

With small villages of stone houses beside fields of highland barley, Gyantse feels far removed from Lhasa, although the drive is only about six hours. Home to two of Tsang's most impressive sights—the massive tiered Gyantse Kumbum at Pelkor Chode Monastery and the Gyantse Dzong where British soldiers defeated Tibetans in 1904—Gyantse is an essential stop on the journey toward Everest. Tourist dollars have transformed what was once a small village into a small one bustling with hotels, restaurants, and Internet cafés. However, the sites remain impressive, and the journey to get here over the Yong-la Pass is unforgettable.

### GETTING HERE AND AROUND

Coming from Lhasa, don't let your driver take the longer but faster route through Shigatse to reach Gyantse. Insist on being taken via the dirt road over the Yong-la Pass, where the views are absolutely stunning. Few tourists take this route, and the locals will be genuinely surprised to see you. Once in Gyantse, don't feel the need to rush on to Shigatse the same day; you can spend the night and see the sights in the morning without significantly throwing off your touring schedule.

### SAFETY AND PRECAUTIONS

At 12,959 feet above sea level, visitors to Gyantse may find the altitude difficult to handle. Take it easy and seek medical assistance if necessary.

# A Once-Mighty Empire

The Tibet Autonomous Region (TAR) bears only a passing resemblance to what was once a massive empire that encompassed all of Tibet, Qinghai (except for the area around Xining), western Sichuan, and parts of northern Yunnan. Historically, despite their modern-day reputation for being a peaceful people, Tibetans were known as fierce warriors and feared by their neighbors. They even sacked the Chinese capital of Chang'an, now Xi'an, in the 8th century.

When the Mongols conquered China in the 13th century and founded the Yuan Dynasty, they also took control of Tibet, adopting Tibetan Buddhism as their official religion. This relationship came back to haunt Tibetans—it was used by China's successive dynasties and governments to legitimize the nation's claim to Tibet. In 1950, with almost 10 years of experience fighting first the Japanese and then the Nationalist government, the People's Liberation Army entered Tibet and quickly crushed all resistance.

**TIMING**

Most visitors spend a full day and night in Gyantse in preparation for Everest Base Camp and to allow enough time to see the town's attractions.

**EXPLORING**

Gyantse is easily navigable on foot. The Pelkor Chode Monastery is 10 minutes' walking northwest of the fortress; both can easily be visited and toured over the course of about three hours.

**Gyantse Dzong** (江孜镇 *Jiāngzī xiàn*). In the 14th and 15th centuries Gyantse rose to political power along with the rise of the Sakyapa monastic order. To get an idea of the amount of construction during this period, make the steep 20-minute climb to the top of this old fortress on the northern edge of town. The building isn't in great shape, but you'll be treated to staggering views of the town and the surrounding Nyang Chu Valley. Signs reading "Jump Off Cliff" aren't making a suggestion, but pointing to the location where Tibetan warriors jumped to their deaths rather than surrender to British troops in 1904. The best way to see everything here is to wind around the fortress clockwise toward the top, using the long concrete staircase to descend. Be careful, as there's a slippery bit of concrete at the bottom of the stairs. The **Anti-British Imperialist Museum,** just inside the front gate, is worth a visit for a distorted yet amusing account of the British invasion, sprinkled with obvious propaganda. ⊠ *North end of Yingxiong Lu* ☎ *0892/817–2263* ⊡ *Y40* ⊙ *Daily 9–6:30.*

Fodor's Choice ★ **Pelkor Chode Monastery** (白居寺 *Báijū sì*). One of the few multidenominational monastic complexes in Tibet—housing Gelugpa, Sakyapa, and Bupa monks—Pelkor Chode is home to the **Gyantse Kumbum.** Built in 1427, this building with its glittering golden dome and four sets of spellbinding eyes rising over uniquely tiered circular architecture is one of the most beautiful in Tibet. Inside there are six floors, each a labyrinth of small chapels adorned with Nepalese-influenced murals and

11

statues. A steep ladder at the rear of the fifth floor provides access to the roof. Impressive in itself, you'll appreciate this complex even more after you've seen it from the heights of Gyantse Dzong. ⊠ *Northwest end of Pelkor Lu* ☎ *0892/817–2680* 💳 *Y60* ⏱ *Daily 9–7.*

## SHIGATSE

*4½ hrs (280 km [170 miles]) west of Lhasa by jeep. 1½ hrs (90 km [55 miles]) northwest of Gyantse. 6 hrs (240 km [150 miles]) northeast of Shegar.*

Tibet's second-largest city, Shigatse, is the traditional capital of Tsang and home to the Tashilhunpo Monastery, Tibet's largest functioning monastic institution. The Tsang kings once ruled over the region from the fortress north of town. Most people spend only a day in Shigatse, visiting the monastery and wandering up and down the city's Walking Street, a tourist-friendly section of Qingdao Lu. The city is divided up into a traditional Tibetan quarter and brand-new Chinese town. Shigatse is quite pleasant, but you haven't traveled all the way to Tibet to see another unremarkable city.

### GETTING HERE AND AROUND
The perfectly smooth road from Lhasa to Shigatse travels alongside the picturesque Tsangpo River beneath the towering walls of Nimo Gorge. Rather than stopping in Shigatse the first time you pass through, consider visiting the city on the way back from Everest Base Camp. Driving from Gyantse all the way to Shegar in a single day will maximize the time you have to spend at the mountain by getting a significant chunk of driving out of the way.

### SAFETY AND PRECAUTIONS
Shigaste saw some major rioting during the disturbances in 2008, and there has been a police and army presence here and at Tashilhunpo Monastery ever since.

### TIMING
A day is sufficient to walk around the town and see the monastery.

### EXPLORING
Everything of interest to foreign visitors, including most hotels and restaurants, is on the stretch of road between the monastery and the fortress, namely Walking Street, which you can recognize by the Chinese-style gates on either end.

**Tashilhunpo Monastery** (扎什倫布寺 *Zhāshílúnbù sì*). One of the six great Gelugpa institutions, this monastery is the seat of the Panchen Lama and one of the few religious sites in Tibet not destroyed during the Cultural Revolution. The Chapel of Maitreya houses an 85-foot-high statue of the Future Buddha—the largest in the world—covered with 600 pounds of gold. More than 1,000 more images are painted on the surrounding walls. You will also be able to visit the Panchen Lama tombs, many of which are lined with photos and sculptures of their later reincarnations. The beautiful stupa of the 10th Panchen Lama, built in 1990 after his death in 1989, is topped with a remarkable likeness of his unmistakable fat, jocular face done in pure gold. As this is the largest functioning monastery in Tibet, the police presence can be a bit heavy at times, especially since the 2008 riots. Refrain from discussing politics or the Dalai Lama. Camera fees are Y75 per temple. Don't try to take unauthorized photos, as monks here have been known to manhandle those unwilling to pay for a snapshot. ⊠ *Qingdai Xi Lu* ☎ *0892/882–5220* ⊒ *Y80* ⊘ *Daily 9:30–5 (closed to tourists noon–2).*

## SHEGAR

*6 hrs (240 km [150 miles]) southwest of Shigatse. 3½ hrs (110 km [70 miles]) northeast of Rongbuk Monastery and Everest Base Camp.*

There isn't much of anything to see in Shegar—which also goes by the name New Tingri—a town so small that its two intersecting streets don't even have names. Nevertheless, it's the best place to spend the night before heading down to Rongbuk Monastery for the hike to Everest Base Camp. Supplies in Shegar are more expensive than in Shigatse, but the gouging here is nothing compared to what you'll find closer to Everest.

### GETTING HERE AND AROUND

The long drive from Shigatse to Shegar is necessary if you want to maximize your time at Everest Base Camp. On the way to Mount Everest, you'll encounter a border area checkpoint about 15 minutes outside of town, so don't forget to bring your passport. About 45 minutes later you'll reach Bang-la Pass on the Friendship Highway, with perhaps the world's best view of the Himalayas. On a clear day you can see four of the world's 10 highest peaks, including Everest, Lhotse, Makalu, and Cho Oyu.

### SAFETY AND PRECAUTIONS

The standard advice at being at this altitude applies here; if you feel very ill, you must descend to a lower level immediately.

### TIMING

Most visitors here will be very anxious to reach Everest Base Camp as soon as they can, and there is no need to hang out here for more than a night to get acclimatized.

## EVEREST BASE CAMP

*14 hrs (670 km [420 miles]) southwest of Lhasa by jeep. 3 hrs (110 km [70 miles]) southwest of Shegar (New Tingri).*

"Because it's there," mountaineer George Mallory quipped in 1922 when asked why he wanted to climb the tallest mountain on the planet. The fabled peak is located in the world's highest national park, Qomolangma Nature Reserve, which is a visual delight that alone is worth the trek from Lhasa. After the monsoon rains in June the hillsides are covered with a variety of blooming flowers and butterflies. Even from April to June the light snow blanketing the rugged ground and along babbling brooks is striking.

The scenery is more spectacular than the accommodations at Everest Base Camp.

### GETTING HERE AND AROUND

If you only have eyes for Everest, you can make it here from Lhasa and back in three days. But you spend about 10 hours driving every day, skip all the sights along the way, and hang out for only an hour or so at Everest Base Camp. Most people make this a five-day trip. Not included in the price of your tour will be the Y180 per person entrance fee for the national park, plus Y400 per land cruiser or Y600 per van, usually split among the passengers, and an extra Y180 for the guide's admission. You are not allowed to drive direct to the Base Camp. There is a car park very close to Rongbuk Monastery, and mini-buses (Y25) take you from the car park the rest of the way. Have your passport with you.

### SAFETY AND PRECAUTIONS

As everywhere in Tibet, altitude sickness is common here, and your body needs time to recover. Roughly one out of every 20 visitors needs to be flown out and back down to lower altitudes. If you become ill, you will want to be evacuated to Lhasa as soon as possible. Also, proper clothing and sunscreen are essential. Bring antibacterial hand wash, since it doesn't require water.

### TIMING

Your time at Everest Base Camp is very much dependent on the weather; it can be demoralizing to travel so far and not see the highest mountains in the world because of cloud cover. With this in mind, it's worth planning to stay for at least a couple of days. The best time to enjoy the area is April, May, and June. Avoid traveling here from October to April, as it's cold. July and August is the rainy season, and it's almost impossible to see Mount Everest though the mist.

## TOURS

Snowlion Tours and Tibetan Connections run several tours that include a trip to Everest Base Camp. Trekking tours are possible but they are not cheap. An eight-day tour can cost you Y2,000 per day (including accommodations, food, transportation, camping gear, entrance fees, and English-speaking guide).

**Rongbuk Monastery** (绒布寺修道院 *Róngbù sì xiūdàoyuàn*). You can visit the world's highest monastery, Rongbuk Monastery, on your way to Base Camp. There were once 500 monks living here, but now there are only 20 monks and 10 nuns, who delight in the company of visitors. It is 8 km (5 miles) along a dirt road from the monastery to Base Camp. The 15-minute drive from the monastery is no longer officially allowed, but plenty of jeeps get through with a little cajoling and perhaps a bit of cash. It's more thrilling, however, to make the three-hour walk, even if it is just to say that you trekked the Everest region. Horse-drawn carts are also available for Y30 per person one way, making the trip in about an hour. 🎫 Y35.

# UNDERSTANDING CHINA

**CHINA AT A GLANCE**

**VOCABULARY**

# CHINA AT A GLANCE

## FAST FACTS

- Capital: Beijing
- National anthem: "March of the Volunteers"
- Type of government: Communist
- Administrative divisions: 23 provinces (including Taiwan), 5 autonomous regions, 4 municipalities, 2 special administrative regions (Hong Kong and Macau)
- Independence: October 1, 1949
- Constitution: December 4, 1982
- Legal system: A mix of custom and statute, largely criminal law, with rudimentary civil code
- Voting: 18 years of age
- Legislature: Unicameral National People's Congress; 2,985 members elected by municipal, regional, and provincial people's congresses to serve five-year terms; the last elections were in 2008.
- Population: 1.3 billion; the largest in the world
- Population density: 138 people per square km (361 people per square mile)
- Median age: Female 36.6, male 35.2
- Life expectancy: Female 77.1, male 72.8
- Infant mortality rate: 15.6 deaths per 1,000 live births
- Literacy: 92.2%
- Language: Standard Chinese or Mandarin (official), Yue (Cantonese), Wu (Shanghainese), Minbei (Fuzhou), Minnan (Hokkien-Taiwanese), Xiang, Gan, Hakka dialects
- Ethnic groups: Han Chinese 92%; Zhuang, Uygur, Hui, Yi, Tibetan, Miao, Manchu, Mongol, Buyi, Korean, and other nationalities 8%
- Religion: Officially atheist, but Taoism, Buddhism, Christianity, and Islam are practiced.
- Discoveries and Inventions: Decimal system (1400 BC), paper (100 BC), seismograph (AD 100), compass (200), matches (577), gunpowder (700), paper money (800), movable type (1045)

## GEOGRAPHY AND ENVIRONMENT

- Land area: 9.3 million square km (3.6 million square miles), the fourth-largest country in the world, and slightly smaller than the United States
- Coastline: 14,500 km (9,010 miles) on the Yellow Sea, the East China Sea, and the South China Sea
- Terrain: Mostly mountains, high plateaus, deserts in west; plains, deltas, and hills in east
- Islands: Hainan, Taiwan, many smaller islands along the coast
- Natural resources: Aluminum, antimony, coal, hydropower, iron ore, lead, magnetite, manganese, mercury, molybdenum, natural gas, petroleum, tin, tungsten, uranium, vanadium, zinc
- Natural hazards: Droughts, earthquakes, floods, land subsidence, tsunamis, typhoons
- Environmental issues: Air pollution (greenhouse gases, sulfur dioxide particulates), especially from China's reliance on coal, which is used to generate 68% of the country's electric power. Acid rain is another consequence of burning high-sulfur coal, particularly in the north. Deforestation, soil erosion, and economic development have destroyed one-fifth of agricultural land since 1949. Water pollution from untreated wastes and water shortages are other problems.

*China is an attractive piece of meat coveted by all . . . but very tough, and for years no one has been able to bite into it.*

*— Zhou Enlai,*

*Chinese Premier, 1973*

# ECONOMY

- Currency: Yuan
- Exchange rate: Y6.14=$1
- GDP: $7.318 trillion
- Inflation: 2.61%
- Per capita income: Y52,252 ($8,400)
- Unemployment: 6.5%
- Workforce: 795.5 million (agriculture 36.7%; industry 28.7%; services 34.6%)
- Debt: $656.3 billion
- Major industries: Armaments, automobiles, cement, chemical fertilizers, coal, consumer electronics, food processing, footwear, iron and steel, machine building, petroleum, telecommunications, textiles and apparel, toys
- Agricultural products: Barley, cotton, fish, millet, oilseed, peanuts, pork, potatoes, rice, sorghum, tea, wheat
- Exports: $1.9 trillion
- Major export products: electrical and other machinery, including data processing equipment, apparel, textiles, iron and steel, optical and medical equipment
- Export partners: U.S. 17.1%; Hong Kong 14.1%; Japan 7.8%; South Korea 4.4%; Germany 4%
- Imports: $1.7 trillion
- Major import products: Chemicals, iron and steel, machinery and equipment, mineral fuels, plastics
- Import partners: Japan 11.2%; South Korea 9.3%; U.S. 6.8%; Germany 5.3%; Australia 4.6%

## POLITICAL CLIMATE

Since the Chinese Communist Party (CCP) took control of the government in 1949, it has shown little tolerance for outside views. Other major political parties are banned and the government is quick to crack down on movements that it doesn't approve of, most recently the Falun Gong. China's size and diversity complicate national politics, with party control weaker in rural areas, where most of the population lives. Successful politicians have sought support from local and regional leaders and must work to keep influential nonparty members from creating a stir.

The decade-long struggle for democracy, which ended in the bloody Tiananmen Square protests of 1989, has fragmented and lost much of its momentum. The party blamed its rise on foreign agitators and reminds the population that political stability is essential for China's economic growth. There is increasing frustration among the Chinese people over political corruption at the local and national levels, prompting urgent calls for government reform. Always alert to domestic discontent, the Chinese government maintains tight control over media, Internet, and other forms of communication to prevent dissent.

## DID YOU KNOW?

- China spent $52 billion on renewable energy in 2012, leading the United States, Germany, Italy, and India.
- China has approximately 3.4 million active military personnel.
- There are about 100,000 mass protests every year in China, largely in rural areas.
- China consumes more steel than the U.S., Europe, and Japan combined.
- During the Holocaust, Shanghai was the only port that would accept Jews without an entry visa or passport.
- Tsingtao Beer makes up more than 50% of China's beer exports.
- The 2008 Olympic Games in Beijing cost $40 billion, the most expensive in history.

# CHINESE VOCABULARY

| | CHINESE | ENGLISH EQUIVALENT | CHINESE | ENGLISH EQUIVALENT |
|---|---|---|---|---|
| CONSONANTS | | | | |
| | b | **b**oat | p | **p**ass |
| | m | **m**ouse | f | **f**lag |
| | d | **d**ock | t | **t**ongue |
| | n | **n**est | l | **l**ife |
| | g | **g**oat | k | **k**eep |
| | h | **h**ouse | j | and **y**et |
| | q | chi**ck**en | x | **sh**ort |
| | zh | ju**dg**e | ch | chur**ch** |
| | sh | **sh**eep | r* | **r**ead |
| | z | see**ds** | c | do**ts** |
| | s | **s**eed | | |
| VOWELS | | | | |
| | ü | **You** | ia | **ya**rd |
| | üe | y**ou** + **e** | ian | **yen** |
| | a | f**a**ther | iang | **young** |
| | ai | **K**i**te** | ie | **yet** |
| | ao | n**ow** | o | **a**ll |
| | e | **ea**rn | ou | g**o** |
| | ei | **Day** | u | w**oo**d |
| | er | c**ur**ve | ua | **wa**ft |
| | i | **yi**eld | uo | **wa**ll |
| | i (after z, c, s, zh, ch, sh) | **th**un**der** | | |

### WORD ORDER
The basic Chinese sentence structure is the same as in English, following the pattern of subject-verb-object:

He took my pen.       Tā ná le wǒ de bǐ.

s    v        o            s    v        o

### NOUNS
There are no articles in Chinese, although there are many "counters," or "measure words," which are used when a certain number of something is specified. Various attributes of a noun—such as size, shape, or use—determine which counter is used with that noun. Chinese does not distinguish between singular and plural.

| a pen | yìzhī bǐ |
| a book | yìběn shū |

### VERBS

Chinese verbs are not conjugated, and they do not have tenses. Instead, a system of word order, word repetition, and the addition of a number of adverbs serves to indicate the tense of a verb, whether the verb is a suggestion or an order, or even whether the verb is part of a question. Tāzaì ná wǒ de bǐ. (He is taking my pen.) Tā ná le wǒ de bǐ. (He took my pen.) Tā you méi you ná wǒ de bǐ? (Did he take my pen?) Tā yào ná wǒ de bǐ. (He will take my pen.)

### TONES

In English, intonation patterns can indicate whether a sentence is a statement (He's hungry.), a question (He's hungry?), or an exclamation (He's hungry!). In Chinese, words have a particular tone value, and these tones are important in determining the meaning of a word. In the following examples, the words look similar but each is said with one of the four tones found in standard Chinese: mā (high, steady tone) means mother; má (rising tone, like a question) means fiber; mǎ (dipping tone) means horse; and mà (dropping tone) means swear.

### PHRASES

You don't need to master the entire Chinese language to spend a week in China, but taking charge of a few key phrases in the language can aid you in just getting by.

## COMMON GREETINGS

| | |
|---|---|
| Hello/Good morning | Nǐ hǎo/Zǎoshàng hǎo |
| Good evening | Wǎnshàng hǎo |
| Good-bye | Zàijiàn |
| Title for a married woman or an older unmarried woman | Tàitai/Fūrén |
| Title for a young and unmarried woman | Xiǎojiě |
| Title for a man | Xiānshēng |
| How are you? | Nǐ hǎo ma? |
| Fine, thanks. And you? | Hěn hǎo. Xièxiè. Nǐ ne? |
| What is your name? | Nǐ jiào shénme míngzi? |
| My name is... | Wǒ jiào... |
| Nice to meet you | Hěn gāoxìng rènshì nǐ |
| I'll see you later. | Huítóu jiàn. |

## POLITE EXPRESSIONS

| | |
|---|---|
| Please. | Qǐng. |
| Thank you. | Xièxiè. |
| Thank you very much. | Duōxiè. |
| You're welcome. | Búkèqi |
| Yes, thank you. | Shì de, xièxiè. |
| No, thank you. | Bù, xièxiè. |
| I beg your pardon. | Qǐng yuánliàng. |
| I'm very sorry. | Hěn bàoqiàn. |
| Pardon me. | Dùibùqǐ. |
| That's okay. | Méi shénme. |
| It doesn't matter. | Méi guānxi. |
| Do you speak English? | Nǐ hui shuō Yīngyǔ ma? |
| Yes. | Shì de. |
| No. | Bù. |
| Maybe. | Bù yī dìng |
| I can speak a little. | Wǒ néng shuō yī diǎnr. |
| I understand a little. | Wǒ dǒng yì diǎnr. |
| I don't understand. | Wǒ bù dǒng. |
| I don't speak Chinese very well. | Wǒ Zhōngwén shuō de bù hǎo. |
| Would you repeat that, please? | Qǐng zài shuō yíbiàn? |
| I don't know. | Wǒ bù zhīdaò. |

**COMMON GREETINGS**

| No problem. | Méi wèntí. |
| It's my pleasure. | Méi guānxi. |

**NEEDS AND QUESTION WORDS**

| I'd like... | Wǒ xiǎng... |
| I need... | Wǒ xūyào... |
| What would you like? | Nǐ yaò shénme? |
| Please bring me... | Qǐng gěi wǒ... |
| I'm looking for... | Wǒ zài zhǎo... |
| I'm hungry. | Wǒ è le. |
| I'm thirsty. | Wǒ kǐukě. |
| It's important. | Hěn zhòngyào. |
| It's urgent. | Hěn jǐnjí. |
| How? | Zěnmeyàng? |
| How much? | Duōshǎo? |
| How many? | Duōshǎo gè? |
| Which? | Nǎ yí gè? |
| What? | Shénme? |
| What kind of? | Shénme yàng de? |
| Who? | Shuí? |
| Where? | Nǎli? |
| When? | Shénme shíhòu? |
| What does this mean? | Zhè shì shénme yìsi? |
| What does that mean? | Nà shì shénme yìsi? |
| How do you say...in Chinese? | ...yòng Zhōngwén zěnme shūo? |

**AT THE AIRPORT**

| Where is... | ...zài nǎr? |
| customs? | hǎigūan |
| passport control? | hùzhào jiānyàn |
| the information booth? | wènxùntái |
| the ticketing counter? | shòupiàochù |
| the baggage claim? | xínglǐchù |
| the ground transportation? | dìmìan jiāotōng |
| Is there a bus to the city? | yǒu qù chéng lǐ de gōnggòng qìchē ma? |
| Where are... | ...zài nǎr? |

## COMMON GREETINGS

| | |
|---|---|
| the international departures? | guójì hángbĕn chūfĕ diăn? |
| the international arrivals? | guójì hángbĕn dàodá diăn? |
| What is your nationality? | Nĭ shì nĕi guó rén? |
| I am an American. | Wŏ shì Mĕiguó rén. |
| I am Canadian. | Wŏ shì Jiĕnádà rén. |

### AT THE HOTEL, RESERVING A ROOM

| | |
|---|---|
| I would like a room... | Wŏ yào yí ge fángjiān. |
| for one person | yìjiān dānrén |
| for two people | yìjiān shuāngrén |
| for tonight | jīntīan wănshàng |
| for two nights | liăng gè wănshàng |
| for a week | yí ge xīngqī |
| Do you have a different room? | Nĭ hái yŏu biéde fángjiān ma? |
| with a bath | dài yùshì de fángjiān |
| with a shower | dài línyù de fángjiān |
| with a toilet | dài cèsuĭ de fángjiān |
| with air-conditioning | yŏu kōngtiáo de fángjiān |
| How much is it? | Duōshăo qián? |
| My bill, please. | Qĭng jiézhàng. |

### AT THE RESTAURANT

| | |
|---|---|
| Where can we find a good restaurant? | Zài năr kĕyĭ zhăodào yìjiē hăo cānguăn? |
| We'd like a(n)...restaurant. | Wŏmen xiăng qù yì gè... cānguăn. |
| elegant | gāo jí |
| fast-food | kuàicān |
| inexpensive | piányì de |
| seafood | hăixiān |
| vegetarian | Sushi |
| café | kāfeī diàn |
| A table for two | liăng wèi |
| Waiter, a menu, please. | Fúwùyuán, qĭng gĕi wŏmen càidān. |
| The wine list, please. | Qĭng gĕi wŏmen jiŭdān. |
| Appetizers | kāiwèi cài |
| Main course | zhŭ cài |

**COMMON GREETINGS**

| | |
|---|---|
| Dessert | tiándiǎn |
| What would you like? | Nǐ yào shénme cài? |
| What would you like to drink? | Nǐ yào hē shénme yǐnliào? |
| Can you recommend a good wine? | Nǐ néng tūijiàn yí ge hǎo jiǔ ma? |
| Wine, please. | Qǐng lǎi diǎn jiǔ |
| Beer, please. | Qǐng lǎi diǎn píjiǔ. |
| I didn't order this. | Wǐ méiyǒu diǎn zhè gè. |
| That's all, thanks. | Jiù zhèxie, xièxiè. |
| The check, please. | Qǐng jiézhàng. |
| Cheers!/Bottoms Up! | Gānbēi! |
| To your health! | Zhù nǐ shēntì jiànkāng. |

**OUT ON THE TOWN**

| | |
|---|---|
| Where can I find... | Nǎr yǒu... |
| an art museum? | yìshù bówùguǎn? |
| a museum of natural history? | zìránlìshǐ bówùguǎn? |
| a history museum? | lìshǐ bówuguǎn? |
| a gallery? | huàláng? |
| interesting architecture? | yǒuqù de jiànzhùwù? |
| a church? | jiàotáng? |
| the zoo? | dòngwùyuán? |
| I'd like... | Wǒ xiǎng... |
| to see a play. | kàn xì. |
| to see a movie. | kàn diànyǐng. |
| to see a concert. | qù yīnyuèhuì. |
| to see the opera. | kàn gējù. |
| to go sightseeing. | qù guānguāng. |
| to go on a bike ride. | qí zixíngchē. |

**SHOPPING**

| | |
|---|---|
| Where is the best place to go shopping for... | Mǎi...zuì hǎo qù nǎr? |
| clothes? | yīfu? |
| food? | shíwù? |
| souvenirs? | jìniànpǐn? |
| furniture? | jīajù? |
| fabric? | bùliào? |

**COMMON GREETINGS**

| | |
|---|---|
| antiques? | gǔdǐng? |
| books? | shūjí? |
| sporting goods? | yùndòng wùpǐn? |
| electronics? | diànqì? |
| computers? | diànnǎo? |

**DIRECTIONS**

| | |
|---|---|
| Excuse me. Where is... | Duìbùqǐ... zài nǎr? |
| the bus stop? | qìchēzhàn? |
| the subway station? | dìtiězhàn? |
| the restroom? | xǐshǐujiān? |
| the taxi stand? | chūzū chēzhàn? |
| the nearest bank? | zùijìn de yínháng? |
| the hotel? | lǚˇguǎn? |
| To the right | Zài yòubiān. |
| To the left. | Zài zuǐbiān. |
| Straight ahead. | Wǎng qián zǒu. |
| It's near here. | Jiuzài zhè fùjìn. |
| Go back. | Wǎng húi zǒu. |
| Next to... | Jǐnkào... |

**TIME**

| | |
|---|---|
| What time is it? | Xiànzài jǐdiǎn? |
| It is noon. | Zhōngwǔ. |
| It is midnight. | Bànyè. |
| It is 9 am | Shàngwǔ jǐu diǎn. |
| It is 1 pm | Xiàwǔ yì diǎn. |
| It is 3 o'clock. | Sān diǎn (zhōng). |
| 5:15 | Wǔ diǎn shíwǔ fēn. |
| 7:30 | Qī diǎn sānshí (bàn). |
| 9:45 | Jǐu diǎn sìshíwǔ. |
| Now | Xiànzài |
| Later | Wǎn yì diǎnr |
| Immediately | Mǎshàng |
| Soon | Hěn kuài |

## COMMON GREETINGS

### DAYS OF THE WEEK

| | |
|---|---|
| Monday | Xīngqī yī |
| Tuesday | Xīngqī èr |
| Wednesday | Xīngqī sān |
| Thursday | Xīngqī sì |
| Friday | Xīngqī wǔ |
| Saturday | Xīngqī liu |
| Sunday | Xīngqī rì (tiān) |

### MODERN CONNECTIONS

| | |
|---|---|
| Where can I find... | Zài nǎr kěyǐ shǐ yòng... |
| a telephone? | diànhuà? |
| a fax machine? | chuánzhēnjī? |
| an Internet connection? | guójì wǎnglù? |
| How do I call the United States? | Gěi Měiguó dǎ diànhuà zěnme dǎ? |
| I need... | Wǒ xūyào... |
| a fax sent. | fā chuánzhēn. |
| a hookup to the Internet. | yǔ guójì wǎnglù liánjiē. |
| a computer. | diànnǎo. |
| a package sent overnight. | liányè bǎ bāoguǒ jìchū. |
| some copies made. | fùyìn yìxiē wénjiàn. |
| a DVD player | yǐngdié jī |
| an overhead projector and markers. | huàndēngjī he biāoshìqì. |

### EMERGENCIES AND SAFETY

| | |
|---|---|
| Help! | Jiùmìng a! |
| Fire! | Jiùhuǐ a! |
| I need a doctor. | Wǒ yào kàn yīshēng. |
| Call an ambulance! | Mǎshàng jiào jiuhùchē! |
| What happened? | Fāshēng le shénme shì? |
| I am/My wife is/My husband is/ | Wǒ/Wǒ qīzi/Wǒ Zhàngfu/ |
| My friend is/Someone is... | Wǒ péngyǒu/Yǒu rén... |
| having a heart attack. | bìng de hěn lìhài. |
| choking. | yēzhù le. |
| losing consciousness. | yūndǎo le. |
| about to vomit. | yào ǒutùwù le. |

## COMMON GREETINGS

| | |
|---|---|
| having a seizure. | yǒu fābìng le. |
| stuck. | bèi kǎ zhù le. |
| I can't breathe. | Wǒ bù néng hūxī. |
| I tripped and fell. | Wǒ bàn dǎo le. |
| I cut myself. | Wǒ gē shěng le. |
| I drank too much. | Wǒ jiǔ hē de tài duō le. |
| I don't know. | Wǒ bù zhīdào. |
| I've injured my... | Wǒ de...shòushěng le. |
| head | toú |
| neck | bózi |
| back | bèi |
| arm | gē bèi |
| leg | tuǐ |
| foot | jiǎo |
| eye(s) | yǎnjīng |
| I've been robbed. | Wǒ bèi qiǎng le. |

## NUMBERS

| | |
|---|---|
| 0 | Líng |
| 1 | Yī |
| 2 | Èr, liǎng |
| 3 | Sān |
| 4 | Sì |
| 5 | Wǔ |
| 6 | Liù |
| 7 | Qī |
| 8 | Bā |
| 9 | Jiǔ |
| 10 | Shí |
| 11 | Shíyī |
| 12 | Shí'èr |
| 13 | Shísān |
| 14 | Shísì |
| 15 | Shíwǔ |
| 16 | Shíliù |
| 17 | Shíqī |

**COMMON GREETINGS**

| | |
|---|---|
| 18 | Shíbā |
| 19 | Shíjiŭ |
| 20 | Èrshí |
| 21 | Èrshíyī |
| 22 | Èrshí'èr |
| 23 | Èrshísān |
| 30 | Sānshí |
| 40 | Sìshí |
| 50 | Wŭshí |
| 60 | Liùshí |
| 70 | Qīshí |
| 80 | Bāshí |
| 90 | Jiŭshí |
| 100 | Yìbăi |
| 1,000 | Yìqiān |
| 1,100 | Yìqiān yìbăi |
| 2,000 | Liăngqiān |
| 10,000 | Yíwàn |
| 100,000 | Shíwàn |
| 1,000,000 | Băiwàn |

# TRAVEL SMART CHINA

Visit Fodors.com for advice, updates, and bookings

# GETTING HERE AND AROUND

Make no mistake: This is one HUGE country. China's efficient train system is a great way of getting around, especially with the high-speed rail lines linking major cities like Beijing, Guangzhou, and Shanghai. The growing network of domestic flights is also a good option, although for some routes high-speed rail can be cheaper and faster, saving you the two-hour check-in time at most airports.

China's capital, Beijing, is in the northeast, while the financial capital of Shanghai is halfway down the east coast. The historic city of Nanjing is upriver from Shanghai; head much farther inland and you'll hit the erstwhile capital Xi'an, home to the Terracotta Warriors.

Limestone mountains surround the Guilin area, in southern China. The region's hubs are Guangzhou, capital of Guangdong Province, and Shenzhen, an industrial boomtown on the border with Hong Kong. Though part of China, Hong Kong is a Special Administrative Region, and functions as if it were another country.

Smack bang in the middle of China is Sichuan province. Its capital, Chengdu, is a lively financial center and an important transport hub connecting eastern and western China. Kunming is the capital of the southwestern province of Yunnan. Once the gateway to the Silk Road, it now leads to the bordering countries of Myanmar, Laos, and Vietnam.

Despite ongoing international controversy, Tibet, in the far west of the country, remains a Special Autonomous Region. Its capital, Lhasa, the historic center of Tibetan Buddhism, is a mind-blowing 3,650 meters (11,975 feet) above sea level in the northern Himalayas.

Vast deserts and grassy plains make up much of northwest China. Here the autonomous Xinjiang region is home to a largely Muslim population. Its capital city, Ürümqi, is the world's farthest inland city. Nei Mongol, or Inner Mongolia, is a great swath of (mostly barren) land that runs across much of northern China.

Maps with street names in Pinyin are available in most Chinese cities, though they're not always up to date. A few crucial words of Chinese can help decode street names. *Lu* means road, *jie* means street, *dalu* is a main road, and *dajie* is a main street. Those endings are often preceded by a compass point: *bei* (north), *dong* (east), *nan* (south), *xi* (west), and *zhong* (middle). These distinguish different sections of long streets. So, if you're looking for Beijing Xi Lu, it's the western end of Beijing Road.

| TRAVEL TIMES FROM BEIJING | | |
|---|---|---|
| To | By Air | By Train |
| Shanghai | 2¼ hours | 5–20 hours |
| Xi'an | 2 hours | 5–19 hours |
| Guangzhou | 3 hours | 9–29 hours |
| Hong Kong | 3¾ hours | 24–27 hours |
| Guilin | 3¼ hours | 22–27 hours |
| Kunming | 3¼ hours | 38–47 hours |
| Nanjing | 1¾ hours | 3–15 hours |
| Lhasa | 6 hours | 45 hours |
| Ürümqi | 4 hours | 34 hours |
| Chengdu | 3¾ hours | 25–31 hours |

## ▌ AIR TRAVEL

If you are flying to China on a SkyTeam airline (Delta, for example), consider the Go Greater China Pass, which covers 148 destinations in China, including Hong Kong, Macao, and Taiwan. After you purchase your international ticket to mainland China or Taiwan on a SkyTeam member airline, you can fly within China on China Airlines, China Southern, or China Eastern. If you are a member of a frequent-flier program, these flights will count toward miles. The price of the pass is between $270 and $1,300, depending upon the distance you plan to fly.

Beijing, Xiamen, and Hong Kong are three of the cities included in the One-World Alliance Visit Asia Pass. Cities are grouped into zones, and a flat rate is levied for each flight based on the zone in which the city is located. It doesn't include flights from the United States, however. Inquire through American Airlines, Cathay Pacific, or any other OneWorld member. It won't be the cheapest way to get around, but you'll be flying on some of the world's best airlines.

**Air Pass Info Go Greater China Pass** ☎ 800/221-1212 ⊕ www.skyteam.com. **Visit Asia Pass** ☎ 800/233-2742 ⊕ www.oneworld. com.

Beijing, Shanghai, and Hong Kong are China's three major international hubs. You can catch nonstop or one-stop flights to Beijing from New York (13¾), Chicago (13–14 hours), San Francisco (11½–12½ hours), Los Angeles (11½–13 hours), London (10½–11½ hours), and Sydney (14–16 hours). Though most airlines say that reconfirming your return flight is unnecessary, some local airlines cancel your seat if you don't reconfirm.

**Airlines and Airports Airline and Airport Links.com.** Airline and Airport Links. com has links to the websites of many of the world's airlines and airports. ⊕ www. airlineandairportlinks.com.

**Airline Security Issues Transportation Security Administration.** Transportation Security Administration answers almost every question about US airline security and travel regulations that you may have. ⊕ www.tsa.gov.

## AIRPORTS

Northern China's main hub is the frenetic Beijing Capital International Airport (PEK), 20 miles northeast of the Beijing city center. Plans are underway to have a new airport built in Beijing by October 2018. Shanghai has two airports: Pudong International Airport (PVG) is newer and flashier than Hongqiao International Airport (SHA), but Hongqiao is more efficient and closer to downtown. The main hub in southern China is the sleek and modern Hong Kong International Airport (HKG), also known as Chek Lap Kok.

There are also international airports at Guangzhou (CAN), Kunming (KMG), Xiamen (XMN), Shenzhen (SZX), Xi'an (XIY), Chengdu (CTU), and Guilin (KWL), among others.

Clearing customs and immigration in China can take a while, especially in the morning, so arrive at least two hours before your scheduled flight time.

While you're wandering through Chinese airports, someone may approach you offering to carry your luggage, or even just give you directions. Be aware that this "helpful" stranger will almost certainly expect payment. Many of the X-ray machines used for large luggage items aren't film-safe, so keep film in your carry-on if you're still using a nondigital camera.

**Airport Information Beijing Capital International Airport** ☎ 010/6454-1100 ⊕ www. en.bcia.com.cn. **Chengdu Shuangliu International Airport** ☎ 028/8520-5555 ⊕ www. cdairport.com. **Guangzhou Baiyun International Airport** ☎ 020/3606-6999 ⊕ www. guangzhouairportonline.com. **Guilin Liangjiang International Airport** ☎ 0773/284-5114. **Hong Kong International Airport** ☎ 852/2261-2727 ⊕ www.hongkongairport. com. **Kunming Changsui International Airport** ☎ 871/96566 ⊕ www.kmgairport.com. **Shanghai Hongqiao International Airport** ☎ 021/96990 ⊕ www.shanghaiairport.com. **Shanghai Pudong International Airport** ☎ 021/96990 ⊕ www.shanghaiairport.com. **Shenzhen Bao'an International Airport** ☎ 0755/2777-2000 ⊕ www.eng.szairport. com. **Xi'an Xianyang International Airport** ☎ 029/0500-2327 ⊕ www.xxia.com.cn/ en. **Xiamen Gaoqi International Airport** ☎ 0592/570-6078 ⊕ www.xiagc.com.cn/en.

**FLIGHTS**

**TO AND FROM CHINA**

Air China is China's flagship carrier. It operates nonstop flights from Beijing and Shanghai to various North American and European cities. Although it once had a sketchy safety record, the situation has improved dramatically, and it is now part of the Star Alliance of airlines worldwide. Don't confuse it with the similarly named China Airlines, which is operated out of Taiwan.

Air Canada has daily flights to Beijing and Shanghai from Toronto, and daily flights to Hong Kong from Toronto, Calgary, Edmonton, and Vancouver. Cathay Pacific flies to Beijing via Hong Kong. China Eastern and China Southern airlines fly from China to the West Coast of the United States. Japan Airlines and All Nippon fly to Beijing via Tokyo. United flies to Beijing and Shanghai.

**WITHIN CHINA**

Air China is the major carrier for domestic routes, flying to more than 180 cities in China. Its main rivals are China Southern and China Eastern. Smaller Shanghai Airlines has a growing number of national routes, mostly out of Shanghai.

The service on most Chinese airlines is on a par with low-cost American airlines—be prepared for limited legroom, iffy food, and possibly no personal TV. Always arrive at least two hours before departure, as chronic overbooking means latecomers just don't get on. In southern China typhoons often ground airplanes, so be prepared for delays if you are traveling between July and October.

You can make reservations and buy tickets for flights within China through airline websites or with travel agencies. It's worth contacting a travel agency to compare prices.

**Airline Contacts Air China** ☎ 800/882–8122 ⊕ www.airchina.com. **China Eastern** ☎ 626/583–1500 ⊕ www.flychinaeastern.us. **China Southern** ☎ 888/338–8988 ⊕ www.flychinasouthern.com.

**BEST FOOT FORWARD**

Foot-massage spas are all the rage in China, but if you thought this was a new trend brought on by an upwardly mobile (and naturally more footsore) Chinese populace, think again. While Western medicine sees the foot as mere locomotion, practitioners of traditional Chinese reflexology think that bodily health is reflected in the sole. Each organ is connected to a specific reflex point on the foot. With precise and skillful manipulation of these points, vital functions can be stimulated, toxins eliminated, blood circulation improved, and nerves soothed. If your masseur is skilled, he'll be able to give you a fairly accurate health diagnosis after just a few minutes of looking at your feet. A smoker? Have indigestion? Sleeping poorly? Your feet tell all.

**▌ BIKE TRAVEL**

Bicycles are still the primary form of transport for millions of Chinese people, although the proliferation of cars and smog make biking in the cities a chore. Large cities like Beijing, Chengdu, Xi'an, Shanghai, and Guilin have well-defined bike lanes, often separated from other traffic. Travel by bike is common in the countryside around places like Guilin, for locals and tourists alike. Locals don't use gears much—take your cue from them and just roll along at a leisurely pace. Note that bikes have to give way to motorized vehicles at intersections. If a flat tire or sudden brake failure strikes, seek out the nearest street-side mechanic (they're everywhere), easily identified by their bike parts and pumps.

In major cities, some lower-end hotels and hostels rent bikes. Street-side bike rental stations are also proliferating. Otherwise, inquire at bike shops, hotels, or even corner shops. The going rental rate is Y15 to Y30 a day, plus a refundable deposit. Check the seat and wheels carefully.

Most rental bikes come with a lock, but they're usually pretty low quality. Instead, leave your wheels at an attended bike park—peace of mind costs a mere Y0.50. Helmets are nearly unheard of in China, though upmarket rental companies catering to foreign tourists usually stock them. They charge much more for their bikes, but they're usually in better condition.

If you're planning a lot of cycling, note that for about Y150 to Y200 you can buy your own basic bike, though expect to pay three or four times that for a mountain bike with all the bells and whistles or for a "Flying Pigeon," the classic heavy-duty model.

U.S.-based Backroads has a China bike tour suitable for families. Bike China Adventures organizes trips of varying length and difficulty all over China.

**BIKES IN FLIGHT**

Most airlines accommodate bikes as luggage, provided they are dismantled and boxed; check with individual airlines about packing requirements. Some airlines sell bike boxes, which are often free at bike shops, for about $20 (bike bags can be considerably more expensive).

**Tour Operators Backroads** ☎ *800/462–2848* ⊕ *www.backroads.com.* **Bike China Adventures** ☎ *800/818–1778* ⊕ *www.bikechina.com.*

## ▮ BOAT TRAVEL

Trains and planes are fast replacing China's boat and ferry services. The China-Japan International Ferry Company operates a ferry every Tuesday between Kobe or Osaka and Shanghai. The Shanghai Ferry Company has a weekly ferry to Osaka. Both companies maintain English-language websites with timetables.

Four- to seven-day cruises along the Yangtze River are the most popular, and thus the most touristy of the domestic boat rides. Both local and international companies run these tours, but shop around, as prices vary drastically. *See chapter 8 for detailed information on Yangtze River cruises.*

**Ferry Information China-Japan International Ferry Company** ⊠ *908 Dongdaming Lu, Shanghai* ☎ *021/6325–7642* ⊕ *www. shinganjin.com/index_e.php.* **Shanghai Ferry Company** ⊠ *500 Dongdaming Lu, Shanghai* ☎ *021/6181–8000* ⊕ *www.shanghai-ferry. co.jp/english.*

## ▮ BUS TRAVEL

China has some reasonably comfortable long-distance buses running between most major cities. These luxury coaches are equipped with air-conditioning, soft seats, and screens playing nonstop movies, usually at deafening levels. Bring earplugs if you can't stand the noise.

Buying tickets can be complicated if you don't speak Chinese—you may end up on one of the cramped, old-fashioned buses, much like school buses (or worse). The conditions on sleeper buses are especially dire. Taking a train or an internal flight is much easier and safer, especially in rural areas where bad road conditions make for dangerous rides.

Big cities often have more than one bus terminal, and some companies have their own private depots. Buses usually depart and arrive punctually, and service is frequent. You can buy tickets for a small surcharge through your hotel.

## ▮ CAR TRAVEL

Driving yourself is not a possibility in mainland China, as the only valid driver's licenses are Chinese ones. However, this restriction should be cause for relief, as city traffic is terrible, drivers manic and maniacal, and getting lost inevitable for first-timers. Conditions in Hong Kong aren't much better, but you can drive there using a U.S. or international license.

A far better idea is to put yourself in the experienced hands of a local driver. All the same, consider your itinerary carefully before doing so—in big cities, taking the subway or walking is often far quicker.

Reserve the car for excursions farther afield.

The quickest way to arrange for a car and driver is to flag down a taxi. If you're happy with a driver you've used for trips around town, ask if you can hire him for the day. After some negotiating, expect to pay between Y350 and Y600, depending on the type of car. Most hotels can make arrangements for you, though they often charge you double that rate.

Another alternative is American car-rental agency Avis, which includes mandatory chauffeurs as part of all rental packages. A car and driver usually cost Y740 to Y850 ($118 to $136) per day. The company's headquarters are in Shanghai, with locations in Beijing, Hong Kong, Shanghai, Guangzhou, Shenzhen, and Chengdu.

**Information**

**Avis** ☎ 021/6229–1118 ⊕ www.avischina.com.

# ▌ TRAIN TRAVEL

China's enormous rail network is one of the world's busiest. Trains are usually safe, efficient, and run strictly to schedule. The high-speed rail system makes getting around the country very easy. In late 2012, the Beijing-Guangzhou line opened, cutting travel time between the two cities from 30 hours to about 9 hours. At 1,428 miles, the line is the longest in the world.

There are certain intricacies to buying tickets, which usually have to be purchased in your departure city. You can buy most tickets up to 18 days in advance; three to four days ahead is usually enough time, except during the three national holidays—Chinese New Year (two days in mid-January–February), Labor Day (May 1), and National Day (October 1).

The cheapest place to purchase tickets is the train station, where they only accept cash and English is rarely spoken. In larger cities like Shanghai or Beijing, there is a special ticket window for foreigners with a staff that speaks some English. There are also train booking offices scattered

**SERIOUS TRAINING**

The most dramatic Chinese train experience is the six-day trip between Beijing and Moscow, often referred to as the Trans-Siberian railway, though that's actually the service that runs between Moscow and Vladivostok. Two weekly services cover the 8,047 km (5,000 miles) between Moscow and Beijing. The Trans-Manchurian is a Russian train that goes through northeast China, whereas the Trans-Mongolian is a Chinese train that goes through the Great Wall and crosses the Gobi Desert. Both have first-class compartments with four berths or luxury two-berth compartments. Trains leave from Beijing Station—the cheapest place to buy tickets, though it's easier to get them through CITS.

around most cities. Fighting the crowds in train stations can be a headache—most travel agents or hotels will book your tickets for a small surcharge. Consider it money well spent! Travel China Guide has an online booking service that caters to foreigners. The company will deliver the tickets to your hotel or arrange for you to pick them up at the train station. Avoid the scruffy-looking individuals who try to sell you tickets outside the stations—these tickets are inevitably fake and could land you in trouble with the authorities.

The train system offers a glimpse of old-fashioned socialist euphemisms. There are four classes, but instead of first class and second class, in China you talk about hard and soft. Hard seats (*yingzuo*) are often rigid benches guaranteed to numb the buttocks within seconds; soft seats (*ruanzuo*), common on short day trips, are more like the seats in long-distance American trains. For overnight journeys, the cheapest option is the hard sleeper (*yingwo*), open bays of six bunks, in two tiers of three. They're cramped, but not uncomfortable; though you take your own bedding and share the toilet with everyone in the wagon. Soft sleepers (*ruanwo*) are more comfortable: the closed compartments have four beds with bedding. Trains between Beijing, Shanghai, Hong Kong, and Xi'an also have a deluxe class, with only two berths per compartment and private bathrooms. The nonstop Z-series trains are even more luxurious. Train types are identifiable by the letter preceding the route number: Z is for nonstop, T is for a normal express, and C, G, and D are high-speed trains.

Overpriced dining cars serve meals that are often inedible, so do as the locals do and use the massive thermoses of boiled water in each compartment for your own noodles or instant soup. Trains are always crowded, but you are guaranteed your designated seat, though not always the overhead luggage rack. When you board a train, the staff will take away your ticket and give you a plastic card with your seat or bed number. When you disembark you give the plastic card to the attendant and receive your ticket back. Note that theft on trains is increasing; on overnight trains, sleep with your valuables or keep them on the inside of the bunk.

You can find out just about everything about Chinese train travel at Seat 61's comprehensive website. China Highlights has a searchable online timetable for major train routes.

**Information China Highlights** ⊕ *www. chinahighlights.com.* **Seat 61** ⊕ *www.seat61. com/china.htm.* **Travel China Guide** ⊕ *www. travelchinaguide.com/china-trains.*

# ESSENTIALS

### GREETINGS

Chinese people aren't very touchy-feely with one another, even less so with strangers. Stick to handshakes and low-key greetings when first meeting local people. Always use a person's title and surname until you're invited to do otherwise.

### SIGHTSEEING

By and large, the Chinese are a rule-abiding bunch. Follow their lead and avoid doing anything signs advise against. Although you won't be banned from entering any sightseeing spots for reason of dress, you'd do well to avoid overly skimpy or casual clothes.

China is a crowded country; pushing, nudging, and line-jumping are commonplace. It may be hard to accept, but avoid reacting (even verbally) if you're accidentally shoved.

### OUT ON THE TOWN

It's a great honor to be invited to someone's house, so explain at length if you can't go. Arrive punctually with a small gift for the hosts; remove your shoes outside if you see other guests doing so. Eating lots is the biggest compliment you can pay the food (and the cook).

Smoking is one of China's greatest vices. No-smoking sections in restaurants used to be nonexistent, but they are becoming more common in cities like Beijing and Shanghai.

Holding hands in public is OK, but keep passionate embraces for the hotel room.

### DOING BUSINESS

Time is of the essence when doing business in China. Make appointments well in advance and be extremely punctual, as this shows respect. Chinese people have a keen sense of hierarchy in the office: if you're visiting in a group, the senior member should lead proceedings.

Suits are still the norm in China, regardless of the outside temperature. Women should avoid plunging necklines, heavy makeup, overly short skirts, and high heels. Pants are completely acceptable. Women can expect to be treated as equals in business dealings.

Never say anything that will make people look bad, especially in front of superiors. Avoid being pushy or overly familiar when negotiating: respect silences in conversation, and don't hurry things or interrupt someone who is speaking. When entertaining, local businesspeople may insist on paying: after a slight protest, accept graciously.

Business cards are a big deal: not having one is like not having a personality. If possible, have yours printed in English on one side and Chinese on the other (your hotel can usually arrange this in a matter of hours). Proffer your card with both hands and receive the other person's in the same way, then read it carefully and make an admiring comment.

Many gifts, like clocks and cutting implements, are considered unlucky in China. Food—especially presented in a showy basket—is always a good gift choice, as are imported spirits. Avoid giving four of anything, as the number is associated with death. Offer gifts with both hands, and don't expect people to open them in your presence.

### LANGUAGE

Nearly everyone in mainland China speaks Putonghua (*putōnghuà,* the "common language") another name for Mandarin Chinese. It's written using ideograms, or characters; in 1949 the government introduced a phonetic writing system that uses the Roman alphabet. Known as Pinyin, it's widely used to label public buildings and station names. Even if you don't speak or read Chinese, you can easily compare Pinyin names with a map. For a little help, try Julie Mazel Sussman's *I Can Read That! A Traveler's Introduction to Chinese Characters.*

In Hong Kong the main language spoken is Cantonese, although many people also speak English. There are many other local Chinese dialects. Some use the same characters as Putonghua for writing, but the pronunciation is so different as to be unintelligible to a Putonghua speaker. There are several non-Chinese languages (such as Mongolian, Uyghur, and Tibetan) spoken by China's ethnic minorities.

Chinese grammar is simple, but a complex tonal system of pronunciation means it usually takes a long time for foreigners to learn Chinese. Making yourself understood can be tricky; however, the Chinese will appreciate your making the effort to speak a few phrases understood almost everywhere. Try "Hello"—*"Ní hǎo"* (nee how); "Thank you"—*"Xiè xiè"* (shee-yeh shee-yeh); and "Good-bye"—*"Zai jian"* (dzai djan). When pronouncing words written in Pinyin, remember that "q" and "x" are pronounced like "ch" and "sh," respectively; "zh" is pronounced like the "j" in "just"; "c" is pronounced like "ts."

English isn't widely spoken, though the staff in most hotels, travel agencies, and upscale restaurants in major cities is the exception. If you're lost and need help, look first to someone under 30, who may have studied some English in school. In shops, calculators and hand gestures do most of the talking.

A great place to start learning online before your trip is ChinesePod.com, which has free podcasts you can download and listen to any time.

# ▌ ACCOMMODATIONS

The forums on Fodors.com are a great place to start your hotel investigations.

Location is the first thing you should consider. Chinese cities are usually big, and there's no point schlepping halfway across town for one particular hotel when a similar option is available more conveniently.

In major urban centers, many four- or five-star hotels belong to familiar international

chains, and are usually a safe—if pricey—bet. You can expect swimming pools, Internet access, and business services. Hard-as-a-board beds are a trademark of Chinese hotels, even in luxury chains.

Locally owned hotels with four stars or fewer have erratic standards both inside and outside big cities, as bribery plays a big part in star acquisition. However, air-conditioning, color TVs, and private bathrooms are the norm for three to four stars, and even lone-star hotels have private bathrooms, albeit with a squatter toilet. All hotels, from pricey to cheap, will provide you with an electric kettle or a thermos for making tea.

When checking into a hotel, make sure your room isn't above or below the karaoke room, usually located on the second or third floor. Otherwise you may be in for some sleepless nights.

## APARTMENT AND HOUSE RENTALS

There's an abundance of furnished properties for short- and long-term rentals in Beijing, Guangzhou, Hong Kong, Shanghai, and some other cities. Prices vary wildly. At the top end are luxury apartments and villas, usually far from the city center and accessible by (chauffeur-driven) car. Usually described as "serviced apartments" or "villas," these often include gyms and pools, and rates are usually well over $2,000 a month.

There are a lot of well-located mid-range properties in new apartment blocks. They're usually clean and nicely furnished, and rents start at $500 a month. What you get for your money fluctuates, so shop around. For longer, cheaper stays, there are normal local apartments. These are firmly off the tourist circuit and often cost a third of the price of the mid-range properties. The plumbing and electricity may not be up to code, and amenities may be lacking. It helps to bring a Chinese friend along to negotiate on your behalf.

Property sites like Asian Expat, Move and Stay, and Sublet.com have hundreds of apartments in major cities. The online classified pages in local English-language magazines or on expat websites are good places to look for cheaper properties.

**Contacts Asia Expat** ⊕ *www.asiaxpat.com.* **Move and Stay** ⊕ *www.moveandstay.com.* **Sublet.com** ⊕ *www.sublet.com.*

## HOMESTAYS

Single travelers can arrange homestays (often in combination with language courses) through the Lotus Education Foundation. Rates vary according to your length of stay, starting at about $200 a week. Make sure to ask for references before handing over your hard-earned cash.

**Contacts Lotus Education Foundation** ☎ *408/996–1929* ⊕ *www.lotuseducation.org.*

## HOTELS

When checking into a hotel, you need to show your passport—the desk clerk records the number before you're given a room. In smaller hotels, unmarried couples may occasionally have problems staying together in the same room, but simply wearing a wedding band is one way to avoid this complication. Friends or couples of the same sex, especially women, shouldn't have a problem getting a room together. It's normal for hotels to post "visitor hours" for nonguests.

All hotels listed have private bath unless otherwise noted. Remember that water is a precious resource in China, and use it accordingly.

## ▌ BUSINESS SERVICES AND FACILITIES

Your hotel (or a mid- to high-end hotel nearby) is the best place to start looking for business services, including translation. Most are up to speed with the needs of business travelers, and if they don't offer a service they can put you in touch with a company that does. Regus and the Executive Centre are international business-services companies with several office locations in Beijing, Shanghai, and Hong Kong. They provide secretarial services, meeting and conference facilities, and office rentals.

**Contacts Executive Centre** ☎ *852/2297– 2292* ⊕ *www.executivecentre.com.* **Regus** ☎ *400/120–1205* ⊕ *www.regus.cn.*

## ▌ COMMUNICATIONS

### INTERNET

In China's major cities you shouldn't have any trouble getting online. Wi-Fi is growing exponentially—many hotels offer it for free. Many also have computer terminals in their business centers that you can use if you didn't bring along a laptop. Internet cafés are ubiquitous in big cities, and are rapidly spreading to smaller destinations. Known as *wang ba* in Chinese, they're not usually signposted in English, so ask your hotel to recommend one nearby. Prices (and cleanliness) vary considerably, but start at about Y3 to Y10 per hour.

Remember that there is strict government control of the Internet in China. Authorities frequently shut down Internet cafés, citing "spiritual pollution." There's usually no problem with accessing your email, but you may be unable to access news sites and even some blogs. To get around the restrictions, you can subscribe to a Virtual Private Network or use proxy servers to access certain sites. AnchorFree offers a free service called Hotspot Shield, although it includes annoying pop-up ads. More reliable VPN services, like those from WiTopia, cost about $40 a year for safe, fast surfing. If you're going to be in China for a while, investing in a VPN is worthwhile.

## PHONES

The country code for China is 86; the city code for Beijing is 10, and the city code for Shanghai is 21. Hong Kong has its own country code: 852. To call China from the United States or Canada, dial the international access code (011), followed by the country code (86), the area or city code, and the eight-digit phone number.

Numbers beginning with 800 within China are toll-free. Note that a call from China to a toll-free number in the United States or Hong Kong is a full-tariff international call. If you need to call home, use your computer and a service like Skype. Be sure to download the U.S. version of Skype, because the Chinese TOM-Skype is constantly monitored by the government.

### CALLING WITHIN CHINA

The Chinese phone system is cheap and efficient. Local calls are usually free, and long-distance rates are very low. Calling from your hotel room is a good option, as hotels can only add a 15% service charge.

Chinese phone numbers have eight digits—that's usually all you need to dial these when calling somewhere within the city. To call another city, dial 0, the city code, and the eight-digit phone number.

For directory assistance, dial 114. If you want information for other cities, dial the city code followed by 114 (this is considered a long-distance call). For example, if you're in Beijing and need directory assistance for Shanghai, dial 021–114. The operators do not speak English, so if you don't speak Chinese you're best off asking your hotel for help.

### CALLING OUTSIDE CHINA

To make an international call from within China, dial 00 (the international access code) and then the country code, area code, and phone number. The United States country code is 1.

IDD (international direct dialing) service is available at all hotels, post offices, major shopping centers, and airports. Simply dial 108 (the local operator) and the local access codes from China: 11 (southern China) or 888 (northern China) for AT&T, 12 for MCI, and 13 for Sprint. Dialing instructions in English will follow.

**Access Codes AT&T Direct** ☎ *800/874–4000, 108–888 from northern China, 108–11 from southern China.* **MCI WorldPhone** ☎ *800/444–4444, 108–12 from China.* **Sprint International Access** ☎ *800/793–1153, 108–13 from China.*

### CALLING CARDS

Calling cards are a key part of the Chinese phone system. There are two kinds: the IC card (integrated circuit; *àicei ka*), for local and domestic long-distance calls on pay phones; and the IP card (Internet protocol; *aipi ka*) for international calls from any phone. You can buy both at post offices, convenience stores, and street vendors.

IC cards come in denominations of Y20, Y50, and Y100, and can be used in any pay phone with a card slot—most urban pay phones have them. Local calls using them cost around Y0.30 a minute, and less on weekends and after 6 pm.

IP cards come with face values of Y20, Y30, Y50, and Y100. The going rate for them might be half that, so bargain with the vendors. To use IP cards, first dial a local access number. You then enter a card number and a PIN, and finally the phone number, complete with international dial codes. There are countless different card brands; China Mobile, China Unicom, and China Telecom are usually reliable.

### CELL PHONES

If you have a tri-band GSM or a CDMA phone, pick up a local SIM card (*sim ka*) from any branch of China Mobile or China Unicom: there are often branches at international airports. You'll be presented with a list of possible phone numbers, with varying prices—an "unlucky" phone number (one with lots of 4s) could be as cheap as Y50, whereas an auspicious one (full of 8s) could fetch Y300 or more. You then buy prepaid cards to charge minutes onto your SIM—do this straightaway, as you need credit to receive calls. Local calls to landlines cost Y0.25 per minute, and Y0.60 to cell phones. Rates can vary depending on the services you sign up for or add to your SIM. International calls from cell phones are very expensive.

Remember to bring an adapter for your phone charger. You can also buy cheap handsets from China Mobile—if you're planning to stay even a couple of days this is probably cheaper than renting a phone.

**Contacts Cellular Abroad.** Cellular Abroad rents and sells GMS phones and SIM card packages that work in many countries. ☎ 800/287–5072 ⊕ www.cellularabroad.com. **Mobal.** Mobal rents cell phones and sells GSM phones (starting at $49) that will operate in 170 countries. Per-call rates vary throughout the world. ☎ 888/888–9162 ⊕ www.mobalrental.com.

## ▌ CUSTOMS AND DUTIES

Except for the usual prohibitions against narcotics, explosives, plant and animal material, firearms, and ammunition, you can take anything into China that you plan to take away with you. Cameras, video recorders, GPS equipment, laptops, and the like should pose no problems. However, China is very sensitive about printed matter deemed seditious, such as religious, pornographic, and political texts, especially articles, books, and pictures of Tibet or Xinjiang. All the same, small amounts of English-language reading matter aren't generally a problem. Customs officials are for the most part easygoing, and visitors are rarely searched. It's not necessary to fill in customs declaration forms, but if you carry in a large amount of cash, say several thousand dollars, you should declare it upon arrival.

You're not allowed to remove any antiquities dating to before 1795. Antiques from between 1795 and 1949 must have

an official red seal attached—quality antiques shops know this and arrange it.

**U.S. Information U.S. Customs and Border Protection** ☎ 877/227–5511 ⊕ www.cbp.gov.

## ▌ EATING OUT

In China meals are really a communal event, so food in a Chinese home or restaurant is always shared—you usually have a small bowl or plate and take food from central platters. Although Western-style cutlery is often available, it won't hurt to brush up on your use of chopsticks, the utensil of choice.

The standard eating procedure is to hold the bowl close to your mouth and shovel in the contents without any qualms. Noisily slurping up soup and noodles is the norm. Place bones or seeds in a small dish or on the table beside your bowl. It's considered bad manners to point or play with your chopsticks, or to place them on top of your rice bowl when you're finished eating (place the chopsticks horizontally on the table or plate). Avoid leaving your chopsticks standing up in a bowl of rice—they look like the two incense sticks burned at funerals.

If you're invited to a formal Chinese meal, be prepared for great ceremony, endless toasts and speeches, and a grand variety of elaborate dishes. Your host will be seated at the "head" of the round table, which is the seat that faces the door. Wait to be instructed where to sit. Don't start eating until the host takes the first bite, and then simply help yourself as the food comes around, but don't take the last piece on a platter. Always let the food touch your plate before bringing it up to your mouth; eating directly from the serving dish is bad form.

### MEALS AND MEALTIMES

Food is a central part of Chinese culture, and so eating should be a major activity on any trip to China. Breakfast is not usually a big deal—congee, or rice porridge (*zhou*), is the standard dish. Most mid- and upper-end hotels do big buffet spreads, whereas café chains in major cities serve lattes and croissants.

Snacks are a food group in themselves. There's no shortage of street stalls selling grilled meats, bowls of noodle soup, and the ubiquituous *baozi* (steamed buns stuffed with meat or veggies). Many visitors are hesitant to eat from stalls—you'd be missing out on some of the best nibbles around, though. Pick a place where lots of locals are eating to be on the safe side, and bring along your own chopsticks.

The food in hotel restaurants is usually acceptable but vastly overpriced. Restaurants frequented by locals always serve tastier fare at better prices. Don't pass by establishments without an English menu—a good phrase book and lots of pointing can usually get you what you want.

If you're craving Western food (or sushi or curry), rest assured that big cities have plenty of international chain restaurants. Most higher-end Chinese restaurants have a Western menu, but you're usually safer sticking to the Chinese food.

Meals in China are served early: breakfast until 9 am, lunch between 11 and 2, and dinner from 5 to 9.

Unless otherwise noted, the restaurants listed in this guide are open daily for lunch and dinner.

### PAYING

At most restaurants you ask for the bill (mai dan) at the end of the meal, as you do back home. At cheap noodle bars and street stands you often pay up front. Only very upmarket restaurants accept credit cards.

### RESERVATIONS AND DRESS

Regardless of where you are, it's a good idea to make a reservation if you can. In some places (Hong Kong, for example), it's expected. We only mention them specifically when reservations are essential (there's no other way you'll ever get a table) or when they are not accepted. For popular restaurants, book as far ahead as you can (often 30 days), and reconfirm as soon as you arrive. (Large parties should always call ahead to check the reservations policy.) We mention dress only when men are required to wear a jacket or a jacket and tie.

### WINES, BEER, AND SPIRITS

Forget tea, today the people's drink of choice is beer. Massively popular among Chinese men, it's still a bit of a no-no for Chinese women, however. Tsingtao, China's most popular brew, is a 4% lager that comes in liter bottles and is usually cheaper than water. Many regions have their own local breweries, and international brands are available.

When you see "wine" on the menu, it's usually referring to sweet fruit wines or distilled rice wine. The most famous brand of Chinese liquor is Maotai, a distilled liquor ranging in strength from 35% to 53% proof. Like most firewaters, it's an acquired taste.

There are basically no licensing laws in China, so you can drink anywhere, and at any time, provided you can find a place to serve you.

## ▌ ELECTRICITY

The electrical current in China is 220 volts and 50 cycles alternating current (AC), so most American appliances can't be used without a transformer. A universal adapter is especially useful in China, as wall outlets come in a bewildering variety of configurations: two- and three-pronged round plugs, as well as two-pronged flat sockets. Although blackouts are rare in Chinese cities, villages occasionally lose power for short periods of time.

Consider making a small investment in a universal adapter, which has several types of plugs in one lightweight, compact unit. Most laptops and cell-phone chargers are dual voltage (i.e., they operate equally well on 110 and 220 volts), so require only an adapter. These days the same is true of small appliances such as hair dryers. Always check labels and manufacturer instructions to be sure. Don't use 110-volt outlets marked for shavers, only for high-wattage appliances such as hair dryers.

**Contacts Steve Kropla's Help for World Travelers.** Steve Kropla's Help for World Travelers has information on electrical and telephone plugs around the world. ⊕ www.kropla. com. **Walkabout Travel Gear.** Walkabout Travel Gear has a good coverage of electricity under "adapters." ☎ 800/852–7085 ⊕ www. walkabouttravelgear.com.

## ▮ EMERGENCIES

If you lose your passport, contact your embassy immediately. Embassy officials can also advise you on how to proceed in case of other emergencies. The staff at your hotel may be able to provide an interpreter if you need to report an emergency or crime to doctors or the police. Most police officers and hospital staff members don't speak English, though you may find one or two people who do.

Ambulances generally offer just a means of transport, not medical aid; taking a taxi is quicker, and means you can choose the hospital you want to go to. Where possible, go to a private clinic catering to expats—prices are sky-high, but so are their hygiene and medical standards. Most have reliable 24-hour pharmacies.

**U.S. Embassy and Consulate United States Consulate** ✉ 1469 Huaihai Zhong Lu, Xuhui District, Shanghai ☎ 021/3271–4650, 021/6433–3936 for after-hours emergencies

⊕ www.shanghai.usembassy-china.org. cn ✉ Citizen Services Section, Westgate Mall, 1038 Nanjing Xi Lu, 8th fl., Shanghai ☎ 021/3217–4650, 021/6433–3936 for emergencies. **United States Embassy** ✉ 55 Anjialou Lu, Chaoyang District, Beijing ☎ 010/8531–3000, 010/8531–4000 for emergencies ⊕ www.beijing.usembassy-china.org.cn. **United States Citizens Services** ✉ 4 Ling Shi Guan Rd., Chengdu ☎ 028/8558–3992 ⊕ www. chengdu.usembassy-china.org.cn ✉ 1 South Shamian St., Guangzhou ☎ 020/8518–7605, 020/8121–6077 for after-hours emergencies ⊕ www.guangzhou.usembassy-china.org.cn.

**General Emergency Contacts Ambulance** ☎ 120. **Fire** ☎ 119. **Police** ☎ 110.

## ▮ HEALTH

The most common types of illnesses are caused by contaminated food and water. Especially in developing countries, drink only bottled, boiled, or purified water and drinks; don't drink from public fountains or ask for beverages without ice. You should even consider using bottled or boiled water to brush your teeth. Make sure food has been thoroughly cooked and is served to you fresh and hot; avoid vegetables and fruits that you haven't washed (in bottled or purified water) or peeled yourself. If you have problems, mild cases of traveler's diarrhea may respond to Imodium (known generically as loperamide) or Pepto-Bismol. Be sure to drink plenty of fluids; if you can't keep fluids down, seek medical help immediately. Tap water in major cities like Beijing and Shanghai is safe for brushing teeth, but buy bottled water to drink and check to see that the bottle is sealed.

Infectious diseases can be airborne or passed via mosquitoes and ticks and through direct or indirect physical contact with animals or people. Some, including Norwalk-like viruses that affect your digestive tract, can be passed along through contaminated food. If you are traveling in an area where malaria is prevalent, use a repellant containing DEET and take malaria-prevention medication before, during, and after your trip as directed by your physician. Condoms can help prevent most sexually transmitted diseases, but they aren't absolutely reliable, and their quality varies from country to country. Speak with your physician and/or check the CDC or World Health Organization websites for health alerts, particularly if you're pregnant, traveling with children, or have a chronic illness.

### SHOTS AND MEDICATIONS
No immunizations are required for entry into China, but it's a good idea to be immunized against typhoid and Hepatitis A and B before traveling, as well as to get routine tetanus-diphtheria and measles boosters. In winter a flu vaccination is also smart, especially if you're infection-prone or are a senior citizen. ■TIP→ **In summer months malaria is a risk in tropical and rural areas, especially Hainan and Yunnan provinces—consult your doctor four to six weeks before your trip, as preventive treatments vary.** The risk of contracting malaria in cities is small.

**Health Warnings National Centers for Disease Control & Prevention** (*CDC*). ☎ *800/232–4636 international travelers' health line* ⊕ *www.cdc.gov/travel/destinations/china.htm.* **World Health Organization** (*WHO*). ⊕ *www.who.int.*

### SPECIFIC ISSUES IN CHINA
At China's public hospitals, foreigners need to pay fees to register, to see a doctor, and then for all tests and medication. Prices are cheap compared to the fancy foreigner clinics in major cities, where you pay $100 to $150 just for a consultation. However, most doctors at public hospitals don't speak English, and hygiene standards are low—all the more reason to take out medical insurance.

Hong Kong has excellent public and private health care. Foreigners have to pay for both, so insurance is a good idea. Even for lesser complaints, private doctors charge a fortune: head to a public hospital if money is tight. In an emergency you'll always receive treatment first and get the bill afterward—Y570 is the standard ER charge.

The best place to start looking for a suitable doctor is through your hotel concierge, then the local Public Security Bureau. If you become seriously ill or are injured, it is best to fly home, or at least to Hong Kong, as quickly as possible. In Hong Kong, English-speaking doctors are widely available.

Pneumonia and influenza are common among travelers returning from China—talk to your doctor about inoculations before you leave. If you need to buy prescription drugs, try to go to the pharmacies of reputable private hospitals or to bigger chain stores like Watsons.

### OVER-THE-COUNTER REMEDIES
Most pharmacies in big Chinese cities carry over-the-counter Western medicines and traditional Chinese medicines. You usually need to ask for the generic name of the drug you're looking for, not a brand name. Acetominophen—or Tylenol—is often known as paracetomol in Hong Kong. In big cities reputable pharmacies like Watsons are always a better bet than no-name ones.

# ▌ HOURS OF OPERATION

Most banks and government offices are open weekdays 9 to 5 or 6, although close for lunch (sometime between noon and 2). Some bank branches keep longer hours and are open Saturday (and occasionally Sunday) mornings. Many hotel currency-exchange desks stay open 24 hours. Museums open from roughly 9 to 6, six or seven days a week. Everything in China grinds to a halt for the first two or three days of Chinese New Year (sometime in mid-January to February), and opening hours are often reduced for the rest of that season.

Pharmacies are open daily from 8:30 or 9 to 6 or 7. Some large pharmacies stay open until 9 or even later. Shops and department stores are generally open daily 8 to 8; some stores stay open even later in summer, in popular tourist areas, or during peak tourist season.

## HOLIDAYS

National holidays in mainland China include New Year's Day (January 1); Spring Festival aka Chinese New Year (late January/early February); Qingming Jie (April 4); International Labor Day (May 1); Dragon Boat Festival (late May/ early June); anniversary of the founding of the Communist Party of China (July 1); anniversary of the founding of the Chinese People's Liberation Army (August 1); and National Day—founding of the People's Republic of China in 1949 (October 1); Chongyang Jie or Double Ninth Festival (ninth day of ninth lunar month). Hong Kong celebrates most of these festivals, and also has public holidays at Easter and for Christmas and Boxing Day (December 25 and 26).

## MAIL

Sending international mail from China is extremely reliable. Airmail letters to any place in the world should take five to 14 days. Express Mail Service (EMS) is available to many international destinations. Letters sent within any city arrive the next day, and mail to the rest of China takes a day or two longer. Domestic mail can be subject to search, so don't send sensitive materials such as religious or political literature, as you might cause the recipient trouble.

Service is more reliable if you mail letters from post offices rather than mailboxes. Buy envelopes here, too, as there are standardized sizes in China. You need to glue stamps onto envelopes, as they're not self-adhesive. Most post offices are open daily between 8 am and 7 pm; many keep longer hours. Your hotel can usually send letters for you, too.

You can use the Roman alphabet to write an address. Do not use red ink, which has a negative connotation. You must also include a six-digit zip code for mail within China. Sending airmail postcards costs Y4.50 and letters Y5 to Y7.

Long-term guests can receive mail at their hotels. Otherwise, the best place to receive mail is at the American Express office. Most major Chinese cities have American Express offices with client-mail service. Be sure to bring your American Express card, as the staff will not give you the mail without seeing it.

## SHIPPING PACKAGES

It's easy to ship packages home from China. Take what you want to send *unpacked* to the post office—everything will be sewn up officially into satisfying linen-bound packages, a service that costs a few yuan. You have to fill in lengthy forms—enclosing a photocopy of receipts for the goods inside isn't a bad idea, as they may be opened by customs along the line. Large antiques stores often offer reliable shipping services that take care of customs in China.

International courier services operating in China include DHL, Federal Express, and UPS—next-day delivery for a 1-kilogram (2.2-pound) package starts at about Y300. Your hotel can also arrange shipping parcels, but there's usually a hefty markup.

**Express Services DHL** ☎ *800/810–8000*
⊕ *www.cn.dhl.com/en.html.* **FedEx**
🖷 *800/463–3339* ⊕ *www.fedex.com.* **UPS**
🖷 *800/820–8388* ⊕ *www.ups.com.*

| ITEM | AVERAGE COST |
|---|---|
| Cup of coffee at Starbucks | Y25–Y30 |
| Glass of local beer | Y15 |
| Cheapest subway ticket | Y3 |
| Starting rate for taxi ride in Beijing or Shanghai | Y10 |
| Set lunch in a cheap restaurant | Y30 |
| Half-hour foot massage | Y50 |
| Movie ticket | Y99 |

# ▌ MONEY

China is a cheap destination by most North Americans' standards, but expect your dollar to do more for you in smaller cities than in pricey Shanghai or Beijing. The exception to the rule is Hong Kong, where eating and sleeping prices are on a par with those in the United States.

In mainland China, the best places to convert your dollars into yuan are your hotel's front desk or a branch of a major bank, such as Bank of China, CITIC, or HSBC. These charge standardized government rates—anything cheaper is illegal, and thus risky. You need to present your passport to change money.

Prices throughout this guide are given for adults. Substantially reduced fees are almost always available for children, students, and senior citizens.

Although credit cards are gaining ground in China, for day-to-day transactions cash is definitely king.

**Currency Conversion Google** ⊕ *www.google.com.* **Oanda.com** ⊕ *www.oanda.com.* **XE.com** ⊕ *www.xe.com/cc.*

## ATMS AND BANKS

Your own bank will probably charge a fee for using ATMs abroad; the foreign bank you use may also charge a fee. Nevertheless, you'll usually get a better rate of exchange at an ATM than you will at a currency-exchange office or even when changing money in a bank.

▮ TIP→ **PINs with more than four digits are not recognized at ATMs in many countries. If yours has five or more, remember to change it before you leave.**

ATMs are widespread in major Chinese cities. The most reliable ATMs are at HSBC, which also have the highest withdrawal limit, which offsets transaction charges. Of the Chinese banks, your best bet for ATMs is the Bank of China, which accepts most foreign cards. That said, machines frequently refuse to give cash for mysterious reasons—move on and try another. On-screen instructions appear automatically in English.

ATMs are everywhere throughout Hong Kong—most carry the sign ETC instead of ATM. Subway stations are a good place to look.

## CREDIT CARDS

American Express, MasterCard, and Visa are accepted at most hotels and a growing number of upmarket stores and restaurants. Diners Club is less widely accepted.

It's a good idea to inform your credit-card company before you travel. Otherwise, the credit-card company might put a hold on your card owing to unusual activity—not a good thing halfway through your trip. Record all your credit-card numbers—as well as the phone numbers to call if your cards are lost or stolen—in a safe place, so you're prepared should something go wrong. Both MasterCard and Visa have general numbers you can call (collect if you're abroad) if your card is lost, but you're better off calling the number of your issuing bank, since MasterCard and Visa usually just transfer you to your bank; your bank's number is usually printed on your card.

If you plan to use your credit card for cash advances, you'll need to apply for a PIN at least two weeks before your trip. Although it's usually cheaper (and safer) to use a credit card abroad for large purchases (so you can cancel payments or be reimbursed if there's a problem), note that some credit-card companies *and* the banks that issue them add substantial percentages to all foreign transactions, whether they're in a foreign currency or not. Check on these fees before leaving home, so there won't be any surprises when you get the bill.

■TIP→ Before you charge something, ask the merchant whether or not he or she plans to do a dynamic currency conversion (DCC). In such a transaction the credit-card processor (shop, restaurant, or hotel, not Visa or MasterCard) converts the currency and charges you in dollars. In most cases you'll pay the merchant a 3% fee for this service in addition to any credit-card company and issuing-bank foreign-transaction surcharges.

Dynamic currency conversion programs are becoming increasingly widespread. Merchants who participate in them are supposed to ask whether you want to be charged in dollars or the local currency, but they don't always do so. And even if they do offer you a choice, they may well avoid mentioning the additional surcharges. The good news is that you *do* have a choice. And if this practice really gets your goat, you can avoid it entirely thanks to American Express; with its cards, DCC simply isn't an option.

**Reporting Lost Cards American Express** ☎ 800/528–4800 in the U.S., 336/393–1111 collect from abroad ⊕ www.americanexpress. com. **Diners Club** ☎ 800/234–6377 in the U.S., 514/881–3735 collect from abroad ⊕ www.dinersclub.com. **MasterCard** ☎ 800/307–7309 in the U.S., 636/722–7111 collect from abroad, 800/110–7309 in China ⊕ www.mastercard.com. **Visa** ☎ 800/847– 2911 in the U.S., 303/967–1096 collect from abroad, 800/711–2911 or 110-2911 in China ⊕ www.visa.com.

**CURRENCY AND EXCHANGE**

The Chinese currency is officially called the yuan (Y), and is also known as *renminbi* (RMB), or "People's Money." You may also hear it called *kuai,* an informal expression like "buck."

Old and new styles of bills circulate in China, and many denominations have both coins and bills. The Bank of China issues bills in denominations of 1 (burgundy), 2 (green), 5 (brown or purple), 10 (turquoise), 20 (brown), 50 (blue or occasionally yellow), and 100 (red). There are 1-yuan coins, too. The yuan subdivides into 10-cent units called *jiao* or *mao;* these come in bills and coins of 1, 2, and 5. The smallest denomination is the *fen,* which comes in coins (and occasionally tiny notes) of 1, 2, and 5. Counterfeiting is rife in China, and even small stores inspect notes with ultraviolet lamps. Change can be a problem—don't expect much success paying for a Y3 purchase with a Y100 note.

Exchange rates in China are fixed by the government daily, so it's equally good at branches of the Bank of China, at big department stores, or at your hotel's exchange desk. Any lower rates are illegal, so you're exposing yourself to scams. A passport is required. Hold on to your exchange receipt, which you need to convert your extra yuan back into dollars.

In Hong Kong the only currency used is the Hong Kong dollar, divided into 100 cents. Three local banks (HSBC, Standard Chartered, and the Bank of China) all issue bills and each has its own designs. At this writing the Hong Kong dollar was pegged to the U.S. dollar at approximately 7.75 Hong Kong dollars to 1 U.S. dollar. There are no currency restrictions in Hong Kong. You can exchange currency at the airport, in hotels, in banks, and through private money changers scattered through the tourist areas. Banks usually have the best rates, but as they charge a flat HK$50 fee for non-account holders, it's better to change large sums infrequently. Currency-exchange offices have no fees, but they offset that with poor rates. Stick to ATMs whenever you can.

■TIP➜ **Even if a currency-exchange booth has a sign promising no commission, rest assured that there's some kind of huge, hidden fee. (Oh . . . that's right. The sign didn't say no fee.) And as for rates, you're almost always better off getting foreign currency at an ATM or exchanging money at a bank.**

| GENERAL REQUIREMENTS FOR MAINLAND CHINA | |
|---|---|
| Passport | Must be valid for six months after date of arrival |
| Visa | Required for U.S. citizens ($130) |
| Required Vaccinations | None |
| Recommended Vaccinations | Hepatitis A and B, typhoid, influenza, booster for tetanus-diphtheria |
| Driving | Chinese driver's license required |

# ■ PASSPORTS AND VISAS

All U.S. citizens, even infants, need a valid passport with a tourist visa stamped in it to enter China (except for Hong Kong, where you only need a valid passport). It's always best to have at least six months' validity on your passport before traveling to Asia.

Getting a tourist visa to China (known as an "L" visa) in the United States is straightforward. Standard visas are for single-entry stays of up to 30 days, and are valid for 90 days from the day of issue (NOT the day of entry), so don't get your visa too far in advance. The cost for a tourist visa issued to a U.S. citizen is $130; citizens of other countries can expect to pay between $30 and $90.

Travel agents in Hong Kong can also issue visas to visit mainland China—though regulations can change during times of unrest. Note: The visa application will ask your occupation. The Chinese government doesn't look favorably upon those who work in publishing or the media. People in these professions routinely give "teacher" as their occupation. Before you go, contact the embassy or consulate of the People's Republic of China to gauge the current mood.

**Hong Kong Travel Agents China Travel Service.** China Travel Service has 36 branches in Hong Kong and Macau. ⊠ *78-83 Connaught Rd., Hong Kong* ☎ *852/2998–7888* ⊕ *www. ctshk.com.*

Children traveling with only one parent do not need a notarized letter of permission to enter China. However, as these kinds of policies can change, being overprepared isn't a bad idea.

Under no circumstances should you overstay your visa. To extend your visa, stop by the Entry and Exit Administration Office of the local branch of the Public Security Bureau a week before your visa expires. The office is known as the PSB or the Foreigner's Police; most are open weekdays 9 to 11:30 and 1:30 to 4:30. The process is extremely bureaucratic, but it's usually no problem to get a month's extension on a tourist visa. You need to bring your registration of temporary residency from your hotel and your passport, which you generally need to leave for five to seven days (so do any transactions requiring it beforehand). If you are trying to extend a business visa, you'll need the above items as well as a letter from the business that originally invited you to China saying it would like to extend your stay for work reasons. Rules are always changing, so you will probably need to go to the office at least twice to get all your papers in order.

**Chinese Visa Information Chinese Consulate** ☎ *212/868–2078* ⊕ *www.nyconsulate. prchina.org.* **Chinese Embassy Visa Office** ☎ *202/495–2266* ⊕ *www.china-embassy.org.*

# PACKING

Most Chinese people dress for comfort, so you can plan to do the same. There's little risk of offending people with your dress: Westerners tend to attract attention regardless of their attire. Fashion capitals Hong Kong and Shanghai are the exceptions to the comfort rule: slop around in flip-flops and worn denims and you *will* feel that there's a neon "tourist" sign over your head. Opt for your smarter jeans or capri pants for sightseeing there.

Sturdy, comfortable walking shoes are a must: go for closed shoes over sandals, as dust and toe-stomping crowds make them impractical. Northern Chinese summers are dusty and baking hot, so slacks, capris, and sturdy shorts are best. A raincoat, especially a light Goretex one or a fold-up poncho, is useful for an onset of rainy weather, especially in Southern China. During the harsh winters, thermal long johns and thick socks are a lifesaver—especially in low-star hotel rooms.

That said, in urban centers you can prepare to be unprepared: big Chinese cities are a clothes shopper's paradise. If a bulky jacket's going to put you over the airline limit, buy one in China and leave it behind when you go. All the other woollies—and silkies, the local insulator of choice—you'll need go for a song, as do brand-name jackets. Scarves, gloves, and hats, all musts, are also easy to find.

Most good hotels have reliable overnight laundry services, though costs can rack up on a long trip. Look outside your hotel for cheaper laundries, and bring some concentrated travel detergent for small or delicate items. Note that it's often cheaper to buy things than have your own laundered, so if you're even a little interested in shopping, consider bringing an extra, foldable bag for carting purchases home.

Keep packets of tissues and antibacterial hand wipes in your day pack—paper isn't a feature of many Chinese restrooms, and you often can't buy it in smaller towns. A small flashlight with extra batteries is also

**WORD OF MOUTH**

"I am grateful that we went to China during the winter and consider it a terrific option for people like us who really love to escape the crowds. Be prepared for the cold—pack more than you think you need and make sure you've got insulated shoes. It will make a huge difference in making the most of your trip." —Partmtn

useful. The brands in Chinese pharmacies are limited, so take adequate stocks of your potions and lotions, feminine-hygiene products (tampons are especially hard to find), and birth control. All of these things are easy to get in Hong Kong.

In your carry-on luggage, pack an extra pair of eyeglasses or contact lenses and enough of any medication you take to last a few days longer than the entire trip.

If you're planning a longer trip or will be using local tour guides, bring a few inexpensive items from your home country as gifts. Popular gifts are candy, T-shirts, and small cosmetic items such as lipstick and nail polish—double-check that none were made in China. Be wary about giving American magazines and books as gifts, as these can be considered propaganda and get your Chinese friends in trouble.

# RESTROOMS

Public restrooms abound in mainland China—the street, parks, restaurants, department stores, and major tourist attractions are all likely locations. Most charge a small fee (usually less than Y1), but seldom provide Western-style facilities or private booths. Instead, expect squat toilets, open troughs, and rusty spigots; WC signs at intersections point the way to these facilities. Toilet paper is a rarity, so carry tissues and antibacterial hand wipes. The restrooms in the newest shopping plazas, fast-food outlets, and deluxe restaurants catering to foreigners are generally on a par with American restrooms. In Hong Kong, public restrooms are well maintained. Alternatively, dip into malls or the lobby of big international hotels to use their loos.

**Find a Loo The Bathroom Diaries.** The Bathroom Diaries is flush with unsanitized info on restrooms the world over—each one located, reviewed, and rated. ⊕ *www. thebathroomdiaries.com.*

## ▌ SAFETY

There is little violent crime against tourists in China, partly because the penalties are severe for those who are caught—China's yearly death-sentence tolls run into the thousands. Single women can move about without too much hassle. Handbag-snatching and pickpocketing do happen in markets and on crowded buses or trains—keep an eye open and your money safe, and you should have no problems. Use the lockbox in your hotel room to store any valuables, but always carry your passport with you for identification purposes.

China is full of people looking to make a quick buck. The most common scam involves people persuading you to go with them for a tea ceremony, which is often so pleasant that you don't smell a rat until several hundred dollars appear on your credit-card bill. "Art students" who pressure you into buying work is another common scam. The same rules that apply to hostess bars worldwide are also true in China. Avoiding such scams is as easy as refusing *all* unsolicited services—be it from taxi or pedicab drivers, tour guides, or potential "friends."

▌TIP➡ **Distribute your cash, credit cards, IDs, and other valuables between a deep front pocket, an inside jacket or vest pocket, and a hidden money pouch. Don't reach for the money pouch once you're in public.**

Chinese traffic is as manic as it looks, and survival of the fittest (or the biggest) is the main rule. Crossing streets can be an extreme sport. Drivers rarely give pedestrians the right-of-way, and don't even look for pedestrians when making a right turn on a red light. Cyclists have less power but are just as aggressive.

The severely polluted air of China's big cities can bring on, or aggravate, respiratory problems. If you're a sufferer, take the cue from locals, who wear surgical masks, or a scarf or bandana as protection.

**Contact Transportation Security Administration** (*TSA;*). ☎ 866/289–9673 ⊕ *www.tsa. gov.*

## ▌ TAXES

There is no sales tax in China or Hong Kong. Mainland hotels charge a 5% tax; bigger, joint-venture hotels also add a 10% to 15% service fee. Some restaurants charge a 10% service fee.

## ▌ TIME

The whole of China is 8 hours ahead of London, 13 hours ahead of New York, 14 hours ahead of Chicago, and 16 hours ahead of Los Angeles. There's no daylight saving time, so subtract an hour in summer.

**Time Zones Timeanddate.com.** Timeanddate. com can help you figure out the correct time anywhere in the world. ⊕ *www.timeanddate. com/worldclock.*

## ▌ TIPPING

Tipping is a tricky issue in China. It's officially forbidden by the government, and locals simply don't do it. In general, follow their lead without qualms. Nevertheless, the practice is beginning to catch on, especially among tour guides, who often expect Y10 a day. Official CTS representatives aren't allowed to accept tips, but you can give them candy, T-shirts, and other small gifts. You don't need to tip in restaurants or in taxis.

In Hong Kong, hotels and major restaurants usually add a 10% service charge; this money rarely goes to waiters and waitresses. Add on up to 10% more for good service. Tipping restroom attendants is common, but it is generally not the custom to leave an additional tip in taxis and hair salons.

# ▮ TOURS

Most guided tours to China take in three or four major cities, often combined with a Yangtze River cruise or a visit to far-flung Tibet. You get a day or two in each place, with the same sights featured in most tours. If you want to explore a given city in any kind of depth, you're better doing it by yourself or getting a private guide.

Shopping stops plague China tours, so inquire before booking as to when, where, and how many to expect. Although you're never obliged to buy anything, they can take up big chunks of your valuable travel time, and the products offered are always ridiculously overpriced. Even on the best tours, you can count on having to sit through at least one or two.

Small groups and excellent guides are what Overseas Adventure Travel takes pride in. The Adventure Center has a huge variety of China packages, including trekking, cycling, and family tours. China Focus Travel has 10 different China tours—it squeezes in a lot for your money. Ritz Tours is a mid-range agency specializing in East Asian tours. R. Crusoe & Son is an offbeat company that organizes small group or tailor-made private tours. For something more mainstream, try Pacific Delight.

Not all of the companies we list include air travel in their packages. Check this when you're researching your trip.

**Recommended Companies China Focus Travel** ☎ 800/868–7244 ⊕ www. chinafocustravel.com. **Overseas Adventure Travel** ☎ 800/493–6824 ⊕ www.oattravel.com. **Pacific Delight** ☎ 800/221–7179 ⊕ www. pacificdelighttours.com. **R. Crusoe & Son** ☎ 800/585–8555 ⊕ www.rcrusoe.com. **Ritz Tours** ☎ 888/345–7489 ⊕ www.ritztours.com.

**Adventure Center** ☎ 866/338–8735 ⊕ www. adventurecenter.com.

## SPECIAL-INTEREST TOURS
### CULTURE

Local guides are often creative when it comes to history and culture, so having an expert with you can make a big difference. Learning is the focus of Smithsonian Journeys' small-group tours, which are led by university professors. China experts also lead National Geographic's trips, though all that knowledge doesn't come cheap.

Wild China is a local company with some of the most unusual trips around, including visits to ethnic minority groups, Tibet, and little-known Xinjiang province, as well as more conventional historical trips and journeys focusing on traditional festivals. Ethnic folk art and the Silk Road are two of the focuses of Wild China's art and architecture tours.

**Contacts National Geographic Expeditions** ☎ 888/966–8687 ⊕ www. nationalgeographicexpeditions.com. **Smithsonian Journeys** ☎ 855/330–1542 ⊕ www. smithsonianjourneys.org. **Wild China** ☎ 888/902–8808 ⊕ www.wildchina.com.

### CULINARY

Artisans of Leisure's culinary tour takes in Shanghai and Beijing from the cities' choicest establishments, with prices to match. Intrepid Travel is an Australian company specializing in budget, independent travel. Their China Gourmet Traveler tour includes market visits, cooking demonstrations, and lots of eating at down-to-earth restaurants. Imperial Tours Culinary Tour combines sightseeing with cooking lectures and demonstrations, and lots of five-star dining.

**Contacts Artisans of Leisure** ☎ 800/214–8144 ⊕ www.artisansofleisure.com. **Imperial Tours** ☎ 888/888–1970 ⊕ www.imperialtours. net. **Intrepid Travel** ☎ 800/970–7299 ⊕ www. intrepidtravel.com.

**GOLF**

China Highlights organizes short golf packages that combine sightseeing with golfing in Beijing, Shanghai, Kunming, Guangzhou, and Guilin.

**Contacts China Highlights** ☎ *800/268–2918* ⊕ *www.chinahighlights.com.*

**HIKING**

Adventure Center's China hikes include an eight-day walk along the Great Wall, a three-week walk along the route of the Communists' 1934 Long March, and a trip that combines mild hikes with Yangtze cruises and sightseeing.

**Contacts The Adventure Center** ☎ *866/338–8735* ⊕ *www.adventurecenter.com.*

# ▌ VISITOR INFORMATION

For general information before you go, including advice on tours, insurance, and safety, call or visit the website of the China National Tourist Office.

The two best-known Chinese travel agencies are the state-run China International Travel Service (CITS) and China Travel Service (CTS), both under the same government ministry. Although they have some tourist information, they are businesses, so don't expect endless resources if you're not purchasing a tour or flight. In theory, CTS offices offer local sightseeing tours, and CITS arranges packages from overseas; in reality, their services overlap.

The Hong Kong Tourism Board has stacks of online information about events, sightseeing, shopping, and dining in Hong Kong. They also organize tour packages from the United States, and local sightseeing tours.

**Contacts China International Travel Service** ☎ *626/568–8993* ⊕ *www.citsusa.com.* **China National Tourist Office** ☎ *212/760–8218* ⊕ *www.cnto.org.* **China Travel Service** ☎ *800/899–8618* ⊕ *www.chinatravelservice. com.* **Hong Kong Tourist Board** ⊕ *www. discoverhongkong.com.*

**ONLINE TRAVEL TOOLS**

The websites listed in this book are in English. If you come across a Chinese-language site you think might be useful, copy the URL into Google, then click the "Translate this page" link. Translations are literal, but generally work for finding out information like opening hours or prices.

**ALL ABOUT CHINA**

The excellent *China Digital Times* tracks China-related news and culture. The Oriental List has extremely reliable information about travel in China. A detailed database on Chinese art, film, literature, and more is available at Chinese Culture. Information about all of Hong Kong's arts and cultural programs is available at the Hong Kong Leisure and Cultural Services Department.

**China Digital Times** ⊕ *www.chinadigitaltimes. net.***Chinese Culture** ⊕ *www.chinaculture. org.***Hong Kong Leisure and Cultural Services Department** ⊕ *www.lcsd.gov.hk.* **The Oriental List** ⊕ *www.datasinica.com.*

**BUSINESS**

China Business Weekly is published by the *China Daily* newspaper.

**China Business Weekly** ⊕ *www.chinadaily. com.cn/english/bw/bwtop.html.*

**LOCAL INSIGHT**

Asia Expat gives advice and listings from foreigners living in Beijing, Hong Kong, Guangzhou, and Shanghai. Asia City is an online version of quirky weekly rags that give the lowdown on everything happening in Shanghai and Hong Kong.

**Asia Expat** ⊕ *www.asiaxpat.com.* **Asia City** ⊕ *www.asia-city.com.*

**NEWSPAPERS**

*China Daily* is the leading English-language daily. The English edition of China's most popular—and most propagandistic—daily is called the *People's Daily*. Hong Kong's leading English-language daily is the *South China Morning Post.*

*China Daily* ⊕ *www.chinadaily.com.cn.* *People's Daily* ⊕ *www.english.peopledaily.com.cn.* *South China Morning Post* ⊕ *www.scmp.com.*

## GREAT CHINESE READS

**Big Name Fiction:** 2012 Nobel Peace Prize winner Mo Yan's *Life and Death Are Wearing Me Out*; *Wolf Totem* by Jiang Rong; *The Civil Servant's Notebook* by Wang Xiaofang; *Northern Girls* by Sheng Keyi; Gao Xingjian's *Soul Mountain.*

**China 101:** *The China Reader: The Reform Era,* edited by Orville Schell and David Shambaugh; *The Search for Modern China,* by Jonathan Spence; and *A History of Hong Kong,* by Frank Welsh.

**How about Mao:** Dr. Li Zhisui's *The Private Life of Chairman Mao* or Jung Chang's *Mao The Unknown Story.*

# INDEX

## PHOTO CREDITS

Front cover: Peter Adams/JAI/Corbis [Description: Girls of Long Horn Miao tribe dancing, Sugao, Guizhou Province]. 1, Boaz Rottem/age fotostock. 2-3, Alvaro Leiva / age fotostock. 5, lu linsheng/ iStockphoto. Chapter 1: Experience China. 8-9, José Fuste Raga/age fotostock. 10, Holly Peabody, Fodors.com member. 11 (left), Hong Kong Tourism Board. 11 (right), DK.samco/Shutterstock. 12, Iain Masterton / age fotostock. 13, SEUX Paule / age fotostock. 14, Brian Jeffery Beggerly/Flickr. 15 (left), Hong Kong Tourism Board. 15 (right), Hotel G Beijing. 16 (left), Jarno Gonzalez Zarraonandia/iStock-photo. 16 (top), fotohunter/Shutterstock. 16 (bottom), Jonathan Larsen/Shutterstock. 17 (top left), Hung Chung Chih/Shutterstock. 17 (bottom left), Peter Mukherjee/iStockphoto. 17 (right), loong/Shut-terstock. 18 (left), Chunni4691/Shutterstock. 18 (top right), Holger Mette/iStockphoto. 18 (bottom right), George Clerk/iStockphoto. 19 (top left), richliy/Shutterstock. 19 (bottom left), Hung Chung Chih/Shutterstock. 19 (right), Ivan Walsh/Flickr. 20, John Leung/Shutterstock. 21 (left), Eastimages/ Shutterstock. 21 (right), gary718/Shutterstock. 22, Marc van Vuren/Shutterstock. 23 (left), Gretchen Winters, Fodors.com member. 23 (right), Steve Slawsky. 24, Sze Kit Poon/iStockphoto. 25 (left), oksana.perkins/Shutterstock. 25 (right), Andrew Kerr/Shutterstock. 34, bbobo, Fodors.com member. 35, qingqing/Shutterstock. 36 (left), Kowloonese/Wikimedia Commons. 36 (top right), Daniel Shich-man & Yael Tauger/Wikimedia Commons. 36 (bottom right), Wikimedia Commons. 37 (left), Hung Chung Chih/Shutterstock. 37 (right), rodho/Shutterstock. 38, (left), Chinneeb/Wikimedia Commons. 38 (top right), B_cool/Wikimedia Commons. 38 (bottom right), Imperial Painter/Wikimedia Commons. 39 (left and bottom right), Wikimedia Commons. 39 (top right), Joe Brandt/iStockphoto. 40 (top left, bottom left, and top right), Wikimedia Commons. 40 (bottom right), K.T. Thompson/wikipedia.org. 41 (top right), Wikimedia Commons. 41 (bottom left), ImagineChina. 41 (right), tomislav domes/Flickr. 42, TAO IMAGES/age fotostock. Chapter 2: Beijing. 43, TAO IMAGES/age fotostock. 44, claudio zac-cherini/Shutterstock. 45 (left), yxm2008/Shutterstock. 45 (right), Johann 'Jo' Guzman, Fodors.com member. 46, sanglei slei/iStockphoto. 49, TAO IMAGES/age fotostock. 54, lu linsheng/iStockphoto. 55 (top), TAO IMAGES/age fotostock. 55 (bottom), Bob Balestri/iStockphoto. 56, Lance Lee | AsiaPhoto. com/iStockphoto. 57 (left), Jiping Lai/iStockphoto. 57 (right 1), May Wong/Flickr. 57 (right 2), William Perry/iStockphoto. 57 (right 3), bing liu/iStockphoto. 57 (right 4), William Perry/iStockphoto. 58 (bot-tom left and right), Wikimedia Commons. 58 (top), Helena Lovincic/iStockphoto. 59 (top), rehoboth foto/Shutterstock. 59 (bottom left and right), Wikimedia Commons. 63, P. Narayan/age fotostock. 67, Jose Fuste Raga/age fotostock. 69, Lim Yong Hian/Shutterstock. 77, TAO IMAGES/age fotostock. 83, TAO IMAGES/age fotostock. 90, patrick frilet/age fotostock. 96 (top), Red Capital Residence. 96, (bot-tom left), Hotel G Beijing. 96 (bottom right), Epoque Hotels. 101 (top), Hyatt Hotels. 101 (bottom), Starwood Hotels and Resorts. 107, Werner Bachmeier/age fotostock. 110-11, Sylvain Grandadam/age fotostock. 114, Christian Kober/age fotostock. 121, TAO IMAGES/age fotostock. 128, John W. War-den/age fotostock. 129, Wikimedia Commons. 130-31, Liu Jianmin/age fotostock. 134, Alan Crawford/ iStockphoto. 135, Eugenia Kim/iStockphoto. 136, Jarno Gonzalez/iStockphoto. 137, Chris Ronneseth/ iStockphoto. 138, JTB Photo/age fotostock. Chapter 3: Beijing to Shanghai. 141, Steve Vidler/age foto-stock. 142, Chi King/Flickr. 143 (left), www.seefarseeeast.com/Flickr. 143 (right), Gina Smith/iStock-photo. 144, suecan1/Flickr. 151, richliy/Shutterstock. 154, View Stock/age fotostock. 161, David Lyons/age fotostock. 164, Karl Johaentges/age fotostock. 171, (c) Bjmcse | Dreamstime.com. 178, nozo-miiqel/Flickr. 185, Charles Bowman / age fotostock. 188, JTB Photo/age fotostock. 193, White Star / Spierenb/age fotostock. 197, suecan1/Flickr. 206, Karl Johaentges/age fotostock. 210, hxdyl/Shutter-stock. Chapter 4: Shanghai. 213, Lucas Vallecillos/age foto stock. 214, hxdyl/Shutterstock. 215 (right), (c) Hel080808 Dreamstime.com. 215 (left), claudio zaccherini/Shutterstock. 216, Augapfel/Flickr. 221, Gaby Wojciech / age fotostock. 226, claudio zaccherini/Shutterstock. 231, José Fuste Raga/age fotos-tock. 234-35, c) Pixattitude | Dreamstime.com. 243, SALDARI/age fotostock. 249, Karl Johaentges/age fotostock. 252, JTB Photo/age fotostock. 257, Hippo/age fotostock. 266 (top), Starwood Hotels & Resorts. 266 (bottom), JIA Shanghai. 269 (top), URBN Hotels. 269 (bottom left), Shangri-La Hotels and Resorts. 269 (bottom right), Starwood Hotels & Resorts. 274, 279, and 285, Karl Johaentges/age fotostock. Chapter 5: Eastern China. 287, TAO IMAGES/age fotostock. 288, Jon Mullen/iStockphoto. 289 (left), robert van beets/iStockphoto. 289 (right), hxdbzxy/Shutterstock. 290, China National Tour-ist Office. 297, SuperStock/age fotostock. 300, and 305, JTB Photo/age fotostock. 306, TAO IMAGES/ age fotostock. 309, JTB Photo/age fotostock. 317, Christian Kober/age fotostock. 318, SuperStock/age fotostock. 319 (top), TAO IMAGES/age fotostock. 319 (bottom), Mark52/Shutterstock. 320, Shigeki Tanaka/age fotostock. 321 (left), Yuan yanwu - Imaginechina. 321 (top right), Huiping Zhu/iStock-photo. 321 (bottom right), richliy/Shutterstock. 329, Shigeki Tanaka/age foto stock. Chapter 6: Hong Kong. 331, Hemis / Alamy. 332, Hong Kong Tourism Board. 333, Ella Hanochi/iStockphoto. 334, Laoshi/iStockphoto. 338, Amanda Hall / age fotostock. 343, Dallas & John Heaton / age fotostock.

354, Ron Yue / Alamy. 357, Raga Jose Fuste / age fotostock. 369, BrokenSphere/wiki-pedia.org. 377 (top and bottom), Michael Weber. 380 (top), InterContinental Hong Kong/fl ickr. 380 (bottom left), bryangeek/fl ickr. 380 (bottom right), The Luxe Manor. 385, Fumio Okada / age fotostock. 390 and 398, Hong Kong Tourism Board. 405, Iain Masterton / Alamy. 412, Steve Vidler / age fotostock. 418, Christian Goupi / age fotostock. Chapter 7: Pearl River Delta. 421, José Fuste Raga/age fotostock. 422, J Aaron Farr/Flickr. 423 (left), Hector Joseph Lumang/iStockphoto. 423 (right), Mission Hills. 424, Rüdiger Meier/Wikimedia Commons. 431, View Stock/age fotostock. 432, Charles Bowman/age fotostock. 442, Steve Vidler/age fotostock. 446, (c) Huating | Dreamstime.com. 449, TAO IMAGES/age fotostock. 453, Robert Francis/age fotostock. 454, Mission Hills. Chapter 8: The Southwest. 457, Philippe Michel/age fotostock. 458, Jakrit Jiraratwaro/Shutterstock. 459 (bottom), Christophe Cerisier/iStockphoto. 459 (top), Anthon Jackson/Shutterstock. 460, Edwin Lee/Flickr. 463, Christian Kober/age fotostock. 468, Li Xin/age fotostock. 470-71, KingWu/iStockphoto. 476, EcoPrint/Shutterstock. 483 (top), Huang jinguo - Imaginechina. 483 (bottom), disc picture/Shutterstock. 484, Dave Bartruff/age fotostock. 485, YinYang/iStockphoto. 486 (top left), Wikimol/Wikimedia Commons. 486 (bottom), Natallia Yaumenenka/iStockphoto. 486 (top right), Christopher Noble/iStockphoto. 487, Wikimedia Commons. 488 (top), christine gonsalves/iStockphoto. 488 (left), dem10/iStockphoto. 488 (middle), Jason Fasi/Wikimedia Commons. 488 (right), jacus/iStockphoto. 489 (left), Iateasquirrel/Wikimedia Commons. 489 (middle), Juanmonino/iStockphoto. 489 (right), annastock/Shutterstock. 492, JTB Photo/age fotostock. 495, SEUX Paule/age fotostock. 500, CINTRACT Romain/age fotostock. 503, Stefan Auth/age fotostock. 510, c) Elifranssens | Dreamstime.com. 513, Andrea Pistolesi/age fotostock. 518, Michele Falzone/age fotostock. 522, Angelo Cavallii/age fotostock. 523, Dennis Cox/age fotostock. Chapter 9: Sichuan and Chongqing. 525, Karl Johaentges/age fotostock. 526 and 527 (top), fenghui/Shutterstock. 527 (bottom), JingAiping/Shutterstock. 528, loong/Shutterstock. 532, Hung Chung Chih/Shutterstock. 536, Jose Fuste Raga/age foto stock. 543, Manfred Bail/age fotostock. 546, José Fuste Raga/age fotostock. 551, Jane Sweeney/age fotostock. 555, FOTOSEARCH RM/age fotostock. 556 (bottom), FotoosVanRobin/Wikimedia Commons. 556 (top), Chubykin Arkady/Shutterstock. 557 (left), ImagineChina. 557 (top right), hywit dimyadi/iStockphoto. 557 (bottom right), Maria Ly/Flickr. 558 (bottom left), Hannamariah/Shutterstock. 558 (top right), zkruger/iStockphoto. 559 (top left), Ritesh Man Tamrakar/Wikimedia Commons. 559 (middle left), Rjanag/Wikimedia Commons. 559 (bottom left), Craig Lovell / Eagle Visions Photography / Alamy. 559 (right), Cephas Picture Library / Alamy. 560 (top left), Eneri LLC/iStockphoto. 560 (bottom left), Man Haan Chung/iStockphoto. 560 (top right), Holger Gogolin/iStockphoto. 560 (bottom right), Eneri LLC/iStockphoto. 568, View Stock/age fotostock. Chapter 10: The Silk Road. 571, TORRIONE Stefano/age fotostock. 572 (bottom), Amy Nichole Harris/Shutterstock. 572 (top), Stuart Taylor/Shutterstock. 573 (top), Dada/Flickr. 573 (bottom), Alica Q/Shutterstock. 574, loong/Shutterstock. 580, William Fawcett fotoVoyager.com/iStockphoto. 586 (left), John Goulter/age fotostock. 586-87, Greg Knudsen, Fodors.com member. 588, hanhanpeggy/iStockphoto. 589 (top), Wikimedia Commons. 589 (bottom), André Viegas/Shutterstock. 590 (top), Amy Nichole Harris/Shutterstock. 590 (bottom), zhuda/Shutterstock. 590-91, Martin Puddy/age fotostock. 591 (top inset), Yan Vugenfi rer/Shutterstock. 591 (bottom inset), Ke Wang/Shutterstock. 592 (top), Lukas Hlavac/Shutterstock. 592 (bottom), Olaf Schubert /age fotostock. 593, xxapril/iStockphoto. 601, vito arcomano/age fotostock. 607, Aldo Pavan/age fotostock. 611, TAO IMAGES/age fotostock. 614, José Fuste Raga/age fotostock. 617, Mark Henley/age fotostock. 623, JTB Photo/age fotostock. 630-31, Philippe Michel/age fotostock. Chapter 11: Tibet. 633, TAO IMAGES/age fotostock. 634 (bottom), Tian Zhan/iStockphoto. 634 (top), Hung Chung Chih/Shutterstock. 635, Terraxplorer/iStockphoto. 636, Helena Lovincic/iStockphoto. 643, Stefan Auth /age fotostock. 646-47, Colin Monteath/age fotostock. 652, McPHOTOs /age fotostock. 655, Angelo Cavalli /age fotostock. 657, Bjorn Svensson/age fotostock. 661, Meiqianbao/Shutterstock. Back cover (from left to right): Hung Chung Chih/Shutterstock; fenghui/Shutterstock; Holger Mette/iStockphoto. Spine: Nicha/Shutterstock.

# NOTES

# NOTES

# NOTES

# NOTES

# NOTES

# ABOUT OUR WRITERS

Sophie Friedman is a transplanted New Yorker living in Shanghai. She has previously worked at *Time Out New York* and *The Huffington Post* and is a contributor to *Condé Nast Traveler, The South China Morning Post, The Wall Street Journal,* and CNN. She hopes that the ever-evolving, sometimes-astounding places listed in the Shanghai chapter will provide you with as many wonderful experiences and memories as they have her.

Daniel Garber has called China home for nearly five years. After finishing a degree in journalism from New York University, he moved to a small village in Eastern China, bought a tiny pug, and became addicted to Longjing green tea, learning Mandarin and exploring China on an electric motorbike. Along with Dana Kaufman, Daniel updated the Sichuan and Chongqing chapter.

A resident of China for seven years, Kit Gillet is a former staff writer for *The South China Morning Post*. Now a freelance journalist for *The Economist, The New York Times, The Guardian, The Wall Street Journal, The Los Angeles Times* and *Monocle*, he updated the Silk Road and Tibet chapters.

Julie Grundvig is a professional writer, editor, and China arts specialist with more than 20 years of experience living, working, and traveling throughout China. She holds an MA from the University of British Columbia in Classical Chinese Studies. Her writings on Chinese art, travel and cultural heritage have been published worldwide. Julie updated our Experience China, Understanding China, and Travel Smart chapters.

Dana Kaufman moved to China in 2005, and has held a number of jobs ranging from teacher to chef to entrepreneur. In addition to learning Chinese calligraphy, Dana enjoys photographing Asia's most remote and fascinating faces and landscapes. Dana and Daniel Garber now own and operate an American restaurant and martini bar in Chengdu. Along with Daniel, Dana updated the Sichuan and Chongqing chapter.

Tom O'Malley has lived and worked in Beijing since 2008, writing about China travel and food for *The Guardian, The South China Morning Post, Travel & Leisure,* and *Time Out,* in between working as a restaurant consultant, food critic, and DJ. He updated our Beijing to Shanghai chapter.

Kate Springer is an American journalist based in Hong Kong. She focuses on travel, lifestyle, and environmental reporting, and her work has appeared in *Time, HK Magazine, Forbes Travel Guide,* and *Smart Travel Asia*. When she's not ambling around Asia, you'll find her teaching English, dabbling in photography, and devouring *xiao long bao* dumplings. She updated our Eastern China chapter and portions of Hong Kong.

Sander Van de Moortel first landed in Yunnan in 2011 after taking a wrong turn on a bike trip through Vietnam. Comfortably trapped in Kunming by his linguistic ambitions and his somewhat complicated relationship with China, he has been further exploring the region's colorful patchwork by bicycle. Sander updated the Southwest chapter.

A native New Yorker, Amy Wu found her way to Hong Kong after college in 1996 to cover the handover, and returned in 2010 to pursue a teaching career in journalism. She's worked for *Time* and *The Deal* and regularly contributes columns to *The South China Morning Post* and *The Huffington Post*. When she isn't traveling, Amy enjoys trying new cuisines, taking pictures, and swimming. Amy updated the Pearl River Delta chapter.

## Beijing Contributors

Sky Canaves is a writer whose work has been focused on China since the late '90s, when she spent an academic year studying in Nanjing. She was reporter for *The Wall Street Journal* in Hong Kong and Beijing, where she covered the 2008

Summer Olympic Games and launched the publication's China Real Time blog. After nine years in Asia, she recently returned to her hometown, New York City. For this edition, Sky updated the Exploring and Where to Eat sections.

Gareth Clark has worked in magazines for nearly a decade, the bulk of which he spent writing for *Time Out* publications in the Middle East and Asia. In 2009 he moved to China, where he became the editor of local listings bible *Time Out Beijing* before going freelance. He loves nothing more than eating a hot baozi on a smoggy day. Gareth updated the Shopping and Side Trips sections.

Born in Beijing, Ami Li grew up in the U.S. Luckily, her parents forced her to go to Chinese school every weekend for the first 15 years of her life because she ultimately parlayed her native-level Mandarin into her current job at Split Works, an independent music and festival promoter in her home city. Before finding her calling as a music promoter, Ami honed her translation skills by working for *The New York Times* Beijing bureau and wrote for publications such as *City Weekend* and *China Music Radar*. Ami updated the Nightlife & Arts section.

Adrian Sandiford is a PTC and MDJA award-winning magazine journalist based in Beijing. Previously on staff at *Esquire* in London, he moved east in 2008 to become the editor of *Time Out Beijing*, where he is now editor-at-large. He spent years uncovering the best that China's capital has to offer and his work has since covered everything from writing about trends in the local food scene for *The Times of London* to editing a series of books on contemporary Chinese art for leading critic and curator Karen Smith. He is also the author of the *Wallpaper\* City Guide: Guangzhou* and *Wallpaper\* City Guide: Beijing*. Adrian updated the Experience and Where Stay sections.

## Hong Kong Contributors

After earning her MFA from the Writing Division at Columbia University, Doretta Lau worked for *Time Out Hong Kong* and *HK* magazines. She is currently a contributor to Artforum.com, where she reports on events and writes exhibition reviews. As a freelance journalist and writer, she has worked in print and radio for media outlets in Hong Kong, Canada, the United States, and England. Doretta updated Hong Kong and Kowloon neighborhoods.

Born and raised in Hong Kong, Samantha Leese was educated at Stanford University and the London School of Journalism. Sam is a contributing editor at *Glass* and *Prestige* magazines, and writes on arts, culture, and travel for CNN, *The Spectator*, and *Asia Tatler*, among other titles. She lives by the beach in Hong Kong. Samantha updated the Nightlife section.

Maloy Luakian moved to Hong Kong after watching *Chungking Express* in 1999 and, aside from a few years in Italy, has lived there ever since. She has written travel articles for both print and online newspapers and magazines, focusing mostly on food, architecture, and alternative activities for travelers, such as ghost hunting in Manila or visiting abandoned parks and cities in China.

Dorothy So studied in Los Angeles, where she developed a passion for exploring different food cultures. Honing in on her interest in food, she moved back to her home city of Hong Kong in 2009 to work as a dining journalist. Her writing has appeared in many publications, including *HK*, *Time Out*, and *The South China Morning Post*. Dorothy updated the Where to Eat and Experience sections.

Jason Spotts is a food and lifestyle writer born and raised in Hong Kong. He has spent years exploring both the colonial and local sides of Hong Kong's unique culture. Jason's work has appeared in *The South China Morning Post*, *Hong Kong Tatler*, *Crave*, and *Time Out*.